PARIS

ÉMILE ZOLA

PARIS

TRANSLATED BY ERNEST ALFRED VIZETELLY

ALAN SUTTON

First published in 1896

First published in this edition in the United Kingdom in 1993
Alan Sutton Publishing Ltd
Phoenix Mill · Far Thrupp · Stroud · Gloucestershire

First published in this edition in the United States of America in 1993
Alan Sutton Publishing Inc · 83 Washington Street · Dover · NH 03820

British Library Cataloguing in Publication Data
A catalogue record for this book is available from the British Library

ISBN 0-7509-0450-X

Library of Congress Cataloging in Publication Data applied for

Cover picture: On the Banks of the Seine *by Jean Beraud (Photograph: Fine Art Photographic
Library Ltd)*

Typeset in 9/10 Bembo.
Typesetting and origination by
Alan Sutton Publishing Limited.
Printed in Great Britain by
The Guernsey Press Company Limited,
Guernsey, Channel Islands.

'In the Twentieth Century there will be an extraordinary nation. This nation will be great, but its greatness will not prevent it from being free. It will be illustrious, wealthy, thoughtful, pacific, cordial to the rest of mankind. . . . The capital of this nation will be Paris, but its country will not be known as France. In the Twentieth Century its country will be called Europe, and in after centuries, as it still and ever develops, it will be called Mankind. . . . Before possessing its nation, Europe possesses its city. The nation does not yet exist, but its capital is already here. This may seem a prodigy, yet it is a law. Embryonic development, whether nation or creature be in question, always begins with the head. . . . Throughout historical times the world has ever had a city which has been The City. The brain is a necessity. Nothing can be accomplished without the organ whence come both initiative and will. Acephalous civilisation is beyond conception. It is from three cities, Jerusalem, Athens, Rome, that the modern world has been evolved. They did their work. Of Jerusalem there now remains but a gibbet, Calvary ; of Athens, a ruin, the Parthenon ; of Rome, a phantom, its empire. Are these cities dead, then ? No. A broken eggshell does not necessarily imply that the egg has been destroyed ; it rather signifies that the bird has come forth from it, and lives. From out of those shells lying yonder—Rome, Athens, and Jerusalem—the human ideal has sprung and soared. From Rome has come power ; from Athens, Art ; from Jerusalem, freedom : the great, the beautiful, the true. . . . And they live anew in Paris, which in one way has resuscitated Rome, in another Athens, and in another Jerusalem ; for from the cry of Golgotha came the principle of the Rights of Man. And Paris also has its crucified ; one that has been crucified for eighteen hundred years—the People. . . . But the function of Paris is to spread ideas. Its never-ending duty is to scatter truths over the world, a duty it incessantly discharges. Paris is a sower, sowing the darkness with sparks of light. It is Paris which, without a pause, stirs up the fire of progress. It casts superstition and fanaticism, and hatred and folly and prejudice on to this fire, and from all such darkness comes a blaze of light. . . . Moreover, Paris is like the centre of our nervous system; each of its quivers is felt throughout the world. . . . And, further, it is like a ship sailing on through storms and whirlpools to unknown Atlantides, and ever towing the fleet of mankind in its wake. There can be no greater ecstasy than that which comes from perception of the universal advance, when one hears the echoes of the receding tempests, the creaking of the rigging and the panting of the toiling crew, when one feels the straining of the timbers, and realises the speed with which, in spite of all, one happily travels onward. Search the whole world through; it is ever upon the deck of Paris that one may best hear the flapping and quivering of the full-spread, invisible sails of human Progress.'

VICTOR HUGO.

CONTENTS

BOOK I

BOOK II

BOOK III

BOOK IV

BOOK V

INTRODUCTION

In 1893, after twenty-five years' involvement, Zola brought his cycle of *Rougon-Macquart* novels to a triumphant and no doubt relieved conclusion. The task of remaining referentially accurate and avoiding anachronisms in his depiction of the historical period of the Second Empire (1852–70) had become increasingly difficult under the pressure of contemporary events, with novels such as *Au Bonheur des Dames, Germinal* and *L'Argent* showing signs of the need felt by the author to synthesize more recent stages of development in mass merchandising, revolutionary syndicalism and financial market manipulation. A dozen years earlier, Zola had predicted to his friend Paul Alexis that after the *Rougon-Macquart* he might occupy himself with a history of French literature, write children's stories, or even do nothing at all. But the undermining of previously held convictions, such as his belief in social Darwinism, led him to think again, and to address social problems of immediate relevance to the final decade of the century.

That a substantial body of readers should be eager to see the new direction his thoughts were taking in *Lourdes*, the novel on the documentary research for which he was known to be proceeding in his usual assiduous fashion, was greatly to the credit of a man whose failure to obtain the enabling *baccalauréat* meant that he lacked credible academic qualifications. Émile Zola was born near the Paris Bourse in 1840, to a Venetian engineer father and a French mother from the grain-growing plain of the Beauce, to the south-west of the city. The family moved in 1843 to Aix-en-Provence, where Francesco was involved in a bold project to ensure the town's water supply via an aqueduct, but died in 1847, leaving them in a state of

poverty relieved only by the gentle climate. They returned to
Paris in 1858, thereby disrupting Émile's secondary school
studies at a critical time; after failing his exams, he was obliged
to find low-grade clerical employment and, abandoning this, led
an impecunious bohemian existence in a succession of dismal
apartments. Here he read omnivorously, penned epic poetry
and contemplated other literary projects.

At length he was found a post in the publicity department of
the progressive publishing house of Hachette. His job
description in 1862 included menial tasks such as the packing
and despatch of books, but his natural talent for writing blurbs
and synopses soon flourished, and he made personal contact
with distinguished authors and standard-bearers of scientific
positivism such as Michelet, Taine and Sainte-Beuve. He began
to write reviews and art criticism for newspapers, championing
the objectivity and modernity of painters like Manet and
novelists like the Goncourts, and to find publishers willing to
print his fiction, beginning with a volume of short stories,
Contes à Ninon. The sexual frankness of his novels, particularly
Thérèse Raquin (1867), led to brushes with imperial censorship,
and his political outspokenness would have landed him in court
for incitement to military disobedience if the Franco–Prussian
War of 1870 had not intervened.

The *débâcle* of Sedan and Emperor Napoléon III's flight from
France provided Zola with the 'terrible but necessary ending'
he had openly wished for the cycle of novels that he had offered
two years earlier to the publisher Lacroix. This was to become
Les Rougon-Macquart, a natural and social history of a family
during the Second Empire, in which the two major scientific
determinants of heredity and environment were to be seen in
their effect on the legitimate issue of Adélaïde Fouque's
marriage to Rougon, a solid citizen, and the illegitimate
progeny of her liaison with a criminal degenerate, Macquart.
The original plan provided for the opening *La Fortune des
Rougon* and another nine novels, but soon it was expanded to a
list of seventeen, and the ultimate total of twenty could have
been higher but for a somewhat uneasy conflation of subject-
matter in *La Bête Humaine*. The novels enjoyed unremarkable

sales until 1877, when the seventh in the series, *L'Assommoir*, his first total immersion in a study of working-class life, gave Zola both commercial and critical success. Fame and fortune then allowed him to buy his house at Médan, today a Zola museum, where he entertained the young writers, including Huysmans and Maupassant, who were to immortalize the setting in the anthology of antimilitaristic short stories, *Les Soirées de Médan* (1880).

This collection owed much of its acclaim to a by now well-oiled publicity machine that had given maximum exposure to Zola's theories on literary and dramatic naturalism, most trenchantly and truculently formulated in the collection of essays, *Le Roman Expérimental*, which appeared in the same year. His sustained polemical comparison between the novelist's craft and the experimental scientist's pursuit of working hypotheses provoked lively controversy on the intellectual scene in France. Bold paradoxes such as 'the Republic will be naturalist, or will not exist' commended his ideas to the attention of arch-opponents such as Brunetière, and Balzac, Stendhal and Flaubert were lauded in essays reprinted under the title of *Les Romanciers Naturalistes* that established them as forebears of Zola's movement, through the honour more properly belonged to the Goncourt brothers, whose *Soeur Philomène* (1861) and *Germinie Lacerteux* (1864) had been a major influence on the uncompromisingly deterministic *Thérèse Raquin*.

The year 1880 was also marked by a series of bereavements: the writer Duranty was followed by Flaubert, and finally Zola's mother. Depression, insomnia and psychosomatic disorders overcame the author, and Lazare of *La Joie de Vivre* (1883) seems an uncomfortably close fictional incarnation. But such Schopenhauerian pessimism was more constant in Maupassant than in Zola: his robust secular faith in human qualities that triumph over biological determinism suffuses the endings of *Germinal* (1885), *La Terre* (1887), *L'Argent* (1890), *La Débâcle* (1892) and *Le Docteur Pascal* (1893). It is a faith that, respectfully rather than arrogantly asserted, continues to be manifest in the *Three Cities* (1894–8), but one that was to be put to the severest of tests by the Dreyfus Affair. Zola's brave crusade was a result of the unjust conviction and deportation of a French officer accused of spying, mainly on the grounds that he was Jewish whereas the more circumstantially guilty Esterhazy was not. In *J'Accuse* (*L'Aurore*, 13 January 1898), an open letter condemning the anti-Semitic prejudice of those who had engineered this travesty of justice, the accusation of libel was deliberately provoked in the hope that aspects of the case would be reopened during the consequent criminal proceedings. After a second trial Zola was convicted and, while the appeal was pending, forced to flee to England, where he stayed for nearly a year until moves to obtain a pardon for Dreyfus had gained momentum. It was in exile that he began to write the *Four Gospels*, which are notable because, in spite of all that could have caused him personally to despair, such matters are regarded as but a minor setback in the victorious forward march of mankind, described with visionary enthusiasm in scenarios anticipating the ultimate defeat of retrograde obscurantism in all its forms. Only the first three of these – *Fécondité, Travail,* and *Vérité* – had been completed before his untimely death by carbon monoxide poisoning in 1902. A few preparatory notes exist for the last, and its title – *Justice* – denotes Zola's greatest desire, and one shared by the central protagonist of the *Three Cities*.

F.W.J. Hemmings notes that up to *Nana*, the ninth of the *Rougon-Macquart* cycle, Zola's novels are gratuitous, almost decorative, with the twin goals of environmental reconstruction and precise historical depiction predominating. After this, though, they become functional, beginning to address themselves to more specific and timeless dilemmas and problems without descending to the special pleading or the artificial, allegorical construction of the *roman à thèse*, and hence displaying both social consciousness and creative vitality in a delicate balancing act. But strain was already apparent in *Le Docteur Pascal*, that bends beneath the burden of recapitulation, and the *Three Cities* and the *Four Gospels* will subsequently prove to be fairly mechanically assembled, with plot subservient to ideas. Characters now tend to be stereotypes or mouthpieces, and to recur not in the Balzacian sense – from novel to novel – but at regular and predictable intervals within each.

The boundless confidence in science of the mid-1860s had given way, by the 1890s, to a 'moral and intellectual uneasiness amidst which the end of the century is struggling' (*Rome*, I, 1). A revival of religious faith was being experienced by a younger generation of intellectuals, stimulated by Pope Leo XIII, whose encyclicals, such as *Rerum Novarum* (1891), sought to reconquer the moral high ground. Brunetière, an adversary who had sought no quarrel with Zola's agnosticism but rather with the unimaginative crudity of his naturalist aesthetics, was ostentatiously converted to Catholicism; in the *Revue des Deux Mondes* of 1 January 1895, he claimed to have done so because of the 'bankruptcy of science'. More pertinently to Zola, perhaps, the greater depth of the Russian novel, with its spiritually tormented protagonists such as Dostoevsky's Alyosha (*The Brothers Karamazov*), had been proclaimed in influential critical essays by Count Eugène-Melchior de Vogüé. Religious preoccupations had not been absent from the *Rougon-Macquart* novels (*La Conquête de Plassans, La Faute de l'Abbé Mouret, La Joie de Vivre, Le Rêve*), but it could be argued that the triumph of scientific rationalism over narrow dogmatism had been hitherto unproblematical. The one-off novel about Lourdes developed into a cities trilogy, in which Zola endeavoured to sustain his appeal to the following generation by asserting his naturalist principles in a more tender and humanitarian way.

The third and final study, *Paris* (1898), is obviously not so much about a voyage as a return to the capital of France where Zola had lived for the whole of his working life. After the lack of comprehension shown him by the Pope three years earlier, l'Abbé Pierre Froment's abandonment of his priestly vocation is almost complete, but he continues to seek an outlet for his love of mankind in the exercise of practical charity; until, that is, he recoils in disgust from the bureaucratic formalities that send him on fruitless errands around Paris while an old man lies dying. He is reunited with his elder brother Guillaume, a chemist after his father's heart, but one who is willing to allow the high explosives he invents to be used to further anarchist campaigns of propaganda by the deed. The inclusion of a terrorist such as

Souvarine in *Germinal* was slightly anachronistic for a novel set
in the years 1866–7, but Prince Kropotkin, one of Guillaume's
models, is of most direct relevance to the France of the 1890s,
shaken by a series of bomb outrages in the metropolis. The trial
of one of Froment's accomplices, Salvat, reflects real-life ones
involving Vaillant and Ravachol, and the public spectacle of
guillotining that takes place at the gates of La Roquette prison
is described with humanitarian distaste, but documentary
accuracy. Many of the anarchists' ideals would not be
disavowed by Pierre; he too, for instance, is appalled by the
'monstrous carbuncle' of the Basilica of the Sacré-Coeur, built
both in glorification of a tasteless cult and in atonement for
France's war guilt, the hubristic meddling in the Hohenzollern
candidacy that provoked the 1870 conflict with Prussia. Never,
though, would he approve of the way publicity for a cause is to
be gained from a cataclysmic destruction that involves the
random slaughter of innocents.

Parliament is a hive of corruption, rocked by an 'African
Railways' financial scandal resembling the Panama affair, and
with the majority of its members cowering in fear of power-
broking political journalists such as Sagnier, whose anti-Semitic
broadsheet, *La Voix du Peuple*, has a clear documentary
counterpart in Édouard Drumont's *La Libre Parole*. The time-
biding Monferrand, a *député* from the Corrèze department, has
some fortuitous similarities with the present-day Jacques Chirac:
plus ça change . . . What institution, then, and what philosophy
remain in which Pierre may place his hope and trust?

The answer to the former is matrimony, but by a civil rather
than a religious contract. Marie, the fiancée of Guillaume, is by
age and temperament more suited to the younger brother, but
he must conquer his initial apparent aversion for an
emancipated woman (the relationship, being one of ideological
necessity, is not developed with any degree of psychological
penetration), and discard his encumbering cassock. As for the
latter, a chorus of spokesmen corresponding closely to
contemporary figures, from the eternal political prisoner and
exile Barthès (supposedly Cipriani, but vocally reminiscent
of Barbès, and biographically of the hard-line socialist and

perennial prisoner, Blanqui) to the chemist Bertheroy (modelled on Berthelot), appear at regular intervals to utter substantial disquisitions on varieties of left-wing political philosophy. The one most acceptable to Zola is that of the moderate Bertheroy: science is the only true revolutionary.

The exalted and millenarian conclusion of the work finds the potentially lethal explosive more gainfully employed in the chambers of the internal combustion engine. The small experimental prototype, in its disregard of Carnot's second principle of thermodynamics regarding energy depletion, situates the *Three Cities* in polar opposition to the bleak verisimilitude of the *Rougon-Macquart* cycle, summarized by Michel Serres as: 'Things burn too fast: an epic of entropy'. The concluding vision of Paris as the newly sown field, bearing the rich harvest of rationalistic enlightenment that will be borne to the furthermost points of the globe, could almost have occurred to Michelet, from whom Zola's ideas had shown considerable mid-career digression.

Ernest Alfred Vizetelly's translation is perfectly satisfactory for a novel whose saturation with didactic pronouncements presents few stylistic challenges. An unexpected bonus in the English version is that the triumph of rationalism extends to female apparel: 'rationals', an 1890s' word (always in helpful inverted commas) denoting knickerbockers or culottes, are Marie's fashion tip for bicycle rides! We have had to wait until now for a female protagonist of the *Three Cities* to be portrayed without a degree of chauvinist prejudice, making this gender variant on *sartor resartus* both refreshing and welcome.

GEOFF WOOLLEN

PARIS

BOOK I

I

THE PRIEST AND THE POOR

THAT morning, one towards the end of January, Abbé Pierre Froment, who had a mass to say at the Sacred Heart at Montmartre, was on the height, in front of the basilica, already at eight o'clock. And before going in he gazed for a moment upon the immensity of Paris spread out below him.

After two months of bitter cold, ice and snow, the city was steeped in a mournful, quivering thaw. From the far-spreading, leaden-hued heavens a thick mist fell like a mourning shroud. All the eastern portion of the city, the abodes of misery and toil, seemed submerged beneath ruddy steam, amid which the panting of workshops and factories could be detected; while westwards, towards the districts of wealth and enjoyment, the fog broke and lightened, becoming but a fine and motionless veil of vapour. The curved line of the horizon could scarcely be divined; the expanse of houses, which nothing bounded, appeared like a chaos of stone, studded with stagnant pools, which filled the hollows with pale steam; whilst against them the summits of the edifices, the house-tops of the loftier streets, showed black like soot. It was a Paris of mystery, shrouded by clouds, buried as it were beneath the ashes of some disaster, already half-sunken in the suffering and the shame of that which its immensity concealed.

Thin and sombre in his flimsy cassock, Pierre was looking on, when Abbé Rose, who seemed to have sheltered himself behind a pillar of the porch on purpose to watch for him, came forward : ' Ah ! it's you at last, my dear child,' said he ; ' I have something to ask you.'

He seemed embarrassed and anxious, and glanced round distrustfully to make sure that nobody was near. Then, as if the solitude thereabouts did not suffice to reassure him, he led Pierre some distance away, through the icy, biting wind, which he himself did not seem to feel. ' This is the matter,' he resumed ; ' I have been told that a poor fellow, a former house-painter, an old man of seventy, who naturally can work no more, is dying of hunger in a hovel in the Rue des Saules. So, my dear child, I thought of you. I thought you would consent to take him these three francs from me, so that he may at least have some bread to eat for a few days.'

' But why don't you take him your alms yourself ? '

At this Abbé Rose again grew anxious, and cast vague, frightened glances about him. ' Oh, no, oh, no ! ' he said, ' I can no longer do that after all the worries that have befallen me. You know that I am watched, and should get another scolding if I were caught giving alms like this, scarcely knowing to whom I give them. It is true that I had to sell something to get these three francs. But, my dear child, render me this service, I pray you.'

Pierre, with heart oppressed, stood contemplating the old priest, whose locks were quite white, whose full lips spoke of infinite kindliness, and whose eyes shone clear and child-like in his round and smiling face. And he bitterly recalled the story of that lover of the poor, the semi-disgrace into which he had fallen through the sublime candour of his charitable goodness. His little ground-floor of the Rue de Charonne, which he had turned into a refuge where he offered shelter to all the wretchedness of the streets, had ended by giving cause for scandal. His *naïveté* and innocence had been abused ; and abominable things had gone on under his roof without his knowledge. Vice had turned the asylum into a meeting-place ; and at last, one night, the police had descended upon it to arrest a young girl accused of infanticide. Greatly concerned by this scandal, the diocesan authorities had forced Abbé Rose to close his shelter, and had removed him from the church of Ste. Marguerite to that of St. Pierre of

Montmartre, where he now again acted as curate. Truth to tell, it was not a disgrace but a removal to another spot. However, he had been scolded and was watched, as he said; and he was much ashamed of it, and very unhappy at being only able to give alms by stealth, much like some hare-brained prodigal who blushes for his faults.

Pierre took the three francs. 'I promise to execute your commission, my friend, oh! with all my heart,' he said.

'You will go after your mass, won't you? His name is Laveuve; he lives in the Rue des Saules in a house with a courtyard, just before reaching the Rue Marcadet. You are sure to find it. And if you want to be very kind you will tell me of your visit this evening at five o'clock, at the Madeleine, where I am going to hear Monseigneur Martha's address. He has been so good to me! Won't you also come to hear him?'

Pierre made an evasive gesture. Monseigneur Martha, Bishop of Persepolis and all powerful at the archiepiscopal palace, since, like the genial propagandist he was, he had been devoting himself to increasing the subscriptions for the basilica of the Sacred Heart, had indeed supported Abbé Rose; in fact, it was by his influence that the Abbé had been kept in Paris, and placed once more at St. Pierre de Montmartre.

'I don't know if I shall be able to hear the address,' said Pierre, 'but in any case I will go there to meet you.'

The north wind was blowing, and the gloomy cold penetrated both of them on that deserted summit amidst the fog which changed the vast city into a misty ocean. However, some footsteps were heard, and Abbé Rose, again mistrustful, saw a man go by, a tall and sturdy man, who wore clogs and was bareheaded, showing his thick and closely cut white hair. 'Is not that your brother?' asked the old priest.

Pierre had not stirred. 'Yes, it is my brother Guillaume,' he quietly responded. 'I have found him again since I have been coming occasionally to the Sacred Heart. He owns a house close by, where he has been living for more than twenty years, I think. When we meet we shake hands, but I have never even been to his house. Oh! all is quite dead between us; we have nothing more in common, we are parted by worlds.'

Abbé Rose's tender smile again appeared, and he waved his hand as if to say that one must never despair of love. Guillaume Froment, a savant of lofty intelligence, a chemist

who lived apart from others, like one who rebelled against
the social system, was now a parishioner of the Abbé's, and
when the latter passed the house where Guillaume lived with
his three sons—a house all alive with work—he must often
have dreamt of leading him back to God.

'But, my dear child,' he resumed, 'I am keeping you here
in this dark cold, and you are not warm. Go and say your
mass. Till this evening, at the Madeleine.' Then, in
entreating fashion, after again making sure that none could
hear them, he added, still with the air of a child at fault:
'And not a word to anybody about my little commission—it
would again be said that I don't know how to conduct
myself.'

Pierre watched the old priest as he went off towards the
Rue Cartot, where he lived on a damp ground-floor, enlivened
by a strip of garden. The veil of disaster, which was submerging Paris, now seemed to grow thicker under the gusts
of the icy north wind. And at last Pierre entered the
basilica, his heart upset, overflowing with the bitterness
stirred up by the recollection of Abbé Rose's story—that
bankruptcy of charity, the frightful irony of a holy man
punished for bestowing alms, and hiding himself that he
might still continue to bestow them. Nothing could calm
the smart of the wound reopened in Pierre's heart—neither
the warm peacefulness into which he entered, nor the silent
solemnity of the broad, deep fabric, whose new stonework was
quite bare, without a single painting or any kind of decoration;
the nave being still half-barred by the scaffoldings which
blocked up the unfinished dome. At that early hour the
masses of entreaty had already been said at several altars,
under the grey light falling from the high and narrow
windows, and the tapers of entreaty were burning in the
depths of the apse. So Pierre made haste to go to the
sacristy, there to assume his vestments in order that he might
say his mass in the chapel of St. Vincent de Paul.

But the floodgates of memory had been opened, and his
only thoughts were for his distress whilst in mechanical
fashion he performed the rites and made the customary
gestures. Since his return from Rome three years previously
he had been living in the very worst anguish that can fall on
man. At the outset, in order to recover his lost faith, he had
essayed a first experiment: he had gone to Lourdes, there to
seek the innocent belief of the child who kneels and prays,

the primitive faith of young nations bending beneath the terror born of ignorance; but he had rebelled yet more than ever in presence of what he had witnessed at Lourdes: that glorification of the absurd, that collapse of common-sense; and was convinced that salvation, the peace of men and nations nowadays, could not lie in such puerile relinquishment of reason. And afterwards, again yielding to the need of loving whilst yet allowing reason, so hard to satisfy, her share in his intellect, he had staked his final peace on a second experiment, and had gone to Rome to see if Catholicism could there be renewed, could revert to the spirit of primitive Christianity and become the religion of the democracy, the faith which the modern world, upheaving and in danger of death, was awaiting in order to calm down and live. And he had found there naught but ruins, the rotted trunk of a tree that could never put forth another springtide; and he had heard there naught but the supreme rending of the old social edifice, near to its fall. Then it was that, relapsing into boundless doubt, total negation, he had been recalled to Paris by Abbé Rose in the name of their poor, and had returned thither that he might forget and immolate himself and believe in them—the poor—since they and their frightful sufferings alone remained certain. And then it was, too, that for three years he had come in contact with that collapse, that very bankruptcy of goodness itself: charity a derision, charity useless and flouted.

Those three years had been lived by Pierre amidst ever-growing torments, in which his whole being had ended by sinking. His faith was for ever dead; dead, too, even his hope of utilising the faith of the multitudes for the general salvation. He denied everything, he anticipated nothing but the final, inevitable catastrophe: revolt, massacre and conflagration, which would sweep away a guilty and condemned world. Unbelieving priest that he was, yet watching over the faith of others, honestly, chastely discharging his duties, full of haughty sadness at the thought that he had been unable to renounce his mind as he had renounced his flesh and his dream of being a saviour of the nations, he withal remained erect, full of fierce yet solitary grandeur. And this despairing, denying priest, who had dived to the bottom of nothingness, retained such a lofty and grave demeanour, perfumed by such pure kindness, that in his parish of Neuilly he had acquired the reputation of being a young saint, one beloved by Providence, whose prayers wrought miracles. He was but a personification of the rules of the Church ; of the priest he retained only the gestures ; he was like an empty sepulchre in which not even the ashes of hope remained ; yet grief-stricken, weeping women worshipped him and kissed his cassock ; and it was a tortured mother whose infant was in danger of death, who had implored him to come and ask that infant's cure of Jesus, certain as she felt that Jesus would grant her the boon in that sanctuary of Montmartre, where blazed the prodigy of His heart, all burning with love.

Clad in his vestments, Pierre had reached the Chapel of St. Vincent de Paul. He there ascended the altar-step and began the mass ; and when he turned round with hands spread out to bless the worshippers he showed his hollow cheeks, his gentle mouth contracted by bitterness, his loving eyes darkened by suffering. He was no longer the young priest whose countenance had glowed with tender fever on the road to Lourdes, whose face had been illumined by apostolic fervour when he started for Rome. The two hereditary influences which were ever at strife within him—that of his father to whom he owed his impregnable, towering brow, that of his mother who had given him his love-thirsting lips—were still waging war, the whole human battle of sentiment and reason, in that now ravaged face of his, whither in moments of forgetfulness ascended all the chaos of internal suffering. The lips still confessed that unquenched thirst for love, self-bestowal and life, which he well thought he could never more content, whilst the solid brow, the citadel which made him suffer, obstinately refused to capitulate, whatever might be the assaults of error. But he stiffened himself, hid the horror of the void in which he struggled, and showed himself superb, making each gesture, repeating each word in sovereign fashion. And gazing at him through her tears, the mother who was there among the few kneeling women, the mother who awaited a supreme intercession from him, who thought him in communion with Jesus for the salvation of her child, beheld him radiant with angelic beauty like some messenger of the Divine grace.

When, after the offertory, Pierre uncovered the chalice he felt contempt for himself. The shock had been too great, and he thought of those things in spite of all. What puerility there had been in his two experiments at Lourdes and Rome, the *naïveté* of a poor distracted being, consumed by a desire to love and believe. To have imagined that present-day science would in his person accommodate itself to the faith of the year One Thousand, and in particular to have foolishly believed that he, petty priest that he was, would be able to indoctrinate the Pope and prevail on him to become a saint and change the face of the world! It all filled him with shame ; how people must have laughed at him! Then, too, his idea of a schism made him blush. He again beheld himself at Rome, dreaming of writing a book by which he would violently sever himself from Catholicism to preach the new religion of the democracies, the purified, human and living Gospel. But what ridiculous folly! A schism? He had known in Paris an abbé of great heart and mind who had attempted to bring about that famous, predicted, awaited schism. Ah! the poor man, the sad, the ludicrous labour in the midst of universal incredulity, the icy indifference of some, the mockery and the reviling of others! If Luther were to come to France in our days he would end, forgotten and dying of hunger, on a Batignolles fifth-floor. A schism cannot succeed among a people that no longer believes, that has ceased to take all interest in the Church, and set its hope elsewhere. And it was all Catholicism, in fact all Christianity, that would be swept away, for, apart from certain moral maxims, the Gospel no longer supplied a possible code for society. And this conviction increased Pierre's torment on the days when his cassock weighed more heavily on his shoulders, when he ended by feeling contempt for himself at thus celebrating the Divine mystery of the mass, which for him had become but the formula of a dead religion.

Having half-filled the chalice with wine from the vase, Pierre washed his hands, and again perceived the mother with her face of ardent entreaty. Then he thought it was for her that, with the charitable leanings of a vow-bound man, he had remained a priest, a priest without belief, feeding the belief of others with the bread of illusion. But this heroic conduct, the haughty spirit of duty in which he imprisoned himself, was not practised by him without growing anguish. Did not elementary probity require that he should cast aside the cassock and return into the midst of men? At certain times the falsity of his position filled him with disgust for his useless heroism; and he asked himself if it were not cowardly and dangerous to leave the masses in superstition.

Certainly the theory of a just and vigilant Providence, of a future paradise where all the sufferings of the world would receive compensation, had long seemed necessary to the wretchedness of mankind ; but what a trap lay in it, what a pretext for the tyrannical grinding down of nations ; and how far more virile it would be to undeceive the nations, however brutally, and give them courage to live the real life, even if it were in tears. If they were already turning aside from Christianity, was not this because they needed a more human ideal, a religion of health and joy which should not be a religion of death ? On the day when the idea of charity should crumble, Christianity would crumble also, for it was built upon the idea of Divine charity correcting the injustice of fate, and offering future rewards to those who might suffer in this life. And it was crumbling ; for the poor no longer believed in it, but grew angry at the thought of that deceptive paradise, with the promise of which their patience had been beguiled so long, and demanded that their share of happiness should not always be put off until the morrow of death. A cry for justice arose from every lip, for justice upon this earth, justice for those who hunger and thirst, whom alms are weary of relieving after eighteen hundred years of Gospel teaching, and who still and ever lack bread to eat.

When Pierre, with his elbows on the altar, had emptied the chalice after breaking the sacred wafer, he felt himself sinking into yet greater distress. And so a third experiment was beginning for him, the supreme battle of justice against charity, in which his heart and his mind would struggle together in that great Paris, so full of terrible, unknown things. The need for the divine still battled within him against domineering intelligence. How among the masses would one ever be able to content the thirst for the mysterious ? Leaving the *élite* on one side, would science suffice to pacify desire, lull suffering, and satisfy the dream ? And what would become of himself in the bankruptcy of that same charity, which for three years had alone kept him erect by occupying his every hour, and giving him the illusion of self-devotion, of being useful to others ? It seemed, all at once, as if the ground sank beneath him, and he heard nothing save the cry of the masses, silent so long, but now demanding justice, growling and threatening to take their share, which was withheld from them by force and ruse. Nothing more, it seemed, could delay the inevitable catastrophe, the fratricidal class warfare that would sweep away the olden world, which was condemned to disappear beneath the mountain of its crimes. Every hour with frightful sadness he expected the collapse, Paris steeped in blood, Paris in flames. And his horror of all violence froze him; he knew not where to seek the new belief, which might dissipate the peril. Fully conscious though he was that the social and religious problems are but one, and are alone in question in the dreadful daily labour of Paris, he was too deeply troubled himself, too far removed from ordinary things by his position as a priest, and too sorely rent by doubt and powerlessness, to tell as yet where might be truth, and health, and life. Ah! to be healthy and to live, to content at last both heart and reason in peace, in the certain, simply honest labour which man has come to accomplish upon this earth!

The mass was finished, and Pierre descended from the altar, when the weeping mother, near whom he passed, caught hold of a corner of the chasuble with her trembling hands, and kissed it with wild fervour, as one may kiss some relic of a saint from whom one expects salvation. She thanked him for the miracle which he must have accomplished, certain as she felt that she would find her child cured. And he was deeply stirred by that love, that ardent faith of hers, in spite of the sudden and yet keener distress which he felt at being in no wise the sovereign minister that she thought him, the minister able to obtain a respite from Death. But he dismissed her consoled and strengthened, and it was with an ardent prayer that he entreated the unknown but conscious Power to succour the poor creature. Then, when he had divested himself in the sacristy, and found himself again out of doors before the basilica, lashed by the keen wintry wind, a mortal shiver came upon him, and froze him, while through the mist he looked to see if a whirlwind of anger and justice had not swept Paris away: that catastrophe which must some day destroy it, leaving only the pestilential quagmire of its ruins under the leaden heavens.

Pierre wished to fulfil Abbé Rose's commission immediately. He followed the Rue des Norvins, on the crest of Montmartre; and, reaching the Rue des Saules, descended by its steep slope, between mossy walls, to the other side of Paris. The three francs which he was holding in his cassock pocket filled him at once with gentle emotion and covert anger

against the futility of charity. But as he gradually descended
by the sharp declivities and interminable storeys of steps,
the mournful nooks of misery which he espied took possession
of him, and infinite pity wrung his heart. A whole new
district was here being built alongside the broad thoroughfares
opened since the great works of the Sacred Heart had begun.
Lofty middle-class houses were already rising among ripped-up
gardens and plots of vacant land, still edged with palings.
And these houses with their substantial frontages, all new
and white, lent a yet more sombre and leprous aspect to such
of the old shaky buildings as remained, the low pothouses
with blood-coloured walls, the *cités* of workmen's dwellings,
those abodes of suffering with black, soiled buildings, in which
human cattle were piled. Under the low-hanging sky that
day the pavement, dented by heavily laden carts, was covered
with mud ; the thaw soaked the walls with an icy dampness,
whilst all the filth and destitution brought terrible sadness to
the heart.

After going as far as the Rue Marcadet Pierre retraced his
steps ; and in the Rue des Saules, certain that he was not
mistaken, he entered the courtyard of a kind of barracks or
hospital, encompassed by three irregular buildings. This
court was a quagmire, where filth must have accumulated
during the two months of terrible frost ; and now all was melting,
and an abominable stench arose. The buildings were half
falling, the gaping vestibules looked like cellar holes, strips
of paper streaked the cracked and filthy window-panes, and
vile rags hung about like flags of death. Inside a shanty
which served as the doorkeeper's abode Pierre only saw an
infirm man rolled up in a tattered strip of what had once
been a horse-cloth.

'You have an old workman named Laveuve here,' said
the priest. ' Which staircase is it, which floor ? '

The man did not answer, but opened his anxious eyes,
like a scared idiot. The doorkeeper, no doubt, was in the
neighbourhood. For a moment the priest waited ; then,
seeing a little girl on the other side of the courtyard, he
risked himself, crossed the quagmire on tiptoe, and asked :
' Do you know an old workman named Laveuve in the house,
my child ? '

The little girl, who only had a ragged gown of pink cotton
stuff about her meagre figure, stood there shivering, her
hands covered with chilblains. She raised her delicate face,

which looked pretty though nipped by the cold : ' Laveuve,' said she, ' no, don't know, don't know.' And with the unconscious gesture of a beggar child she put out one of her poor, numbed and disfigured hands. Then, when the priest had given her a little bit of silver, she began to prance through the mud like a joyful goat, singing the while in a shrill voice : ' Don't know, don't know.'

Pierre decided to follow her. She vanished into one of the gaping vestibules, and, in her rear, he climbed a dark and fetid staircase, whose steps were half-broken and so slippery, on account of the vegetable parings strewn over them, that he had to avail himself of the greasy rope by which the inmates hoisted themselves upwards. But every door was closed ; he vainly knocked at several of them, and only elicited, at the last, a stifled growl, as though some despairing animal were confined within. Returning to the yard he hesitated, then made his way to another staircase, where he was deafened by piercing cries, as of a child who is being butchered. He climbed on hearing this noise, and at last found himself in front of an open room where an infant, who had been left alone, tied in his little chair, in order that he might not fall, was howling without drawing breath. Then Pierre went down again, upset, frozen by the sight of so much destitution and abandonment.

But a woman was coming in, carrying three potatoes in her apron, and on being questioned by him she gazed distrustfully at his cassock. ' Laveuve, Laveuve, I can't say,' she replied. ' If the doorkeeper were there she might be able to tell you. There are five staircases, you see, and we don't all know each other. Besides, there are so many changes. Still, try over there ; at the far end.'

The staircase at the back of the yard was yet more abominable than the others, its steps warped, its walls slimy, as if soaked with the sweat of anguish. At each successive floor the drain-sinks exhaled a pestilential stench, whilst from every lodging came moans, or a noise of quarrelling, or some frightful sign of misery. A door swung open, and a man appeared dragging a woman by the hair, whilst three youngsters sobbed aloud. On the next floor, Pierre caught a glimpse of a room where a young girl in her teens, racked by coughing, was hastily carrying an infant to and fro to quiet it, in despair that all the milk of her breast should be exhausted. Then, in an adjoining lodging, came the poignant spectacle of three

beings, half clad in shreds, apparently sexless and ageless,
who, amidst the dire bareness of their room, were gluttonously
eating from the same earthen pan some pottage which even
dogs would have refused. They barely raised their heads to
growl, and did not answer Pierre's questions.

He was about to go down again, when right atop of the
stairs, at the entry of a passage, it occurred to him to make a
last try by knocking at a door. It was opened by a woman
whose uncombed hair was already getting grey, though she
could not be more than forty ; while her pale lips, and dim
eyes set in a yellow countenance, expressed utter lassitude, the
shrinking, the constant dread of one whom wretchedness has
pitilessly assailed. The sight of Pierre's cassock disturbed her,
and she stammered anxiously : ' Come in, come in, Monsieur
l'Abbé.'

However, a man whom Pierre had not at first seen—a
workman also of some forty years, tall, thin, and bald, with
scanty moustache and beard of a washed-out, reddish hue—
made an angry gesture, a threat as it were, to turn the
priest out of doors. But he calmed himself, sat down near a
rickety table, and pretended to turn his back. And as there
was also a child present—a fair-haired girl, eleven or twelve
years old, with a long and gentle face and that intelligent and
somewhat aged expression which great misery imparts to
children—he called her to him and held her between his
knees, doubtless to keep her away from the man in the
cassock.

Pierre—whose heart was oppressed by his reception, and
who realised the utter destitution of this family by the sight
of the bare, fireless room and the distressed mournfulness of
its three inmates—decided all the same to repeat his question : ' Madame, do you know an old workman named
Laveuve in the house ? '

The woman—who now trembled at having admitted him,
since it seemed to displease her man—timidly tried to arrange
matters. ' Laveuve, Laveuve ; no, I don't. But Salvat, you
hear ? Do you know a Laveuve here ? '

Salvat merely shrugged his shoulders ; but the little girl
could not keep her tongue still : ' I say, mamma Théodore, it's
p'r'aps the Philosopher.'

' A former house-painter,' continued Pierre, ' an old man
who is ill and past work.'

Madame Théodore was at once enlightened. ' In that

case it's him, it's him. We call him the Philosopher, a nick-
name folks have given him in the neighbourhood. But there's
nothing to prevent his real name from being Laveuve.'

With one of his fists raised towards the ceiling, Salvat
seemed to be protesting against the abomination of a world
and a Providence that allowed old toilers to die of hunger
just like broken-down beasts. However, he did not speak,
but relapsed into the savage, heavy silence, the bitter medita-
tion in which he had been plunged when the priest arrived.
He was a journeyman engineer, and gazed obstinately at the
table where lay his little leather tool-bag, bulging with something it contained—something, perhaps, which he had to
take back to a workshop. He might have been thinking of a
long, enforced spell of idleness, of a vain search for any kind
of work during the two previous months of that terrible
winter. Or perhaps it was the coming bloody reprisals of
the starvelings that occupied the fiery reverie which set his
large, strange, vague blue eyes aglow. All at once he noticed
that his daughter had taken up the tool-bag and was trying
to open it to see what it might contain. At this he quivered
and at last spoke, his voice kindly, yet bitter with sudden
emotion, which made him turn pale. 'Céline, you must
leave that alone. I forbade you to touch my tools,' said he;
then, taking the bag, he deposited it with great precaution
against the wall behind him.

'And so, madame,' asked Pierre, 'this man Laveuve lives
on this floor?'

Madame Théodore directed a timid, questioning glance at
Salvat. She was not in favour of hustling priests when they
took the trouble to call, for at times there was a little money
to be got from them. And when she realised that Salvat, who
had once more relapsed into his black reverie, left her free to
act as she pleased, she at once tendered her services. 'If
Monsieur l'Abbé is agreeable, I will conduct him. It's just at
the end of the passage. But one must know the way, for there
are still some steps to climb.'

Céline, finding a pastime in this visit, escaped from her
father's knees and likewise accompanied the priest. And
Salvat remained alone in that den of poverty and suffering,
injustice and anger, without a fire, without bread, haunted by
his burning dream, his eyes again fixed upon his bag, as if
there, among his tools, he possessed the wherewithal to heal
the ailing world.

It indeed proved necessary to climb a few more steps; and then following Madame Théodore and Céline, Pierre found himself in a kind of narrow garret under the roof, a loft a few yards square, where one could not stand erect. There was no window, only a skylight, and as the snow still covered it one had to leave the door wide open in order that one might see. And the thaw was entering the place, the melting snow was falling drop by drop, and coursing over the tiled floor. After long weeks of intense cold, dark dampness poured quivering over all. And there, lacking even a chair, even a plank, Laveuve lay in a corner on a little pile of filthy rags spread upon the bare tiles; he looked like some animal dying on a dung-heap.

'There!' said Céline in her sing-song voice, 'there he is, that's the Philosopher!'

Madame Théodore had bent down to ascertain if he still lived. 'Yes, he breathes; he's sleeping, I think. Oh! if he only had something to eat every day he would be well enough. But what would you have? He has nobody left him, and when one gets to seventy the best is to throw oneself into the river. In the house-painting line it often happens that a man has to give up working on ladders and scaffoldings at fifty. He at first found some work to do on the ground level. Then he was lucky enough to get a job as night watchman. But that's over; he's been turned away from everywhere, and, for two months now he's been lying in this nook waiting to die. The landlord hasn't dared to fling him into the street as yet, though not for want of any inclination that way. We others sometimes bring him a little wine and a crust of course; but when one has nothing oneself how can one give to others?'

Pierre, terrified, gazed at that frightful remnant of humanity, that remnant into which fifty years of toil, misery and social injustice had turned a man. And he ended by distinguishing Laveuve's white, worn, sunken, deformed head. Here, on a human face, appeared all the ruin following upon hopeless labour. Laveuve's unkempt beard straggled over his features, suggesting an old horse that is no longer cropped; his toothless jaws were quite askew, his eyes were vitreous, and his nose seemed to plunge into his mouth. But above all else one noticed his resemblance to some beast of burden, deformed by hard toil, lamed, worn to death, and now only good for the knackers.

'Ah! the poor fellow,' muttered the shuddering priest,

'And he is left to die of hunger, all alone, without any succour? And not a hospital, not an asylum has given him shelter?'

'Well,' resumed Madame Théodore in her sad yet resigned voice, 'the hospitals are built for the sick, and he isn't sick, he's simply finishing off, with his strength at an end. Besides, he isn't always easy to deal with. People came again only lately to put him in an asylum, but he won't be shut up. And he speaks coarsely to those who question him, not to mention that he has the reputation of liking drink and talking badly about the gentlefolks. But, thank Heaven, he will now soon be delivered.'

Pierre had leant forward on seeing Laveuve's eyes open, and he spoke to him tenderly, telling him that he had come from a friend with a little money to enable him to buy what he might most pressingly require. At first, on seeing Pierre's cassock, the old man growled some coarse words; but, despite his extreme feebleness, he still retained the pert chaffing spirit of the Parisian artisan: 'Well, then, I'll willingly drink a drop,' he said distinctly, 'and have a bit of bread with it, if there's the needful; for I've lost taste of both for a couple of days past.'

Céline offered her services, and Madame Théodore sent her to fetch a loaf and a quart of wine with Abbé Rose's money. And in the interval she told Pierre how Laveuve was at one moment to have entered the Asylum of the Invalids of Labour, a charitable enterprise whose lady patronesses were presided over by Baroness Duvillard. However, the usual regulation inquiries had doubtless led to such an unfavourable report that matters had gone no further.

'Baroness Duvillard! But I know her, and will go to see her to-day!' exclaimed Pierre, whose heart was bleeding. 'It is impossible for a man to be left in such circumstances any longer.'

Then, as Céline came back with the loaf and the wine, the three of them tried to make Laveuve more comfortable, raised him on his heap of rags, gave him to eat and to drink, and afterwards left the remainder of the wine and the loaf—a large four-pound loaf—near him, recommending him to wait awhile before he finished the bread, as otherwise he might stifle.

'Monsieur l'Abbé ought to give me his address in case I

should have any news to send him,' said Madame Théodore
when she again found herself at her door.

Pierre had no card with him, and so all three went into
the room. But Salvat was no longer alone there. He stood
talking in a low voice very quickly, and almost mouth to
mouth, with a young fellow of twenty. The latter, who was
slim and dark, with a sprouting beard and hair cut in brush
fashion, had bright eyes, a straight nose, and thin lips set in
a pale and slightly freckled face, betokening great intelligence.
With stern and stubborn brow, he stood shivering in his well-
worn jacket.

'Monsieur l'Abbé wants to leave me his address for the
Philosopher's affair,' gently explained Madame Théodore,
annoyed to find another there with Salvat.

The two men had glanced at the priest and then looked at
each other, each with terrible mien. And they suddenly
ceased speaking in the bitter cold which fell from the ceiling.
Then, again with infinite precaution, Salvat went to take his
tool-bag from alongside the wall.

'So you are going down, you are again going to look for
work?' asked Madame Théodore.

He did not answer, but merely made an angry gesture, as
if to say that he would no longer have anything to do with
work, since work for so long a time had not cared to have
anything to do with him.

'All the same,' resumed the woman, 'try to bring something back with you, for you know there's nothing. At what
time will you be back?'

With another gesture he seemed to answer that he would
come back when he could, perhaps never. And tears rising,
despite all his efforts, to his vague, blue, glowing eyes, he
caught hold of his daughter Céline, kissed her violently,
distractedly, and then went off, with his bag under his arm,
followed by his young companion.

'Céline,' resumed Madame Théodore, 'give Monsieur
l'Abbé your pencil; and, see, Monsieur, seat yourself here, it
will be better for writing.'

When Pierre had installed himself at the table, on the
chair previously occupied by Salvat, she went on talking,
seeking to excuse her man for his scanty politeness: 'He
hasn't a bad heart, but he's had so many worries in life that
he has become a bit cracked. It's like that young man whom
you just saw here, Monsieur Victor Mathis. There's another

for you who isn't happy, a young man who was well brought up, who has a lot of learning, and whose mother, a widow, has only just got the wherewithal to buy bread. So one can understand it, can't one ? It all upsets their heads, and they talk of blowing up everybody. For my part, those are not my notions, but I forgive them, oh ! willingly enough.'

Perturbed, yet interested by all the vague mystery and horror which he could divine around him, Pierre made no haste to write his address, but lingered listening, as if inviting confidence.

'If you only knew, Monsieur l'Abbé, that poor Salvat was a forsaken child, without father or mother, and had to scour the roads and try every trade at first to get a living. Then afterwards he became a mechanician, and a very good workman, I assure you, very skilful and very painstaking. But he already had those ideas of his, and quarrelled with people, and tried to bring his mates over to his views; and so he was unable to stay anywhere. At last, when he was thirty, he was stupid enough to go to America with an inventor, who traded on him to such a point that after six years of it he came back ill and penniless. I must tell you that he had married my younger sister, Léonie, and that she died before he went to America, leaving him little Céline, who was only a year old. I myself was then living with my husband, Théodore Labitte, a mason; and it's not to brag that I say it, but however much I wore out my eyes with needlework he used to beat me till he left me half-dead on the floor. But he ended by deserting me and going off with a young woman of twenty, which, after all, caused me more pleasure than grief. And naturally when Salvat came back he sought me out, and found me alone with his little Céline, whom he had left in my charge when he went away, and who called me mamma. And we've all three been living together since then——.'

She became somewhat embarrassed, and then, as if to show that she did not altogether lack some respectable family connections, she went on to say : 'For my part I've had no luck; but I've another sister, Hortense, who's married to a clerk, Monsieur Chrétiennot, and lives in a pretty lodging on the Boulevard Rochechouart. There were three of us born of my father's second marriage, Hortense, who's the youngest, Léonie, who's dead, and myself, Pauline, the eldest. And of my father's first marriage I've still a brother, Eugène

Toussaint, who is ten years older than me and is an engineer
like Salvat, and has been working ever since the war in the
same establishment, the Grandidier factory, only a hundred
steps away in the Rue Marcadet. The misfortune is that he
had a stroke lately. As for me, my eyes are done for; I
ruined them by working ten hours a day at fine needlework.
And now I can no longer even try to mend anything without
my eyes filling with water till I can't see at all. I've tried to
find charwoman's work, but I can't get any; bad luck always
follows us. And so we are in need of everything; we've
nothing but black misery, two or three days sometimes going
by without a bite, so that it's like the chance life of a dog
that feeds on what it can find. And with these last two
months of bitter cold to freeze us, it's sometimes made us
think that one morning we should never wake up again.
But what would you have? I've never been happy. I was
beaten to begin with, and now I'm done for, left in a corner,
living on, I really don't know why.'

Her voice had begun to tremble, her red eyes moistened,
and Pierre could realise that she thus wept through life, a
good enough woman, but one who had no will, and was already
blotted out, so to say, from existence.

'Oh! I don't complain of Salvat,' she went on. 'He's a
good fellow; he only dreams of everybody's happiness, and he
doesn't drink, and he works when he can. Only it's certain
that he'd work more if he didn't busy himself with politics.
One can't discuss things with comrades, and go to public
meetings, and be at the workshop at the same time. In that
he's at fault, that's evident. But all the same he has good
reason to complain, for one can't imagine such misfortunes
as have pursued him. Everything has fallen on him, everything has beaten him down. Why, a saint even would have
gone mad, so that one can understand that a poor beggar who
has never had any luck should get quite wild. For the last
two months he has only met one good heart, a learned gentleman who lives up yonder on the height, Monsieur Guillaume
Froment, who has given him a little work, just something to
enable us to have some soup now and then.'

Much surprised by this mention of his brother, Pierre
wished to ask certain questions; but a singular feeling of
uneasiness, in which fear and discretion mingled, checked
his tongue. He looked at Céline, who stood before him,
listening in silence with her grave, delicate air; and Madame

Théodore, seeing him smile at the child, indulged in a final remark: 'It's just the thought of that child,' said she, 'that throws Salvat out of his wits. He adores her, and he'd kill everybody, if he could, when he sees her go supperless to bed. She's such a good girl; she was learning so nicely at the Communal School! But now she hasn't even a shift to go there in.'

Pierre, who had at last written his address, slipped a five-franc piece into the little girl's hand, and, desirous as he was of curtailing any thanks, he hastily said: 'You will know now where to find me if you need me for Laveuve. But I'm going to busy myself about him this very afternoon, and I really hope that he will be fetched away this evening.'

Madame Théodore did not listen, but poured forth all possible blessings; whilst Céline, thunderstruck at seeing five francs in her hand, murmured: 'Oh! that poor papa, who has gone to hunt for money! Shall I run after him to tell him that we've got enough for to-day?'

Then the priest, who was already in the passage, heard the woman answer: 'Oh! he's far away if he's still walking. He'll p'r'aps come back right enough.'

However, as Pierre, with buzzing head and grief-stricken heart, hastily escaped out of that frightful house of suffering, he perceived to his astonishment Salvat and Victor Mathis standing together in a corner of the filthy courtyard, where the stench was so pestilential. They had come downstairs, there to continue their interrupted colloquy. And again they were talking in very low tones, and very quickly, mouth to mouth, absorbed in the violent thoughts which made their eyes flare. But they heard the priest's footsteps, recognised him, and suddenly becoming cold and calm, exchanged an energetic hand-shake without uttering another word. Victor went up towards Montmartre, whilst Salvat hesitated like a man who is consulting destiny. Then, as if trusting himself to stern chance, drawing up his thin figure, the figure of a weary, hungry toiler, he turned into the Rue Marcadet, and walked towards Paris, his tool-bag still under his arm.

For an instant Pierre felt a desire to run and call to him that his little girl wished him to go back again. But the same feeling of uneasiness as before came over the priest—a commingling of discretion and fear, a covert conviction that nothing could stay destiny. And he himself was no longer

calm, no longer experienced the icy, despairing distress of the
early morning. On finding himself again in the street, amidst
the quivering fog, he felt the fever, the glow of charity which
the sight of such frightful wretchedness had ignited, once
more within him. No, no! such suffering was too much; he
wished to struggle still, to save Laveuve and restore a little
joy to all those poor folk. The new experiment presented
itself with that city of Paris which he had seen shrouded as
with ashes, so mysterious and so perturbing beneath the
threat of inevitable justice. And he dreamt of a huge sun
bringing health and fruitfulness, that would make of the
huge city the fertile field where would sprout the better world
of to-morrow.

II

WEALTH AND WORLDLINESS

THAT same morning, as was the case nearly every day, some
intimates were expected to *déjeuner* at the Duvillards', a few
friends who more or less invited themselves. And on that
chilly day, all thaw and fog, the regal mansion in the Rue
Godot-de-Mauroy, near the Boulevard de la Madeleine, bloomed
with the rarest flowers, for flowers were the greatest passion
of the Baroness, who transformed the lofty, sumptuous rooms,
littered with marvels, into warm and odoriferous conservatories,
whither the gloomy, livid light of Paris penetrated caressingly
with infinite softness.

The great reception rooms were on the ground floor,
looking on to the spacious courtyard, and preceded by a little
winter garden, which served as a vestibule where two footmen
in liveries of dark green and gold were invariably on duty.
A famous gallery of paintings, valued at millions of francs,
occupied the whole of the northern side of the house. And
the grand staircase, of a sumptuousness which also was
famous, conducted to the apartments usually occupied by the
family—a large red drawing-room, a small blue and silver
drawing-room, a study whose walls were hung with old
stamped leather, and a dining-room in pale green with English
furniture, not to mention the various bedchambers and
dressing-rooms. Built in the time of Louis XIV., the mansion
retained an aspect of noble grandeur, subordinated to the
epicurean tastes of the triumphant *bourgeoisie*, which for a

century now had reigned by virtue of the omnipotence of money.

Noon had not yet struck, and Baron Duvillard, contrary to custom, found himself the first in the little blue and silver *salon*. He was a man of sixty, tall and sturdy, with a large nose, full cheeks, broad, fleshy lips, and wolfish teeth, which had remained very fine. He had, however, become bald at an early age, and dyed the little hair that was left him. Moreover, since his beard had turned white he had kept his face clean-shaven. His grey eyes bespoke his audacity, and in his laugh there was a ring of conquest, while the whole of his face expressed the fact that this conquest was his own, that he wielded the sovereignty of an unscrupulous master, who used and abused the power stolen and retained by his caste.

He took a few steps, and then halted in front of a basket of wonderful orchids near the window. On the mantelpiece and table tufts of violets sent forth their perfume, and in the warm, deep silence which seemed to fall from the hangings, the Baron sat down and stretched himself in one of the large armchairs, upholstered in blue satin striped with silver. He had taken a newspaper from his pocket, and began to re-peruse an article it contained, whilst all around him the entire mansion proclaimed his immense fortune, his sovereign power, the whole history of the century which had made him the master. His grandfather, Jérome Duvillard, son of a petty advocate of Poitou, had come to Paris as a notary's clerk in 1788, when he was eighteen; and very keen, intelligent and hungry, he had gained the family's first three millions—at first in trafficking with the *émigrés'* estates when they were confiscated and sold as national property, and later, in contracting for supplies to the imperial army. His father, Grégoire Duvillard, born in 1805, and the real great man of the family—he who had first reigned in the Rue Godot-de-Mauroy, after King Louis Philippe had granted him the title of Baron—remained one of the recognised heroes of modern finance by reason of the scandalous profits which he had made in every famous thieving speculation of the July Monarchy and the Second Empire, such as mines, railroads, and the Suez Canal. And he, the present Baron, Henri by name, and born in 1836, had only seriously gone into business on Baron Grégoire's death soon after the Franco-German War. However, he had done so with such a rageful appetite, that in a quarter of a century he had again doubled the family fortune. He rotted and

devoured everything that he touched; and at the same time
he was the tempter personified—the man who bought all
consciences that were for sale — having fully understood
the new era and its tendencies in presence of the democracy, which in its turn had become hungry and impatient. Inferior though he was both to his father and his
grandfather, being a man of enjoyment, caring less for the
work of conquest than the division of the spoil, he nevertheless
remained a terrible fellow, a sleek triumpher, whose operations
were all certainties, who amassed millions at each stroke, and
treated with governments on a footing of equality, able as he
was to place, if not France, at least a ministry, in his pocket.
In one century and three generations royalty had become
embodied in him : a royalty already threatened, already
shaken by the tempest close ahead. And at times his figure
grew and expanded till it became, as it were, an incarnation
of the whole *bourgeoisie*—that *bourgeoisie* which at the
division of the spoils in 1789 appropriated everything, and has
since fattened on everything at the expense of the masses,
and refuses to restore anything whatever.

The article which the Baron was re-perusing in a half-
penny newspaper interested him. 'La Voix du Peuple' was
a noisy sheet which, under the pretence of defending outraged
justice and morality, set a fresh scandal circulating every
morning in the hope of thereby increasing its sales. And
that day, in big type on its front page, this sub-title was
displayed : 'The Affair of the African Railways. Five Millions
spent in Bribes : Two Ministers Bought, Thirty Deputies and
Senators Compromised.' Then in an article of odious violence
the paper's editor, the famous Sagnier, announced that he
possessed and intended to publish the list of the thirty-two
members of Parliament, whose support Baron Duvillard had
purchased at the time when the Chambers had voted the bill
for the African Railway Lines. Quite a romantic story was
mingled with all this—the adventures of a certain Hunter,
whom the Baron had employed as his go-between, and who
had now fled. The Baron, however, re-perused each sentence
and weighed each word of the article very calmly ; and
although he was alone he shrugged his shoulders and spoke
aloud with the tranquil assurance of a man whose responsibility is covered and who is, moreover, too powerful to be
molested.

'The idiot!' he said; ' he knows even less than he pretends.'

Just then, however, a first guest arrived, a man of barely four-and-thirty, elegantly dressed, dark and good looking, with a delicately shaped nose, and curly hair and beard. As a rule, too, he had laughing eyes, and something giddy, flighty, bird-like in his demeanour; but that morning he seemed nervous, anxious even, and smiled in a scared way.

'Ah! it's you, Duthil,' said the Baron, rising. 'Have you read this?' And he showed the new comer the 'Voix du Peuple,' which he was folding up to replace it in his pocket.

'Why, yes, I've read it. It's amazing. How can Sagnier have got hold of the list of names? Has there been some traitor?'

The Baron looked at his companion quietly, amused by his secret anguish. Duthil, the son of a notary of Angoulême, almost poor and very honest, had been sent to Paris as deputy for that town whilst yet very young, thanks to the high reputation of his father; and he there led a life of pleasure and idleness, even as he had formerly done when a student. However, his pleasant bachelor's quarters in the Rue de Suresnes, and his success as a handsome man in the whirl of women among whom he lived, cost him no little money; and gaily enough, devoid as he was of any moral sense, he had already glided into all sorts of compromising and lowering actions, like a light-headed, superior man, a charming, thoughtless fellow, who attached no importance whatever to such trifles.

'Bah!' said the Baron at last. 'Has Sagnier even got a list? I doubt it, for there was none; Hunter wasn't so foolish as to draw one up. And besides, it was merely an ordinary affair; nothing more was done than is always done in such matters of business.'

Duthil, who for the first time in his life had felt anxious, listened like one that needs to be reassured. 'Quite so; eh?' he exclaimed. 'That's what I thought. There isn't a cat to be whipped in the whole affair.'

He tried to laugh as usual, and no longer exactly knew how it was that he had received some ten thousand francs in connection with the matter—whether it were in the shape of a vague loan, or else under some pretext of publicity, puffery, or advertising, for Hunter had acted with extreme adroitness, so as to give no offence to the susceptibilities of even the least virginal consciences.

'No, there's not a cat to be whipped' repeated Duvillard, who decidedly seemed amused by the face which Duthil was pulling. 'And besides, my dear fellow, it's well known that cats always fall on their feet. But have you seen Silviane?'

'I have just left her. I found her in a great rage with you. She learnt this morning that her affair of the Comédie is off.'

A rush of anger suddenly reddened the Baron's face. He, who could scoff so calmly at the threat of the African Railways scandal, lost his balance and felt his blood boiling directly there was any question of Silviane, the last, imperious passion of his sixtieth year. 'What! off?' said he. 'But at the Fine Arts Office they gave me almost a positive promise only the day before yesterday.'

He referred to a stubborn caprice of Silviane d'Aulnay, who, although she had hitherto only reaped a success of beauty on the stage, obstinately sought to enter the Comédie Française and make her *début* there in the part of ' Pauline ' in Corneille's ' Polyeucte,' which part she had been studying desperately for several months past. Her idea seemed an insane one, and all Paris laughed at it ; but the young woman, with superb assurance, kept herself well to the front, and imperiously demanded the *rôle*, feeling sure that she would conquer.

'It was the minister! who wouldn't have it,' explained Duthil.

The Baron was choking. 'The minister! the minister! Ah! well, I will soon have that minister sent to the right-about.'

However he had to cease speaking, for at that moment Baroness Duvillard came into the little drawing-room. At forty-six years of age she was still very beautiful. Very fair and tall, having hitherto put on but little superfluous fat, and retaining perfect arms and shoulders, with speckless silky skin, it was only her face that was spoiling—colouring slightly with reddish blotches. And these blemishes were her torment, her hourly thought and worry. Her Jewish origin was revealed by her somewhat long and strangely charming face, with blue and softly voluptuous eyes. As indolent as an Oriental slave, disliking to have to move, walk, or even speak, she seemed intended for a harem life, especially as she was for ever tending her person. That day she was all in white, gowned in a white silk toilette of delicious and lustrous simplicity.

Duth complimented her, and kissed her hand with an enraptured air. 'Ah! madame, you set a little springtide in my heart. Paris is so black and muddy this morning.'

However, a second guest entered the room, a tall and handsome man of five or six and thirty; and the Baron, still disturbed by his passion, profited by this opportunity to make his escape. He carried Duthil away into his study, saying, 'Come here an instant, my dear fellow. I have a few more words to say to you about the affair in question. Monsieur de Quinsac will keep my wife company for a moment.'

The Baroness, as soon as she was alone with the new comer, who, like Duthil, had most respectfully kissed her hand, gave him a long, silent look, while her soft eyes filled with tears. Deep silence, tinged with some slight embarrassment, had fallen, but she ended by saying in a very low voice: 'How happy I am, Gérard, to find myself alone with you for a moment. For a month past I have not had that happiness.'

The circumstances in which Henri Duvillard had married the younger daughter of Justus Steinberger, the great Jew banker, formed quite a story, which was often recalled. The Steinbergers—after the fashion of the Rothschilds—were originally four brothers—Justus, residing in Paris, and the three others at Berlin, Vienna, and London, a circumstance which gave their secret association most formidable power in the financial markets of Europe. Justus, however, was the least wealthy of the four, and in Baron Grégoire Duvillard he had a redoubtable adversary, against whom he was compelled to struggle each time that any large prey was in question. And it was after a terrible encounter between the pair, after the eager sharing of the spoils, that the crafty idea had come to Justus of giving his younger daughter, Eve, in marriage, by way of *douceur*, to the Baron's son, Henri. So far the latter had only been known as an amiable fellow, fond of horses and club life; and no doubt Justus's idea was that, at the death of the redoubtable Baron, who was already condemned by his physicians, he would be able to lay his hands on the rival banking-house, particularly if he only had in front of him a son-in-law whom it was easy to conquer. As it happened, Henri had been mastered by a violent passion for Eve's blonde beauty, which was then dazzling. He wished to marry her, and his father, who knew him, consented, in reality greatly amused to think that Justus was making an execrably bad stroke of business. The enterprise became indeed disastrous for Justus when Henri succeeded his father, and the man of prey appeared from beneath the man of pleasure and carved himself his own huge share in exploiting the unbridled appetites of the middle-class democracy, which had at last secured possession of power. Not only did Eve fail to devour Henri, who in his turn had become Baron Duvillard, the all-powerful banker, more and more master of the market; but it was the Baron who devoured Eve, and this in less than four years' time. After she had borne him a daughter and a son in turn, he suddenly drew away from her, neglected her, as if she were a mere toy that he no longer cared for. She was at first both surprised and distressed by the change, especially on learning that he was resuming his bachelor's habits, and had set his fickle if ardent affections elsewhere. Then, however, without any kind of recrimination, any display of anger, or even any particular effort to regain her ascendency over him, she, on her side, imitated his example. She could not live without love, and assuredly she had only been born to be beautiful, to fascinate, and reap adoration. To the lover whom she chose when she was five-and-twenty she remained faithful for more than fifteen years, as faithful as she might have been to a husband; and when he died her grief was intense—it was like real widowhood. Six months later, however, having met Count Gérard de Quinsac, she had again been unable to resist her imperative need of adoration, and an intrigue had followed.

'Have you been ill, my dear Gérard?' she inquired, noticing the young man's embarrassment. 'Are you hiding some worry from me?'

She was ten years older than he was; and she clung desperately to this last passion of hers, revolting at the thought of growing old, and resolved upon every effort to keep the young man beside her.

'No, I am hiding nothing, I assure you,' replied the Count. 'But my mother has had much need of me recently.'

She continued looking at him, however, with anxious passion, finding him so tall and aristocratic of mien, with his regular features and dark hair, and moustaches which were always most carefully tended. He belonged to one of the oldest families of France, and resided on a ground floor in the Rue St. Dominique with his widowed mother, who had been ruined by her adventurously inclined husband,

and had at most an income of some fifteen thousand francs[1]
to live upon. Gérard, for his part, had never done anything.
Contenting himself with his one year of obligatory military
service, he had renounced the profession of arms in the same
way as he had renounced that of diplomacy, the only one that
offered him an opening of any dignity. He spent his days in
that busy idleness common to all young men who lead ' Paris
life.' And his mother, haughtily severe though she was,
seemed to excuse this, as if in her opinion a man of his birth
was bound by way of protest to keep apart from official life
under a Republic. However, she no doubt had more intimate,
more disturbing reasons for indulgence. She had nearly
lost him when he was only seven, through an attack of brain
fever. At eighteen he had complained of his heart, and the
doctors had recommended that he should be treated gently in
all respects. She knew, therefore, what a lie lurked behind his
proud demeanour, within his lofty figure, that haughty *façade*
of his race. He was but dust, ever threatened with illness
and collapse. In the depths of his seeming virility there was
merely girlish *abandon*; and he was simply a weak, good-
natured fellow, liable to every stumble. It was on the
occasion of a visit which he had paid with his mother to the
Asylum of the Invalids of Labour that he had first seen Eve,
whom he continued to meet; his mother, closing her eyes to
this culpable connection in a sphere of society which she
treated with contempt, in the same way as she had closed
them to so many other acts of folly, which she had forgiven
because she regarded them as the mere lapses of an ailing
child. Moreover, Eve had made a conquest of Madame de
Quinsac, who was very pious, by an action which had recently
amazed society. It had been suddenly learnt that she had
allowed Monseigneur Martha to convert her to the Roman
Catholic faith. This thing, which she had refused to do when
solicited by her lawful husband, she had since done in the hope
of ensuring herself a lover's eternal affection. And all Paris
was still stirred by the magnificence exhibited at the
Madeleine, on the occasion of the baptism of that Jewess of
five-and-forty, whose beauty and whose tears had upset every
heart.

Gérard, on his side, was still flattered by the deep and
touching tenderness shown to him; but weariness was coming,
and he had already sought to break off the connection by

[1] £600.

avoiding any further assignations. He well understood Eve's glances and her tears, and though he was moved at sight of them, he tried to excuse himself. ' I assure you,' said he, ' my mother has kept me so busy that I could not get away.' But she, without a word, still turned her tearful glance on him, and weak, like herself, in despair that he should have been left alone with her in this fashion, he yielded, unable to continue refusing. ' Well, then,' said he, ' this afternoon at four o'clock, Rue Matignon, if you are free.'

He had lowered his voice in speaking, but a slight rustle made him turn his head and start like one in fault. It was the Baroness's daughter Camille entering the room. She had heard nothing ; but by the smile which the others had exchanged, by the very quiver of the air, she understood everything—an assignation for that very day and at the very spot which she suspected. Some slight embarrassment followed, an exchange of anxious and evil glances.

Camille, at three-and-twenty, was a very dark young woman, short of stature and somewhat deformed, with her left shoulder higher than the right. There seemed to be nothing of her father or mother in her. Her case was one of those unforeseen accidents in family heredity which make people wonder whence they can arise. Her only pride lay in her beautiful black eyes and superb black hair, which, short as she was, would, said she, have sufficed to clothe her. But her nose was long, her face deviated to the left, and her chin was pointed. Her thin, witty and malicious lips bespoke all the rancour and perverse anger stored in the heart of this uncomely creature, whom the thought of her uncomeliness enraged. However, the one whom she most hated in the whole world was her own mother—that *amorosa* who was so little fitted to be a mother, who had never loved her, never paid attention to her, but had abandoned her to the care of servants from her very infancy. In this wise real hatred had grown up between the two women, mute and frigid on the one side, and active and passionate on the other. The daughter hated her mother because she found her beautiful, because she had not been created in the same image : beautiful with the beauty with which her mother crushed her. Day by day she suffered at being sought by none, at realising that the adoration of one and all still went to her mother. As she was amusing in her maliciousness, people listened to her and laughed ; however, the glances of all the men—even, and indeed especially, the younger ones—soon reverted to her triumphant mother, who seemingly defied old age. In part for this reason Camille, with ferocious determination, had decided that she would dispossess her mother of her last lover, Gérard, and marry him herself, conscious that such a loss would doubtless kill the Baroness. Thanks to her promised dowry of five millions of francs, the young woman did not lack suitors; but, little flattered by their advances, she was accustomed to say, with her malicious laugh: 'Oh! of course; why, for five millions they would take a wife from a madhouse.' However, she herself had really begun to love Gérard, who, good-natured as he was, evinced much kindness towards this suffering young woman whom nature had treated so harshly. It worried him to see her forsaken by everyone, and little by little he yielded to the grateful tenderness which she displayed towards him, happy, handsome man that he was, at being regarded as a demi-god and having such a slave. Indeed, in his attempt to quit the mother there was certainly a thought of allowing the daughter to marry him, which would be an agreeable ending to it all; though he did not as yet acknowledge this, ashamed as he felt and embarrassed by his illustrious name and all the complications and tears which he foresaw.

The silence continued. Camille with her piercing glance, as sharp as any knife, had told her mother that she knew the truth; and then with another and pain-fraught glance she had complained to Gérard. He, in order to re-establish equilibrium, could only think of a compliment: 'Good morning, Camille. Ah! that havana-brown gown of yours looks nice! It's astonishing how well rather sombre colours suit you.'

Camille glanced at her mother's white robe, and then at her own dark gown, which scarcely allowed her neck and wrists to be seen. 'Yes,' she replied, laughing, 'I only look passable when I don't dress as a young girl.'

Eve, ill at ease, worried by the growth of a rivalry, in which she did not as yet wish to believe, changed the conversation. 'Isn't your brother there?' she asked.

'Why, yes, we came down together.'

Hyacinthe, who came in at that moment, shook hands with Gérard in a weary way. He was twenty, and had inherited his mother's pale blond hair, and her long face full of Oriental languor; while from his father he had derived his grey eyes and thick lips, expressive of unscrupulous appetites. A wretched scholar, regarding every profession with the same contempt, he had decided to do nothing. Spoilt by his father, he took some little interest in poetry and music, and lived in an extraordinary circle of artists, low women, madmen and bandits; boasting himself of all sorts of crimes and vices, professing the very worst philosophical and social ideas, invariably going to extremes—becoming in turn a Collectivist, an Individualist, an Anarchist, a Pessimist, a Symbolist, and what not besides; without, however, ceasing to be a Catholic, as this conjunction of Catholicity with something else seemed to him the supreme *bon ton.* In reality he was simply empty and rather a fool. In four generations the vigorous hungry blood of the Duvillards, after producing three magnificent beasts of prey, had, as if exhausted by the contentment of every passion, ended in this sorry, emasculated creature, who was incapable alike of great knavery or great debauchery.

Camille, who was too intelligent not to realise her brother's nothingness, was fond of teasing him; and looking at him as he stood there, tightly buttoned in his long frock-coat with pleated skirt—a resurrection of the romantic period, which he carried to exaggeration—she resumed : 'Mamma has been asking for you, Hyacinthe. Come and show her your gown. You are the one who would look nice dressed as a young girl.'

However, he eluded her without replying. He was covertly afraid of her, though they lived together in great intimacy, frankly exchanging confidences respecting their perverse views of life. And he directed a glance of disdain at the wonderful basket of orchids, which seemed to him past the fashion, far too common nowadays. For his part he had left the lilies of life behind him, and reached the ranunculus, the flower of blood.

The two last guests who were expected now arrived almost together. The first was the investigating magistrate Amadieu, a little man of five-and-forty, who was an intimate of the household and had been brought into notoriety by a recent Anarchist affair. Between a pair of fair, bushy whiskers he displayed a flat, regular, judicial face, to which he tried to impart an expression of keenness by wearing a single eyeglass, behind which his glance sparkled. Very worldly, moreover, he belonged to the new judicial school, being a

distinguished psychologist and having written a book in reply
to the abuses of criminalist physiology. And he was also a
man of great, tenacious ambition, fond of notoriety, and ever
on the look-out for those resounding legal affairs which bring
glory. Behind him at last appeared General de Bozonnet,
Gérard's uncle on the maternal side, a tall, lean old man
with a nose like an eagle's beak. Chronic rheumatism had
recently compelled him to retire from the service. Raised
to a colonelcy after the Franco-German war in reward for his
gallant conduct at St. Privat, he had, in spite of his extremely
monarchical connections, kept his sworn faith to Napoleon
III. And he was excused in his own sphere of society for
this species of military Bonapartism, on account of the
bitterness with which he accused the Republic of having
ruined the army. Worthy fellow that he was, extremely
fond of his sister, Madame de Quinsac, it seemed as though
he acted in accordance with some secret desire of hers in
accepting the invitations of Baroness Duvillard, by way of
rendering Gérard's constant presence in her house more natural
and excusable.

However, the Baron and Duthil now returned from the
study, laughing loudly in an exaggerated way, doubtless to
make the others believe that they were quite easy in mind.
And one and all passed into the large dining-room, where a
big wood fire was burning, its gay flames lighting like a
ray of springtide the fine mahogany furniture of English
make laden with silver and crystal. The room, of a soft
mossy green, had an unassuming charm in the pale light;
and the table, which in the centre displayed the richness of
its covers and the immaculate whiteness of its linen adorned
with Venetian point, seemed to have flowered miraculously
with a wealth of large tea roses, most admirable blooms for
the season, and of delicious perfume.

The Baroness seated the General on her right and Amadieu
on her left. The Baron on his right placed Duthil, and on
his left Gérard. Then the young people installed themselves
at either end, Camille between Gérard and the General, and
Hyacinthe between Duthil and Amadieu. And forthwith,
from the moment of starting on the scrambled eggs and truffles,
conversation began—the usual conversation of Parisian
déjeuners, when every event, great or little, of the morning
or the day before is passed in review: the truths and the
falsehoods current in every social sphere, the financial scandal

and the political adventure of the hour, the novel that has just appeared, the play that has just been produced, the stories which should only be retailed in whispers, but which are repeated aloud. And beneath all the light wit which circulates, beneath all the laughter, which often has a false ring, each retains his or her particular worry or distress of mind, at times so acute that it becomes perfect agony.

With his quiet and wonted impudence, the Baron, bravely enough, was the first to speak of the article in the 'Voix du Peuple.' 'I say, have you read Sagnier's article this morning? It's a good one; he has *verve*, you know, but what a dangerous lunatic he is!'

This set everybody at ease, for the article would certainly have weighed upon the *déjeuner* had no one mentioned it.

'It's the "Panama" dodge over again!' cried Duthil. 'But no, no, we've had quite enough of it!'

'Why,' resumed the Baron, 'the affair of the African Railway Lines is as clear as spring water! All those whom Sagnier threatens may sleep in peace. The truth is that it's a scheme to upset Barroux's ministry. Leave to interpellate will certainly be asked for this afternoon. You'll see what a fine uproar there'll be in the Chamber.'

'That libellous, scandal-seeking press,' said Amadieu gravely, 'is a dissolving agent which will bring France to ruin. We ought to have laws against it.'

The General made an angry gesture: 'Laws! What's the use of them, since nobody has the courage to enforce them?'

Silence fell. With a light, discreet step the house-steward presented some grilled mullet. So noiseless was the service amid the cheerful perfumed warmth that not even the faintest clatter of crockery was heard. Without anyone knowing how it had come about, however, the conversation had suddenly changed; and somebody inquired, 'So the revival of the piece is postponed?'

'Yes,' said Gérard, 'I heard this morning that "Polyeucte" wouldn't get its turn till April at the earliest.'

At this Camille, who hitherto had remained silent, watching the young Count and seeking to win him back, turned her glittering eyes upon her father and mother. It was a question of that revival in which Silviane was so stubbornly determined to make her *début*. However, the Baron and the Baroness evinced perfect serenity, having long been acquainted with all that concerned each other. More-

over, Eve was too much occupied with her own passion to
think of anything else, and the Baron too busy with the fresh
application which he intended to make in tempestuous fashion
at the Ministry of Fine Arts, so as to wrest Silviane's engagement from those in office. He contented himself with
saying: 'How would you have them revive pieces at the
Comédie? They have no actresses left there.'

'Oh, by the way,' the Baroness on her side simply remarked, 'yesterday, in that play at the Vaudeville, Delphine
Vignot wore such an exquisite gown. She's the only one too
who knows how to arrange her hair.'

Thereupon Duthil, in somewhat veiled language, began to
relate a story about Delphine and a well-known senator. And
then came another scandal, the sudden and almost suspicious
death of a lady friend of the Duvillards'; whereupon the
General, without any transition, broke in to relieve his bitter
feelings by denouncing the idiotic manner in which the army
was now-a-days organised. Meantime the old Bordeaux
glittered like ruby blood in the delicate crystal glasses. A
truffled fillet of venison had just cast its somewhat sharp scent
amidst the dying perfume of the roses, when some asparagus
made its appearance, a *primeur* which once had been so rare,
but which no longer caused any astonishment.

'Now-a-days we get it all through the winter,' said the
Baron with a gesture of disenchantment.

'And so,' asked Gérard at the same moment, 'the Princess
de Harn's *matinée* is for this afternoon?'

Camille quickly intervened. 'Yes, this afternoon. Shall
you go?'

'No, I don't think so, I sha'n't be able,' replied the young
man in embarrassment.

'Ah! that little Princess, she's really deranged, you know,'
exclaimed Duthil. 'You are aware that she calls herself a
widow? But the truth, it seems, is that her husband, a real
Prince, connected with a royal house and very handsome, is
travelling about the world in the company of a singer. She, with
her vicious, urchin-like face, preferred to come and reign in Paris,
in that mansion of the Avenue Hoche, which is certainly the
most extraordinary Noah's ark imaginable, with its swarming
of cosmopolitan society indulging in every extravagance!'

'Be quiet, you malicious fellow,' the Baroness gently interrupted. 'We, here, are very fond of Rosemonde, who is a
charming woman.'

'Oh! certainly,' Camille again resumed. 'She invited us; and we are going to her place by-and-by, are we not, mamma?'

To avoid replying, the Baroness pretended that she did not hear; whilst Duthil, who seemed to be well-informed concerning the Princess, continued to make merry over her intended *matinée*, at which she meant to produce some Spanish dancing-girls whose performance was so very indecorous that all Paris, forewarned of the circumstance, would certainly swarm to her house. And he added: 'You've heard that she has given up painting? Yes, she busies herself with chemistry? Her *salon* is full of Anarchists now— and, by the way, it seemed to me that she had cast her eyes on you, my dear Hyacinthe.'

Hyacinthe had hitherto held his tongue, as if he took no interest in anything. 'Oh! she bores me to death,' he now condescended to reply. 'If I'm going to her *matinée*, it's simply in the hope of meeting my friend young Lord George Eldrett, who wrote to me from London to give me an appointment at the Princess's. And I admit that hers is the only *salon* where I find somebody to talk to.'

'And so,' asked Amadieu in an ironical way, 'you have now gone over to Anarchism?'

With his air of lofty elegance Hyacinthe imperturbably confessed his creed: 'But it seems to me, monsieur, that in these times of universal baseness and ignominy, no man of any distinction can be other than an Anarchist.'

A laugh ran round the table. Hyacinthe was very much spoilt, and considered very entertaining. His father in particular was immensely amused by the notion that he of all men should have an Anarchist for a son. However, the General, in his rancorous moments, talked anarchically enough of blowing up a society which was so stupid as to let itself be led by half a dozen disreputable characters. And, indeed, the investigating magistrate, who was gradually making a specialty of Anarchist affairs, proved the only one who opposed the young man, defending threatened civilisation and giving terrifying particulars concerning what he called the army of devastation and massacre. The others, while partaking of some delicious duck's-liver *pâté*, which the house-steward handed them, continued smiling. There was so much misery, said they; one must take everything into account; things would surely end by righting themselves.

And the Baron himself declared, in a conciliatory manner: 'It's certain that one might do something, though nobody knows exactly what. As for all sensible and moderate claims, oh! I agree to them in advance. For, instance, the lot of the working classes may be ameliorated, charitable enterprises may be undertaken, such, for instance, as our Asylum for the Invalids of Labour, which we have reason to be proud of. But we must not be asked for impossibilities.'

With the dessert came a sudden spell of silence; it was as if, amidst the restless fluttering of the conversation, and the dizziness born of the copious meal, each one's worry or distress was again wringing the heart and setting an expression of perturbation on the countenance. The nervous absent-mindedness of Duthil, threatened with denunciation, was seen to revive; so, too, the anxious anger of the Baron, who was meditating how he might possibly manage to content Silviane. That woman was this sturdy, powerful man's taint, the secret sore which would perhaps end by eating him away and destroying him. But it was the frightful drama in which the Baroness, Camille and Gérard were concerned that flitted by most visibly across the faces of all three of them: that hateful rivalry of mother and daughter, contending for the man they loved. And, meantime, the silver-gilt blades of the dessert-knives were delicately peeling choice fruit. And there were bunches of golden grapes looking beautifully fresh, and a procession of sweetmeats and little cakes—an infinity of dainties, over which the most satiated appetites lingered complacently.

Then, just as the finger-glasses were being served, a footman came and bent over the Baroness, who answered in an undertone, 'Well, show him into the *salon*; I will join him there.' And aloud to the others she added: 'It's Monsieur l'Abbé Froment, who has called and asks most particularly to see me. He won't be in our way; I think that almost all of you know him. Oh! he's a genuine saint, and I have much sympathy for him.'

For a few minutes longer they loitered round the table, and then at last quitted the dining-room, which was full of the odours of viands, wines, fruits, and roses; quite warm, too, with the heat thrown out by the big logs of firewood, which were falling into embers amidst the somewhat jumbled brightness of all the crystal and silver, and the pale, delicate light which fell upon the disorderly table.

Pierre had remained standing in the centre of the little blue and silver *salon*. Seeing a tray on which the coffee and the liqueurs were in readiness, he regretted that he had insisted upon being received. And his embarrassment increased when the company came in rather noisily, with bright eyes and rosy cheeks. However, his charitable fervour had revived so ardently within him that he overcame this embarrassment, and all that remained to him of it was a slight feeling of discomfort at bringing the whole frightful morning which he had just spent amid such scenes of wretchedness, such darkness and cold, such filth and hunger, into this bright, warm, perfumed affluence, where the useless and the super-fluous overflowed around those folk who seemed so gay at having made a delightful meal.

However, the Baroness at once came forward with Gérard ; for it was through the latter, whose mother he knew, that the priest had been presented to the Duvillards at the time of the famous conversion. And as he apologised for having called at such an inconvenient hour, the Baroness responded : 'But you are always welcome, Monsieur l'Abbé. You will allow me just to attend to my guests, won't you ? I will be with you in an instant.'

She thereupon returned to the table on which the tray had been placed, in order to serve the coffee and the liqueurs, with her daughter's assistance. Gérard, however, remained with Pierre ; and, so it chanced, began to speak to him of the Asylum for the Invalids of Labour, where they had met one another at the recent laying of the foundation-stone of a new pavilion which was being erected, thanks to a handsome donation of 100,000 francs made by Baron Duvillard. So far, the enterprise only comprised four pavilions out of the fourteen which it was proposed to erect on the vast site given by the City of Paris on the peninsula of Gennevilliers ;[1] and so the subscription fund remained open. And, indeed, no little noise was made over this charitable enterprise, which was regarded as a complete and peremptory reply to the accusa-tions of those evilly disposed persons who charged the satiated *bourgeoisie* with doing nothing for the workers. But the truth was that a magnificent chapel, erected in the centre of the site, had absorbed two-thirds of the funds hitherto collected. Numerous lady patronesses, chosen from all the

---

[1] This so-called peninsula lies to the north-west of Paris, and is formed by the windings of the Seine.—*Trans.*

'worlds' of Paris—the Baroness Duvillard, the Countess de Quinsac, the Princess Rosemonde de Harn, and a score of others—were entrusted with the task of keeping the enterprise alive by dint of collections and fancy bazaars. But success had been chiefly obtained thanks to the happy idea of ridding the ladies of all the weighty cares of organisation by choosing as managing director a certain Fonsègue, who, besides being a deputy and editor of the 'Globe' newspaper, was a prodigious promoter of all sorts of enterprises. And the 'Globe' never paused in its propaganda, but answered the attacks of the revolutionaries by extolling the inexhaustible charity of the governing classes in such wise that at the last elections the enterprise had served as a victorious electoral weapon.

However, Camille was walking about with a steaming cup of coffee in her hand. 'Will you take some coffee, Monsieur l'Abbé?' she inquired.

'No, thank you, mademoiselle.'

'A glass of Chartreuse then?'

'No, thank you.'

Then, everybody being served, the Baroness came back and said amiably: 'Well, Monsieur l'Abbé, what do you desire of me?'

Pierre began to speak almost in an undertone, his throat contracting and his heart beating with emotion. 'I have come, madame, to appeal to your great kindness of heart. This morning, in a frightful house in the Rue des Saules, behind Montmartre, I beheld a sight which utterly upset me. You can have no idea what an abode of misery and suffering it was; its inmates without fire or bread, the men reduced to idleness because there is no work, the mothers having no more milk for their babes, the children barely clad, coughing and shivering. And among all these horrors I saw the worst, the most abominable of all—an old workman, laid on his back by age, dying of hunger, huddled on a heap of rags, in a nook which a dog would not even accept as a kennel.'

He tried to recount things as discreetly as possible, frightened by the very words he spoke, the horrors he had to relate in that sphere of superlative luxury and enjoyment, before those happy ones who possessed all the gifts of this world; for—to use a slang expression—he fully realised that he sang out of tune, and in most uncourteous fashion. What a strange idea of his to have called at the hour when one has just finished *déjeuner*, when the aroma of hot coffee flatters

happy digestion ! Nevertheless he went on, and even ended
by raising his voice, yielding to the feeling of revolt which
gradually stirred him ; going to the end of his terrible narrative, naming Laveuve, insisting on the unjust abandonment
in which the old man was left, and asking for succour in the
name of human compassion. And the whole company
approached to listen to him ; he could see the Baron and
the General, and Duthil and Amadieu in front of him, sipping
their coffee, in silence, without a gesture.

'Well, madame,' he concluded, 'it seemed to me that
one could not leave that old man an hour longer in such a
frightful position, and that this very evening you would have
the extreme goodness to have him admitted into the Asylum
of the Invalids of Labour, which is, I think, the proper and
only place for him.'

Tears had moistened Eve's beautiful eyes. She was in
consternation at so sad a story coming to her to spoil her
afternoon, when she was looking forward to her assignation
with Gérard. Weak and indolent as she was, lacking all
initiative, too much occupied moreover with her own person,
she had only accepted the presidency of the committee on
the condition that all administrative worries were to fall on
Fonsègue. 'Ah ! Monsieur l'Abbé,' she murmured, 'you rend
my heart. But I can do nothing, nothing at all, I assure
you. Moreover, I believe that we have already inquired into
the affair of that man Laveuve. With us, you know, there
must be the most serious guarantees with regard to every
admission. A reporter is chosen who has to give us full information. Wasn't it you, Monsieur Duthil, who were charged
with this man Laveuve's affair ? '

The deputy was finishing a glass of Chartreuse. 'Yes, it
was I. That fine fellow played you a comedy, Monsieur
l'Abbé. He isn't at all ill, and if you left him any money you
may be sure he went down to drink it as soon as you were
gone. For he is always drunk ; and, besides that, he has the
most hateful disposition imaginable, crying out from morning
till evening against the *bourgeois*, and saying that if he had
any strength left in his arms he would undertake to blow up
the whole show. And, moreover, he won't go into the asylum ;
he says that it's a real prison, where one's guarded by Beguins
who force one to hear mass, a dirty convent where the gates
are shut at nine in the evening ! And there are so many of
them like that, who rather than be succoured prefer their

liberty, with cold and hunger and death. Well, then, let the Laveuves die in the street, since they refuse to be with us, and be warm, and eat in our asylums!'

The General and Amadieu nodded their heads approvingly. But Duvillard showed himself more generous. 'No, no, indeed! A man's a man after all, and should be succoured in spite of himself.'

Eve, however, in despair at the idea that she would be robbed of her afternoon, struggled and sought for reasons. 'I assure you that my hands are altogether tied. Monsieur l'Abbé does not doubt my heart or my zeal. But how can I possibly assemble the committee without a few days' delay? And I have particular reasons for coming to no decision, especially in an affair which has already been inquired into and pronounced upon, without the committee's sanction.' Then, all at once she found a solution : ' What I advise you to do, Monsieur l'Abbé, is to go at once to see Monsieur Fonsègue, our managing director. He alone can act in an urgent case, for he knows that the ladies have unlimited confidence in him and approve everything he does.'

'You will find Fonsègue at the Chamber,' added Duthil smiling; ' only the sitting will be a warm one, and I doubt whether you will be able to have a comfortable chat with him.'

Pierre, whose heart had contracted yet more painfully, insisted on the subject no further, but at once made up his mind to see Fonsègue, and in any event obtain from him a promise that the wretched Laveuve should be admitted to the Asylum that very evening. Then he lingered in the *salon* for a few minutes listening to Gérard, who obligingly pointed out to him how he might best convince the deputy, which was by alleging how bad an effect such a story might have should it be brought to light by the revolutionary newspapers. However, the guests were beginning to take their leave. The General, as he went off, came to ask his nephew if he should see him that afternoon at his mother's, Madame de Quinsac, whose 'day' it was: a question which the young man answered with an evasive gesture when he noticed that both Eve and Camille were looking at him. Then came the turn of Amadieu, who hurried off saying that a serious affair required his presence at the Palace of Justice. And Duthil soon followed him in order to repair to the Chamber.

'I'll see you between four and five at Silviane's, eh?' said the Baron as he conducted him to the door. 'Come and

tell me what occurs at the Chamber in consequence of that
odious article of Sagnier's. I must at all events know. For
my part I shall go to the Fine Arts Office, to settle that
affair of the Comédie; and besides, I've some calls to make,
some contractors to see, and a big launching and advertisement affair to settle.'

'It's understood then, between four and five, at Silviane's,'
said the deputy, who went off again mastered by his vague
uneasiness, his anxiety as to what turn that nasty affair of
the African Railway Lines might take.

And all of them had forgotten Laveuve, the miserable
wretch who lay at death's door; and all of them were
hastening away to their business or their passions, caught in
the toils, sinking under the grindstone and whisked away by
that rush of all Paris, whose fever bore them along, throwing
one against another in an ardent scramble, in which the
sole question was who should pass over the others and crush
them.

'And so, mamma,' said Camille, who continued to
scrutinise her mother and Gérard, 'you are going to take us
to the Princess's *matinée*.'

'By-and-by, yes. Only I sha'n't be able to stay there
with you. I received a telegram from Salmon about my
corsage this morning, and I must absolutely go to try it on
at four o'clock.'

By the slight trembling of her mother's voice the girl
felt certain that she was telling a falsehood, 'Oh!' said
she, 'I thought you were only going to try it on to-morrow.
In that case I suppose we are to go and call for you at
Salmon's with the carriage on leaving the *matinée*?'

'Oh no, my dear! One never knows when one will be
free; and besides, if I have a moment, I shall call at the
modiste's.'

Camille's secret rage brought almost a murderous glare
to her dark eyes. The truth was evident. But however
passionately she might desire to set some obstacle across
her mother's path, she could not, dared not carry matters
any further. In vain had she attempted to implore Gérard
with her eyes. He was waiting to take his leave, and
averted his gaze. Pierre, who had become acquainted
with many things since he had frequented the house, noticed
how all three of them quivered, and divined thereby the
mute and terrible drama.

At this moment, however, Hyacinthe, stretched in an arm-chair, and munching an ether capsule, the only liqueur in which he indulged, raïsed his voice : ' For my part, you know, I'm going to the Exposition du Lis. All Paris is swarming there. There's one painting in particular, "The Rape of a Soul," which it's absolutely necessary for one to have seen.'

' Well, but I don't refuse to drive you there,' resumed the Baroness. ' Before going to the Princess's we can look in at that exhibition.'

' That's it, that's it,' hastily exclaimed Camille, who, though she harshly derided the symbolist painters as a rule, now doubtless desired to delay her mother. Then, forcing herself to smile, she asked : ' Won't you risk a look-in at the Exposition du Lis with us, Monsieur Gérard ? '

' Well, no,' replied the Count, ' I want to walk. I shall go with Monsieur l'Abbé Froment as far as the Chamber.'

Thereupon he took leave of mother and daughter, kissing the hand of each in turn. It had just occurred to him that to while away his time he also might call for a moment at Silviane's, where, like the others, he had his *entrées*. On reaching the cold and solemn courtyard he said to the priest, ' Ah ! it does one good to breathe a little cool air. They keep their rooms too hot, and all those flowers, too, give one the headache.'

Pierre for his part was going off with his brain in a whirl, his hands feverish, his senses oppressed by all the luxury which he left behind him, like the dream of some glowing, perfumed paradise where only the elect have their abode. At the same time his reviving thirst for charity had become keener than ever, and without listening to the Count, who was speaking very affectionately of his mother, he reflected as to how he might obtain Laveuve's admission to the Asylum from Fonsègue. However, when the door of the mansion had closed behind them and they had taken a few steps along the street, it occurred to Pierre that a moment previously a sudden vision had met his gaze. Had he not seen a workman carrying a tool-bag, standing and waiting on the foot pave-ment across the road, gazing at that monumental door, closed upon so much fabulous wealth—a workman in whom he fancied he had recognised Salvat, that hungry fellow who had gone off that morning in search of work ? At this thought Pierre hastily turned round. Such wretchedness in face of so much affluence and enjoyment made him feel anxious. But the workman, disturbed in his contemplation, and possibly fearing that he had been recognised, was going off with dragging step. And now, getting only a back view of him, Pierre hesitated, and ended by thinking that he must have been mistaken.

III

RANTERS AND RULERS

WHEN Abbé Froment was about to enter the Palais-Bourbon he remembered he had no admission card, and he was making up his mind that he would simply ask for Fonsègue, though he was not known to him, when, on reaching the vestibule, he perceived Mège, the Collectivist deputy, with whom he had become acquainted in his days of militant charity in the poverty-stricken Charonne district.

'What! you here? You surely have not come to evangelise us?' said Mège.

'No, I've come to see Monsieur Fonsègue on an urgent matter, about a poor fellow who cannot wait.'

'Fonsègue? I don't know if he has arrived. Wait a moment.' And stopping a short, dark young fellow with a sharp, sly air, Mège said to him : 'Massot, here's Monsieur l'Abbé Froment, who wants to speak to your governor at once.'

'The governor? But he isn't here. I left him at the office of the paper, where he'll be detained for another quarter of an hour. However, if Monsieur l'Abbé likes to wait he will surely see him here.'

Thereupon Mège ushered Pierre into the large waiting-hall, the Salle des Pas Perdus, which in other moments looked so vast and cold with its bronze Minerva and Laocoon, and its bare walls on which the pale mournful winter light fell from the glass doors communicating with the garden. Just then, however, it was crowded, and warmed, so to say, by the feverish agitation of the many groups of men that had gathered here and there, and the constant coming and going of those who hastened through the throng. Most of these were deputies, but there were also numerous journalists and inquisitive visitors. And a growing uproar prevailed : colloquies now in undertones, now in loud voices, exclama-

tions and bursts of laughter, amidst no little passionate
gesticulation. Mège's return into the tumult seemed to fan
it. He was tall, apostolically thin, and somewhat neglectful
of his person, looking already old and worn for his age, which
was but five and forty, though his eyes still glowed with
youth behind the glasses which never left his beak-like nose.
And he had a warm but grating voice, and had always been
known to cough, living on solely because he was bitterly intent
on doing so in order to realise the dream of social reorganisation
which haunted him. The son of a poorly circumstanced
medical man of a northern town, he had come to Paris when
very young, living there during the Empire on petty newspaper and other unknown work, and first making a reputation
as an orator at the public meetings of the time. Then, after
the war, having become the chief of the Collectivist party,
thanks to his ardent faith and the extraordinary activity of
his fighting nature, he had at last managed to enter the
Chamber, where, brimful of information, he fought for
his ideas with fierce determination and obstinacy, like a
doctrinaire who has decided in his own mind what the world
ought to be, and who regulates in advance, and bit by bit, the
whole dogma of Collectivism. However, since he had taken
pay as a deputy the outside Socialists had looked upon him
as a mere rhetorician, an aspiring dictator who only tried to
cast society in a new mould for the purpose of subordinating
it to his personal views and ruling it.

'You know what is going on?' he said to Pierre. 'This
is another nice affair, is it not? But what would you have?
We are in mud to our very ears.'

He had formerly conceived genuine sympathy for the
priest, whom he had found so gentle with all who suffered,
and so desirous of social regeneration. And the priest himself
had ended by taking an interest in this authoritarian dreamer,
who was resolved to make men happy in spite even of themselves. He knew that he was poor, and led a retired life with
his wife and four children, to whom he was devoted.

'You can well understand that I am no ally of Sagnier's,'
Mège resumed. 'But as he chose to speak out this morning and
threaten to publish the names of all those who have taken
bribes, we can't allow ourselves to pass as accomplices any
further. It has long been said that there was some nasty
jobbery in that suspicious affair of the African Railways. And
the worst is that two members of the present Cabinet are in

question; for three years ago, when the Chambers dealt with Duvillard's scheme, Barroux was at the Home Department, and Monferrand at that of Public Works. Now that they have come back again, Monferrand at the Home Department, and Barroux at that of Finance, with the Presidency of the Council, it isn't possible, is it? for us to do otherwise than compel them to enlighten us, in their own interest even, about their former goings-on. No, no, they can no longer keep silence, and I've announced that I intend to interpellate them this very day.'

It was the announcement of Mège's interpellation, following the terrible article of the 'Voix du Peuple,' which thus set the lobbies in an uproar. And Pierre remained rather scared at this big political affair falling into the midst of his scheme to save a wretched pauper from hunger and death. Thus he listened without fully understanding the explanations which the Socialist deputy was passionately giving him, while all around them the uproar increased, and bursts of laughter rang out, testifying to the astonishment which the others felt at seeing Mège in conversation with a priest.

'How stupid they are!' said Mège disdainfully. 'Do they think, then, that I eat a cassock for *déjeuner* every morning? But I beg your pardon, my dear Monsieur Froment. Come, take a place on that seat and wait for Fonsègue.'

Then he himself plunged into all the turmoil, and Pierre realised that his best course was to sit down and wait quietly. His surroundings began to influence and interest him, and he gradually forgot Laveuve for the passion of the Parliamentary crisis amidst which he found himself cast. The frightful Panama adventure was scarcely over; he had followed the progress of that tragedy with the anguish of a man who every night expects to hear the tocsin sound the last hour of olden, agonising society. And now a little Panama was beginning, a fresh cracking of the social edifice, an affair such as had been frequent in all parliaments in connection with big financial questions, but one which acquired mortal gravity from the circumstances in which it came to the front. That story of the African Railway Lines, that little patch of mud, stirred up and exhaling a perturbing odour, and suddenly fomenting so much emotion, fear, and anger in the Chamber, was after all but an opportunity for political strife, a field on which the voracious appetites of the various 'groups' would take exercise and sharpen; and, at bottom, the sole question was that of overthrowing the ministry and replacing it by another. Only, behind all that lust of power, that continuous onslaught of ambition, what a distressful prey was stirring—the whole people with all its poverty and its sufferings!

Pierre noticed that Massot—'little Massot,' as he was generally called—had just seated himself on the bench beside him. With his lively eye and ready ear listening to everything and noting it, gliding everywhere with his ferret-like air, Massot was not there in the capacity of a gallery man, but had simply scented a stormy debate, and come to see if he could not pick up material for some occasional 'copy.' And this priest lost in the midst of the throng doubtless interested him.

'Have a little patience, Monsieur l'Abbé,' said he, with the amiable gaiety of a young gentleman who makes fun of everything. 'The governor will certainly come, for he knows well enough that they are going to heat the oven here. You are not one of his constituents from La Corrèze, are you?'

'No, no! I belong to Paris; I've come on account of a poor fellow whom I wish to get admitted into the Asylum of the Invalids of Labour.'

'Oh! all right. Well, I'm a child of Paris, too.'

Then Massot laughed. And indeed he was a child of Paris, son of a chemist of the St. Denis district, and an ex-dunce of the Lycée Charlemagne, where he had not even finished his studies. He had failed entirely, and at eighteen years of age had found himself cast into journalism with barely sufficient knowledge of orthography for that calling. And for twelve years now, as he often said, he had been a rolling stone, wandering through all spheres of society, confessing some and guessing at others. He had seen everything, and become disgusted with everything, no longer believing in the existence of great men, or of truth, but living peacefully enough on universal malice and folly. He naturally had no literary ambition—in fact he professed a deliberate contempt for literature. Withal, he was not a fool, but wrote in accordance with no matter what views in no matter what newspaper, having neither conviction nor belief, but quietly claiming the right to say whatever he pleased to the public, on condition that he either amused or impassioned it.

'And so,' said he, 'you know Mège, Monsieur l'Abbé? What a study in character, eh? A big child, a dreamer of dreams in the skin of a terrible sectarian! Oh! I have had a deal of intercourse with him; I know him thoroughly. You are no doubt aware that he lives on with the everlasting conviction that he will attain to power in six months' time, and that between evening and morning he will have established that famous Collectivist community which is to succeed capitalist society, just as day follows night. And, by the way, as regards his interpellation to-day, he is convinced that in overthrowing the Barroux ministry he'll be hastening his own turn. His system is to use up his adversaries. How many times haven't I heard him making his calculations : there's such an one to be used up, then such an one, and then such an one, so that he himself may at last reign. And it's always to come off in six months at the latest. The misfortune is, however, that others are always springing up, and so his turn never comes at all.'

Little Massot openly made merry over it. Then, slightly lowering his voice, he asked : 'And Sagnier, do you know him ? No ? Do you see that red-haired man with the bull's neck—the one who looks like a butcher ? That one yonder, who is talking in a little group of frayed frock-coats.'

Pierre at last perceived the man in question. He had broad red ears, a hanging under-lip, a large nose, and big, projecting dull eyes.

'I know that one thoroughly as well,' continued Massot ; 'I was on the "Voix du Peuple" under him before I went on the "Globe." The one thing that nobody is exactly aware of is whence Sagnier first came. He long dragged out his life in the lower depths of journalism, doing nothing at all brilliant, but wild with ambition and appetite. Perhaps you remember the first hubbub he made—that rather dirty affair of a new Louis XVII. which he tried to launch, and which made him the extraordinary Royalist that he still is. Then it occurred to him to espouse the cause of the masses, and he made a display of vengeful Catholic socialism, attacking the Republic and all the abominations of the times in the name of justice and morality, under the pretext of curing them. He began with a series of sketches of financiers, a mass of dirty, uncontrolled, unproved tittle-tattle, which ought to have led him to prison, but which met, as you know, with such wonderful success when gathered together in a volume. And he goes on in the same style in the "Voix du Peuple," which he himself made a success at the time of the Panama affair by dint of denunciation and scandal, and which to-day is like a sewer-pipe pouring forth all the filth of the times. And whenever the stream slackens, why, he invents things just to satisfy his craving for that hubbub on which both his pride and his pocket subsist.'

Little Massot spoke without bitterness; indeed, he had even begun to laugh again. Beneath his thoughtless ferocity he really felt some respect for Sagnier. 'Oh! he's a bandit,' he continued, 'but a clever fellow all the same. You can't imagine how full of vanity he is. Lately it occurred to him to get himself acclaimed by the populace, for he pretends to be a kind of King of the Markets, you know. Perhaps he has ended by taking his fine judge-like airs in earnest, and really believes that he is saving the people and helping the cause of virtue. What astonishes me is his fertility in the arts of denunciation and scandalmongering. Never a morning comes but he discovers some fresh horror, and delivers fresh culprits over to the hatred of the masses. No! the stream of mud never ceases; there is an incessant, unexpected spurt of infamy, an increase of monstrous fancies each time that the disgusted public shows any sign of weariness. And, do you know, there's genius in that, Monsieur l'Abbé; for he is well aware that his circulation goes up as soon as he threatens to speak out and publish a list of traitors and bribe-takers. His sales are certain now for some days to come.'

Listening to Massot's gay, bantering voice, Pierre began to understand certain things the exact meaning of which had hitherto escaped him. He ended by questioning the young journalist, surprised as he was that so many deputies should be in the lobbies when the sitting was in progress. Oh! the sitting, indeed. The gravest matters, some bill of national interest, might be under discussion, yet every member fled from it at the sudden threat of an interpellation which might overturn the ministry. And the passion stirring there was the restrained anger, the growing anxiety of the present ministry's clients, who feared that they might have to give place to others; and it was also the sudden hope, the eager hunger of all who were waiting—the clients of the various possible ministries of the morrow.

Massot pointed to Barroux, the head of the Cabinet, who, though he was out of his element in the Department of Finance, had taken it simply because his generally recognised integrity was calculated to reassure public opinion after the Panama crisis. Barroux was chatting in a corner with the Minister of Public Instruction, Senator Taboureau, an old university man with a shrinking, mournful air, who was extremely honest, but totally ignorant of Paris, coming as he did from some far-away provincial faculty. Barroux for his part was of decorative aspect, tall, and with a handsome, clean-shaven face, which would have looked quite noble had not his nose been rather too small. Although he was sixty, he still had a profusion of curly snow-white hair to complete the somewhat theatrical majesty of his appearance, which he was wont to turn to account when in the tribune. Coming of an old Parisian family, well-to-do, an advocate by profession, then a Republican journalist under the Empire, he had reached office with Gambetta, showing himself at once honest and romantic, loud of speech, and somewhat stupid, but at the same time very brave and very upright, and still clinging with ardent faith to the principles of the great Revolution. However, his Jacobinism was getting out of fashion—he was becoming an 'ancestor,' as it were, one of the last props of the middle-class Republic, and the new comers, the young politicians with long teeth, were beginning to smile at him. Moreover, beneath the ostentation of his demeanour and the pomp of his eloquence there was a man of hesitating, sentimental nature, a good fellow who shed tears when re-perusing the verses of Lamartine.

However, Monferrand, the minister for the Home Department, passed by and drew Barroux aside to whisper a few words in his ear. He, Monferrand, was fifty, short and fat, with a smiling, fatherly air; nevertheless a look of keen intelligence appeared at times on his round and somewhat common face, fringed by a beard which was still dark. In him one divined a man of government, with hands which were fitted for difficult tasks, and which never released a prey. Formerly mayor of the town of Tulle, he came from La Corrèze, where he owned a large estate. He was certainly a force in motion, one whose constant rise was anxiously watched by keen observers. He spoke simply and quietly, but with extraordinary power of conviction. Having apparently no ambition, affecting indeed the greatest disinterestedness, he nevertheless harboured the most ferocious appetites. Sagnier had written that he was a thief and a murderer, having strangled two of his aunts in order to inherit their property. But even if he were a murderer, he was certainly not a vulgar one.

Then, too. came another personage of the drama which

was about to be performed—deputy Vignon, whose arrival excited the various groups. The two ministers looked at him, whilst he, at once surrounded by his friends, smiled at them from a distance. He was not yet thirty-six. Slim, and of average height, very fair, with a fine blonde beard, of which he took great care, a Parisian by birth, having rapidly made his way in the government service, at one time Prefect at Bordeaux, he now represented youth and the future in the Chamber. He had realised that new men were needed in the direction of affairs in order to accomplish the more urgent, indispensable reforms; and very ambitious and intelligent as he was, knowing many things, he already had a programme, the application of which he was quite capable of attempting, in part at any rate. However, he evinced no haste, but was full of prudence and shrewdness, convinced that his day would dawn, strong in the fact that he was as yet compromised in nothing, but had all space before him. At bottom he was merely a first-class administrator, clear and precise in speech, and his programme only differed from Barroux's by the more up-to-date phraseology of its formulas, although the advent of a Vignon ministry in place of a Barroux one appeared an event of importance. And it was of Vignon that Sagnier had written that he aimed at the Presidency of the Republic, even should he have to march through blood to reach the Elysée Palace.

'*Mon Dieu!*' Massot was explaining, 'it's quite possible that Sagnier isn't lying this time, and that he has really found a list of names in some pocket-book of Hunter's that has fallen into his hands. I myself have long known that Hunter was Duvillard's vote-recruiter in the affair of the African Railways. But to understand matters one must first realise what his mode of proceeding was—the skill and the kind of amiable delicacy that he showed, which were far from the brutal corruption and dirty trafficking that people imagine. One must be such a man as Sagnier to picture a parliament as an open market, where every conscience is for sale and is impudently knocked down to the highest bidder. Oh! things happened in a very different way indeed; and they are explainable, and at times even excusable. Thus the article is levelled in particular against Barroux and Monferrand, who are designated in the clearest possible manner although they are not named. You are no doubt aware that at the time of the vote Barroux was at the Home

Department and Monferrand at that of Public Works, and
so now they are accused of having betrayed their trusts, the
blackest of all social crimes. I don't know into what political
combinations Barroux may have entered, but I am ready to
swear that he put nothing in his pocket, for he is the most
honest of men. As for Monferrand, that's another matter ;
he's a man to carve himself his share, only I should be much
surprised if he had put himself in a bad position. He's
incapable of a blunder, particularly a stupid one like that of
taking money and leaving a receipt for it lying about.'

Massot paused, and with a jerk of his head called Pierre's
attention to Duthil, who, feverish, but nevertheless smiling,
stood in a group which had just collected around the two
ministers. 'There ! do you see that young man yonder, that
dark handsome fellow whose beard looks so triumphant ? '

'I know him,' said Pierre.

'Oh ! you know Duthil. Well, he's one who most certainly
took money. But he's a mere bird. He came to us from
Angoulême to lead the pleasantest of lives here, and he has
no more conscience, no more scruples, than the pretty finches
of his native part, who are ever love-making. Ah ! for
Duthil, Hunter's money was like manna due to him, and he
never even paused to think that he was dirtying his fingers.
You may be quite sure he feels astonished that people should
attach the slightest importance to the matter.'

Then Massot designated another deputy in the same
group, a man of fifty or thereabouts, of slovenly aspect and
lachrymose mien, lanky, too, like a maypole, and somewhat
bent by the weight of his head, which was long and suggestive of a horse's. His scanty, straight, yellowish hair, his
drooping moustaches, in fact the whole of his countenance,
expressed everlasting distress.

'And Chaigneux, do you know him ?' continued Massot,
referring to the deputy in question. 'No ? Well, look at him,
and ask yourself if it isn't quite as natural that he, too,
should have taken money. He came from Arras. He was a
solicitor there. When his division elected him he let politics
intoxicate him, and sold his practice to make his fortune in
Paris, where he installed himself with his wife and his three
daughters. And you can picture his bewilderment amidst
those four women—terrible women, ever busy with finery,
receiving and paying visits, and running after marriageable
men who flee away. It's ill-luck with a vengeance, the daily

defeat of a poor devil of mediocre attainments, who imagined that his position as a deputy would facilitate money-making, and who is drowning himself in it all. And so, how can Chaigneux have done otherwise than take money, he who is always hard up for a five-hundred-franc note ? I admit that originally he wasn't a dishonest man. But he's become one.'

Massot was now fairly launched, and went on with his portraits, the series which he had, at one moment, dreamt of writing under the title of ' Deputies for Sale.' There were the simpletons who fell into the furnace, the men whom ambition goaded to exasperation, the low minds that yielded to the temptation of an open drawer, the company-promoters who grew intoxicated and lost ground by dint of dealing with big figures. At the same time, however, Massot admitted that these men were relatively few in number, and that black sheep were to be found in every parliament of the world. Then Sagnier's name cropped up again, and Massot remarked that only Sagnier could regard the French Chambers as mere dens of thieves.

Pierre, meantime, felt most interested in the tempest which the threat of a ministerial crisis was stirring up before him. Not only the men like Duthil and Chaigneux, pale at feeling the ground tremble beneath them, and wondering whether they would not sleep at the Mazas prison that night, were gathered round Barroux and Monferrand; all the latter's clients were there, all who enjoyed influence or office through them, and who would collapse and disappear should they happen to fall. And it was something to see the anxious glances and the pale dread amidst all the whispered chatter, the bits of information and tittle-tattle which were carried hither and thither. Then, in a neighbouring group formed round Vignon, who looked very calm and smiled, were the other clients, those who awaited the moment to climb to the assault of power, in order that they, in their turn, might at last possess influence or office. Eyes glittered with covetousness, hopeful delight could be read in them, pleasant surprise at the sudden opportunity now offered. Vignon avoided replying to the over-direct questions of his friends, and simply announced that he did not intend to intervene. Evidently enough his plan was to let Mège interpellate and overthrow the ministry, for he did not fear him, and in his own estimation would afterwards simply have to stoop to pick up the fallen portfolios.

'Ah! Monferrand now,' little Massot was saying, 'there's a rascal who trims his sails! I knew him as an anti-clerical, a devourer of priests, Monsieur l'Abbé, if you will allow me so to express myself; however, I don't say this to be agreeable to you, but I think I may tell you for certain that he has become reconciled to religion. At least, I have been told that Monseigneur Martha, who is a great converter, now seldom leaves him. This is calculated to please one in these new times, when science has become bankrupt, and religion blooms afresh with delicious mysticism on all sides, whether in art, literature, or society itself.'

Massot was jesting, according to his wont; but he spoke so amiably that the priest could not do otherwise than bow. However, a great stir had set in before them; it was announced that Mège was about to ascend the tribune, and thereupon all the deputies hastened into the assembly hall, leaving only the inquisitive visitors and a few journalists in the Salle des Pas Perdus.

'It's astonishing that Fonsègue hasn't yet arrived,' resumed Massot; 'he's interested in what's going on. However he's so cunning, that when he doesn't behave as others do, one may be sure he has his reasons for it. Do you know him?' And as Pierre gave a negative answer, Massot went on: 'Oh! he's a man of brains and real power—I speak with all freedom, you know, for I don't possess the bump of veneration; and as for my editors, well, they're the very puppets that I know the best and pick to pieces with the most enjoyment. Fonsègue, also, is clearly designated in Sagnier's article. Moreover, he's one of Duvillard's usual clients. There can be no doubt that he took money, for he takes money in everything. Only he always protects himself, and takes it for reasons which may be acknowledged—as payment or commission on account of advertising, and so forth. And if I left him just now looking, as it seemed to me, rather disturbed, and if he delays his arrival here to establish, as it were, a moral alibi, the truth must be that he has committed the first imprudent action in his life.'

Then Massot rattled on, telling all there was to tell about Fonsègue. He, too, came from the department of La Corrèze, and had quarrelled for life with Monferrand after some unknown underhand affairs. Formerly an advocate at Tulle, his ambition had been to conquer Paris; and he had really conquered it, thanks to his big morning newspaper, 'Le Globe,' of which he was both founder and director. He now resided in a luxurious mansion in the Avenue du Bois de Boulogne, and no enterprise was launched but he carved himself a princely share in it. He had a genius for 'business,' and employed his newspaper as a weapon to enable him to reign over the market. But how very carefully he had behaved, what long and skilful patience he had shown before attaining to the reputation of a really serious man, who guided authoritatively the most virtuous and respected of the organs of the press! Though in reality he believed neither in God nor in Devil, he had made this newspaper the supporter of order, property, and family ties; and though he had become a Conservative Republican, since it was to his interest to be such, he had remained outwardly religious, affecting a Spiritualism which reassured the *bourgeoisie*. And amidst all his accepted power, to which others bowed, he nevertheless had one hand deep in every available money-bag.

'Ah! Monsieur l'Abbé,' said Massot, 'see to what journalism may lead a man! There you have Sagnier and Fonsègue: just compare them a bit. In reality they are birds of the same feather; each has a quill and uses it. But how different the systems and the results. Sagnier's print is really a sewer which rolls him along and carries him to the cesspool; while the other's paper is certainly an example of the best journalism one can have, most carefully written, with a real literary flavour, a treat for readers of delicate minds, and an honour to the man who directs it. But at the bottom, good heavens! in both cases the farce is precisely the same!'

Massot burst out laughing, well pleased with this final thrust. Then all at once: 'Ah! here's Fonsègue at last!' said he.

Quite at his ease, and still laughing, he forthwith introduced the priest. 'This is Monsieur l'Abbé Froment, my dear *patron*, who has been waiting more than twenty minutes for you. I'm just going to see what is happening inside. You know that Mège is interpellating the government.'

The new comer started slightly: 'An interpellation!' said he. 'All right, all right, I'll go to it.'

Pierre was gazing at him. He was about fifty years of age, short of stature, thin and active, and still young-looking, without a grey hair in his black beard. He had sparkling eyes, too, but his mouth, said to be a terrible one, was hidden

by his moustaches. And withal he looked a pleasant companion, full of wit to the tip of his little pointed nose, the
nose of a sporting dog that is ever scenting game. 'What
can I do for you, Monsieur l'Abbé?' he inquired.

Then Pierre briefly presented his request, recounting his
visit to Laveuve that morning, giving every heartrending
particular, and asking for the poor wretch's immediate admittance to the Asylum.

'Laveuve!' said the other; 'but hasn't his affair been
examined? Why, Duthil drew up a report on it, and things
appeared to us of such a nature that we could not vote for
the man's admittance.'

But the priest insisted: 'I assure you, monsieur, that
your heart would have burst with compassion had you been
with me this morning. It is revolting that an old man should
be left in such frightful abandonment even for another hour.
He must sleep at the Asylum to night.'

Fonsègue began to protest. 'To-night! But it's impossible, altogether impossible! There are all sorts of indispensable formalities to be observed. And besides, I alone
cannot take such responsibility. I haven't the power. I am
only the manager; all that I do is to execute the orders of
the committee of lady patronesses.'

'But it was precisely Baroness Duvillard who sent me to
you, monsieur, telling me that you alone had the necessary
authority to grant immediate admittance in an exceptional
case.'

'Oh! it was the Baroness who sent you. Ah! that is
just like her, incapable of coming to any decision herself, and
far too desirous of her own quietude to accept any responsibility. Why is it that she wants me to have the worries?
No, no, Monsieur l'Abbé, I certainly won't go against all our
regulations; I won't give an order which would perhaps
embroil me with all those ladies. You don't know them, but
they become positively terrible directly they attend our
meetings.'

He was growing lively, defending himself with a jocular
air, whilst in secret he was fully determined to do nothing.
However, just then Duthil abruptly reappeared, hastening,
bareheaded, from lobby to lobby in order to recruit absent
members, particularly those who were interested in the grave
debate at that moment beginning. 'What, Fonsègue!' he

cried; 'are you still here? Go, go to your seat at once; it's serious!' And thereupon he disappeared.

His colleague evinced no haste, however. It was as if the suspicious affair which was impassioning the Chamber had no concern for him. And he still smiled, although a slight feverish quiver made him blink. 'Excuse me, Monsieur l'Abbé,' he said at last. 'You see that my friends have need of me. I repeat to you that I can do absolutely nothing for your *protégé*.'

But Pierre would not accept this reply as a final one. 'No, no, monsieur,' he rejoined; 'go to your affairs, I will wait for you here. Don't come to a decision without full reflection. You are wanted, and I feel that your mind is not sufficiently at liberty for you to listen to me properly. By-and-by, when you come back and give me your full attention, I am sure that you will grant me what I ask.'

And although Fonsègue, as he went off, repeated that he could not alter his decision, the priest stubbornly resolved to make him do so, and sat down on the bench again, prepared, if needful, to stay there till the evening. The Salle des Pas Perdus was now almost quite empty, and looked yet more frigid and mournful with its Laocoon and its Minerva, and its bare commonplace walls like those of a railway-station waiting-room, between which all the scramble of the century passed, though apparently without even warming the lofty ceiling. Never had paler and more callous light entered by the large glazed doors, behind which one espied the little, slumberous garden with its meagre, wintry lawns. And not an echo of the tempest of the sitting near at hand reached the spot; from the whole heavy pile there fell but death-like silence, and a covert quiver of distress that had come from far away, perhaps from the entire country.

It was that which now haunted Pierre's reverie. The whole ancient, envenomed sore spread out before his mind's eye, with its poison and virulence. Parliamentary rottenness had slowly increased till it had begun to attack society itself. Above all the low intrigues and the rush of personal ambition there certainly remained the loftier struggle of the contending principles, with history on the march, clearing the past away and seeking to bring more truth, justice, and happiness in the future. But in practice, if one only considered the horrid daily *cuisine* of the sphere, what an unbridling of egotistical appetite one beheld, what an absorbing passion to strangle

one's neighbour and triumph oneself alone! Among the
various groups one found but an incessant battle for power
and the satisfactions that it gives. 'Left,' 'Right,'
'Catholics,' 'Republicans,' 'Socialists,' the names given to
the parties of twenty different shades, were simply labels
classifying forms of the one burning thirst to rule and
dominate. All questions could be reduced to a single one,
that of knowing whether this man, that man, or that other
man should hold France in his grasp, to enjoy it, and dis-
tribute its favours among his creatures. And the worst was
that the outcome of the great parliamentary battles, the days
and the weeks lost in setting this man in the place of that
man, and that other man in the place of this man, was simply
stagnation, for not one of the three men was better than his
fellows, and there were but vague points of difference between
them; in such wise that the new master bungled the very
same work as the previous one had bungled, forgetful, perforce, of programmes and promises as soon as ever he began
to reign.

However, Pierre's thoughts invincibly reverted to Laveuve,
whom he had momentarily forgotten, but who now seized
hold of him again with a quiver as of anger and death. Ah!
what could it matter to that poor old wretch, dying of
hunger on his bed of rags, whether Mège should overthrow
Barroux's ministry, and whether a Vignon ministry should
ascend to power or not? At that rate a century, two
centuries, would be needed before there would be bread in
the garrets where groan the lamed sons of labour, the old,
broken-down beasts of burden. And behind Laveuve there
appeared the whole army of misery, the whole multitude of
the disinherited and the poor, who agonised and asked for
justice whilst the Chamber, sitting in all pomp, grew
furiously impassioned over the question as to whom the
nation should belong to, as to who should devour it. Mire
was flowing on in a broad stream, the hideous, bleeding,
devouring sore displayed itself in all impudence, like some
cancer which preys upon an organ and spreads to the
heart. And what disgust, what nausea must such a
spectacle inspire; and what a longing for the vengeful
knife that would bring health and joy!

Pierre could not have told for how long he had been
plunged in this reverie, when uproar again filled the hall.
People were coming back, gesticulating and gathering in

groups. And suddenly he heard little Massot exclaim near him : ' Well, if it isn't down it's not much better off. I wouldn't give four sous for its chance of surviving.'

He referred to the ministry, and began to recount the sitting to a fellow-journalist who had just arrived. Mège had spoken very eloquently, with extraordinary fury of indignation against the rotten *bourgeoisie*, which rotted everything it touched ; but, as usual, he had gone much too far, alarming the Chamber by his very violence. And so, when Barroux had ascended the tribune to ask for a month's adjournment of the interpellation, he had merely had occasion to wax indignant, in all sincerity be it said, full of lofty anger that such infamous campaigns should be carried on by a certain portion of the press. Were the shameful Panama scandals about to be renewed ? Were the national representatives going to let themselves be intimidated by fresh threats of denunciation ? It was the Republic itself which its adversaries were seeking to submerge beneath a flood of abominations. No, no, the hour had come for one to collect one's thoughts, and work in quietude without allowing those who hungered for scandal to disturb the public peace. And the Chamber, impressed by these words, fearing, too, lest the electorate should at last grow utterly weary of the continuous overflow of filth, had adjourned the interpellation to that day month. However, although Vignon had not personally intervened in the debate, the whole of his group had voted against the ministry, with the result that the latter had merely secured a majority of two votes—a mockery.

' But in that case they will resign,' said somebody to Massot.

' Yes, so it's rumoured. But Barroux is very tenacious. At all events, if they show any obstinacy they will be down before a week is over, particularly as Sagnier, who is quite furious, declares that he will publish the list of names to-morrow.'

Just then, indeed, Barroux and Monferrand were seen to pass, hastening along with thoughtful, busy mien, and followed by their anxious clients. It was said that the whole Cabinet was about to assemble to consider the position and come to a decision. And then Vignon, in his turn, reappeared amidst a stream of friends. He, for his part, was radiant, with a joy which he sought to conceal, calming his friends in his desire not to cry victory too soon. However, the eyes of the band glittered, like those of a pack of hounds when the moment draws near for the offal of the quarry to be distributed. And even Mège also looked triumphant. He had all but over-thrown the ministry. That made another one that was worn out, and by-and-by he would wear out Vignon's, and at last govern in his turn.

'The devil!' muttered little Massot, 'Chaigneux and Duthil look like whipped dogs. And see, there's nobody who is worth the governor. Just look at him, how superb he is, that Fonsègue! But good-bye; I must now be off!'

Then he shook hands with his brother-journalist, unwilling as he was to remain any longer, although the sitting still continued, some bill of public importance again being debated before rows of empty seats.

Chaigneux, with his desolate mien, had gone to lean against the pedestal of the high figure of Minerva; and never before had he been more bowed down by his needy distress, the everlasting anguish of his ill-luck. On the other hand, Duthil, in spite of everything, was perorating in the centre of a group with an affectation of scoffing unconcern; never-theless nervous twitches made his nose pucker and distorted his mouth, while the whole of his handsome face was becoming moist with fear. And even as Massot had said, there really was only Fonsègue who showed composure and bravery, ever the same with his restless little figure, and his eyes beaming with wit, though at times they were just faintly clouded by a shadow of uneasiness.

Pierre had risen to renew his request; but Fonsègue fore-stalled him, vivaciously exclaiming: 'No, no, Monsieur l'Abbé, I repeat that I cannot take on myself such an infraction of our rules. There was an inquiry, and a decision was arrived at. How would you have me overrule it?'

'Monsieur,' said the priest, in a tone of deep grief, 'it is a question of an old man who is hungry and cold, and in danger of death if he be not succoured.'

With a despairing gesture, the director of 'Le Globe' seemed to take the very walls as witnesses of his powerlessness. No doubt he feared some nasty affair for his newspaper, in which he had employed the Invalids of Labour enterprise as an electoral weapon. Perhaps, too, the secret terror into which the sitting of the Chamber had just thrown him was hardening his heart. 'I can do nothing,' he repeated. 'But naturally

I don't ask better than to have my hands forced by the ladies of the committee. You already have the support of Baroness Duvillard; secure that of some others.'

Pierre, who was determined to fight on to the very end, saw in this suggestion a supreme chance. 'I know the Countess de Quinsac,' he said; 'I can go to see her at once.'

'Quite so! An excellent idea, the Countess de Quinsac! Take a cab and go to see the Princess de Harn as well. She bestirs herself a great deal, and is becoming very influential. Secure the approval of those ladies, go back to the Baroness's at seven, get a letter from her to cover me, and then call on me at the office of my paper. That done, your man shall sleep at the Asylum at nine o'clock!'

He evinced in speaking a kind of joyous good nature, as though he no longer doubted of success now that he ran no risk of compromising himself. And great hope again came back to the priest: 'Ah! thank you, monsieur,' he said; 'it is a work of salvation that you will accomplish.'

'But you surely know that I ask nothing better. Ah! if we could only cure misery, prevent hunger and thirst by a mere word. However, make haste, you have not a minute to lose.'

They shook hands, and Pierre at once tried to get out of the throng. This, however, was no easy task, for the various groups had grown larger as all the anger and anguish, roused by the recent debate, ebbed back there amid a confused tumult. It was as when a stone, cast into a pool, stirs the ooze below, and causes hidden, rotting things to rise once more to the surface. And Pierre had to bring his elbows into play and force a passage athwart the throng, betwixt the shivering cowardice of some, the insolent audacity of others, and the smirchings which sullied the greater number, given the contagion which inevitably prevailed. However, he carried away a fresh hope, and it seemed to him that if he should save a life, make but one man happy that day, it would be like a first instalment of redemption, a sign that a little forgiveness would be extended to the many follies and errors of that egotistical and all-devouring political world.

On reaching the vestibule a final incident detained him for a moment longer. Some commotion prevailed there, following upon a quarrel between a man and an usher, the latter of whom had prevented the former from entering on finding that the admission ticket which he tendered was an

old one, with its original date scratched out. The man, very
rough at the outset, had then refrained from insisting—as if
indeed sudden timidity had come upon him. And in this
ill-dressed fellow Pierre was astonished to recognise Salvat,
the journeyman engineer, whom he had seen going off in
search of work that same morning. This time it was certainly
he, tall, thin and ravaged, with dreamy yet flaming eyes,
which set his pale starveling's face aglow. He no longer
carried his tool-bag; his ragged jacket was buttoned up and
distended on the left side by something that he carried in a
pocket, doubtless some hunk of bread. And on being repulsed
by the ushers he walked away, taking the Concorde Bridge,
slowly, as if chancewise, like a man who knows not whither
he is going.

IV

SOCIAL SIDELIGHTS

In her old faded drawing-room—a Louis Seize *salon* with
grey woodwork—the Countess de Quinsac sat near the
chimney-piece in her accustomed place. She was singularly
like her son, with a long and noble face, her chin somewhat
stern, but her eyes still beautiful beneath her fine snowy hair,
which was arranged in the antiquated style of her youth.
And whatever her haughty coldness, she knew how to be
amiable, with perfect, kindly graciousness.

Slightly waving her hand after a long silence, she resumed,
addressing herself to the Marquis de Morigny, who sat on the
other side of the chimney, where for long years he had always
taken the same armchair: 'Ah! you are right, my friend.
Providence has left us here forgotten, in a most abominable
epoch.'

'Yes, we passed by the side of happiness and missed it,'
the Marquis slowly replied, 'and it was your fault, and doubtless mine as well.'

Smiling sadly, she stopped him with another wave of her
hand. And the silence fell once more; not a sound from the
streets reached that gloomy ground floor at the rear of the
courtyard of an old mansion in the Rue St. Dominique,
almost at the corner of the Rue de Bourgogne.

The Marquis was an old man of seventy-five, nine years
older than the Countess. Short and thin though he was,

he none the less had a distinguished air, with his clean-shaven face, furrowed by deep, aristocratic wrinkles. He belonged to one of the most ancient families of France, and remained one of the last hopeless Legitimists, of very pure and lofty views, zealously keeping his faith to the dead monarchy amidst the downfall of everything. His fortune, still estimated at several millions of francs, remained, as it were, in a state of stagnation through his refusal to invest it in any enterprise of the century. It was known that in all discretion he had loved the Countess, even when M. de Quinsac was alive, and had, moreover, offered marriage after the latter's death, at the time when the widow had sought a refuge on that damp ground floor with merely an income of some 15,000 francs, saved with great difficulty from the wreck of the family fortune. But she, who adored her son Gérard, then in his tenth year, and of delicate health, had sacrificed everything to the boy from a kind of maternal chasteness and a super-stitious fear that she might lose him should she set another affection and another duty in her life. And the Marquis, while bowing to her decision, had continued to worship her with his whole soul, ever paying his court as on the first evening when he had seen her, still gallant and faithful after a quarter of a century had passed. There had never been anything between them, not even the exchange of a kiss.

Seeing how sad she looked, he feared that he might have displeased her, and so he asked : ' I should have liked to render you happy, but I didn't know how, and the fault can certainly only rest with me. Is Gérard giving you any cause for anxiety ? '

She shook her head, and then replied : ' As long as things remain as they are we cannot complain of them, my friend, since we accepted them.'

She referred to her son's culpable connection with Baroness Duvillard. She had ever shown much weakness with regard to that son whom she had had so much trouble to rear, for she alone knew what exhaustion, what racial collapse was hidden behind his proud bearing. She tolerated his idleness, the apathe-tic disgust which, man of pleasure that he was, had turned him from the profession of diplomacy as from that of arms. How many times had she not repaired his acts of folly and paid his petty debts, keeping silent concerning them, and refusing all pecuniary help from the Marquis, who no longer dared offer his millions, so stubbornly intent she was on living upon the

remnants of her own fortune. And thus she had ended by
closing her eyes to her son's scandalous love intrigue, divining
in some measure how things had happened, through self-
abandonment and lack of conscience—the man weak, unable
to resume possession of himself, and the woman holding and
retaining him. The Marquis, however, strangely enough, had
only forgiven the intrigue on the day when Ève had allowed
herself to be converted.

'You know, my friend, how good-natured Gérard is,' the
Countess resumed. 'In that lie both his strength and
weakness. How would you have me scold him when he
weeps over it all with me? He will tire of that woman.'

M. de Morigny wagged his head. 'She is still very
beautiful,' said he. 'And then there's the daughter. It would
be graver still if he were to marry her——'

'But the daughter's infirm?'

'Yes, and you know what would be said: A Quinsac
marrying a monster for the sake of her millions.'

This was their mutual terror. They knew everything that
went on at the Duvillards'—the affectionate friendship of the
uncomely Camille and the handsome Gérard, the seeming
idyll beneath which lurked the most awful of dramas. And
they protested with all their indignation. 'Oh! that—no, no,
never!' the Countess declared. 'My son in that family?—no,
I will never consent to it.'

Just at that moment General de Bozonnet entered. He
was much attached to his sister and came to keep her company
on the days when she received, for the old circle had gradually
dwindled down till now only a few faithful ones ventured into
that grey, gloomy *salon*, where one might have fancied oneself
thousands of leagues from present-day Paris. And forthwith, in order to enliven the room, he related that he had been
to *déjeuner* at the Duvillards', and named the guests, Gérard
among them. He knew that he pleased his sister by going
to the banker's house, whence he brought her news—a house,
too, which he cleansed in some degree by conferring on it the
great honour of his presence. And he himself in nowise felt
bored there, for he had long been gained over to the century
and showed himself of a very accommodating disposition in
everything that did not pertain to military art.

'That poor little Camille worships Gérard,' said he; 'she
was devouring him with her eyes at table.'

But M. de Morigny gravely intervened: 'There lies the

danger ; a marriage would be absolutely monstrous from every point of view.'

The General seemed astonished : 'Why, pray ? She isn't beautiful, but it's not only the beauties who marry ! And there are her millions. However, our dear child would only have to put them to a good use. True, there is also the mother ; but, *mon Dieu !* such things are so common now-a-days in Paris society ? '

This revolted the Marquis, who made a gesture of utter disgust. What was the use of discussion when all collapsed ? How could one answer a Bozonnet, the last surviving representative of such an illustrious family, when he reached such a point as to excuse the infamous morals that prevailed under the Republic ; after denying his king, too, and serving the Empire, faithfully and passionately attaching himself to the fortunes and memory of Cæsar ? However, the Countess also became indignant : 'Oh ! what are you saying, brother ? I will never authorise such a scandal ; I swore so only just now.'

'Don't swear, sister,' exclaimed the General ; 'for my part, I should like to see our Gérard happy. That's all. And one must admit that he's not good for much. I can understand that he didn't go into the army, for that profession is done for. But I do not so well understand why he did not enter the diplomatic profession, or accept some other occupation. It is very fine, no doubt, to run down the present times and declare that a man of our sphere cannot possibly do any clean work in them. But, as a matter of fact, it is only idle fellows who still say that. And Gérard has but one excuse, his lack of aptitude, will, and strength.'

Tears had risen to the mother's eyes. She ever trembled, well knowing how deceitful were appearances : a mere chill might carry her son off, however tall and strong he might look. And was he not indeed a symbol of that old-time aristocracy, still so lofty and proud in appearance, though at bottom it is but dust ?

'Well,' continued the General, 'he's thirty-six now ; he's constantly hanging on your hands, and he must make an end of it all.'

However, the Countess silenced him and turned to the Marquis : 'Let us put our confidence in God, my friend,' said she. 'He cannot but come to my help, for I have never willingly offended Him.'

'Never!' replied the Marquis, who in that one word set an expression of all his grief, all his affection and worship for that woman whom he had adored for so many years.

But another faithful friend came in and the conversation changed. M. de Larombière, Vice-President of the Appeal Court, was an old man of seventy-five, thin, bald, and clean-shaven but for a pair of little white whiskers. And his grey eyes, compressed mouth, and square and obstinate chin lent an expression of great austerity to his long face. The grief of his life was that, being afflicted with a somewhat childish lisp, he had never been able to make his full merits known when a public prosecutor, for he esteemed himself to be a great orator. And this secret worry rendered him morose. In him appeared an incarnation of that old royalist France which sulked and only served the Republic against its heart, that old stern magistracy which closed itself to all evolution, to all new views of things and beings. Of petty 'gown' nobility, originally a Legitimist, but now supporting Orleanism, he believed himself to be the one man of wisdom and logic in that *salon*, where he was very proud to meet the Marquis.

They talked of the last events; but with them political conversation was soon exhausted, amounting as it did to a mere bitter condemnation of men and occurrences, for all three were of one mind as to the abominations of the Republican *régime*. They themselves, however, were only ruins, the remnants of the old parties now all but utterly powerless. The Marquis for his part soared on high, yielding in nothing, ever faithful to the dead past; he was one of the last representatives of that lofty, obstinate *noblesse* which dies where it finds itself without an effort to escape its fate. The judge, who at least had a pretender living, relied on a miracle, and demonstrated the necessity of one, if France were not to sink into the depths of misfortune and completely disappear. And as for the General, all that he regretted of the two Empires was their great wars; he left the faint hope of a Bonapartist restoration on one side to declare that by not contenting itself with the Imperial military system, and by substituting therefor obligatory service, the nation in arms, the Republic had killed both warfare and the country.

When the Countess's one man-servant came to ask her if she would consent to receive Abbé Froment, she seemed somewhat surprised. 'What can he want of me? Show him in,' she said.

She was very pious, and having met Pierre in connection with various charitable enterprises, she had been touched by his zeal as well as by the saintly reputation which he owed to his Neuilly parishioners.

He, absorbed by his fever, felt intimidated directly he crossed the threshold. He could at first distinguish nothing, but fancied he was entering some place of mourning, a shadowy spot where human forms melted away and voices were never raised above a whisper. Then, on perceiving the persons who were present, he felt yet more out of his element, for they seemed so sad, so far removed from the world whence he had just come, and whither he was about to return. And when the Countess had made him sit dowr beside her in front of the chimney-piece, it was in a low voice that he told her the lamentable story of Laveuve, and asked her support to secure the man's admittance to the Asylum for the Invalids of Labour.

'Ah! yes,' said she, 'that enterprise which my son wished me to belong to. But, Monsieur l'Abbé, I have never once attended the committee meetings. So how could I intervene, having assuredly no influence whatever?'

Again had the figures of Eve and Gérard arisen before her, for it was at this asylum that the pair had first met. And influenced by her sorrowful maternal love she was already weakening, although it was regretfully that she had lent her name to one of those noisy charitable enterprises, which people abused to further their selfish interests in a manner she condemned.

'But, madame,' Pierre insisted, 'it is a question of a poor starving old man. I implore you to be compassionate.'

Although the priest had spoken in a low voice, the General drew near. 'It's for your old revolutionary that you are running about, is it not?' said he. 'Didn't you succeed with the manager, then? The fact is that it's difficult to feel any pity for fellows who, if they were the masters, would, as they themselves say, sweep us all away.'

M. de Larombière jerked his chin approvingly. For some time past he had been haunted by the Anarchist peril. But Pierre, distressed and quivering, again began to plead his cause. He spoke of all the frightful misery, the homes where there was no food, the women and children shivering with cold, and the fathers scouring muddy, wintry Paris in search of a bit of bread. All that he asked for was a line on a visiting card, a kindly word from the Countess, which he would at once carry to Baroness Duvillard to prevail on her to set the regulations aside. And in that mournful *salon* his words, tremulous with stifled tears, fell one by one, like sounds from afar, dying away in a dead world where there was no echo left.

Madame de Quinsac turned towards M. de Morigny, but he seemed to take no interest in it at all. He was gazing fixedly at the fire, with the haughty air of a stranger who was indifferent to the things and beings in whose midst an error of time compelled him to live. But feeling that the glance of the woman he worshipped was fixed upon him, he raised his head ; and then their eyes met for a moment with an expression of infinite gentleness, the mournful gentleness of their heroic love.

'*Mon Dieu !*' said she, 'I know your merits, Monsieur l'Abbé, and I won't refuse my help to one of your good works.'

Then she withdrew for a moment, and returned with a card on which she had written that she supported with all her heart Monsieur l'Abbé Froment in the steps he was taking. And he thanked her and went off delighted, as if he carried yet a fresh hope of salvation from that drawing-room, where, as he retired, gloom and silence once more seemed to fall on that old lady and her last faithful friends gathered around the fire, last relics of a world that was soon to disappear.

Once outside, Pierre joyfully climbed into his cab again, after giving the Princess de Harn's address in the Avenue Kléber. If he could also obtain her approval he would no longer doubt of success. However, there was such a crush on the Concorde Bridge that the driver had to walk his horse. And, on the foot-pavement, Pierre again saw Duthil, who, with a cigar between his lips, was smiling at the crowd, with his amiable bird-like heedlessness, happy as he felt at finding the pavement dry and the sky blue on leaving that worrying sitting of the Chamber. Seeing how gay and triumphant he looked, a sudden inspiration came to the priest, who said to himself that he ought to win over this young man, whose report had had such a disastrous effect. As it happened, the cab having been compelled to stop altogether, the deputy had just recognised him and was smiling at him.

'Where are you going, Monsieur Duthil?' Pierre asked.

'Close by, in the Champs-Elysées.'

'I'm going that way, and, as I should much like to speak to you for a moment, it would be very kind of you to take a seat beside me. I will set you down wherever you like.'

'Willingly, Monsieur l'Abbé. It won't inconvenience you if I finish my cigar?'

'Oh! not at all.'

The cab found its way out of the crush, crossed the Place de la Concorde, and began to ascend the Champs Elysées. And Pierre, reflecting that he had very few minutes before him, at once attacked Duthil, quite ready for any effort to convince him. He remembered what a *sortie* the young deputy had made against Laveuve at the Baron's; and thus he was astonished to hear him interrupt and say quite pleasantly, enlivened as he seemed by the bright sun, which was again beginning to shine: 'Ah, yes! your old drunkard! So you didn't settle his business with Fonsègue? And what is it you want? To have him admitted to-day? Well, you know I don't oppose it?'

'But there's your report.'

'My report?—oh, my report! But questions change according to the way one looks at them. And if you are so anxious about your Laveuve I won't refuse to help you.'

Pierre gazed at him in astonishment, at bottom extremely well pleased. And there was no further necessity even for him to speak.

'You didn't take the matter in hand properly,' continued Duthil, leaning forward with a confidential air. 'It's the Baron who's the master at home, for reasons which you may divine, which you may very likely know. The Baroness does all that he asks without even discussing the point; and this morning, instead of starting on a lot of useless visits, you only had to gain his support, particularly as he seemed to be very well disposed. And she would then have given way immediately.' Duthil began to laugh. 'And so,' he continued, 'do you know what I'll do? Well, I'll gain the Baron over to your cause. Yes, I am this moment going to a house where he is, where one is certain to find him every day at this time.' Then he laughed more loudly. 'And perhaps you are not ignorant of it, Monsieur l'Abbé. When he is there you may be certain he never gives a refusal. I promise you I'll make him swear that he will compel his wife to grant your man admission this very evening. Only it will, perhaps, be rather late. '

Then all at once, as if struck by a fresh idea, Duthil went on : ' But why shouldn't you come with me ? You secure a line from the Baron, and thereupon, without losing a minute, you go in search of the Baroness. Ah ! the character of the house worries you a little ? I understand it. Well, would you like to see only the Baron there ? You can wait for him in a little *salon* downstairs ; I will bring him to you. '

This proposal made Duthil altogether merry ; but Pierre, quite scared, hesitated at the idea of thus going to Silviane d'Aulnay's. It was hardly a place for him. However, to achieve his purpose he would have descended into the very dwelling of the fiend, and had already done so sometimes with Abbé Rose, when there was hope of assuaging wretchedness. So he turned to Duthil and consented to accompany him.

Silviane d'Aulnay's little mansion, a very luxurious one, displaying, so to say, the luxury of a temple, refined but suggestive of gallantry, stood in the Avenue d'Antin, near the Champs-Elysées. The inmate of this sanctuary, where the orfrays of old dalmaticas glittered in the mauve reflections from the windows of stained glass, had just completed her twenty-fifth year. Short and slim she was, of an adorable, dark beauty, and all Paris was acquainted with her delicious, virginal countenance of a gentle oval, her delicate nose, her little mouth, her candid cheeks and artless chin, above all which she wore her black hair in thick, heavy bands, which hid her low brow. Her notoriety was due precisely to her pretty air of astonishment, the infinite purity of her blue eyes, the whole expression of chaste innocence which she assumed when it so pleased her—an expression which contrasted powerfully with her true nature, shameless creature that she really was, of the most monstrous, confessed, and openly-displayed perversity ; such as, in fact, often spring up from the rotting soil of great cities. Extraordinary things were related about Silviane's tastes and fancies. Some said that she was a doorkeeper's, others a doctor's, daughter. In any case she had managed to acquire instruction and manners, for when occasion required she lacked neither wit, nor style, nor deportment. She had been rolling through the theatres for ten years or so, applauded for her beauty's sake, and she had even ended by obtaining some pretty little successes in such parts as those of very pure young maidens or loving and persecuted young wives. Since there had been a question, however, of her entering the Comédie Française to play the *rôle* of Pauline in 'Polyeucte,' some people had waxed indignant and others had roared with laughter, so ridiculous did the idea appear, so outrageous for the majesty of classic tragedy. She, however, quiet and stubborn, wished this thing to be, was resolved that it should be, certain as she was that she would secure it, and insolent like a creature to whom men had never yet been able to refuse anything.

That day, at three o'clock, Gérard de Quinsac, not knowing how to kill the time pending the appointment he had given Eve in the Rue Matignon, had thought of calling at Silviane's, which was in the neighbourhood. She was an old caprice of his, and even nowadays he would sometimes linger at the little mansion if its pretty mistress felt bored. However, he had this time found her in a fury ; and, reclining in one of the deep armchairs of the *salon* where 'old gold' formed the predominant colour, he was listening to her complaints. She, standing before him in a white gown, white indeed from head to foot, like Eve herself at the *déjeuner*, was speaking passionately, and fast convincing him. Won over indeed by so much youth and beauty, he unconsciously compared her to his other flame, already regretting his coming assignation, and so mastered by supineness, both moral and physical, that he would have preferred to remain all day in the depths of that armchair.

' You hear me, Gérard ! ' she at last exclaimed ; ' I'll have nothing whatever to do with him unless he brings me my nomination.'

Just then Baron Duvillard came in, and forthwith she changed to ice and received him like some sorely offended young queen who awaits an explanation ; whilst he, who foresaw the storm and brought moreover disastrous tidings, forced a smile though very ill at ease. She was the stain, the blemish attaching to that man who was yet so sturdy and so powerful amidst the general decline of his race. And she was also the beginning of justice and punishment, taking all his piled-up gold from him by the handful, and avenging by her cruelty those who shivered and who starved. And it was pitiful to see that feared and flattered man, beneath whom states and governments trembled, here turn pale with anxiety, bend low in all humility, and relapse into senile, stammering infancy under the spur of acute passion.

'Ah! my dear friend,' said he, 'if you only knew how I have been rushing about. I had a lot of worrying business, some contractors to see, a big advertisement affair to settle, and I feared that I should never be able to come and kiss your hand.'

He kissed it, but she let her arm fall, coldly, indifferently, contenting herself with looking at him, waiting for what he might have to say to her, and embarrassing him to such a point that he began to perspire and stammer, unable to express himself. 'Of course,' he began, 'I also thought of you, and went to the Fine Arts Office, where I had received a positive promise. Oh! they are still very much in your favour at the Fine Arts Office! Only, just fancy, it's that idiot of a minister, that Taboureau,[1] an old professor from the provinces who knows nothing about our Paris, that has expressly opposed your nomination, saying that as long as he is in office you shall not appear at the Comédie.'

Erect and rigid, she spoke but two words: 'And then?'

'And then—well, my dear, what would you have me do? One can't, after all, overthrow a ministry to enable you to play the part of Pauline.'

'Why not?'

He pretended to laugh, but his blood rushed to his face, and the whole of his sturdy figure quivered with anguish. 'Come, my little Silviane,' said he, 'don't be obstinate. You can be so nice when you choose. Give up the idea of that *début*. You, yourself, would risk a great deal in it, for what would be your worries if you were to fail? You would weep all the tears in your body. And besides, you can ask me for so many other things which I should be so happy to give you. Come now, at once make a wish, and I will gratify it immediately.'

In a frolicsome way he sought to take her hand again. But she drew back with an air of much dignity. 'No, you hear me, my dear fellow, I will have nothing whatever to do with you—nothing, so long as I don't play Pauline.'

---

[1] Taboureau is previously described as Minister of Public Instruction. It should be pointed out, however, that although under the present Republic the Ministries of Public Instruction and Fine Arts have occasionally been distinct departments, at other times they have been united—one minister, as in Taboureau's case, having charge of both.— *Trans.*

He understood her fully, and he knew her well enough to realise how rigorously she would treat him. Only a kind of grunt came from his contracted throat, though he still tried to treat the matter in a jesting way. 'Isn't she bad-tempered to-day!' he resumed at last, turning towards Gérard. 'What have you done to her that I find her in such a state?'

However, the young man, who kept very quiet for fear lest he himself might be bespattered in the course of the dispute, continued to stretch himself out in a languid way and gave no answer.

But Silviane's anger burst forth. 'What has he done to me? He has pitied me for being at the mercy of such a man as you—so egotistical, so insensible to the insults heaped upon me. Ought you not to be the first to bound with indignation? Ought you not to have exacted my admittance to the Comédie as a reparation for the insult? For, after all, it is a defeat for you; if I'm considered unworthy, you are struck at the same time as I am. And so I'm a drab, eh? Say at once that I'm a creature to be driven away from all respectable houses.'

She went on in this style, coming at last to vile words, the abominable words which, in moments of anger, always ended by returning to her innocent-looking lips. The Baron, who well knew that a syllable from him would only increase the foulness of the overflow, vainly turned an imploring glance on the Count to solicit his intervention. Gérard, with his keen desire for peace and quietness, often brought about a reconciliation, but this time he did not stir, feeling too lazy and sleepy to interfere. And Silviane all at once came to a finish, repeating her trenchant, severing words : 'Well, manage as you can—secure my *début*, or I'll have nothing more to do with you, nothing!'

'All right! all right!' Duvillard at last murmured, sneering, but in despair ; 'we'll arrange it all.'

However, at that moment a servant came in to say that M. Duthil was downstairs and wished to speak to the Baron in the smoking-room. Duvillard was astonished at this, for Duthil usually came up as though the house were his own. Then he reflected that the deputy had doubtless brought him some serious news from the Chamber which he wished to impart to him confidentially. So he followed the servant, leaving Gérard and Silviane together.

In the smoking-room, an apartment communicating with

the hall by a wide bay, the curtain of which was drawn up, Pierre stood with his companion, waiting and glancing curiously around him. What particularly struck him was the almost religious solemnness of the entrance, the heavy hangings, the mystic gleams of the stained glass, the old furniture steeped in chapel-like gloom amidst scattered perfumes of myrrh and incense. Duthil, who was still very gay, tapped a low divan with his cane and said: ' She has a nicely furnished house, eh? Oh! she knows how to look after her interests.'

Then the Baron came in, still quite upset and anxious. And without even perceiving the priest, desirous as he was of tidings, he began: ' Well, what did they do? Is there some very bad news then?'

' Mège interpellated and applied for a declaration of urgency so as to overthrow Barroux. You can imagine what his speech was.'

' Yes, yes, against the *bourgeois*, against me, against you. It's always the same thing—— And then?'

' Then—well, urgency wasn't voted, but, in spite of a very fine defence, Barroux only secured a majority of two votes.'

' Two votes—the devil! Then he's down, and we shall have a Vignon ministry next week.'

' That's what everybody said in the lobbies.'

The Baron frowned, as if he were estimating what good or evil might result to the world from such a change. Then, with a gesture of displeasure, he said: ' A Vignon ministry! The devil! That would hardly be any better. Those young democrats pretend to be virtuous, and a Vignon ministry wouldn't admit Silviane to the Comédie.'

This, at first, was his only thought in presence of the crisis which made the political world tremble. And so the deputy could not refrain from referring to his own anxiety. ' Well, and we others—what is our position in it all?'

This brought Duvillard back to the situation. With a fresh gesture, this time a superbly proud one, he expressed his full and impudent confidence. ' We others?—why, we remain as we are; we've never been in peril I imagine. Oh! I am quite at ease; Sagnier can publish his famous list if it amuses him to do so. If we haven't long since bought Sagnier and his list, it's because Barroux is a thoroughly honest man, and for my part I don't care to throw money out of window. I repeat to you that we fear nothing.'

Then, as he at last recognised Abbé Froment, who had remained in the shade, Duthil explained what service the priest desired of him. And Duvillard in his state of emotion, his heart still rent by Silviane's sternness, must have felt a secret hope that a good action might bring him luck; so he at once consented to intervene in favour of Laveuve's admission. Taking a card and a pencil from his pocket-book he drew near to the window. 'Oh! whatever you desire, Monsieur l'Abbé,' he said, 'I shall be very happy to participate in this good work. Here, this is what I have written: "My dear, please do what M. l'Abbé Froment solicits in favour of this unfortunate man, since our friend Fonsègue only awaits a word from you to take proper steps."'

At this moment through the open bay Pierre caught sight of Gérard, whom Silviane, calm once more, and inquisitive no doubt to know why Duthil had called, was escorting into the hall. And the sight of the young woman filled him with astonishment, so simple and gentle did she seem to him, full of the immaculate candour of a virgin. Never had he dreamt of a lily of more modest yet delicious bloom in the whole garden of innocence.

'Now,' continued Duvillard, 'if you wish to hand this card to my wife at once, you must go to the Princess de Harn's, where there is a *matinée*——'

'I was going there, Monsieur le Baron.'

'Very good. You will certainly find my wife there; she is to take the children there.' Then he paused, for he too had just seen Gérard; and he called him: 'I say, Gérard, my wife said that she was going to that *matinée*, didn't she? You feel sure—don't you?—that Monsieur l'Abbé will find her there?'

Although the young man was then going to the Rue Matignon, there to wait for Eve, it was in the most natural manner possible that he replied: 'If Monsieur l'Abbé makes haste, I think he will find her there, for she was certainly going there before trying on a corsage at Salmon's.'

Then he kissed Silviane's hand, and went off with the air of a handsome, indolent man, who knows no malice, and is even weary of pleasure.

Pierre, feeling rather embarrassed, was obliged to let Duvillard introduce him to the mistress of the house. He bowed in silence, whilst she, likewise silent, returned his bow with modest reserve, the tact appropriate to the occasion,

such as no *ingenue*, even at the Comédie, was then capable
of.   And while the Baron accompanied the priest to the
door, she returned to the *salon* with Duthil, who was
scarcely screened by the door-curtain before he passed his
arm round her waist.

When Pierre, who at last felt confident of success, found
himself, still in his cab, in front of the Princess de Harn's
mansion in the Avenue Kléber, he suddenly relapsed into
great embarrassment.   The avenue was crowded with
carriages brought thither by the musical *matinée*, and such
a throng of arriving guests pressed round the entrance,
decorated with a kind of tent with scallopings of red velvet,
that he deemed the house unapproachable.   How could he
manage to get in?   And how in his cassock could he reach
the Princess, and ask for a minute's conversation with
Baroness Duvillard?   Amidst all his feverishness he had
not thought of these difficulties.   However, he was
approaching the door on foot, asking himself how he might
glide unperceived through the throng, when the sound of a
merry voice made him turn: 'What, Monsieur l'Abbé! Is it
possible!   So now I find you here!'

It was little Massot who spoke.   He went everywhere,
witnessed ten sights a day—a parliamentary sitting, a funeral,
a wedding, any festive or mourning scene—when he wanted
a good subject for an article.   'What! Monsieur l'Abbé,' he
resumed, 'and so you have come to our amiable Princess's
to see the Mauritanians dance!'

He was jesting, for the so-called Mauritanians were simply
six Spanish dancing-girls, who by the sensuality of their
performance were then making all Paris rush to the Folies-
Bergère.   For drawing-room entertainments these girls
reserved yet more indecorous dances—dances of such a
character indeed that they would certainly not have been
allowed in a theatre.   And the *beau monde* rushed to see
them at the houses of the bolder lady-entertainers, the
eccentric and foreign ones like the Princess, who in order to
draw society recoiled from no 'attraction.'

However, when Pierre had explained to little Massot that
he was still running about on the same business, the
journalist obligingly offered to pilot him.   He knew the
house, obtained admittance by a back door, and brought
Pierre along a passage into a corner of the hall, near the
very entrance of the grand drawing-room.   Lofty green

plants decorated this hall, and in the spot selected Pierre was virtually hidden. 'Don't stir, my dear Abbé,' said Massot, 'I will try to ferret out the Princess for you. And you shall know if Baroness Duvillard has already arrived.'

What surprised Pierre was that every window-shutter of the mansion was closed, every chink stopped up so that daylight might not enter, and that every room flared with electric lamps, an illumination of supernatural intensity. The heat was already very great, the atmosphere heavy with a violent perfume of flowers and *odore di femina*. And to Pierre, who felt both blinded and stifled, it seemed as if he were entering one of those luxurious, unearthly Dens of the Flesh such as the pleasure-world of Paris conjures from dreamland. By rising on tiptoes, as the drawing-room entrance was wide open, he could distinguish the backs of the women who were already seated, rows of necks crowned with fair or dark hair. The Mauritanians were doubtless executing their first dance. He did not see them, but he could divine the lascivious passion of the dance from the quiver of all those women's necks, which swayed as beneath a great gust of wind. Then laughter arose and a tempest of bravos, quite a tumult of enjoyment.

'I can't put my hand on the Princess; you must wait a little,' Massot returned to say. 'However, I met Janzen, and he promised to bring her to me. Don't you know Janzen?'

Then, in part because his profession willed it, and in part for pleasure's sake, he began to gossip. The Princess was a good friend of his. He had described her first *soirée* during the previous year, when she had made her *début* at that mansion on her arrival in Paris. He knew the real truth about her, so far as it could be known. Rich? yes, perhaps she was, for she spent enormous sums. Married she must have been, and to a real prince, too; no doubt she was still married to him, in spite of her story of widowhood. Indeed, it seemed certain that her husband, who was as handsome as an archangel, was travelling about with a vocalist. As for having a bee in her bonnet, that was beyond discussion, as clear as noon-day. Whilst showing much intelligence, she constantly and suddenly shifted. Incapable of any prolonged effort, she went from one thing that had awakened her curiosity to another, never attaching herself anywhere. After ardently busying herself with painting, she had lately become impassioned for chemistry, and was now letting poetry master her.

'And so you don't know Janzen,' continued Massot. 'It was he who threw her into chemistry, into the study of explosives especially, for, as you may imagine, the only interest in chemistry for her is its connection with Anarchism. She, I think, is really an Austrian, though one must always doubt anything she herself says. As for Janzen, he calls himself a Russian, but he's probably German. Oh ! he's the most unobtrusive, enigmatical man in the world, without a home, perhaps without a name—a terrible fellow with an unknown past. I myself hold proofs which make me think that he took part in that frightful crime at Barcelona. At all events, for nearly a year now I've been meeting him in Paris, where the police are no doubt watching him. And nothing can rid me of the idea that he merely consented to become our lunatic Princess's lover in order to throw the detectives off the scent. He pretends to live a mere life of pleasure, but he has introduced to the house some extraordinary people, Anarchists of all nationalities and shades—for instance, one Raphanel, that fat, jovial little man yonder, a Frenchman he is, and his companions would do well to mistrust him. Then there's a Bergaz, a Spaniard, I think, an obscure jobber at the Bourse, whose sensual, blobber-lipped mouth is so disquieting. And there are others and others, adventurers and bandits from the four corners of the earth ! ... Ah ! the foreign colonies of our Parisian pleasure-world ! There are a few spotless fine names, a few real great fortunes among them but, as for the rest, ah ! what a herd ! '

Rosemonde's own drawing-room was summed up in those words : resounding titles, real millionaires, then, down below, the most extravagant medley of international imposture and turpitude. And Pierre thought of that internationalism, that cosmopolitanism, that flight of foreigners which, ever denser and denser, swooped down upon Paris. Most certainly it came thither to enjoy it, as to a city of adventure and delight, and it helped to rot it a little more. Was it then a necessary thing, that decomposition of the great cities which have governed the world, that affluxion of every passion, every desire, every gratification, that gathering together of reeking soil from all parts of the world, there where, in beauty and intelligence, blooms the flower of civilisation ?

However, Janzen appeared, a tall, thin fellow of about thirty, very fair, with grey, pale, harsh eyes, and a pointed beard and flowing curly hair which elongated his livid, cloudy face. He spoke indifferent French in a low voice and without a gesture. And he declared that the Princess could not be found; he had looked for her everywhere. Possibly, if somebody had displeased her, she had shut herself up in her room and gone to bed, leaving her guests to amuse themselves in all freedom in whatever way they might choose.

'Why, but here she is!' suddenly said Massot.

Rosemonde was indeed there, in the vestibule, watching the door as if she expected somebody. Short, slight, and strange rather than pretty, with her delicate face, her sea-green eyes, her small quivering nose, her rather large and over-ruddy mouth, which was parted so that one could see her superb teeth, she that day wore a sky-blue gown spangled with silver; and she had silver bracelets on her arms and a silver circlet in her pale brown hair, which rained down in curls and frizzy, straggling locks as though waving in a perpetual breeze.

'Oh! whatever you desire, Monsieur l'Abbé,' she said to Pierre as soon as she knew his business. 'If they don't take your old man in at our asylum, send him to me; I'll take him, I will; I will sleep him somewhere here.'

However, she remained fidgety, and continually glanced towards the door. And on the priest asking if Baroness Duvillard had yet arrived: 'Why, no!' she cried, 'and I am much surprised at it. She is to bring her son and daughter. Yesterday, Hyacinthe positively promised me that he would come.'

He was her new caprice. If her passion for chemistry was giving way to a budding taste for decadent, symbolical verse, it was because one evening, whilst discussing Occultism with Hyacinthe, she had discovered an extraordinary beauty in him: the astral beauty of Nero's wandering soul! At least, said she, the signs of it were certain.

And all at once she quitted Pierre: 'Ah, at last!' she cried, feeling relieved and happy. Then she darted forward: Hyacinthe was at that moment coming in with his sister Camille.

On the very threshold, however, he had just met the friend on whose account he was there, young Lord George Eldrett, a pale and languid stripling with the hair of a girl; and he scarcely condescended to notice the tender greeting of Rosemonde, for he professed to regard woman as an impure and degrading creature. Distressed by such coldness, she followed the two young men, returning in their rear into the reeking, blinding furnace of the drawing-room.

Massot, however, had been obliging enough to stop Camille and bring her to Pierre, who at the first words they exchanged relapsed into despair. 'What, mademoiselle! has not madame your mother accompanied you here?'

The girl, clad according to her wont in a dark gown, this time of peacock-blue, was nervous, with wicked eyes and sibilant voice. And as she ragefully drew up her little figure, her deformity, the unequal height of her two shoulders, became more apparent than ever. 'No,' she rejoined, 'she was unable. She had something to try on at her dressmaker's. We stopped too long at the Exposition du Lis, and she requested us to set her down at Salmon's door on our way here.'

It was Camille herself who had skilfully prolonged the visit to the art show, still hoping to prevent her mother from meeting Gérard. And her rage arose from the ease with which her mother had got rid of her, thanks to that falsehood of having something to try on.

'But,' ingenuously said Pierre, 'if I went at once to this person, Salmon, I might perhaps be able to send up my card.'

Camille gave a shrill laugh, so funny did the idea appear to her. Then she retorted: 'Oh! who knows if you would still find her there? She had another pressing appointment, and is no doubt already keeping it!'

'Well, then, I will wait for her here. She will surely come to fetch you, will she not?'

'Fetch us? Oh no! since I tell you that she has other important affairs to attend to. The carriage will take us home alone, my brother and I.'

The girl's pain-fraught irony was becoming yet more bitter. Didn't that priest understand her, then, that he asked such naïve questions which were like dagger-thrusts in her heart? Yet he must know, since everybody knew the truth.

'Ah! how worried I am,' Pierre resumed, so grieved indeed that tears almost came to his eyes. 'It's still on account of that poor man about whom I have been busying myself since this morning. I have a line from your father, and Monsieur Gérard told me——' But at this point he paused in confusion, and amidst all his thoughtlessness of the world, absorbed as he was in the one passion of charity, he suddenly divined the truth. 'Yes,' he added mechanically, 'I just now saw your father again with Monsieur de Quinsac.'

'I know, I know,' replied Camille, with the suffering yet scoffing air of a girl who is ignorant of nothing. 'Well, Monsieur l'Abbé, if you have a line from papa for mamma, you must wait till mamma has finished her business. You might come to the house about six o'clock, but I doubt if you'll find her there, as she may well be detained.'

While Camille thus spoke her murderous eyes glistened, and each word she uttered, simple as it seemed, became instinct with ferocity, as if it were a knife, which she would have liked to plunge into her mother's breast. In all certainty she had never before hated her mother to such a point as this in her envy of her beauty and her happiness in being loved. And the irony which poured from the girl's virgin lips, before that simple priest, was like a flood of mire with which she sought to submerge her rival.

Just then, however, Rosemonde came back again, feverish and flurried as usual. And she led Camille away: 'Ah, my dear, make haste. They are extraordinary, delightful, intoxicating!'

Janzen and little Massot also followed the Princess. All the men hastened from the adjoining rooms, scrambled and plunged into the *salon* at the news that the Mauritanians had again begun to dance. That time it must have been the frantic, lascivious gallop that Paris whispered about, for Pierre saw the rows of necks and heads, now fair, now dark, wave and quiver as beneath a violent wind. With every window-shutter closed, the conflagration of the electric lamps turned the place into a perfect brazier, reeking with human effluvia. And there came a spell of rapture, fresh laughter and bravos, all the delight of an overflowing orgie.

When Pierre again found himself on the footwalk, he remained for a moment bewildered, blinking, astonished to be in broad daylight once more. Half-past four would soon strike, but he had nearly two hours to wait before calling at the house in the Rue Godot-de-Mauroy. What should he do? He paid his driver; preferring to descend the Champs Elysées on foot, since he had some time to lose. A walk, moreover, might calm the fever which was burning his hands, in the passion of charity which ever since the morning had been mastering him more and more, in proportion as he encountered fresh and fresh obstacles. He now had but one pressing

desire : to complete his good work, since success henceforth
seemed certain. And he tried to restrain his steps and walk
leisurely down the magnificent avenue, which had now been
dried by the bright sun, and was enlivened by a concourse of
people, while overhead the sky was again blue, lightly blue,
as in springtime.

Nearly two hours to lose while, yonder, the wretched
Laveuve lay with life ebbing from him on his bed of rags, in
his icy den ! Sudden feelings of revolt, of well-nigh irresistible
impatience ascended from Pierre's heart, making him quiver
with desire to run off and at once find Baroness Duvillard, so
as to obtain from her the all-saving order. He felt sure that
she was somewhere near, in one of those quiet neighbouring
streets, and great was his perturbation, his dolorous anger
at having to wait in this wise to save a human life until she
should have attended to those affairs of hers, of which her
daughter spoke with such murderous glances ! He seemed to
hear a formidable cracking : the family life of the *bourgeoisie*
was collapsing : the father was at a hussy's house, the mother
with a lover ; the son and daughter knew everything, the
former gliding to idiotic perversity, the latter enraged, and
dreaming of stealing her mother's lover to make an husband
of him. And meantime the splendid equipages descended the
triumphal avenue, and the crowd with its luxury flowed
along the side-walks, one and all joyous and superb, seemingly
with no idea that somewhere at the far end there was a
gaping abyss wherein every one of them would fall and be
annihilated !

When Pierre got as far as the Summer Circus he was
much surprised at again seeing Salvat, the journeyman
engineer, on one of the avenue seats. He must have sunk
down there, overcome by weariness and hunger, after many a
vain search. However, his jacket was still distended by
something he carried in or under it, some bit of bread, no
doubt, which he meant to take home with him. And leaning
back, with his arms hanging listlessly, he was watching with
dreamy eyes the play of some very little children, who, with
the help of their wooden spades, were laboriously raising
mounds of sand, and then destroying them by dint of kicks.
As he looked at them his red eyelids moistened, and a very
gentle smile appeared on his poor discoloured lips. This
time Pierre, feeling really anxious, wished to approach
and question him. But Salvat distrustfully rose and went

off in the direction of the Circus, where a concert was then finishing. And he prowled around the entrance of that festive edifice, where two thousand happy people, piled up together, were listening to music.

V

FROM RELIGION TO ANARCHY

As Pierre was reaching the Place de la Concorde he suddenly remembered the appointment which Abbé Rose had given him for five o'clock at the Madeleine, and which he was forgetting in the feverishness born of his repeated steps to save Laveuve. And at thought of it he hastened on, well pleased at having something to occupy and keep him patient.

When he entered the church he was surprised to find it so dark. There were only a few candles burning, huge shadows were flooding the nave, and amidst the semi-obscurity a very loud, clear voice spoke on with a ceaseless streaming of words. All that one could at first distinguish of the numerous congregation was a pale, vague mass of heads, motionless with extreme attention. In the pulpit stood Monseigneur Martha, finishing his third address on the New Spirit. The two former ones had re-echoed far and wide, and so what is called ' all Paris ' was there—women of society, politicians, and writers, who were captivated by the speaker's artistic oratory, his warm, skilful language, and his broad, easy gestures, worthy of a great actor.

Pierre did not wish to disturb the solemn attention, the quivering silence, above which the prelate's voice alone rang out. Accordingly he resolved to wait before seeking Abbé Rose, and remained standing near a pillar. A parting gleam of daylight fell obliquely on Monseigneur Martha, who looked tall and sturdy in his white surplice, and scarcely showed a grey hair, although he was more than fifty. He had handsome features : black, keen eyes, a commanding nose, a mouth and chin of the greatest firmness of contour. What more particularly struck one, however, what gained the heart of every listener, was the expression of extreme amiability and anxious sympathy which softened the imperious haughtiness of the prelate's face.

Pierre had formerly known him as Curé, or parish priest,

of Ste Clotilde. He was doubtless of Italian origin, but he had
been born in Paris, and had quitted the seminary of St. Sul-
pice with the best possible record. Very intelligent and very
ambitious, he had evinced an activity which even made his
superiors anxious. Then, on being appointed Bishop of
Persepolis, he had disappeared, gone to Rome, where he had
spent five years engaged in work of which very little was
known. However, since his return he had been astonishing
Paris by his brilliant propaganda, busying himself with the
most varied affairs, and becoming much appreciated and very
powerful at the archiepiscopal residence. He devoted himself
in particular, and with wonderful results, to the task of increasing the subscriptions for the completion of the basilica
of the Sacred Heart. He recoiled from nothing, neither from
journeys, nor lectures, nor collections, nor applications to
Government, nor even endeavours among Israelites and Free-
masons. And at last, again enlarging his sphere of action, he
had undertaken to reconcile Science with Catholicism, and to
bring all Christian France to the Republic, by on all sides ex-
pounding the policy of Pope Leo XIII., in order that the
Church might finally triumph.

However, in spite of the advances of this influential and
amiable man, Pierre scarcely liked him. He only felt grateful to him for one thing, the appointment of good Abbé Rose
as curate at St. Pierre de Montmartre, which appointment he
had secured for him no doubt in order to prevent such a
scandal as the punishment of an old priest for showing himself too charitable. On thus finding and hearing the prelate
in that renowned pulpit of the Madeleine, still and ever
pursuing his work of conquest, Pierre remembered how he
had seen him at the Duvillards' during the previous spring,
when, with his usual *maestria*, he had achieved his greatest
triumph—the conversion of Eve to Catholicism. That
church, too, had witnessed her baptism, a wonderfully
pompous ceremony, a perfect gala offered to the public which
figures in all the great events of Parisian life. Gérard had
knelt down, moved to tears, whilst the Baron triumphed like
a good-natured husband who was happy to find religion
establishing perfect harmony in his household. It was
related among the spectators that Eve's family, and particularly old Justus Steinberger, her father, was not in
reality much displeased by the affair. The old man sneer-
ingly remarked, indeed, that he knew his daughter well

enough to wish her to belong to his worst enemy. In the banking business there is a class of security which one is pleased to see discounted by one's rivals. With the stubborn hope of triumph peculiar to his race, Justus, consoling himself for the failure of his first scheme, doubtless considered that Eve would prove a powerful dissolving agent in the Christian family which she had entered, and thus help to make all wealth and power fall into the hands of the Jews.

However, Pierre's vision faded. Monseigneur Martha's voice was rising with increase of volume, celebrating, amidst the quivering of the congregation, the benefits that would accrue from the New Spirit, which was at last about to pacify France and restore her to her due rank and power. Were there not certain signs of this resurrection on every hand? The New Spirit was the revival of the Ideal, the protest of the soul against degrading materialism, the triumph of spirituality over filthy literature; and it was also Science accepted, but set in its proper place, reconciled with Faith, since it no longer pretended to encroach on the latter's sacred domain; and it was further the Democracy welcomed in fatherly fashion, the Republic legitimated, recognised in her turn as Eldest Daughter of the Church. A breath of poetry passed by. The Church opened her heart to all her children, there would henceforth be but concord and delight if the masses, obedient to the New Spirit, would give themselves to the Master of love as they had given themselves to their kings, recognising that the Divinity was the one unique power, absolute sovereign of both body and soul.

Pierre was now listening attentively, wondering where it was that he had previously heard almost identical words. And suddenly he remembered; and could fancy that he was again at Rome, listening to the last words of Monsignor Nani, the Assessor of the Holy Office. Here, again he found the dream of a democratic Pope, ceasing to support the compromised monarchies, and seeking to subdue the masses. Since Cæsar was down, or nearly so, might not the Pope realise the ancient ambition of his forerunners and become both emperor and pontiff, the sovereign, universal divinity on earth? This, too, was the dream in which Pierre himself, with apostolic naïveté, had indulged when writing his book, 'New Rome': a dream from which the sight of the real Rome had so roughly roused him. At bottom it was merely a policy of hypocritical falsehood, the priestly policy which relies on time, and is ever tenacious, carrying on the work of conquest with extraordinary suppleness, resolved to profit by everything. And what an evolution it was, the Church of Rome making advances to Science, to the Democracy, to the Republican *régimes*, convinced that it would be able to devour them if only it were allowed the time! Ah! yes, the New Spirit was simply the Old Spirit of Domination, incessantly reviving and hungering to conquer and possess the world.

Pierre thought that he recognised among the congregation certain deputies whom he had seen at the Chamber. Wasn't that tall gentleman with the fair beard, who listened so devoutly, one of Monferrand's creatures? It was said that Monferrand, once a devourer of priests, was now smilingly coquetting with the clergy. Quite an underhand evolution was beginning in the sacristies, orders from Rome flitted hither and thither; it was a question of accepting the new form of government, and absorbing it by dint of invasion. France was still the Eldest Daughter of the Church, the only great nation that had sufficient health and strength to place the Pope in possession of his temporal power once more. So France must be won; it was well worth one's while to espouse her, even if she were Republican. In the eager struggle of ambition the bishop made use of the minister, who thought it to his interest to lean upon the bishop. But which of the two would end by devouring the other? And to what a *rôle* had religion sunk; it was either an electoral weapon, an element in a parliamentary majority, or a secret reason for obtaining or retaining a ministerial portfolio! Of divine charity, the basis of religion, there was no thought, and Pierre's heart filled with bitterness as he remembered the recent death of Cardinal Bergerot, the last of the great saints and pure minds of the French episcopacy, which now seemed to be merely a set of intriguers and fools.

However, the address was drawing to a close. In a glowing peroration, which evoked the basilica of the Sacred Heart dominating Paris with the saving symbol of the Cross from the sacred Mount of the Martyrs,[1] Monseigneur Martha showed the great city Christian once more and master of the world, thanks to the moral omnipotence conferred upon it by the divine breath of the New Spirit. Unable to applaud, the congregation gave utterance to a murmur of approving rap-

[1] Montmartre.

ture, delighted as it was with this miraculous finish which
reassured both pocket and conscience. Then Monseigneur
Martha quitted the pulpit with a noble step, whilst a loud
noise of chairs broke upon the dark peacefulness of the
church, where the few lighted candles glittered like the first
stars in the evening sky. A long stream of men, vague,
whispering shadows, glided away. The women alone remained, praying on their knees.

Pierre, still in the same spot, was rising on tip-toes, looking for Abbé Rose, when a hand touched him. It was that of
the old priest, who had seen him from a distance. 'I was
yonder near the pulpit,' said he, 'and I saw you plainly, my
dear child. Only I preferred to wait so as to disturb nobody.
What a beautiful address dear Monseigneur delivered!'

He seemed, indeed, much moved. But there was deep
sadness about his kindly mouth and clear childlike eyes, whose
smile as a rule illumined his good, round white face. 'I was
afraid you might go off without seeing me,' he resumed, 'for
I have something to tell you. You know that poor old man
to whom I sent you this morning and in whom I asked you
to interest yourself? Well, on getting home I found a lady
there, who sometimes brings me a little money for my poor.
Then I thought to myself that the three francs I gave you
were really too small a sum, and this worried me like a kind
of remorse, so that I couldn't resist the impulse, but went this
afternoon to the Rue des Saules myself.'

He lowered his voice from a feeling of respect, in order not
to disturb the deep, sepulchral silence of the church. Covert
shame, moreover, impeded his utterance, shame at having
again relapsed into the sin of blind, imprudent charity, as his
superiors reproachfully said. And, quivering, he concluded
in a very low voice indeed: 'And so, my child, picture my
grief. I had five francs more to give the poor old man, and I
found him dead.'

Pierre suddenly shuddered. But he was unwilling to understand: 'What, dead!' he cried. 'That old man dead!
Laveuve dead?'

'Yes, I found him dead—ah! amidst what frightful
wretchedness, like an old animal that has laid itself down for
the finish on a heap of rags in the depths of a hole. No
neighbours had assisted him in his last moments; he had
simply turned himself towards the wall. And ah! how bare
and cold and deserted it was! And what a pang for a poor

creature to go off like that without a word, a caress. Ah!
my heart bounded within me and it is still bleeding!'

Pierre in his utter amazement at first made but a gesture
of revolt against imbecile social cruelty. Had the bread left
near the unfortunate wretch, and devoured too eagerly,
perhaps, after long days of abstinence, been the cause of his
death? Or was not this rather the fatal *dénouement* of an ended
life, worn away by labour and privation? However, what
did the cause signify? Death had come and delivered the
poor man. 'It isn't he that I pity,' Pierre muttered at last;
'it is we—we who witness all that, we who are guilty of these
abominations.'

But good Abbé Rose was already becoming resigned, and
would only think of forgiveness and hope. 'No, no, my child,
rebellion is evil. If we are all guilty we can only implore
Providence to forget our faults. I had given you an appointment here hoping for good news; and it's I who come to
tell you of that frightful thing. Let us be penitent and
pray.'

Then he knelt upon the flagstones near the pillar, in the
rear of the praying women, who looked black and vague in
the gloom. And he inclined his white head, and for a long
time remained in a posture of humility.

But Pierre was unable to pray, so powerfully did revolt
stir him. He did not even bend his knees, he remained
erect and quivering. His heart seemed to have been crushed;
not a tear came to his ardent eyes. So Laveuve had died
yonder, stretched on his litter of rags, his hands clenched in
his obstinate desire to cling to his life of torture, whilst he,
Pierre, again glowing with the flame of charity, consumed
by apostolic zeal, had been scouring Paris to find him for the
evening a clean bed on which he might be saved. Ah!
the atrocious irony of it all! He must have been at the
Duvillards' in the warm *salon*, all blue and silver, whilst the
old man was expiring; and it was for a wretched corpse that
he had then hastened to the Chamber of Deputies, to the
Countess de Quinsac's, to that creature Silviane's, and to that
creature Rosemonde's. And it was for that corpse, freed
from life, escaped from misery as from prison, that he had
worried people, broken in upon their egotism, disturbed the
peace of some, threatened the pleasures of others! What
was the use of hastening from the parliamentary den to the
cold *salon* where the dust of the past was congealing; of

going from the sphere of middle-class debauchery to that of cosmopolitan extravagance, since one always arrived too late, and saved people when they were already dead? How ridiculous to have allowed himself to be fired once more by that blaze of charity, that final conflagration, only the ashes of which he now felt within him? This time he thought he was dead himself; he was nought but an empty sepulchre.

And all the frightful void and chaos which he had felt that morning at the basilica of the Sacred Heart after his mass became yet deeper, henceforth unfathomable. If charity were illusory and useless the Gospel crumbled, the end of the Book was nigh. After centuries of stubborn efforts, Redemption through Christianity failed, and another means of salvation was needed by the world in presence of the exasperated thirst for justice which came from the duped and wretched nations. They would have no more of that deceptive paradise, the promise of which had so long served to prop up social iniquity; they demanded that the question of happiness should be decided upon this earth. But how? By means of what new religion, what combination between the sentiment of the Divine and the necessity for honouring life in its sovereignty and its fruitfulness? Therein lay the grievous, torturing problem, into the midst of which Pierre was sinking; he, a priest, severed by vows of chastity and superstition from the rest of mankind.

He had ceased to believe in the efficacy of alms; it was not sufficient that one should be charitable, henceforth one must be just. Given justice, indeed, horrid want would disappear, and no such thing as charity would be needed. Most certainly there was no lack of compassionate hearts in that grievous city of Paris; charitable foundations sprouted forth there like green leaves at the first warmth of springtide. There were some for every age, every peril, every misfortune. Through the concern shown for mothers children were succoured even before they were born; then came infant and orphan asylums lavishly provided for all sorts of classes; and, afterwards, man was followed through his life, help was tendered on all sides, particularly as he grew old, by a multiplicity of asylums, almshouses, and refuges. And there were all the hands stretched out to the forsaken ones, the disinherited ones, even the criminals, all sorts of associations to protect the weak, societies for the prevention of crime, homes that offered hospitality to those who repented.

Whether as regards the propagation of good deeds, the
support of the young, the saving of life, the bestowal of
pecuniary help, or the promotion of guilds, pages and pages
would have been needed merely to particularise the extraordinary vegetation of charity that sprouted between the
paving-stones of Paris with so fine a vigour, in which
goodness of soul was mingled with social vanity. Still that
could not matter, since charity redeemed and purified all.
But how terrible the proposition that this charity was a
useless mockery ! What ! after so many centuries of Christian
charity not a sore had healed ! Misery had only grown and
spread, irritated even to rage. Incessantly aggravated, the
evil was reaching the point when it would be impossible to
tolerate it for another day, since social injustice was neither
arrested nor even diminished thereby. And besides, if only
one single old man died of cold and hunger, did not the
social edifice, raised on the theory of charity, collapse ? But
one victim, and society was condemned, thought Pierre.

He now felt such bitterness of heart that he could remain
no longer in that church where the shadows ever slowly fell,
blurring the sanctuaries and the large pale images of Christ
nailed upon the Cross. All was about to sink into darkness,
and he could hear nothing beyond an expiring murmur of
prayers, a plaint from the women who were praying on their
knees, in the depths of the shrouding gloom.

At the same time he hardly liked to go off without saying
a word to Abbé Rose, who in his entreaties born of simple
faith left the happiness and peace of mankind to the good pleasure of the Invisible. However, fearing that he might disturb
him, Pierre was making up his mind to retire, when the old priest
of his own accord raised his head. 'Ah, my child,' said he,
'how difficult it is to be good in a reasonable manner.
Monseigneur Martha has scolded me again, and but for the
forgiveness of God I should fear for my salvation.'

For a moment Pierre paused under the porticus of the
Madeleine, on the summit of the great flight of steps which,
rising above the railings, dominates the Place. Before him
was the Rue Royale dipping down to the expanse of the Place
de la Concorde, where rose the obelisk and the pair of plashing
fountains. And, farther yet, the paling colonnade of the
Chamber of Deputies bounded the horizon. It was a vista of
sovereign grandeur under that pale sky over which twilight
was slowly stealing. The thoroughfares seemed to expand,

the edifices receded, and assumed a quivering, soaring aspect like that of the palaces of dreamland. No other capital in the world could boast a scene of such airy pomp, such grandiose magnificence, at that hour of vagueness, when falling night imparts to cities a dreamy semblance, the infinite of human immensity.

Motionless and hesitating in presence of the opening expanse, Pierre distressfully pondered as to whither he should go now that all which he had so passionately sought to achieve since the morning had suddenly crumbled away. Was he still bound for the Duvillard mansion in the Rue Godot-de-Mauroy? He no longer knew. Then the exasperating remembrance, with its cruel irony, returned to him. Since Laveuve was dead, of what use was it for him to kill time and perambulate the pavements pending the arrival of six o'clock? The idea that he had a home, and that the most simple course would be to return to it, did not even occur to him. He felt as if there were something of importance left for him to do, though he could not possibly tell what it might be. It seemed to him to be everywhere and yet very far away, to be so vague and difficult of accomplishment that he would certainly never be in time or have sufficient power to do it. However, with heavy feet, and tumultuous brain he descended the steps and, yielding to some obstinate impulse, began to walk through the flower-market, a late winter market where the first azaleas were opening with a little shiver. Some women were purchasing Nice roses and violets; and Pierre looked at them as if he were interested in all that soft, delicate, perfumed luxury. But suddenly he felt a horror of it and went off, starting along the Boulevards.

He walked straight before him without knowing why or whither. The falling darkness surprised him as if it were an unexpected phenomenon. Raising his eyes to the sky he felt astonished at seeing its azure gently pale between the slender black streaks of the chimneys. And the huge golden letters by which names or trades were advertised on every balcony also seemed to him singular in the last gleams of the daylight. Never before had he paid attention to the motley tints seen on the house-fronts, the painted mirrors, the blinds, the coats of arms, the posters of violent hues, the magnificent shops, like drawing-rooms and boudoirs open to the full light. And then, both in the roadway and along the foot-pavements between the blue, red or yellow columns and kiosks, what mighty traffic there was, what an extraordinary crowd ! The vehicles rolled along in a thundering stream : upon all sides billows of cabs were parted by the ponderous tacking of huge omnibuses, which suggested lofty, bright-hued battle-ships. And on either hand, and farther and farther, and even among the wheels, the flood of passengers rushed on incessantly, with the conquering haste of ants in a state of revolution. Whence came all those people, and whither were all those vehicles going ? How stupefying and torturing it all was.

Pierre was still walking straight ahead, mechanically, carried on by his gloomy reverie. Night was approaching, the first gas-burners were being lighted ; it was the dusk of Paris, the hour when real darkness has not yet come, when the electric lights flame in the dying day. Lamps shone forth upon all sides, the shop-fronts were fast being illumined. Soon, moreover, right along the Boulevards the vehicles would carry their vivid starry lights, like a milky way on the march betwixt the foot pavements all glowing with lanterns and cordons and girandoles, a dazzling profusion of radiance akin to sunlight. And the shouts of the drivers and the jostling of the foot passengers re-echoed the parting haste of the Paris which is all business or passion, which is absorbed in the merciless struggle for love and for money. The hard day was over, and now the Paris of Pleasure was lighting up, for its night of *fête*. The cafés, the wine shops, the restaurants flared and displayed their bright metal bars, and their little white tables behind their clear and lofty windows, whilst near their doors, by way of temptation, were oysters and choice fruits. And the Paris which was thus awaking with the first flashes of the gas was already full of the gaiety of enjoyment, already yielding to an unbridled appetite for whatsoever may be purchased.

However, Pierre had a narrow escape of being knocked down. A flock of newspaper hawkers came out of a side street, and darted through the crowd shouting the titles of the evening journals. A fresh edition of the ' Voix du Peuple ' gave rise, in particular, to a deafening clamour, which ascended above all the rumbling of wheels. At regular intervals hoarse voices raised and repeated the cry : ' Ask for the " Voix du Peuple "—the new scandal of the African Railway Lines, the repulse of the ministry, the

thirty-two bribe-takers of the Chamber and the Senate!'
And these announcements, set in huge type, could be read
on the copies of the paper, which the hawkers flourished
like banners. Accustomed as it was to such filth, saturated
with infamy, the crowd continued on its way without paying
much attention. Still a few men paused and bought the
paper, while painted women, who had come down to the
Boulevards in search of a dinner, trailed their skirts and
waited for some chance lover, glancing interrogatively at the
outside customers of the cafés. And meantime the dis-
honouring shout of the newspaper hawkers, that cry in
which there was both smirch and buffet, seemed like the
last knell of the day, ringing the nation's funeral at the
outset of the night of pleasure which was beginning.

Then Pierre once more remembered his morning and that
frightful house in the Rue des Saules, where so much want
and suffering were heaped up. He again saw the yard filthy
like a quagmire, the evil-smelling staircases, the sordid, bare,
icy rooms, the families fighting for messes which even stray
dogs would not have eaten ; the mothers, with exhausted
breasts, carrying screaming children to and fro ; the old men
who fell in corners like brute beasts, and died of hunger amidst
filth. And then came his other hours with the magnificence
or the quietude or the gaiety of the *salons* through which he
had passed, the whole insolent display of financial Paris, and
political Paris, and society Paris. And at last he came to
the dusk, and to that Paris-Sodom and Paris-Gomorrah before
him, which was lighting itself up for the night, for the
abominations of that accomplice night which, like fine dust,
was little by little submerging the expanse of roofs. And the
hateful monstrosity of it all howled aloud under the pale sky
where the first pure, twinkling stars were gleaming.

A great shudder swept through Pierre as he thought of all
that mass of iniquity and suffering, of all that went on below
amid want and crime, and all that went on above amid wealth
and vice. The *bourgeoisie*, wielding power, would relinquish
nought of the sovereignty which it had conquered, wholly
stolen, while the people, the eternal dupe, silent so long,
clenched its fists and growled, claiming its legitimate share.
And it was that frightful injustice which filled the growing
gloom with anger. From what dark-breasted cloud would
the thunderbolt fall ? For years he had been waiting for that
thunderbolt which low rumbles announced on all points of

the horizon. And if he had written a book full of candour
and hope, if he had gone in all innocence to Rome, it was to
avert that thunderbolt and its frightful consequences. But
all hope of the kind was dead within him; he felt that the
thunderbolt was inevitable, that nothing henceforth could
stay the catastrophe. And never before had it seemed to be
so near, amidst the smiling impudence of some, and the
exasperated distress of others. Aye, it was gathering, and it
would surely fall over that Paris, all lust and bravado, which,
when evening came, thus stirred up its furnace.

Tired out and distracted, Pierre raised his eyes as he
reached the Place de l'Opéra. Where was he then? The
heart of the great city seemed to beat on that spot, in that vast
expanse where met so many thoroughfares, as if from every
point the blood of distant districts flowed thither along
triumphal avenues. Right away to the horizon stretched the
great gaps of the Avenue de l'Opéra, the Rue du Quatre-
Septembre, and the Rue de la Paix, still showing clearly in a
final glimpse of daylight, but already starred with swarming
sparks. The torrent of the Boulevard traffic poured across
the Place where clashed, too, all that from the neighbouring
streets, with a constant turning and eddying which made the
spot the most dangerous of whirlpools. In vain did the police
seek to impose some little prudence, the stream of pedestrians
still rushed on, wheels became entangled and horses reared
amidst all the uproar of the human tide, which was as loud,
as incessant as the tempest voice of an ocean. Then there
was the detached mass of the opera-house, slowly steeped in
gloom and rising huge and mysterious like a symbol, its lyre-
bearing figure of Apollo, right aloft, showing a last reflection
of daylight amidst the livid sky. And all the windows of the
house-fronts began to shine, gaiety sprang from those thousands of lamps which coruscated one by one, a universal
longing for ease and free gratification of each desire spread
with the growing dusk; whilst, at long intervals, the
large globes of the electric lights shone as brightly as the
moons of the city's cloudless nights.

But why was he, Pierre, there, he asked himself, irritated
and wondering. Since Laveuve was dead he had but to go
home, bury himself in his nook, and close up door and windows, like one who was henceforth useless, who had neither
belief nor hope, and awaited nought save annihilation. It
was a long journey from the Place de l'Opéra to his little
house at Neuilly. Still, however great his weariness, he

would not take a cab, but retraced his steps, turning towards
the Madeleine again, and plunging into the scramble of the
pavements, amidst the deafening uproar from the roadway,
with a bitter desire to aggravate his wound and saturate himself with revolt and anger. Was it not yonder at the corner
of that street, at the end of that Boulevard, that he would
find the expected abyss into which that rotten world, whose
old society he could hear rending at each step, must soon
assuredly topple?

However, when Pierre wished to cross the Rue Scribe a
block in the traffic made him halt. In front of a luxurious
café two tall, shabbily-clad and very dirty fellows were alternately offering the ' Voix du Peuple ' with its account of the
scandals and the bribe-takers of the Chamber and the Senate,
in voices so suggestive of cracked brass that passers-by
clustered around them. And here, in a hesitating, wandering
man, who after listening drew near to the large café and peered
through its windows, Pierre was once again amazed to recognise
Salvat. This time the meeting struck him forcibly, filled
him with suspicion to such a point that he also stopped and
resolved to watch the journeyman engineer. He did not
expect that one of such wretched aspect, with what seemed to be
a hunk of bread distending his old ragged jacket, would enter and
seat himself at one of the café's little tables amidst the warm
gaiety of the lamps. However, he waited for a moment, and then
saw him wander away with slow and broken steps as if the
café, which was nearly empty, did not suit him. What could
he have been seeking, whither had he been going since the
morning, ever on a wild, solitary chase through the Paris of
wealth and enjoyment while hunger dogged his steps? It was
only with difficulty that he now dragged himself along, his
will and energy seemed to be exhausted. As if quite overcome, he drew near to a kiosk, and for a moment leant against
it. Then, however, he drew himself up again, and walked on
further, still as it were in search of something.

And now came an incident which brought Pierre's emotion
to a climax. A tall sturdy man on turning out of the Rue
Caumartin caught sight of Salvat, and approached him. And
just as the new-comer without false pride was shaking the
workman's hand, Pierre recognised him as his brother
Guillaume. Yes, it was indeed he, with his thick bushy hair
already white like snow, though he was but seven-and-forty.
However, his heavy moustaches had remained quite dark
without a silver thread, thus lending an expression of

vigorous life to his full face with its lofty towering brow. It was from his father that he had inherited that brow of impregnable logic and reason, similar to that which Pierre himself possessed. But the lower part of the elder brother's countenance was fuller than that of his junior; his nose was larger, his chin was square, and his mouth broad and firm of contour. A pale scar, the mark of an old wound, streaked his left temple. And his physiognomy, though it might at first seem very grave, rough, and unexpansive, beamed with masculine kindliness whenever a smile revealed his teeth, which had remained extremely white.

While looking at his brother, Pierre remembered what Madame Théodore had told him that morning. Guillaume, touched by Salvat's dire want, had arranged to give him a few days' employment. And this explained the air of interest with which he now seemed to be questioning him, while the engineer, whom the meeting disturbed, stamped about as if eager to resume his mournful ramble. For a moment Guillaume appeared to notice the other's perturbation, by the embarrassed answers which he obtained from him. Still they at last parted as if each were going his way. Then, however, almost immediately, Guillaume turned round again and watched the other, as with harassed stubborn mien he went off through the crowd. And the thoughts which had come to Guillaume must have been very serious and very pressing, for he all at once began to retrace his steps and follow the workman from a distance, as if to ascertain for certain what direction he would take.

Pierre had watched the scene with growing disquietude. His nervous apprehension of some great unknown calamity, the suspicions born of his frequent and inexplicable meetings with Salvat, his surprise at now seeing his brother mingled with the affair, all helped to fill him with a pressing desire to know, witness, and perhaps prevent. So he did not hesitate, but followed the others in a prudent way.

Fresh perturbation came upon him when first Salvat and then Guillaume suddenly turned into the Rue Godot-de-Mauroy. What destiny was thus bringing him back to that street whither a little time previously he had wished to return in feverish haste, and whence only the death of Laveuve had kept him? And his consternation increased yet further when after losing sight of Salvat for a moment, he saw him standing in front of the Duvillard mansion, on the same spot where he had fancied he recognised him that morning. As it happened the carriage entrance of the mansion was wide open. Some repairs had been made to the paving of the porch, and although the workmen had now gone off, the doorway remained gaping, full of the falling night. The narrow street, running from the glittering Boulevard, was steeped in bluish gloom, starred at long intervals by a gas-lamp. Some women went by compelling Salvat to step off the foot pavement. But he returned to it again, lighted the stump of a cigar, some remnant which he had found under a table outside a café, and then resumed his watch, patient and motionless, in front of the mansion.

Disturbed by his dim conjectures, Pierre gradually grew frightened, and asked himself if he ought not to approach that man. The chief thing that detained him was the presence of his brother whom he had seen disappear into a neighbouring doorway, whence he also was observing the engineer, ready to intervene. And so Pierre contented himself with not losing sight of Salvat, who was still waiting and watching, merely taking his eyes from the mansion in order to glance towards the Boulevard as though he expected someone or something from that direction. And at last, indeed, the Duvillards' landau appeared, with coachman and footman in livery of green and gold—a closed landau to which a pair of tall horses of superb build was harnessed in stylish fashion.

Contrary to custom, however, the carriage, which at that hour usually brought the father and mother home, was only occupied that evening by the son and daughter, Hyacinthe and Camille. Returning from the Princess de Harn's *matinée*, they were chatting freely, with that calm immodesty by which they sought to astonish one another. Hyacinthe, yielding to his perverted ideas, was attacking women, whilst Camille openly counselled him to respond to the Princess's advances. However, she was visibly irritated and feverish that evening, and, suddenly changing the subject, she began to speak of their mother and Gérard de Quinsac.

'But what can it matter to you?' quietly retorted Hyacinthe; and, seeing that she almost bounded from the seat at the remark, he continued: 'Are you still in love with him then? Do you still want to marry him?'

'Yes, I do, and I will!' she cried with all the jealous rage of an uncomely girl, who suffered so acutely at seeing herself spurned whilst her yet beautiful mother stole from her the man she wanted.

'You will, you will!' resumed Hyacinthe, well pleased to have an opportunity of teasing his sister whom he somewhat feared. 'But you won't unless *he* is willing—— And he doesn't care for you.'

'He does!' retorted Camille in a fury. 'He's kind and pleasant with me, and that's enough.'

Her brother felt afraid as he noticed the blackness of her glance, and the clenching of her weak little hands whose fingers bent like claws. And after a pause he asked: 'And papa, what does he say about it?'

'Oh, papa! All that he cares about is the other one.'

Then Hyacinthe began to laugh.

But the landau, with its tall horses trotting on sonorously, had turned into the street and was approaching the house, when a slim fair-haired girl of sixteen or seventeen, a modiste's errand girl with a large bandbox on her arm, hastily crossed the road in order to enter the arched doorway before the carriage. She was bringing a new hat for the Baroness, and had come all along the Boulevard musing, with her soft blue eyes, her pinky nose, and her mouth which ever laughed in the most adorable little face that one could see. And it was at this same moment that Salvat, after another glance at the landau, sprang forward and entered the doorway. An instant afterwards he reappeared, flung his lighted cigar stump into the gutter; and without undue haste went off, slinking into the depths of the vague gloom.

And then what happened? Pierre, later on, remembered that a dray of the Western Railway Company in coming up stopped and delayed the landau for a moment, whilst the young errand girl entered the doorway. And with a heart-pang beyond description he saw his brother Guillaume in his turn spring forward and rush into the mansion as though impelled to do so by some revelation, some sudden certainty. He, Pierre, though he understood nothing clearly, could divine the approach of some frightful horror. But when he would have run, when he would have shouted, he found himself as if nailed to the pavement, and felt his throat clutched as by a hand of lead. Then suddenly came a thunderous roar, a formidable explosion, as if the earth was opening, and the lightning-struck mansion was being annihilated. Every window-pane of the neighbouring houses was shivered, the glass raining down with the loud clatter of hail. For a moment a hellish flame fired the street, and the dust and the smoke were such that the few passers-by were blinded and howled with affright, aghast at toppling, as they thought, into that fiery furnace.

And that dazzling flare brought Pierre enlightenment. He once more saw the bomb distending the tool-bag which lack of work had emptied and rendered useless. He once more saw it under the ragged jacket, a protuberance caused, he had fancied, by some hunk of bread, picked up in a corner and treasured that it might be carried home to wife and child. After wandering and threatening all happy Paris, it was there that it had flared, there that it had burst with a thunder-clap, there on the threshold of the sovereign *bourgeoisie* to whom all wealth belonged. He, however, at that moment thought only of his brother Guillaume, and flung himself into that porch where a volcanic crater seemed to have opened. And at first he distinguished nothing, the acrid smoke streamed over all. Then he perceived the walls split, the upper floor rent open, the paving broken up, strewn with fragments. Outside, the landau which had been on the point of entering, had escaped all injury ; neither of the horses had been touched, nor was there even a scratch on any panel of the vehicle. But the young girl, the pretty, slim, fair-haired errand girl, lay there on her back, her stomach ripped open, whilst her delicate face remained intact, her eyes clear, her smile full of astonishment, so swiftly and lightning-like had come the catastrophe. And near her, from the fallen band-box, whose lid had merely come unfastened, had rolled the new hat, a very fragile pink hat, which still looked charming in its flowery freshness.

By a prodigy Guillaume was alive and already on his legs again. His left hand alone streamed with blood, a projectile seemed to have broken his wrist. His moustaches moreover had been burnt, and the explosion by throwing him to the ground had so shaken and bruised him, that he shivered from head to feet as with intense cold. Nevertheless, he recognised his brother without even feeling astonished to see him there, as indeed often happens after great disasters, when the unexplained becomes providential. That brother, of whom he had so long lost sight, was there, naturally enough, because it was necessary that he should be there. And Guillaume, amidst the wild quivers by which he was shaken, at once cried to him : 'Take me away! take me away! To your house at Neuilly, oh! take me away!'

Then, for sole explanation, and referring to Salvat, he stammered : ' I suspected that he had stolen a cartridge from me; only one most fortunately, for otherwise the whole district would have been blown to pieces. Ah ! the wretched fellow ! I wasn't in time to set my foot upon the match.'

With perfect lucidity of mind, such as danger sometimes imparts, Pierre, neither speaking nor losing a moment, remembered that the mansion had a back entrance fronting the Rue Vignon. He had just realised in what serious peril his brother would be if he were found mixed up in that affair. And with all speed, when he had led him into the gloom of the Rue Vignon, he tied his handkerchief round his wrist, which he bade him press to his chest, under his coat, which would conceal it.

But Guillaume, still shivering and haunted by the horror he had witnessed, repeated : ' Take me away—to your place at Neuilly—not to my home.'

' Of course, of course, be easy. Come, wait here a second, I will stop a cab.'

In his eagerness to procure a conveyance, Pierre had brought his brother down to the Boulevard again. But the terrible thunder-clap of the explosion had upset the whole neighbourhood, horses were still rearing, and people were running demented, hither and thither. And numerous police-men had hastened up, and a rushing crowd was already blocking the lower part of the Rue Godot-de-Mauroy, which was now as black as a pit, every light in it having been ex-tinguished ; whilst on the Boulevard a hawker of the ' Voix du Peuple ' still stubbornly vociferated : ' The new scandal of the African Railway Lines ! The thirty-two bribe-takers of the Chamber and the Senate ! The approaching fall of the Ministry ! '

Pierre was at last managing to stop a cab when he heard a person who ran by say to another, ' The Ministry ? Ah, well ! that bomb will mend it right enough ! '

Then the brothers seated themselves in the cab, which carried them away. And now, over the whole of rumbling Paris black night had gathered, an unforgiving night, in which the stars foundered amidst the mist of crime and anger that had risen from the house-roofs. The great cry of justice swept by amidst the same terrifying flapping of wings which Sodom and Gomorrah once heard bearing down upon them from all the black clouds of the horizon.

BOOK II

I

REVOLUTIONISTS

IN that out of the way street at Neuilly, along which nobody passed after dusk, Pierre's little house was now steeped in deep slumber under the black sky; each of its shutters closed, and not a ray of light stealing forth from within. And one could divine, too, the profound quietude of the little garden in the rear, a garden empty and lifeless, benumbed by the winter cold.

Pierre had several times feared that his brother would faint away in the cab in which they were journeying. Leaning back, and often sinking down, Guillaume spoke not a word. And terrible was the silence between them—a silence fraught with all the questions and answers which they felt it would be useless and painful to exchange at such a time. However, the priest was anxious about the wound, and wondered to what surgeon he might apply, desirous as he was of admitting only a sure, staunch man into the secret, for he had noticed with how keen a desire to disappear his brother had sought to hide himself.

Until they reached the Arc de Triomphe the silence remained unbroken. It was only there that Guillaume seemed to emerge from the prostration of his reverie. 'Mind Pierre,' said he, 'no doctor. We will attend to this together.'

Pierre was on the point of protesting, but he realised that it would be useless to discuss the subject at such a moment, and so he merely waved his hand to signify that he should act in spite of the prohibition were it necessary. In point of fact, his anxiety had increased, and when the cab at last drew up before the house it was with real relief that he saw his brother alight without evincing any marked feebleness. He

himself quickly paid the driver, well-pleased, too, at finding
that nobody, not even a neighbour, was about. And having
opened the door with his latch key, he helped the injured man
to ascend the steps.

A little night lamp glimmered faintly in the vestibule.
On hearing the door open, Pierre's servant, Sophie, had at
once emerged from the kitchen. A short, thin, dark woman
of sixty, she had formed part of the household for more than
thirty years, having served the mother before serving the son.
She knew Guillaume, having seen him when he was a young
man, and doubtless she now recognised him, although well-
nigh ten years had gone by since he had last crossed that
threshold. Instead of evincing any surprise, she seemed to
consider his extraordinary return quite natural, and remained
as silent and discreet as usual. She led, indeed, the life of a
recluse, never speaking unless her work absolutely required it.
And thus she now contented herself with saying : ' Monsieur
l'Abbé, Monsieur Bertheroy is in the study, and has been
waiting there for a quarter of an hour.'

At this Guillaume intervened, as if the news revived him.
' Does Bertheroy still come here, then ? I'll see him
willingly. His is one of the best, the broadest, minds of
these days. He has still remained my master.'

A former friend of their father—the illustrious chemist,
Michel Froment—Bertheroy had now, in his turn, become one
of the loftiest glories of France, one to whom chemistry owed
much of the extraordinary progress that has made it the
mother-science, by which the very face of the earth is being
changed. A member of the Institute, laden with offices and
honours, he had retained much affection for Pierre, and
occasionally visited him in this wise before dinner, by way
of relaxation, he would say.

' You showed him into the study ? All right, then, we
will go there,' said the Abbé to the servant. ' Light a lamp
and take it into my room, and get my bed ready so that my
brother may go to bed at once.'

While Sophie, without a word or sign of surprise, was
obeying these instructions, the brothers went into their father's
former laboratory, of which the priest had now made a
spacious study. And it was with a cry of joyous astonishment
that the *savant* greeted them on seeing them enter the room
side by side, the one supporting the other. ' What, together ! '
he exclaimed. ' Ah ! my dear children, you could not have

caused me greater pleasure! I who have so often deplored your painful misunderstanding.'

Bertheroy was a tall and lean septuagenarian with angular features. His yellow skin clung like parchment to the projecting bones of his cheeks and jaw. Moreover, there was nothing imposing about him; he looked like some old shop-keeping herbalist. At the same time he had a fine, broad, smooth brow, and his eyes still glittered brightly beneath his tangled hair.

'What, have you injured yourself, Guillaume?' he continued, as soon as he saw the bandaged hand.

Pierre remained silent, so as to let his brother tell the story as he chose. Guillaume had realised that he must confess the truth, but in simple fashion, without detailing the circumstances. 'Yes, in an explosion,' he answered, 'and I really think that I have my wrist broken.'

At this, Bertheroy, whose glance was fixed upon him, noticed that his moustaches were burnt, and that there was an expression of bewildered stupor, such as follows a catastrophe, in his eyes. Forthwith the *savant* became grave and circumspect; and without seeking to compel confidence by any questions, he simply said: 'Indeed! an explosion! Will you let me see the injury? You know that before letting chemistry ensnare me I studied medicine, and am still somewhat of a surgeon.'

On hearing these words Pierre could not restrain a heart-cry: 'Yes, yes, master! Look at the injury—I was very anxious, and to find you here is unhoped-for good fortune!'

The *savant* glanced at him, and divined that the hidden circumstances of the accident must be serious. And then, as Guillaume, smiling, though paling with weakness, consented to the suggestion, Bertheroy retorted that before anything else he must be put to bed. The servant just then returned to say the bed was ready, and so they all went into the adjoining room, where the injured man was soon undressed and helped between the sheets.

'Light me, Pierre,' said Bertheroy, 'take the lamp; and let Sophie give me a basin full of water and some cloths.' Then, having gently washed the wound, he resumed: 'The devil! The wrist isn't broken, but it's a nasty injury. I am afraid there must be a lesion of the bone. Some nails passed through the flesh, did they not?'

Receiving no reply, he relapsed into silence. But his

surprise was increasing, and he closely examined the hand, which the flame of the explosion had scorched, and even sniffed the shirt cuff as if seeking to understand the affair better. He evidently recognised the effects of one of those new explosives which he himself had studied, almost created. In the present case, however, he must have been puzzled, for there were characteristic signs and traces the significance of which escaped him.

'And so,' he at last made up his mind to ask, carried away by professional curiosity, 'and so it was a laboratory explosion which put you in this nice condition. What devilish powder were you concocting then?'

Guillaume, ever since he had seen Bertheroy thus studying his injury, had, in spite of his sufferings, given marked signs of annoyance and agitation. And as if the real secret which he wished to keep lay precisely in the question now put to him, in that powder, the first experiment with which had thus injured him, he replied with an air of restrained ardour, and a straight frank glance: 'Pray do not question me, master. I cannot answer you. You have, I know, sufficient nobility of nature to nurse me and care for me without exacting a confession.'

'Oh! certainly, my friend,' exclaimed Bertheroy; 'keep your secret. Your discovery belongs to you if you have made one; and I know that you are capable of putting it to the most generous use. Besides, you must be aware that I have too great a passion for truth to judge the actions of others, whatever their nature, without knowing every circumstance and motive.'

So saying, he waved his hand as if to indicate how broadly tolerant and free from error and superstition was that lofty sovereign mind of his, which in spite of all the orders that bedizened him, in spite of all the academical titles that he bore as an official *savant*, made him a man of the boldest and most independent views, one whose only passion was truth, as he himself said.

He lacked the necessary appliances to do more than dress the wound, after making sure that no fragment of any projectile had remained in the flesh. Then he at last went off, promising to return at an early hour on the morrow; and, as the priest escorted him to the street door, he spoke some comforting words: if the bone had not been deeply injured all would be well.

On returning to the bedside, Pierre found his brother still sitting up and seeking fresh energy in his desire to write home and tranquillise his loved ones. So the priest, after providing pen and paper, again had to take up the lamp and light him. Guillaume fortunately retained full use of his right hand, and was thus able to pen a few lines to say that he would not be home that night. He addressed the note to Madame Leroi, the mother of his deceased mistress, who, since the latter's death, had remained with him and had reared his three sons. Pierre was aware also that the household at Montmartre included a young woman of five- or six-and-twenty, the daughter of an old friend to whom Guillaume had given shelter on her father's death, and whom he was soon to marry, in spite of the great difference in their ages. For the priest, however, all these were vague, disturbing things, condemnable features of disorderly life, and he had invariably pretended to be ignorant of them.

'So you wish this note to be taken to Montmartre at once?' he said to his brother.

'Yes, at once. It is scarcely more than seven o'clock now, and it will be there by eight. And you will choose a reliable man, won't you?'

'The best course will be for Sophie to take a cab. We need have no fear with her. She won't chatter. Wait a moment, and I will settle everything.'

Sophie, on being summoned, at once understood what was wanted of her, and promised to say, in reply to any questions, that M. Guillaume had come to spend the night at his brother's, for reasons which she did not know. And without indulging in any reflections herself, she left the house, saying simply: 'Monsieur l'Abbé's dinner is ready; he will only have to take the broth and the stew off the stove.'

However, when Pierre this time returned to the bedside to sit down there, he found that Guillaume had fallen back with his head resting on both pillows. And he looked very weary and pale, and showed signs of fever. The lamp, standing on a corner of a side table, cast a soft light around, and so deep was the quietude that the big clock in the adjoining dining-room could be heard ticking. For a moment the silence continued around the two brothers, who, after so many years of separation, were at last reunited and alone together. Then the injured man brought his right hand to the edge of the sheet, and the priest grasped it, pressed it tenderly in his own.

And the clasp was a long one, those two brotherly hands remained locked, one in the other.

'My poor little Pierre,' Guillaume faintly murmured, 'you must forgive me for falling on you in this fashion. I've invaded the house and taken your bed, and I'm preventing you from dining.'

'Don't talk, don't tire yourself any more,' interrupted Pierre. 'Is not this the right place for you when you are in trouble?'

A warmer pressure came from Guillaume's feverish hand, and tears gathered in his eyes. 'Thanks, my little Pierre. I've found you again, and you are as gentle and loving as you always were. Ah! you cannot know how delightful it seems to me.'

Then the priest's eyes also were dimmed by tears. Amidst the deep quietude, the great sense of comfort which had followed their violent emotion, the brothers found an infinite charm in being together once more in the home of their childhood.[1] It was there that both their father and mother had died—the father tragically, struck down by an explosion in his laboratory; the mother piously, like a very saint. It was there, too, in that same bed, that Guillaume had nursed Pierre, when, after their mother's death, the latter had nearly died; and it was there now that Pierre in his turn was nursing Guillaume. All helped to bow them down and fill them with emotion: the strange circumstances of their meeting, the frightful catastrophe which had caused them such a shock, the mysteriousness of the things which remained unexplained between them. And now that after so long a separation they were tragically brought together again, they both felt their memory awaking. The old house spoke to them of their childhood, of their parents dead and gone, of the far-away days when they had loved and suffered there. Beneath the window lay the garden, now icy cold, which once, under the sunbeams, had re-echoed with their play. On the left was the laboratory, the spacious room where their father had taught them to read. On the right, in the dining-room, they could picture their mother cutting bread and butter for them, and looking so gentle with her big, despairing eyes—those of a believer mated to an infidel. And the feeling that they were now alone in that home, and the pale, sleepy gleam of the lamp, and the deep silence of the garden and

[1] See M. Zola's 'Lourdes,' Day I., Chapter II.

the house, and the very past itself, all filled them with the softest of emotion blended with the keenest bitterness.

They would have liked to talk and unbosom themselves. But what could they say to one another? Although their hands remained so tightly clasped, did not the most impassable of chasms separate them? In any case, they thought so. Guillaume was convinced that Pierre was a saint, a priest of the most robust faith, without a doubt, without aught in common with himself, whether in the sphere of ideas or in that of practical life. A hatchet-stroke had parted them, and each lived in a different world. And in the same way Pierre pictured Guillaume as one who had lost caste, whose conduct was most suspicious, who had never even married the mother of his three children, but was on the point of marrying that girl who was far too young for him, and who had come nobody knew whence. In him, moreover, were blended the passionate ideas of a *savant* and a revolutionist, ideas in which one found negation of everything, acceptance and possibly provocation of the worst forms of violence, with a glimpse of the vague monster of Anarchism underlying all. And so, on what basis could there be any understanding between them, since each retained his prejudices against the other, and saw him on the opposite side of the chasm, without possibility of any plank being thrown across it to enable them to unite? Thus, all alone in that room, their poor hearts bled with distracted brotherly love.

Pierre knew that, on a previous occasion, Guillaume had narrowly escaped being compromised in an Anarchist affair. He asked him no questions, but he could not help reflecting that he would not have hidden himself in this fashion had he not feared arrest for complicity. Complicity with Salvat? Was he really an accomplice? Pierre shuddered, for the only materials on which he could found a contrary opinion were, on one hand, the words that had escaped his brother after the crime, the cry he had raised accusing Salvat of having stolen a cartridge from him; and, on the other hand, his heroic rush into the doorway of the Duvillard mansion in order to extinguish the match. A great deal still remained obscure; but if a cartridge of that frightful explosive had been stolen from Guillaume the fact must be that he manufactured such cartridges and had others at home. Of course, even if he were not an accomplice, the injury to his wrist had made it needful for him to disappear. Given his bleeding hand, and the previous suspicions levelled against him, he would never have convinced anybody of his innocence. And yet, even allowing for these surmises, the affair remained wrapt in darkness: a crime on Guillaume's part seemed a possibility, and to Pierre it was all dreadful to think of.

Guillaume, by the trembling of his brother's moist, yielding hand, must in some degree have realised the prostration of his poor mind, already shattered by doubt and finished off by this calamity. Indeed, the sepulchre was empty now, the very ashes had been swept out of it.

'My poor little Pierre,' the elder brother slowly said. 'Forgive me if I do not tell you anything. I cannot do so. And besides, what would be the use of it? We should certainly not understand one another. . . . So let us keep from saying anything, and let us simply enjoy the delight of being together and loving one another in spite of all.'

Pierre raised his eyes, and for a long time their glances lingered, one fixed on the other. 'Ah!' stammered the priest, 'how frightful it all is!'

Guillaume, however, had well understood the mute inquiry of Pierre's eyes. His own did not waver but replied boldly, beaming with purity and loftiness: 'I can tell you nothing. Yet, all the same, let us love each other, my little Pierre.'

And then Pierre for a moment felt that his brother was above all base anxiety, above the guilty fear of the man who trembles for himself. In lieu thereof he seemed to be carried away by the passion of some great design, the noble thought of concealing some sovereign idea, some secret which it was imperative for him to save. But, alas! this was only the fleeting vision of a vague hope; for all vanished, and again came the doubt, the suspicion of a mind dealing with one that it knew nothing of.

And all at once a souvenir, a frightful spectacle, arose before Pierre's eyes and distracted him: 'Did you see, brother,' he stammered, 'did you see that fair-haired girl lying under the archway, ripped open, with a smile of astonishment on her face?'

Guillaume in his turn quivered, and in a low and dolorous voice replied: 'Yes, I saw her! Ah, poor little thing! Ah! the atrocious necessities, the atrocious errors of justice!'

Then, amidst the frightful shudder that seemed to sweep

by, Pierre, with his horror of all violence, succumbed, and let his face sink upon the counterpane at the edge of the bed. And he sobbed distractedly: a sudden attack of weakness, overflowing in tears, cast him there exhausted, with no more strength than a child. It was as if all his sufferings since the morning, the deep grief with which universal injustice and woe inspired him, were bursting forth in that flood of tears which nothing now could stay. And Guillaume who, to calm his little brother, had set his hand upon his head, in the same way as he had often caressingly stroked his hair in childhood's days, likewise felt upset and remained silent, unable to find a word of consolation, resigned, as he was, to the eruption which in life is always possible, the cataclysm by which the slow evolution of nature is always liable to be precipitated. But how hard a fate for the wretched ones whom the lava sweeps away in millions! And then his tears also began to flow amidst the profound silence.

'Pierre,' he gently exclaimed at last, 'you must have some dinner. Go, go and have some. And screen the lamp; leave me by myself, and let me close my eyes. It will do me good.'

Pierre had to content him. However, he left the dining-room door open; and weak for want of food, though he had not hitherto noticed it, he ate standing, with his ears on the alert, listening lest his brother should complain or call him. And the silence seemed to have become yet more complete, the little house sank, as it were, into annihilation, instinct with all the melancholy charm of the past.

At about half-past eight, when Sophie returned from her errand to Montmartre, Guillaume heard her step, light though it was. And he at once became restless and wanted to know what news she brought. It was Pierre, however, who enlightened him. 'Don't be anxious. Sophie was received by an old lady who, after reading your note, merely answered, "Very well." She did not even ask Sophie a question, but remained quite composed without sign of curiosity.'

Guillaume, realising that this fine serenity perplexed his brother, thereupon replied with similar calmness: 'Oh! it was only necessary that grandmother should be warned. She knows well enough that if I don't return home it is because I can't.'

However, from that moment it was impossible for the

injured man to rest. Although the lamp was hidden away in
a corner, he constantly opened his eyes, glanced round him,
and seemed to listen, as if for sounds from the direction of
Paris. And it at last became necessary for the priest to
summon the servant and ask her if she had noticed anything
strange on her way to or from Montmartre. She seemed
surprised by the question, and answered that she had noticed
nothing. Besides, the cab had followed the outer boulevards,
which were almost deserted. A slight fog had again begun
to fall, and the streets were steeped in icy dampness.

By the time it was nine o'clock Pierre realised that his
brother would never be able to sleep if he were thus left
without news. Amidst his growing feverishness the injured
man experienced keen anxiety, a haunting desire to know if
Salvat were arrested and had spoken out. He did not confess
this; indeed he sought to convey the impression that he had
no personal disquietude, which was doubtless true. But his
great secret was stifling him; he shuddered at the thought
that his lofty scheme, all his labour and all his hope, should
be at the mercy of that unhappy man whom want had filled
with delusions and who had sought to set justice upon earth
by the aid of a bomb. And in vain did the priest try to make
Guillaume understand that nothing certain could yet be
known. He perceived that his impatience increased every
minute, and at last resolved to make some effort to satisfy
him.

But where could he go, of whom could he inquire?
Guillaume, while talking and trying to guess with whom
Salvat might have sought refuge, had mentioned Janzen,
the Princess de Harn's mysterious lover; and for a moment
he had even thought of sending to this man for information.
But he reflected that if Janzen had heard of the explosion he
was not at all the individual to wait for the police at home.

Meantime Pierre repeated: 'I will willingly go to buy the
evening papers for you—but there will certainly be nothing in
them. Although I know almost everyone in Neuilly I can
think of nobody who is likely to have any information, unless
perhaps it were Bache——'

'You know Bache, the municipal councillor?' interrupted
Guillaume.

'Yes, we have both had to busy ourselves with charitable
work in the neighbourhood.'

'Well, Bache is an old friend of mine, and I know no

safer man. Pray go to him and try to bring him back with you.'

A quarter of an hour later Pierre returned with Bache, who resided in a neighbouring street. And it was not only Bache whom he brought with him, for, much to his surprise, he had found Janzen at Bache's house. As Guillaume had suspected, Janzen, while dining at the Princess de Harn's, had heard of the crime, and had consequently refrained from returning to his little lodging in the Rue des Martyrs, where the police might well have set a trap for him. His connections were known, and he was aware that he was watched and was liable at any moment to arrest or expulsion as a foreign Anarchist. And so he had thought it prudent to solicit a few days' hospitality of Bache, a very upright and obliging man, to whom he entrusted himself without fear. He would never have remained with Rosemonde, that adorable lunatic who for a month past had been exhibiting him as her lover, and whose useless and dangerous extravagance of conduct he fully realised.

Guillaume was so delighted on seeing Bache and Janzen that he wished to sit up in bed again. But Pierre bade him remain quiet, rest his head on the pillows, and speak as little as possible. Then, while Janzen stood near, erect and silent, Bache took a chair and sat down by the bedside with many expressions of friendly interest. He was a stout man of sixty with a broad, full face, a large white beard and long white hair. His little, gentle eyes had a dim, dreamy expression, while a pleasant, hopeful smile played round his thick lips. His father, a fervent St. Simonian, had brought him up in the doctrines of that belief. While retaining due respect for it, however, his personal inclinations towards orderliness and religion had led him to espouse the ideas of Fourier, in such wise that one found in him a succession and an abridgment, so to say, of two doctrines. Moreover, when he was about thirty, he had busied himself with spiritualism. Possessed of a comfortable little fortune, his only adventure in life had been his connection with the Paris Commune of 1871. How or why he had become a member of it he could now scarcely tell. Condemned to death by default, although he had sat among the Moderates, he had resided in Belgium until the amnesty; and since then Neuilly had elected him as its representative on the Paris Municipal Council, less by way of glorifying in him a victim of reaction than as a reward for his worthiness, for he was really esteemed by the whole district.

Guillaume, with his desire for tidings, was obliged to confide in his two visitors, tell them of the explosion and Salvat's flight, and how he himself had been wounded while seeking to extinguish the match. Janzen, with curly beard and hair, and a thin, fair face such as painters often attribute to the Christ, listened coldly, as was his wont, and at last said slowly in a gentle voice : 'Ah! so it was Salvat! I thought it might be little Mathis—I'm surprised that it should be Salvat —for he hadn't made up his mind.' Then, as Guillaume anxiously inquired if he thought that Salvat would speak out, he began to protest ; 'Oh! no ; oh! no.'

However, he corrected himself with a gleam of disdain in his clear, harsh eyes : 'After all, there's no telling. Salvat is a man of sentiment.'

Then Bache, who was quite upset by the news of the explosion, tried to think how his friend Guillaume, to whom he was much attached, might be extricated from any charge of complicity should he be denounced. And Guillaume, at sight of Janzen's contemptuous coldness, must have suffered keenly, for the other evidently believed him to be trembling, tortured by the one desire to save his own skin. But what could he say, how could he reveal the deep concern which rendered him so feverish without betraying the secret which he had hidden even from his brother ?

However, at this moment Sophie came to tell her master that M. Théophile Morin had called with another gentleman. Much astonished by this visit at so late an hour, Pierre hastened into the next room to receive the new-comers. He had become acquainted with Morin since his return from Rome, and had helped him to introduce a translation of an excellent scientific manual, prepared according to the official programmes, into the Italian schools.[1] A Franc-Comtois by birth, a compatriot of Proudhon, with whose poor family he had been intimate at Besançon, Morin, himself the son of a journeyman clockmaker, had grown up with Proudhonian ideas, full of affection for the poor and an instinctive hatred of property and wealth. Later on, having come to Paris as a school teacher, impassioned by study, he had given his whole mind to Auguste Comte. Beneath the fervent Positivist, however, one might yet find the old Proudhonian, the pauper

[1] See M. Zola's 'Rome,' Chapters IV. and XVI.

who rebelled and detested want. Moreover, it was scientific Positivism that he clung to; in his hatred of all mysticism he would have nought to do with the fantastic religious leanings of Comte in his last years. And in Morin's brave, consistent, somewhat mournful life, there had been but one page of romance : the sudden feverish impulse which had carried him off to fight in Sicily by Garibaldi's side. Afterwards he had again become a petty professor in Paris, obscurely earning a dismal livelihood.

When Pierre returned to the bedroom he said to his brother in a tone of emotion : ' Morin has brought me Barthès, who fancies himself in danger and asks my hospitality.'

At this Guillaume forgot himself and became excited : ' Nicholas Barthès, a hero with a soul worthy of antiquity. Oh ! I know him ; I admire and love him. You must set your door open wide for him.'

Bache and Janzen, however, had glanced at one another smiling. And the latter with his cold ironical air, slowly remarked : ' Why does Monsieur Barthès hide himself? A great many people think he is dead ; he is simply a ghost who no longer frightens anybody.'

Four-and-seventy years of age as he now was, Barthès had spent nearly half a century in prison. He was the eternal prisoner, the hero of liberty whom each successive Government had carried from citadel to fortress. Since his youth he had been marching on amidst his dream of fraternity, fighting for an ideal Republic based on truth and justice, and each and every endeavour had led him to a dungeon ; he had invariably finished his humanitarian reverie under bolts and bars. Carbonaro, Republican, evangelical sectarian, he had conspired at all times and in all places, incessantly struggling against the Power of the day whatever it might be. And when the Republic at last had come, that Republic which had cost him so many years of gaol, it had, in its own turn, imprisoned him, adding fresh years of gloom to those which already had lacked sunlight. And thus he remained the martyr of freedom : freedom which he still desired in spite of everything ; freedom, which, strive as he might, never came, never existed.

' But you are mistaken,' replied Guillaume, wounded by Janzen's raillery. ' There is again a thought of getting rid of Barthès, whose uncompromising rectitude disturbs our politicians ; and he does well to take his precautions ! '

Nicholas Barthès came in, a tall, slim, withered old man, with a nose like an eagle's beak, and eyes that still burned in their deep sockets, under white and bushy brows. His mouth, toothless but still refined, was lost to sight between his moustaches and snowy beard ; and his hair, crowning him whitely like an aureola, fell in curls over his shoulders. Behind him with all modesty came Théophile Morin with his grey whiskers, his grey, brush-like hair, his spectacles, and his yellow, weary mien—that of an old professor exhausted by years of teaching. Neither of them seemed astonished or awaited an explanation on finding that man in bed with an injured wrist. And there were no introductions, those who were acquainted merely smiled at one another.

Barthès, for his part, stooped and kissed Guillaume on both cheeks. ' Ah ! ' said the latter, almost gaily, ' it gives me courage to see you.'

However, the new-comers had brought a little information. The boulevards were in an agitated state, the news of the crime had spread from café to café, and everybody was anxious to see a late edition which one paper had published giving a very incorrect account of the affair, full of the most extraordinary details. Briefly, nothing positive was as yet known.

On seeing Guillaume turn pale Pierre compelled him to lie down again, and even talked of taking the visitors into the next room. But the injured man gently replied : ' No, no, I promise you that I won't stir again, that I won't open my mouth. But stay there and chat together. I assure you that it will do me good to have you near me and hear you.'

Then, under the sleepy gleams of the lamp, the others began to talk in undertones. Old Barthès, who considered that bomb to be both idiotic and abominable, spoke of it with the stupefaction of one who, after fighting like a hero through all the legendary struggles for liberty, found himself belated, out of his element, in a new era, which he could not understand. Did not the conquest of freedom suffice for everything ? he added. Was there any other problem beyond that of founding the real Republic ? Then, referring to Mège and his speech in the Chamber that afternoon, he bitterly arraigned Collectivism, which he declared to be one of the democratic forms of tyranny. Théophile Morin, for his part, also spoke against the Collectivist enrolling of the social forces, but he professed yet greater hatred of the odious

violence of the Anarchists; for it was only by evolution that
he expected progress, and he felt somewhat indifferent as to
what political means might bring about the scientific society
of to-morrow. And in like way Bache did not seem to be
particularly fond of the Anarchists, though he was touched by
the idyllic dream, the humanitarian hope, whose germs lay
beneath their passion for destruction. And, like Barthès, he
also flew into a passion with Mège, who since entering the
Chamber had become, said he, a mere rhetorician and
theorist, dreaming of dictatorship. Meantime Janzen, still
erect, his face frigid and his lips curling ironically, listened to
all three of them, and vented a few trenchant words to express
his own Anarchist faith; the uselessness of drawing distinc-
tions, and the necessity of destroying everything in order
that everything might be rebuilt on fresh lines.

Pierre, who had remained near the bed, also listened with
passionate attention. Amidst the downfall of his own beliefs,
the utter void which he felt within him, here were these four
men, who represented the cardinal points of this century's
ideas, debating the very same terrible problem which brought
him so much suffering, that of the new belief which the
democracy of the coming century awaits. And, ah! since the
days of the immediate ancestors, since the days of Voltaire
and Diderot and Rousseau, how incessantly had billows of
ideas followed and jostled one another, the older ones giving
birth to new ones, and all breaking and bounding in a
tempest in which it was becoming so difficult to distinguish
anything clearly! Whence came the wind, and whither
was the ship of salvation going, for what port ought one to
embark? Pierre had already thought that the balance-sheet
of the century ought to be drawn up, and that, after accepting
the legacies of Rousseau and the other precursors, he ought
to study the ideas of St. Simon, Fourier, and even Cabet; of
Auguste Comte, Proudhon and Karl Marx as well, in order,
at any rate, to form some idea of the distance that had been
travelled, and of the cross-ways which one had now reached.
And was not this an opportunity, since chance had gathered
those men together in his house, living exponents of the
conflicting doctrines which he wished to examine?

On turning round, however, he perceived that Guillaume
was now very pale and had closed his eyes. Had even he,
with his faith in science, felt the doubt which is born of

contradictory theories, and the despair which comes when one sees the fight for truth resulting in growth of error?

'Are you in pain?' the priest anxiously inquired.

'Yes, a little. But I will try to sleep.'

At this they all went off with silent handshakes. Nicholas Barthès alone remained in the house and slept in a room on the first floor which Sophie had got ready for him. Pierre, unwilling to quit his brother, dozed off upon a sofa. And the little house relapsed into its deep quietude, the silence of solitude and winter, through which passed the melancholy quiver of the souvenirs of childhood.

In the morning, as soon as it was seven o'clock, Pierre had to go for the newspapers. Guillaume had passed a bad night and intense fever had set in. Nevertheless, his brother was obliged to read him the endless articles on the explosion. There was an amazing medley of truths and inventions, of precise information lost amidst unexpected extravagance. Sagnier's paper, the 'Voix du Peuple,' distinguished itself by its sub-titles in huge print and a whole page of particulars jumbled together chancewise. It had at once decided to postpone the famous list of the thirty-two deputies and senators compromised in the African Railways affair; and there was no end to the details it gave of the aspect of the entrance to the Duvillard mansion after the explosion: the pavement broken up, the upper floor rent open, the huge doors torn away from their hinges. Then came the story of the Baron's son and daughter preserved as by a miracle, the landau escaping the slightest injury, while the banker and his wife, it was alleged, owed their preservation to the circumstance that they had lingered at the Madeleine after Monseigneur Martha's remarkable address there. An entire column was given to the one victim, the poor, pretty, fair-haired errand girl, whose identity did not seem to be clearly established although a flock of reporters had rushed first to the *modiste* employing her, in the Avenue de l'Opéra, and next to the upper part of the Faubourg St. Denis, where it was thought her grandmother resided. Then, in a gravely worded article in 'Le Globe,' evidently inspired by Fonsègue, an appeal was made to the Chamber's patriotism to avoid giving cause for any ministerial crisis in the painful circumstances through which the country was passing. Thus the ministry might last, and live in comparative quietude, for a few weeks longer.

Guillaume, however, was struck by one point only : the culprit was not known ; Salvat, it appeared certain, was neither arrested nor even suspected. It seemed, indeed, as if the police were starting on a false scent—that of a well-dressed gentleman wearing gloves, whom a neighbour swore he had seen entering the mansion at the moment of the explosion. Thus Guillaume became a little calmer. But his brother read to him from another paper some particulars concerning the engine of destruction that had been employed. It was a preserved-meat can, and the fragments of it showed that it had been comparatively small. And Guillaume relapsed into anxiety on learning that people were much astonished at the violent ravages of such a sorry appliance, and that the presence of some new explosive of incalculable power was already suspected.

At eight o'clock Bertheroy put in an appearance. Although he was sixty-eight he showed as much briskness and spright-liness as any young sawbones calling in a friendly way to perform a little operation. He had brought an instrument case, some linen bands and some lint. However, he became angry on finding the injured man nervous, flushed and hot with fever.

' Ah ! I see that you haven't been reasonable, my dear child,' said he. ' You must have talked too much, and have bestirred and excited yourself.' Then, having carefully probed the wound, he added, while dressing it : ' The bone is injured, you know, and I won't answer for anything unless you behave better. Any complications would make amputation necessary.'

Pierre shuddered, but Guillaume shrugged his shoulders, as if to say that he might just as well be amputated since all was crumbling around him. Bertheroy, who had sat down, lingering there for another moment, scrutinised both brothers with his keen eyes. He now knew of the explosion, and must have thought it over. ' My dear child,' he resumed in his brusque way, ' I certainly don't think that you committed that abominable act of folly in the Rue Godot-de-Mauroy. But I fancy that you were in the neighbourhood—no, no, don't answer me, don't defend yourself. I know nothing and desire to know nothing, not even the formula of that devilish powder of which your shirt-cuff bore traces, and which has wrought such terrible havoc.'

And then as the brothers remained surprised, turning cold with anxiety, in spite of his assurances, he added with a sweeping gesture : ' Ah ! my friends, I regard such an action as even more useless than criminal ! I only feel contempt for the vain agitation of politics, whether they be revolutionary or conservative. Does not science suffice ? Why hasten the times when one single step of science brings humanity nearer to the goal of truth and justice than do a hundred years of politics and social revolt ? Why, it is science alone which sweeps away dogmas, casts down gods, and creates light and happiness. And I, Member of the Institute as I am, decorated and possessed of means, I am the only true Revolutionist.'

Then he began to laugh and Guillaume realised all the good-natured irony of his laugh. While admiring him as a great *savant*, he had hitherto suffered at seeing him lead such a *bourgeois* life, accepting whatever appointments and honours were offered him, a Republican under the Republic, but quite ready to serve science under no matter what master. But now, from beneath this opportunist, this hieratical *savant*, this toiler who accepted wealth and glory from all hands, there appeared a quiet yet terrible evolutionist, who certainly expected that his own work would help to ravage and renew the world !

However, Bertheroy rose and took his leave : ' I'll come back ; behave sensibly, and love one another as well as you can.'

When the brothers again found themselves alone, Pierre seated at Guillaume's bedside, their hands once more sought each other and met in a burning clasp instinct with all their anguish. How much threatening mystery and distress there was both around and within them ! The grey wintry daylight came into the room, and they could see the black trees in the garden, while the house remained full of quivering silence, save that overhead a faint sound of footsteps was audible. They were the steps of Nicholas Barthès, the heroic lover of freedom, who, rising at daybreak, had, like a caged lion, resumed his wonted promenade, the incessant coming and going of one who had ever been a prisoner. And as the brothers ceased listening to him their eyes fell on a news-paper which had remained open on the bed, a newspaper soiled by a sketch in outline which pretended to portray the poor dead errand girl, lying, ripped open, beside the band-box and the hat it had contained. It was so frightful, so atrociously hideous a scene, that two big tears again fell upon Pierre's cheeks, whilst Guillaume's blurred, despairing eyes gazed wistfully far away, seeking for the Future.

II

A HOME OF INDUSTRY

THE little house in which Guillaume had dwelt for so many years, a home of quietude and hard work, stood in the pale light of winter up yonder at Montmartre, peacefully awaiting his return. He reflected, however, after *déjeuner* that it might not be prudent for him to go back thither for some weeks, and he therefore thought of sending Pierre to explain the position of affairs. 'Listen, brother,' he said. 'You must render me this service. Go and tell them the truth—that I am here, slightly injured, and do not wish them to come to see me, for fear lest somebody should follow them and discover my retreat. After the note I wrote them last evening they would end by getting anxious if I did not send them some news.' Then, yielding to the one worry which, since the previous night, had disturbed his clear, frank glance, he added: 'Just feel in the right-hand pocket of my waistcoat; you will find a little key there. Good! that's it. Now you must give it to Madame Leroi, my mother-in-law, and tell her that if any misfortune should happen to me, she is to do what is agreed between us. That will suffice, she will understand you.'

At the first moment Pierre had hesitated; but he saw how even the slight effort of speaking exhausted his brother, so he silenced him, saying: 'Don't talk, but put your mind at ease. I will go and reassure your people, since you wish that this commission should be undertaken by me.'

Truth to tell, the errand was so distasteful to Pierre that he had at first thought of sending Sophie in his place. All his old prejudices were reviving; it was as if he were going to some ogre's den. How many times had he not heard his mother say 'that creature!' in referring to the woman with whom her elder son cohabited. Never had she been willing to kiss Guillaume's boys; the whole connection had shocked her, and she was particularly indignant that Madame Leroi, the woman's mother, should have joined the household for the purpose of bringing up the little ones. Pierre retained so strong a recollection of all this that even nowadays, when he went to the basilica of the Sacred Heart and passed the little house on his way, he glanced at it distrustfully, and kept

as far from it as he could, as if it were some abode of vice and
error. Undoubtedly, for ten years now, the boys' mother had
been dead, but did not another scandal-inspiring creature
dwell there, that young orphan girl to whom his brother had
given shelter, and whom he was going to marry, although a
difference of twenty years lay between them ? To Pierre all
this was contrary to propriety, abnormal, and revolting, and
he pictured a home given over to social rebellion, where lack
of principle led to every kind of disorder.

However, he was leaving the room to start upon his
journey, when Guillaume called him back. 'Tell Madame
Leroi,' said he, 'that if I should die you will let her know of
it, so that she may immediately do what is necessary.'

'Yes, yes,' answered Pierre. 'But calm yourself, and
don't move about. I'll say everything. And in my absence
Sophie will stop here with you in case you should need her.'

Having given full instructions to the servant, Pierre set
out to take a tramcar, intending to alight from it on the
Boulevard de Rochechouart, and then climb the height on
foot. And on the road, lulled by the gliding motion of the
heavy vehicle, he began to think of his brother's past life and
connexions, with which he was but vaguely, imperfectly
acquainted. It was only at a later date that details of everything came to his knowledge. In 1850 a young professor
named Leroi, who had come from Paris to the college of
Montauban with the most ardent republican ideas, had
there married Agathe Dagnan, the youngest girl of an
old Protestant family from the Cévennes. Young Madame
Leroi was *enceinte* when her husband, threatened with arrest
for contributing some violent articles to a local newspaper,
immediately after the 'Coup d'Etat,' found himself obliged to
seek refuge at Geneva. It was there that the young couple's
daughter, Marguerite, a very delicate child, was born in 1852.
For seven years, that is until the Amnesty of 1859, the household struggled with poverty, the husband giving but a few ill-
paid lessons, and the wife absorbed in the constant care which
the child required. Then, after their return to Paris, their
ill-luck became even greater. For a long time the ex-professor
vainly sought regular employment ; it was denied him on
account of his opinions, and he had to run about giving
lessons in private houses. When he was at last on the point
of being received back into the University a supreme blow, an
attack of paralysis, fell upon him. He lost the use of both

legs. And then came utter misery, every kind of sordid drudgery, the writing of articles for dictionaries, the copying of manuscripts, and even the addressing of newspaper wrappers, on the fruits of which the household barely contrived to live, in a little lodging in the Rue Monsieur-le-Prince.

It was there that Marguerite grew up. Leroi, embittered by injustice and suffering, predicted the advent of a Republic which would avenge the follies of the Empire, and a reign of science which would sweep away the deceptive and cruel divinity of religious dogmas. On the other hand, Agathe's religious faith had collapsed at Geneva, at sight of the narrow and imbecile practices of Calvinism, and all that she retained of it was the old Protestant leaven of rebellion. She had become at once the head and the arm of the house; she went for her husband's work, took it back when completed, and even did much of it herself, whilst, at the same time, performing her house duties, and rearing and educating her daughter. The latter, who attended no school, was indebted for all she learnt to her father and mother, on whose part there was never any question of religious instruction. Through contact with her husband, Madame Leroi had lost all belief, and her Protestant heredity inclining her to free inquiry and examination, she had arranged for herself a kind of peaceful atheism, based on paramount principles of human duty and justice, which she applied courageously, irrespective of all social conventionalities. The long iniquity of her husband's fate, the undeserved misfortunes which struck her through him and her daughter, ended by endowing her with wonderful fortitude and devotion, which made her, whether as a judge, a manager, or a consoler, a woman of incomparable energy and nobleness of character.

It was in the Rue Monsieur-le-Prince that Guillaume became acquainted with the Leroi family, after the war of 1870. On the same floor as their little lodging he occupied a large room, where he devoted himself passionately to his studies. At the outset there was only an occasional bow, for Guillaume's neighbours were very proud and very grave, leading their life of poverty in fierce silence and retirement. Then intercourse began with the rendering of little services, such as when the young man procured the ex-professor a commission to write a few articles for a new encyclopædia. But all at once came the catastrophe: Leroi died in his armchair one evening while his daughter was wheeling him

from his table to his bed. The two distracted women had
not even the money to bury him. The whole secret of their
bitter want flowed forth with their tears, and they were
obliged to accept the help of Guillaume, who, from that
moment, became the necessary confidant and friend. And
the thing which was bound to happen did happen, in the
most simple and loving manner, permitted by the mother
herself, who, full of contempt for a social system which
allowed those of good hearts to die of hunger, refused to
admit the necessity of any social tie, Thus there was no
question of a regular marriage. One day Guillaume, who
was twenty-three years old, found himself mated to Marguerite, who was twenty ; both of them handsome, healthy,
and strong, adoring one another, loving work, and full of hope
in the future.

From that moment a new life began. Since his father's
death, Guillaume, who had broken off all intercourse with his
mother, had been receiving an allowance of two hundred
francs (£8) a month. This just represented daily bread ;
however, he was already doubling the amount by his work as
a chemist : his analyses and researches, which tended to
the employment of certain chemical products in industry.
So he and Marguerite installed themselves on the very
summit of Montmartre in a little house, at a rental of
eight hundred francs a year, the great convenience of the
place being a strip of garden, where one might, later
on, erect a wooden workshop. In all tranquillity Madame
Leroi took up her abode with the young people, helping them,
and sparing them the necessity of keeping a second servant.
And at successive intervals of two years, her three grand-
children were born, three sturdy boys ; first Thomas, then
François, and then Antoine. And in the same way as she
had devoted herself to her husband and daughter, and then
to Guillaume, so did she now devote herself to the children.
She became 'Mère-Grand'—an emphatic and affectionate way
of expressing the term 'grandmother'—for all who lived in
the house, the older as well as the younger ones. She there
personified sense, and wisdom, and courage ; it was she who
was ever on the watch, who directed everything, who was
consulted about everything, and whose opinion was always
followed. Indeed, she reigned there like an all-powerful
queen-mother.

For fifteen years this life went on, a life of hard work and

peaceful affection, while the strictest economy was observed
in contenting every need of the modest little household. Then
Guillaume lost his mother, took his share of the family in-
heritance, and was able to satisfy his old desire, which was to
buy the house he lived in, and build a spacious workshop in
the garden. He was even able to build it of bricks, and add
an upper story to it. But the work was scarcely finished, and
life seemed to be on the point of expanding and smiling on
them all, when misfortune returned, and typhoid fever, with
brutal force, carried off Marguerite, after a week's illness.
She was then five-and-thirty, and her eldest boy, Thomas,
was fourteen. Thus Guillaume, distracted by his loss, found
himself a widower at thirty-eight. The thought of introducing
any unknown woman into that retired home, where all hearts
beat in tender unison, was so unbearable to him that he determined to take no other mate. His work absorbed him, and
he would know how to quiet both his heart and his flesh.
Mère-Grand, fortunately, was still there, erect and courageous ;
the household retained its queen, and in her the children
found a manageress and teacher, schooled in adversity and
heroism.

Two years passed ; and then came an addition to the
family. A young woman, Marie Couturier, the daughter of
one of Guillaume's friends, suddenly entered it. Couturier
had been an inventor, a madman with some measure of
genius, and had spent a fairly large fortune in attempting all
sorts of fantastic schemes. His wife, a very pious woman,
had died of grief at it all ; and although on the rare occasions
when he saw his daughter, he showed great fondness for her
and loaded her with presents, he had first placed her in a
boarding college, and afterwards left her in the charge of
a poor female relative. Remembering her only on his death-
bed, he had begged Guillaume to give her an asylum, and find
her a husband. The poor relation, who dealt in ladies' and
babies' linen, had just become a bankrupt. So, at nineteen,
the girl, Marie, found herself a penniless outcast, possessed of
nothing save a good education, health and courage. Guillaume would never allow her to run about giving lessons. He
took her, in quite a natural way, to help Mère-Grand, who was
no longer so active as formerly. And the latter approved the
arrangement, well pleased at the advent of youth and gaiety,
which would somewhat brighten the household, whose life
had been one of much gravity ever since Marguerite's death.

Marie would simply be an elder sister; she was too old for
the boys, who were still at college, to be disturbed by her
presence. And she would work in that house where everybody worked. She would help the little community pending
the time when she might meet and love some worthy fellow
who would marry her.

Five more years elapsed without Marie consenting to quit
that happy home. The sterling education she had received
was lodged in a vigorous brain, which contented itself with the
acquirement of knowledge. Yet she had remained very pure
and healthy, even very *naïve*, maidenly by reason of her natural
rectitude. And she was also very much a woman, beautifying
and amusing herself with a mere nothing, and ever showing
gaiety and contentment. Moreover, she was in no wise of a
dreamy nature, but very practical, always intent on some work
or other, and only asking of life such things as life could give,
without anxiety as to what might lie beyond it. She lovingly
remembered her pious mother, who had prepared her for her
first Communion in tears, imagining that she was opening
heaven's portals to her. But since she had been an orphan
she had of her own accord ceased all practice of religion; her
good sense revolting and scorning the need of any moral
police regulations to make her do her duty. Indeed, she considered such regulations dangerous and destructive of true
health. Thus, like Mère-Grand, she had come to a sort of
quiet and almost unconscious atheism, not after the fashion
of one who reasons, but simply like the brave, healthy girl she
was, one who had long endured poverty without suffering
from it, and believed in nothing save the necessity of effort.
She had been kept erect, indeed, by her conviction that happiness was to be found in the normal joys of life, lived
courageously. And her happy equilibrium of mind had ever
guided and saved her; in such wise that she willingly listened
to her natural instinct, saying, with her pleasant laugh, that
this was, after all, her best adviser. She rejected two offers of
marriage, and on the second occasion as Guillaume pressed
her to accept, she grew astonished, and inquired if he had had
enough of her in the house. She found herself very comfortable, and she rendered service there. So why should she
leave and run the risk of being less happy elsewhere, particularly as she was not in love with anybody?

Then, by degrees, the idea of a marriage between Marie
and Guillaume presented itself; and indeed what could have

been more reasonable and advantageous for all ? If Guillaume had not mated again it was for his sons' sake, because he feared that by introducing a stranger to the house he might impair its quietude and gaiety. But now there was a woman among them who already showed herself maternal towards the boys, and whose bright youth had ended by disturbing his own heart. He was still in his prime, and had always held that it was not good for man to live alone, although, personally, thanks to his ardour for work, he had hitherto escaped excessive suffering in his bereavement. However, there was the great difference of ages to be considered ; and he would have bravely remained in the background and have sought a younger husband for Marie, if his three big sons and Mère-Grand herself had not conspired to effect his happiness by doing all they could to bring about a marriage which would strengthen every home-tie and impart, as it were, a fresh springtide to the house. As for Marie, touched and grateful to Guillaume for the manner in which he had treated her for five years past, she immediately consented with an impulse of sincere affection, in which, she fancied, she could detect love. And at all events, could she act in a more sensible, reasonable way, base her life on more certain prospects of happiness? So the marriage had been resolved upon ; and about a month previously it had been decided that it should take place during the ensuing spring, towards the end of April.

When Pierre, after alighting from the tramcar, began to climb the interminable flights of steps leading to the Rue St.-Eleuthère, a feeling of uneasiness again came over him at the thought that he was about to enter that suspicious ogre's den where everything would certainly wound and irritate him. Given the letter which Sophie had carried thither on the previous night, announcing that the master would not return, how anxious and upset must all its inmates be ! However, as Pierre ascended the final flight and nervously raised his head, the little house appeared to him right atop of the hill, looking very serene and quiet under the bright wintry sun, which had peered forth as if to bestow upon the modest dwelling an affectionate caress.

There was a door in the old garden wall alongside the Rue St.-Eleuthère, almost in front of the broad thorough-fare conducting to the basilica of the Sacred Heart ; but to reach the house itself one had to skirt the wall and climb to the

Place du Tertre, where one found the façade and the entrance. Some children were playing on the Place, which, planted as it was with a few scrubby trees, and edged with humble shops— a fruiterer's, a grocer's, and a baker's—looked like some square in a small provincial town. In a corner, on the left, Guillaume's dwelling, which had been whitewashed during the previous spring, showed its bright frontage and five lifeless windows, for all its life was on the other, the garden side, which overlooked Paris and the far horizon.

Pierre mustered his courage, and pulling a brass knob which glittered like gold, rang the bell. There came a gay, distant jingle; but for a moment nobody appeared, and he was about to ring again, when the door was thrown wide open, revealing a passage which ran right through the house, beyond which appeared the ocean of Paris, the endless sea of house roofs bathed in sunlight. And against this spacious, airy background, stood a young woman of twenty-six, clad in a simple gown of black woollen stuff, half covered by a large blue apron. She had her sleeves rolled up above her elbows, and her arms and hands were still moist with water which she had but imperfectly wiped away.

A moment's surprise and embarrassment ensued. The young woman who had hastened to the door with laughing mien, became grave and covertly hostile at sight of the visitor's cassock. The priest thereupon realised that he must give his name : ' I am Abbé Pierre Froment.'

At this the young woman's smile of welcome came back to her. ' Oh ! I beg your pardon, monsieur—I ought to have recognised you, for I saw you wish Guillaume good day one morning as you passed.'

She said Guillaume ; she, therefore, must be Marie. And Pierre looked at her in astonishment, finding her very different from what he had imagined. She was only of average height, but she was vigorously, admirably built, broad of hip and broad of shoulder, with the small firm bosom of an amazon. By her erect and easy step, instinct with all the adorable grace of woman in her prime, one could divine that she was strong, muscular, and healthy. A brunette, but very white of skin, she had a heavy helm of superb black hair, which she fastened in a negligent way, without any show of coquetry. And under her dark locks, her pure, intelligent brow, her delicate nose and gay eyes appeared full of intense life ; whilst the somewhat heavier character of her lower features, her fleshy lips, and full chin, bespoke her quiet kindliness. She had surely come on earth as a promise of every form of tenderness, every form of devotion. In a word, she was a true mate for man.

However, with her heavy, straying hair and superb arms, so ingenuous in their nudity, she only gave Pierre an impression of superfluous health and extreme self-assurance. She displeased him and even made him feel somewhat anxious, as if she were a creature different from all others.

'It is my brother Guillaume who has sent me,' he said.

At this her face again changed; she became grave and hastened to admit him to the passage. And when the door was closed she answered: 'You have brought us news of him then! I must apologise for receiving you in this fashion. The servants have just finished some washing, and I was making sure if the work had been well done. Pray excuse me, and come in here for a moment; it is perhaps best that I should be the first to know the news.'

So saying, she led him past the kitchen to a little room which served as scullery and wash-house. A tub full of soapy water stood there, and some dripping linen hung over some wooden bars. 'And so, Guillaume?' she asked.

Pierre then told the truth in simple fashion; that his brother's wrist had been injured; that he himself had witnessed the accident, and that his brother had then sought an asylum with him at Neuilly, where he wished to remain and get cured of his injury in peace and quietness, without even receiving a visit from his sons. While speaking in this fashion, the priest watched the effect of his words on Marie's face: first fright and pity, and then an effort to calm herself and judge things reasonably.

'His letter quite froze me last night,' she ended by replying. 'I felt sure that some misfortune had happened. But one must be brave and hide one's fear from others. His wrist injured, you say—it is not a serious injury, is it?'

'No; but it is necessary that every precaution should be taken with it.'

She looked him well in the face with her big frank eyes, which dived into his own as if to reach the very depths of his being, though at the same time she plainly sought to restrain the score of questions which rose to her lips. 'And that is all, he was injured in an accident,' she resumed; 'he didn't ask you to tell us anything further about it?'

'No; he simply desires that you will not be anxious.'

Thereupon she insisted no further; but showed herself obedient and respectful of the decision which Guillaume had arrived at. It sufficed that he should have sent a messenger to reassure the household—she did not seek to learn any more. And even as she had returned to her work in spite of the secret anxiety in which the letter of the previous evening had left her, so now with her air of quiet strength, she recovered an appearance of serenity, a quiet smile and clear brave glance.

'Guillaume only gave me one other commission,' resumed Pierre, 'that of handing a little key to Madame Leroi.'

'Very good,' Marie answered, 'Mère-Grand is here; and, besides, the children must see you. I will take you to them.'

Once more quite tranquil, she examined Pierre without managing to conceal her curiosity, which seemed of rather a kindly nature blended with an element of vague pity. Her fresh white arms had remained bare. In all candour she slowly drew down her sleeves; then took off the large blue apron, and showed herself with her rounded figure, at once robust and elegant, in her modest black gown. He meanwhile looked at her, and most certainly he did not find her to his liking. On seeing her there before him, so natural, healthy, and courageous, quite a feeling of revolt arose within him, though he knew not why.

'Will you please follow me, Monsieur l'Abbé?' she said. 'We must cross the garden.'

On the ground-floor of the house, across the passage, and facing the kitchen and the scullery, there were two other rooms, a library overlooking the Place du Tertre, and a dining-room whose windows opened into the garden. The four rooms on the first floor served as bedchambers for the father and the three boys. As for the garden, originally but a small one, it had now been reduced to a kind of gravelled yard by the erection of the large workshop at one end of it. Of the former greenery, however, there still remained two huge plumtrees with old knotted trunks, as well as a big clump of lilac bushes, which every spring were covered with bloom. And in front of the latter Marie had arranged a broad flower-bed, in which she amused herself with growing a few roses, some wallflowers, and some mignonette.

With a wave of her hand as she went past, she called Pierre's attention to the black plumtrees and the lilacs and roses, which showed but a few greenish spots, for winter still held the little nook in sleep. 'Tell Guillaume,' she said, ' that he must make haste to get well and be back for the first shoots.'

Then, as Pierre at that moment glanced at her, she all at once flushed purple. Much to her distress, sudden and involuntary blushes would in this wise occasionally come upon her, even at the most innocent remarks. She found it ridiculous to feel such childish emotion when she had so brave a heart. But her pure maidenly blood had retained exquisite delicacy, such natural and instinctive modesty that she yielded to it perforce. And doubtless she had merely blushed because she feared that the priest might think she had referred to her marriage in speaking of the spring.

' Please go in, Monsieur l'Abbé. The children are there, all three.' And forthwith she ushered him into the workshop.

It was a very spacious place, over sixteen feet high, with a brick flooring and bare walls painted an iron grey. A sheet of light, a streaming bath of sunshine, spread to every corner through a huge window facing the south, where lay the immensity of Paris. The Venetian shutters often had to be lowered in the summer to attenuate the great heat. From morn till night the whole family lived here, closely and affectionately united in work. Each was installed as fancy listed, having a particular chosen place. One half of the building was occupied by the father's chemical laboratory with its stove, experiment tables, shelves for apparatus, glass cases and cupboards for phials and jars. Near all this Thomas, the eldest son, had installed a little forge, an anvil, a vice bench, in fact everything necessary to a working mechanician, such as he had become since taking his bachelor's degree, from his desire to remain with his father and help him with certain researches and inventions. Then, at the other end, the younger brothers, François and Antoine, got on very well together on either side of a broad table which stood amidst a medley of portfolios, nests of drawers and revolving book-stands. François, laden with academical laurels, first on the pass list for the École Normale, had entered that college where young men are trained for university professorships, and was there preparing for his Licentiate degree, while Antoine, who on reaching the third class at the Lycée Condorcet had taken a dislike to classical

studies, now devoted himself to his calling as a wood-engraver.
And, in the full light under the window, Mère-Grand and
Marie likewise had their particular table, where needlework,
embroidery, all sorts of *chiffons* and delicate things lay about
near the somewhat rough jumble of retorts, tools, and big
books.

Marie, however, on the very threshold called out in her
calm voice, to which she strove to impart a gay and cheering
accent: ' Children! children! here is Monsieur l'Abbé with
news of father! '

Children, indeed! Yet what motherliness she already set
in the word as she applied it to those big fellows whose elder
sister she had long considered herself to be! At three-and-
twenty Thomas was quite a colossus, already bearded and
extremely like his father. But although he had a lofty brow
and energetic features, he was somewhat slow both in mind
and body. And he was also taciturn, almost unsociable,
absorbed in filial devotion, delighted with the manual toil
which made him a mere workman at his master's orders.
François, two years younger than Thomas, and nearly as tall,
showed a more refined face, though he had the same large
brow and same firm mouth, a perfect blending of health and
strength, in which the man of intellect, the scientific
Normalian could only be detected by the brighter and more
subtle sparkle of the eyes. The youngest of the brothers,
Antoine, who for his eighteen years was almost as strong as
his elders, and promised to become as tall, differed from them
by his lighter hair and soft, blue dreamy eyes, which he had
inherited from his mother. It had been difficult, however,
to distinguish one from the other when all three were school-
boys at the Lycée Condorcet ; and even nowadays people
made mistakes unless they saw them side by side, so as to
detect the points of difference which were becoming more
marked as age progressed.

On Pierre's arrival the brothers were so absorbed in their
work that they did not even hear the door open. And again,
as in the case of Marie, the priest was surprised by the discipline and firmness of mind, which amidst the keenest
anxiety gave the young fellows strength to take up their
daily task. Thomas, who stood at his vice-bench in a blouse,
was carefully filing a little piece of copper with rough but
skilful hands. François, leaning forward, was writing in a
bold, firm fashion, whilst on the other side of the table,

Antoine, with a slender graver between his fingers, finished a block for an illustrated newspaper.

However, Marie's clear voice made them raise their heads : ' Children, father has sent you some news ! '

Then all three with the same impulse hurriedly quitted their work and came forward. One could tell that directly there was any question of their father they were drawn together, blended one with the other, so that but one and the same heart beat in their three broad chests. However, a door at the far end of the work-room opened at that moment, and Mère-Grand, coming from the upper floor where she and Marie had their bedrooms, made her appearance. She had just absented herself to fetch a skein of wool ; and she gazed fixedly at the priest, unable to understand the reason of his presence.

Marie had to explain matters. ' Mère-Grand,' said she, ' this is Monsieur l'Abbé Froment, Guillaume's brother ; he has come from him.'

Pierre on his side was examining the old lady, astonished to find her so erect and full of life at seventy. Her former beauty had left a stately charm on her rather long face ; youthful fire still lingered in her brown eyes ; and very firm was the contour of her pale lips, which in parting showed that she had retained all her teeth. A few white hairs alone silvered her black tresses, which were arranged in old-time fashion. Her cheeks had but slightly withered, and her deep, symmetrical wrinkles gave her countenance an expression of much nobility, a sovereign air as of a queen-mother, which, tall and slight of stature as she was, and invariably gowned in black woollen stuff, she always retained, no matter how humble her occupation.

' So Guillaume sent you, monsieur ? ' she said ; ' he is injured, is he not ? '

Surprised by this proof of intuition, Pierre repeated his story. ' Yes, his wrist is injured—but oh ! it's not a serious matter so far.'

On the part of the three sons, he had divined a sudden quiver, an impulse of their whole beings to rush to the help and defence of their father. And for their sakes he sought words of comfort : ' He is with me at Neuilly. And with due care it is certain that no dangerous complications will arise. He sent me to tell you to be in no wise uneasy about him.'

Mère-Grand for her part evinced no fears, but preserved
great calmness, as if the priest's tidings contained nothing
beyond what she had known already. If anything, she
seemed rather relieved, freed from anxiety which she had
confided to none. ' If he is with you, monsieur,' she
answered, ' he is evidently as comfortable as he can be, and
sheltered from all risks. We were surprised, however, by his
letter last night, as it did not explain why he was detained,
and we should have ended by feeling frightened. But now
everything is satisfactory.'

Mère-Grand and the three sons, following Marie's example,
sought no further explanation. On a table near by, Pierre
noticed several morning newspapers lying open and displaying
column after column of particulars about the crime. The
sons had certainly read those papers, and had feared lest their
father should be compromised in that frightful affair. How
far did their knowledge of the latter go ? They must be
ignorant of the part played by Salvat. It was surely impossible for them to piece together all the unforeseen circumstances which had brought about their father's meeting with
the workman, and then the crime. Mère-Grand, no doubt,
was in certain respects better informed than the others. But
they, the sons and Marie, neither knew nor sought to know
anything. And thus what a wealth of respect and affection
there was in their unshakable confidence in the father, in
the tranquillity they displayed directly he sent them word
that they were not to be anxious about him !

' Madame,' Pierre resumed, ' Guillaume told me to give
you this little key, and to remind you of what he charged
you to do, if any misfortune should befall him.'

She started, but so slightly that it was scarcely perceptible ;
and taking the key, she answered as if some ordinary wish on
the part of a sick person were alone in question. ' Very well.
Tell him that his wishes shall be carried out.' Then she
added, ' But pray take a seat, monsieur.'

Pierre, indeed, had remained standing. However, he now
felt it necessary to accept a chair, desirous as he was of hiding
the embarrassment which he still felt in this house, although
he was *en famille* there. Marie, who could not live without
occupation for her fingers, had just returned to some embroidery, some of the fine needlework which she persisted
in executing for an establishment dealing in baby-linen and
bridal *trousseaux* ; for she wished at any rate to earn her

own pocket-money, she often said with a laugh. Mère-Grand, too, from habit, which she followed even when visitors were present, had once more started on her perpetual stocking-mending; while François and Antoine had again seated themselves at their table; and Thomas alone remained on his legs, leaning against his bench. All the charm of industrious intimacy pervaded the spacious, sun-lit room.

'But we'll all go to see father to-morrow,' Thomas suddenly exclaimed.

Before Pierre could answer Marie raised her head. 'No, no,' said she, 'he does not wish any of us to go to him; for if we should be watched and followed we should betray the secret of his retreat. Isn't that so, Monsieur l'Abbé?'

'It would indeed be prudent of you to deprive yourselves of the pleasure of embracing him until he himself can come back here. It will be a matter of some two or three weeks,' answered Pierre.

Mère-Grand at once expressed approval of this. 'No doubt,' said she. 'Nothing could be more sensible.'

So the three sons did not insist, but bravely accepted the secret anxiety in which they must for a time live, renouncing the visit which would have caused them so much delight because their father bade them do so and because his safety depended perhaps on their obedience.

However, Thomas resumed: 'Then, Monsieur l'Abbé, will you please tell him that as work will be interrupted here, I shall return to the factory during his absence. I shall be more at ease there for some researches on which we are engaged.'

'And please tell him from me,' put in François, 'that he mustn't worry about my examination. Things are going very well. I feel almost certain of success.'

Pierre promised that he would forget nothing. However, Marie raised her head, smiling and glancing at Antoine, who had remained silent with a far-away look in his eyes. 'And you, little one,' said she, 'don't you send him any message?'

Emerging from a dream, the young fellow also began to smile. 'Yes, yes, a message that you love him dearly, and that he's to be quick back for you to make him happy.'

At this they all became merry, even Marie, who in lieu of embarrassment showed a tranquil gaiety born of confidence in the future. Between her and the young men there was nought but happy affection. And a grave smile appeared

even on the pale lips of Mère-Grand, who likewise approved
of the happiness which life seemed to be promising.

Pierre wished to stay a few minutes longer. They all
began to chat, and his astonishment increased. He had gone
from surprise to surprise in this house where he had expected
to find equivocal, disorderly life and rebellion against social
laws, such as destroys morality. But instead of this he
had found loving serenity, and such strong discipline that
life there partook of the gravity, almost the austerity of convent life, tempered by youth and gaiety. The vast room was
redolent of industry and quietude, warm with bright sunshine.
However, what most particularly struck him was the Spartan
training, the bravery of mind and heart among those sons
who allowed nothing to be seen of their personal feelings, and
did not presume to judge their father, but remained content
with his message, ready to await events, stoical and silent,
while carrying on their daily tasks. Nothing could be more
simple, more dignified, more lofty. And there was also the
smiling heroism of Mère-Grand and Marie, those two women
who slept over that laboratory where terrible preparations
were manipulated, and where an explosion was always
possible.

However, such courage, orderliness, and dignity merely surprised Pierre, without touching him. He had no cause for complaint, he had received a polite greeting if not an affectionate
one, but then he was as yet only a stranger there, a priest.
In spite of everything, however, he remained hostile, feeling
that he was in a sphere where none of his own torments
could be shared or even guessed. How did those folks manage
to be so calm and happy amidst their religious unbelief, their
exclusive faith in science, in presence of that terrifying Paris
which spread before them the boundless sea, the growling
abomination of its injustice and its want? As this thought
came to him he turned his head and gazed at the city through
the huge window, whence it stretched away, ever present,
ever living its giant life. And at that hour, under the oblique
sunrays of the winter afternoon, all Paris was speckled with
luminous dust, as if some invisible sower, hidden amidst the
glory of the planet, were fast scattering seed which fell upon
every side in a stream of gold. The whole field was covered
with it; for the endless chaos of house roofs and edifices
seemed to be land in tilth, furrowed by some gigantic plough.
And Pierre in his uneasiness, stirred despite everything by

an invincible need of hope, asked himself if this was not
a good sowing, the furrows of Paris strewn with light by the
divine sun for the great future harvest, that harvest of truth
and justice of whose advent he had despaired.

At last he rose and took his leave, promising to return at
once, if there should be any bad news. It was Marie who
showed him to the front door. And there another of those
childish blushes which worried her so much suddenly rose
to her face, when she, in her turn, wished to send her
loving message to the injured man. However, with her gay,
candid eyes fixed on those of the priest, she bravely spoke the
words: ' Good-bye, *Monsieur l'Abbé*. Tell Guillaume that I
love him and await him.'

III

PENURY AND TOIL

THREE days went by, and every morning Guillaume, confined
to his bed and consumed by fever and impatience, experienced
fresh anxiety directly the newspapers arrived. Pierre had
tried to keep them from him, but Guillaume then worried
himself the more, and so the priest had to read him column
by column all the extraordinary articles that were published
respecting the crime.

Never before had so many rumours inundated the press.
Even the ' Globe,' usually so grave and circumspect, yielded
to the general *furore*, and printed whatever statements reached
it. But the more unscrupulous papers were the ones to read.
The ' Voix du Peuple ' made all possible use of the public
feverishness to increase its sales. Each morning it employed
some fresh device, and printed some frightful story of a
nature to drive people mad with terror. It related that
not a day passed without Baron Duvillard receiving threatening letters of the coarsest description, announcing that his
wife, his son, and his daughter would all be killed, that he
himself would be butchered in turn, and that do what he
might his house would none the less be blown up. And as a
measure of precaution the house was guarded day and night
by a perfect army of plain-clothes officers. Then another
article contained an amazing piece of invention. Some

Anarchists, after carrying barrels of powder into a sewer near the Madeleine, were said to have undermined the whole district, planning a perfect volcano there, into which one-half of Paris would sink. And at another time it was alleged that the police were on the track of a terrible plot which embraced all Europe, from the depths of Russia to the shores of Spain. The signal for putting it into execution was to be given in France, and there would be a three days' massacre, with grape shot sweeping every one off the Boulevards, and the Seine running red, swollen by a torrent of blood. Thanks to these able and intelligent devices of the Press, terror now reigned in the city; frightened foreigners fled from the hotels *en masse*; and Paris had become a mere mad-house, where the most idiotic delusions at once found credit.

It was not all this, however, that worried Guillaume. He was only anxious about Salvat and the various new 'clues' which the newspaper reporters attempted to follow up. The engineer was not yet arrested, and, so far indeed, there had been no statement in print to indicate that the police were on his track. At last, however, Pierre one morning read a paragraph which made the injured man turn pale.

'Dear me! It seems that a tool has been found among the rubbish at the entrance of the Duvillard mansion. It is a bradawl, and its handle bears the name of Grandidier, which is that of a man who owns some well-known metal works. He is to appear before the investigating magistrate to-day.'

Guillaume made a gesture of despair. 'Ah!' said he, 'they are on the right track at last. That tool must certainly have been dropped by Salvat. He worked at Grandidier's before he came to me for a few days. And from Grandidier they will learn all that they need to know in order to follow the scent.'

Pierre then remembered that he had heard the Grandidier factory mentioned at Montmartre. Guillaume's eldest son, Thomas, had served his apprenticeship there, and even worked there occasionally nowadays.

'You told me,' resumed Guillaume, 'that during my absence Thomas intended to go back to the factory. It's in connection with a new motor which he's planning, and has almost hit upon. If there should be an investigation there, he may be questioned, and may refuse to answer, in order to guard his secret. So he ought to be warned of this, warned at once!'

Without trying to extract any more precise statement from his brother, Pierre obligingly offered his services. ' If you like,' said he, ' I will go to see Thomas this afternoon. Perhaps I may come across Monsieur Grandidier himself and learn how far the affair has gone, and what was said at the investigating magistrate's.'

With a moist glance and an affectionate grasp of the hand, Guillaume at once thanked Pierre. ' Yes, yes, brother, go there, it will be good and brave of you.'

' Besides,' continued the priest, ' I really wanted to go to Montmartre to-day. I haven't told you so, but something has been worrying me. If Salvat has fled he must have left the woman and the child all alone up yonder. On the morning of the day when the explosion took place I saw the poor creatures in such a state of destitution that I can't think of them without a heart-pang. Women and children so often die of starvation when the man is no longer there.'

At this, Guillaume, who had kept Pierre's hand in his own, pressed it more tightly, and in a trembling voice exclaimed : ' Yes, yes, and that will be good and brave too. Go there, brother, go there.'

That house of the Rue des Saules, that horrible home of want and agony, had lingered in Pierre's memory. To him it was like an embodiment of the whole filthy *cloaca* in which the poor of Paris suffer unto death. And on returning thither that afternoon, he found the same slimy mud around it ; its yard littered with the same filth, its dark, damp stairways redolent of the same stench of neglect and poverty, as before. In winter time, while the fine central districts of Paris are dried and cleansed, the far-away districts of the poor remain gloomy and miry, beneath the everlasting tramp of the wretched ones who dwell in them.

Remembering the staircase which conducted to Salvat's lodging, Pierre began to climb it amidst a loud screaming of little children, who suddenly became quiet, letting the house sink into death-like silence once more. Then the thought of Laveuve, who had perished up there like a stray dog, came back to Pierre. And he shuddered when, on the top landing, he knocked at Salvat's door, and profound silence alone answered him. Not a breath was to be heard.

However, he knocked again, and as nothing stirred he began to think that nobody could be there. Perhaps Salvat had returned to fetch the woman and the child, and perhaps they had followed him to some humble nook abroad. Still this would have astonished him; for the poor seldom quit their homes, they die where they have suffered. So he gave another and a gentle knock.

And at last a faint sound, the light tread of little feet was heard amidst the silence. Then a weak, childish voice ventured to inquire: 'Who is there?'

'Monsieur l'Abbé.'

The silence fell again, nothing more stirred. There was evidently hesitation on the other side.

'Monsieur l'Abbé who came the other day,' said Pierre again.

This evidently put an end to all uncertainty, for the door was set ajar and little Céline admitted the priest. 'I beg your pardon, Monsieur l'Abbé,' said she, 'but Mamma Théodore has gone out, and she told me not to open the door to anyone.'

Pierre had, for a moment, imagined that Salvat himself was hiding there. But with a glance he took in the whole of the small bare room, where man, woman, and child dwelt together. At the same time, Madame Théodore doubtless feared a visit from the police. Had she seen Salvat since the crime? Did she know where he was hiding? Had he come back there to embrace and tranquillise them both?

'And your papa, my dear,' said Pierre to Céline, 'isn't he here either?'

'Oh! no, monsieur, he has gone away.'

'What, gone away?'

'Yes, he hasn't been home to sleep, and we don't know where he is.'

'Perhaps he's working.'

'Oh, no! he'd send us some money if he was.'

'Then he's gone on a journey, perhaps?'

'I don't know.'

'He wrote to Mamma Théodore, no doubt?'

'I don't know.'

Pierre asked no further questions. In fact, he felt somewhat ashamed of his attempt to extract information from this child of eleven, whom he thus found alone. It was quite possible that she knew nothing, that Salvat, in a spirit of prudence, had even refrained from sending any tdings of himself. Indeed, there was an expression of truthfulness on the child's fair, gentle, and intelligent face, which was grave with the gravity that extreme misery imparts to the young.

'I am sorry that Mamma Théodore isn't here,' said Pierre, 'I wanted to speak to her.'

'But perhaps you would like to wait for her, Monsieur l'Abbé. She has gone to my Uncle Toussaint's in the Rue Marcadet; and she can't stop much longer, for she's been away more than an hour.'

Thereupon Céline cleared one of the chairs on which lay a handful of scraps of wood, picked up on some waste ground.

The bare and fireless room was assuredly also a breadless one. Pierre could divine the absence of the bread-winner, the disappearance of the man who represents will and strength in the home, and on whom one still relies even when weeks have gone by without work. He goes out and scours the city, and often ends by bringing back the indispensable crust which keeps death at bay. But with his disappearance comes complete abandonment, the wife and child in danger, destitute of all prop and help.

Pierre, who had sat down and was looking at that poor, little, blue-eyed girl, to whose lips a smile returned in spite of everything, could not keep from questioning her on another point. 'So you don't go to school, my child?' said he.

She faintly blushed and answered : 'I've no shoes to go in.'

He glanced at her feet, and saw that she was wearing a pair of ragged old list-slippers, from which her little toes protruded, red with cold.

'Besides,' she continued, 'Mamma Théodore says that one doesn't go to school when one's got nothing to eat. Mamma Théodore wanted to work but she couldn't, because her eyes got burning hot and full of water. And so we don't know what to do, for we've had nothing left since yesterday, and if Uncle Toussaint can't lend us twenty sous it'll be all over.'

She was still smiling in her unconscious way, but two big tears had gathered in her eyes. And the sight of the child shut up in that bare room, apart from all the happy ones of earth, so upset the priest that he again felt his anger with want and misery awakening. Then, another ten minutes having elapsed, he became impatient, for he had to go on to the Grandidier works before returning home.

' I don't know why Mamma Théodore doesn't come back,'
repeated Céline, ' Perhaps she's chatting.' Then, an idea
occurring to her she continued : ' I'll take you to my Uncle
Toussaint's, Monsieur l'Abbé, if you like, It's close by, just
round the corner.'

' But you have no shoes, my child.'

' Oh ! that don't matter, I walk all the same.'

Thereupon he rose from the chair and said simply : ' Well,
yes, that will be better, take me there. And I'll buy you
some shoes.'

Céline turned quite pink, and then made haste to follow
him after carefully locking the door of the room like a good
little housewife, though, truth to tell, there was nothing worth
stealing in the place.

In the meantime it had occurred to Madame Théodore
that before calling on her brother Toussaint to try to borrow
a franc from him, she might first essay her luck with her
younger sister, Hortense, who had married little Chrétiennot,
a clerk, and occupied a flat of four rooms on the Boulevard
de Rochechouart. This was quite an experiment, however,
and the poor woman only made the venture because Céline
had been fasting since the previous day.

Eugène Toussaint, the mechanician, a man of fifty, was
her step-brother, by the first marriage contracted by her
father. A young dressmaker, whom the latter had subsequently wedded, had borne him three daughters, Pauline,
Léonie, and Hortense. And on his death, his son Eugène,
who already had a wife and child of his own, had found himself for a short time with his stepmother and sisters on his
hands. The stepmother, fortunately, was an active and
intelligent woman, and knew how to get out of difficulties.
She returned to her former workroom where her daughter
Pauline was already apprenticed, and she next placed Léonie
there ; so that, Hortense, the youngest girl, who was a spoilt
child, prettier and more delicate than her sisters, was alone
left at school. And, later on—after Pauline had married
Labitte the stonemason, and Léonie, Salvat the journeyman-
engineer—Hortense, while serving as assistant at a con-
fectioner's in the Rue des Martyrs, had there become acquainted
with Chrétiennot, a clerk, who married her. Léonie had
died young, only a few weeks after her mother ; Pauline,
forsaken by her husband, lived with her brother-in-law
Salvat, and Hortense alone wore a light silk gown on

Sundays, resided in a new house, and ranked as a 'lady,' at the price, however, of interminable worries and great privation.

Madame Théodore knew that her sister was generally short of money towards the month's end, and therefore felt rather ill at ease in thus venturing to apply for a loan. Chrétiennot, moreover, embittered by his own mediocrity, had of late years accused his wife of being the cause of their spoilt life, and had ceased all intercourse with her relatives. Toussaint, no doubt, was a decent workman; but that Madame Théodore who lived in misery with her brother-in-law, and that Salvat who wandered from workshop to workshop like an incorrigible ranter whom no employer would keep; those two with their want and dirt and rebellion, had ended by incensing the vain little clerk, who was not only a great stickler for the proprieties, but was soured by all the difficulties he encountered in his own life. And thus he had forbidden Hortense to receive her sister.

All the same, as Madame Théodore climbed the carpeted staircase of the house on the Boulevard Rochechouart, she experienced a certain feeling of pride at the thought that she had a relation living in such luxury. The Chrétiennots' rooms were on the third floor, and overlooked the courtyard. Their *femme-de-ménage*—a woman who goes out by the day or hour charring, cleaning, and cooking—came back every afternoon about four o'clock to see to the dinner, and that day she was already there. She admitted the visitor, though she could not conceal her anxious surprise at her boldness in calling in such slatternly garb. However, on the very threshold of the little *salon*, Madame Théodore stopped short in wonderment herself, for her sister Hortense was sobbing and crouching on one of the armchairs, upholstered in blue repp, of which she was so proud.

'What is the matter? What has happened to you?' asked Madame Théodore.

Her sister, though scarcely two-and-thirty, was no longer 'the beautiful Hortense' of former days. She retained a doll-like appearance, with a tall slim figure, pretty eyes, and fine, fair hair. But she who had once taken so much care of herself, had now come down to dressing-gowns of doubtful cleanliness. Her eyelids, too, were reddening, and blotches were appearing on her skin. She had begun to fade after giving birth to two daughters, one of whom was now nine and the other seven years of age. Very proud and egotistical, she herself now regretted her marriage, for she had formerly considered herself a real beauty, worthy of the palaces and equipages of some Prince Charming. And at this moment she was plunged in such despair that her sister's sudden appearance on the scene did not even astonish her: 'Ah! it's you,' she gasped. 'Ah! if you only knew what a blow's fallen on me in the middle of all our worries!'

Madame Théodore at once thought of the children, Lucienne and Marcelle. 'Are your daughters ill?' she asked.

'No, no, our neighbour has taken them for a walk on the Boulevard. But the fact is, my dear, I'm *enceinte*, and when I told Chrétiennot of it after lunch, he flew into a most fearful passion, saying the most dreadful, the most cruel things!'

Then she again sobbed. Gentle and indolent by nature, desirous of peace and quietness before anything else, she was incapable of deceiving her husband, as he well knew. But the trouble was that an addition to the family would upset the whole economy of the household.

'*Mon Dieu!*' said Madame Théodore at last, 'you brought up the others, and you'll bring up this one too.'

At this an explosion of anger dried the other's eyes; and she rose, exclaiming: 'You are good, you are! One can see that our purse isn't yours. How are we to bring up another child when we can scarcely make both ends meet, as it is?'

And thereupon, forgetting the pride and vanity which usually prompted her to silence or falsehood, she freely explained their embarrassment, the horrid pecuniary worries which made their life perpetual misery. Their rent amounted to 700 francs,[1] so that out of the 3,000 francs[2] which the husband earned at his office, barely a couple of hundred were left them every month. And how were they to manage with that little sum, provide food and clothes, keep up their rank and so forth? There was the indispensable black coat for monsieur, the new dress which madame must have at regular intervals, under penalty of losing caste, the new boots which the children required almost every month, in fact, all sorts of things that could not possibly be dispensed with. One might strike a dish or two out of the bill of fare, and

[1] £28.   [2] £120.

even go without wine; but evenings came when it was absolutely necessary to take a cab. And, apart from all this, one had to reckon with the wastefulness of the children, the disorder in which the discouraged wife left the house, and the despair of the husband, who was convinced that he would never extricate himself from his difficulties, even should his salary some day be raised to as high a figure as 4,000 francs. Briefly one here found the unbearable penury of the petty clerk, with consequences as disastrous as the dire want of the artisan: the mock façade and lying luxury; all the disorder and suffering which lie behind intellectual pride at not earning one's living at a bench or on a scaffolding.

'Well, well,' repeated Madame Théodore, 'you can't kill the child.'

'No, of course not; but it's the end of everything,' answered Hortense, sinking into the armchair again. 'What will become of us, *mon Dieu!* What will become of us!' Then she collapsed in her unbuttoned dressing gown, tears once more gushing from her red and swollen eyes.

Much vexed that circumstances should be so unpropitious, Madame Théodore nevertheless ventured to ask for the loan of twenty sous; and this brought her sister's despair and confusion to a climax. 'I really haven't a centime in the house,' said she, 'just now I borrowed ten sous for the children from the servant. I had to get ten francs from the Mont de Piété on a little ring the other day. And it's always the same at the end of the month. However, Chrétiennot will be paid to-day, and he's coming back early with the money for dinner. So if I can I will send you something to-morrow.'

At this same moment the servant hastened in with a distracted air, being well aware that monsieur was in no wise partial to madame's relatives. 'Oh madame, madame!' said she; 'here's master coming up the stairs.'

'Quick then, quick, go away!' cried Hortense, 'I should only have another scene if he met you here. To-morrow, if I can, I promise you.'

To avoid Chrétiennot who was coming in, Madame Théodore had to hide herself in the kitchen. As he passed, she just caught sight of him, well dressed as usual in a tight-fitting frock coat. Short and lean, with a thin face and long and carefully tended beard, he had the bearing of one who is both vain and quarrelsome. Fourteen years of office life had withered him, and now the long evening hours which he spent at a neighbouring café were finishing him off.

When Madame Théodore had quitted the house she turned with dragging steps towards the Rue Marcadet where the Toussaints resided. Here, again, she had no great expectations, for she well knew what ill-luck and worry had fallen upon her brother's home. During the previous autumn Toussaint, though he was but fifty, had experienced an attack of paralysis which had laid him up for nearly five months. Prior to this mishap he had borne himself bravely, working steadily, abstaining from drink, and bringing up his three children in true fatherly fashion. One of them, a girl, was now married to a carpenter, with whom she had gone to Le Havre, while of the others, both boys—one, a soldier, had been killed in Tonquin, and the other, Charles, after serving his time in the army, had become a working mechanician. However, Toussaint's long illness had exhausted the little money which he had in the Savings' Bank, and now that he had been set on his legs again, he had to begin life once more without a copper in pocket.

Madame Théodore found her sister-in-law alone in the cleanly kept room which she and her husband occupied. Madame Toussaint was a portly woman, whose corpulence increased in spite of everything, whether it were worry or fasting. She had a round puffy face with bright little eyes; and was a very worthy woman, whose only faults were an inclination for gossiping and a fondness for good cheer. Before Madame Théodore even opened her mouth she understood the object of her visit. 'You've come on us at a bad moment, my dear,' she said, 'we're stumped. Toussaint wasn't able to go back to the works till the day before yesterday, and he'll have to ask for an advance this evening.'

As she spoke, she looked at the other with no great sympathy, hurt as she felt by her slovenly appearance. 'And Salvat,' she added, 'is he still doing nothing?'

Madame Théodore doubtless foresaw the question, for she quietly lied: 'He isn't in Paris; a friend has taken him off for some work over Belgium way, and I'm waiting for him to send us something.'

Madame Toussaint still remained distrustful, however: 'Ah!' she said, 'it's just as well that he shouldn't be in Paris; for with all those bomb affairs we couldn't help thinking of him, and saying that he was quite mad enough to mix himself up in them.'

The other did not even blink. If she knew anything she kept it to herself.

'But you, my dear, can't you find any work?' continued Madame Toussaint.

'Well, what would you have me do with my poor eyes? It's no longer possible for me to sew.'

'That's true. Every seamstress gets done for. When Toussaint was laid up here I myself wanted to go back to my old calling as a needlewoman. But there! I spoilt everything and did no good. Charring's about the only thing that one can always do. Why don't you get some jobs of that kind?'

'I'm trying, but I can't find any.'

Little by little Madame Toussaint was softening at sight of the other's miserable appearance. She made her sit down, and told her that she would give her something if Toussaint should come home with money. Then, yielding to her partiality for gossiping, since there was somebody to listen to her, she started telling stories. The one affair, however, on which she invariably harped was the sorry business of her son Charles and a servant girl at a wine shop over the way. Before going into the army Charles had been a most hardworking and affectionate son, invariably bringing his pay home to his mother. And certainly he still worked and showed himself good-natured; but military service, while sharpening his wits, had taken away some of his liking for ordinary manual toil. It wasn't that he regretted army life, for he spoke of his barracks as a prison. Only his tools had seemed to him rather heavy when, on quitting the service, he had been obliged to take them in hand once more.

'And so, my dear,' continued Madame Toussaint, 'it's all very well for Charles to be kind-hearted, he can do no more for us. I knew that he wasn't in a hurry to get married, as it costs money to keep a wife. And he was always very prudent too, with girls. But what would you have? There was that moment of folly with that Eugénie over the road, a regular baggage who's already gone off with another man, and left her baby behind. Charles has put it out to nurse, and pays for it every month. And a lot of expense it is too, perfect ruination. Yes, indeed, every possible misfortune has fallen on us.'

In this wise Madame Toussaint rattled on for a full half-hour. Then seeing that waiting and anxiety had made her sister-in-law turn very pale, she suddenly stopped short. 'You're losing patience, eh?' she exclaimed. 'The fact is, that Toussaint won't be back for some time. Shall we go to the works together? I'll easily find out if he's likely to bring any money home.'

They then decided to go down, but at the bottom of the stairs they lingered for another quarter of an hour chatting with a neighbour who had lately lost a child. And just as they were at last leaving the house they heard a call: 'Mamma! mamma!'

It came from little Céline, whose face was beaming with delight. She was wearing a pair of new shoes, and devouring a cake. 'Mamma,' she resumed, 'Monsieur l'Abbé who came the other day wants to see you. Just look! he bought me all this!'

On seeing the shoes and the cake, Madame Théodore understood matters. And when Pierre, who was behind the child, accosted her she began to tremble and stammer thanks. Madame Toussaint on her side had quickly drawn near, not indeed to ask for anything herself, but because she was well pleased at such a God-send for her sister-in-law, whose circumstances were worse than her own. And when she saw the priest slip ten francs into Madame Théodore's hand she explained to him that she herself would willingly have lent something had she been able. Then she promptly started on the stories of Toussaint's attack and her son Charles's ill-luck.

But Céline broke in: 'I say, mamma, the factory where papa used to work is here in this street, isn't it? Monsieur l'Abbé has some business there.'[1]

'The Grandidier factory,' resumed Madame Toussaint; 'well, we were just going there, and we can show Monsieur l'Abbé the way.'

It was only a hundred steps off. Escorted by the two women and the child, Pierre slackened his steps and tried to extract some information about Salvat from Madame

---

[1] Although the children of the French peasantry almost invariably address their parents as 'father' and 'mother,' those of the working classes of Paris, and some other large cities usually employ the terms 'papa' and 'mamma.' I mention this because some readers, mindful of the customs of the English working-classes, might think it strange that Céline should make use of the latter appellations.—*Trans.*

Théodore. But she at once became very prudent. She had
not seen him again, she declared; he must have gone with a
mate to Belgium, where there was a prospect of some work.
From what she said, it appeared to the priest that Salvat
had not dared to return to the Rue des Saules since his
crime, in which all had collapsed, both his past life of toil
and hope, and his recent existence with its duties towards the
woman and the child.

'There's the factory, Monsieur l'Abbé,' suddenly said
Madame Toussaint, 'my sister-in-law won't have to wait now,
since you've been kind enough to help her. Thank you for
her and for us.'

Madame Théodore and Céline likewise poured forth their
thanks, standing beside Madame Toussaint in the everlasting
mud of that populous district, amidst the jostling of the
passers-by. And lingering there as if to see Pierre enter,
they again chatted together and repeated that, after all, some
priests were very kind.

The Grandidier works covered an extensive plot of ground.
Facing the street there was only a brick building with
narrow windows and a great archway, through which one
espied a long courtyard. But, in the rear, came a suite of
habitations, workshops, and sheds, above whose never-ending
roofs arose the two lofty chimneys of the furnaces. From
the very threshold one detected the rumbling and quivering
of machinery, all the noise and bustle of work. Black
water flowed by at one's feet, and up above white vapour
spurted from a slender pipe with a regular strident puff, as if
it were the very breath of that huge, toiling hive.

Bicycles were now the principal output of the works. When
Grandidier had taken them on leaving the Dijon Arts and
Trades School, they were declining under bad management,
slowly building some little motive engines by the aid of
antiquated machinery. Foreseeing the future, however, he
had induced his elder brother, one of the managers of the
Bon Marché, to finance him, on the promise that he would
supply that great emporium with excellent bicycles at
150 francs a-piece. And now quite a big venture was in
progress, for the Bon Marché was already bringing out the
new popular machine 'La Lisette,' the 'Bicycle for the
Million,' as the advertisements asserted. Nevertheless,
Grandidier was still in all the throes of a great struggle, for
his new machinery had cast a heavy burden of debt on him.

At the same time each month brought its effort, the perfecting or simplifying of some part of the manufacture, which meant a saving in the future. He was ever on the watch; and even now was thinking of reverting to the construction of little motors, for he thought he could foresee in the near future the triumph of the motor-car.

On asking if M. Thomas Froment were there, Pierre was led by an old workman to a little shed, where he found the young fellow in the linen jacket of a mechanician, his hands black with filings. He was adjusting some piece of mechanism, and nobody would have suspected him to be a former pupil of the Lycée Condorcet, one of the three clever Froments who had there rendered the name famous. But his only desire had been to act as his father's faithful servant, the arm that forges, the embodiment of the manual toil by which conceptions are realised. And, a giant of three-and-twenty, ever attentive and courageous, he was likewise a man of patient, silent, and sober nature.

On catching sight of Pierre he quivered with anxiety and sprang forward. 'Father is no worse?' he asked.

'No, no. But he read in the papers a story of a bradawl found in the Rue Godot-de-Mauroy, and it made him anxious, because the police may make a perquisition here.'

Thomas, his own anxiety allayed, began to smile. 'Tell him he may sleep quietly,' he responded. 'To begin with, I've unfortunately not yet arranged our little motor such as I want it to be. In fact, I haven't yet put it together. I'm keeping the pieces at our house, and nobody knows exactly what I come to do at the factory. So the police may search, they will find nothing here. Our secret runs no risk.'

Pierre promised to repeat these words to Guillaume, so as to dissipate his fears. However, when he tried to sound Thomas, and ascertain the position of affairs, what the factory people thought of the discovery of the bradawl, and whether there was as yet any suspicion of Salvat, he once more found the young man taciturn, and elicited merely a 'yes' or a 'no' in answer to his inquiries. The police had not been there as yet? No. But the men must surely have mentioned Salvat? Yes, of course, on account of his Anarchist opinions. But what had Grandidier, the master, said on returning from the investigating magistrate's? As for that Thomas knew nothing. He had not seen Grandidier that day.

'But here he comes!' the young man added. 'Ah!

poor fellow, his wife, I fancy, had another attack this morning.'

He alluded to a frightful story which Guillaume had already recounted to Pierre. Grandidier, falling in love with a very beautiful girl, had married her; but for five years now she had been insane: the result of puerperal fever and the death of an infant son. Her husband, with his ardent affection for her, had been unwilling to place her in an asylum, and had accordingly kept her with him in a little pavilion, whose windows, overlooking the courtyard of the factory, always remained closed. She was never seen; and never did he speak of her to anybody. It was said that she was usually like a child, very gentle and very sad, and still beautiful, with queenly golden hair. At times, however, attacks of frantic madness came upon her, and he then had to struggle with her, and often hold her for hours in his arms to prevent her from splitting her head against the walls. Fearful shrieks would ring out for a time, and then death-like silence would fall once more.

Grandidier came into the shed where Thomas was working. A handsome man of forty, with an energetic face, he had a dark and heavy moustache, brush-like hair, and clear eyes. He was very partial to Thomas, and during the young fellow's apprenticeship there, had treated him like a son. And he now let him return thither whenever it pleased him; and placed his appliances at his disposal. He knew that he was trying to devise a new motor, a question in which he himself was extremely interested; still he evinced the greatest discretion, never questioning Thomas, but awaiting the result of his endeavours.

'This is my uncle, Abbé Froment, who looked in to wish me good day,' said the young man, introducing Pierre.

An exchange of polite remarks ensued. Then Grandidier sought to cast off the sadness which made people think him stern and harsh, and exclaimed in a bantering tone: 'I didn't tell you, Thomas, of my business with the investigating magistrate. If I hadn't enjoyed a good reputation we should have had all the spies of the Prefecture here. The magistrate wanted me to explain the presence of that bradawl in the Rue Godot-de-Mauroy, and I at once realised that, in his opinion, the culprit must have worked here. For my part I immediately thought of Salvat. But I don't denounce people. The magistrate has my hiring-book, and as for Salvat I simply answered that he worked here for nearly three months last autumn, and then disappeared. They can look for him themselves! Ah! that magistrate! you can picture him: a little fellow with fair hair and cat-like eyes, very careful of his appearance, a society man evidently, but quite frisky at being mixed up in this affair.'

' Isn't he Monsieur Amadieu?' asked Pierre.

' Yes, that's his name. Ah! he's certainly delighted with the present which those Anarchists have made him, with that crime of theirs.'

The priest listened in deep anxiety. As his brother had feared, the true scent, the first conducting wire had now been found. And he looked at Thomas to see if he also were disturbed. But the young man was either ignorant of the ties which linked Salvat to his father, or else he possessed great power of self-control, for he merely smiled at Grandidier's sketch of the magistrate.

Then, as Grandidier went to look at the piece of mechanism which Thomas was finishing, and they began to speak about it, Pierre drew near to an open doorway which communicated with a long workshop where engine lathes were rumbling, and the beams of press-drills falling quickly and rhythmically. Leather gearing spun along with a continuous gliding, and there was ceaseless bustle and activity amidst the odoriferous dampness of all the steam. Scores of perspiring workmen, grimy with dust and filings, were still toiling. Still this was the final effort of the day. And as three men approached a water-tap near Pierre to wash their hands, he listened to their talk, and became particularly interested in it when he heard one of them, a tall ginger-haired fellow, call another, Toussaint, and the third, Charles.

Toussaint, a big, square-shouldered man with knotty arms, only showed his fifty years on his round, scorched face, which besides being roughened and wrinkled by labour, bristled with grey hairs, which nowadays he was content to shave off once a week. It was only his right arm that was affected by paralysis, and moved rather sluggishly. As for Charles, a living portrait of his father, he was now in all the strength of his six-and-twentieth year, with splendid muscles distending his white skin and a full face barred by a heavy black moustache. The three men, like their employer, were speaking of the explosion at the Duvillard mansion, of the bradawl found there, and of Salvat, whom they all now suspected.

'Why only a brigand would do such a thing!' said Toussaint. 'That Anarchism disgusts me. I'll have none of it. But all the same it's for the *bourgeois* to settle matters. If the others want to blow them up, it's their concern. It's they who brought it about.'

This indifference was undoubtedly the outcome of a life of want and social injustice; it was the indifference of an old toiler, who weary of struggling and hoping for improvements, was now quite ready to tolerate the crumbling of a social system, which threatened him with starvation in his impotent old age.

'Well, you know,' rejoined Charles, 'I've heard the Anarchists talking, and they really say some very true and sensible things. And just take yourself, father; you've been working for thirty years, and isn't it abominable that you should have had to pass through all that you did pass through recently, liable to go off like some old horse that's slaughtered at the first sign of illness? And, of course, it makes me think of myself, and I can't help feeling that it won't be at all amusing to end like that. And may the thunder of God kill me if I'm wrong, but one feels half inclined to join in their great flare-up if it's really to make everybody happy!'

He certainly lacked the flame of enthusiasm, and if he had come to these views it was solely from impatience to lead a less toilsome life, for compulsory military service had given him ideas of equality among all men—a desire to struggle, raise himself, and obtain his legitimate share of life's enjoyments. It was, in fact, the inevitable step which carries each generation a little more forward. There was the father, who, deceived in his hope of a fraternal republic, had grown sceptical and contemptuous; and there was the son advancing towards a new faith, and gradually yielding to violent ideas, since political liberty had failed to redeem its promises.

However, as the big, ginger-haired fellow grew angry, and shouted that if Salvat were guilty, he ought to be caught and guillotined at once, without waiting for judges, Toussaint ended by endorsing his opinion. 'Yes, yes, he may have married one of my sisters, but I renounce him. . . . And yet, you know, it would astonish me to find him guilty, for he isn't wicked at heart. I'm sure he wouldn't kill a fly.'

'But what would you have?' put in Charles. 'When a man's driven to extremities he goes mad.'

They had now washed themselves; but Toussaint, on perceiving his employer, lingered there in order to ask him for an advance. As it happened, Grandidier, after cordially shaking hands with Pierre, approached the old workman of his own accord, for he held him in esteem. And, after listening to him, he gave him a line for the cashier on a card. As a rule, he was altogether against the practice of advancing money, and his men disliked him, and said he was over rigid, though in point of fact he had a good heart. But he had his position as an employer to defend, and to him concessions meant ruin. With such keen competition on all sides, with the capitalist system entailing a terrible and incessant struggle, how could one grant the demands of the workers, even when they were legitimate?

Sudden compassion came upon Pierre when, after quitting Thomas, he saw Grandidier, who had finished his round, crossing the courtyard in the direction of the closed pavilion, where all the grief of his heart-tragedy awaited him. Here was that man waging the battle of life, defending his fortune, with the risk that his business might melt away amidst the furious warfare between capital and labour; and at the same time, in lieu of evening repose, finding nought but anguish at his hearth: a mad wife, an adored wife, who had sunk back into infancy, and was for ever dead to love! How incurable was his secret despair! Even on the days when he triumphed in his workshops, disaster awaited him at home. And could any more unhappy man, any man more deserving of pity, be found even among the poor who died of hunger, among those gloomy workers, those vanquished sons of labour who hated and who envied him?

When Pierre found himself in the street again he was astonished to see Madame Toussaint and Madame Théodore still there with little Céline. With their feet in the mud, like bits of wreckage against which beat the ceaseless flow of wayfarers, they had lingered there, still and ever chatting, loquacious and doleful, lulling their wretchedness to rest beneath a deluge of tittle-tattle. And when Toussaint, followed by his son, came out, delighted with the advance he had secured, he also found them on the same spot. Then he told Madame Théodore the story of the bradawl, and the idea which had occurred to him and all his mates that Salvat might well be the culprit. She, however, though turning very pale, began to protest, concealing both what she knew, and what she really thought.

'I tell you I haven't seen him for several days,' said she. 'He must certainly be in Belgium. And as for a bomb, that's rubbish. You say-yourself that he's very gentle and wouldn't harm a fly!'

A little later as Pierre journeyed back to Neuilly in a tramcar he fell into a deep reverie. All the stir and bustle of that working class district, the buzzing of the factory, the overflowing activity of that hive of labour, seemed to have lingered within him. And for the first time, amidst his worries, he realised the necessity of work. Yes, it was fatal, but it also gave health and strength. In effort which sustains and saves, he at last found a solid basis on which all might be reared. Was this, then, the first gleam of a new faith? But ah! what mockery! Work an uncertainty, work hopeless, work always ending in injustice! And then want ever on the watch for the toiler, strangling him as soon as slack times came round, and casting him into the streets like a dead dog immediately old age set in.

On reaching Neuilly, Pierre found Bertheroy at Guillaume's bedside. The old *savant* had just dressed the injured wrist, and was not yet certain that no complications would arise. 'The fact is,' he said to Guillaume, 'you don't keep quiet. I always find you in a state of feverish emotion which is the worst possible thing for you. You must calm yourself, my dear fellow, and not allow anything to worry you.'

A few minutes later, however, just as he was going away, he said with his pleasant smile: 'Do you know that a newspaper writer came to interview me about that explosion? Those reporters imagine that scientific men know everything! I told the one who called on me that it would be very kind of *him* to enlighten *me* as to what powder was employed. And, by the way, I am giving a lesson on explosives at my laboratory to-morrow. There will be just a few persons present. You might come as well, Pierre, so as to give an account of it to Guillaume; it would interest him.'

At a glance from his brother, Pierre accepted the invitation. Then, Bertheroy having gone, he recounted all he had learnt during the afternoon, how Salvat was suspected, and how the investigating magistrate had been put on the right scent. And at this news, burning fever again came

over Guillaume, who with his head buried in the pillow, and
his eyes closed, stammered as if in a kind of nightmare:
' Ah ! then, this is the end ! Salvat arrested, Salvat interrogated ! Ah ! that so much toil and so much hope should
crumble ! '

IV

CULTURE AND HOPE

On the morrow, punctually at one o'clock, Pierre reached the
Rue d'Ulm, where Bertheroy resided in a fairly large house,
which the State had placed at his disposal, in order that he
might install in it a laboratory for study and research. Thus
the whole first floor had been transformed into one spacious
apartment, where, from time to time, the illustrious chemist
was fond of receiving a limited number of pupils and
admirers, before whom he made experiments, and explained
his new discoveries and theories.

For these occasions a few chairs were set out before a
long and massive table, which was covered with jars and
appliances. In the rear one saw a furnace, while all
around were glass cases, full of vials and specimens. The
persons present were, for the most part, fellow *savants*, with
a few young men, and even a lady or two, and, of course, an
occasional journalist. The whole made up a kind of family
gathering, the visitors chatting with the master in all
freedom.

Directly Bertheroy perceived Pierre he came forward,
pressed his hand, and seated him on a chair beside Guillaume's son François, who had been one of the first arrivals.
The young man was completing his third year at the École
Normale, close by, so he only had a few steps to take to call
upon his master Bertheroy, whom he regarded as one of the
firmest minds of the age. Pierre was delighted to meet his
nephew, for he had been greatly impressed in his favour on
the occasion of his visit to Montmartre. François, on his
side, greeted his uncle with all the cordial expansiveness of
youth. He was, moreover, well pleased to obtain some news
of his father.

However, Bertheroy began. He spoke in a familiar and
sober fashion, but frequently employed some very happy

expressions. At first he gave an account of his own extensive labours and investigations with regard to explosive substances, and related with a laugh that he sometimes manipulated powders which would have blown up the entire district. But, said he, in order to reassure his listeners, he was always extremely prudent. At last he turned to the subject of that explosion in the Rue Godot-de-Mauroy, which, for some days, had filled Paris with dismay. The remnants of the bomb had been carefully examined by experts, and one fragment had been brought to him, in order that he might give his opinion on it. The bomb appeared to have been prepared in a very rudimentary fashion; it had been charged with small pieces of iron, and fired by means of a match, such as a child might have devised. The extraordinary part of the affair was the formidable power of the central cartridge, which, although it must have been a small one, had wrought as much havoc as any thunder-bolt. And the question was this: What incalculable power of destruction might one not arrive at if the charge were increased ten, twenty, or a hundredfold! Embarrassment began, and divergencies of opinion clouded the issue directly one tried to specify what explosive had been employed. Of the three experts who had been consulted, one pronounced himself in favour of dynamite pure and simple; but the two others, although they did not agree together, believed in some combination of explosive matters. He, Bertheroy, had modestly declined to adjudicate, for the fragment submitted to him bore traces of so slight a character, that analysis became impossible. Thus he was unwilling to make any positive pronouncement. But his opinion was that one found oneself in presence of some unknown powder, some new explosive, whose power exceeded anything that had hitherto been dreamt of. He could picture some unknown *savant*, or some ignorant but lucky inventor, discovering the formula of this explosive under mysterious conditions. And this brought him to the point he wished to reach, the question of all the explosives which are so far unknown, and of the coming discoveries which he could foresee. In the course of his investigations he himself had found cause to suspect the existence of several such explosives, though he had lacked time and opportunity to prosecute his studies in that direction. However, he indicated the field which should be explored, and the best way of proceeding. In his opinion it

was there that lay the future. And in a broad and eloquent peroration, he declared that explosives had hitherto been degraded
by being employed in idiotic schemes of vengeance and destruction; whereas it was in them possibly that lay the liberating
force which science was seeking, the lever which would change
the face of the world, when they should have been so domesticated and subdued as·to be only the obedient servants of
man.

Throughout this familiar discourse Pierre could feel that
François was growing impassioned, quivering at thought of
the vast horizon which the master opened up. He himself had become extremely interested, for he could not
do otherwise than notice certain allusions, and connect
what he heard with what he had guessed of Guillaume's
anxiety regarding that secret which he feared to see at the
mercy of an investigating magistrate. And so as he, Pierre,
before going off with François, approached Bertheroy to wish
him good-day, he pointedly remarked: 'Guillaume will be
very sorry that he was unable to hear you unfold those
admirable ideas.'

The old *savant* smiled. 'Pooh!' said he; 'just give him
a summary of what I said. He will understand. He knows
more about the matter than I do.'

In presence of the illustrious chemist, François preserved
the silent gravity of a respectful pupil, but when he and
Pierre had taken a few steps down the street, he suddenly
remarked: 'What a pity it is that a man of such broad
intelligence, free from all superstition, and anxious for the
sole triumph of truth, should have allowed himself to be
classified, ticketed, bound round with titles and academical
functions! How greatly our affection for him would increase
if he took less State pay, and freed himself from all the grand
cordons which tie his hands.'

'What would you have!' rejoined Pierre, in a conciliatory
spirit. 'A man must live! At the same time I believe that
he does not regard himself as tied by anything.'

Then, as they had reached the entrance of the École
Normale, the priest stopped, thinking that his companion was
going back to the college. But François, raising his eyes and
glancing at the old place, remarked: 'No, no, to-day's Thursday, and I'm at liberty! Oh! we have a deal of liberty, perhaps too much. But for my part I'm well pleased at it,
for it often enables me to go to Montmartre and work at my

own little table. It's only there that I feel any real strength and clearness of mind.'

His preliminary examinations had entitled him to admission at either the École Polytechnique or the École Normale,[1] and he had chosen the latter, entering its scientific section with No. 1 against his name. His father had wished him to make sure of an avocation, that of professor, even if circumstances should allow him to remain independent and follow his own bent, on leaving the college. François, who was very precocious, was now preparing for his last examination there, and the only rest he took was in walking to and from Montmartre, or in strolling through the Luxembourg gardens.

From force of habit he now turned towards the latter, accompanied by Pierre and chatting with him. One found the mildness of spring-time there that February afternoon; for pale sunshine streamed between the trees which were still leafless. It was indeed one of those first fine days which draw little green gems from the branches of the lilac bushes.

The École Normale was still the subject of conversation and Pierre remarked: 'I must own that I hardly like the spirit that prevails there. Excellent work is done no doubt, and the only way to form professors is to teach men the trade by cramming them with the necessary knowledge. But the worst is that although all the students are trained for the teaching profession, many of them don't remain in it, but go out into the world, take to journalism, or make it their business to control the arts, literature and society. And those who do this are for the most part unbearable. After swearing by Voltaire they have gone back to spiritualism and mysticism, the last drawing-room craze. Now that a firm faith in science is regarded as brutish and inelegant, they fancy that they rid themselves of their caste by feigning amiable doubt, and ignorance and innocence. What they most fear is that they may carry a scent of the schools about with them, so they put on extremely Parisian airs, venture on somersaults and slang, and assume all the grace of dancing bears in their eager desire to please. From that desire spring the sarcastic shafts which they aim at science, they who pretend that they know everything but who go back to the belief

---

[1] The purposes of the École Normale have been referred to on p. 127. At the École Polytechnique young men receive much of the preliminary training which they require to become either artillery officers, or military, naval, or civil engineers.—*Trans.*

of the humble, the naïve idealism of Biblical legends, just because they think the latter to be more distinguished.'

François began to laugh : ' The portrait is perhaps a little overdrawn,' said he, ' still there's truth in it, a great deal of truth.'

' I have known several of them,' continued Pierre, who was growing animated. ' And among them all I have noticed that a fear of being duped leads them to reaction against the entire effort, the whole work of the century. Disgust with liberty, distrust of science, denial of the future, that is what they now profess. And they have such a horror of the commonplace that they would rather believe in nothing or the incredible. It may of course be commonplace to say that two and two make four, yet it's true enough ; and it is far less foolish for a man to say and repeat it than to believe, for instance, in the miracles of Lourdes.'

François glanced at the priest in astonishment. The other noticed it and strove to restrain himself. Nevertheless, grief and anger carried him away whenever he spoke of the educated young people of the time, such, as in his despair, he imagined them to be. In the same way as he had pitied the toilers dying of starvation in the districts of misery and want, so here he overflowed with contempt for the young men who lacked bravery in the presence of knowledge, and harked back to the consolation of deceptive spirituality, the promise of an eternity of happiness in death, which last was longed for and exalted as the very sum of life. Was not the cowardly thought of refusing to live for the sake of living, so as to discharge one's simple duty in being and making one's effort, equivalent to absolute assassination of life ? However, the *Ego* was always the mainspring, each one sought personal happiness. And Pierre was grieved to think that those young people, instead of discarding the past and marching on to the truths of the future, were relapsing into shadowy metaphysics through sheer weariness and idleness, due in part perhaps to the excessive exertion of the century which had been overladen with human toil.

However, François had begun to smile again. ' But you are mistaken,' said he, ' we are not all like that at the École Normale. You only seem to know the Normalians of the Section of Letters, and your opinions would surely change if you knew those of the Section of Sciences. It is quite true that the reaction against Positivism is making itself felt among our literary fellow students, and that they, like others, are haunted by the idea of that famous bankruptcy of Science. This is perhaps due to their masters, the neo-spiritualists and dogmatical rhetoricians into whose hands they have fallen. And it is still more due to fashion, the whim of the times which, as you have very well put it, regards scientific truth as bad taste, something graceless and altogether too brutal for light and distinguished minds. Consequently, a young fellow of any shrewdness who desires to please is perforce won over to the new spirit.'

'The new spirit!' interrupted Pierre, unable to restrain himself. 'Oh! that is no mere innocent, passing fashion, it is a tactical device and a terrible one, an offensive return of the powers of darkness against those of light, of servitude against free thought, truth and justice.'

Then, as the young man again looked at him with growing astonishment, he relapsed into silence. The figure of Monseigneur Martha had risen before his eyes, and he fancied he could again hear the prelate at the Madeleine, striving to win Paris over to the policy of Rome, to that spurious neo-Catholicism which, with the object of destroying democracy and science, accepted such portions of them as it could adapt to its own views. This was indeed the supreme struggle. Thence came all the poison poured forth to the young. Pierre knew what efforts were being made in religious circles to help on this revival of mysticism, in the mad hope of hastening the rout of science. Monseigneur Martha, who was all-powerful at the Catholic University, said to his intimates, however, that three generations of devout and docile pupils would be needed before the Church would again be absolute sovereign of France.

·'Well, as for the École Normale,' continued François, 'I assure you that you are mistaken. There are a few narrow bigots there no doubt. But even in the Section of Letters the majority of the students are sceptics at bottom—sceptics of discreet and good-natured average views. Of course they are professors before everything else, though they are a trifle ashamed of it; and, as professors, they judge things with no little pedantic irony, devoured by a spirit of criticism, and quite incapable of creating anything themselves. I should certainly be astonished to see the man of genius whom we await come out of their ranks. To my thinking indeed, it would be preferable that some barbarian genius, neither well

read nor endowed with critical faculty, or power of weighing
and shading things, should come and open the next century
with a hatchet stroke, sending up a fine flare of truth and
reality. . . . However, as for my comrades of the Scientific
Section, I assure you that neo-Catholicism and Mysticism and
Occultism, and every other branch of the fashionable phan-
tasmagoria trouble them very little indeed. They are not
making a religion of science, they remain open to doubt on
many points; but they are mostly men of very clear and firm
minds whose passion is the acquirement of certainty, and who
are ever absorbed in the investigations which continue
throughout the whole vast field of human knowledge. They
haven't flinched, they have remained Positivists, or Evolu-
tionists, or Determinists, and have set their faith in observation
and experiment to help on the final conquest of the world.'

François himself was growing excited, as he thus confessed his faith while strolling along the quiet sunlit garden
paths. 'The young indeed!' he resumed. 'Do people know
them? It makes us laugh when we see all sorts of apostles
fighting for us, trying to attract us, and saying that we are
white or black or gray, according to the hue which they require for the triumph of their particular ideas! The real young
men are in the schools, laboratories and libraries. It's
they who work and who'll bring to-morrow to the world. It's
not the young fellows of dinner and supper clubs, who issue
manifestoes and indulge in all sorts of extravagance. The
latter make a great deal of noise, no doubt; in fact, they
alone are heard. But if you knew of the ceaseless efforts and
passionate striving of the others, those who remain silent,
absorbed in their tasks. And I know many of them, they
are with their century, they have rejected none of its hopes,
but are marching on to the coming century, resolved to pursue
the work of their forerunners, ever going towards more light
and more equity. And just speak to *them* of the bankruptcy
of science. They'll shrug their shoulders at the mere idea,
for they know well enough that science has never before in-
flamed so many hearts or achieved greater conquests! It is
only if the schools, laboratories and libraries were closed,
and the social soil radically changed, that one would have
cause to fear a fresh growth of error such as weak hearts and
narrow minds hold so dear!'

At this point François's fine flow of eloquence was
interrupted. A tall young fellow stopped to shake hands

with him; and Pierre was surprised to recognise Baron Duvillard's son Hyacinthe, who bowed to him in very correct style. 'What! you here in our old quarter,' exclaimed François.

'My dear fellow, I'm going to Jonas's, over yonder, behind the Observatory. Don't you know Jonas? Ah! my dear fellow, he's a delightful sculptor, who has succeeded in doing away with matter almost entirely. He has carved a figure of Woman, no bigger than the finger, and entirely soul, free from all baseness of form, and yet complete. All Woman, indeed, in her essential symbolism! Ah! it's grand, it's over-powering. A perfect scheme of æsthetics, a real religion!'

François smiled as he looked at Hyacinthe, buttoned up in his long, pleated frock-coat, with his made-up face, and carefully cropped hair and beard. 'And yourself?' said he, 'I thought you were working, and were going to publish a little poem, shortly?'

'Oh! the task of creating is so distasteful to me, my dear fellow! A single line often takes me weeks. . . . Still, yes, I have a little poem on hand, "The End of Woman." And you see, I'm not so exclusive as some people pretend, since I admire Jonas, who still believes in Woman. His excuse is sculpture, which, after all, is at best such a gross materialistic art. But in poetry, good heavens, how we've been overwhelmed with Woman, always Woman! It's surely time to drive her out of the temple, and cleanse it a little. Ah! if we were all pure and lofty enough to do without Woman, and renounce all those horrid sexual questions, so that the last of the species might die childless, eh? The world would then at least finish in a clean and proper manner!'

Thereupon, Hyacinthe walked off with his languid air, well pleased with the effect which he had produced on the others.

'So you know him?' said Pierre to François.

'He was my school-fellow at Condorcet, we were in the same classes together. Such a funny fellow he was! A perfect dunce! And he was always making a parade of Father Duvillard's millions, while pretending to disdain them, and act the revolutionist, for ever saying that he'd use his cigarette to fire the cartridge which was to blow up the world! He was Schopenhauer, and Nietzsche, and Tolstoi, and Ibsen, rolled into one ! And you can see what he has become with it all : a humbug with a diseased mind ! '

' It's a terrible symptom,' muttered Pierre, ' when through *ennui* or lassitude, or the contagion of destructive fury, the sons of the happy and privileged ones start doing the work of the demolishers.'

François had resumed his walk, going down towards the ornamental water, where some children were sailing their boats. ' That fellow is simply grotesque,' he replied ; ' but how would you have sane people give any heed to that mysticism, that awakening of spirituality which is alleged by the same *doctrinaires* who started the bankruptcy of science cry, when after so brief an evolution it produces such insanity, both in art and literature ? A few years of in-fluence have sufficed ; and now Satanism, Occultism, and other absurdities are flourishing ; not to mention that, ac-cording to some accounts, the Cities of the Plains are reconciled with new Rome. Isn't the tree judged by its fruits ? And isn't it evident that, instead of a renascence, a far-spreading social movement bringing back the past, we are simply witnessing a transitory reaction, which many things explain ? The old world would rather not die, and is strug-gling in a final convulsion, reviving for a last hour before it is swept away by the overflowing river of human knowledge, whose waters ever increase. And yonder, in the future, lies the new world, which the real young men will bring into existence, those who work, those who are not known, who are not heard. And yet, just listen ! Perhaps you will hear them, for we are among them, in their " quarter." This deep silence is that of the labour of all the young fellows who are leaning over their work-tables, and day by day carrying forward the conquest of truth.'

So saying François waved his hand towards all the day-schools and colleges and high schools beyond the Luxembourg garden, towards the Faculties of Law and Medicine, the Institute and its five Academies, the innumerable libraries and museums which made up the broad domain of intellectual labour. And Pierre, moved by it all, shaken in his theories of negation, thought that he could indeed hear a low but far-spreading mur-mur of the work of thousands of active minds, rising from laboratories, studies and class, reading and lecture rooms. It was not like the jerky, breathless trepidation, the loud clamour of factories where manual labour toils and chafes. But here too there were sighs of weariness, efforts as killing, exertion as fruitful in its results. Was it indeed true that the cultured young were still and ever in their silent forge, renouncing no hope, relinquishing no conquest, but in full freedom of mind forging the truth and justice of to-morrow with the invincible hammers of observation and experiment?

François, however, had raised his eyes to the Palace clock to ascertain the time. 'I'm going to Montmartre,' he said; 'will you come part of the way with me?'

Pierre assented, particularly as the young man added that on his way he meant to call for his brother Antoine at the Museum of the Louvre. That bright afternoon the Louvre picture galleries were steeped in warm and dignified quietude, which one particularly noticed on coming from the tumult and scramble of the streets. The majority of the few people one found there were copyists working in deep silence, which only the wandering footsteps of an occasional tourist disturbed. Pierre and François found Antoine at the end of the gallery assigned to the Primitive masters. With scrupulous, almost devout care he was making a drawing of a figure by Mantegna. The Primitives did not impassion him by reason of any particular mysticism and ideality, such as fashion pretends to find in them, but on the contrary, and justifiably enough, by reason of the sincerity of their ingenuous realism, their respect and modesty in presence of nature, and the minute fidelity with which they sought to transcribe it. He spent days of hard work in copying and studying them, in order to learn strictness and probity of drawing from them—all that lofty distinction of style which they owe to their candour as honest artists.

Pierre was struck by the pure glow which a sitting of good hard work had set in Antoine's light blue eyes. It imparted warmth and even feverishness to his fair face, which was usually all dreaminess and gentleness. His lofty forehead now truly looked like a citadel armed for the conquest of truth and beauty. He was only eighteen, and his story was simply this: as he had grown disgusted with classical studies and been mastered by a passion for drawing, his father had let him leave the Lycée Condorcet when he was in the third class there. Some little time had then elapsed while he felt his way and the deep originality within him was being evolved. He had tried etching on copper, but had soon come to wood-engraving, and had attached himself to it in spite of the discredit into which it had fallen, lowered as it had been to the level of a mere trade. Was there not here an entire art to restore and enlarge? For his own part he dreamt of engraving his own drawings, of being at once the brain which conceives and the hand which executes, in such wise as to obtain new effects of great intensity both as regards perception and touch. To comply with the wishes of his father, who desired each of his sons to have a trade, he earned his bread like other engravers by working for the illustrated newspapers. But, in addition to this current work, he had already engraved several blocks instinct with wonderful power and life. They were simply copies of real things, scenes of everyday existence, but they were accentuated, elevated so to say, by the essential line, with a maestria which on the part of so young a lad fairly astonished one.

'Do you want to engrave that?' François asked him, as he placed his copy of Mantegna's figure in his portfolio.

'Oh! no, that's merely a dip into innocence, a good lesson to teach one to be modest and sincere. Life is very different nowadays.'

Then, while walking along the streets—for Pierre, who felt growing sympathy for the two young fellows, went with them in the direction of Montmartre, forgetful of all else—Antoine, who was beside him, spoke expansively of his artistic dreams.

'Colour is certainly a power, a sovereign source of charm, and one may, indeed, say that without colour nothing can be completely represented. Yet, singularly enough, it isn't indispensable to me. It seems to me that I can picture life as intensely and definitely with mere black and white, and I even fancy that I shall be able to do so in a more essential manner, without any of the dupery which lies in colour. But what a task it is! I should like to depict the Paris of nowadays in a few scenes, a few typical figures, which would serve as testimony for all time. And I should like to do it with great fidelity and candour, for an artist only lives by reason of his candour, his humility and steadfast belief in Nature, which is ever beautiful. I've already done a few figures; I will show them to you. But ah! if I only dared to tackle my blocks with the graver, at the outset, without drawing my subject beforehand. For that generally takes away one's fire. However, what I do with the pencil is a mere sketch; for with the graver I may come upon a

find, some unexpected strength or delicacy of effect. And so
I'm draughtsman and engraver all in one, in such a way that
my blocks can only be turned out by myself. If the drawings
on them were engraved by another, they would be quite
lifeless. . . . Yes, life may spring from the fingers just as
well as from the brain, when one really possesses creative
power.'

They walked on, and when they found themselves below
Montmartre, and Pierre spoke of taking a tram-car to
return to Neuilly, Antoine, quite feverish with artistic
passion, asked him if he knew Jahan, the sculptor, who was
working for the Sacred Heart. And on receiving a negative
reply, he added : ' Well, come and see him for a moment.
He has a great future before him. You'll see an angel of his
which has been declined.'

Then, as François began to praise the angel in question,
Pierre agreed to accompany them. On the summit of the
height, among all the sheds which the building of the
basilica necessitated, Jahan had been able to set up a glazed
workshop large enough for the huge angel ordered of him.
His three visitors found him there in a blouse, watching a
couple of assistants, who were rough-hewing the block of
stone whence the angel was to emerge. Jahan was a sturdy
man of thirty-six, with dark hair and beard, a large, ruddy
mouth, and fine bright eyes. Born in Paris, he had studied
at the Fine Art School, but his impetuous temperament had
constantly landed him in trouble there.

' Ah ! yes,' said he, ' you've come to see my angel, the one
which the Archbishop wouldn't take. Well, there it is.'

The clay model of the figure, some three feet high, and
already drying, looked superb in its soaring posture, with its
large, outspread wings expanding as if with passionate desire
for the infinite. The body, barely draped, was that of a slim
yet robust youth, whose face beamed with the rapture of his
ascent to heaven.

' They found him too human,' said Jahan. ' And after all
they were right. There's nothing so difficult to imagine as
an angel. One even hesitates as to the sex ; and when faith
is lacking one has to take the first model one finds and copy
it and spoil it. For my part, while I was modelling that one,
I tried to imagine a beautiful youth suddenly endowed with
wings, and carried by the intoxication of his flight into all
the joy of the sunshine. But it upset them, they wanted

something more religious, they said ; and so then I concocted that wretched thing over there. After all, one has to earn one's living, you know.'

So saying he waved his hand towards another model, the one for which his assistants were preparing the stone. And this model represented an angel of the correct type, with symmetrical wings like those of a goose, a figure of neither sex, and commonplace features, expressing the silly ecstasy that tradition requires.

'What would you have ? ' continued Jahan. 'Religious art has sunk to the most disgusting triteness. People no longer believe ; churches are built like barracks, and decorated with saints and virgins fit to make one weep. The fact is that genius is only the fruit of the social soil ; and a great artist can only send up a blaze of the faith of the time he lives in. For my part I'm the grandson of a Beauceron peasant. My father came to Paris to set himself up in business as a marble worker for tombstones and so forth, just at the top of the Rue de la Roquette. It was there I grew up. I began as a workman, and all my childhood was spent among the masses, in the streets, without ever a thought even of setting foot in a church. So few Parisians think of going to church nowadays. And so what's to become of art since there's no belief left in the Divinity or even in beauty ? We're forced to go forward to the new faith, which is the faith in life and work and fruitfulness, in all that labours and produces.'

Then suddenly breaking off he exclaimed : 'By the way, I've been doing some more work to my figure of Fecundity, and I'm fairly well pleased with it. Just come with me and I'll show it you.'

Thereupon he insisted on taking them to his private studio which was near by, just below Guillaume's little house. It was entered by way of the Rue du Calvaire, a street which is simply a succession of ladder-like flights of steps. The door opened on to one of the little landings, and one found oneself in a spacious well-lighted apartment littered with models and casts, fragments and figures, quite an overflow of sturdy, powerful talent. On a stool was the unfinished model of Fecundity swathed in wet clothes. These Jahan removed, and then she stood forth with her rounded figure, her broad hips and her wifely, maternal bosom, full of the milk which nourishes and redeems.

'Well, what do you think of her?' asked Jahan. 'Built as she is, I fancy that her children ought to be less puny than the pale, languid, æsthetic fellows of nowadays!'

While Antoine and François were admiring the figure, Pierre for his part took most interest in a young girl who had opened the door to them, and who had now wearily re-seated herself at a little table to continue a book she was reading. This was Jahan's sister, Lise. A score of years younger than himself, she was but sixteen, and had been living alone with him since their father's death. Very slight and delicate looking, she had a most gentle face, with fine light hair which suggested pale gold-dust. She was almost a cripple, with legs so weak that she only walked with difficulty; and her mind also was belated, still full of childish *naïveté*. At first this had much saddened her brother, but with time he had grown accustomed to her innocence and languor. Busy as he always was, ever in a transport, over-flowing with new plans, he somewhat neglected her by force of circumstances, letting her live beside him much as she listed.

Pierre had noticed, however, the sisterly impulsiveness with which she had greeted Antoine. The latter, after congratulating Jahan on his statue, came and sat down beside her, questioned her and wished to see the book which she was reading. During the last six months the most pure and affectionate intercourse had sprung up between them. He, from his father's garden, up yonder on the Place du Tertre, could see her through the huge window of that studio where she led so innocent a life. And noticing that she was always alone, as if forsaken, he had begun to take an interest in her. Then had come acquaintance; and delighted to find her so simple and so charming, he had conceived the design of rousing her to intelligence and life, by loving her, by becoming at once the mind and the heart whose power fructifies. Weak plant that she was, in need of delicate care, sunshine and affection, he became for her all that her brother had, through circumstances, failed to be. He had already taught her to read, a task in which every mistress had previously failed. But him she listened to and understood. And by slow degrees a glow of happiness came to the beautiful clear eyes set in her irregular face. It was love's miracle, the creation of woman beneath the breath of a young lover who gave himself entirely. No doubt she still remained very

delicate, with such poor health that one ever feared she
might expire in a faint sigh; and her legs, moreover, were
still too weak to admit of her walking any distance. But all
the same, she was no longer the little wilding, the little
ailing flower of the previous spring.

Jahan, who marvelled at the incipient miracle, drew near
to the young people. 'Ah!' said he, 'your pupil does you
honour. She reads quite fluently you know, and understands
the fine books you send her. You read to me of an evening
now, don't you, Lise?'

She raised her candid eyes, and gazed at Antoine with a
smile of infinite gratitude. 'Oh! whatever he'll teach me,'
she said, 'I'll learn it, and do it.'

The others laughed gently. Then as the visitors were
going off, François paused before a model which had cracked
while drying. 'Oh! that's a spoilt thing,' said the sculptor.
'I wanted to model a figure of Charity. It was ordered of
me by a philanthropic institution. But try as I might, I could
only devise something so commonplace that I let the clay
spoil. Still I must think it over and endeavour to take the
matter in hand again.'

When they were outside, it occurred to Pierre to go as far
as the basilica of the Sacred Heart, in the hope of finding
Abbé Rose there. So the three of them went round by way
of the Rue Gabrielle and climbed the steps of the Rue Chape.
And just as they were reaching the summit where the basilica
reared its forest of scaffoldings beneath the clear sky, they
encountered Thomas, who on leaving the factory had gone
to give an order to a founder in the Rue Lamarck.

He, who as a rule was so silent and discreet, now happened
to be in an expansive mood, which made him look quite
radiant. 'Ah! I'm so pleased,' he said, addressing Pierre; 'I
fancy that I've found what I want for our little motor. Tell
father that things are going on all right, and that he must
make haste to get well.'

At these words his brothers, François and Antoine, drew
close to him with a common impulse. And they stood there
all three, a valiant little group, their hearts uniting and beating with one and the same delight at the idea that their
father would be gladdened, that the good news they were
sending him would help him towards recovery. As for
Pierre, who, now that he knew them, was beginning to love
them and judge them at their worth, he marvelled at the sight

of these three young giants, each so strikingly like the other, and drawn together so closely and so promptly, directly their filial affection took fire.

'Tell him that we are waiting for him, and will come to him at the first sign if we are wanted.'

Then each in turn shook the priest's hand vigorously. And while he remained watching them as they went off towards the little house, whose garden he perceived over the wall of the Rue Saint-Eleuthère, he fancied he could there detect a delicate silhouette, a white, sunlit face under a helm of dark hair. It was doubtless the face of Marie, examining the buds on her lilac bushes. At that evening hour, however, the diffuse light was so golden that the vision seemed to fade in it as in a halo. And Pierre, feeling dazzled, turned his head, and on the other side saw nought but the overwhelming, chalky mass of the basilica, whose hugeness shut out all view of the horizon.

For a moment he remained motionless on that spot, so agitated by conflicting thoughts and feelings that he could read neither heart nor mind clearly. Then, as he turned once more he saw all Paris spread out at his feet, a limpid, lightsome Paris, beneath the pink glow of that spring-like evening. The endless billows of house-roofs showed forth with wonderful distinctness, and one could have counted the chimney stacks and the little black streaks of the windows by the million. The edifices rising into the calm atmosphere seemed like the anchored vessels of some fleet arrested in its course, with lofty masting which glittered at the sun's farewell. And never before had Pierre so distinctly observed the divisions of that human ocean. Eastward and northward was the city of manual toil with the rumbling and the smoke of its factories. Southward, beyond the river, was the city of study, of intellectual labour, so calm, so perfectly serene. And on all sides the passion of trade ascended from the central districts, where the crowds rolled and scrambled amidst an everlasting uproar of wheels; while westward, the city of the happy and powerful ones, those who fought for sovereignty and wealth, spread out its piles of palaces amidst the slowly reddening flare of the declining planet.

And then, from the depths of his negation, the chaos into which his loss of faith had plunged him, Pierre felt a delicious freshness pass like the vague advent of a new faith. So vague it was that he could not have expressed even his

hope of it in words. But already among the rough factory
workers, manual toil had appeared to him necessary and re-
demptive, in spite of all the misery and abominable injustice
to which it led. And now the young men of intellect of whom
he had despaired, that generation of the morrow which he had
thought spoilt, relapsing into ancient error and rottenness,
had appeared to him full of virile promise, resolved to prosecute the work of those who had gone before, and effect, by
the aid of Science only, the conquest of absolute truth and
absolute justice.

V

PROBLEMS

A FULL month had already gone by since Guillaume had
taken refuge at his brother's little house at Neuilly. His
wrist was now nearly healed. He had long ceased to keep
his bed, and often strolled through the garden. In spite of his
impatience to go back to Montmartre, join his loved ones,
and resume his work there, he was each morning prompted
to defer his return by the news he found in the newspapers.
The situation was ever the same. Salvat, whom the police
now suspected, had been perceived one evening near the
central markets, and then again lost sight of. Every day,
however, his arrest was said to be imminent. And in that
case what would happen? Would he speak out, and would
fresh perquisitions be made?

For a whole week the press had been busy with the
bradawl found under the entrance of the Duvillard mansion.
Nearly every reporter in Paris had called at the Grandidier
factory and interviewed both workmen and master. Some
had even started on personal investigations, in the hope of
capturing the culprit themselves. There was no end of
jesting about the incompetence of the police, and the hunt
for Salvat was followed all the more passionately by the
general public, as the papers overflowed with the most
ridiculous concoctions, predicting further explosions, and
declaring even that all Paris would some morning be blown
into the air. The 'Voix du Peuple' set a fresh shudder
circulating every day by its announcements of threatening
letters, incendiary placards, and mysterious far-reaching plots.

And never before had so base and foolish a spirit of contagion wafted insanity through a civilised city.

Guillaume, for his part, no sooner awoke of a morning than he was all impatience to see the newspapers, quivering at the idea that he would at last read of Salvat's arrest. In his state of nervous expectancy, the wild campaign which the press had started, the idiotic and the ferocious things which he found in one or another journal, almost drove him crazy. A number of 'suspects' had already been arrested in a kind of chance razzia, which had swept up the usual Anarchist herd, together with sundry honest workmen and bandits, *illuminés* and lazy devils—in fact, a most singular, motley crew, which investigating magistrate Amadieu was endeavouring to turn into a gigantic association of evil-doers. One morning, moreover, Guillaume found his own name mentioned in connection with a perquisition at the residence of a re-volutionary journalist, who was a friend of his. At this his heart bounded with revolt, but he was forced to the con-clusion that it would be prudent for him to remain patient a little longer, in his peaceful retreat at Neuilly, since the police might at any moment break into his home at Montmartre, to arrest him should it find him there.

Amidst all this anxiety the brothers led a most solitary and gentle life. Pierre himself now spent most of his time at home. The first days of March had come, and precocious springtide imparted delightful charm and warmth to the little garden. Guillaume, however, since quitting his bed, had more particularly installed himself in his father's old laboratory, now transformed into a spacious study. All the books and papers left by the illustrious chemist were still there, and among the latter Guillaume found a number of unfinished essays, the perusal of which greatly excited his interest, and often absorbed him from morning till night. It was this which largely enabled him to bear his voluntary seclusion patiently. Seated on the other side of the big table, Pierre also mostly occupied himself with reading; but at times his eyes would quit his book and wander away into gloomy reverie, into all the chaos into which he still and ever sank. For long hours the brothers would in this wise remain side by side, without speaking a word. Yet they knew they were together; and occasionally, when their eyes met, they would exchange a smile. The strong affection of former days was again springing up within them; their childhood, their home, their parents, all seemed to live once more in the quiet atmosphere they breathed. However, the bay window overlooked the garden in the direction of Paris, and often, when they emerged from their reading or their reverie, it was with a sudden feeling of anxiety, and in order to lend ear to the distant rumbling, the increased clamour of the great city.

On other occasions they paused as if in astonishment at hearing a continuous footfall overhead. It was that of Nicholas Barthès, who still lingered in the room above. He seldom came downstairs, and scarcely ever ventured into the garden, for fear, said he, that he might be perceived and recognised from a distant house whose windows were concealed by a clump of trees. One might laugh at the old conspirator's haunting thought of the police. Nevertheless, the caged-lion restlessness, the ceaseless promenade of that perpetual prisoner who had spent two-thirds of his life in the dungeons of France in his desire to secure the liberty of others, imparted to the silence of the little house a touching melancholy, the very rhythm as it were of all the great good things which one hoped for, but which would never perhaps come.

Very few visits drew the brothers from their solitude. Bertheroy came less frequently now that Guillaume's wrist was healing. The most assiduous caller was certainly Théophile Morin, whose discreet ring was heard every other day at the same hour. Though he did not share the ideas of Barthès he worshipped him as a martyr; and would always go upstairs to spend an hour with him. However, they must have exchanged few words, for not a sound came from the room. Whenever Morin sat down for a moment in the laboratory with the brothers, Pierre was struck by his seeming weariness, his ashen grey hair and beard and dismal countenance, from which all life appeared to have been effaced by long years spent in the teaching profession. Indeed, it was only when the priest mentioned Italy that he saw his companion's resigned eyes blaze up like live coals. One day when he spoke of the great patriot Orlando Prada, Morin's companion of victory in Garibaldi's days, he was amazed by the sudden flare of enthusiasm which lighted up the other's lifeless features. However, these were but transient flashes ; the old professor soon reappeared, and all that one found in Morin was the friend of Proudhon and the subsequent dis-

ciple of Auguste Comte. Of his Proudhonian principles he
had retained all a pauper's hatred of wealth, and a desire for a
more equitable partition of fortune. But the new times dismayed him, and neither principle nor temperament allowed
him to follow Revolutionism to its utmost limits. Comte
had imparted unshakable convictions to him in the sphere
of intellectual questions, and he contented himself with the
clear and decisive logic of Positivism, rejecting all meta-
physical hypotheses as useless, persuaded as he was that the
whole human question, whether social or religious, would be
solved by science alone. This faith, firm as it had remained,
was, however, coupled with secret bitterness, for nothing
seemed to advance in a sensible manner towards its goal.
Comte himself had ended in the most cloudy mysticism;
great *savants* recoiled from truth in terror; and now bar-
barians were threatening the world with fresh night; all of
which made Morin almost a reactionist in politics, already
resigned to the advent of a dictator, who would set things
somewhat in order, so that humanity might be able to complete its education.

Other visitors who occasionally called to see Guillaume
were Bache and Janzen, who invariably came together at
night-time. Every now and then they would linger chatting with Guillaume in the spacious study until two o'clock
in the morning. Bache, who was fat and had a fatherly air,
with his little eyes gently beaming amidst all the snowy
whiteness of his hair and beard, would talk on slowly,
unctuously, and interminably as soon as he had begun to
explain his views. He would address merely a polite bow to
Saint-Simon, the initiator, the first to lay down the law that
work was a necessity for one and all according to their
capacities; but on coming to Fourier his voice softened and
he confessed his whole religion. To his thinking, Fourier
had been the real messiah of modern times, the saviour of
genius who had sown the good seed of the future world, by
regulating society such as it would certainly be organised
to-morrow. The law of harmony had been promulgated;
human passions, liberated and utilised in healthy fashion,
would become the requisite machinery; and work, rendered
pleasant and attractive, would prove the very function of life.
Nothing could discourage Bache; if merely one parish began
by transforming itself into a *phalansterium*, the whole department would soon follow, then the adjacent departments,

and finally all France. Moreover, Bache even favoured the schemes of Cabet, whose Icaria, said he, had in no wise been such a foolish idea. Further, he recalled a motion he had made, when member of the Commune in 1871, to apply Fourier's ideas to the French Republic ; and he was apparently convinced that the troops of Versailles had delayed the triumph of Communism for half a century. Whenever people nowadays talked of table-turning he pretended to laugh, but at bottom he had remained an impenitent 'spiritist.' Since he had been a municipal councillor he had been travelling from one socialist sect to another, according as their ideas offered points of resemblance to his old faith. And he was fairly consumed by his need of faith, his perplexity as to the Divine, which he was now occasionally inclined to find in the legs of some piece of furniture, after denying its presence in the churches.

Janzen, for his part, was as taciturn as his friend Bache was garrulous. Such remarks as he made were brief, but they were as galling as lashes, as cutting as sabre-strokes. At the same time his ideas and theories remained somewhat obscure, partly by reason of this brevity of his, and partly on account of the difficulty he experienced in expressing himself in French. He was from over yonder, from some far away land—Russia, Poland, Austria or Germany, nobody exactly knew ; and it mattered little, for he acknowledged no country, but wandered far and wide with his dream of blood-shedding fraternity. Whenever, with his wonted frigidity, he gave utterance to one of those terrible remarks of his which, like a scythe in a meadow, cut away all before him, little else than the necessity of thus mowing down nations, in order to sow the earth afresh with a young and better community, became apparent. At each proposition unfolded by Bache, such as labour rendered agreeable by police regulations, *phalansteria* organised like barracks, religion transformed into pantheist or spiritist deism, he gently shrugged his shoulders. What could be the use of such childishness, such hypocritical repairing, when the house was falling and the only honest course was to throw it to the ground, and build up the substantial edifice of to-morrow with entirely new materials ? On the subject of propaganda by deeds, bomb-throwing and so forth, he remained silent, though his gestures were expressive of infinite hope. He evidently approved that course. The legend which made him one of the perpetrators of the crime of Barcelona set a gleam of horrible glory in his mysterious past. One day when Bache, while speaking to him of his friend Bergaz, the shadowy Bourse jobber who had already been compromised in some piece of thieving, plainly declared that the aforesaid Bergaz was a bandit, Janzen contented himself with smiling, and replying quietly that theft was merely forced restitution. Briefly, in this man of culture and refinement, in whose own mysterious life one might perhaps have found various crimes but not a single act of base improbity, one could divine an implacable, obstinate theorician, who was resolved to set the world ablaze for the triumph of his ideas.

On certain evenings when a visit from Théophile Morin coincided with one from Bache and Janzen, and they and Guillaume continued chatting until far into the night, Pierre would listen to them in despair from the shadowy corner where he remained motionless, never once joining in the discussions. Distracted by his own unbelief and thirst for truth, he had at the outset taken a passionate interest in these debates, desirous as he was of drawing up a balance-sheet of the century's ideas, so as to form some notion of the distance that had been travelled, and the profits that had accrued. But he recoiled from all this in fresh despair, on hearing the others argue each from his own standpoint and without possibility of concession and agreement. After the repulses he had encountered at Lourdes and Rome, he well realised that in this fresh experiment which he was making with Paris, the whole brain of the century was in question, the new truths, the expected gospel which was to change the face of the world. And, burning with inconsiderate zeal, he went from one belief to another, which other he soon rejected in order to adopt a third. If he had first felt himself to be a Positivist with Morin, an Evolutionist and Determinist with Guillaume, he had afterwards been touched by the fraternal dream of a new golden age which he had found in Bache's humanitarian Communism. And indeed even Janzen had momentarily shaken him by his fierce confidence in the theory of liberative Individualism. But afterwards he had found himself out of his depth ; and each and every theory had seemed to him but part of the chaotic contradictions and incoherences of humanity on its march. It was all a continuous piling up of dross, amidst which he lost himself. Although Fourier had sprung from Saint-Simon he denied him in part ;

and if Saint-Simon's doctrine ended in a kind of mystical
sensuality, the other's conducted to an inacceptable regimenting of society. Proudhon, for his part, demolished
without rebuilding anything. Comte, who created method
and declared science to be the one and only sovereign, had
not even suspected the advent of the social crisis which
now threatened to sweep all away, and had finished personally
as a mere worshipper of love, overpowered by woman.
Nevertheless, these two, Comte and Proudhon, entered the
lists and fought against the others, Fourier and Saint-
Simon; the combat between them or their disciples becoming
so bitter and so blind that the truths common to them all
were obscured and disfigured beyond recognition. Thence
came the extraordinary muddle of the present hour; Bache
with Saint-Simon and Fourier, and Morin with Proudhon and
Comte, utterly failing to understand Mège, the Collectivist
deputy, whom they held up to execration, him and his State
Collectivism, in the same way, moreover, as they thundered
against all the other present-time Socialist sects, without
realising that these also, whatever their nature, had more or
less sprung from the same masters as themselves. And all
this seemingly indicated that Janzen was right when he declared that the house was past repair, fast crumbling amidst
rottenness and insanity, and that it ought to be levelled to the
ground.

One night, after the three visitors had gone, Pierre, who
had remained with Guillaume, saw him grow very gloomy as
he slowly walked to and fro. He, in his turn, had doubtless
felt that all was crumbling. And though his brother alone
was there to hear him he went on speaking. He expressed
all his horror of the Collectivist State as imagined by Mège,
a Dictator-State re-establishing ancient servitude on yet
closer lines. The error of all the Socialist sects was their
arbitrary organisation of Labour, which enslaved the individual
for the profit of the community. And, forced to conciliate
the two great currents, the rights of society and the rights of
the individual, Guillaume had ended by placing his whole
faith in free Communism, an anarchical state in which he
dreamt of seeing the individual freed, moving and developing
without restraint, for the benefit both of himself and of all
others. Was not this, said he, the one truly scientific theory,
unities creating worlds, atoms producing life by force of
attraction, free and ardent love? All oppressive minorities

would disappear; and the faculties and energies of one and all would by free play arrive at harmony amidst the equilibrium —which changed according to needs—of the active forces of advancing humanity. In this wise he pictured a nation, knowing no State tutelage, without a master, almost without laws, a happy nation, each citizen of which, completely developed by the exercise of liberty, would, of his free will, come to an understanding with his neighbours with regard to the thousand necessities of life. And thence would spring society, free association, hundreds of associations which would regulate social life; though at the same time they would remain variable, in fact often opposed and hostile to one another. For progress is but the fruit of conflict and struggle; the world has only been created by the battle of opposing forces. And that was all; there would be no more oppressors, no more rich, no more poor; the domain of the earth with its natural treasures and implements of labour would be restored to the people, its legitimate owners, who would know how to enjoy it rightfully and sensibly when nothing abnormal would impede their expansion. Then only would the law of love make its action felt; then would human solidarity, which, among mankind, is the living form of universal attraction, acquire all its power, bringing men closer and closer together, and uniting them in one sole family. A splendid dream it was—the noble and pure dream of absolute freedom —free man in free society. And thither a *savant's* superior mind was fated to come after passing on the road the many Socialist sects which one and all bore the stigma of tyranny. And, assuredly, as thus indulged, the Anarchist idea is the loftiest, the proudest of all ideas. And how delightful to yield to the hope of harmony in life—life which, restored to the full exercise of its natural powers, would of itself create happiness!

When Guillaume ceased speaking, he seemed to be emerging from a dream; and he glanced at Pierre with some dismay, for he feared that he might have said too much and have hurt his feelings. Pierre—moved though he was, for a moment in fact almost won over—had just seen the terrible practical objection, which destroyed all hope, arise before his mind's eye. Why had not harmony asserted itself in the first days of the world, at the time of the earliest forms of society? How was it that tyranny had triumphed, delivering nations over to oppressors? And supposing that the apparently insolvable problem of destroying everything, and beginning everything afresh, should ever be solved, who could promise that mankind, obedient to the same laws, would not again follow the same paths as formerly? After all, mankind, nowadays, is simply what life has made it; and nothing proves that life would again make it other than it is. To begin afresh, ah, yes! but to attain another result! But could that other result really come from man? Was it not rather man himself who should be changed? To start afresh from where one was, to continue the evolution that had begun, undoubtedly meant slow travel and dismal waiting. But how great would be the danger and even the delay, if one went back without knowing by what road across the whole chaos of ruins one might regain all the lost time!

'Let us go to bed,' at last said Guillaume, smiling. 'It's silly of me to weary you with all these things which don't concern you.'

Pierre, in his excitement, was about to reveal his own heart and mind, and the whole torturing battle within him. But a feeling of shame again restrained him. His brother only knew him as a believing priest, faithful to his faith. And so, without answering, he betook himself to his room.

On the following evening, about ten o'clock, while Guillaume and Pierre sat reading in the study, the old servant entered to announce M. Janzen and a friend. The friend was Salvat.

'He wished to see you,' Janzen explained to Guillaume. 'I met him, and when he heard of your injury and anxiety he implored me to bring him here. And I've done so, though it was perhaps hardly prudent of me.'

Guillaume had risen full of surprise and emotion at such a visit; Pierre, however, though equally upset by Salvat's appearance, did not stir from his chair, but kept his eyes upon the workman.

'Monsieur Froment,' Salvat ended by saying, standing there in a timid, embarrassed way, 'I was very sorry indeed when I heard of the worry I'd put you in; for I shall never forget that you were very kind to me when everybody else turned me away.'

As he spoke he balanced himself alternately on either leg, and transferred his old felt hat from hand to hand.

'And so I wanted to come and tell you myself that if I

took a cartridge of your powder one evening when you had your back turned, it's the only thing that I feel any remorse about in the whole business, since it may compromise you. And I also want to take my oath before you that you've nothing to fear from me, that I'll let my head be cut off twenty times, if need be, rather than utter your name. That's all that I had in my heart.'

He relapsed into silence and embarrassment, but his soft, dreamy eyes, the eyes of a faithful dog, remained fixed upon Guillaume with an expression of respectful worship. And Pierre was still gazing at him athwart the hateful vision which his arrival had conjured up, that of the poor, dead errand girl, the fair pretty child lying ripped open under the entrance of the Duvillard mansion! Was it possible that he was there, he, that madman, that murderer, and that his eyes were actually moist!

Guillaume, touched by Salvat's words had drawn near and pressed his hand. 'I am well aware, Salvat,' said he, 'that you are not wicked at heart. But what a foolish and abominable thing you did!'

Salvat showed no sign of anger, but gently smiled. 'Oh! if it had to be done again, Monsieur Froment, I'd do it. It's my idea, you know. And apart from you, all is well; I am content.'

He would not sit down, but for another moment continued talking with Guillaume, while Janzen, as if he washed his hands of the business, deeming this visit both useless and dangerous, sat down and turned over the leaves of a picture book. And Guillaume made Salvat tell him what he had done on the day of the crime; how like a stray dog he had wandered in distraction through Paris, carrying his bomb with him, originally in his tool-bag and then under his jacket; how he had gone a first time to the Duvillard mansion and found its carriage entrance closed; then how he had betaken himself first to the Chamber of Deputies which the ushers had prevented him from entering, and afterwards to the Circus, where the thought of making a great sacrifice of *bourgeois* had occurred to him too late. And finally, how he had at last come back to the Duvillard mansion, as if drawn thither by the very power of destiny. His tool-bag was lying in the depths of the Seine, he said; he had thrown it into the water with sudden hatred of work since it had even failed to give him bread. And he next told the story of his flight; the

explosion shaking the whole district behind him, while, with
delight and astonishment, he found himself some distance off,
in quiet streets where nothing was as yet known. And for a
month past he had been living in chance fashion, how or
where he could hardly tell, but he had often slept in the open,
and gone for a day without food. One evening little Victor
Mathis had given him five francs. Then other comrades had
helped him, taken him in for a night and sent him off at
the first sign of peril. Far-spreading, tacit complicity had
hitherto saved him from the police. As for going abroad,
well, he had, at one moment, thought of doing so; but a
description of his person must have been circulated, the
gendarmes must be waiting for him at the frontiers, and so
would not flight instead of retarding rather hasten his arrest ?
Paris, however, was an ocean ; it was there that he incurred
the least risk of capture. Moreover, he no longer had
sufficient energy to flee. A fatalist as he was after his own
fashion, he could not find strength to quit the pavements
of Paris, but there awaited arrest, like a social waif carried
chancewise through the multitude as in a dream.

'And your daughter, little Céline ? ' Guillaume inquired.
'Have you ventured to go back to see her ? '

Salvat waved his hand in a vague way. 'No, but what
would you have ? She's with Mamma Théodore. Women
always find some help. And then I'm done for, I can do
nothing for anybody. It's as if I were already dead.' However, in spite of these words, tears were rising to his eyes.
'Ah ! the poor little thing ! ' he added, 'I kissed her with all
my heart before I went away. If she and the woman hadn't
been starving so long the idea of that business would perhaps
never have come to me.'

Then, in all simplicity, he declared that he was ready to
die. If he had ended by depositing his bomb at the entrance
of the Duvillards' house, it was because he knew the banker
well, and was aware that he was the wealthiest of those
bourgeois whose fathers at the time of the Revolution had
duped the people, by taking all power and wealth for
themselves : the power and wealth which the sons were
nowadays so obstinately bent on retaining that they would
not even bestow the veriest crumbs on others. As for the
Revolution, he understood it in his own fashion, like an
illiterate fellow who had learnt the little he knew from
newspapers and speeches at public meetings. And he struck

his chest with his fist as he spoke of his honesty, and was particularly desirous that none should doubt his courage because he had fled.

'I've never robbed anybody,' said he, 'and if I don't go and hand myself up to the police, it's because they may surely take the trouble to find and arrest me. I'm very well aware that my affair's clear enough, as they've found that bradawl and know me. All the same, it would be silly of me to help them in their work. Still they'd better make haste, for I've almost had enough of being tracked like a wild beast and no longer knowing how I live.'

Janzen, yielding to curiosity, had ceased turning over the leaves of the picture book and was looking at Salvat. There was a smile of disdain in the Anarchist leader's cold eyes; and in his usual broken French he remarked : 'A man fights and defends himself, kills others and tries to avoid being killed himself. That's warfare.'

These words fell from his lips amidst deep silence. Salvat, however, did not seem to have heard them, but stammered forth his faith in a long sentence laden with fulsome expressions, such as the sacrifice of his life in order that want might cease, and the example of a great action, in the certainty that it would inspire other heroes to continue the struggle. And with this certainly sincere faith and illuminism of his there was blended a martyr's pride, delight at being one of the radiant, worshipped saints of the dawning Revolutionary Church.

As he had come so he went off. When Janzen had led him away, it seemed as if the night which had brought him had carried him back into its impenetrable depths. And then only did Pierre rise from his chair. He was stifling, and threw the large window of the room wide open. It was a very mild but moonless night, whose silence was only disturbed by the subsiding clamour of Paris, which stretched away, invisible, on the horizon.

Guillaume according to his habit had begun to walk up and down. And at last he spoke, again forgetting that his brother was a priest. 'Ah! the poor fellow! How well one can understand that deed of violence and hope! His whole past life of fruitless labour and ever-growing want explains it. Then, too, there has been all the contagion of ideas; the frequentation of public meetings where men intoxicate themselves with words, and of secret meetings among comrades where faith acquires firmness and the mind soars wildly. Ah! I think I know that man well indeed! He's a good workman, sober and courageous. Injustice has always exasperated him. And little by little the desire for universal happiness has cast him out of the realities of life which he has ended by holding in horror. So how can he do otherwise than live in a dream—a dream of redemption, which, from circumstances, has turned to fire and murder as its fitting instruments? As I looked at him standing there, I fancied I could picture one of the first Christian slaves of ancient Rome. All the iniquity of old Pagan society, agonising beneath the rottenness born of debauchery and covetousness, was weighing on his shoulders, bearing him down. He had come from the dark Catacombs where he had whispered words of deliverance and redemption with his wretched brethren. And a thirst for martyrdom consumed him, he spat in the face of Cæsar, he insulted the gods, he fired the pagan temples, in order that the reign of Jesus might come and abolish servitude. And he was ready to die, to be torn to pieces by the wild beasts!'

Pierre did not immediately reply. He had already been struck, however, by the fact that there were undoubted points of resemblance between the secret propaganda and militant faith of the Anarchists, and certain practices of the first Christians. Both sects embrace a new faith in the hope that the lowly may thereby at last reap justice. Paganism disappears through weariness of the flesh and the need of a more lofty and pure faith. That dream of a Christian paradise opening up a future life with a system of compensations for the ills endured on earth, was the outcome of young hope dawning at its historic hour. But to-day, when eighteen centuries have exhausted that hope, when the long experiment is over and the toiler finds himself duped and still and ever a slave, he once more dreams of setting happiness upon this earth, particularly as each day Science tends more and more to show him that the happiness of the spheres beyond is a lie. And in all this there is but the eternal struggle of the poor and the rich, the eternal question of bringing more justice and less suffering to the world.

'But surely,' Pierre at last replied, 'you can't be on the side of those bandits, those murderers whose savage violence horrifies me! I let you talk on yesterday, when you dreamt of a great and happy people, of ideal anarchy in which each would be free amidst the freedom of all. But what abomination, what disgust both for mind and heart when one passes from theory to propaganda and practice! If yours is the brain that thinks, whose is the hateful hand that acts, that kills children, breaks doors open and empties drawers? Do you accept that responsibility? With your education, your culture, the whole social heredity behind you, does not your entire being revolt at the idea of stealing and murdering?'

Guillaume halted before his brother, quivering. 'Steal and murder! no! no! I will not. But one must say everything and fully understand the history of the evil hour through which we are passing. It is madness sweeping by: and to tell the truth, everything necessary to provoke it has been done. At the very dawn of the Anarchist theory, at the very first innocent actions of its partisans, there was such stern repression, the police so grossly ill-treating the poor devils that fell into its hands, that little by little came anger and rage leading to the most horrible reprisals. It is the Terror initiated by the *bourgeois* that has produced Anarchist savagery. And would you know whence Salvat and his crime have come? Why, from all our centuries of impudence and iniquity, from all that the nations have suffered, from all the sores which are now devouring us, the impatience for enjoyment, the contempt of the strong for the weak, the whole monstrous spectacle which is presented by our rotting society!'

Guillaume was again slowly walking to and fro; and as if he were reflecting aloud he continued: 'Ah! to reach the point I have attained, through how much thought, through how many battles have I not passed! I was merely a Positivist, a *savant* devoted to observation and experiment, accepting nothing apart from proven facts. Scientifically and socially, I admitted that simple evolution had slowly brought humanity into being. But both in the history of the globe and that of human society, I found it necessary to make allowance for the volcano, the sudden cataclysm, the sudden eruption, by which each geological phase, each historical period has been marked. In this wise one ends by ascertaining that no forward step has ever been taken, no progress ever accomplished in the world's history, without the help of horrible catastrophes. Each advance has meant the sacrifice of millions and millions of human lives. This of course revolts us, given our narrow ideas of justice, and we regard nature as a most barbarous mother; but, if we cannot excuse the volcano, we ought to deal with it when it bursts forth, like wise men forewarned of its possibility. . . . And then, ah, then! well, perhaps, I'm a dreamer like others, but I have my own notions.'

With a sweeping gesture he confessed what a social dreamer there was within him beside the methodical and scrupulous *savant*. His constant endeavour was to bring all back to science, and he was deeply grieved at finding in nature no scientific sign of equality or even justice, such as he craved for in the social sphere. His despair indeed came from this inability to reconcile scientific logic with apostolic love, the dream of universal happiness and brotherhood and the end of all iniquity.

Pierre, however, who had remained near the open window, gazing into the night towards Paris, whence ascended the last sounds of the evening of passionate pleasure, felt the whole flood of his own doubt and despair stifling him. It was all too much: that brother of his who had fallen upon him with his scientific and apostolic beliefs, those men who came to discuss contemporary thought from every standpoint, and finally that Salvat who had brought thither the exasperating memory of his mad deed. And Pierre, who had listened to them all without a word, without a gesture, who had hidden his secrets from his brother, seeking refuge in his supposed priestly views, suddenly felt such bitterness stirring his heart that he could lie no longer.

'Ah! brother, if you have your dream, I have my sore which has eaten into me and left me void! Your Anarchy, your dream of just happiness, for which Salvat works with bombs, why it is the final burst of insanity which will sweep everything away! How is it that you can't realise it? The century is ending in ruins. I've been listening to you all for a month past. Fourier destroyed Saint-Simon, Proudhon and Comte demolished Fourier, each in turn piling up incoherences and contradictions, leaving mere chaos behind them, which nobody dares to sort out. And since then, Socialist sects have been swarming and multiplying, the more sensible of them leading simply to dictatorship, while the others indulge in most dangerous reveries. And after such a tempest of ideas there could indeed come nothing but your Anarchy, which undertakes to bring the old world to a finish by reducing it to dust . . . . Ah! I expected it, I was waiting for it—that final catastrophe, that fratricidal madness, the inevitable class warfare in which our civilisation was destined to collapse! Everything announced it: the want and misery below, the egotism up above, all the cracking of the old human habitation, borne down by too great a weight of crime and grief. When I went to Lourdes it was to see if the divinity of simple minds would work the awaited miracle, and restore the belief of the early ages to the people which rebelled through excess of suffering. And when I went to Rome it was in the naïve hope of there finding the new religion required by our democracies, the only one that could pacify the world by bringing back the brotherliness of the golden age. But how foolish of me all that was! Both here and there, I simply lighted on nothingness. There where I so ardently dreamt of finding the salvation of others, I only sank myself, going down a-peak like a ship not a timber of which is ever found again. One tie still linked me to my fellow men, that of charity, the dressing, relieving and perhaps, in the long run, healing of wounds and sores; but that last cable has now been severed. Charity, to my mind, appears futile and derisive by the side of justice, to whom all supremacy belongs, and whose advent has become a necessity and can be stayed by none. And so it is all over, I am mere ashes, an empty grave as it were. I no longer believe in anything, anything, anything whatever!'

Pierre had risen to his full height, with arms outstretched as if to let all the nothingness within his heart and mind fall from them. And Guillaume, distracted by the sight of such a fierce denier, such a despairing Nihilist as was now revealed to him, drew near, quivering: 'What are you saying, brother! I thought you so firm, so calm in your belief! A priest to be admired, a saint worshipped by the whole of this parish! I was unwilling even to discuss your faith, and now it is you who deny all, and believe in nothing whatever!'

Pierre again slowly stretched out his arms. 'There is nothing; I tried to learn all, and only found the atrocious grief born of the nothingness that overwhelms me.'

'Ah! how you must suffer, Pierre, my little brother! Can religion, then, be even more withering than science, since it has ravaged you like that, while I have yet remained an old madman, still full of fancies?'

Guillaume caught hold of Pierre's hands and pressed them, full of terrified compassion in presence of all the grandeur and horror embodied in that unbelieving priest who watched over the belief of others, and chastely, honestly discharged his duty amidst the haughty sadness born of his falsehood. And how heavily must that falsehood have weighed upon his conscience for him to confess himself in that fashion, amidst an utter collapse of his whole being! A month previously, in the unexpansiveness of his proud solitude, he would never have taken such a course. To speak out it was necessary that he should have been stirred by many things, his reconciliation with his brother, the conversations he had heard of an evening, the terrible drama in which he was mingled, as well as his reflections on labour struggling against want, and the vague hope with which the sight of intellectual youth had inspired him. And, indeed, amid the very excess of his negation was there not already the faint dawn of a new faith?

This Guillaume must have understood, on seeing how he quivered with unsatisfied tenderness as he emerged from the fierce silence which he had preserved so long. He made him sit down near the window, and placed himself beside him without releasing his hands. 'But I won't have you suffer, my little brother!' he said, 'I won't leave you, I'll nurse you. For I know you much better than you know yourself. You would never have suffered were it not for the battle between your heart and your mind, and you will cease to suffer on the day when they make peace, and you love what you understand.' And in a lower voice, with infinite affection, he went on: 'You see, it's our poor mother and our poor father continuing their painful struggle in you. You were too young at the time, you couldn't know what went on. But I knew them both very wretched: he, wretched through her, who treated him as if he were one of the damned; and she suffering through him, tortured by his irreligion. When he died, struck down by an explosion in this very room, she took it to be the punishment of God. Yet, what an honest man he was, with a good, great heart, what a worker, seeking for truth alone, and desirous of the love and happiness of all! Since we have spent our evenings here, I have felt him coming back, reviving as it were both around and within us;

and she, too, poor, saintly woman, is ever here, enveloping us with love, weeping, and yet stubbornly refusing to understand. It is they, perhaps, who have kept me here so long, and who at this very moment are present to place your hands in mine.'

And, indeed, it seemed to Pierre as if he could feel the spirit of vigilant affection which Guillaume evoked passing over them both. There was again a revival of all the past, all their youth, and nothing could have been more delightful.

'You hear me, brother,' Guillaume resumed. 'You must reconcile them, for it is only in you that they can be reconciled. You have his firm, lofty brow, and her mouth and eyes of unrealisable tenderness. So, try to bring them to agreement, by some day contenting, as your reason shall allow, the everlasting thirst for love, and self-bestowal, and life, which for lack of satisfaction is killing you. Your frightful wretchedness has no other cause. Come back to life, love, bestow yourself, be a man !'

Pierre raised a dolorous cry : 'No, no, the death born of doubt has swept through me, withering and shattering everything, and nothing more can live in such cold dust !'

'But, come,' resumed Guillaume, 'you cannot have reached such absolute negation. No man reaches it. Even in the most disabused of minds there remains a nook of fancy and hope. To deny charity, devotion, the prodigies which love may work, ah ! for my part I do not go so far as that. And now that you have shown me your sore, why should I not tell you my dream, the wild hope which keeps me alive ! It is strange ; but, are *savants* to be the last childish dreamers, and is faith only to spring up nowadays in chemical laboratories ?'

Intense emotion was stirring Guillaume ; there was battle waging in both his brain and his heart. And at last, yielding to the deep compassion which filled him, vanquished by his ardent affection for his unhappy brother, he spoke out. But he had drawn yet closer to Pierre, even passed one arm around him ; and it was thus embracing him that he, in his turn, made his confession, lowering his voice as if he feared that someone might overhear his secret. 'Why should you not know it ?' he said. 'My own sons are ignorant of it. But you are a man and my brother, and since there is nothing of the priest left in you, it is to the brother I will

confide it. This will make me love you the more, and
perhaps it may do you good.'

Then he told him of his invention, a new explosive, a
powder of such extraordinary force that its effects were
incalculable. And he had found employment for this powder
in an engine of warfare, a special cannon, hurling bombs
which would assure the most overwhelming victory to the
army using them. The enemy's forces would be destroyed in
a few hours, and besieged cities would fall into dust at the
slightest bombardment. He had long searched and doubted,
calculated, recalculated, and experimented; but everything
was now ready : the precise formula of the powder, the
drawings for the cannon and the bombs, a whole packet of
precious papers stored in a safe spot. And after months of
anxious reflection he had resolved to give his invention to
France, so as to ensure her a certainty of victory in her
coming, inevitable war with Germany !

At the same time, he was not a man of narrow patriotism ;
on the contrary he had a very broad, international conception
of the future liberative civilisation. Only he believed in the
initiatory mission of France, and particularly in that of Paris,
which, even as it is to-day, was destined to be the world's
brain to-morrow, whence all science and justice would
proceed. The great idea of liberty and equality had already
soared from it at the prodigious blast of the Revolution ; and
from its genius and valour the final emancipation of man
would also take its flight. Thus it was necessary that Paris
should be victorious in the struggle in order that the world
might be saved.

Pierre understood his brother, thanks to the lecture on
explosives which he had heard at Bertheroy's. And the
grandeur of this scheme, this dream, particularly struck him
when he thought of the extraordinary future which would open
for Paris amidst the effulgent blaze of the bombs. Moreover,
he was struck by all the nobility of soul which had lain behind
his brother's anxiety for a month past. If Guillaume had
trembled it was simply with fear that his invention might be
divulged in consequence of Salvat's crime. The slightest
indiscretion might compromise everything ; and that little
stolen cartridge, whose effects had so astonished *savants*,
might reveal his secret. He felt it necessary to act in
mystery, choosing his own time, awaiting the proper hour,
until when the secret would slumber in its hiding-place,

confided to the sole care of Mère-Grand, who had her orders and knew what she was to do, should he, in any sudden accident, disappear.

'And, now,' said Guillaume in conclusion, 'you know my hopes and my anguish, and you can help me and even take my place if I am unable to reach the end of my task. Ah! to reach the end! Since I have been shut up here, reflecting, consumed by anxiety and impatience, there have been hours when I have ceased to see my way clearly! There is that Salvat, that wretched fellow for whose crime we are all of us responsible, and who is now being hunted down like a wild beast! There is also that insensate and unsatiable *bourgeoisie*, which will let itself be crushed by the fall of the shaky old house, rather than allow the least repair to it! And there is further that cupid, that abominable Parisian press, so harsh towards the weak and little, so fond of insulting those who have none to defend them, so eager to coin money out of public misfortune, and ready to spread insanity on all sides, simply to increase its sales! Where, therefore, shall one find truth and justice, the hand endowed with logic and health that ought to be armed with the thunder-bolt? Would Paris the conqueror, Paris the master of the nations, prove the justiciar, the saviour that men await! Ah! the anguish of believing oneself to be the master of the world's destinies, and to have to choose and decide.'

He had risen again quivering, full of anger and fear that human wretchedness and baseness might prevent the realisation of his dream. And amidst the heavy silence which fell in the room, the little house suddenly resounded with a regular, continuous footfall.

'Ah, yes! to save men and love them, and wish them all to be equal and free,' murmured Pierre bitterly. 'But just listen! Barthès' footsteps are answering you, as if from the everlasting dungeon into which his love of liberty has thrown him!'

However, Guillaume had already regained possession of himself, and coming back in a transport of his faith, he once more took Pierre in his loving, saving arms, like an elder brother who gives himself without restraint. 'No, no, I'm wrong, I'm blaspheming,' he exclaimed, 'I wish you to be with me, full of hope and full of certainty. You must work, you must love, you must revive to life. Life alone can give you back peace and health.'

Tears returned to the eyes of Pierre, who was penetrated to the heart by this ardent affection. 'Ah! how I should like to believe you,' he faltered, 'and try to cure myself. True, I have already felt, as it were, a vague revival within me. And yet to live again, no, I cannot; priest that I am I can be nought but an empty tomb.'

He was shaken by so frightful a sob that Guillaume could not restrain his own tears. And clasped in one another's arms the brothers wept on, their hearts full of the softest emotion in that home of their youth, whither the dear shadows of their parents ever returned, hovering around until they should be reconciled and restored to the peace of the earth. And all the darkness and mildness of the garden streamed in through the open window, while yonder, on the horizon, Paris had fallen asleep in the mysterious gloom, beneath a very peaceful sky which was studded with stars.

BOOK III

I

THE RIVALS

On the Wednesday preceding the mid-Lent Thursday, a great charity bazaar was held at the Duvillard mansion, for the benefit of the Asylum of the Invalids of Labour. The ground-floor reception rooms, three spacious Louis Seize *salons*, whose windows overlooked the bare and solemn court-yard, were given up to the swarm of purchasers; five thousand admission cards having been distributed among all sections of Parisian society. And the opening of the bombarded mansion in this wise to thousands of visitors was regarded as quite an event, a demonstration, although some people whispered that the Rue Godot-de-Mauroy and the adjacent streets were guarded by an army of police agents.

The idea of the bazaar had come from Duvillard himself, and at his bidding his wife had resigned herself to all this worry for the benefit of the enterprise over which she presided with such distinguished nonchalance. On the previous day the 'Globe' newspaper, inspired by its director Fonsègue, who was also the general manager of the asylum, had published a very fine article, announcing the bazaar, and pointing out how noble, and touching, and generous was the initiative of the Baroness, who still gave her time, her money, and even her home to charity, in spite of the abominable crime which had almost reduced that home to ashes. Was not this the magnanimous answer of the spheres above to the hateful passions of the spheres below? And was it not also a peremptory answer to those who accused the capitalists of doing nothing for the wage-earners, the disabled and broken-down sons of toil?

The drawing-room doors were to be opened at two o'clock, and would only close at seven, so that there would be five full hours for the sales. And at noon, when nothing was as yet ready downstairs, when workmen and women were still decorating the stalls, and sorting the goods amidst a final scramble, there was, as usual, a little friendly *déjeuner*, to which a few guests had been invited, in the private rooms on the first floor. However, a scarcely expected incident had given a finishing touch to the general excitement of the house; that very morning Sagnier had resumed his campaign of denunciation in the matter of the African Railway Lines. In a virulent article in the ' Voix du Peuple,' he had inquired if it were the intention of the authorities to beguile the public much longer with the story of that bomb and that Anarchist whom the police did not arrest. And this time, while undertaking to publish the names of the thirty-two corrupt senators and deputies in a very early issue, he had boldly named Minister Barroux as one who had pocketed a sum of 200,000 francs. Mège would therefore certainly revive his interpellation, which might become dangerous, now that Paris had been thrown into such a distracted state by terror of the Anarchists. At the same time it was said that Vignon and his party had resolved to turn circumstances to account, with the object of overthrowing the Ministry. Thus a redoubtable crisis was inevitably at hand. Fortunately, the Chamber did not meet that Wednesday; in fact, it had adjourned until the Friday, with the view of making mid-Lent a holiday. And so forty-eight hours were left one to prepare for the onslaught.

Eve, that morning, seemed more gentle and languid than ever, rather pale too, with an expression of sorrowful anxiety in the depths of her beautiful eyes. She set it all down to the very great fatigue which the preparations for the bazaar had entailed on her. But the truth was that Gérard de Quinsac, after shunning any further assignation, had for five days past avoided her in an embarrassed way. Still she was convinced that she would see him that morning, and so she had again ventured to wear the white silk gown which made her look so much younger than she really was. At the same time, beautiful as she had remained, with her delicate skin, superb figure, and noble and charming countenance, her six-and-forty years were asserting themselves in her blotchy complexion and the little creases which were appearing about her lips, eyelids, and temples.

Camille, for her part, though her position as daughter of

the house made it certain that she would attract much
custom as a saleswoman, had obstinately persisted in wearing
one of her usual dresses, a dark 'carmelite' gown, an old
woman's frock as she herself called it with a cutting laugh.
However, her long and wicked looking face beamed with some
secret delight; such an expression of wit and intelligence
wreathing her thin lips and shining in her big eyes that
one lost sight of her deformity and thought her almost
pretty.

Eve experienced a first deception in the little blue and
silver sitting-room where, accompanied by her daughter, she
awaited the arrival of her guests. General de Bozonnet, whom
Gérard was to have brought with him, came in alone, explaining that Madame de Quinsac had felt rather poorly that
morning, and that Gérard, like a good and dutiful son, had
wished to remain with her. Still he would come to the
bazaar directly after *déjeuner*. While the Baroness listened
to the General, striving to hide her disappointment and her
fear that she would now be unable to obtain any explanation
from Gérard that day, Camille looked at her with eager, devouring eyes. And a certain covert instinct of the misfortune
threatening her must at that moment have come to Eve, for
in her turn she glanced at her daughter and turned pale as if
with anxiety.

Then Princess Rosemonde de Harn swept in like a whirlwind. She also was to be one of the saleswomen at the stall
chosen by the Baroness, who liked her for her very turbu-
lence, the sudden gaiety which she generally brought with her.
Gowned in satin of a fiery hue—red shot with yellow—looking
very eccentric with her curly hair and thin boyish figure,
she laughed and talked of an accident by which her carriage
had almost been cut in halves. Then, as Baron Duvillard and
Hyacinthe came in from their rooms, late as usual, she took
possession of the young man and scolded him, for on the
previous evening she had vainly waited for him till ten o'clock
in the expectation that he would keep his promise to escort
her to a tavern at Montmartre, where some horrible things
were said to occur. Hyacinthe, looking very bored, quietly
replied that he had been detained at a *séance* given by some
adepts in the new Magic, in the course of which the soul
of St. Theresa had descended from heaven to recite a love
sonnet.

However, Fonsègue was now coming in with his wife, a

tall, thin, silent, and generally insignificant woman, whom he
seldom took about with him. On this occasion he had been
obliged to bring her, as she was one of the lady-patronesses
of the asylum, and he himself was coming to lunch with the
Duvillards in his capacity as general manager. To the
superficial observer he looked quite as gay as usual; but he
blinked nervously, and his first glance was a questioning one
in the direction of Duvillard, as if he wished to know how
the latter bore the fresh thrust directed at him by Sagnier.
And when he saw the banker looking perfectly composed, as
superb, as rubicund as usual, and chatting in a bantering
way with Rosemonde, he also put on an easy air, like a
gamester who had never lost but had always known how to
compel good luck, even in hours of treachery. And by way
of showing his unconstraint of mind he at once addressed the
Baroness on managerial matters: ' Have you now succeeded
in seeing M. l'Abbé Froment for the affair of that old man
Laveuve, whom he so warmly recommended to us ? All the
formalities have been gone through, you know, and he can be
brought to us at once, as we have had a bed vacant for three
days past.'

' Yes, I know,' replied Eve; ' but I can't imagine what
has become of Abbé Froment, for he hasn't given us a sign
of life for a month past. However, I made up my mind to
write to him yesterday, and beg him to come to the bazaar
to-day. In this manner I shall be able to acquaint him with
the good news myself.'

' It was to leave you the pleasure of doing so,' said
Fonsègue, ' that I refrained from sending him any official
communication. He's a charming priest, is he not ? '

' Oh ! charming, we are very fond of him.'

However, Duvillard now intervened to say that they need
not wait for Duthil, as he had received a telegram from him
stating that he was detained by sudden business. At this
Fonsègue's anxiety returned, and he once more questioned
the Baron with his eyes. Duvillard smiled, however, and reassured him in an undertone : ' It's nothing serious. Merely
a commission for me, about which he'll only be able to bring
me an answer by-and-bye.' Then, taking Fonsègue on one
side, he added : ' By the way, don't forget to insert the
paragraph I told you of.'

' What paragraph ? Oh ! yes, the one about that *soirée*
at which Silviane recited a piece of verse. Well, I wanted to

speak to you about it. It worries me a little, on account of the excessive praise it contains.'

Duvillard, but a moment before so full of serenity, with his lofty, conquering, disdainful mien, now suddenly became pale and agitated. 'But I absolutely want it to be inserted, my dear fellow! You would place me in the greatest embarrassment if it were not to appear, for I promised Silviane that it should.'

As he spoke his lips trembled, and a scared look came into his eyes, plainly revealing his dismay.

'All right, all right,' said Fonsègue, secretly amused, and well pleased at this complicity. 'As it's so serious the paragraph shall go in, I promise you.'

The whole company was now present, since neither Gérard nor Duthil was to be expected. So they went into the dining-room amidst a final noise of hammering in the sale rooms below. The meal proved somewhat of a scramble, and was on three occasions disturbed by female attendants, who came to explain difficulties and ask for orders. Doors were constantly slamming, and the very walls seemed to shake with the unusual bustle which filled the house. And feverish as they all were in the dining-room, they talked in desultory, haphazard fashion on all sorts of subjects, passing from a ball given at the Ministry of the Interior on the previous night, to the popular mid-Lent festival which would take place on the morrow, and ever reverting to the bazaar, the prices that had been given for the goods which would be on sale, the prices at which they might be sold, and the probable figure of the full receipts, all this being interspersed with strange anecdotes, witticisms, and bursts of laughter. On the General mentioning magistrate Amadieu, Eve declared that she no longer dared to invite him to *déjeuner,* knowing how busy he was at the Palace of Justice. Still, she certainly hoped that he would come to the bazaar and contribute something. Then Fonsègue amused himself with teasing Princess Rosemonde about her fire-hued gown, in which, said he, she must already feel roasted by the flames of hell; a suggestion which secretly delighted her, as Satanism had now become her momentary passion. Meantime, Duvillard lavished the most gallant politeness on that silent creature, Madame Fonsègue, while Hyacinthe, in order to astonish even the Princess, explained in a few words how the New Magic could transform a young man of absolute chasteness into a sexless angel. And Camille, who seemed very happy and very excited, from time to time darted a hot glance at her mother, whose anxiety and sadness increased as she found the other more and more aggressive, and apparently resolved upon open and merciless warfare.

At last, just as the dessert was coming to an end, the Baroness heard her daughter exclaim in a piercing, defiant voice : 'Oh ! don't talk to me of the old ladies who still seem to be playing with dolls, and paint themselves, and dress as if they were about to be confirmed ! All such ogresses ought to retire from the scene ! I hold them in horror ! '

At this, Eve nervously rose from her seat, and exclaimed apologetically : ' You must forgive me for hurrying you like this. But I'm afraid that we shall hardly have time to drink our coffee in peace, though perhaps we may be able to draw breath a little.'

The coffee was served in the little blue and silver sitting-room, where bloomed some lovely yellow roses, testifying to the Baroness's keen passion for flowers, which made the house an abode of perpetual spring. Duvillard and Fonsègue, however, carrying their cups of steaming coffee with them, at once went into the former's private room to smoke a cigar there and chat in freedom. Still the door remained wide open, and one could hear their gruff voices more or less distinctly. Meantime, General de Bozonnet, delighted to find in Madame Fonsègue a serious, submissive person, who listened without interrupting, began to tell her a very long story of an officer's wife who had followed her husband through every battle of the war of 1870. Then Hyacinthe, who took no coffee—contemptuously declaring it to be a beverage only fit for doorkeepers—managed to rid himself of Rosemonde, who was sipping some kummel, in order to come and whisper to his sister : 'I say, it was very stupid of you to taunt mamma in the way you did just now. I don't care a rap about it myself. But it ends by being noticed and, I warn you candidly, it shows ill breeding.'

Camille gazed at him fixedly with her black eyes. ' Pray don't *you* meddle with my affairs,' said she.

At this he felt frightened, scented a storm, and decided to take Rosemonde into the adjoining red drawing-room in order to show her a picture which his father had lately purchased. And the General, on being called by him, likewise conducted Madame Fonsègue thither.

The mother and daughter then suddenly found themselves alone and face to face. Eve was leaning on a pier-table, as if overcome; and indeed the least sorrow bore her down, so weak at heart she was, ever ready to weep in her naïve and perfect egotism. Why was it that her daughter thus hated her, and did her utmost to disturb that last happy spell of love in which her heart lingered? She looked at Camille, grieved rather than irritated; and the unfortunate idea came to her of making a remark about her dress at the very moment when the girl was on the point of following the others into the larger drawing-room.

'It's quite wrong of you, my dear,' said she, 'to persist in dressing like an old woman. It doesn't improve you a bit.'

As Eve spoke, her soft eyes, those of one who had ever been courted and worshipped, expressed sudden compassion for that ugly, deformed girl, whom she had never been able to regard as a daughter. Was it possible that she, with her sovereign beauty, that beauty which she herself had ever adored and nursed, making it her one care, her one religion—was it possible that she had given birth to such a graceless creature, with a dark goatish profile, one shoulder higher than the other, and a pair of endless arms such as hunchbacks often have? All her grief and all her shame at having had such a child became apparent in the quivering of her voice.

Camille, however, had stopped short, as if struck in the face with a whip. Then she came back to her mother and the horrible explanation began with these simple words spoken in an undertone: 'You consider that I dress badly? Well, you ought to have paid some attention to me, have seen that my gowns suited your taste, and have taught me your secret of looking beautiful!'

Eve, with her dislike of all painful feeling, all quarrelling and bitter words, was already regretting her attack. So she sought to effect a retreat, particularly as time was flying and they would soon be expected downstairs: 'Come, be quiet, and don't show your bad temper when all those people can hear us. I have loved you——'

But with a quiet yet terrible laugh Camille interrupted her. 'You've loved me! Oh! my poor mamma, what a comical thing to say! Have you ever loved *anybody*? You want others to love *you*, but that's another matter. As for your child, any child, do you even know how it ought to be loved?

You have always neglected me, thrust me on one side, deeming me so ugly, so unworthy of you! And besides you have not had days and nights enough to love yourself! Oh! don't deny it, my poor mamma, but even now you're looking at me as if I were some loathsome monster that's in your way.'

From that moment the abominable scene was bound to continue to the end. With their teeth set, their faces close together, the two women went on speaking in feverish whispers.

'Be quiet, Camille, I tell you! I will not allow such language!'

'But I won't be quiet when you do all you can to wound me. If it's wrong of me to dress like an old woman, perhaps somebody we know is rather ridiculous in dressing like a girl, like a bride.'

'Like a bride? I don't understand you.'

'Oh! yes, you do. However, I would have you know that everybody doesn't find me so ugly as you try to make them believe.'

'If you look amiss it is because you don't dress properly, that is all I said.'

'I dress as I please, and no doubt I do so well enough, since I'm loved as I am.'

'What, really! Does someone love you? Well, let him inform us of it and marry you.'

'Yes—certainly, certainly! It will be a good riddance, won't it? And you'll have the pleasure of seeing me as a bride!'

Their voices were rising in spite of their efforts to restrain them. However, Camille paused and drew breath before hissing out the words: 'Gérard is coming here to ask for my hand in a day or two.'

Eve, livid, with wildly staring eyes, did not seem to understand. 'Gérard! why do you tell me that?'

'Why, because it's Gérard who loves me and who is going to marry me! You drive me to extremities; you're for ever repeating that I'm ugly; you treat me like a monster whom nobody will ever care for. So I'm forced to defend myself and tell you the truth, in order to prove to you that everybody is not of your opinion.'

Silence fell, the frightful thing which had risen between them seemed to have arrested the quarrel. But there was neither mother nor daughter left there. They were simply two tortured, defiant rivals. Eve in her turn drew a long breath and glanced anxiously towards the adjoining room to ascertain if anyone were coming in or listening to them. And then in a tone of resolution she made answer:

'You cannot marry Gérard.'

'Pray, why not?'

'Because I won't have it; because it's impossible.'

'That isn't a reason, give me a reason.'

'The reason is that the marriage is impossible—that is all.'

'No, no, I'll tell you the reason since you force me to it. The reason is that Gérard is your lover! But what does that matter since I know it and am willing to take him all the same?'

And to this retort Camille's flaming eyes added the words: 'And it is particularly on that account that I want him.' All the long torture born of her infirmities, all her rage at having always seen her mother beautiful, courted and adored, was now stirring her and seeking vengeance in cruel triumph. At last then she was snatching from her rival the lover of whom she had so long been jealous!

'You wretched girl!' stammered Eve, wounded in the heart and almost sinking to the floor. 'You don't know what you say or what you make me suffer.'

However, she again had to pause, draw herself erect, and smile; for Rosemonde and Hyacinthe hastened in from the adjoining room with the news that she was wanted downstairs. The doors were about to be opened, and it was necessary she should be at her stall. Yes, Eve answered, she would be down in another moment. Still even as she spoke she leant more heavily on the pier-table behind her in order that she might not fall.

Hyacinthe had drawn near to his sister: 'You know,' said he, 'it's simply idiotic to quarrel like that. You would do much better to come downstairs.'

But Camille harshly dismissed him: 'Just *you* go off, and take the others with you. It's quite as well that they shouldn't be about our ears.'

Hyacinthe glanced at his mother, like one who knew the truth and considered the whole affair ridiculous. And then, vexed at seeing her so deficient in energy in dealing with that little pest his sister, he shrugged his shoulders, and leaving them to their folly, conducted the others away. One could hear Rosemonde laughing as she went off below, while the General, descending the stairs with Madame Fonsègue, began to tell her another story. However, at the moment when the mother and daughter at last fancied themselves alone once more, other voices reached their ears, those of Duvillard and Fonsègue, who were still near at hand. The Baron from his room might well overhear the dispute.

Eve felt that she ought to have gone off. But she had lacked the strength to do so; it had been a sheer impossibility for her after those words which had smote her like a buffet amidst her distress at the thought of losing her lover.

'Gérard cannot marry you,' she said, 'he does not love you.'

'He does.'

'You fancy it because he has good-naturedly shown some kindness to you, on seeing others pay you such little attention. But he does not love you.'

'He does. He loves me first because I'm not such a fool as many others are, and particularly because I'm young.'

This was a fresh wound for the Baroness; one inflicted with mocking cruelty in which rang out all the daughter's triumphant delight at seeing her mother's beauty at last ripening and waning. 'Ah! my poor mamma, you no longer know what it is to be young. If I'm not beautiful, at all events I'm young; my eyes are clear and my lips are fresh. And my hair's so long too, and I've so much of it that it would suffice to gown me if I chose. You see, one's never ugly when one's young. Whereas, my poor mamma, everything is ended when one gets old. It's all very well for a woman to have been beautiful, and to strive to keep so, but in reality there's only ruin left, and shame, and disgust.'

She spoke those words in such a sharp, ferocious voice that each of them entered her mother's heart like a knife. Tears rose to the eyes of the wretched woman, again stricken in her bleeding wound. Ah! it was true, she remained without weapons against youth. And all her anguish came from the consciousness that she was growing old, from the feeling that love was departing from her now that like a fruit she had ripened and fallen from the tree.

'But Gérard's mother will never let him marry you,' she said.

'He will prevail on her, that's his concern. I've a dowry of two millions, and two millions can settle many things.'

'Do you now want to libel him, and say that he's marrying you for your money?'

'No, indeed! Gérard's a very nice and honest fellow. He loves me and he's marrying me for myself. But, after all, he isn't rich, he still has no assured position, although he's thirty-six; and there may well be some advantage in a wife who brings you wealth as well as happiness. For, you hear, mamma, it's happiness I'm bringing him, real happiness, love that's shared and is certain of the future.'

Once again their faces drew close together. The hateful scene, interrupted by sounds around them, postponed, and then resumed, was dragging on, becoming a perfect drama full of murderous violence, although they never shouted, but spoke the whole time in low and gasping voices. Neither gave way to the other, though at every moment they were liable to some surprise; for as all the doors were open, the servants might come in, and moreover the Baron's voice still rang out gaily, close at hand.

'He loves you, he loves you'—continued Eve. 'That's what you say. But *he* never told you so.'

'He has told me so twenty times, he repeats it every time that we are alone together!'

'Yes, just as one says it to a little girl by way of amusing her. But he has never told you that he meant to marry you.'

'He told it me the last time he came. And it's settled. I'm simply waiting for him to get his mother's consent and make his formal offer.'

'You lie, you lie, you wretched girl! You simply want to make me suffer, and you lie, you lie!'

Eve's grief at last burst forth in that cry of protest. She no longer knew that she was a mother, and was speaking to her daughter. The woman, the *amorosa*, alone remained in her, outraged and exasperated by a rival. And with a sob she confessed the truth: 'It is I he loves! Only the last time I spoke to him, he swore to me—you hear me?—he swore upon his honour that he did not love you, and that he would never marry you!'

A faint, sharp laugh came from Camille. Then, with an air of derisive compassion, she replied: 'Ah! my poor mamma, you really make me sorry for you! What a child you are! Yes, really, you are the child, not I. What! you who ought to have so much experience, you still allow your-

self to be duped by a man's protests! That one really has
no malice; and, indeed, that's why he swears whatever you
want him to swear, just to please and quiet you, for at heart
he's a little bit of a coward.'

'You lie, you lie!'

'But just think matters over. If he no longer comes
here, if he didn't come to lunch this morning, it is simply
because he's had enough of you. He has left you for good,
just have the courage to realise it. Of course he's still polite
and amiable, because he's a well-bred man, and doesn't know
how to break off. The fact is that he takes pity on you.'

'You lie, you lie!'

'Well, question him then. Have a frank explanation with
him. Ask him his intentions in a friendly way. And then
show some good-nature yourself, and realise that if you care
for him you ought to give him me at once in his own interest.
Give him back his liberty, and you will soon see that I'm the
one he loves.'

'You lie, you lie! You wretched child, you only want to
torture and kill me!'

Then, in her fury and distress, Eve remembered that she was
the mother, and that it was for her to chastise that unworthy
daughter. There was no stick near her, but from a basket of
the yellow roses, whose powerful scent intoxicated both of
them, she plucked a handful of blooms, with long and spiny
stalks, and smote Camille across the face. A drop of blood
appeared on the girl's left temple, near her eyelid.

But she sprang forward, flushed and maddened by this
correction, with her hand raised, and ready to strike back.
'Take care, mother! I swear I'd beat you like a gipsy! And
now just put this into your head: I mean to marry Gérard,
and I will; and I'll take him from you, even if I have to
raise a scandal, should you refuse to give him to me with
good grace.'

Eve, after her one act of angry vigour, had sunk into an
armchair, overcome, distracted. And all the horror of
quarrels, which sprang from her egotistical desire to be happy,
caressed, flattered, and adored, was returning to her. But
Camille, still threatening, still unsatiated, showed her heart
as it really was, her stern, black, unforgiving heart, intoxicated with cruelty. There came a moment of supreme
silence, while Duvillard's gay voice again rang out in the
adjoining room.

The mother was gently weeping, when Hyacinthe, coming upstairs at a run, swept into the little *salon*. He looked at the two women, and made a gesture of indulgent contempt. 'Ah! you're no doubt satisfied now! But what did I tell you? It would have been much better for you to have come downstairs at once! Everybody is asking for you. It's all idiotic. I've come to fetch you.'

Eve and Camille would not yet have followed him, perhaps, if Duvillard and Fonsègue had not at that moment come out of the former's room. Having finished their cigars they also spoke of going downstairs. And Eve had to rise and smile and show dry eyes, while Camille, standing before a looking-glass, arranged her hair, and stanched the little drop of blood that had gathered on her temple, with her handkerchief.

There was already quite a number of people below, in the three huge saloons adorned with tapestry and plants. The stalls had been draped with red silk, which set a gay, bright glow around the goods. And no ordinary bazaar could have put forth such a show, for there was something of everything among the articles of a thousand different kinds, from sketches by recognised masters, and the autographs of famous writers, down to socks, pins, and combs. The haphazard way in which things were laid out was in itself an attraction; and, in addition, there was a buffet, where the whitest of beautiful hands poured out champagne, and two lotteries, one for an organ and another for a pony-drawn village cart, the tickets for which were sold by a bevy of charming girls, who had scattered through the throng. As Duvillard had expected, however, the great success of the bazaar lay in the delightful little shiver which the beautiful ladies experienced as they passed through the entrance where the bomb had exploded. The rougher repairing work was finished, the walls and ceilings had been doctored, in part reconstructed. However, the painters had not yet come, and here and there white patches of stone and plaster work showed like fresh scars left by all the terrible gashes. It was with mingled anxiety and rapture, that pretty heads emerged from the carriages which, arriving in a continuous stream, made the flagstones of the court re-echo. In the three saloons, beside the stalls, there was no end to the lively chatter: 'Ah! my dear, did you see all those marks? How frightful! The whole house was almost blown up. And to think it might begin again while we are here! One really needs some courage to come, but then, that asylum is such a deserving institution, and money is badly wanted to build a new wing. And besides, those monsters will see that we are not frightened, whatever they do.'

When the Baroness at last came down to her stall with Camille she found the saleswomen feverishly at work already under the direction of Princess Rosemonde, who on occasions of this kind evinced the greatest cunning and rapacity, robbing her customers in the most impudent fashion. 'Ah! here you are,' she exclaimed. 'Beware of a number of higglers who have come to secure bargains. I know them! They watch for their opportunities, turn everything topsy-turvy and wait for us to lose our heads and forget prices, so as to pay even less than they would in a real shop. But I'll get good prices from them, you shall see!'

At this, Eve, who for her own part was a most incapable saleswoman, had to laugh with the others. And in a gentle voice she made a pretence of addressing certain recommendations to Camille, who listened with a smiling and most submissive air. In point of fact the wretched mother was sinking with emotion, particularly at the thought that she would have to remain there till seven o'clock, and suffer in secret before all those people, without possibility of relief. And thus it was almost like a respite when she suddenly perceived Abbé Froment sitting and waiting for her on a settee, covered with red velvet, near her stall. Her legs were failing her, so she took a place beside him.

'You received my letter then, Monsieur l'Abbé. I am glad that you have come, for I have some good news to give you, and wished to leave you the pleasure of imparting it to your *protégé*, that man Laveuve, whom you so warmly recommended to me. Every formality has now been fulfilled, and you can bring him to the Asylum to-morrow.'

Pierre gazed at her in stupefaction. 'Laveuve? Why, he is dead!'

In her turn she became astonished. 'What, dead! But you never informed me of it! If I told you of all the trouble that has been taken, of all that had to be undone and done again, and the discussions, and the papers and the writing! Are you quite sure that he is dead?'

'Oh! yes, he is dead. He has been dead a month.'

'Dead a month! Well, we could not know, you yourself

gave us no sign of life. Ah! good heavens! what a worry that he should be dead. We shall now be obliged to undo everything again!'

'He is dead, madame. It is true that I ought to have informed you of it. But that doesn't alter the fact—he is dead.'

Dead! that word which kept on returning, the thought too that for a month past she had been busying herself for a corpse, quite froze her, brought her to the very depths of despair like an omen of the cold death into which she herself must soon descend, in the shroud of her last passion. And, meantime, Pierre, despite himself, smiled bitterly at the atrocious irony of it all. Ah! that lame and halting Charity, which proffers help when men are dead!

The priest still lingered on the settee when the Baroness rose. She had seen magistrate Amadieu hurriedly enter, as if he wished just to show himself, purchase some trifle or other and then return to the Palace of Justice. However, he was also perceived by little Massot, the 'Globe' reporter, who was prowling round the stalls, and who at once bore down upon him, eager for information. And he hemmed him in and forthwith interviewed him respecting the affair of that mechanician Salvat, who was accused of having deposited the bomb at the entrance of the house. Was this simply an invention of the police, as some newspapers pretended? Or was it really correct? And if so would Salvat soon be arrested? In self-defence Amadieu answered correctly enough that the affair did not as yet concern him; and would only come within his attributions if Salvat should be arrested and the investigation placed in his hands. At the same time, the air of pomposity and shrewdness which the magistrate assumed suggested that he already knew everything to the smallest details, and that, had he chosen, he could have promised some great events for the morrow. A circle of ladies had gathered round him as he spoke; quite a number of pretty women, feverish with curiosity, jostling one another in their eagerness to hear that brigand tale which sent a little shiver coursing under their skins. However, Amadieu managed to slip off after paying Rosemonde twenty francs for a cigarette case, which was perhaps worth thirty sous.

Massot, on recognising Pierre, came up to shake hands with him. 'Don't you agree with me, Monsieur l'Abbé,

that Salvat must be a long way off by now if he's got good
legs? Ah! the police will always make me laugh!'

However, Rosemonde brought Hyacinthe up to the
journalist. 'Monsieur Massot,' said she, 'you who go everywhere, I want you to be judge. That Chamber of Horrors
at Montmartre, that tavern where Legras sings the "Flowers
of the Pavement" '——

'Oh! a delightful spot, madame,' interrupted Massot, 'I
wouldn't take even a gendarme there.'

'No, don't jest, Monsieur Massot, I'm talking seriously.
Isn't it quite allowable for a respectable woman to go there
when she's accompanied by a gentleman?' And, without
allowing the journalist time to answer her she turned towards Hyacinthe: 'There! you see that Monsieur Massot
doesn't say no! You've got to take me there this evening,
it's sworn, it's sworn.'

Then she darted away to sell a packet of pins to an old
lady, while the young man contented himself with remarking in
the voice of one who has no illusions left: 'She's quite
idiotic with her Chamber of Horrors!'

Massot philosophically shrugged his shoulders. It was
only natural that a woman should want to amuse herself.
And when Hyacinthe had gone off, passing with perverse
contempt beside the lovely girls who were selling lottery
tickets, the journalist ventured to murmur: 'All the same,
it would do that youngster good if a woman were to take him
in hand.'

Then, again addressing Pierre, he resumed: 'Why here
comes Duthil! What did Sagnier mean this morning by
saying that Duthil would sleep at Mazas to-night?'

In a great hurry apparently, and all smiles, Duthil was
cleaving his way through the crowd in order to join Duvillard
and Fonsègue, who still stood talking near the Baroness's
stall. And he waved his hand to them in a victorious way,
to imply that he had succeeded in the delicate mission entrusted to him. This was nothing less than a bold manœuvre
to hasten Silviane's admission to the Comédie Française.
The idea had occurred to her of making the Baron give a
dinner at the Café Anglais in order that she might meet at it
an influential critic, who, according to her statements, would
compel the authorities to throw the doors wide open for her as
soon as he should know her. It did not seem easy, however,
to secure the critic's presence, as he was noted for his stern

and grumbling disposition. And, indeed, after a first repulse, Duthil had for three days past been obliged to exert all his powers of diplomacy, and bring even the remotest influence into play. But he was radiant now, for he had conquered.

'It's for this evening, my dear Baron, at half-past seven,' he exclaimed. 'Ah! dash it all, I've had more trouble than I should have had to secure a concession vote!' Then he laughed with the pretty impudence of a man of pleasure, whom political conscientiousness did not trouble. And, indeed, his allusion to the fresh denunciations of the 'Voix du Peuple' hugely amused him.

'Don't jest,' muttered Fonsègue, who for his part wished to divert himself by frightening the young deputy. 'Things are going very badly!'

Duthil turned pale, and a vision of the police and Mazas rose before his eyes. In this wise abject terror came over him from time to time. However, with his lack of all moral sense, he soon felt reassured and began to laugh. 'Oh!' he retorted gaily, winking towards Duvillard, 'the governor's there to pilot the barque!'

The Baron, who was extremely pleased, had pressed his hands, thanked him, and called him an obliging fellow. And now turning towards Fonsègue he exclaimed: 'I say, you must make one of us this evening. Oh! it's necessary. I want something imposing round Silviane. Duthil will represent the Chamber, you journalism, and I finance——' But he suddenly paused on seeing Gérard, who, with a somewhat grave expression, was leisurely picking his way through the sea of skirts. 'Gérard, my friend,' exclaimed the Baron after beckoning to him, 'I want you to do me a service.' And forthwith he told him what was in question; how the influential critic had been prevailed upon to attend a dinner which would decide Silviane's future; and how it was the duty of all her friends to rally round her.

'But I can't,' the young man answered in embarrassment. 'I have to dine at home with my mother, who was rather poorly this morning.'

'Oh! a sensible woman like your mother will readily understand that there are matters of exceptional importance. Go home and excuse yourself. Tell her some story, tell her that a friend's happiness is in question.' And as Gérard began to weaken, Duvillard added: 'The fact is that I really want you, my dear fellow; I must have a society man.

Society, you know, is a great force in theatrical matters; and if Silviane has society with her, her triumph is certain.'

Gérard promised, and then chatted for a moment with his uncle, General de Bozonnet, who was quite enlivened by that throng of women, among whom he had been carried hither and thither like an old rudderless ship. After acknowledging the amiability with which Madame Fonsègue had listened to his stories, by purchasing an autograph of Monseigneur Martha from her for a hundred francs, he had quite lost himself amid the bevy of girls who had passed him on, one to another. And now, on his return from them, he had his hands full of lottery tickets: 'Ah! my fine fellow,' said he, 'I don't advise you to venture among all those young persons. You would have to part with your last copper. But, just look! there's Mademoiselle Camille beckoning to you!'

Camille, indeed, from the moment she had perceived Gérard, had been smiling at him and awaiting his approach. And when their glances met he was obliged to go to her, although, at the same moment, he felt that Eve's despairing and entreating eyes were fixed upon him. The girl, who fully realised that her mother was watching her, at once made a marked display of amiability, profiting by the licence which charitable fervour authorised, to slip a variety of little articles into the young man's pockets, and then place others in his hands, which she pressed within her own, showing the while all the sparkle of youth, and indulging in fresh, merry laughter, which quite tortured her rival.

So extreme was Eve's suffering, that she wished to intervene and part them. But it so chanced that Pierre barred her way, for he wished to submit an idea to her before leaving the bazaar. 'Madame,' said he, 'since that man Laveuve is dead, and you have taken so much trouble with regard to the bed which you now have vacant, will you be so good as to keep it vacant until I have seen our venerable friend, Abbé Rose? I am to see him this evening, and he knows so many cases of want, and would be so glad to relieve one of them, and bring you some poor *protégé* of his.'

'Yes, certainly,' stammered the Baroness, 'I shall be very happy—I will wait a little, as you desire—of course, of course, Monsieur l'Abbé.'

She was trembling all over, she no longer knew what she was saying; and, unable to conquer her passion, she turned aside from the priest, unaware even that he was still there, when Gérard, yielding to the dolorous entreaty of her eyes, at last managed to escape from Camille and join her.

'What a stranger you are becoming, my friend!' she said aloud, with a forced smile. 'One never sees you now.'

'Why, I have been poorly,' he replied, in his amiable way. 'Yes, I assure you I have been ailing a little.'

He, ailing! She looked at him with maternal anxiety, quite upset. And, indeed, however proud and lofty his figure, his handsome regular face did seem to her paler than usual. It was as if the nobility of the façade had, in some degree, ceased to hide the irreparable dilapidation within. And given his real good-nature, it must have been true that he suffered— suffered by reason of his useless, wasted life, on account of all the money he cost his impoverished mother, and of the needs that were at last driving him to marry that wealthy deformed girl, whom at first he had merely pitied. And so weak did he seem to Eve, so like a piece of wreckage tossed hither and thither by a tempest, that, at the risk of being overheard by the throng, she let her heart flow forth in a low but ardent, entreating murmur: 'If you suffer, ah! what sufferings are mine!—Gérard we must see one another, I will have it so.'

'No, I beg you, let us wait,' he stammered in embarrassment.

'It must be, Gérard: Camille has told me your plans. You cannot refuse to see me. I insist on it.'

He made yet another attempt to escape the cruel explanation. 'But it's impossible at the usual place,' he answered quivering. 'The address is known.'

'Then to-morrow, at four o'clock, at that little restaurant in the Bois where we have met before.'

He had to promise, and they parted. Camille had just turned her head and was looking at them. Moreover, quite a number of women had besieged the stall; and the Baroness began to attend to them with the air of a ripe and nonchalant goddess, while Gérard rejoined Duvillard, Fonsègue and Duthil, who were quite excited at the prospect of their dinner that evening.

Pierre had heard a part of the conversation between Gérard and the Baroness. He knew what skeletons the house concealed, what physiological and moral torture and wretchedness lay beneath all the dazzling wealth and power. There was here an envenomed, bleeding sore, ever spreading, a cancer eating into father, mother, daughter, and son, who one

and all had thrown social bonds aside. However, the priest
made his way out of the *salons*, half stifling amidst the
throng of lady-purchasers who were making quite a triumph
of the bazaar. And yonder, in the depths of the gloom he
could picture Salvat running and running on till he disappeared from sight; while the corpse of Laveuve seemed to
him like a buffet of atrocious irony dealt to noisy and delu-
sive charity.

· II

SPIRIT AND FLESH

How delightful was the quietude of the little ground floor
overlooking a strip of garden in the Rue Cortot, where
good Abbé Rose resided! Hereabouts there was not even a
rumble of wheels, or an echo of the panting breath of Paris,
which one heard on the other side of the height of Montmartre. The deep silence and sleepy peacefulness were
suggestive of some distant provincial town.

Seven o'clock had struck, the dusk had gathered slowly,
and Pierre was in the humble dining-room, waiting for the
femme-de-ménage to place the soup upon the table. Abbé
Rose, anxious at having seen so little of him for a month
past, had written asking him to come to dinner, in order that
they might have a quiet chat concerning their affairs. From
time to time Pierre still gave his friend money for charitable
purposes; in fact, ever since the days of the asylum in the
Rue de Charonne, they had had accounts together, which
they periodically settled. So that evening after dinner they
were to talk of it all, and see if they could not do even
more than they had hitherto done. The good old priest was
quite radiant at the thought of the peaceful evening
which he was about to spend in attending to the affairs of
his beloved poor; for therein lay his only amusement, the
sole pleasure to which he persistently and passionately returned, in spite of all the worries that his inconsiderate
charity had already so often brought him.

Glad to be able to procure his friend this pleasure, Pierre,
on his side, grew calmer, and found relief and momentary
repose in sharing the other's simple repast and yielding to all
the kindliness around him, far from his usual worries. He

remembered the vacant bed at the Asylum, which Baroness
Duvillard had promised to keep in reserve until he should
have asked Abbé Rose if he knew of any case of destitution
particularly worthy of interest; and so before sitting down
to table he spoke of the matter.

'Destitution worthy of interest!' replied Abbé Rose,
'ah! my dear child, every case is worthy of interest. And
when it's a question of old toilers without work the only
trouble is that of selection, the anguish of choosing one and
leaving so many others in distress.' Nevertheless, painful
though his scruples were, he strove to think and come to some
decision. 'I know the case which will suit you,' he said at
last. 'It's certainly one of the greatest suffering and
wretchedness; and, so humble a one, too—an old carpenter
of seventy-five, who has been living on public charity during
the eight or ten years that he has been unable to find work.
I don't know his name, everybody calls him "the big Old'un."
There are times when he does not come to my Saturday
distributions for weeks together. We shall have to look for
him at once. I think that he sleeps at the Night Refuge in
the Rue d'Orsel when lack of room there doesn't force him
to spend the night crouching behind some palings. Shall we
go down the Rue d'Orsel this evening?'

Abbé Rose's eyes beamed brightly as he spoke, for this
proposal of his signified a great debauch, the tasting of
forbidden fruit. He had been reproached so often and so
roughly with his visits to those who had fallen to the deepest
want and misery, that in spite of his overflowing, apostolic
compassion, he now scarcely dared to go near them. However,
he continued: 'Is it agreed, my child? Only this once?
Besides, it is our only means of finding the big Old'un. You
won't have to stop with me later than eleven. And I should
so like to show you all that! You will see what terrible
sufferings there are! And perhaps we may be fortunate
enough to relieve some poor creature or other.'

Pierre smiled at the juvenile ardour displayed by this old
man with snowy hair. 'It's agreed, my dear Abbé,' he
responded, 'I shall be very pleased to spend my whole evening
with you, for I feel it will do me good to follow you once more
on one of those rambles which used to fill our hearts with
grief and joy.'

At this moment the servant brought in the soup; however,
just as the two priests were taking their seats a discreet ring

was heard, and when Abbé Rose learnt that the visitor was a neighbour, Madame Mathis, who had come for an answer, he gave orders that she should be shown in.

'This poor woman,' he explained to Pierre, 'needed an advance of ten francs to get a mattress out of pawn ; and I didn't have the money by me at the time. But I've since procured it. She lives in the house, you know, in silent poverty, on so small an income that it hardly keeps her in bread.'

'But hasn't she a big son of twenty ?' asked Pierre, suddenly remembering the young man he had seen at Salvat's.

'Yes, yes. Her parents, I believe, were rich people in the provinces. I've been told that she married a music master, who gave her lessons, at Nantes ; and who ran away with her and brought her to Paris, where he died. It was quite a doleful love-story. By selling the furniture and realising every little thing she possessed, she scraped together an income of about two thousand francs a year, with which she was able to send her son to college and live decently herself. But a fresh blow fell on her ; she lost the greater part of her little fortune, which was invested in doubtful securities. So now her income amounts at the utmost to eight hundred francs ; two hundred of which she has to expend in rent. For all her other wants she has to be content with fifty francs a month. About eighteen months ago her son left her so as not to be a burden on her, and he is trying to earn his living somewhere, but without success, I believe.'

Madame Mathis, a short, dark woman, with a sad, gentle, retiring face, came in. Invariably clad in the same black gown, she showed all the anxious timidity of a poor creature whom the storms of life perpetually assailed. When Abbé Rose had handed her the ten francs discreetly wrapped in paper, she blushed and thanked him, promising to pay him back as soon as she received her month's money, for she was not a beggar and did not wish to encroach on the share of those who starved.

'And your son, Victor, has he found any employment ?' asked the old priest.

She hesitated, ignorant as she was of what her son might be doing, for nowadays she did not see him for weeks together. And finally, she contented herself with answering : 'He has a good heart, he is very fond of me. It is a great misfortune that we should have been ruined before he could enter the

École Normale. It was impossible for him to prepare for the examination. But at the Lycée he was such a diligent and intelligent pupil!'

'You lost your husband when your son was ten years old, did you not?' said Abbé Rose.

At this she blushed again, thinking that her husband's story was known to the two priests. 'Yes, my poor husband never had any luck,' she said. 'His difficulties embittered and excited his mind, and he died in prison. He was sent there through a disturbance at a public meeting, when he had the misfortune to wound a police officer. He had also fought at the time of the Commune. And yet he was a very gentle man and extremely fond of me.'

Tears had risen to her eyes; and Abbé Rose, much touched, dismissed her: 'Well, let us hope that your son will give you satisfaction, and be able to repay you for all you have done for him.'

With a gesture of infinite sorrow, Madame Mathis discreetly withdrew. She was quite ignorant of her son's doings, but fate had pursued her so relentlessly that she ever trembled.

'I don't think that the poor woman has much to expect from her son,' said Pierre, when she had gone, 'I only saw him once, but the gleam in his eyes was as harsh and trenchant as that of a knife.'

'Do you think so?' the old priest exclaimed, with his kindly *naïveté*. 'Well, he seemed to me very polite, perhaps a trifle eager to enjoy life; but, then, all the young folks are impatient nowadays. Come, let us sit down to table, for the soup will be cold.'

Almost at the same hour, on the other side of Paris, night had in like fashion slowly fallen in the drawing-room of the Countess de Quinsac, on the dismal, silent ground-floor of an old mansion in the Rue St. Dominique. The Countess was there, alone with her faithful friend, the Marquis de Morigny, she on one side, and he on the other side of the chimney-piece, where the last embers of the wood fire were dying out. The servant had not yet brought the lamp, and the Countess refrained from ringing, finding some relief from her anxiety in the falling darkness, which hid from view all the unconfessed thoughts that she was afraid she might show on her weary face. And it was only now, before that dim hearth, and in that black room, where never a sound of wheels disturbed the silence of the slumberous past, that she dared to speak.

'Yes, my friend,' she said, 'I am not satisfied with Gérard's health. You will see him yourself, for he promised to come home early and dine with me. Oh! I'm well aware that he looks big and strong; but to know him properly one must have nursed and watched him as I have done! What trouble I had to rear him! In reality he is at the mercy of any petty ailment. His slightest complaint becomes serious illness. And the life he leads does not conduce to good health.'

She paused and sighed, hesitating to carry her confession further.

'He leads the life he can,' slowly responded the Marquis de Morigny, of whose delicate profile, and proud, yet loving bearing, little could be seen in the gloom. 'As he was unable to endure military life, and as even the fatigues of diplomacy frighten you, what would you have him do? He can only live apart pending the final collapse, while this abominable Republic is dragging France to the grave.'

'No doubt, my friend. And yet it is just that idle life which frightens me. He is losing in it all that was good and healthy in him. I don't refer merely to the *liaisons* which we have had to tolerate. The last one, which I found so much difficulty in countenancing at the outset, so contrary did it seem to all my ideas and beliefs, has since seemed to me to exercise almost a good influence. Only he is now entering his thirty-sixth year, and can he continue living in this fashion without object or duties? If he is ailing it is perhaps precisely because he does nothing, holds no position, and serves no purpose.' Her voice again quavered. 'And then, my friend, since you force me to tell you everything, I must own that I am not in good health myself. I have had several fainting fits of late, and have consulted a doctor. The truth is, that I may go off at any moment.'

With a quiver, Morigny leant forward in the still deepening gloom, and tried to take hold of her hands. 'You! what, am I to lose you, my last affection!' he faltered, 'I who have seen the old world I belong to crumble away, I who only live in the hope that you at all events will still be here to close my eyes!'

But she begged him not to increase her grief: 'No, no, don't take my hands, don't kiss them! Remain there in the shade, where I can scarcely see you. . . . We have loved one another so long without aught to cause shame or regret; and that will prove our strength—our divine strength—till we reach the grave. . . . And if you were to touch me, if I were to feel you too near me I could not finish, for I have not done so yet.'

As soon as he had relapsed into silence and immobility, she continued: 'If I were to die to-morrow, Gérard would not even find here the little fortune which he still fancies is in my hands. The dear child has often cost me large sums of money without apparently being conscious of it. I ought to have been more severe, more prudent. But what would you have? Ruin is at hand, I have always been too weak a mother. And do you now understand in what anguish I live? I ever have the thought that if I die Gérard will not even possess enough to live on, for he is incapable of effecting the miracle which I renew each day, in order to keep the house up on a decent footing. . . . Ah! I know him, so supine, so sickly, in spite of his proud bearing, unable to do anything, even conduct himself. And so what will become of him, will he not fall into the most dire distress?'

Then her tears flowed freely, her heart opened and bled, for she foresaw what must happen after her death: the collapse of her race and of a whole world in the person of that big child. And the Marquis, still motionless but distracted, feeling that he had no title to offer his own fortune, suddenly understood her, foresaw in what disgrace this fresh disaster would culminate.

'Ah! my poor friend!' he said at last in a voice trembling with revolt and grief. 'So you have agreed to that marriage —yes, that abominable marriage with that woman's daughter! Yet you swore it should never be! You would rather witness the collapse of everything, you said. And now you are consenting, I can feel it!'

She still wept on in that black, silent drawing-room before the chimney-piece where the fire had died out. Did not Gérard's marriage to Camille mean a happy ending for herself, a certainty of leaving her son wealthy, loved, and seated at the banquet of life? However, a last feeling of rebellion arose within her. 'No, no,' she exclaimed, 'I don't consent, I swear to you that I don't consent as yet. I am fighting with my whole strength, waging an incessant battle, the torture of which you cannot imagine.'

Then, in all sincerity, she foresaw the likelihood of defeat.
'If I should some day give way, my friend, at all events
believe that I feel, as fully as you do, how abominable such a
marriage must be. It will be the end of our race and our
honour !'

This cry profoundly stirred the Marquis, and he was unable
to add a word. Haughty and uncompromising Catholic and
Royalist that he was, he, on his side also, expected nothing but
the supreme collapse. Yet how heart-rending was the
thought that this noble woman, so dearly and so purely loved,
would prove one of the victims of the catastrophe ! And
in the shrouding gloom he found courage to kneel before
her, take her hand, and kiss it.

Just as the servant was at last bringing a lighted lamp
Gérard made his appearance. The past-century charm of the
old Louis XVI. drawing-room, with its pale woodwork, again
became apparent in the soft light. In order that his mother
might not be over-saddened by his failure to dine with her
that evening the young man had put on an air of brisk
gaiety ; and when he had explained that some friends were
waiting for him, she at once released him from his promise,
happy as she felt at seeing him so merry.

'Go, go, my dear boy,' said she, 'but mind you do not tire
yourself too much. . . . I am going to keep Morigny ; and the
General and Larombière are coming at nine o'clock. So be
easy, I shall have someone with me, to keep me from fretting
and feeling lonely.'

In this wise Gérard after sitting down for a moment and
chatting with the Marquis was able to slip away, dress and
betake himself to the Café Anglais.

When he reached it women in fur cloaks were already
climbing the stairs, fashionable and merry parties were filling
the private rooms, the electric lights shone brilliantly, and
the walls vibrated with the stir of feverish pleasure and
debauchery. In the room which Baron Duvillard had
engaged the young man found an extraordinary display, the
most superb flowers, and a profusion of plate and crystal as
for a royal gala. The pomp with which the six covers were
laid called forth a smile ; while the bill of fare and the
wine-list promised marvels, all the rarest and most expensive
things that could be selected.

'It's stylish, isn't it ?' exclaimed Silviane, who was already
there with Duvillard, Fonsègue and Duthil. 'I just wanted

to make your influential critic open his eyes a little ! When one treats a journalist to such a dinner as this, he has got to be amiable, hasn't he ? '

In her desire to conquer it had occurred to the young woman to array herself in the most amazing fashion. Her gown of yellow satin, covered with old Alençon lace, was cut low at the neck ; and she had put on all her diamonds, a necklace, a diadem, shoulder-knots, bracelets and rings. With her candid, girlish face, she looked like some Virgin in a missal, a Queen-Virgin, laden with the offerings of all Christendom.

' Well, well, you look so pretty,' said Gérard, who sometimes jested with her, ' that I think it will do all the same.'

' Ah ! ' she replied with equanimity. ' You consider me a bit vulgar, I see. Your opinion is that a simple little dinner and a modest gown would have shown better taste. But ah ! my dear fellow, you don't know the way to get round men ! '

Duvillard signified his approval, for he was delighted to be able to show her in all her glory, adorned like an idol. Fonsègue, for his part, talked of diamonds, saying that they were now doubtful investments, as the day when they would become articles of current manufacture was fast approaching, thanks to the electrical furnace and other inventions. Meantime Duthil, with an air of ecstasy and the dainty gestures of a lady's maid, hovered around the young woman, either smoothing a rebellious bow or arranging some fold of her lace.

' But I say,' resumed Silviane, ' your critic seems to be an ill-bred man, for he's keeping us waiting.'

Indeed, the critic arrived a quarter of an hour late, and while apologising, he expressed his regret that he should be obliged to leave at half-past nine, for he was absolutely compelled to put in an appearance at a little theatre in the Rue Pigalle. He was a big fellow of fifty with broad shoulders and a full, bearded face. His most disagreeable characteristic was the narrow dogmatic pedantry which he had acquired at the École Normale, and had never since been able to shake off. All his herculean efforts to be sceptical and frivolous, and the twenty years he had spent in Paris mingling with every section of society, had failed to rid him of it. *Magister* he was, and *magister* he remained, even in his most strenuous flights of imagination and audacity. From the moment of his arrival he tried to show himself enraptured with Silviane. Naturally enough, he already knew her by sight, and had even criticised her on one occasion in five or six contemptuous lines. However, the sight of her there, in full beauty, clad like a queen, and presented by four influential protectors, filled him with emotion; and he was struck with the idea that nothing would be more Parisian and less pedantic than to assert she had some talent and give her his support.

They had seated themselves at table, and the repast proved a magnificent one, the service ever prompt and assiduous, an attendant being allotted to each diner. While the flowers scattered perfume through the room, and the plate and crystal glittered on the snowy cloth, an abundance of delicious and unexpected dishes was handed round—a sturgeon from Russia, prohibited game, truffles as big as eggs, and hothouse fruit as full of flavour as if it were naturally matured. It was money flung out of window, simply for the pleasure of wasting more than other people, and eating what they could not procure. The influential critic, though he displayed the ease of a man accustomed to every sort of festivity, really felt astonished at it all, and became servile, promising his support, and pledging himself far more than he really wished to. Moreover, he showed himself very gay, found some witty remarks to repeat, and even some rather ribald jests. But when the champagne appeared after the roast and the grand burgundies, his over-excitement brought him back perforce to his real nature. The conversation had now turned on Corneille's 'Polyeucte' and the part of 'Pauline,' in which Silviane wished to make her *début* at the Comédie Française. This extraordinary caprice, which had quite revolted the influential critic a week previously, now seemed to him simply a bold enterprise in which the young woman might even prove victorious if she consented to listen to his advice. And, once started, he delivered quite a lecture on the part, boldly asserting that no actress had ever yet understood it properly, for at the outset Pauline was simply a well-meaning little *bourgeoise*, and the beauty of her conversion at the finish arose from the working of a miracle, a stroke of heavenly grace which endowed her with something divine. This was not the opinion of Silviane, who from the first lines regarded Pauline as the ideal heroine of some symbolical legend. However, as the critic talked on and on,

she had to feign approval; and he was delighted at finding
her so beautiful and docile beneath his ferrule. At last, as
ten o'clock was striking, he rose and tore out of the hot and
reeking room in order to attend to his work.

'Ah! my dears,' cried Silviane, 'he's a nice bore is that
critic of yours! What a fool he is with his idea of Pauline
being a little *bourgeoise*! I would have given him a fine
dressing if it weren't for the fact that I have some need of
him. Ah! no, it's too idiotic! Pour me out a glass of champagne, I want something to set me right after all that!'

The *fête* then took quite an intimate turn between the
four men who remained and that bare-armed, bare-breasted
girl, covered with diamonds. From the neighbouring
passages and rooms came bursts of laughter and sounds of
kissing, all the stir and mirth of the debauchery now filling
the house; while beneath the windows torrents of vehicles
and pedestrians streamed along the Boulevards where reigned
the wild fever of pleasure and harlotry.

'No, don't open it, or I shall catch cold!' resumed
Silviane, addressing Fonsègue as he stepped towards the
window. 'Are you so very warm then? I'm just comfortable. . . . But, Duvillard, my good fellow, please order some
more champagne. It's wonderful what a thirst your critic has
given me!'

Amidst the blinding glare of the lamps and the perfume of
the flowers and wines, one almost stifled in the room. And
Silviane was seized with an irresistible desire for a spree, a
desire to tipple and amuse herself in some vulgar fashion, as
in her bygone days. A few glasses of champagne brought
her to full pitch, and she showed the boldest and giddiest
gaiety. The others, who had never before seen her so lively,
began on their side to feel much amused. As Fonsègue was
obliged to go to his office she embraced him 'like a daughter,'
as she expressed it. However, on remaining alone with the
others she indulged in great freedom of speech, which became
more and more marked as her intoxication increased. And
to the class of men with whom she consorted her great
attraction, as she was well aware, lay in the circumstance
that with her virginal countenance and her air of ideal purity
was coupled the most monstrous perversity ever displayed by
any shameless woman. Despite her innocent blue eyes and
lily-like candour, she would give rein, particularly when
she was drunk, to the most diabolical of fancies.

Duvillard let her drink on, but she guessed his thoughts, like she guessed those of the others, and simply smiled while concocting impossible stories and descanting fantastically in the language of the gutter. And seeing her there in her dazzling gown fit for a queenly virgin, and hearing her pour forth the vilest words, they thought her most wonderfully droll. However, when she had drunk as much champagne as she cared for and was half crazy, a novel idea suddenly occurred to her.

'I say, my children,' she exclaimed, 'we are surely not going to stop here. It's so precious slow! You shall take me to the Chamber of Horrors—eh? just to finish the evening. I want to hear Legras sing "La Chemise," that song which all Paris is running to hear him sing.'

But Duvillard indignantly rebelled: 'Oh! no,' said he; 'most certainly not. It's a vile song and I'll never take you to such an abominable place.'

However, she did not appear to hear him. She had already staggered to her feet and was arranging her hair before a looking-glass. 'I used to live at Montmartre,' she said, 'and it'll amuse me to go back there. And, besides, I want to find out if this Legras is a Legras that I knew, oh! ever so long ago! Come, up you get, and let us be off!'

'But my dear girl,' pleaded Duvillard, 'we can't take you into that den dressed as you are! Just fancy your entering that place in a low-necked gown and covered with diamonds! Why everyone would jeer at us! Come, Gérard, just tell her to be a little reasonable.'

Gérard, equally offended by the idea of such a freak, was quite willing to intervene. But she closed his mouth with her gloved hand and repeated with the gay obstinacy of intoxication: 'Pooh, it will be all the more amusing if they do jeer at us! Come, let us be off, let us be off, quick!'

Thereupon, Duthil who had been listening with a smile and the air of a man of pleasure whom nothing astonishes or displeases, gallantly took her part. 'But, my dear Baron, everybody goes to the Chamber of Horrors,' said he. 'Why I myself have taken the noblest ladies there, and precisely to hear that song of Legras, which is no worse than anything else.'

'Ah! you hear what Duthil says!' cried Silviane. 'He's

a deputy, he is, and he wouldn't go there if he thought it would compromise his honorability ! '

Then, as Duvillard still struggled on in despair at the idea of exhibiting himself with her in such a scandalous place, she became all the merrier : ' Well, my dear fellow, please yourself. I don't need you. You and Gérard can go home if you like. But I'm going to Montmartre with Duthil. You'll take charge of me, won't you, Duthil, eh ? '

However, the Baron was in no wise disposed to let the evening finish in that fashion. The mere idea of it gave him a shock, and he had to resign himself to the girl's stubborn caprice. The only consolation he could think of was to secure Gérard's presence, for the young man, with some lingering sense of decorum still obstinately refused to make one of the party. So the Baron took his hands and detained him, repeating in urgent tones that he begged him to come as an essential mark of friendship. And at last the wife's lover and daughter's sister had to give way to the man who was the former's husband and the latter's father.

Silviane was immensely amused by it all, and, indiscreetly thee-ing and thou-ing Gérard, suggested that he at least owed the Baron some little compliance with his wishes.

Duvillard pretended not to hear her. He was listening to Duthil, who told him that there was a sort of box in a corner of the Chamber of Horrors, in which one could in some measure conceal oneself. And then, as Silviane's carriage— a large closed landau, whose coachman, a sturdy handsome fellow, sat waiting impassively on his box—was down below, they started off.

The Chamber of Horrors was installed in premises on the Boulevard de Rochechouart, formerly occupied by a café whose proprietor had become bankrupt.[1] It was a suffocating place, narrow, irregular, with all sorts of twists, turns, and secluded nooks, and a low and smoky ceiling. And nothing could have been more rudimentary than its decorations. The walls had simply been placarded with posters of violent hues,

[1] Those who know Paris will identify the site selected by M. Zola as that where ' Colonel ' Lisbonne of the Commune installed his den the ' Bagne ' some years ago. However, such places as the ' Chamber of Horrors ' nowadays abound in the neighbourhood of Montmartre, and it must be admitted that whilst they are frequented by certain classes of Frenchmen they owe much of their success in a pecuniary sense to the patronage of foreigners. Among the latter, Englishmen are particularly conspicuous.—*Trans.*

some of the crudest character, showing the barest of female
figures. Behind a piano at one end there was a little platform reached by a curtained doorway. For the rest, one
simply found a number of bare wooden forms set alongside the veriest pot-house tables, on which the glasses
containing various beverages left round and sticky marks.
There was no luxury, no artistic feature, no cleanliness even.
Globeless gas burners flared freely, heating a dense mist
compounded of tobacco smoke and human breath. Perspiring, apoplectical faces could be perceived through this
veil, and an acrid odour increased the intoxication of the
assembly, which excited itself with louder and louder
shouts at each fresh song. It had been sufficient for an
enterprising fellow to set up these boards, bring out
Legras, accompanied by two or three girls, make him sing
his frantic and abominable songs, and in two or three
evenings overwhelming success had come, all Paris being
enticed and flocking to the place, which for ten years or so
had failed to pay as a mere café, where by way of amusement petty cits had been simply allowed their daily games
at dominoes.

And the change had been caused by the passion for filth,
the irresistible attraction exercised by all that brought
shame and disgust. The Paris of enjoyment, the *bourgeoisie* which held all wealth and power, which would
relinquish nought of either, though it was surfeited and
gradually wearying of both, simply hastened to the place in
order that obscenity and insult might be flung in its face.
Hypnotised, as it were, while staggering to its fall, it felt a
need of being spat upon. And what a frightful symptom
there lay in it all: those condemned ones rushing upon dirt
of their own accord, voluntarily hastening their own decomposition by that unquenchable thirst for the vile, which
attracted men, reputed to be grave and upright, and lovely
women of the most perfect grace and luxury, to all the beastli-
ness of that low den !

At one of the tables nearest the stage sat little Princess
Rosemonde de Harn, with wild eyes and quivering nostrils,
delighted as she felt at now being able to satisfy her curiosity
regarding the depths of Paris life. Young Hyacinthe had
resigned himself to the task of bringing her, and correctly
buttoned up in his long frock-coat, he was indulgent enough
to refrain from any marked expression of boredom. At a

neighbouring table they had found a shadowy Spaniard of their acquaintance, a so-called Bourse jobber, Bergaz, who had been introduced to the Princess by Janzen, and usually attended her entertainments. They virtually knew nothing about him, not even if he really earned at the Bourse all the money which he sometimes spent so lavishly, and which enabled him to dress with affected elegance. His slim, lofty figure was not without a certain air of distinction, but his red lips spoke of strong passions, and his bright eyes were those of a beast of prey. That evening he had two young fellows with him, one Rossi, a short, swarthy Italian, who had come to Paris as a painter's model, and had soon glided into the lazy life of certain disreputable callings, and the other, Sanfaute, a born Parisian blackguard, a pale, beardless, vicious and impudent stripling of La Chapelle, whose long, curly hair fell down upon either side of his bony cheeks.

'Oh ! pray now !' feverishly said Rosemonde to Bergaz ; ' as you seem to know all these horrid people, just show me some of the celebrities. Aren't there some thieves and murderers among them ? '

He laughed shrilly, and in a bantering way replied : ' But you know these people well enough, madame. That pretty, pink, delicate-looking woman over yonder is an American lady, the wife of a consul, whom, I believe, you receive at your house. That other on the right, that tall brunette who shows such queenly dignity, is a Countess, whose carriage passes yours every day in the Bois. And the thin one yonder, whose eyes glitter like those of a she-wolf, is the particular friend of a high official, who is well known for his reputation of austerity.'

But she stopped him, in vexation : 'I know, I know. But the others, those of the lower classes, those whom one comes to see.'

Then she went on asking questions, and seeking for terrifying and mysterious countenances. At last, two men seated in a corner ended by attracting her attention ; one of them a very young fellow with a pale, pinched face, and the other an ageless individual who, besides being buttoned up to his neck in an old coat, had pulled his cap so low over his eyes, that one saw little of his face beyond the beard which fringed it. Before these two stood a couple of mugs of beer, which they drank slowly and in silence.

'You are making a great mistake, my dear,' said Hyacinthe with a frank laugh, 'if you are looking for brigands in disguise. That poor fellow with the pale face, who surely doesn't have food to eat every day, was my schoolfellow at Condorcet!'

Bergaz expressed his amazement. 'What! you knew Mathis at Condorcet! After all, though, you're right, he received a college education. Ah! and so you know him. A very remarkable young man he is, though want is throttling him. But, I say, the other one, his companion, you don't know *him*?'

Hyacinthe, after looking at the man with the cap-hidden face, was already shaking his head, when Bergaz suddenly gave him a nudge as a signal to keep quiet, and by way of explanation he muttered: 'Hush! Here's Raphanel. I've been distrusting him for some time past. Whenever he appears anywhere, the police are not far off.'

Raphanel was another of the vague, mysterious Anarchists whom Janzen had presented to the Princess by way of satisfying her momentary passion for revolutionism. This one, though he was a fat, gay, little man, with a doll-like face and childish nose, which almost disappeared between his puffy cheeks, had the reputation of being a thorough desperado; and at public meetings he certainly shouted for fire and murder with all his lungs. However, although he had already been compromised in various affairs, he had invariably managed to save his own bacon, whilst his companions were kept under lock and key; and this they were now beginning to think somewhat singular.

He at once shook hands with the Princess in a jovial way, took a seat near her without being invited, and forthwith denounced the dirty *bourgeoisie* which came to wallow in places of ill fame. Rosemonde was delighted, and encouraged him, but others near by began to get angry, and Bergaz examined him with his piercing eyes, like a man of energy who acts, and lets others talk. Now and then, too, he exchanged quick glances of intelligence with his silent lieutenants, Sanfaute and Rossi, who plainly belonged to him, both body and soul. They were the ones who found their profit in Anarchy, practising it to its logical conclusions, whether in crime or in vice.

Meantime, pending the arrival of Legras with his 'Flowers of the Pavement,' two female vocalists had followed one another on the stage, the first fat and the second thin, one chirruping some silly love songs with an under-current of dirt, and the other shouting the coarsest of refrains, in a most violent, fighting voice. She had just finished amidst a storm of bravos, when the assembly, stirred to merriment and eager for a laugh, suddenly exploded once more. Silviane was entering the little box at one end of the hall. When she appeared erect in the full light, with bare arms and shoulders, looking like a planet in her gown of yellow satin and her blazing diamonds, there arose a most formidable uproar, shouts, jeers, hisses, laughter and growls mingled with ferocious applause. And the scandal increased, and the vilest expressions flew about as soon as Duvillard, Gérard and Duthil also showed themselves, looking very serious and dignified with their white ties and spreading shirt fronts.

'We told you so!' muttered Duvillard, who was much annoyed with the affair, while Gérard tried to conceal himself in a dim corner.

She, however, smiling and enchanted, faced the public, accepting the storm with the candid bearing of a foolish virgin, much as one inhales the vivifying air of the open when it bears down upon one in a squall. And, indeed, she herself had sprung from the sphere before her, its atmosphere was her native air.

'Well, what of it?' she said replying to the Baron who wanted her to sit down. 'They are merry. It's very nice. Oh! I'm really amusing myself!'

'Why yes, it's very nice,' declared Duthil, who in like fashion set himself at his ease. 'Silviane is right, people naturally like a laugh now and then!'

Amidst the uproar which did not cease, little Princess Rosemonde rose enthusiastically to get a better view. 'Why it's your father who's with that woman, Silviane;' she said to Hyacinthe, 'just look at them! Well, he certainly has plenty of bounce to show himself here with her!'

Hyacinthe, however, refused to look. It didn't interest him, his father was an idiot, only a child would lose his head over a girl in that fashion. And with his contempt for woman the young man became positively insulting.

'You try my nerves, my dear fellow,' said Rosemonde as she sat down. 'You are the child with your silly ideas about us. And as for your father he does quite right to love that girl. I find her very pretty indeed, quite adorable!'

Then all at once the uproar ceased, those who had risen resumed their seats, and the only sound was that of the feverish throb which coursed through the assembly. Legras had just appeared on the platform. He was a pale sturdy fellow with a round and carefully shaven face, stern eyes, and the powerful jaws of a man who compels the adoration of women by terrorising them. He was not deficient in talent, he sang true, and his ringing voice was one of extra-ordinary penetration and pathetic power. However, his success was chiefly due to his so-called 'Flowers of the Pavement'; for all the foulness and suffering of the lower spheres, the whole abominable sore of the social hell created by the rich, shrieked aloud in these songs in words of filth and fire and blood.

A prelude was played on the piano, and Legras standing there in his velvet jacket sang 'La Chemise,' the horrible song which brought all Paris to hear him. All the lust and vice that crowd the streets of the great city appeared with their filth and their poison; and amid the spectacle of Woman stripped, degraded, ill-treated, dragged through the mire and cast into a cesspool, there rang out the crime of the *bourgeoisie*. But the scorching insult of it all was less in the words themselves than in the manner in which Legras cast them in the faces of the rich, the happy, the beautiful ladies who came to listen to him. Under the low ceiling, amidst the smoke from the pipes, in the blinding glare of the gas, he sent his lines flying through the assembly like expectorations, projected by a whirlwind of furious contempt. And when he had finished there came delirium; the beautiful ladies did not even think of wiping away the many affronts they had received but applauded frantically. The whole assembly stamped and shouted, and wallowed, distracted, in its ignominy.

'Bravo! bravo!' the little Princess repeated in her shrill voice. 'It's astonishing, astonishing, prodigious!'

And Silviane, whose intoxication seemed to have increased since she had been there, in the depths of that fiery furnace, made herself particularly conspicuous by the manner in which she clapped her hands and shouted: 'It's he, it's my Legras! I really must kiss him, he's pleased me so much!'

Duvillard, now fairly exasperated, wished to take her off by force. But she clung to the hand-rest of the box, and shouted yet more loudly, though without any show of temper. It became necessary to parley with her. Yes, she was willing to go off and let them drive her home; but, first of all, she must embrace Legras, who was an old friend of hers. 'Go and wait for me in the carriage!' she said, 'I will be with you in a moment.'

Just as the assembly was at last becoming calmer, Rosemonde perceived that the box was emptying; and her own curiosity being satisfied, she thought of prevailing on Hyacinthe to see her home. He, who had listened to Legras in a languid way without even applauding, was now talking of Norway with Bergaz, who pretended that he had travelled in the North. Oh! the fiords! oh! the ice-bound lakes! oh! the pure lily-white, chaste coldness of the eternal winter! It was only amid such surroundings, said Hyacinthe, that he could understand woman and love, like a kiss of the very snow itself.

'Shall we go off there to-morrow?' exclaimed the Princess with her vivacious effrontery. 'I'll shut up my house and slip the key under the door.'

Then she added that she was jesting, of course. But Bergaz knew her to be quite capable of such a freak; and at the idea that she might shut up her little mansion and perhaps leave it unprotected he exchanged a quick glance with Sanfaute and Rossi, who still smiled in silence. Ah! what an opportunity for a fine stroke! What an opportunity to get back some of the wealth of the community appropriated by the blackguard *bourgeoisie*!

Meantime Raphanel, after applauding Legras, was looking all round the place with his little grey, sharp eyes. And at last young Mathis and his companion, the ill-clad individual, of whose face only a scrap of beard could be seen, attracted his attention. They had neither laughed nor applauded; they seemed to be simply a couple of tired fellows who were resting, and in whose opinion one is best hidden in the midst of a crowd.

Then, all at once Raphanel turned towards Bergaz, saying: 'That's surely little Mathis over yonder. But who's that with him?'

Bergaz made an evasive gesture; he did not know. However, he no longer took his eyes from Raphanel. And he saw the other feign indifference at what followed, and finish his beer and take his leave, with the jesting remark that he had an appointment with a lady at a neighbouring omnibus office. No sooner had he gone than Bergaz rose, sprang over some of the forms and jostled people in order to reach little Mathis, in whose ear he whispered a few words. And the young man at once left his table, taking his companion and pushing him outside through an occasional exit. It was all so rapidly accomplished that none of the general public paid attention to the flight.

' What is it ? ' said the Princess to Bergaz, when he had quietly resumed his seat between Rossi and Sanfaute.

'Oh ! nothing, I merely wished to shake hands with Mathis as he was going off.'

Thereupon Rosemonde announced that she meant to do the same. Nevertheless, she lingered a moment longer and again spoke of Norway on perceiving that nothing could impassion Hyacinthe except the idea of the eternal snow, the intense, purifying cold of the polar regions. In his poem on the 'End of Woman,' a composition of some thirty lines, which he hoped he should never finish, he thought of introducing a forest of frozen pines by way of final scene. However, the Princess had risen and was gaily reverting to her jest, declaring that she meant to take him home to drink a cup of tea and arrange their trip to the Pole, when an involuntary exclamation fell from Bergaz, who, while listening, had kept his eyes on the doorway.

' Mondésir ! I was sure of it ! '

There had appeared at the entrance a short, sinewy, broad-backed little man, about whose round face, bumpy forehead and snub nose there seemed to be much military roughness. One might have thought him a non-commissioned officer in civilian attire. He gazed over the whole room, and seemed at once dismayed and disappointed.

Bergaz, however, wishing to account for his exclamation, resumed in an easy way : ' Ah ! I said there was a smell of the police here ! You see that fellow, don't you ?—he's a detective, a very clever one, named Mondésir, who had some trouble when he was in the army. Just look at him, sniffing like a dog that has lost scent ! Well, well, my brave fellow, if you've been told of any game you may look and look for it, the bird's flown already ! '

Once outside, when Rosemonde had prevailed on Hyacinthe to see her home, they hastened to get into the brougham, which was waiting for them, for near at hand they perceived Silviane's landau, with the majestic coachman

motionless on his box, while Duvillard, Gérard, and Duthil
still stood waiting on the kerbstone. They had been there
for nearly twenty minutes already, in the semi-darkness of
that outer boulevard, where all the vices of the poor districts
of Paris were on the prowl. They were roughly jostled by
drunkards; and shadowy women brushed against them as
they went by whispering beneath the oaths and blows of
bullies. And there were couples seeking the darkness under
the trees, and lingering on the benches there; while all
around were low taverns and dirty lodging-houses, and places
of ill-fame. All the human degradation which till break of
day swarms in the black mud of this part of Paris, enveloped
the three men, giving them the horrors, and yet neither the
Baron nor Gérard nor Duthil was willing to go off. Each
hoped that he would tire out the others, and escort Silviane
home when she should at last appear.

The Baron was the first to grow impatient, and he suddenly
said to the coachman: ' Jules, go and see why madame doesn't
come.'

' But the horses, Monsieur le Baron? '

' Oh! they will be all right, we are here.'

A fine drizzle had begun to fall; and the wait went on
again as if it would never finish. However, an unexpected
meeting gave them momentary occupation. A shadowy
form, something which seemed to be a thin, black-skirted
woman brushed against them. And all of a sudden they were
surprised to find it was a priest.

' What! is it you, Monsieur l'Abbé Froment? ' exclaimed
Gérard. ' At this time of night—and in this part of Paris? '

Thereupon Pierre, without venturing either to express his
own astonishment at finding them there themselves, or to ask
them what they were doing, explained that he had been
belated through accompanying Abbé Rose on a visit to a night
refuge. Ah! to think of all the frightful want which at last
drifted to those pestilential dormitories where the stench had
almost made him faint! To think of all the weariness and
despair which there sank into the slumber of utter prostration,
like that of beasts falling to the ground to sleep off the
abominations of life! No name could be given to the
promiscuity; poverty and suffering were there in heaps,
children and men, young and old, beggars in sordid rags
beside shamefaced paupers in threadbare frock-coats, all the
waifs and strays of the daily shipwrecks of Paris life, all the

laziness and vice, and ill-luck and injustice which the torrent
rolls on, and throws off like scum.   Some slept as if quite
annihilated, with the faces of corpses.   Others, lying on their
backs with mouths agape, snored loudly as if still venting the
plaint of their sorry life.   And others tossed restlessly, still
struggling in their slumber against fatigue and cold and
hunger, which pursued them like nightmares of monstrous
shape.   And from all those human beings, stretched there
like wounded after a battle, from all that ambulance of life
reeking with a stench of rottenness and death, there ascended
a nausea born of revolt, the vengeance-prompting thought of
all the happy chambers where, at that same hour, the wealthy
loved or rested in fine linen and costly lace.[1]

In vain had Pierre and Abbé Rose passed all the poor wretches
in review while seeking the big Old 'un, the former carpenter,
so as to rescue him from that cesspool of misery, and send him
to the Asylum on the morrow.   He had presented himself at the refuge that evening, but there was no room left, for,
horrible to say, even the shelter of that hell could only be
granted to early comers.   And so he must now be leaning
against a wall, or lying behind some palings.   This had greatly
distressed poor Abbé Rose and Pierre, but it was impossible
for them to search every dark, suspicious corner ; and so the
former had returned to the Rue Cortot, while the latter was
seeking a cab to convey him back to Neuilly.

The fine drizzling rain was still falling and becoming
almost icy, when Silviane's coachman, Jules, at last reappeared and interrupted the priest, who was telling the Baron

---

[1] Even the oldest Paris night-refuges, which are the outcome of private
philanthropy—L'Œuvre de l'Hospitalité de Nuit—have only been in
existence some fourteen or fifteen years.   Before that time, and from the
period of the great Revolution forward, there was absolutely no place, either
refuge, asylum, or workhouse, in the whole of that great city of wealth
and pleasure, where the houseless poor could crave a night's shelter.
The various royalist, imperialist, and republican governments and
municipalities of modern France have often been described as 'paternal,'
but no governments and municipalities in the whole civilised world have
done less for the very poor.   The official Poor Relief Board—L'Assistance Publique—has for fifty years been a by-word, a mockery, and a
sham, in spite of its large revenue.   And this neglect of the very poor
has been an important factor in every French Revolution.   Each of
these—even that of 1870—had its purely economic side, though many
superficial historians are content to ascribe economic causes to the one
Revolution of 1789, and to pass them by in all other instances.—*Trans.*

and the others how his visit to the refuge still made him shudder.

'Well, Jules—and madame?' asked Duvillard, quite anxious at seeing the coachman return alone.

Impassive and respectful, with no other sign of irony than a slight involuntary twist of the lips, Jules answered: 'Madame sends word that she is not going home; and she places her carriage at the gentlemen's disposal if they will allow me to drive them home.'

This was the last straw, and the Baron flew into a passion. To have allowed her to drag him to that vile den, to have waited there hopefully so long, and to be treated in this fashion for the sake of a Legras! No, no, he, the Baron, had had enough of it, and she should pay dearly for her abominable conduct! Then he stopped a passing cab and pushed Gérard inside it, saying, 'You can set me down at my door.'

'But she's left us the carriage!' shouted Duthil, who was already consoled, and inwardly laughed at the termination of it all. 'Come here, there's plenty of room for three. No? you prefer the cab? Well, just as you like, you know.'

For his part he gaily climbed into the landau and drove off lounging on the cushions, while the Baron, in the jolting old cab, vented his rage without a word of interruption from Gérard, whose face was hidden by the darkness. To think of it! that she, whom he had overwhelmed with gifts, who had already cost him two millions of francs, should in this fashion insult him, the master who could dispose both of fortunes and of men! Well, she had chosen to do it, and he was delivered! Then Duvillard drew a long breath like a man released from the galleys.

For a moment Pierre watched the two vehicles go off; then he took his own way under the trees, so as to shelter himself from the rain until a vacant cab should pass. Full of distress and battling thoughts he had begun to feel icy cold. The whole monstrous night of Paris, all the debauchery and woe that sobbed around him made him shiver. Phantom-like women who, when young, had led lives of infamy in wealth, and who now, old and faded, led lives of infamy in poverty, were still and ever wandering past him in search of bread, when suddenly a shadowy form grazed him, and a voice murmured in his ear: 'Warn your brother, the police are on Salvat's track, he may be arrested at any moment.'

The shadowy figure was already going its way, and as a gas ray fell upon it, Pierre thought that he recognised the pale, pinched face of Victor Mathis. And at the same time, yonder in Abbé Rose's peaceful dining-room, he fancied he could again see the gentle countenance of Madame Mathis, so sad and so resigned, living on solely by the force of the last trembling hope which she had unhappily set in her son.

III

PLOT AND COUNTERPLOT

ALREADY at eight o'clock on that holiday-making mid-Lent Thursday, when all the offices of the Home Department were empty, Monferrand, the Minister, sat alone in his private room. A single usher guarded his door, and in the first ante-chamber there were only a couple of messengers.

The Minister had experienced, on awaking, the most unpleasant of emotions. The ' Voix du Peuple,' which on the previous day had revived the African Railway scandal, by accusing Barroux of having pocketed 200,000 francs, had that morning published its long promised list of the bribe-taking senators and deputies. And at the head of this list Monferrand had found his own name set down against a sum of 80,000 francs, while Fonsègue was credited with 50,000. Then a fifth of the latter amount was said to have been Duthil's share, and Chaigneux had contented himself with the beggarly sum of 3,000 francs—the lowest price paid for any one vote, the cost of each of the others ranging from 5 to 20,000.

It must be said that there was no anger in Monferrand's emotion. Only he had never thought that Sagnier would carry his passion for uproar and scandal so far as to publish this list—a page which was said to have been torn from a memorandum-book belonging to Duvillard's agent, Hunter, and which was covered with incomprehensible hieroglyphics that ought to have been discussed and explained, if, indeed, the real truth was to be arrived at. Personally, Monferrand felt quite at ease, for he had written nothing, signed nothing, and knew that one could almost always extricate oneself from a mess by dint of audacity, and denial. Neverthe-

less, what a commotion it would all cause in the parliamentary
duck-pond! He at once foresaw the inevitable consequence,
the ministry overthrown and swept away by this fresh whirlwind of denunciation and tittle-tattle. Mège would renew
his interpellation on the morrow, Vignon and his friends
would at once lay siege to the posts they coveted; and he,
Monferrand, could picture himself driven out of that
ministerial sanctum where, for eight months past, he had
been taking his ease, not with any foolish vainglory, but
with the pleasure of feeling that he was in his proper place
as a born ruler, who believed he could tame and lead the
multitude.

Having thrown the newspapers aside with a disdainful
gesture, he rose and stretched himself, growling the while
like a plagued lion. And then he began to walk up and
down the spacious room, which showed all the faded official
luxury of mahogany furniture and green damask hangings.
Stepping to and fro, with his hands behind his back, he no
longer wore his usual fatherly, good-natured air. He
appeared as he really was, a born wrestler, short, but broad
shouldered, with sensual mouth, fleshy nose, and stern eyes,
that all proclaimed him to be unscrupulous, of iron will, and
fit for the greatest tasks. Still, in this case, in what direction
lay his best course? Must he let himself be dragged down
with Barroux? Perhaps his personal position was not
absolutely compromised? And yet how could he part
company from the others, swim ashore, and save himself
while they were being drowned? It was a grave problem,
and with his frantic desire to retain power, he made
desperate endeavours to devise some suitable manœuvre.

But he could think of nothing, and began to swear at the
virtuous fits of that silly Republic, which, in his opinion,
rendered all government impossible. To think of such
foolish fiddle-faddle stopping a man of his acumen and
strength! How indeed can anybody govern a nation if he is
denied the use of money, that sovereign means of sway?
Then he laughed bitterly; for the idea of an idyllic country
where all great enterprises would be carried out in an absolutely honest manner seemed to him the height of absurdity.
At last, however, unable as he was to come to a determination, it occurred to him to confer with Baron Duvillard,
whom he had long known, and whom he regretted not
having seen sooner so as to urge him to purchase Sagnier's

silence. At first he thought of sending the Baron a brief
note by a messenger; but he disliked committing anything
to paper, for the veriest scrap of writing may prove dangerous;
so he preferred to employ the telephone which had been
installed for his private use near his writing table.

'It is Baron Duvillard who is speaking to me? . . . Quite
so. It's I, the Minister, Monsieur Monferrand. I shall be
much obliged if you will come to see me at once. . . . Quite
so, quite so, I will wait for you.'

Then again he walked to and fro and meditated. That
fellow Duvillard was as clever a man as himself, and might be
able to give him an idea. For his own part he was still trying
to devise some scheme, when the usher entered saying that
Monsieur Gascogne, the Chief of the Detective Police, particularly wished to speak to him. Monferrand's first thought
was that the Prefecture of Police desired to know his views
respecting the steps which ought to be taken to ensure
public order that day; for two mid-Lent processions—one of
the Washerwomen and the other of the Students—were
to march through Paris, whose streets would certainly be
crowded.

'Show Monsieur Gascogne in,' he said.

A tall, slim, dark man, looking like an artisan in his
Sunday best, then stepped into the ministerial sanctum.
Fully acquainted with the under-currents of Paris life, this
Chief of the Detective Force had a cold dispassionate nature
and a clear and methodical mind. Professionalism slightly
spoilt him, however; he would have possessed more intelligence if he had not credited himself with so much.

He began by apologising for his superior the Prefect, who
would certainly have called in person had he not been suffering from indisposition. However, it was perhaps best that
he, Gascogne, should acquaint Monsieur le Ministre with
the grave affair which brought him, for he knew every
detail of it. Then he revealed what the grave affair was.

'I believe, Monsieur le Ministre, that we at last hold
the perpetrator of the crime in the Rue Godot-de-Mauroy.'

At this, Monferrand, who had been listening impatiently,
became quite impassioned. The fruitless searches of the
police, the attacks and the jeers of the newspapers were a
source of daily worry to him. 'Ah!—Well so much the
better for you, Monsieur Gascogne,' he replied with brutal

frankness : 'You would have ended by losing your post. The man is arrested ? '

'Not yet, Monsieur le Ministre ; but he cannot escape, and it is merely an affair of a few hours.'

Then the Chief of the Detective Force told the whole story : how Detective Mondésir on being warned by a secret agent that the Anarchist Salvat was in a tavern at Montmartre, had reached it just as the bird had flown ; then how chance had again set him in presence of Salvat at a hundred paces or so from the tavern, the rascal having foolishly loitered there to watch the establishment ; and afterwards how Salvat had been stealthily shadowed in the hope that they might catch him in his hiding-place with his accomplices. In this wise, he had been tracked to the Porte-Maillot, where realising, no doubt, that he was pursued he had suddenly bolted into the Bois de Boulogne. It was there that he had been hiding since two o'clock in the morning in the drizzle which had not ceased to fall. They had waited for daylight in order to organise a *battue* and hunt him down like some animal, whose weariness must necessarily ensure capture. And so, from one moment to another, he would be caught.

'I know the great interest you take in the arrest, Monsieur le Ministre,' added Gascogne, 'and it occurred to me to ask your orders. Detective Mondésir is over there, directing the hunt. He regrets that he did not apprehend the man on the Boulevard de Rochechouart ; but, all the same, the idea of following him was a capital one, and Mondésir can only be reproached with having forgotten the Bois de Boulogne in his calculations.'

Salvat arrested ! That fellow Salvat whose name had filled the newspapers for three weeks past. This was a most fortunate stroke which would be talked of far and wide ! In the depths of Monferrand's eyes one could divine a world of thoughts, with a sudden determination to turn this incident which chance had brought him to his own personal advantage. In his own mind a link was already forming between this arrest and that African Railways interpellation which was likely to overthrow the ministry on the morrow. The first outlines of a scheme already rose before him. Was it not his good star that had sent him what he had been seeking—a means of fishing himself out of the troubled waters of the approaching crisis ?

'But tell me, Monsieur Gascogne,' said he, 'are you quite sure that this man Salvat committed the crime?'

'Oh! perfectly sure, Monsieur le Ministre. He'll confess everything in the cab before he reaches the Prefecture.'

Monferrand again walked to and fro with a pensive air, and ideas came to him as he spoke on in a slow, meditative fashion. 'My orders! well, my orders, they are, first, that you must act with the very greatest prudence. Yes, don't gather a mob of promenaders together. Try to arrange things so that the arrest may pass unperceived—and if you secure a confession keep it to yourself, don't communicate it to the newspapers. Yes, I particularly recommend that point to you, don't take the newspapers into your confidence at all—and finally, come and tell me everything, and observe secrecy, absolute secrecy with everybody else.'

Gascogne bowed and would have withdrawn, but Monferrand detained him to say that not a day passed without his friend Monsieur Lehmann, the Public Prosecutor, receiving letters from Anarchists who threatened to blow him up with his family; in such wise that, although he was by no means a coward, he wished his house to be guarded by plain clothes officers. A similar watch was already kept upon the house where investigating magistrate Amadieu resided. And if the latter's life was precious, that of Public Prosecutor Lehmann was equally so, for he was one of those political magistrates, one of those shrewd talented Israelites who make their way in very honest fashion by invariably taking the part of the Government in office.

Then Gascogne in his turn remarked: 'There is also the Barthès affair, Monsieur le Ministre.—We are still waiting. Are we to arrest Barthès at that little house at Neuilly?'

One of those chances which sometimes come to the help of detectives and make people think them men of genius had revealed to him the circumstance that Barthès had found a refuge with Abbé Pierre Froment. Ever since the Anarchist terror had thrown Paris into dismay a warrant had been out against the old man, not for any precise offence, but simply because he was a suspicious character and might, therefore, have had some intercourse with the Revolutionists. However, it had been repugnant to Gascogne to arrest him at the house of a priest whom the whole district venerated as a saint; and the Minister, whom he had consulted on the point, had not only approved of his reserve, since a member of the clergy was in question, but had undertaken to settle the affair himself.

'No, Monsieur Gascogne,' he now replied, 'don't move in the matter. You know what my feelings are, that we ought to have the priests with us and not against us. I have had a letter written to Abbé Froment in order that he may call here this morning, as I shall have no other visitors. I will speak to him myself, and you may take it that the affair no longer concerns you.'

Then he was about to dismiss him when the usher came back saying that the President of the Council was in the ante-room.[1]

'Barroux!—Ah! dash it, then, Monsieur Gascogne, you had better go out this way. It is as well that nobody should meet you, as I wish you to keep silent respecting Salvat's arrest. It's fully understood, is it not? I alone am to know everything; and you will communicate with me here direct, by the telephone, if any serious incident should arise.'

The Chief of the Detective Police had scarcely gone off, by way of an adjoining *salon*, when the usher reopened the door communicating with the ante-room and announced: 'Monsieur le Président du Conseil.'

With a nicely adjusted show of deference and cordiality, Monferrand stepped forward, his hands outstretched: 'Ah! my dear President, why did you put yourself out to come here? I would have called on you if I had known that you wished to see me.'

But with an impatient gesture Barroux brushed aside all question of etiquette. 'No, no! I was taking my usual stroll in the Champs Elysées, and the worries of the situation impressed me so keenly that I preferred to come here at once. You yourself must realise that we can't put up with what is taking place. And pending to-morrow morning's council, when we shall have to arrange a plan of defence, I felt that there was good reason for us to talk things over.'

He took an arm-chair, and Monferrand on his side rolled another forward so as to seat himself with his back to the light. Whilst Barroux, the elder of the pair by ten years, blanched and solemn, with a handsome face, snowy whiskers,

[1] The title of President of the Council is given to the French prime minister. I mention this because English readers might confound it with that of 'Lord President of the Council,' which nowadays is but a secondary post in English administrations.—*Trans.*

clean shaven chin and upper lip, retained all the dignity of power, the bearing of a Conventionnel of romantic views, who sought to magnify the rectitude of his rather foolish but good-hearted *bourgeois* nature into something great; the other, beneath his heavy common countenance and feigned frankness and simplicity, concealed unknown depths, the unfathomable soul of a shrewd enjoyer and despot who was alike pitiless and unscrupulous in attaining his ends.

For a moment Barroux drew breath, for in reality he was greatly moved, his blood rising to his head, and his heart beating with indignation and anger at the thought of all the vulgar insults which the 'Voix du Peuple' had heaped upon him again that morning. 'Come, my dear colleague,' said he, 'one must stop that scandalous campaign. Moreover, you must know what awaits us at the Chamber to-morrow. Now that the famous list has been published we shall have every malcontent up in arms; Vignon is bestirring himself already——'

'Ah! you have news of Vignon?' exclaimed Monferrand, becoming very attentive.

'Well, as I passed his door just now, I saw a string of cabs waiting there. All his creatures have been on the move since yesterday, and at least twenty persons have told me that the band is already dividing the spoils. For, as you must know, the fierce and ingenuous Mège is again going to pull the chestnuts out of the fire for others. Briefly, we are dead, and the others claim that they are going to bury us in mud before they fight over our leavings.' With his arm outstretched Barroux made a theatrical gesture, and his voice resounded as if he were in the tribune. Nevertheless, his emotion was real, tears even were coming to his eyes. 'To think that I who have given my whole life to the Republic, I who founded it, who saved it, should be covered with insults in this fashion, and obliged to defend myself against abominable charges! To say that I abused my trust! that I sold myself and took 200,000 francs from that man Hunter, simply to slip them into my pocket! Well, certainly there *was* a question of 200,000 francs between us. But how and under what circumstances? They were doubtless the same as in your case, with regard to the 80,000 francs that he is said to have handed you——'

But Monferrand interrupted his colleague in a clear trenchant voice: 'He never handed me a centime.'

The other looked at him in astonishment, but found that the features of his big, rough head were steeped in shadow: 'Ah! But I thought you had business relations with him, and knew him particularly well.'

'No, I simply knew Hunter as everyone knew him. I was not even aware that he was Baron Duvillard's agent in the African Railways matter; and there was never any question of that affair between us.'

This was so improbable, so contrary to everything which Barroux knew of the business, that for a moment he felt quite scared. Then he waved his hand as if to say that others might as well look after their own affairs, and reverted to himself. 'Oh! as for me,' he said, 'Hunter called on me more than ten times, and made me quite sick with his talk of the African Railways. It was at the time when the Chamber was asked to authorise the issue of lottery stock.[1] And, by the way, my dear fellow, I was then here at the Home Department, while you had just taken that of Public Works. I can remember sitting at that very writing-table, while Hunter was in the same arm-chair that I now occupy. That day he wanted to consult me about the employment of the large sum which Duvillard's house proposed to spend in advertising; and on seeing what big amounts were set down against the Royalist journals, I became quite angry, for I realised with perfect accuracy that this money would simply be used to wage war against the Republic. And so, yielding to Hunter's entreaties, I also drew up a list allotting 200,000 francs among the friendly Republican newspapers, which were paid through me, I admit it. And that's the whole story.'[2]

Then he sprang to his feet and struck his chest, whilst his voice again rose: 'Well, I've had more than enough of all

---

[1] This kind of stock is common enough in France. A part of it is extinguished annually at a public 'drawing,' when all such shares or bonds that are drawn become entitled to redemption at 'par'; a percentage of them also securing prizes of various amounts. City of Paris Bonds issued on this system are very popular among French people with small savings; but, on the other hand, many ventures, whose lottery stock has been authorised by the Legislature, have come to grief and ruined investors.—*Trans.*

[2] All who are acquainted with recent French history will be aware that Barroux's narrative is simply a passage from the life of the late M. Floquet, slightly modified to suit the requirements of M. Zola's story.—*Trans.*

that calumny and falsehood! And to-morrow I shall simply tell the Chamber my story. It will be my only defence. An honest man does not fear the truth!'

But Monferrand, in his turn, had sprung up with a cry which was a complete confession of his principles: 'It's ridiculous, one never confesses; you surely won't do such a thing!'

'I shall,' retorted Barroux with superb obstinacy. 'And we shall see if the Chamber won't absolve me by acclamation.'

'No, you will fall beneath an explosion of hisses, and drag all of us down with you.'

'What does it matter? We shall fall with dignity, like honest men!'

Monferrand made a gesture of furious anger, and then suddenly became calm. Amidst all the anxious confusion in which he had been struggling since daybreak, a gleam now dawned upon him. The vague ideas suggested by Salvat's approaching arrest took shape, and expanded into an audacious scheme. Why should he prevent the fall of that big ninny Barroux? The only thing of importance was that he, Monferrand, should not fall with him, or any rate that he should rise again. So he protested no further, but merely mumbled a few words, in which his rebellious feelings seemingly died out. And at last, putting on his good-natured air once more, he said: 'Well, after all you are perhaps right. One must be brave. Besides, you are our leader, my dear President, and we will follow you.'

They had now again sat down face to face, and their conversation continued till they came to a cordial agreement respecting the course which the Government should adopt in view of the inevitable interpellation on the morrow.

Meantime, Baron Duvillard was on his way to the ministry. He had scarcely slept that night. When on the return from Montmartre Gérard had set him down at his door in the Rue Godot-de-Mauroy, he had at once gone to bed, like a man who is determined to compel sleep, so that he may forget his worries and recover self-control. But slumber would not come, for hours and hours he vainly sought it. The manner in which he had been insulted by that creature Silviane was so monstrous! To think that she, whom he had enriched, whose every desire he had contented, should have cast such mud at him, the master, who flattered himself that he held Paris and the Republic in his hands, since he bought up and controlled consciences just as others might make corners in wool or leather for the purposes of Bourse speculation. And the dim consciousness that Silviane was the avenging sore, the cancer preying on him who preyed on others, completed his exasperation. In vain did he try to drive away his haunting thoughts, remember his business affairs, his appointments for the morrow, his millions which were working in every quarter of the world, the financial omnipotence which placed the fate of nations in his grasp. Ever, and in spite of all, Silviane rose up before him, splashing him with mud. In despair he tried to fix his mind on a great enterprise which he had been planning for months past, a Trans-Saharian railway, a colossal venture which would set millions of money at work, and revolutionise the trade of the world. And yet Silviane appeared once more, and smacked him on both cheeks with her dainty little hand which she had dipped in the gutter. It was only towards daybreak that he at last dozed off, while vowing in a fury that he would never see her again, that he would spurn her, and order her away, even should she come and drag herself at his feet.

However, when he awoke at seven, still tired and aching, his first thought was for her, and he almost yielded to a fit of weakness. The idea came to him to ascertain if she had returned home, and if so make his peace. But he jumped out of bed, and after his ablutions all his courage came back to him. She was a wretch, and he this time thought himself for ever cured of his passion. To tell the truth, he forgot it as soon as he opened the morning newspapers. The publication of the list of bribe-takers in the ' Voix du Peuple ' quite upset him, for he had hitherto thought it unlikely that Sagnier held any such list. However, he judged the document at a glance, at once separating the few truths it contained from a mass of foolishness and falsehood. And this time also he did not consider himself personally in danger. There was only one thing that he really feared: the arrest of his intermediary, Hunter, whose trial might have drawn him into the affair. As matters stood, and as he did not cease to repeat with a calm smile, he had merely done what every banker does when he launches a company; that is, pay the press for advertisements and puffery, employ brokers, and reward services discreetly rendered to the enterprise. It was all a business matter, and for him that expression summed up everything. Moreover, he played the game of life bravely, and spoke with indignant contempt of a banker who, driven to extremities by blackmailing, had imagined that he would bring a recent scandal to an end by killing himself; whereas from all the mire and blood of that pitiful tragedy, the scandal had sprouted afresh with the most luxuriant and indestructible vegetation. No, no! suicide was not the course to follow, a man ought to remain erect, and struggle on to his very last copper, and the very end of his energy.

When at about nine o'clock a ringing brought Duvillard to the telephone installed in his private room, his folly took possession of him again; for he thought it must be Silviane who wished to speak to him. She often amused herself by thus disturbing him amidst his greatest cares. No doubt she had just returned home, understood that she had carried things too far on the previous evening, and desired to be forgiven. However, when he found that the call was from Monferrand who wished him to go to the ministry he shivered slightly, like a man saved from an abyss beside which he is travelling. And forthwith he called for his hat and stick, desirous as he was of walking and reflecting in the open air. And again he became absorbed in the intricacies of the scandalous business which was about to stir all Paris and the legislature. Kill himself! ah, no, that would be foolish and cowardly. A gust of terror might be sweeping past; nevertheless, for his part he felt quite firm, superior to events, and resolved to defend himself without relinquishing aught of his power.

As soon as he entered the ante-rooms of the ministry he realised that the gust of terror was becoming a tempest. The publication of the terrible list in the 'Voix du Peuple' had chilled the guilty ones to the heart; and, pale and distracted, feeling the ground give way beneath them they had come to take counsel of Monferrand who, they hoped, might save them. The first whom Duvillard perceived was Duthil, looking extremely upset, biting his moustaches, and constantly making grimaces in his efforts to force a smile. The banker scolded him for coming, saying that it was a great mistake to have done so, particularly with such a scared face. The deputy, however, his spirits already cheered by these rough words, began to defend himself, declaring that he had not even read Sagnier's article, and had simply come to recom-

mend a lady friend to the minister. Thereupon the Baron
undertook this business for him and sent him away with the
wish that he might spend a merry mid-Lent. However, the
one who most roused Duvillard's pity was Chaigneux, whose
figure swayed about as if bent by the weight of his long
equine head, and who looked so shabby and untidy that one
might have taken him for an old pauper. On recognising
the banker he darted forward, and bowed to him with
obsequious eagerness.

'Ah! Monsieur le Baron,' said he, 'how wicked some
men must be! They are killing me, I shall die of it all; and
what will become of my wife, what will become of my three
daughters who have none but me to help them?'

The whole of his woeful story lay in that lament. A
victim of politics, he had been foolish enough to quit Arras
and his business there as a solicitor, in order to seek triumph in
Paris with his wife and daughters, whose menial he had
then become—a menial dismayed by the constant rebuffs and
failures which his mediocrity brought upon him. An honest
deputy! ah, good heavens! yes, he would have liked to be
one; but was he not perpetually 'hard-up,' ever in search
of a hundred-franc note, and thus, perforce, a deputy for sale?
And withal he led such a pitiable life, so badgered by the
women folk about him, that to satisfy their demands he
would have picked up money no matter where or how.

'Just fancy, Monsieur le Baron, I have at last found a
husband for my eldest girl. It is the first bit of luck that I have
ever had; there will only be three women left on my hands if
it comes off. But you can imagine what a disastrous impression such an article as that of this morning must create
in the young man's family. So I have come to see the
Minister to beg him to give my future son-in-law a prefectoral
secretaryship. I have already promised him the post, and if
I can secure it things may yet be arranged.'

He looked so terribly shabby and spoke in such a doleful
voice that it occurred to Duvillard to do one of those good actions
on which he ventured at times when they were likely to prove
remunerative investments. It is, indeed, an excellent plan to
give a crust of bread to some poor devil whom one can turn,
if necessary, into a valet or an accomplice. So the banker
dismissed Chaigneux, undertaking to do his business for him
in the same way as he had undertaken to do Duthil's. And
he added that he would be pleased to see him on the morrow

and have a chat with him, as he might be able to help him in the matter of his daughter's marriage.

At this Chaigneux, scenting a loan, collapsed into the most lavish thanks. ' Ah! Monsieur le Baron, my life will not be long enough to enable me to repay such a debt of gratitude.'

As Duvillard turned round he was surprised to see Abbé Froment waiting in a corner of the ante-room. Surely that one could not belong to the batch of *suspects*, although by the manner in which he was pretending to read a newspaper, it seemed as if he were trying to hide some keen anxiety. At last the Baron stepped forward, shook hands, and spoke to him cordially. And Pierre thereupon related that he had received a letter requesting him to call on the Minister that day. Why, he could not tell, in fact, he was greatly surprised, he said, putting on a smile in order to conceal his disquietude. He had been waiting a long time already, and hoped that he would not be forgotten on that bench.

Just then the usher appeared, and hastened up to the banker. 'The Minister,' said he, 'was at that moment engaged with the President of the Council ; but he had orders to admit the Baron as soon as the President withdrew.' Almost immediately afterwards Barroux came out, and as Duvillard was about to enter he recognised and detained him. And he spoke of the denunciations very bitterly, like one indignant with all the slander. Would not he, Duvillard, should occasion require it, testify that he, Barroux, had never taken a centime for himself ? Then, forgetting that he was speaking to a banker, and that he was Minister of Finances, he proceeded to express all his disgust of money. Ah! what poisonous, murky, and defiling waters were those in which money-making went on! However, he repeated that he would chastise his insulters, and that a statement of the truth would suffice for the purpose.

Duvillard listened and looked at him. And all at once the thought of Silviane came back, and took possession of the Baron, without any attempt on his part to drive it away. He reflected that if Barroux had chosen to give him a helping hand when he had asked for it, Silviane would now have been at the Comédie Française, in which case the deplorable affair of the previous night would not have occurred ; for he was beginning to regard himself as guilty in the matter ; if he had only contented Silviane's whim she would never have dismissed him in so vile a fashion.

'You know, I owe you a grudge,' he said, interrupting Barroux.

The other looked at him in astonishment. 'And why, pray?' he asked.

'Why, because you never helped me in the matter of that friend of mine who wishes to make her *début* in "Polyeucte."'

Barroux smiled, and with amiable condescension replied: 'Ah! yes, Silviane d'Aulnay! But, my dear sir, it was Taboureau who put spokes in the wheel. The Fine Arts are his department, and the question was entirely one for him. And I could do nothing; for that very worthy and honest gentleman, who came to us from a provincial faculty, was full of scruples. For my own part I'm an old Parisian, I can understand anything, and I should have been delighted to please you.'

At this fresh resistance offered to his passion Duvillard once more became excited, eager to obtain that which was denied him. 'Taboureau, Taboureau!' said he, 'he's a nice deadweight for you to load yourself with! Honest! isn't everybody honest? Come, my dear Minister, there's still time, get Silviane admitted, it will bring you good luck for to-morrow.'

This time Barroux burst into a frank laugh: 'No, no, I can't cast Taboureau adrift at this moment—people would make too much sport of it—a ministry wrecked or saved by a Silviane question!'

Then he offered his hand before going off. The Baron pressed it, and for a moment retained it in his own, whilst saying very gravely and with a somewhat pale face: 'You do wrong to laugh, my dear Minister. Governments have fallen or set themselves erect again through smaller matters than that. And should you fall to-morrow I trust that you will never have occasion to regret it.'

Wounded to the heart by the other's jesting air, exasperated by the idea that there was something he could not achieve, Duvillard watched Barroux as he withdrew. Most certainly the Baron did not desire a reconciliation with Silviane, but he vowed that he would overturn everything if necessary in order to send her a signed engagement for the Comédie, and this

simply by way of vengeance, as a slap, so to say, yes, a slap
which would make her tingle! That moment spent with
Barroux had been a decisive one.

However, whilst still following Barroux with his eyes,
Duvillard was surprised to see Fonsègue arrive and manœuvre
in such a way as to escape the Prime Minister's notice. He
succeeded in doing so, and then entered the ante-room with
an appearance of dismay about the whole of his little figure,
which was, as a rule, so sprightly. It was the gust of terror,
still blowing, that had brought him thither.

'Didn't you see your friend Barroux?' the Baron asked
him, somewhat puzzled.

'Barroux? No!'

This quiet lie was equivalent to a confession of everything.
Fonsègue was so intimate with Barroux that he thee'd and
thou'd him, and for ten years had been supporting him in his
newspaper, having precisely the same views, the same political
religion. But with a smash-up threatening, he doubtless
realised, thanks to his wonderfully keen scent, that he must
change his friendships if he did not wish to remain under the
ruins himself. If he had, for long years, shown so much
prudence and diplomatic virtue in order to firmly establish
the most dignified and respected of Parisian newspapers, it
was not for the purpose of letting that newspaper be compromised by some foolish blunder on the part of an honest man.

'I thought you were on bad terms with Monferrand,'
resumed Duvillard. 'What have you come for here?'

'Oh! my dear Baron, the director of a leading newspaper
is never on bad terms with anybody. He's at the country's
service.'

In spite of his emotion, Duvillard could not help smiling.
'You are quite right, Fonsègue,' he responded. 'Besides,
Monferrand is really an able man, whom one can support
without fear.'

At this Fonsègue began to wonder whether his anguish
of mind was visible. He, who usually played the game of
life so well, with his own hand under thorough control, had
been terrified by the article in the 'Voix du Peuple.' For the
first time in his career he had perpetrated a blunder, and felt
that he was at the mercy of some denunciation, for with unpardonable imprudence he had written a very brief but compromising note. He was not anxious concerning the 50,000
francs which Barroux had handed him out of the 200,000

destined for the Republican press. But he trembled lest another affair should be discovered, that of a sum of money which he had received as a present. It was only on feeling the Baron's keen glance upon him that he was able to recover some self-possession. How silly it was to lose the knack of lying and to confess things simply by one's demeanour!

But the usher drew near and repeated that the Minister was now waiting for the Baron; and Fonsègue went to sit down beside Abbé Froment, whom he also was astonished to find there. Pierre repeated that he had received a letter, but had no notion what the Minister might wish to say to him. And the quiver of his hands again revealed how feverishly impatient he was to know what it might be. However, he could only wait, since Monferrand was still busy discussing such grave affairs.

On seeing Duvillard enter, the Minister had stepped forward, offering his hand. However much the blast of terror might shake others, he had retained his calmness and good-natured smile. 'What an affair, eh, my dear Baron!' he exclaimed.

'It's idiotic!' plainly declared the other, with a shrug of his shoulders. Then he sat down in the arm-chair vacated by Barroux, while the Minister installed himself in front of him. These two were made to understand one another, and they indulged in the same despairing gestures and furious complaints, declaring that government, like business, would no longer be possible if men were required to show such virtue as they did not possess. At all times, and under every *régime*, when a decision of the Chambers had been required in connection with some great enterprise, had not the natural and legitimate tactics been for one to do what might be needful to secure that decision? It was absolutely necessary that one should obtain influential and sympathetic support, in a word, make sure of votes. Well, everything had to be paid for, men like other things, some with fine words, others with favours or money, presents made in a more or less disguised manner. And even admitting that, in the present cases, one had gone rather far in the purchasing, that some of the bartering had been conducted in an imprudent way, was it wise to make such an uproar over it; would not a strong government have begun by stifling the scandal, from motives of patriotism, a mere sense of cleanliness even?

'Why, of course! You are right, a thousand times right!'

exclaimed Monferrand. 'Ah! if I were the master you would see what a fine first-class funeral I would give it all!' Then, as Duvillard looked at him fixedly, struck by these last words, he added with his expressive smile : 'Unfortunately I'm not the master, and it was to talk to you of the situation that I ventured to disturb you. Barroux, who was here just now, seemed to me in a regrettable frame of mind.'

'Yes, I saw him, he has such singular ideas at times——' Then, breaking off, the Baron added : 'Do you know that Fonsègue is in the ante-room? As he wishes to make his peace with you, why not send for him? He won't be in the way, in fact, he's a man of good counsel, and the support of his newspaper often suffices to give one the victory.'

'What, is Fonsègue there!' cried Monferrand. 'Why, I don't ask better than to shake hands with him. There were some old affairs between us that don't concern anybody! But, good heavens! if you only knew what little spite I harbour!'

When the usher had admitted Fonsègue the reconciliation took place in the simplest fashion. They had been great friends at college in their native Corrèze, but had not spoken together for ten years past in consequence of some abominable affair the particulars of which were not exactly known. However, it becomes necessary to clear away all corpses when one wishes to have the arena free for a fresh battle.

'It's very good of you to come back the first,' said Monferrand. So it's all over, you no longer bear me any grudge?'

'No, indeed!' replied Fonsègue. 'Why should people devour one another when it would be to their interest to come to an understanding?'

Then, without further explanations, they passed to the great affair, and the conference began. And when Monferrand had announced Barroux's determination to confess and explain his conduct, the others loudly protested. That meant certain downfall, they would prevent him, he surely would not be guilty of such folly. Forthwith they discussed every imaginable plan by which the ministry might be saved, for that must certainly be Monferrand's sole desire. He himself with all eagerness pretended to seek some means of extricating his colleagues and himself from the mess in which they were. However, a faint smile still played around his lips, and at last as if vanquished he sought no further. 'There's no help for it,' said he, 'the ministry's down.'

The others exchanged glances, full of anxiety at the thought of another Cabinet dealing with the African Railways affair. A Vignon Cabinet would doubtless plume itself on behaving honestly.

'Well, then, what shall we do?'

But just then the telephone rang, and Monferrand rose to respond to the summons: 'Allow me.'

He listened for a moment and then spoke into the tube, nothing that he said giving the others any inkling of the information which had reached him. This had come from the Chief of the Detective Police, and was to the effect that Salvat's whereabouts in the Bois de Boulogne had been discovered, and that he would be hunted down with all speed. 'Very good! And don't forget my orders,' replied Monferrand.

Now that Salvat's arrest was certain, the Minister determined to follow the plan which had gradually taken shape in his mind; and returning to the middle of the room he slowly walked to and fro, while saying with his wonted familiarity: 'But what would you have, my friends? It would be necessary for me to be the master. Ah! if I were the master! A Commission of Inquiry, yes! that's the proper form for a first-class funeral to take in a big affair like this, so full of nasty things. For my part, I should confess nothing, and I should have a Commission appointed. And then you would see the storm subside.'

Duvillard and Fonsègue began to laugh. The latter, however, thanks to his intimate knowledge of Monferrand, almost guessed the truth. 'Just listen!' said he, 'even if the ministry falls it doesn't necessarily follow that you must be on the ground with it. Besides, a ministry can be mended when there are good pieces of it left.'

Somewhat anxious at finding his thoughts guessed, Monferrand protested: 'No, no, my dear fellow, I don't play that game. We are jointly responsible, we've got to keep together, dash it all!'

'Keep together! Pooh! Not when simpletons purposely drown themselves! And, besides, if we others have need of you, we have a right to save you in spite of yourself! Isn't that so, my dear Baron?'

Then, as Monferrand sat down, no longer protesting but

waiting, Duvillard, who was again thinking of his passion, full of anger at the recollection of Barroux's refusal, rose in his turn, and exclaimed : 'Why, certainly ! If the ministry's condemned let it fall ! What good can you get out of a ministry which includes such a man as Taboureau ! There you have an old, worn-out professor without any prestige, who comes to Paris from Grenoble, and has never set foot in a theatre in his life ! Yet the control of the theatres is handed over to him, and naturally he's ever doing the most stupid things ! '

Monferrand, who was well informed on the Silviane ques tion, remained grave, and for a moment amused himself by trying to excite the Baron. 'Taboureau,' said he, ' is a some-what dull and old-fashioned University man, but at the department of Public Instruction he's in his proper element.'

'Oh ! don't talk like that, my dear fellow ! You are more intelligent than that, you are not going to defend Taboureau as Barroux did ! It's quite true that I should very much like to see Silviane at the Comédie. She's a very good girl at heart, and she has an amazing lot of talent. Would you stand in her way if you were in Taboureau's place ? '

'I ? Good heavens, no ! A pretty girl on the stage, why, it would please everybody, I'm sure. Only it would be neces-sary to have a man of the same views as mine at the depart-ment of Instruction and Fine Arts.'

His sly smile had returned to his face. The securing of that girl's *début* was not a high price to pay for all the influ-ence of Duvillard's millions. Monferrand therefore turned towards Fonsègue as if to consult him. The other, who fully understood the importance of the affair, was meditating in all seriousness : ' A senator is the proper man for Public Instruc-tion,' said he. ' But I can think of none, none at all, such as would be wanted. A man of broad mind, a real Parisian, and yet one whose presence at the head of the University wouldn't cause too much astonishment.—There's perhaps Dauvergne——'

'Dauvergne ! Who's he ? ' exclaimed Monferrand in surprise. 'Ah ! yes, Dauvergne the senator for Dijon—but he's altogether ignorant of University matters, he hasn't the slightest qualification.'

'Well, as for that,' resumed Fonsègue, ' I'm trying to think. Dauvergne is certainly a good-looking fellow, tall and fair and decorative. Besides, he's immensely rich, has a most charming young wife—which does no harm, on the contrary —and he gives real *fêtes* at his place on the Boulevard St. Germain.'

It was only with hesitation that Fonsègue himself had ventured to suggest Dauvergne. But by degrees his selection appeared to him a real 'find.' 'Wait a bit! I recollect now that in his young days Dauvergne wrote a comedy, a one act comedy in verse, and had it performed at Dijon. And Dijon's a literary town, you know, so that piece of his sets a little perfume of "Belles-Lettres" around him. And then, too, he left Dijon twenty years ago, and is now a most determined Parisian, frequenting every sphere of society. Dauvergne will do whatever one desires. He's the man for us, I tell you.'

Duvillard thereupon declared that he knew him, and considered him a very decent fellow. Besides, he or another, it mattered nothing !

'Dauvergne, Dauvergne,' repeated Monferrand. '*Mon Dieu*, yes! After all, why not ? He'll perhaps make a very good Minister. Let us say Dauvergne.' Then suddenly bursting into a hearty laugh : 'And so we are reconstructing the Cabinet in order that that charming young woman may join the Comédie ! The Silviane cabinet.—Well, and what about the other departments ? '

He jested, well knowing that gaiety often hastens difficult solutions. And, indeed, they merrily continued settling what should be done if the ministry were defeated on the morrow. Although they had not plainly said so the plan was to let Barroux sink, even help him to do so, and then fish Monferrand out of the troubled waters. The latter engaged himself with the two others, because he had need of them—the Baron on account of his financial sovereignty, and the director of 'Le Globe' on account of the press campaign which he could carry on in his favour. And in the same way the others, quite apart from the Silviane business, had need of Monferrand, the strong-handed man of government, who undertook to bury the African Railways scandals by bringing about a Commission of Inquiry, all the strings of which would be pulled by himself. There was soon a perfect understanding between the three men, for nothing draws people more closely together than common interest, fear and need. Accordingly when Duvillard spoke of Duthil's business, the young lady whom he wished to recommend, the Minister declared that it was settled. A very nice fellow was Duthil, they needed a good many like him. And it was also agreed that Chaigneux's future son-in-law should have his secretaryship. Poor Chaigneux! He was so devoted, always ready to undertake any commission, and his four womenfolk led him such a hard life!

'Well, then, it's understood.' And Monferrand, Duvillard, and Fonsègue vigorously shook hands.

However, when the first accompanied the others to the door, he noticed a prelate, in a cassock of fine material, edged with violet, speaking to a priest in the ante-room. Thereupon he, the Minister, hastened forward, looking much distressed. 'Ah! you were waiting Monseigneur Martha! Come in, come in quick!'

But with perfect urbanity the Bishop refused. 'No, no, Monsieur l'Abbé Froment was here before me. Pray receive him first.'

Monferrand had to give way; he admitted the priest, and speedily dealt with him. He who usually employed the most diplomatic reserve when he was in presence of a member of the clergy plumply unfolded the Barthès business. Pierre had experienced the keenest anguish during the two hours that he had been waiting there, for he could only explain the letter he had received by a surmise that the police had discovered his brother's presence in his house. And so when he heard the Minister simply speak of Barthès, and declare that the government would rather see him go into exile than be obliged to imprison him once more, he remained for a moment quite disconcerted. As the police had been able to discover the old conspirator in the little house at Neuilly, how was it that they seemed altogether ignorant of Guillaume's presence there? It was, however, the usual gap in the genius of great detectives.

'Pray what do you desire of me, Monsieur le Ministre?' said Pierre at last, 'I don't quite understand.'

'Why, Monsieur l'Abbé, I leave all this to your sense of prudence. If that man were still at your house in forty-eight hours from now, we should be obliged to arrest him there, which would be a source of grief to us, for we are aware that your residence is the abode of every virtue. So advise him to leave France. If he does that we shall not trouble him.'

Then Monferrand hastily brought Pierre back to the ante-room; and, smiling and bending low, he said: 'Monseigneur,

I am entirely at your disposal. Come in, come in, I beg you.'

The prelate, who was gaily chatting with Duvillard and Fonsègue, shook hands with them, and then with Pierre. In his desire to win all hearts, he that morning displayed the most perfect graciousness. His bright, black eyes were all smiles, the whole of his handsome face wore a caressing expression, and he entered the ministerial sanctum leisurely and gracefully, with an easy air of conquest.

And now only Monferrand and Monseigneur Martha were left, talking on and on in the deserted building. Some people had thought that the prelate wished to become a deputy. But he played a far more useful and lofty part in governing behind the scenes, in acting as the directing mind of the Vatican's policy in France. Was not France still the Eldest Daughter of the Church, the only great nation which might some day restore omnipotence to the Papacy? For that reason he had accepted the Republic, preached the duty of 'rallying' to it, and inspired the new Catholic group in the Chamber. And Monferrand, on his side, struck by the progress of the New Spirit, that reaction of mysticism which flattered itself that it would bury science, showed himself full of amiability, like a strong-handed man who, to ensure his own victory, utilised every force that was offered him.

IV

THE MAN HUNT

On the afternoon of that same day such a keen desire for space and the open air came upon Guillaume, that Pierre consented to accompany him on a long walk in the Bois de Boulogne. The priest, upon returning from his interview with Monferrand, had informed his brother that the government once more wished to get rid of Nicholas Barthès. However, they were so perplexed as to how they should impart these tidings to the old man, that they resolved to postpone the matter until the evening. During their walk they might devise some means of breaking the news in a gentle way. As for the walk this seemed to offer no danger; to all appearance Guillaume was in no wise threatened, so why should he continue hiding? Thus the brothers sallied forth and entered the Bois by the Sablons gate, which was the nearest to them.

The last days of March had now come, and the trees were beginning to show some greenery, so soft and light, however, that one might have thought it was pale moss or delicate lace hanging between the stems and boughs. Although the sky remained of an ashen grey the rain, after falling throughout the night and morning, had ceased; and exquisite freshness pervaded that wood now awakening to life-once more, with its foliage dripping in the mild and peaceful atmosphere. The mid-Lent rejoicings had apparently attracted the populace to the centre of Paris, for in the avenues one only found the fashionable folks of select days, the people of society who come thither when the multitude stops away. There were carriages and gentlemen on horseback; beautiful aristocratic ladies who had alighted from their broughams or landaus; and wet-nurses with streaming ribbons, who carried infants wearing the most costly lace. Of the middle-classes, however, one only found a few matrons living in the neighbourhood, who sat here and there on the benches busy with embroidery or watching their children play.

Pierre and Guillaume followed the Allée de Longchamp as far as the road going from Madrid to the lakes. Then they took their way under the trees, alongside the little Longchamps rivulet. They wished to reach the lakes, pass round them, and return home by way of the Maillot gate. But so charming and peaceful was the deserted plantation through which they passed, that they yielded to a desire to sit down and taste the delight of resting amidst all the budding springtide around them. A fallen tree served them as a bench, and it was possible for them to fancy themselves far away from Paris, in the depths of some real forest. It was, too, of a real forest that Guillaume began to think on thus emerging from his long voluntary imprisonment. Ah! for the space; and for the health-bringing air which courses between that forest's branches, that forest of the world which by right should be man's inalienable domain! However, the name of Barthès, the perpetual prisoner, came back to Guillaume's lips, and he sighed mournfully. The thought that there should be even a single man, whose liberty was thus ever assailed, sufficed to poison the pure atmosphere he breathed.

'What will you say to Barthès?' he asked his brother.

'The poor fellow must necessarily be warned. Exile is at any rate preferable to imprisonment.'

Pierre sadly waved his hand. 'Yes, of course, I must warn him. But what a painful task it is!'

Guillaume made no rejoinder, for at that very moment, in that remote, deserted nook, where they could fancy themselves at the world's end, a most extraordinary spectacle was presented to their view. Something or rather someone leapt out of a thicket and bounded past them. It was assuredly a man, but one who was so unrecognisable, so miry, so woeful and so frightful, that he might have been taken for an animal, a boar that hounds had tracked and forced from his retreat. On seeing the rivulet, he hesitated for a moment, and then followed its course. But, all at once, as a sound of footsteps and panting breath drew nearer, he sprang into the water which reached his thighs, bounded on to the further bank, and vanished from sight behind a clump of pines. A moment afterwards some keepers and policemen rushed by, skirting the rivulet, and in their turn disappearing. It was a man hunt that had gone past, a fierce secret hunt with no display of scarlet or blast of horns athwart the soft, sprouting foliage.

'Some rascal or other,' muttered Pierre. 'Ah! the wretched fellow!'

Guillaume made a gesture of discouragement. 'Gendarmes and prison!' said he. 'They still constitute society's only schooling system!'

Meantime the man was still running on, farther and farther away.

When, on the previous night, Salvat had suddenly escaped from the detectives by bounding into the Bois de Boulogne, it had occurred to him to slip round to the Dauphine gate and there descend into the deep ditch [1] of the city ramparts. He remembered days of enforced idleness which he had spent there, in nooks where, for his own part, he had never met a living soul. Nowhere, indeed, could one find more secret places of retreat, hedged round by thicker bushes, or concealed from view by loftier herbage. Some corners of the ditch, at certain angles of the massive bastions, are favourite dens or nests for thieves and lovers. Salvat, as he made his way

---

[1] This ditch or dry moat is about 30 feet deep and 50 feet wide. The counterscarp by which one may descend into it has an angle of 45 degrees.—*Trans.*

through the thickest of the brambles, nettles and ivy, was lucky enough to find a cavity full of dry leaves, in which he buried himself to the chin. The rain had already drenched him, and after slipping down the muddy slope, he had frequently been obliged to grope his way upon all fours. So those dry leaves proved a boon such as he had not dared to hope for. They dried him somewhat, serving as a blanket in which he coiled himself after his wild race through the dank darkness. The rain still fell, but he now only felt it on his head, and, weary as he was, he gradually sank into deep slumber beneath the continuous drizzle. When he opened his eyes again, the dawn was breaking, and it was probably about six o'clock. During his sleep the rain had ended by soaking the leaves, so that he was now immersed in a kind of chilly bath. Still he remained in it, feeling that he was there sheltered from the police, who must now surely be searching for him. None of those bloodhounds would guess his presence in that hole, for his body was quite buried, and briars almost completely hid his head. So he did not stir, but watched the rise of the dawn.

When at eight o'clock some policemen and keepers came by, searching the ditch, they did not perceive him. As he had anticipated, the hunt had begun at the first glimmer of light. For a time his heart beat violently; however, nobody else passed, nothing whatever stirred the grass. The only sounds that reached him were faint ones from the Bois de Boulogne, the ring of a bicyclist's bell, the thud of a horse's hoofs, the rumble of carriage wheels. And time went by, nine o'clock came, and then ten o'clock. Since the rain had ceased falling, Salvat had not suffered so much from the cold, for he was wearing a thick overcoat which little Mathis had given him. But, on the other hand, hunger was coming back; there was a burning sensation in his stomach, and leaden hoops seemed to be pressing against his ribs. He had eaten nothing for two days; he had been starving already on the previous evening, when he had accepted a glass of beer at that tavern at Montmartre. Nevertheless, his plan was to remain in the ditch until nightfall, and then slip away in the direction of the village of Boulogne, where he knew of a means of egress from the wood. He was not caught yet, he repeated, he might still manage to escape. Then he tried to get to sleep again, but failed, so painful had his sufferings become. By the time it was eleven, everything swam before his eyes. He once nearly fainted, and thought that he was going to die. Then rage gradually mastered him, and, all at once, he sprang out of his leafy hiding-place, desperately hungering for food, unable to remain there any longer, and determined to find something to eat, even should it cost him his liberty and life. It was then noon.

On leaving the ditch he found the spreading lawns of the château of La Muette before him. He crossed them at a run, like a madman, instinctively going towards Boulogne, with the one idea that his only means of escape lay in that direction. It seemed miraculous that nobody paid attention to his helter-skelter flight. However, when he had reached the cover of some trees he became conscious of his imprudence, and almost regretted the sudden madness which had borne him along, eager for escape. Trembling nervously he bent low among some furze bushes, and waited for a few minutes to ascertain if the police were behind him. Then with watchful eye and ready ear, wonderful instinct and scent of danger, he went his way again, in slow and cautious fashion. He hoped to pass between the upper lake and the Auteuil race-course; but there were few trees in that part, and they formed a broad avenue. He therefore had to exert all his skill in order to avoid observation, availing himself of the slenderest stems, the smallest bushes, as screens, and only venturing onward after a lengthy inspection of his surroundings. Before long the sight of a guard in the distance revived his fears and detained him, stretched on the ground behind some brambles, for a full quarter of an hour. Then the approach first of a cab, whose driver had lost his way, and afterwards of a strolling pedestrian, in turn sufficed to stop him. He breathed once more, however, when after passing the Mortemart hillock, he was able to enter the thickets lying between the two roads which lead to Boulogne and St. Cloud. The coppices thereabouts were dense, and he merely had to follow them, screened from view, in order to reach the outlet he knew of, which was now near at hand. So he was surely saved.

But all at once, at a distance of some five-and-thirty yards, he saw a keeper, erect and motionless, barring his way. He turned slightly to the left and there perceived another keeper, who also seemed to be awaiting him. And there were more and more of them; at every fifty paces or so stood a fresh one, the whole forming a *cordon*, the meshes as it were of a huge net. The worst was that he must have been per-

ceived, for a light cry, like the clear call of an owl, rang out,
and was repeated farther and farther off. The hunters were
at last on the right scent, prudence had become superfluous,
and it was only by flight that the quarry might now hope to
escape. Salvat understood this so well that he suddenly began
to run, leaping over all obstacles and darting between the
trees, careless whether he were seen or heard. A few bounds
carried him across the Avenue de St. Cloud into the planta-
tions stretching to the Allée de la Reine Marguerite. There
the undergrowth was very dense; in the whole Bois there are
no more closely set thickets. In summer they become one
vast entanglement of verdure, amidst which, had it been the
leafy season, Salvat might well have managed to secrete himself. For a moment he did find himself alone, and thereupon
he halted to listen. He could neither see nor hear the
keepers now. Had they lost his track then? Profound
quietude reigned under the fresh young foliage. But the
light, owlish cry arose once more, branches cracked, and he
resumed his wild flight, hurrying straight before him. Un-
luckily he found the Allée de la Reine Marguerite guarded by
policemen, so that he could not cross over, but had to skirt it
without quitting the thickets. And now his back was turned
towards Boulogne, he was retracing his steps towards
Paris. However, a last idea came to his bewildered mind;
it was to run on in this wise as far as the shady spots around
Madrid, and then, by stealing from copse to copse, attempt to
reach the Seine. To proceed thither across the bare expanse
of the race-course and training-ground was not for a moment
to be thought of.

So Salvat still ran on and on. But on reaching the Alleé
de Longchamp he found it guarded like the other roads, and
therefore had to relinquish his plan of escaping by way of
Madrid and the river-bank. While he was perforce making a
bend alongside the Pré Catelan, he became aware that the
keepers, led by detectives, were drawing yet nearer to him,
confining his movements to a smaller and smaller area. And
his race soon acquired all the frenzy of despair. Haggard
and breathless he leapt mounds, rushed down slopes, fought
his way past multitudinous obstacles. He forced a passage
through brambles, broke down palings, thrice caught his feet
in wire-work which he had not seen, and fell among nettles,
yet picked himself up and went on again, spurred by the
stinging of his hands and face. It was then that Guillaume

and Pierre saw him pass, unrecognisable and frightful, taking to the muddy water of the rivulet like a stag which seeks to set a last obstacle between itself and the hounds. There came to him a wild idea of getting to the lake, and swimming, unperceived, to the island in the centre of it. That, he madly thought, would be a safe retreat, where he might burrow and hide himself without possibility of discovery. And so he still ran on. But once again the sight of some guards made him retrace his steps, and he was compelled to go back and back in the direction of Paris, chased, forced towards the very fortifications whence he had started that morning. It was now nearly three in the afternoon. For more than two hours and a half he had been running.

At last he saw a soft, sandy ride for horsemen before him. He crossed it, splashing through the mire left by the rain, and reached a little pathway, a delightful lovers' lane, as shady in summer as any arbour. For some time he was able to follow it, concealed from observation, and with his hopes reviving. But it led him to one of those broad, straight avenues where carriages and bicycles, the whole afternoon pageant of society swept past under the mild and cloudy sky. So he returned to the thickets, fell once more upon the keepers, lost all notion of the direction he took, and even all power of thought, becoming a mere thing carried along and thrown hither and thither by the chances of the pursuit which pressed more and more closely upon him. Star-like crossways followed one upon another, and at last he came to a broad lawn, where the full light dazzled him. And there he suddenly felt the hot, panting breath of his pursuers close in the rear. Eager, hungry breath it was, like that of hounds seeking to devour him. Shouts rang out, one hand almost caught hold of him, there was a rush of heavy feet, a scramble to seize him. But with a supreme effort he leapt upon a bank, crawled to its summit, rose again, and once more found himself alone, still running on amid the fresh and quiet greenery.

Nevertheless, this was the end. He almost fell flat upon the ground. His aching feet could no longer carry him; blood was oozing from his ears, and froth had come to his mouth. His heart beat with such violence that it seemed likely to break his ribs. Water and perspiration streamed from him, he was miry and haggard and tortured by hunger, conquered, in fact, more by hunger than by fatigue. And through the mist which seemed to have gathered before his

wild eyes, he suddenly saw an open doorway, the doorway of
a coach-house in the rear of a kind of châlet, sequestered
among trees. Excepting a big white cat which took to flight,
there was not a living creature in the place. Salvat plunged
into it and rolled over on a heap of straw, among some empty
casks. He was scarcely hidden there when he heard the
chase sweep by, the detectives and the keepers losing scent,
passing the châlet and rushing in the direction of the Paris
ramparts. The noise of their heavy boots died away, and
deep silence fell while the hunted man, who had carried both
hands to his heart to stay its beating, sank into the most
complete prostration, with big tears trickling from his closed
eyes.

Whilst all this was going on, Pierre and Guillaume, after a
brief rest, had resumed their walk, reaching the lake and
proceeding towards the crossway of the Cascades, in order to
return to Neuilly by the road beyond the water. However,
a shower fell, compelling them to take shelter under the big
leafless branches of a chestnut tree. Then, as the rain came
down more heavily and they could perceive a kind of châlet,
a little café-restaurant, amid a clump of trees, they hastened
thither for better protection. In a side road, which they
passed on their way, they saw a cab standing, its driver waiting there in philosophical fashion under the falling shower.
Pierre, moreover, noticed a young man stepping out briskly in
front of them, a young man resembling Gérard de Quinsac,
who, whilst walking in the Bois, had no doubt been overtaken
by the rain, and like themselves was seeking shelter in the
châlet. However, on entering the latter's public room, the
priest saw no sign of the gentleman, and concluded that he
must have been mistaken. This public room, which had a
kind of glazed verandah overlooking the Bois, contained a
few chairs and tables, the latter with marble tops. On the
first floor there were four or five private rooms reached by a
narrow passage. Though the doors were open the place had as
yet scarcely emerged from its winter's rest. There was nobody
about, and on all sides one found the dampness common to
establishments which, from lack of custom, are compelled to
close from November until March. In the rear were some
stables, a coach-house, and various mossy, picturesque outbuildings, which painters and gardeners would now soon em-
bellish for the gay pleasure parties which the fine weather
would bring.

'I really think that they haven't opened for the season yet,' said Guillaume as he entered the silent house.

'At all events they will let us stay here till the rain stops,' answered Pierre, seating himself at one of the little tables.

Just then a waiter suddenly made his appearance seemingly in a great hurry. He had come down from the first floor, and eagerly rummaged a cupboard for a few dry biscuits which he laid on a plate. At last he condescended to serve the brothers two glasses of Chartreuse.

In one of the private rooms upstairs Baroness Duvillard, who had driven to the châlet in a cab, had been awaiting her lover Gérard for nearly half an hour. It was there that, during the charity bazaar, they had given each other an appointment. For them the châlet had precious memories; two years previously on discovering that secluded nest, which was so deserted in the early, hesitating days of chilly spring, they had met there under circumstances which they could not forget. And the Baroness, in choosing the house for the supreme assignation of their dying passion, had certainly not merely been influenced by a fear that she might be spied upon elsewhere. She had, indeed, thought of the first kisses that had been showered on her there, and would fain have revived them even if they should now prove the last that Gérard would bestow on her.

But she would also have liked to see some sunlight playing over the youthful foliage. The ashen sky and threatening rain saddened her. And when she entered the private room she did not recognise it, so cold and dim it seemed with its faded furniture. Winter had tarried there, with all the dampness and mouldy smell peculiar to rooms which have long remained closed. Then, too, some of the wall-paper which had come away from the plaster hung down in shreds, dead flies were scattered over the parquetry flooring; and in order to open the shutters the waiter had to engage in quite a fight with their fastenings. However, when he had lighted a little gas stove, which at once flamed up and diffused some warmth, the room became more cosy.

Eve had seated herself on a chair, without raising the thick veil which hid her face. Gowned, gloved and bonneted in black, as if she were already in mourning for her last passion, she showed nought of her own person save her superb fair hair, which glittered like a helm of tawny gold. She had ordered tea for two, and when the waiter brought it with a

little plateful of dry biscuits, left, no doubt, from the previous
season, he found her in the same place, still veiled and motionless, absorbed, it seemed, in a gloomy reverie. If she had
reached the café half an hour before the appointed time it was
because she desired some leisure and opportunity to overcome
her despair and compose herself. She resolved that of all
things she would not weep, that she would remain dignified
and speak calmly, like one who, whatever rights she might
possess, preferred to appeal to reason only. And she was
well pleased with the courage that she found within her.
Whilst thinking of what she should say to dissuade Gérard
from a marriage which to her mind would prove both a
calamity and a blunder, she fancied herself very calm, indeed
almost resigned to whatsoever might happen.

But all at once she started and began to tremble. Gérard
was entering the room.

'What! are you here the first, my dear?' he exclaimed.
'I thought that I myself was ten minutes before the time!
And you've ordered some tea and are waiting for me!'

He forced a smile as he spoke, striving to display the same
delight at seeing her, as he had shown in the early golden
days of their passion. But at heart he was much embarrassed,
and he shuddered at the thought of the awful scene which
he could foresee.

She had at last risen and raised her veil. And looking at
him she stammered: 'Yes, I found myself at liberty earlier
than I expected. . . . I feared some impediment might arise
. . . and so I came.'

Then, seeing how handsome and how affectionate he still
looked, she could not restrain her passion. All her skilful
arguments, all her fine resolutions were swept away. Her
flesh irresistibly impelled her towards him; she loved him,
she would keep him, she would never surrender him to
another. And she wildly flung her arms around his neck.

'Oh! Gérard, Gérard! I suffer too cruelly; I cannot, I
cannot bear it! Tell me at once that you will not marry her,
that you will never marry her!'

Her voice died away in a sob, tears started from her eyes,
Ah! those tears which she had sworn she would never shed!
They gushed forth without cessation, they streamed from her
lovely eyes like a flood of the bitterest grief.

'My daughter, O God! What! you would marry my
daughter! She, here, on your neck where I am now! No,

no, such torture is past endurance, it must not be, I will not have it!'

He shivered as he heard that cry of frantic jealousy raised by a mother who now was but a woman, maddened by the thought of her rival's youth, those five-and-twenty summers which she herself had left far behind. For his part, on his way to the assignation, he had come to what he thought the most sensible decision, that of breaking off the intercourse after the fashion of a well-bred man, with all sorts of fine consolatory speeches. But sternness was not in his nature. He was weak and soft-hearted, and had never been able to withstand a woman's tears. Nevertheless, he endeavoured to calm her, and in order to rid himself of her embrace, he made her sit down upon the sofa. And there, beside her, he replied: 'Come, be reasonable, my dear. We came here to have a friendly chat, did we not? I assure you that you are greatly exaggerating matters.'

But she was determined to obtain a more positive answer from him. 'No, no!' she retorted, 'I am suffering too dreadfully, I must know the truth at once. Swear to me that you will never, never marry her!'

He again endeavoured to avoid replying as she wished him to do. 'Come, come,' he said, 'you will do yourself harm by giving way to such grief as this; you know that I love you dearly.'

'Then swear to me that you will never, never marry her.'

'But I tell you that I love you, that you are the only one I love.'

Then she again threw her arms around him, and kissed him passionately upon the eyes. 'Is it true?' she asked in a transport. 'You love me, you love no one else? Oh! tell me so again, and kiss me, and promise me that you will never belong to her.'

Weak as he was he could not resist her ardent caresses and pressing entreaties. There came a moment of supreme cowardice and passion; her arms were around him and he forgot all but her; again and again repeating that he loved none other, and would never, never marry her daughter. At last he even sank so low as to pretend that he simply regarded that poor, deformed creature with pity. His words of compassionate disdain for her rival were like nectar to Eve, for they filled her with the blissful idea that it was she herself who

would ever remain beautiful in his eyes and whom he would
ever love. . . .

At last silence fell between them, like an inevitable reaction after such a tempest of despair and passion. It disturbed Gérard. 'Won't you drink some tea?' he asked. 'It
is almost cold already.'

She was not listening, however. To her the reaction had
come in a different form; and as though the inevitable
explanation were only now commencing, she began to speak
in a sad and weary voice. 'My dear Gérard, you really
cannot marry my daughter. In the first place it would be so
wrong, and then there is the question of your name, your
position. Forgive my frankness, but the fact is that everybody would say that you had sold yourself—such a marriage
would be a scandal for both your family and mine.'

As she spoke she took hold of his hands, like a mother
seeking to prevent her big son from committing some terrible
blunder. And he listened to her, with bowed head and
averted eyes. She now evinced no anger, no jealous rage;
all such feelings seemed to have departed with the rapture of
her passion.

'Just think of what people would say,' she continued. 'I
don't deceive myself, I am fully aware that there is an
abyss between your circle of society and ours. It is all very
well for us to be rich, but money simply enlarges the gap.
And it was all very fine for me to be converted; my daughter
is none the less "the daughter of the Jewess," as folks so
often say. Ah! my Gérard, I am so proud of you, that it
would rend my heart to see you lowered, degraded almost, by
a marriage for money with a girl who is deformed, who is unworthy of you and whom you could not love.'

He raised his eyes and looked at her entreatingly, anxious
as he was to be spared such painful talk. 'But haven't I
sworn to you, that you are the only one I love?' he said.
'Haven't I sworn that I would never marry her? It's all
over. Don't let us torture ourselves any longer.'

Their glances met and lingered on one another, instinct
with all the misery which they dared not express in words.
Eve's face had suddenly aged; her eyelids were red and
swollen, and blotches marbled her quivering cheeks, down
which her tears again began to trickle. 'My poor, poor
Gérard,' said she, 'how heavily I weigh on you. Oh! do not
deny it! I feel that I am an intolerable burden on your

shoulders, an impediment in your life, and that I may bring irreparable disaster on you by my obstinacy in wishing you to be mine alone.'

He tried to speak, but she silenced him. 'No, no, all is over between us. I am growing ugly, all is ended. And besides, I shut off the future from you. I can be of no help to you, whereas you bestow all on me. And yet the time has come for you to assure yourself a position. At your age you can't continue living without any certainty of the morrow, without a home and hearth of your own; and it would be cowardly and cruel of me to set myself up as an obstacle, and prevent you from ending your life happily, as I should do if I clung to you and dragged you down with me.'

Gazing at him through her tears she continued speaking in this fashion. Like his mother she was well aware that he was weak and even sickly; and she therefore dreamt of arranging a quiet life for him, a life of tranquil happiness free from all fear of want. She loved him so fondly and possessed so much genuine kindness of heart that perhaps it might be possible for her to rise even to renunciation and sacrifice. Moreover, the very egotism born of her beauty suggested that it might be well for her to think of retirement and not allow the autumn of her life to be spoilt by torturing dramas. All this she said to him, treating him like a child whose happiness she wished to ensure even at the price of her own; and he, his eyes again lowered, listened without further protest, pleased indeed to let her arrange a pleasant life for him.

Examining the situation from every aspect she at last began to recapitulate the points in favour of that abominable marriage, the thought of which had so intensely distressed her. 'It is certain,' she said, 'that Camille would bring you all that I should like you to have. With her, I need hardly say it, would come plenty, affluence. And, as for the rest, well, I do not wish to excuse myself or you, but I could name twenty households in which there have been worse things. Besides, I was wrong when I said that money opened a gap between people. On the contrary, it draws them nearer together, it secures forgiveness for every fault; so nobody would dare to blame you, there would only be jealous ones around you, dazzled by your good fortune.'

Gérard rose, apparently rebelling once more. 'Surely,' said he, '*you* don't insist on my marrying your daughter?'

'Ah! no indeed! But I am sensible, and I tell you what I ought to tell you. You must think it all over.'

'I have done so already. It is you that I have loved, and that I love still. What you say is impossible.'

She smiled divinely, rose, and again embraced him. 'How good and kind you are, my Gérard. Ah! if you only knew how *I* love you, how I shall always love you, whatever happens.'

Then she again began to weep, and even he shed tears. Their good faith was absolute ; tender of heart as they were, they sought to delay the painful wrenching and tried to hope for further happiness. But they were conscious that the marriage was virtually an accomplished fact. Only tears and words were left them, while life and destiny were marching on. And if their emotion was so acute it was probably because they felt that this was the last time they would meet as lovers. Still they strove to retain the illusion that they were not exchanging their last farewell, that their lips would some day meet again in a kiss of rapture.

Eve removed her arms from the young man's neck, and they both gazed round the room, at the sofa, the table, the four chairs, and the little hissing gas-stove. The moist, hot atmosphere was becoming quite oppressive.

'And so,' said Gérard, 'you won't drink a cup of tea?'

'No, it's so horrid here,' she answered, while arranging her hair in front of the looking-glass.

At that parting moment the mournfulness of this place where she had hoped to find such delightful memories, filled her with distress, which was turning to positive anguish, when she suddenly heard an uproar of gruff voices and heavy feet. People were hastening along the passage and knocking at the doors. And, on darting to the window, she perceived a number of policemen surrounding the châlet. At this the wildest ideas assailed her. Had her daughter employed somebody to follow her? Did her husband wish to divorce her so as to marry Silviane? The scandal would be awful, and all her plans must crumble! She waited in dismay, white like a ghost ; while Gérard, also paling and quivering, begged her to be calm. At last, when loud blows were dealt upon the door and a Commissary of Police enjoined them to open it, they were obliged to do so. Ah! what a moment, and what dismay and shame!

Meanwhile, down below, Pierre and Guillaume had been

waiting for the rain to cease. Seated in a corner of the glazed verandah they talked in under-tones of Barthès' painful affair, and ultimately decided to ask Théophile Morin to dine with them on the following evening, and inform his old friend that he must again go into exile.

'That is the best course,' repeated Guillaume. 'Morin is very fond of him and will know how to break the news. I have no doubt too that he will go with him as far as the frontier.'

Pierre sadly looked at the falling rain. 'Ah! what a choice,' said he, 'to be ever driven to a foreign land under penalty of being thrust into prison. Poor fellow! how awful it is to have never known a moment of happiness and gaiety in one's life, to have devoted one's whole existence to the idea of liberty, and to see it scoffed at and expire with oneself!'

Then the priest paused, for he saw several policemen and keepers approach the café and prowl round it. Having lost scent of the man they were hunting, they had retraced their steps with the conviction no doubt that he had sought refuge in the châlet. And in order that he might not again escape them, they now took every precaution, exerted all their skill in surrounding the place before venturing on a minute search. Covert fear came upon Pierre and Guillaume when they noticed these proceedings. It seemed to them that it must all be connected with the chase which they had caught a glimpse of some time previously. Still as they happened to be in the châlet they might be called upon to give their names and addresses. At this thought they glanced at one another, and almost made up their minds to go off under the rain. But they realised that anything like flight might only compromise them the more. So they waited; and all at once there came a diversion, for two fresh customers entered the establishment.

A victoria with both its hood and apron raised had just drawn up outside the door. The first to alight from it was a young, well-dressed man with a bored expression of face. He was followed by a young woman who was laughing merrily, as if much amused by the persistence of the downpour. By way of jesting, indeed, she expressed her regret that she had not come to the Bois on her bicycle, whereupon her companion retorted that to drive about in a deluge appeared to him the height of idiocy.

'But we were bound to go somewhere, my dear fellow,'

she gaily answered. 'Why didn't you take me to see the maskers?'

'The maskers, indeed! No, no, my dear. I prefer the Bois, and even the bottom of the lake to them.'

Then, as the couple entered the châlet, Pierre saw that the young woman who made merry over the rain was little Princess Rosemonde, while her companion who regarded the mid-Lent festivities as horrible, and bicycling as an utterly unæsthetic amusement, was handsome Hyacinthe Duvillard. On the previous evening, while they were taking a cup of tea together on their return from the Chamber of Horrors, the young man had responded to the Princess's blandishments by declaring that the only form of attachment he believed in was a mystic union of intellects and souls. And as such a union could only be fittingly arrived at amidst the cold, chaste snow, they had decided that they would start for Christiania on the following Monday. Their chief regret was that by the time they reached the fiords the worst part of the northern winter would be over.

They sat down in the café and ordered some *kummel*, but there was none, said the waiter, so they had to content themselves with common *anisette*. Then Hyacinthe, who had been a schoolfellow of Guillaume's sons, recognised both him and Pierre; and leaning towards Rosemonde told her in a whisper who the elder brother was.

Thereupon, with sudden enthusiasm, she sprang to her feet: 'Guillaume Froment, indeed! the great chemist!' And stepping forward with arm outstretched, she continued: 'Ah! monsieur, you must excuse me, but I really must shake hands with you. I have so much admiration for you! You have done such wonderful work in connection with explosives!' Then, noticing the chemist's astonishment, she again burst into a laugh: 'I am the Princess de Harn; your brother Abbé Froment knows me, and I ought to have asked him to introduce me. However, we have mutual friends, you and I; for instance, Monsieur Janzen, a very distinguished man as you are aware. He was to have taken me to see you, for I am a modest disciple of yours. Yes, I have given some attention to chemistry, oh! from pure zeal for truth and in the hope of helping good causes, not otherwise. So you will let me call on you—won't you?—directly I come back from Christiania, where I am going with my young friend here, just to acquire some experience of unknown emotions.'

In this way she rattled on, never allowing the others an opportunity to say a word. And she mingled one thing with another: her cosmopolitan tastes which had thrown her into Anarchism and the society of shady adventurers; her new passion for mysticism and symbolism; her belief that the ideal must triumph over base materialism; her taste for æsthetic verse; and her dream of some unimagined rapture when Hyacinthe should kiss her with his frigid lips in a realm of eternal snow.

All at once, however, she stopped short and again began to laugh. 'Dear me!' she exclaimed. 'What are those policemen looking for here? Have they come to arrest us? How amusing it would be!'

Police Commissary Dupot and Detective Mondésir had just made up their minds to search the café, as their men had hitherto failed to find Salvat in any of the outbuildings. They were convinced that he was here. Dupot, a thin, bald, short-sighted, spectacled little man, wore his usual expression of boredom and weariness, though in reality he was very wide-awake and extremely courageous. He himself carried no weapons; but, as he anticipated a most violent resistance, such as might be expected from a trapped wolf, he advised Mondésir to have his revolver ready. From considerations of hierarchical respect, however, the detective, who with his snub nose and massive figure had much the appearance of a bull-dog, was obliged to let his superior enter first.

From behind his spectacles the Commissary of Police quickly scrutinised the four customers whom he found in the café: the lady, the priest, and the two other men. And passing them in a disdainful way, he at once made for the stairs, intending to inspect the upper floor. Thereupon, the waiter, frightened by the sudden intrusion of the police, lost his head and stammered: 'But there's a lady and gentleman upstairs in one of the private rooms.'

Dupot quietly pushed him aside. 'A lady and gentleman, that's not what we are looking for. . . . Come, make haste, open all the doors, you mustn't leave a cupboard closed.'

Then climbing to the upper floor, he and Mondésir explored in turn every apartment and corner till they at last reached the room where Eve and Gérard were together. Here the waiter was unable to admit them as the door was bolted inside. 'Open the door!' he called through the key-hole, 'it isn't you that they want!'

At last the bolt was drawn back and Dupot, without even venturing to smile, allowed the trembling lady and gentleman to go downstairs, while Mondésir, entering the room, looked under every article of furniture, and even peeped into a little cupboard in order that no neglect might be imputed to him.

Meantime, in the public room which they had to cross after descending the stairs, Eve and Gérard experienced fresh emotion; for people whom they knew were there, brought together by an extraordinary freak of chance. Although Eve's face was hidden by a thick veil, her eyes met her son's glance and she felt sure that he recognised her. What a fatality! He had so long a tongue and told his sister everything! Then, as the Count, in despair at such a scandal, hurried off with the Baroness to conduct her through the pouring rain to her cab, they both distinctly heard little Princess Rosemonde exclaim: 'Why, that was Count de Quinsac! Who was the lady, do you know?' And as Hyacinthe, greatly put out, returned no answer, she insisted, saying: 'Come, you must surely know her. Who was she, eh?'

'Oh! nobody. Some woman or other,' he ended by replying.

Pierre, who had understood the truth, turned his eyes away to hide his embarrassment. But all at once the scene changed. At the very moment when Commissary Dupot and Detective Mondésir came downstairs again, after vainly exploring the upper floor, a loud shout was raised outside, followed by a noise of running and scrambling. Then Gascogne, the Chief of the Detective Force, who had remained in the rear of the châlet, continuing the search through the outbuildings, made his appearance pushing before him a bundle of rags and mud, which two policemen held on either side. And this bundle was the man, the hunted man, who had just been discovered in the coach-house, inside a staved cask, covered with hay.

Ah! what a whoop of victory there was after that run of two hours' duration, that frantic chase which had left them all breathless and footsore! It had been the most exciting, the most savage of all sports—a man hunt! They had caught the man at last and they pushed him, they dragged him, they belaboured him with blows. And he, the man, what a sorry prey he looked! A wreck, wan and dirty from having spent the night in a hole full of leaves, still soaked to his waist from having waded through a stream, drenched too by the rain, bespattered with mire, his coat and trousers in tatters, his cap a mere shred, his legs and hands bleeding from his terrible rush through thickets bristling with brambles and nettles. There no longer seemed anything human about him; his hair stuck to his moist temples, his bloodshot eyes protruded from their sockets; fright, rage, and suffering were all blended on his wasted, contracted face. Still it was he, the man, the quarry, and they gave him another push, and he sank on one of the tables of the little café, still held and shaken, however, by the rough hands of the policemen.

Then Guillaume shuddered as if thunderstruck, and caught hold of Pierre's hand. At this the priest, who was looking on, suddenly understood the truth and also quivered. Salvat! the man was Salvat! It was Salvat whom they had seen rushing through the wood like a wild boar forced by the hounds. And it was Salvat who was there, now conquered and simply a filthy bundle. Then once more there came to Pierre, amidst his anguish, a vision of the errand girl lying yonder at the entrance of the Duvillard mansion, the pretty fair-haired girl whom the bomb had ripped and killed!

Dupot and Mondésir made haste to participate in Gascogne's triumph. To tell the truth, however, the man had offered no resistance; it was like a lamb that he had let the police lay hold of him. And since he had been in the café, still roughly handled, he had simply cast a weary and mournful glance around him.

At last he spoke, and the first words he uttered in a hoarse, gasping voice were these: 'I am hungry.'

He was sinking from hunger and weariness. This was the third day that he had eaten nothing.

'Give him some bread,' said Commissary Dupot to the waiter. 'He can eat it while a cab is being fetched.'

A policeman went off to find a vehicle. The rain had suddenly ceased falling, the clear ring of a bicyclist's bell was heard in the distance, some carriages drove by, and under the pale sunrays life again came back to the Bois.

Meantime, Salvat had fallen gluttonously upon the hunk of bread which had been given him, and whilst he was devouring it with rapturous animal satisfaction, he perceived the four customers around him. He seemed irritated by the sight of Hyacinthe and Rosemonde, whose faces expressed

the mingled anxiety and delight they felt at thus witnessing
the arrest of some bandit or other. But all at once his
mournful, bloodshot eyes wavered, for to his intense surprise
he had recognised Pierre and Guillaume. When he again
looked at the latter it was with the submissive affection of a
grateful dog, and as if he were once more promising that he
would divulge nothing, whatever should happen.

At last he again spoke, as if addressing himself like a man
of courage, both to Guillaume, from whom he had averted
his eyes, and to others also, his comrades who were not
there : ' It was silly of me to run,' said he, ' I don't know
why I did so. It's best that it should be all ended. I am
ready.'

V

THE GAME OF POLITICS

ON reading the newspapers on the following morning Pierre
and Guillaume were greatly surprised at not finding in them
the sensational accounts of Salvat's arrest which they had
expected. All they could discover was a brief paragraph in a
column of general news, setting forth that some policemen on
duty in the Bois de Boulogne had there arrested an Anarchist,
who was believed to have played a part in certain recent
occurrences. On the other hand the papers gave a deal of
space to the questions raised by Sagnier's fresh denunciations.
There were innumerable articles on the African Railways
scandal, and the great debate which might be expected at the
Chamber of Deputies, should Mège, the Socialist member,
really renew his interpellation, as he had announced his
intention of doing.

As Guillaume's wrist was now fast healing, and nothing
seemed to threaten him, he had already on the previous
evening decided that he would return to Montmartre. The
police had passed him by without apparently suspecting any
responsibility on his part ; and he was convinced that Salvat
would keep silent. Pierre, however, begged him to wait a
little longer, at any rate until the prisoner should have been
interrogated by the investigating magistrate, by which time
they would be able to judge the situation more clearly. Then
too, Pierre, during his long stay at the Home Department on
the previous morning, had caught a glimpse of certain things

and overheard certain words which made him suspect some dim connection between Salvat's crime and the parliamentary crisis; and he therefore desired a settlement of the latter before Guillaume returned to his wonted life.

'Just listen,' he said to his brother. 'I am going to Morin's to ask him to come and dine here this evening, for it is absolutely necessary that Barthès should be warned of the fresh blow which is falling on him. And then I think I shall go to the Chamber, as I want to know what takes place there. After that, since you desire it, I will let you go back to your own home.'

It was not more than half-past one when Pierre reached the Palais-Bourbon. It had occurred to him that Fonsègue would be able to secure him admittance to the meeting-hall, but in the vestibule he met General de Bozonnet, who happened to possess a couple of tickets. A friend of his, who was to have accompanied him, had, at the last moment, been unable to come. So widespread was the curiosity concerning the debate now near at hand, and so general were the predictions that it would prove a most exciting one, that the demand for tickets had been extremely keen during the last twenty-four hours. In fact, Pierre would never have been able to obtain admittance if the General had not good-naturedly offered to take him in. As a matter of fact the old warrior was well pleased to have somebody to chat with. He explained that he had simply come there to kill time, just as he might have killed it at a concert or a charity bazaar. However, like the ex-Legitimist and Bonapartist that he was, he had really come for the pleasure of feasting his eyes on the shameful spectacle of parliamentary ignominy.

When the General and Pierre had climbed the stairs, they were able to secure two front seats in one of the public galleries. Little Massot who was already there, and who knew them both, placed one of them on his right and the other on his left. 'I couldn't find a decent seat left in the press gallery,' said he, 'but I managed to get this place, from which I shall be able to see things properly. It will certainly be a big sitting. Just look at the number of people there are on every side!'

The narrow and badly arranged galleries were packed to overflowing. There were men of every age and a great many women too in the confused, serried mass of spectators, amidst which one only distinguished a multiplicity of pale white faces. The real scene, however, was down below in the meeting-hall, which was as yet empty, and with its rows of seats disposed in semicircular fashion looked like the auditorium of a theatre. Under the cold light which fell from the glazed roofing appeared the solemn, shiny tribune, whence members address the Chamber, whilst behind it, on a higher level, and running right along the rear wall, was what is called the Bureau, with its various tables and seats, including the presidential arm-chair. The Bureau, like the tribune, was still unoccupied. The only persons one saw there were a couple of attendants who were laying out new pens and filling inkstands.

'The women,' said Massot with a laugh, after another glance at the galleries, 'come here just as they might come to a menagerie, that is, in the secret hope of seeing wild beasts devour one another. But, by the way, did you read the article in the "Voix du Peuple" this morning? What a wonderful fellow that Sagnier is! When nobody else can find any filth left, he manages to discover some. He apparently thinks it necessary to add something new every day, in order to send his sales up. And of course it all disturbs the public, and it's thanks to him that so many people have come here in the hope of witnessing some horrid scene.'

Then he laughed again, as he asked Pierre if he had read an unsigned article in the 'Globe,' which in very dignified but perfidious language had called upon Barroux to give the full and frank explanations which the country had a right to demand in that matter of the African Railways. This paper had hitherto vigorously supported the President of the Council, but in the article in question the coldness which precedes a rupture was very apparent. Pierre replied that the article had much surprised him, for he had imagined that Fonsègue and Barroux were linked together by identity of views and long-standing personal friendship.

Massot was still laughing. 'Quite so,' said he. 'And you may be sure that the governor's heart bled when he wrote that article. It has been much noticed, and it will do the government a deal of harm. But the governor, you see, knows better than anybody else what line he ought to follow to save both his own position and the paper's.'

Then he related what extraordinary confusion and emotion reigned among the deputies in the lobbies through which he had strolled before coming upstairs to secure a seat. After an adjournment of a couple of days the Chamber found itself

THE GAME OF POLITICS

confronted by this terrible scandal, which was like one of those conflagrations which, at the moment when they are supposed to be dying out, suddenly flare up again and devour everything. The various figures given in Sagnier's list, the two hundred thousand francs paid to Barroux, the eighty thousand handed to Monferrand, the fifty thousand allotted to Fonsègue, the ten thousand pocketed by Duthil, and the three thousand secured by Chaigneux, with all the other amounts distributed among So-and-so and So-and-so, formed the general subject of conversation. And at the same time some most extraordinary stories were current; there was no end of tittle-tattle in which fact and falsehood were so inextricably mingled that everybody was at sea as to the real truth. Whilst many deputies turned pale and trembled as beneath a blast of terror, others passed by purple with excitement, bursting with delight, laughing with exultation at the thought of coming victory. For, in point of fact, beneath all the assumed indignation, all the calls for parliamentary cleanliness and morality, there simply lay a question of persons—the question of ascertaining whether the government would be overthrown, and in that event of whom the new administration would consist. Barroux no doubt appeared to be in a bad way; but with things in such a muddle one was bound to allow a margin for the unexpected. From what was generally said it seemed certain that Mège would be extremely violent. Barroux would answer him, and the Minister's friends declared that he was determined to speak out in the most decisive manner. As for Monferrand he would probably address the Chamber after his colleague, but Vignon's intentions were somewhat doubtful as, in spite of his delight, he made a pretence of remaining in the background. He had been seen going from one to another of his partisans, advising them to keep calm, in order that they might retain the cold, keen *coup d'œil* which in warfare generally decides the victory. Briefly, such was the plotting and intriguing that never had any witch's cauldron brimful of drugs and nameless abominations been set to boil on a more hellish fire than that of this parliamentary cook-shop.

'Heaven only knows what they will end by serving us,' said little Massot by way of conclusion.

General de Bozonnet for his part anticipated nothing but disaster. If France had only possessed an army, said he, one might have swept away that handful of bribe-taking parliamentarians who preyed upon the country and rotted it. But there was no army left, there was merely an armed nation, a very different thing. And thereupon, like a man of a past age whom the present times distracted, he started on what had been his favourite subject of complaint ever since he had been retired from the service.

'Here's an idea for an article if you want one,' he said to Massot. 'Although France may have a million soldiers she hasn't got an army. I'll give you some notes of mine, and you will be able to tell people the truth.'

Warfare, he continued, ought to be purely and simply a caste occupation, with commanders designated by divine right, leading mercenaries or volunteers into action. By democratising warfare people had simply killed it; a circumstance which he deeply regretted, like a born soldier who regarded fighting as the only really noble occupation that life offered. However, as soon as it became every man's duty to fight, none was willing to do so; and thus compulsory military service—what was called 'the nation in arms'—would, at a more or less distant date, certainly bring about the end of warfare. If France had not engaged in a European war since 1870 this was precisely due to the fact that everybody in France was ready to fight. But rulers hesitated to throw a whole nation against another nation, for the loss both in life and treasure would be tremendous. And so the thought that all Europe was transformed into a vast camp filled the General with anger and disgust. He sighed for the old times when men fought for the pleasure of the thing, just as they hunted; whereas nowadays people were convinced that they would exterminate one another at the very first engagement.

'But surely it wouldn't be an evil if war should disappear,' Pierre gently remarked.

This somewhat angered the General. 'Well, you'll have pretty nations if people no longer fight,' he answered, and then trying to show a practical spirit, he added: 'Never has the art of war cost more money than since war itself has become an impossibility. The present-day defensive peace is purely and simply ruining every country in Europe. One may be spared defeat, but utter bankruptcy is certainly at the end of it all. And in any case the profession of arms is done for. All faith in it is dying out, and it will soon be forsaken, just as men have begun to forsake the priesthood.'

Thereupon he made a gesture of mingled grief and anger,

almost cursing that parliament, that Republican legislature before him, as if he considered it responsible for the future extinction of warfare. Little Massot, however, was wagging his head dubiously, for he regarded the subject as rather too serious a one for him to write upon. And, all at once, in order to turn the conversation into another channel, he exclaimed: 'Ah! there's Monseigneur Martha in the diplomatic gallery beside the Spanish Ambassador. It's denied, you know, that he intends to come forward as a candidate in Morbihan. He's far too shrewd to wish to be a deputy. He already pulls the strings which set most of the Catholic deputies who have "rallied" to the Republican Government in motion.'

Pierre himself had just noticed Monseigneur Martha's smiling face. And, somehow or other, however modest might be the prelate's demeanour, it seemed to him that he really played an important part in what was going on. He could hardly take his eyes from him. It was as if he expected that he would suddenly order men hither and thither, and direct the whole march of events.

'Ah!' said Massot again. 'Here comes Mège. It won't be long now before the sitting begins.'

The hall, down below, was gradually filling. Deputies entered and descended the narrow passages between the benches. Most of them remained standing and chatting in a more or less excited way; but some seated themselves and raised their grey, weary faces to the glazed roof. It was a cloudy afternoon, and rain was doubtless threatening, for the light became quite livid. If the hall was pompous it was also dismal with its heavy columns, its cold allegorical statues, and its stretches of bare marble and woodwork. The only brightness was that of the red velvet of the benches and the gallery hand-rests.

Every deputy of any consequence who entered was named by Massot to his companions. Mège, on being stopped by another member of the little Socialist group, began to fume and gesticulate. Then Vignon, detaching himself from a group of friends and putting on an air of smiling composure, descended the steps towards his seat. The occupants of the galleries, however, gave most attention to the accused members, those whose names figured in Sagnier's list. And these were interesting studies. Some showed themselves quite sprightly, as if they were entirely at their ease; but others had assumed a most grave and indignant demeanour. Chaigneux staggered and hesitated as if beneath the weight of some frightful act of injustice ; whereas Duthil looked perfectly serene save for an occasional twitch of his lips. The most admired, however, was Fonsègue, who showed so candid a face, so open a glance, that his colleagues as well as the spectators might well have declared him innocent. Nobody indeed could have looked more like an honest man.

'Ah ! there's none like the governor,' muttered Fonsègue with enthusiasm. 'But be attentive, for here come the Ministers. One mustn't miss Barroux's meeting with Fonsègue, after this morning's article.'

Chance willed it that as Barroux came along with his head erect, his face pale and his whole demeanour aggressive, he was obliged to pass Fonsègue in order to reach the ministerial bench. In doing so he did not speak to him, but he gazed at him fixedly like one who is conscious of defection, of a cowardly stab in the back on the part of a traitor. Fonsègue, however, seemed quite at ease, and went on shaking hands with one and another of his colleagues as if he were altogether unconscious of Barroux's glance. Nor did he even appear to see Monferrand, who walked by in the rear of the prime minister, wearing a placid good-natured air, as if he knew nothing of what was impending, but was simply coming to some ordinary humdrum sitting. However, when he reached his seat, he raised his eyes and smiled at Monseigneur Martha, who gently nodded to him. Then, well pleased to think that things were going as he wished them to go, he began to rub his hands, as he often did by way of expressing his satisfaction.

'Who is that grey-haired, mournful-looking gentleman on the ministerial bench ?' Pierre inquired of Massot.

'Why, that's Taboureau, the Minister of Public Instruction, the excellent gentleman who is said to have no prestige. One's always hearing of him, and one never recognises him ; he looks like an old, badly-worn coin. Just like Barroux he can't feel very well pleased with the governor this afternoon, for to-day's 'Globe' contained an article pointing out his thorough incapacity in everything concerning the fine arts. It was an article in measured language, but all the more effective for that very reason. It would surprise me if Taboureau should recover from it.'

Just then a low roll of drums announced the arrival of

the President and other officials of the Chamber. A door opened, and a little procession passed by amidst an uproar of exclamations and hasty footsteps. Then, standing at his table, the President rang his bell and declared the sitting open. But few members remained silent, however, whilst one of the secretaries, a dark, lanky young man, with a harsh voice, read the minutes of the previous sitting. When they had been adopted, various letters of apology for non-attendance were read, and a short, unimportant bill was passed without discussion. Then, however, came the big affair, Mège's interpellation, and at once the whole Chamber was in a flutter, while the most passionate curiosity reigned in the galleries above. On the Government consenting to the interpellation, the Chamber decided that the debate should take place at once. And thereupon complete silence fell, save that now and again a brief quiver sped by, in which one could detect the various feelings, passions, and appetites swaying the assembly.

Mège began to speak with assumed moderation, carefully setting forth the various points at issue. Tall and thin, gnarled and twisted like a vine-stock, he rested his hands on the tribune as if to support his bent figure, and his speech was often interrupted by the little dry cough which came from the tuberculosis that was burning him. His eyes, however, sparkled with passion behind his glasses, and little by little his voice rose in piercing accents and he drew his lank figure erect and began to gesticulate vehemently. He reminded the Chamber that some two months previously, at the time of the first denunciations published by the ' Voix du Peuple,' he had asked leave to interpellate the Government respecting that deplorable affair of the African Railways ; and he remarked, truly enough, that if the Chamber had not yielded to certain considerations which he did not wish to discuss, and had not adjourned his proposed inquiries, full light would long since have been thrown on the whole affair, in such wise that there would have been no revival, no increase of the scandal, and no possible pretext for that abominable campaign of denunciation which tortured and disgusted the country. However, it had at last been understood that silence could be maintained no longer. It was necessary that the two Ministers who were so loudly accused of having abused their trusts, should prove their innocence, throw full light upon all they had done ; apart from which the

Chamber itself could not possibly remain beneath the charge
of wholesale venality.

Then he recounted the whole history of the affair, beginning with the grant of a concession for the African lines to
Baron Duvillard; and next passing to the proposals for the
issue of lottery stock, which proposals, it was now said, had
only been sanctioned by the Chamber after the most shameful
bargaining and buying of votes. At this point Mège became
extremely violent. Speaking of that mysterious individual
Hunter, Baron Duvillard's recruiter and go-between, he declared that the police had allowed him to flee from France,
much preferring to spend its time in shadowing Socialist
deputies. Then, hammering the tribune with his fist, he
summoned Barroux to give a categorical denial to the charges
brought against him, and to make it absolutely clear that he
had never received a single copper of the two hundred thousand francs specified in Hunter's list. Forthwith certain
members shouted to Mège that he ought to read the whole
list; but when he wished to do so others vociferated that it
was abominable, that such a mendacious and slanderous
document ought not to be accorded a place in the proceedings
of the French legislature. Mège went on, however, in
frantic fashion, figuratively casting Sagnier into the gutter,
and protesting that there was nothing in common between
himself and such a base insulter. But at the same time he
demanded that justice and punishment should be meted out
equally to one and all, and that if indeed there were any
bribe-takers among his colleagues, they should be sent that
very night to the prison of Mazas.

Meantime the President, erect at his table, rang and rang
his bell without managing to quell the uproar. He was like
a pilot who finds the tempest too strong for him. Among all
the men with purple faces and barking mouths who were
gathered in front of him, the ushers alone maintained imperturbable gravity. At intervals between the bursts of
shouting, Mège's voice could still be heard. By some sudden
transition he had come to the question of a Collectivist
organisation of society such as he dreamt of, and he contrasted it with the criminal capitalist society of the present
day, which alone, said he, could produce such scandals. And
yielding more and more to his apostolic fervour, declaring
that there could be no salvation apart from Collectivism, he
shouted that the day of triumph would soon dawn. He

awaited it with a smile of confidence. In his opinion, indeed, he merely had to overthrow that ministry and perhaps another one, and then he himself would at last take the reins of power in hand, like a reformer who would know how to pacify the nation. As outside Socialists often declared, it was evident that the blood of a dictator flowed in that sectarian's veins. His feverish, stubborn rhetoric ended by exhausting his interruptors, who were compelled to listen to him. When he at last decided to leave the tribune, loud applause arose from a few benches on the Left.

'Do you know,' said Massot to the General, 'I met Mège taking a walk with his three little children in the Jardin des Plantes the other day. He looked after them as carefully as an old nurse. I believe he's a very worthy fellow at heart, and lives in a very modest way.'

But a quiver had now sped through the assembly. Barroux had quitted his seat to ascend the tribune. He there drew himself erect, throwing his head back after his usual fashion. There was a haughty, majestic, slightly sorrowful expression on his handsome face, which would have been perfect had his nose only been a little larger. He began to express his sorrow and indignation in fine flowery language, which he punctuated with theatrical gestures. His eloquence was that of a tribune of the romantic school, and as one listened to him one could divine that in spite of all his pomposity he was really a worthy, tender-hearted, and somewhat foolish man. That afternoon he was stirred by genuine emotion; his heart bled at the thought of his disastrous destiny, he felt that a whole world was crumbling with himself. Ah! what a cry of despair he stifled, the cry of the man who is buffeted and thrown aside by the course of events on the very day when he thinks that his civic devotion entitles him to triumph! To have given himself and all he possessed to the cause of the Republic, even in the dark days of the Second Empire; to have fought and struggled and suffered persecution for that Republic's sake; to have established that Republic amidst the battle of parties, after all the horrors of national and civil war; and then, when the Republic at last triumphed and became a living fact, secure from all attacks and intrigues, to suddenly feel like a survival of some other age, to hear new-comers speak a new language, preach a new ideal, and behold the collapse of all he had loved, all he had reverenced, all that had given him strength to fight and conquer! The mighty artisans of the early hours were no more; it had been meet that Gambetta should die. How bitter it all was for the last lingering old ones to find themselves among the men of the new, intelligent, and shrewd generation, who gently smiled at them, deeming their romanticism quite out of fashion! All crumbled since the ideal of liberty collapsed, since liberty was no longer the one desideratum, the very basis of the Republic, whose existence had been so dearly purchased, after so long an effort!

Erect and dignified Barroux made his confession. The Republic to him was like the sacred ark of life; the very worst deeds became saintly if they were employed to save her from peril. And in all simplicity he told his story, how he had found the great bulk of Baron Duvillard's money going to the opposition newspapers as pretended payment for puffery and advertising, whilst on the other hand the Republican organs received but beggarly, trumpery amounts. He had been Minister of the Interior at the time, and had therefore had charge of the press; so what would have been said of him if he had not endeavoured to re-establish some equilibrium in this distribution of funds, in order that the adversaries of the institutions of the country might not acquire a great increase of strength by appropriating all the sinews of war? Hands had been stretched out towards him on all sides, a score of newspapers, the most faithful, the most meritorious, had claimed their legitimate share. And he had ensured them that share by distributing among them the two hundred thousand francs set down in the list against his name. Not a centime of the money had gone into his own pocket, he would allow nobody to impugn his personal honesty, on that point his word must suffice. At that moment Barroux was really grand. All his emphatic pomposity disappeared; he showed himself as he really was—an honest man, quivering, his heart bared, his conscience bleeding, in his bitter distress at having been among those who had laboured and at now being denied reward.

For, truth to tell, his words fell amidst icy silence. In his childish simplicity he had anticipated an outburst of enthusiasm; a Republican Chamber could but acclaim him for having saved the Republic; and now the frigidity of one and all quite froze him. He suddenly felt that he was all alone, done for, touched by the hand of death. Nevertheless, he continued speaking amidst that terrible silence with the courage of one who is committing suicide, and who, from his love of noble and eloquent attitudes, is determined to die standing. He ended with a final impressive gesture. However, as he came down from the tribune, the general coldness seemed to increase, not a single member applauded. With supreme clumsiness he had alluded to the secret scheming of Rome and the clergy whose one object, in his opinion, was to recover the predominant position they had lost and restore monarchy in France at a more or less distant date.

'How silly of him! Ought a man ever to confess?' muttered Massot. 'He's done for, and the ministry too!'

Amidst the general frigidity, however, Monferrand boldly ascended the tribune-stairs. The prevailing uneasiness was compounded of all the secret fear which sincerity always causes, of all the distress of the bribe-taking deputies who felt that they were rolling into an abyss, and also of the embarrassment which the others felt at thought of the more or less justifiable compromises of politics. Something like relief, therefore, came when Monferrand started with the most emphatic denials, protesting in the name of his outraged honour, and dealing blow after blow on the tribune with one hand, while with the other he smote his chest. Short and thickset, with his face thrust forward, hiding his shrewdness beneath an expression of indignant frankness, he was for a moment really superb. He denied everything. He was not only ignorant of what was meant by that sum of eighty thousand francs set down against his name, but he defied the whole world to prove that he had even touched a single copper of that money. He boiled over with indignation to such a point that he did not simply deny bribe-taking on his own part, he denied it on behalf of the whole assembly, of all present and past French legislatures, as if, indeed, bribe-taking on the part of a representative of the people was altogether too monstrous an idea, a crime that surpassed possibility to such an extent that the mere notion of it was absurd. And thereupon applause rang out; the Chamber, delivered from its fears, thrilled by his words, acclaimed him.

From the little Socialist group, however, some jeers arose, and voices summoned Monferrand to explain himself on the subject of the African Railways, reminding him that he had been at the head of the Public Works Department at the time of the vote, and requiring of him that he should state what he now meant to do, as Minister of the Interior, in order to

reassure the country. He juggled with this question, declaring
that if there were any guilty parties they would be punished,
for he did not require anybody to remind him of his duty.
And then, all at once, with incomparable maestria, he had
recourse to the diversion which he had been preparing since
the previous day. His duty, said he, was a thing which he
never forgot; he discharged it like a faithful soldier of the
nation hour by hour, and with as much vigilance as prudence.
He had been accused of employing the police on he knew not
what base spying work in such wise as to allow the man
Hunter to escape. Well, as for that much-slandered police
force, he would tell the Chamber on what work he had really
employed it the day before, and how zealously it had laboured
for the cause of law and order. In the Bois de Boulogne on
the previous afternoon, it had arrested that terrible scoundrel,
the perpetrator of the crime in the Rue Godot-de-Mauroy,
that Anarchist mechanician Salvat, who for six weeks past had
so cunningly contrived to elude capture. The scoundrel had
made a full confession during the evening, and the law would
now take its course with all despatch. Public morality was
at last avenged, Paris might now emerge in safety from its
long spell of terror, Anarchism would be struck down, annihilated. And that was what he, Monferrand, had done as a
Minister for the honour and safety of his country, whilst
villains were vainly seeking to dishonour him by inscribing
his name on a list of infamy, the outcome of the very basest
political intrigues.

The Chamber listened agape and quivering. This story
of Salvat's arrest, which none of the morning papers had
reported; the present which Monferrand seemed to be
making them of that terrible Anarchist whom many had
already begun to regard as a myth; the whole *mise-en-
scène* of the Minister's speech transported the deputies as if
they were suddenly witnessing the finish of a long interrupted
drama. Stirred and flattered, they prolonged their applause,
while Monferrand went on celebrating his act of energy, how
he had saved society, how crime should be punished, and how
he himself would ever prove that he had a strong arm and
could answer for public order. He even won favour with the
Conservatives and Clericals on the Right by separating
himself from Barroux, addressing a few words of sympathy
to those Catholics who had 'rallied' to the Republic, and
appealing for concord among men of different beliefs in order

that they might fight the common enemy, that fierce, wild socialism which talked of overthrowing everything !

By the time Monferrand came down from the tribune, the trick was played, he had virtually saved himself. Both the Right and Left of the Chamber [1] applauded, drowning the protests of the few Socialists whose vociferations only added to the triumphal tumult. Members eagerly stretched out their hands to the Minister, who for a moment remained standing there and smiling. There was, however, some anxiety in that smile of his ; his success was beginning to frighten him. Had he spoken too well, and saved the entire Cabinet instead of merely saving himself? That would mean the ruin of his plan. The Chamber ought not to vote under the effect of that speech which had thrilled it so powerfully. Thus Monferrand, though he still continued to smile, spent a few anxious moments in waiting to see if anybody would rise to answer him.

His success had been as great among the occupants of the galleries as among the deputies themselves. Several ladies had been seen applauding, and Monseigneur Martha had given unmistakable signs of the liveliest satisfaction. 'Ah, General!' said Massot to Bozonnet in a sneering way. 'Those are our fighting men of the present time. And he's a bold and strong one is Monferrand. Of course it is all what people style "saving one's bacon," but none the less it's very clever work.'

Just then, however, Monferrand to his great satisfaction had seen Vignon rise from his seat in response to the urging of his friends. And thereupon all anxiety vanished from the Minister's smile, which became one of malicious placidity.

The very atmosphere of the Chamber seemed to change with Vignon in the tribune. He was slim, with a fair and

---

[1] Ever since the days of the Bourbon Restoration it has been the practice in the French Chambers for the more Conservative members to seat themselves on the President's right, and for the Radical ones to place themselves on his left. The central seats of the semicircle in which the members' seats are arranged in tiers are usually occupied by men of moderate views. Generally speaking, such terms as Right Centre and Left Centre are applied to groups of Moderates inclining in the first place to Conservatism and in the latter to Radicalism. All this is of course known to readers acquainted with French institutions, but I give the explanation because others, after perusing French news in some daily paper, have often asked me what was meant by 'a deputy of the Right,' and so forth.—*Trans.*

carefully tended beard, blue eyes, and all the suppleness of youth. He spoke, moreover, like a practical man, in simple, straightforward language, which made the emptiness of the others' declamatory style painfully conspicuous. His term of official service as a prefect in the provinces had endowed him with keen insight; and it was in an easy way that he propounded and unravelled the most intricate questions. Active and courageous, confident in his own star, too young and too shrewd to have compromised himself in anything so far, he was steadily marching towards the future. He had already drawn up a rather more advanced political programme than that of Barroux and Monferrand, so that when opportunity offered there might be good reasons for him to take their place. Moreover, he was quite capable of carrying out his programme by attempting some of the long-promised reforms for which the country was waiting. He had guessed that honesty, when it had prudence and shrewdness as its allies, must some day secure an innings. In a clear voice, and in a very quiet, deliberate way, he now said what it was right to say on the subject under discussion, the things that common sense dictated and that the Chamber itself secretly desired should be said. He was certainly the first to rejoice over an arrest which would reassure the country; but he failed to understand what connection there could be between that arrest and the sad business that had been brought before the Chamber. The two affairs were quite distinct and different, and he begged his colleagues not to vote in the state of excitement in which he saw them. Full light must be thrown on the African Railways question, and this one could not expect from the two incriminated Ministers. However, he was opposed to any suggestion of a committee of inquiry. In his opinion the guilty parties, if such there were, ought to be brought immediately before a court of law. And, like Barroux, he wound up with a discreet allusion to the growing influence of the clergy, declaring that he was against all unworthy compromises, and was equally opposed to any state dictatorship and any revival of the ancient theocratic spirit.

Although there was but little applause when Vignon returned to his seat, it was evident that the Chamber was again master of its emotions. And the situation seemed so clear, and the overthrow of the ministry so certain, that Mège, who had meant to reply to the others, wisely abstained.

from doing so. Meantime people noticed the placid demeanour of Monferrand, who had listened to Vignon with the utmost complacency, as if he were rendering homage to an adversary's talent; whereas Barroux, ever since the cold silence which had greeted his speech, had remained motionless in his seat, bowed down and pale as a corpse.

'Well, it's all over,' resumed Massot, amidst the hubbub which arose as the deputies prepared to vote; 'the ministry's done for. Little Vignon will go a long way, you know. People say that he dreams of the Elysée. At all events everything points to him as our next prime minister.'

Then, as the journalist rose, intending to go off, the General detained him: 'Wait a moment, Monsieur Massot,' said he. 'How disgusting all that parliamentary cooking is! You ought to point it out in an article, and show people how the country is gradually being weakened and rotted to the marrow by all such useless and degrading discussions. Why a great battle resulting in the loss of 50,000 men would exhaust us less than ten years of this abominable parliamentary system. You must call on me some morning. I will show you a scheme of military reform, in which I point out the necessity of returning to the limited, professional armies which we used to have, for this present-day national army, as folks call it, which is a semi-civilian affair and at best a mere herd of men, is like a dead weight on us, and is bound to pull us down!'

Pierre, for his part, had not spoken a word since the beginning of the debate. He had listened to everything, at first influenced by the thought of his brother's interests, and afterwards mastered by the feverishness which gradually took possession of everybody present. He had become convinced that there was nothing more for Guillaume to fear; but how curiously did one event fit into another, and how loudly had Salvat's arrest re-echoed in the Chamber! Looking down into the seething hall below him, he had detected all the clash of rival passions and interests. After watching the great struggle between Barroux, Monferrand, and Vignon, he had gazed upon the childish delight of that terrible Socialist Mège, who was so pleased at having been able to stir up the depths of those troubled waters, in which he always unwittingly angled for the benefit of others. Then, too, Pierre had become interested in Fonsègue, who, knowing what had been arranged between Monferrand, Duvillard, and himself,

evinced perfect calmness and strove to reassure Duthil and
Chaigneux, who, on their side, were quite dismayed by the
ministry's impending fall. However, Pierre's eyes always
came back to Monseigneur Martha. He had watched his
serene smiling face throughout the sitting, striving to detect
his impressions of the various incidents that had occurred, as
if in his opinion that dramatic parliamentary comedy had
only been played as a step towards the more or less distant
triumph for which the prelate laboured. And now, while
awaiting the result of the vote, as Pierre turned towards
Massot and the General, he found that they were talking of
nothing but recruiting and tactics and the necessity of a bath
of blood for the whole of Europe. Ah! poor mankind, ever
fighting and ever devouring one another in parliaments as
well as on battle-fields, when, thought Pierre, would it decide
to disarm once and for all, and live at peace according to the
laws of justice and reason!

Then he again looked down into the hall, where the greatest confusion was prevailing among the deputies with regard
to the coming vote. There was quite a rainfall of suggested
'resolutions,' from a very violent one proposed by Mège, to
another, which was merely severe, emanating from Vignon.
The ministry, however, would only accept the 'Order of the
day pure and simple,' a mere decision, that is, to pass to the
next business, as if Mège's interpellation had been unworthy
of attention. And presently the Government was defeated,
Vignon's resolution being adopted by a majority of twenty-
five. Some portion of the Left had evidently joined hands
with the Right and the Socialist group. A prolonged hubbub
followed this result.

'Well, so we are to have a Vignon Cabinet,' said Massot,
as he went off with Pierre and the General. 'All the same,
however, Monferrand has saved himself, and if I were in
Vignon's place I should distrust him.'

That evening there was a very touching farewell scene at
the little house at Neuilly. When Pierre returned thither
from the Chamber, saddened but reassured with regard to
the future, Guillaume at once made up his mind to go home
on the morrow. And as Nicholas Barthès was compelled to
leave, the little dwelling seemed on the point of relapsing
into dreary quietude once more.

Théophile Morin, whom Pierre had informed of the painful
alternative in which Barthès was placed, duly came to dinner;

but he did not have time to speak to the old man before they all sat down to table at seven o'clock. As usual Barthès had spent his day in marching, like a caged lion, up and down the room in which he had accepted shelter after the fashion of a big fearless child, who never worried with regard either to his present circumstances or the troubles which the future might have in store for him. His life had ever been one of unlimited hope, which reality had ever shattered. Although all that he had loved, all that he had hoped to secure by fifty years of imprisonment or exile— liberty, equality and a real brotherly republic—had hitherto failed to come, such as he had dreamt of them, he nevertheless retained the candid faith of his youth, and was ever confident in the near future. He would smile indulgently when new-comers, men of violent ideas, derided him and called him a poor old fellow. For his part, he could make neither head nor tail of the many new sects. He simply felt indignant with their lack of human feeling, and stubbornly adhered to his own idea of basing the world's regeneration on the simple proposition that men were naturally good and ought to be free and brotherly.

That evening at dinner, feeling that he was with friends who cared for him, Barthès proved extremely gay, and showed all his ingenuousness in talking of his ideal which would soon be realised, said he, in spite of everything. He could tell a story well whenever he cared to chat, and on that occasion he related some delightful anecdotes about the prisons through which he had passed. He knew all the dungeons, Ste. Pélagie and Mont St. Michel, Belle-Ile-en-Mer and Clairvaux, to say nothing of temporary gaols, and the evil-smelling hulks on board which political prisoners are often confined. And he still laughed at certain recollections, and related how in the direst circumstances he had always been able to seek refuge in his conscience. The others listened to him quite charmed by his conversation, but full of anguish at the thought that this perpetual prisoner or exile must again rise and take his staff to sally forth, driven from his native land once more.

Pierre did not speak out until they were partaking of dessert. Then he related how the Minister had written to him, and how in a brief interview he had stated that Barthès must cross the frontier within forty-eight hours if he did not wish to be arrested. Thereupon the old man gravely rose, with his white fleece, his eagle beak, and his bright eyes still sparkling with the fire of youth. And he wished to go off at once. 'What!' said he, 'you have known all this since yesterday, and have still kept me here at the risk of my compromising you even more than I had done already! You must forgive me, I did not think of the worry I might cause you, I thought that everything would be satisfactorily arranged. I must thank you both—yourself and Guillaume—for the few days of quietude that you have procured to an old vagabond and madman like myself.'

Then, as they tried to prevail on him to remain until the following morning, he would not listen to them. There would be a train for Brussels about midnight, and he had ample time to take it. He refused to let Morin accompany him. No, no, said he, Morin was not a rich man, and moreover he had work to attend to. Why should he take him away from his duties, when it was so easy, so simple, for him to go off alone? He was going back into exile as into misery and grief which he had long known, like some Wandering Jew of Liberty, ever driven onward through the world.

When he took leave of the others at ten o'clock, in the little sleepy street just outside the house, tears suddenly dimmed his eyes. 'Ah! I'm no longer a young man,' he said; 'it's all over this time. I shall never come back again. My bones will rest in some corner over yonder.' And yet, after he had affectionately embraced Pierre and Guillaume, he drew himself up like one who remained unconquered, and he raised a supreme cry of hope. 'But after all, who knows? Triumph may perhaps come to-morrow. The future belongs to those who prepare it and wait for it!'

Then he walked away, and long after he had disappeared his firm, sonorous footsteps could be heard re-echoing in the quiet night.

BOOK IV

I

PIERRE AND MARIE

On the mild March morning when Pierre left his little house at Neuilly to accompany Guillaume to Montmartre, he was oppressed by the thought that on returning home he would once more find himself alone with nothing to prevent him from relapsing into negation and despair. The idea of this had kept him from sleeping, and he still found it difficult to hide his distress and force a smile.

The sky was so clear and the atmosphere so mild that the brothers had resolved to go to Montmartre on foot by way of the outer boulevards. Nine o'clock was striking when they set out. Guillaume for his part was very gay at the thought of the surprise he would give his family. It was as if he were suddenly coming back from a long journey. He had not warned them of his intentions; he had merely written to them now and again to tell them that he was recovering, and they certainly had no idea that his return was so near at hand.

When Guillaume and Pierre had climbed the sunlit slopes of Montmartre, and crossed the quiet countryfied Place du Tertre, the former, by means of a latchkey, quietly opened the door of his house, which seemed to be asleep, so profound was the stillness both around and within it. Pierre found it the same as on the occasion of his previous and only visit. First came the narrow passage which ran through the ground floor, affording a view of all Paris at the further end. Next there was the garden, reduced to a couple of plum trees and a clump of lilac bushes, the leaves of which had now sprouted. And this time the priest perceived three bicycles leaning against the trees. Beyond them stood the large workshop, so gay,

and yet so peaceful, with its huge window overlooking a sea
of roofs.

Guillaume had reached the workshop without meeting
anybody. With an expression of much amusement he raised
a finger to his lips. 'Attention, Pierre,' he whispered; 'you'll
just see!'

Then having noiselessly opened the door, they remained
for a moment on the threshold.

The three sons alone were there. Near his forge stood
Thomas working a boring machine with which he was making
some holes in a small brass plate. Then François and Antoine
were seated on either side of their large table, the former
reading, and the latter finishing a block. The bright sunshine
streamed in, playing over all the seeming disorder of the room,
where so many callings and so many implements found place.
A large bunch of wallflowers bloomed on the women's work-
table near the window; and absorbed as the young men were
in their respective tasks the only sound was the slight hissing
of the boring-machine each time that the eldest of them drilled
another hole.

However, although Guillaume did not stir, there suddenly
came a quiver, an awakening. His sons seemed to guess his
presence, for they raised their heads, each at the same moment.
From each, too, came the same cry, and a common impulse
brought them first to their feet and then to his arms.

'Father!'

Guillaume embraced them, feeling very happy. And that
was all; there was no long spell of emotion, no useless talk.
It was as if he had merely gone out the day before and, delayed
by business, had now come back. Still, he looked at them
with his kindly smile, and they likewise smiled with their eyes
fixed on his. Those glances proclaimed everything, the closest
affection and complete self-bestowal for ever.

'Come in, Pierre,' called Guillaume, 'shake hands with
these young men.'

The priest had remained near the door, overcome by a
singular feeling of discomfort. When his nephews had
vigorously shaken hands with him, he sat down near the
window apart from them, as if he felt out of his element
there.

'Well, youngsters,' said Guillaume, 'where's Mère-Grand,
and where's Marie?'

Their grandmother was upstairs in her room, they said;

and Marie had taken it into her head to go marketing. This, by the way, was one of her delights. She asserted that she was the only one who knew how to buy new-laid eggs and butter of a nutty odour. Moreover, she sometimes brought some dainty or some flowers home, in her delight at proving herself to be so good a housewife.

' And so things are going on well ? ' resumed Guillaume. ' You are all satisfied, your work is progressing, eh ? '

He addressed brief questions to each of them, like one who, on his return home, at once reverts to his usual habits. Thomas, with his rough face beaming, explained in a couple of sentences that he was now sure of perfecting his little motor ; François, who was still preparing for his examination, jestingly declared that he yet had to lodge a heap of learning in his brain ; and then Antoine produced the block which he was finishing, and which depicted his little friend Lise, Jahan's sister, reading in her garden amidst the sunshine. It was like a florescence of that dear belated creature whose mind had been awakened by his affection.

However, the three brothers speedily went back to their places, reverting to their work with a natural impulse, for discipline had made them regard work as life itself. Then Guillaume, who had glanced at what each was doing, exclaimed : 'Ah ! youngsters, I schemed and prepared a lot of things myself while I was laid up. I even made a good many notes. We walked here from Neuilly, but my papers and the clothes which Mère-Grand sent me will come in a cab by-and-bye. . . . Ah ! how pleased I am to find everything in order here, and to be able to take up my task with you again ! Ah ! I shall polish off some work now, and no mistake ! '

He had already gone to his own corner, the space reserved for him between the window and the forge. He there had a chemical furnace, several glass cases and shelves crowded with appliances, and a long table, one end of which he used for writing purposes. And he once more took possession of that little world. After glancing around with delight at seeing everything in its place, he began to handle one object and another, eager to be at work like his sons.

All at once, however, Mère-Grand appeared, calm, grave and erect in her black gown, at the top of the little staircase which conducted to the bedrooms. ' So it's you, Guillaume,' said she, ' will you come up for a moment ? '

He immediately did so, understanding that she wished
to speak to him alone and tranquillise him. It was a question of the great secret between them, that one thing of
which her sons knew nothing, and which, after Salvat's
crime, had brought him to much anguish, through his fear
that it might be divulged. When he reached Mère-Grand's
room she at once took him to the hiding-place near her bed,
and showed him the cartridges of the new explosive, and
the plans of the terrible engine of warfare which he had
invented. He found them all as he had left them. Before
anyone could have reached them, she would have blown up
the whole place at the risk of perishing herself in the explosion. With her wonted air of quiet heroism, she handed
Guillaume the key which he had sent her by Pierre.

'You were not anxious, I hope,' she said.

He pressed her hands with a commingling of affection
and respect. 'My only anxiety,' he replied, 'was that the
police might come here and treat you roughly. . . . You are
the guardian of our secret, and it would be for you to finish
my work should I disappear.'

While Guillaume and Madame Leroi were thus engaged
upstairs, Pierre, still seated near the window below, felt his
discomfort increasing. The inmates of the house certainly
regarded him with no other feeling than one of affectionate
sympathy; and so how came it that he considered them
hostile? The truth was that he asked himself what would
become of him among those workers, who were upheld by
a faith of their own, whereas he believed in nothing, and
did not work. The sight of those young men, so gaily and
zealously toiling, ended by quite irritating him; and the
arrival of Marie brought his distress to a climax.

Joyous and full of life she came in without seeing him,
a basket on her arm. And she seemed to bring all the sunlight of the spring morning with her, so bright was the
sparkle of her youth. The whole of her pink face, her
delicate nose, her broad intelligent brow, her thick, kindly
lips beamed beneath the heavy coils of her black hair. And
her brown eyes ever laughed with the joyousness which comes
from health and strength.

'Ah!' she exclaimed, 'I have brought such a lot of
things, youngsters. Just come and see them, I wouldn't
unpack the basket in the kitchen.'

It became absolutely necessary for the brothers to draw

round the basket which she had laid upon the table. 'First there's the butter!' said she, 'just smell if it hasn't a nice scent of nuts! It's churned especially for me, you know. Then here are the eggs. They were laid only yesterday, I'll answer for it. And, in fact, that one there is this morning's. And look at the cutlets! They're wonderful, aren't they? The butcher cuts them carefully when he sees me. And then here's a cream cheese, real cream, you know, it will be delicious! Ah! and here's the surprise, something dainty, some radishes, some pretty little pink radishes. Just fancy! radishes in March, what a luxury!'[1]

She triumphed like the good little housewife she was, one who had followed a whole course of cookery and home duties at the Lycée Fénelon. The brothers, as merry as she herself, were obliged to compliment her.

All at once, however, she caught sight of Pierre. 'What! you are there, Monsieur l'Abbé?' she exclaimed, 'I beg your pardon, but I didn't see you. How is Guillaume? Have you brought us some news of him?'

'But father's come home,' said Thomas, 'he's upstairs with Mère-Grand.'

Quite thunderstruck, she hastily placed her purchases in the basket. 'Guillaume's come back, Guillaume's come back!' said she, 'and you don't tell me of it, you let me unpack everything! Well, it's nice of me, I must say, to go on praising my butter and eggs when Guillaume's come back.'

Guillaume, as it happened, was just coming down with Madame Leroi. Marie gaily hastened to him and offered him her cheeks, on which he printed two resounding kisses. Then she, resting her hands on his shoulders, gave him a long look, while saying in a somewhat tremulous voice: 'I am pleased, very pleased to see you, Guillaume. I may confess it now; I thought I had lost you, I was very anxious and very unhappy.'

Although she was still smiling, tears had gathered in her eyes, and he, likewise moved, again kissed her, murmuring: 'Dear Marie! How happy it makes me to find you as beautiful and as affectionate as ever.'

Pierre, who was looking at them, deemed them cold. He had doubtless expected more tears, and a more passionate

---

[1] Pampered Londoners, who nowadays get every kind of vegetable and fruit both in and out of season, will scarcely be of Marie's opinion.—*Trans.*

embrace on the part of an affianced pair, whom so grievous
an accident had separated almost on the eve of their wedding.
Moreover, his feelings were hurt by the disproportion of their
respective ages. No doubt his brother still seemed to him
very sturdy and young, and his feeling of repulsion must
have come from that young woman whom, most decidedly, he
did not like. Ever since her arrival he had experienced
increasing discomfort, a keener and keener desire to go off
and never return.

So acute became his suffering at feeling like a stranger in
his brother's home, that he at last rose and sought to take
his leave, under the pretext that he had some urgent matters
to attend to in town.

'What! you won't stay to *déjeuner* with us!' exclaimed
Guillaume in perfect stupefaction. 'Why, it was agreed!
You surely won't distress me like that! This house is your
own, remember!'

Then as with genuine affection they all protested and
pressed him to stay he was obliged to do so. However, he
soon relapsed into silence and embarrassment, seated on the
same chair as before, and listening moodily to those people
who, although they were his relatives, seemed to be far
removed from him.

As it was barely eleven o'clock they resumed work, but
every now and again there was some merry talk. On one of
the servants coming for the provisions, Marie told the girl to
call her as soon as it should be time to boil the eggs, for she
prided herself on boiling them to a nicety, in such wise as to
leave the whites like creamy milk. This gave an opportunity
for a few jests from François, who occasionally teased her
about all the fine things she had learnt at the Lycée Fénelon,
where her father had placed her when she was twelve years
old. However, she was not afraid of him, but gave him tit
for tat by chaffing him about all the hours which he lost at
the École Normale over a mass of pedagogic trash.

'Ah! you big children!' she exclaimed, while still
working at her embroidery. 'You are all very intelligent,
and you all claim to have broad minds, and yet—confess it
now—it worries you a little that a girl like me should have
studied at college in the same way as yourselves. It's a
sexual quarrel, a question of rivalry and competition, isn't
it?'

They protested the contrary, declaring that they were in

favour of girls receiving as complete an education as possible. She was well aware of this ; however, she liked to tease them in return for the manner in which they themselves plagued her.

'But do you know,' said she, 'you are a great deal behind the times? I am well aware of the reproaches which are levelled at girls' colleges by so-called right-minded people. To begin, there is no religious element whatever in the education one receives there, and this alarms many families which consider religious education to be absolutely necessary for girls, if only as a moral weapon of defence. Then, too, the education at our Lycées is being democratised—girls of all positions come to them. Thanks to the scholarships which are so liberally offered, the daughter of the lady who rents a first floor flat often finds the daughter of her door-keeper among her schoolfellows, and some think this objectionable. It is said also that the pupils free themselves too much from home influence, and that too much opportunity is left for personal initiative. As a matter of fact the extensiveness of the many courses of study, all the learning that is required of pupils at the examinations, certainly does tend to their emancipation, to the coming of the future woman and future society, which you young men are all longing for, are you not ?'

'Of course we are ! ' exclaimed François, ' we all agree on that point.'

She waved her hand in a pretty way, and then quietly continued : ' I'm jesting. My views are simple enough, as you well know, and I don't ask for nearly as much as you do. As for woman's claims and rights, well the question is clear enough ; woman is man's equal so far as nature allows it And the only point is to agree and love one another. At the same time I'm well pleased to know what I do—oh ! not from any spirit of pedantry but simply because I think it has all done me good, and given me some moral as well as physical health.'

It delighted her to recall the days she had spent at the Lycée Fénelon, which of the five State colleges for girls opened in Paris was the only one counting a large number of pupils. Most of these were the daughters of officials or professors, who purposed entering the teaching profession. In this case, they had to win their last diploma at the École Normale of Sèvres, after leaving the Lycée. Marie, for her

part, though her studies had been brilliant, had felt no taste
whatever for the calling of teacher. Moreover, when Guillaume had taken charge of her after her father's death, he
had refused to let her run about giving lessons. To provide
herself with a little money, for she would accept none as a
gift, she worked at embroidery, an art in which she was most
accomplished.

While she was talking to the young men Guillaume had
listened to her without interfering. If he had fallen in love
with her it was largely on account of her frankness and up-
rightness, the even balance of her nature, which gave her so
forcible a charm. She knew all ; but if she lacked the poetry
of the shrinking, lamblike girl who has been brought up in
ignorance, she had gained absolute rectitude of heart and
mind, exempt from all hypocrisy, all secret perversity such as
is stimulated by what may seem mysterious in life. And
whatever she might know, she had retained such childlike
purity, that in spite of her six-and-twenty summers, all the
blood in her veins would occasionally rush to her cheeks in
fiery blushes, which drove her to despair.

'My dear Marie,' Guillaume now exclaimed, 'you know
very well that the youngsters were simply joking. You are
in the right, of course. . . . And your boiled eggs cannot be
matched in the whole world.'

He said this in so soft and affectionate a tone that the
young woman flushed purple. Then, becoming conscious of
it, she coloured yet more deeply, and as the three young men
glanced at her maliciously she grew angry with herself.
'Isn't it ridiculous, Monsieur l'Abbé,' she said, turning
towards Pierre, 'for an old maid like myself to blush in that
fashion ? People might think that I had committed a crime.
It's simply to make me blush, you know, that those children
tease me. I do all I can to prevent it, but it's stronger than
my will.'

At this Mère-Grand raised her eyes from the shirt she
was mending, and remarked : 'Oh ! it's natural enough, my
dear. It is your heart rising to your cheeks in order that we
may see it.'

The *déjeuner* hour was now at hand ; and they decided
to lay the table in the workshop as was occasionally done
when they had a guest. The simple, cordial meal proved
very enjoyable in the bright sunlight. Marie's boiled eggs,
which she herself brought from the kitchen covered with a

napkin, were found delicious. Due honour was also done to the butter and the radishes. The only dessert that followed the cutlets was the cream cheese, but it was a cheese such as nobody else had ever partaken of. And, meantime, while they ate and chatted all Paris lay below them stretching away to the horizon with its mighty rumbling.

Pierre had made an effort to become cheerful, but he soon relapsed into silence. Guillaume, however, was very talkative. Having noticed the three bicycles in the garden, he inquired of Marie how far she had gone that morning. She answered that François and Antoine had accompanied her in the direction of Orgemont. The worry of their excursions was that each time they returned to Montmartre they had to push their machines up the height. From the general point of view, however, the young woman was delighted with bicycling, which had many virtues, said she. Then, seeing Pierre glance at her in amazement, she promised that she would some day explain her opinions on the subject to him. After this bicycling became the one topic of conversation until the end of the meal. Thomas gave an account of the latest improvements introduced into Grandidier's machines; and the others talked of the excursions they had made or meant to make, with all the exuberant delight of school children eager for the open air.

In the midst of the chatter, Mère-Grand, who presided at table with the serene dignity of a queen-mother, leant towards Guillaume, who sat next to her, and spoke to him in an undertone. Pierre understood that she was referring to his marriage, which was to have taken place in April, but must now necessarily be deferred. This sensible marriage, which seemed likely to ensure the happiness of the entire household, was largely the work of Mère-Grand and the three young men, for Guillaume would never have yielded to his heart if she whom he proposed to make his wife had not already been a well-loved member of the family. At the present time the last week in June seemed, for all sorts of reasons, to be a favourable date for the wedding.

Marie, who heard the suggestion, turned gaily towards Mère-Grand.

'The end of June will suit very well, will it not, my dear?' said the latter.

Pierre expected to see a flush rise to the young woman's cheeks, but she remained very calm. She felt deep affection, blended with the most tender gratitude, for Guillaume, and was convinced that in marrying him she would be acting wisely and well both for herself and the others.

'Certainly, the end of June,' she repeated, 'that will suit very well indeed.'

Then the sons, who likewise had heard the proposal, nodded their heads by way of assenting also.

When they rose from table Pierre was absolutely determined to go off. The cordial and simple meal, the sight of that family, which had been rendered so happy by Guillaume's return, and of that young woman who smiled so placidly at life, had brought him keen suffering, though why he could not tell. However, it all irritated him beyond endurance; and he therefore again pretended that he had a number of things to see to in Paris. He shook hands in turn with the young men, Mère-Grand and Marie; both of the women evincing great friendliness but also some surprise at his haste to leave the house. Guillaume, who seemed saddened and anxious, sought to detain him, and failing in this endeavour followed him into the little garden, where he stopped him in order to have an explanation.

'Come,' said he, 'what is the matter with you, Pierre? Why are you running off like this?'

'Oh! there's nothing the matter I assure you; but I have to attend to a few urgent affairs.'

'Oh, Pierre, pray put all pretence aside. Nobody here has displeased you or hurt your feelings, I hope. They will all soon love you as I do.'

'I have no doubt of it, and I complain of nobody excepting perhaps myself.'

Guillaume's sorrow was increasing. 'Ah! brother, little brother,' he resumed, 'you distress me, for I can detect that you are hiding something from me. Remember that new ties have linked us together and that we love one another as in the old days when you were in your cradle and I used to come to play with you. I know you well, remember. I know all your tortures since you have confessed them to me; and I won't have you suffer; I want to cure you, I do!'

Pierre's heart was full, and as he heard those words he could not restrain his tears. 'Oh! you must leave me to my sufferings,' he responded. 'They are incurable. You can do nothing for me; I am beyond the pale of nature, I am a monster.'

'What do you say! Can you not return within nature's pale even if you *have* gone beyond it? One thing that I will not allow is that you should go and shut yourself up in that solitary little house of yours, where you madden yourself by brooding over the fall of your faith. Come and spend your time with us, so that we may again give you some taste for life.'

Ah! the empty little house which awaited him! Pierre shivered at the thought of it, at the idea that he would now find himself all alone there, bereft of the brother with whom he had lately spent so many happy days. Into what solitude and torment must he not now relapse after that companionship to which he had become accustomed? However, the very thought of the latter increased his grief, and confession suddenly gushed from his lips: 'To spend my time here, live with you, oh! no, that is an impossibility. Why do you compel me to speak out, and tell you things that I am ashamed of and do not even understand? Ever since this morning you must have seen that I have been suffering here. No doubt it is because you and your people work, whereas I do nothing, because you love one another and believe in your efforts, whereas I no longer know how to love or believe. I feel out of my element. I'm embarrassed here, and I embarrass you. In fact you all irritate me, and I might end by hating you. There remains nothing healthy in me, all natural feelings have been spoilt and destroyed, and only envy and hatred could sprout up from such ruins. So let me go back to my accursed hole, where death will some day come for me. Farewell, brother!'

But Guillaume, full of affection and compassion, caught hold of his arms and detained him. 'You shall not go, I will not allow you to go without a positive promise that you will come back. I don't wish to lose you again, especially now that I know all you are worth and how dreadfully you suffer. I will save you, if need be, in spite of yourself. I will cure you of your torturing doubts, oh! without catechising you, without imposing any particular faith on you, but simply by allowing life to do its work, for life alone can give you back health and hope. So I beg you, brother, in the name of our affection, come back here, come as often as you can to spend a day with us. You will then see that when folks have allotted themselves a task and work together in unison, they escape excessive unhappiness. A task of any kind—yes, that is what is wanted, together with some great passion and frank acceptance of life, so that it may be lived as it should be and loved.'

'But what would be the use of my living here?' Pierre muttered bitterly. 'I've no task left me, and I no longer know how to love.'

'Well, I will give you a task, and as for love that will soon be awakened by the breath of life. Come, brother, consent, consent!'

Then, seeing that Pierre still remained gloomy and sorrowful, and persisted in his determination to go away and bury himself, Guillaume added: 'Ah! I don't say that the things of this world are such as one might wish them to be. I don't say that only joy and truth and justice exist. For instance, the affair of that unhappy fellow Salvat fills me with anger and revolt. Guilty he is, of course, and yet how many excuses he had, and how I shall pity him if the crimes of all of us are laid at his door, if the various political gangs bandy him from one to another, and use him as a weapon in their sordid fight for power. The thought of it all so exasperates me that at times I am as unreasonable as yourself. But now, brother, just to please me, promise that you will come and spend the day after to-morrow with us.'

Then as Pierre still kept silent Guillaume went on: 'I will have it so. It would grieve me too much to think that you were suffering from martyrdom in your solitary nook. I want to cure and save you.'

Tears again rose to Pierre's eyes, and in a tone of infinite distress he answered: 'Don't compel me to promise. . . . All I can say is that I will try to conquer myself.'

The week he then spent in his little, dark, empty home proved a terrible one. Shutting himself up he brooded over his despair at having lost the companionship of that elder brother whom he once more loved with his whole soul. He had never before been so keenly conscious of his solitude; and he was a score of times on the point of hastening to Montmartre, for he vaguely felt that affection, truth and life were there. But on each occasion he was held back by a return of the discomfort which he had already experienced, discomfort compounded of shame and fear. Priest that he was, cut off from love and the avocations of other men, he would surely find nothing but hurt and suffering among creatures who were all nature, freedom, and health. While he pon-

dered thus, however, there rose before him the shades of his
father and mother, those sad spirits that seemed to wander
through the deserted rooms lamenting and entreating him to
reconcile them in himself, as soon as he should find peace.
What was he to do, deny their prayer, and remain weeping
with them, or go yonder in search of the cure which might
at last lull them to sleep and bring them happiness in death
by the force of his own happiness in life? At last a morning
came when it seemed to him that his father enjoined him
with a smile to betake himself yonder, while his mother consented with a glance of her big soft eyes, in which her sorrow at having made so bad a priest of him yielded to her
desire to restore him to the life of our common humanity.

Pierre did not argue with himself that day; he took a cab
and gave Guillaume's address to the driver for fear lest he
should be overcome on the way and wish to turn back. And
when he again found himself, as in a dream, in the large
workshop, where Guillaume and the young men welcomed
him in a delicately affectionate way, he witnessed an unexpected scene which both impressed and relieved him.

Marie, who had scarcely nodded to him as he entered, sat
there with a pale and frowning face. And Mère-Grand, who
was also grave, said, after glancing at her: 'You must
excuse her, Monsieur l'Abbé; but she isn't reasonable. She
is in a temper with all five of us.'

Guillaume began to laugh. 'Ah! she's so stubborn!' he
exclaimed. 'You can have no idea, Pierre, of what goes on
in that little head of hers when anybody says or does anything
contrary to her ideas of justice. Such absolute and lofty
ideas they are, that they can descend to no compromise. For
instance, we were talking of that recent affair of a father who
was found guilty on his son's evidence; and she maintained
that the son had only done what was right in giving evidence
against his father, and that one ought invariably to tell the
truth, no matter what might happen. What a terrible public
prosecutor she would make, eh?'

Thereupon Marie, exasperated by Pierre's smile, which
seemingly indicated that he also thought her in the wrong,
flew into quite a passion.

'You are cruel, Guillaume!' she cried; 'I won't be
laughed at like this.'

'But you are losing your senses, my dear,' exclaimed
François, while Thomas and Antoine again grew merry. 'We

were only urging a question of humanity, father and I, for we
respect and love justice as much as you do.'

'There's no question of humanity, but simply one of
justice. What is just and right *is* just and right, and you
cannot alter it.'

Then, as Guillaume made a further attempt to state his
views and win her over to them, she rose trembling, in such a
passion that she could scarcely stammer : ' No, no, you are all
too cruel, you only want to grieve me. I prefer to go up into
my own room.'

At this Mère-Grand vainly sought to restrain her. 'My
child, my child ! ' said she, ' reflect a moment ; this is very
wrong, you will deeply regret it.'

' No, no ; you are not just, and I suffer too much.'

Then she wildly rushed upstairs to her room overhead.

Consternation followed. Scenes of a similar character
had occasionally occurred before, but there had never been
so serious a one. Guillaume immediately admitted that he
had done wrong in laughing at her, for she could not bear
irony. Then he told Pierre that, in her childhood and youth
she had been subject to terrible attacks of passion whenever
she witnessed or heard of any act of injustice. As she herself
explained, these attacks would come upon her with irresistible
force, transporting her to such a point that she would sometimes fall upon the floor and rave. Even nowadays she proved
quarrelsome and obstinate whenever certain subjects were
touched upon. And she afterwards blushed for it all, fully
conscious that others must think her unbearable.

Indeed, a quarter of an hour later, she came downstairs
again of her own accord, and bravely acknowledged her fault.
' Wasn't it ridiculous of me ? ' she said. ' To think I accuse
others of being unkind when I behave like that ! Monsieur
l'Abbé must have a very bad opinion of me.' Then, after
kissing Mère-Grand, she added : ' You'll forgive me, won't
you ? Oh ! François may laugh now, and so may Thomas
and Antoine. They are quite right, our differences are merely
laughing matters.'

' My poor Marie,' replied Guillaume, in a tone of deep
affection, ' you see what it is to surrender oneself to the
absolute. If you are so healthy and reasonable it's because
you regard almost every thing from the relative point of view,
and only ask life for such gifts as it can bestow. But when
your absolute ideas of justice come upon you, you lose both

equilibrium and reason. At the same time, I must say that
we are all liable to err in much the same manner.'

Marie, who was still very flushed, thereupon answered in
a jesting way : ' Well, it at least proves that I'm not perfect.'

' Oh, certainly ! And so much the better,' said Guillaume,
' for it makes me love you the more.'

This was a sentiment which Pierre himself would willingly
have re-echoed. The scene had deeply stirred him. Had not
his own frightful torments originated with his desire for the
absolute both in things and beings ? He had sought faith in
its entirety, and despair had thrown him into complete negation.
Again, was there not some evil desire for the absolute and some
affectation of pride and voluntary blindness in the haughty
bearing which he had retained amidst the downfall of his
belief, the saintly reputation which he had accepted when he
possessed no faith at all ? On hearing his brother praise
Marie, because she only asked life for such things as it could
give, it had seemed to him that this was advice for himself.
It was as if a refreshing breath of nature had passed before
his face. At the same time his feelings in this respect were
still vague, and the only well-defined pleasure that he experienced came from the young woman's fit of anger, that
error of hers which brought her nearer to him, by lowering
her in some degree from her pedestal of serene perfection. It
was, perhaps, that seeming perfection which had made him
suffer ; however, he was as yet unable to analyse his feelings.
That day, for the first time, he chatted with her for a little
while, and when he went off he thought her very good-hearted
and very human.

Two days later he again came to spend the afternoon in
the large sunlit workshop overlooking Paris. Ever since he
had become conscious of the idle life he was leading, he had
felt very bored when he was alone, and only found relief
among that gay, hard-working family. His brother scolded
him for not having come to *déjeuner*, and he promised to do
so on the morrow. By the time a week had elapsed, none of
the discomfort and covert hostility which had prevailed
between him and Marie remained ; they met and chatted on
a footing of good-fellowship. Although he was a priest, she
was in no wise embarrassed by his presence. With her quiet
atheism, indeed, she had never imagined that a priest could
be different from other men. Thus her sisterly cordiality
both astonished and delighted Pierre. It was as if he wore

the same garments and held the same ideas as his big
nephews, as if there were nothing whatever to distinguish
him from other men. He was still more surprised, however,
by Marie's silence on all religious questions. She seemed to
live on quietly and happily, without a thought of what
might be beyond life, that terrifying realm of mystery, which
to him had brought such agony of mind.

Now that he came every two or three days to Montmartre
she noticed that he was suffering. What could be the matter
with him, she wondered. When she questioned him in a
friendly manner and only elicited evasive replies, she guessed
that he was ashamed of his sufferings, and that they were
aggravated, rendered well-nigh incurable by the very secrecy
in which he buried them. Thereupon womanly compassion
awoke within her, and she felt increasing affection for that
tall, pale fellow with feverish eyes, who was consumed by
grievous torments which he would confess to none. No doubt
she questioned Guillaume respecting her brother's sadness,
and he must have confided some of the truth to her in order
that she might help him to extricate Pierre from his sufferings, and give him back some taste for life. The poor fellow
always seemed so happy when she treated him like a friend,
a brother !

At last, one evening, on seeing his eyes full of tears as
he gazed upon the dismal twilight falling over Paris, she
herself pressed him to confide his trouble to her. And thereupon he suddenly spoke out, confessing all his torture and the
horrible void which the loss of faith had left within him.
Ah ! to be unable to believe, to be unable to love, to be
nothing but ashes, to know of nothing certain by which he
might replace the faith that had fled from him ! She listened
in stupefaction. Why, he must be mad ! And she plainly
told him so, such was her astonishment and revolt at hearing
such a desperate cry of wretchedness. To despair, indeed,
and believe in nothing and love nothing, simply because a
religious hypothesis had crumbled ! And this, too, when the
whole vast world was spread before one, life with the duty of
living it, creatures and things to be loved and succoured,
without counting the universal labour, the task which one
and all came to accomplish ! Assuredly he must be mad,
mad with the gloomiest madness ; still she vowed she would
cure him.

From that time forward she felt the most compassionate

affection for this extraordinary young man, who had first embarrassed and afterwards astonished her. She showed herself very gentle and gay with him; she looked after him with the greatest skill and delicacy of heart and mind. There had been certain similar features in their childhood; each had been reared in the strictest religious views by a pious mother. But afterwards how different had been their fates! Whilst he was struggling with his doubts, bound by his priestly vows, she had grown up at the Lycée Fénelon, where her father had placed her as soon as her mother died; and there, far removed from all practice of religion, she had gradually reached total forgetfulness of her early religious views. It was a constant source of surprise for him to find that she had thus escaped all distress of mind at the thought of what might come after death, whereas that same thought had so deeply tortured him. When they chatted together and he expressed his astonishment at it, she frankly laughed, saying that she had never felt any fear of Hell, for she was certain that no Hell existed. And she added that she lived in all quietude, without hope of going to any Heaven, her one thought being to comply in a reasonable way with the requirements and necessities of earthly life. It was, perhaps, in some measure a matter of temperament with her; but it was also a matter of education. Yet, whatever that education had been, whatever knowledge she had acquired, she had remained very womanly and very loving. There was nothing stern or masculine about her.

'Ah, my friend,' she said one day to Pierre, 'if you only knew how easy it is for me to remain happy so long as I see those I love free from any excessive suffering. For my own part I can always adapt myself to life. I work and content myself no matter what may happen. Sorrow has only come to me from others, for I can't help wishing that everybody should be fairly happy, and there are some who won't. . . . I was for a long time very poor, but I remained gay. I wish for nothing, except for things that can't be purchased. Still want is the great abomination which distresses me. I can understand that you should have felt everything crumbling when charity appeared to you so insufficient a remedy as to be contemptible. Yet it does bring relief; and, moreover, it is so sweet to be able to give. Some day, too, by dint of reason and toil, by the good and efficient working of life itself, the reign of justice will surely come. But now it's I

that am preaching! Oh! I have little taste for it! It would
be ridiculous for me to try to heal you with big phrases. All
the same, I should like to cure you of your gloomy sufferings.
To do so, all that I ask of you is to spend as much time as
you can with us. You know that this is Guillaume's greatest
desire. We will all love you so well, you will see us all so
affectionately united, and so gay over our common work, that
you will come back to truth by joining us in the school of our
good mother nature. You must live and work, and love and
hope.'

Pierre smiled as he listened. He now came to Montmartre
nearly every day. She was so nice and affectionate when
she preached to him in that way with a pretty assumption of
wisdom. As she had said too, life was so delightful in that
big workroom; it was so pleasant to be all together, and to
labour in common at the same work of health and truth.
Ashamed as Pierre was of doing nothing, anxious as he was
to occupy his mind and fingers, he had first taken an interest
in Antoine's engraving, asking why he should not try something of the kind himself. However, he felt that he lacked
the necessary gift for art. Then, too, he recoiled from
François's purely intellectual labour, for he himself had scarcely
emerged from the harrowing study of conflicting texts. Thus
he was more inclined for manual toil like that of Thomas.
In mechanics he found precision and clearness such as might
help to quench his thirst for certainty. So he placed himself
at the young man's orders, pulled his bellows and held
pieces of mechanism for him. He also sometimes served as
assistant to Guillaume, tying a large blue apron over his
cassock in order to help in the experiments. From that time
he formed part of the workshop, which simply counted a
worker the more.

One afternoon early in April, when they were all busily
engaged there, Marie, who sat embroidering at the table in
front of Mère-Grand, raised her eyes to the window and
suddenly burst into a cry of admiration: 'Oh! look at Paris
under that rain of sunlight!'

Pierre drew near; the play of light was much the same
as that which he had witnessed at his first visit. The sun,
sinking behind some slight purple clouds, was throwing down
a hail of rays and sparks which on all sides rebounded and
leapt over the endless stretch of roofs. It might have been
thought that some great sower, hidden amidst the glory of the

planet, was scattering handfuls of golden grain from one horizon to the other.

Pierre, at sight of it, put his fancy into words : 'It is the sun sowing Paris with grain for a future harvest,' said he. 'See how the expanse looks like ploughed land ; the brownish houses are like soil turned up, and the streets are deep and straight like furrows.'

'Yes, yes, that's true,' exclaimed Marie gaily. 'The sun is sowing Paris with grain. See, how it casts the seed of light and health right away to the distant suburbs ! And yet, how singular ! The rich districts on the west seem steeped in a ruddy mist, whilst the good seed falls in golden dust over the left bank and the populous districts eastward. It is there, is it not, that the crop will spring up ? '

They had all drawn near, and were smiling at the symbol. As Marie had said, it seemed indeed that while the sun slowly sank behind the lacework of clouds, the sower of eternal life scattered his flaming seed with a rhythmical swing of the arm, ever selecting the districts of toil and effort. One dazzling handful of grain fell over yonder on the district of the schools ; and then yet another rained down to fertilise the district of the factories and workshops.

'Ah ! well,' said Guillaume gaily. 'May the crop soon sprout from the good ground of our great Paris, which has been turned up by so many revolutions, and enriched by the blood of so many workers ! It is the only ground in the world where Ideas can germinate and bloom. Yes, yes, Pierre is quite right, it is the sun sowing Paris with the seed of the future world which can only sprout up here ! '

Then Thomas, François, and Antoine who stood behind their father in a row, nodded as if to say that this was also their own conviction ; whilst Mère-Grand gazed afar with dreamy eyes as though she could already behold the splendid future.

'Ah ! but it is only a dream ; centuries must elapse. We shall never see it ! ' murmured Pierre with a quiver.

'But others will ! ' cried Marie. 'And does not that suffice ? '

Those lofty words stirred Pierre to the depths of his being. And all at once there came to him the memory of another Marie [1]—the adorable Marie of his youth, that Marie de Guersaint who had been cured at Lourdes, and the loss of whom

[1] The heroine of M. Zola's *Lourdes*.

had left such a void in his heart. Was that new Marie who stood there smiling at him, so tranquil and so charming in her strength, destined to heal that old-time wound? He felt that he was beginning to live again since she had become his friend.

Meantime, there before them, the glorious sun, with the sweep of its rays, was scattering living golden dust over Paris, still and ever sowing the great future harvest of justice and of truth.

II

TOWARDS LIFE

ONE evening, at the close of a good day's work, Pierre, who was helping Thomas, suddenly caught his foot in the skirt of his cassock and narrowly escaped falling. At this, Marie, after raising a faint cry of anxiety, exclaimed: 'Why don't you take it off?'

There was no malice in her inquiry. She simply looked upon the priestly robe as something too heavy and cumbersome, particularly when one had certain work to perform. Nevertheless, her words deeply impressed Pierre, and he could not forget them. When he was at home in the evening and repeated them to himself they gradually threw him into feverish agitation. Why, indeed, had he not divested himself of that cassock, which weighed so heavily and painfully on his shoulders? Then a frightful struggle began within him, and he spent a terrible, sleepless night, again a prey to all his former torments.

At first sight it seemed a very simple matter that he should cast his priestly gown aside, for had he not ceased to discharge any priestly office? He had not said mass for some time past, and this surely meant renunciation of the priesthood. Nevertheless, so long as he retained his gown it was possible that he might some day say mass again, whereas if he cast it aside, he would, as it were, strip himself, quit the priesthood entirely, without possibility of return. It was a terrible step to take, one that would prove irrevocable; and thus he paced his room for hours, in great anguish of mind.

He had formerly indulged in a superb dream. Whilst believing nothing himself he had resolved to watch, in all loyalty, over the belief of others. He would not so lower himself as to forswear his vows, he would be no base renegade, but however great the torments of the void he felt within him he would remain the minister of man's illusions respecting the Divinity. And it was by reason of his conduct in this respect that he had ended by being venerated as a saint—he who denied everything, who had become a mere empty sepulchre. For a long time his falsehood had never disturbed him, but it now brought him acute suffering. It seemed to him that he would be acting in the vilest manner if he delayed placing his life in accord with his opinions. The thought of it all quite rent his heart.

The question was a very clear one. By what right did he remain the minister of a religion in which he no longer believed? Did not elementary honesty require that he should quit a Church in which he denied the presence of the Divinity? He regarded the dogmas of that Church as puerile errors, and yet he persisted in teaching them as if they were eternal truths. Base work it was, that alarmed his conscience. He vainly sought the feverish glow of charity and martyrdom which had led him to offer himself as a sacrifice, willing to suffer all the torture of doubt and to find his own life lost and ravaged, provided that he might yet afford the relief of hope to the lowly. Truth and nature, no doubt, had already regained too much ascendency over him for those feelings to return. The thought of such a lying apostolate now wounded him; he no longer had the hypocritical courage to call the Divinity down upon the believers kneeling before him, when he was convinced that the Divinity would not descend. Thus all the past was swept away; there remained nothing of the sublime pastoral part he would once have liked to play, that supreme gift of himself which lay in stubborn adherence to the rules of the Church, and such devotion to faith as to endure in silence the torture of having lost it.

What must Marie think of his prolonged falsehood? he wondered, and thereupon he seemed to hear her words again: 'Why not take your cassock off?' His conscience bled as if those words were a stab. What contempt must she not feel for him, she who was so upright, so high minded? Every scattered blame, every covert criticism directed against his conduct, seemed to find embodiment in her. It now sufficed that she should condemn him, and he at once felt guilty. At the same time she had never signified her disapproval to him, in all probability because she did not think she had any right to intervene in a struggle of conscience. The superb calmness and healthiness which she displayed still astonished him. He himself was ever haunted and tortured by thoughts of the unknown, of what the morrow of death might have in store for one; but although he had studied and watched her for days together, he had never seen her give a sign of doubt or distress. This exemption from such sufferings as his own was due, said she, to the fact that she gave all her gaiety, all her energy, all her sense of duty to the task of living, in such wise that life itself proved a sufficiency, and no time was left for mere fancies to terrify and stultify her. Well, then, since she with her air of quiet strength had asked him why he did not take off his cassock, he would take it off —yes, he would divest himself of that robe which seemed to burn and weigh him down.

He fancied himself calmed by this decision, and towards morning threw himself upon his bed; but all at once a stifling sensation, a renewal of his abominable anguish brought him to his feet again. No, no, he could not divest himself of that gown which clung so tightly to his flesh. His skin would come away with his cloth, his whole being would be lacerated! Is not the mark of priesthood an indelible one, does it not brand the priest for ever, and differentiate him from the flock? Even should he tear off his gown with his skin, he would remain a priest, an object of scandal and shame, awkward and impotent, shut off from the life of other men. And so why tear it off, since he would still and ever remain in prison, and a fruitful life of work in the broad sunlight was no longer within his reach? He, indeed, fancied himself irremediably stricken with impotence. Thus he was unable to come to any decision, and when he returned to Montmartre two days later he had again relapsed into a state of torment.

Feverishness, moreover, had come upon the happy home. Guillaume was becoming more and more annoyed about Salvat's affair; not a day elapsing without the newspapers fanning his irritation. He had at first been deeply touched by the dignified and reticent bearing of Salvat, who had declared that he had no accomplices whatever. Of course the inquiry into the crime was what is called a secret one; but magistrate Amadieu, to whom it had been entrusted, conducted it in a very noisy way. The newspapers, which he in some degree took into his confidence, were full of articles and paragraphs about him and his interviews with the prisoner. Thanks to Salvat's quiet admissions, Amadieu had been able to retrace the history of the crime hour by hour, his only remaining doubts having reference to the nature of the powder which had been employed, and the making of the bomb itself. It might after all be true that Salvat had loaded the bomb at a friend's, as he indeed asserted was the case; but he must be lying when he added that the only explosive used was dynamite, derived from some stolen cartridges, for all the experts now declared that dynamite would never have produced such effects as those which had been witnessed. This, then, was the mysterious point which protracted the investigations. And day by day the newspapers profited by it to circulate the wildest stories under sensational headings, which were specially devised for the purpose of sending up their sales.

It was all the nonsense contained in these stories that fanned Guillaume's irritation. In spite of his contempt for Sagnier he could not keep from buying the 'Voix du Peuple.' Quivering with indignation, growing more and more exasperated, he was somehow attracted by the mire which he found in that scurrilous journal. Moreover, the other newspapers, including even the 'Globe,' which was usually so dignified, published all sorts of statements for which no proof could be supplied, and drew from them remarks and conclusions which, though couched in milder language than Sagnier's, were none the less abominably unjust. It seemed indeed as if the whole press had set itself the task of covering Salvat with mud, so as to be able to vilify Anarchism generally. According to the journalists the prisoner's life had simply been one long abomination. He had already earned his living by thievery in his childhood at the time when he had roamed the streets, an unhappy, forsaken vagrant; and later on he had proved a bad soldier and a bad worker. He had been punished for insubordination whilst he was in the army, and he had been dismissed from a dozen workshops because he incessantly disturbed them by his Anarchical propaganda. Later still, he had fled his country and led a suspicious life of adventure in America, where, it was alleged, he must have committed all sorts of unknown crimes. Moreover, there was his horrible immorality, his connection with his sister-in-law, that Madame Théodore who had taken charge of his forsaken child in his absence, and with whom he had cohabited since his return to France. In this wise Salvat's failings and transgressions were pitilessly denounced and magnified without any mention of the causes which had induced them, or of the excuses which lay in the unhappy man's degrading environment. And so Guillaume's feelings of humanity and justice revolted, for he knew the real Salvat—a man of tender heart and dreamy mind, so liable to be impassioned by fancies—a man cast into life when a child without weapon of defence, ever trodden down or thrust aside, then gradually exasperated by the perpetual onslaughts of want, and at last dreaming of reviving the golden age by destroying the old, corrupt world.

Unfortunately for Salvat, everything had gone against him since he had been shut up in strict confinement, at the mercy of the ambitious and worldly Amadieu. Guillaume had learnt from his son, Thomas, that the prisoner could count on no support whatever among his former mates at the Grandidier works. These works were becoming prosperous once more, thanks to their steady output of bicycles; and it was said that Grandidier was only waiting for Thomas to perfect his little motor, in order to start the manufacture of motor-cars on a large scale. However, the success which he was now for the first time achieving, and which scarcely repaid him for all his years of toil and battle, had in certain respects rendered him prudent and even severe. He did not wish any suspicion to be cast upon his business through the unpleasant affair of his former workman Salvat, and so he had dismissed such of his workmen as held Anarchist views. If he had kept the two Toussaints, one of whom was the prisoner's brother-in-law, while the other was suspected of sympathy with him, this was because they had belonged to the works for a score of years, and he did not like to cast them adrift. Moreover, Toussaint, the father, had declared that if he were called as a witness for the defence, he should simply give such particulars of Salvat's career as related to the prisoner's marriage with his sister.

One evening when Thomas came home from the works, to which he returned every now and then in order to try his little motor, he related that he had that day seen Madame

Grandidier, the poor young woman who had become insane
through an attack of puerperal fever following upon the death
of a child. Although most frightful attacks of madness
occasionally came over her, and although life beside her was
extremely painful, even during the intervals when she remained downcast and gentle as a child, her husband had
never been willing to send her to an asylum. He kept her
with him in a pavilion near the works, and as a rule the
shutters of the windows overlooking the yard remained closed.
Thus Thomas had been greatly surprised to see one of these
windows open, and the young woman appear at it amidst the
bright sunshine of that early spring. True, she only remained
there for a moment, vision-like, fair and pretty, with smiling
face ; for a servant who suddenly drew near closed the
window, and the pavilion then again sank into lifeless silence.
At the same time it was reported among the men employed
at the works that the poor creature had not experienced an
attack for well-nigh a month past, and that this was the
reason why the 'governor' looked so strong and pleased, and
worked so vigorously to help on the increasing prosperity of
his business.

'He isn't a bad fellow,' added Thomas, 'but with the
terrible competition that he has to encounter, he is bent on
keeping his men under control. Nowadays, says he, when so
many capitalists and wage earners seem bent on exterminating
one another, the latter—if they don't want to starve—ought
to be well pleased when capital falls into the hands of an
active, fair-minded man. . . . If he shows no pity for Salvat,
it is because he really believes in the necessity of an
example.'

That same day Thomas, after leaving the works and
while threading his way through the toilsome hive-like
Marcadet district, had overtaken Madame Théodore and little
Céline, who were wandering on in great distress. It appeared
that they had just called upon Toussaint, who had been
unable to lend them even such a trifle as ten sous. Since
Salvat's arrest, the woman and the child had been forsaken
and suspected by one and all. Driven forth from their
wretched lodging, they were without food and wandered
hither and thither dependent on chance alms. Never had
greater want and misery fallen on defenceless creatures.

'I told them to come up here, father,' said Thomas, 'for I
thought that one might pay their landlord a month's rent, so

that they might go home again. . . . Ah! there's somebody coming now—it's they, no doubt.'

Guillaume had felt angry with himself whilst listening to his son, for he had not thought of the poor creatures. It was the old story: the man disappears, and the woman and the child find themselves in the streets, starving. Whenever Justice strikes a man her blow travels beyond him, fells innocent beings and kills them.

Madame Théodore came in, humble and timid, scared like a luckless creature whom life never wearies of persecuting. She was becoming almost blind, and little Céline had to lead her. The girl's fair, thin face wore its wonted expression of shrewd intelligence, and even now, however woeful her rags, it was occasionally brightened by a childish smile.

Pierre and Marie, who were both there, felt extremely touched. Near them was Madame Mathis, young Victor's mother, who had come to help Mère-Grand with the mending of some house-linen. She went out by the day in this fashion among a few families, and was thus enabled to give her son an occasional franc or two. However, Guillaume alone questioned Madame Théodore.

'Ah! monsieur,' she stammered, 'who could ever have thought Salvat capable of such a thing, he who's so good and so humane? Still it's true, since he himself has admitted it to the magistrate. . . . For my part I told everybody that he was in Belgium. I wasn't quite sure of it, still I'm glad that he didn't come back to see us; for if he had been arrested at our place I should have lost my senses. . . . Well, now that they have him, they'll sentence him to death, that's certain.'

At this Céline, who had been looking around her with an air of interest, piteously exclaimed: 'Oh! no, oh! no, mamma, they won't hurt him!'

Big tears appeared in the child's eyes as she raised this cry. Guillaume kissed her, and then went on questioning Madame Théodore.

'Well, monsieur,' she answered, 'the child's not old or big enough to work as yet, and my eyes are done for, people won't even take me as a charwoman. And so it's simple enough, we starve. . . . Oh! of course I'm not without relations; I have a sister who married very well. Her husband is a clerk, Monsieur Chrétiennot, perhaps you know him. Unfortunately he's rather proud, and as I don't want any scenes between him and my sister, I no longer go to see her. Besides, she's in despair just now, for she's expecting another baby, which is a terrible blow for a small household, when one already has two girls. . . . That's why the only person I can apply to is my brother Toussaint. His wife isn't a bad sort by any means, but she's no longer the same since she's been living in fear of her husband having another attack. The first one carried off all her savings, and what would become of her if Toussaint should remain on her hands, paralysed? Besides, she's threatened with another burden, for, as you may know, her son Charles got keeping company with a servant at a wine shop, who of course ran away after she had a baby, which she left him to see to. So one can understand that the Toussaints themselves are hard put. I don't complain of them. They've already lent me a little money, and of course they can't go on lending for ever.'

She continued talking in this spiritless, resigned way, complaining only on account of Céline; for, said she, it was enough to make one's heart break to see such an intelligent child obliged to tramp the streets after getting on so well at the Communal School. She could feel too that everybody now kept aloof from them on account of Salvat. The Toussaints didn't want to be compromised in any such business. There was only Charles who had said that he could well understand a man losing his head and trying to blow up the *bourgeois*, because they really treated the workers in a blackguard way.

'For my part, monsieur,' added Madame Théodore, 'I say nothing, for I'm only a woman. All the same though, if you'd like to know what I think, well I think that it would have been better if Salvat hadn't done what he did, for we two, the girl and I, are the real ones to suffer from it. Ah! I can't get the idea into my head, that the little one should be the daughter of a man condemned to death.'

Once more Céline interrupted her, flinging her arms around her neck: 'Oh! mamma, oh! mamma, don't say that, I beg you! It can't be true, it grieves me too much!'

At this Pierre and Marie exchanged compassionate glances, while Mère-Grand rose from her chair, in order to go upstairs and search her wardrobes for some articles of clothing which might be of use to the two poor creatures. Guillaume, who, for his part, had been moved to tears, and felt full of revolt against the social system which rendered such distress possible, slipped some alms into [the child's little hand, and promised Madame Théodore that he would see her landlord so as to get her back her room.

'Ah! Monsieur Froment!' replied the unfortunate woman. 'Salvat was quite right when he said you were a real good man! And as you employed him here for a few days you know too that he isn't a wicked one. . . . Now that he's been put in prison everybody calls him a brigand, and it breaks my heart to hear them.' Then, turning towards Madame Mathis who had continued sewing in discreet silence, like a respectable woman whom none of these things could concern, she went on : 'I know you, madame, but I'm better acquainted with your son, Monsieur Victor, who has often come to chat at our place. Oh! you needn't be afraid, I shan't say it, I shall never compromise anybody; but if Monsieur Victor were free to speak, he'd be the man to explain Salvat's ideas properly.'

Madame Mathis looked at her in stupefaction. Ignorant as she was of her son's real life and views, she experienced a vague dread at the idea of any connection between him and that man Salvat's family. Moreover, she refused to believe it possible.

'Oh! you must be mistaken,' she said, 'Victor told me that he now seldom came to Montmartre, as he was always going about in search of work.'

By the anxious quiver of the widow's voice, Madame Théodore understood that she ought not to have mixed her up in her troubles ; and so in all humility she at once beat a retreat : 'I beg your pardon, Madame, I didn't think I should hurt your feelings. Perhaps, too, I'm mistaken, as you say.'

Madame Mathis had again turned to her sewing as to the solitude in which she lived, that nook of decent misery where she dwelt without companionship and almost unknown, with scarcely sufficient bread to eat. Ah! that dear son of hers, whom she loved so well; however much he might neglect her, she had placed her only remaining hope in him : he was her last dream, and would some day lavish all kinds of happiness upon her!

At that moment Mère-Grand came downstairs again, laden with a bundle of linen and woollen clothing, and Madame Théodore and little Céline withdrew while pouring forth their thanks. For a long time after they had gone Guillaume, unable to resume work, continued walking to and fro in silence, with a frown upon his face.

When Pierre, still hesitating and still tortured by conflicting feelings returned to Montmartre on the following day he witnessed with much surprise a visit of a very different kind. There was a sudden gust of wind, a whirl of skirts and a ring of laughter as little Princess Rosemonde swept in, followed by young Hyacinthe Duvillard, who, on his side, retained a very frigid bearing.

'It's I, my dear master,' exclaimed the Princess, 'I promised you a visit, you remember, for I am such a great admirer of your genius. And our young friend here has been kind enough to bring me. We have only just returned from Norway, and my very first visit is for you.'

She turned as she spoke, and bowed in an easy and gracious way to Pierre and Marie, François and Antoine, who were also there. Then she resumed: 'Oh! my dear master, you have no idea how beautifully virginal Norway is! We all ought to go and drink at that new source of the Ideal, and we should return purified, rejuvenated, and capable of great renunciations!'

As a matter of fact she had been well-nigh bored to death there. To make one's honeymoon journey to the land of the ice and snow, instead of to Italy, the hot land of the sun, was doubtless a very refined idea, which showed that no base materialism formed part of one's affections. It was the soul alone that travelled, and naturally it was fit that only kisses of the soul should be exchanged on the journey. Unfortunately, however, Hyacinthe had carried his symbolism so far as to exasperate Rosemonde, and on one occasion they had come to blows over it and then to tears, when this lover's quarrel had ended as many such quarrels do. Briefly they had no longer deemed themselves pure enough for the companionship of the swans and the lakes of dreamland, and had therefore taken the first steamer that was sailing for France.

As it was altogether unnecessary to confess to everybody what a failure their journey had proved, the Princess abruptly brought her rapturous references to Norway to an end, and then exclaimed: 'By the way, do you know what I found awaiting me on my return? Why, I found my house pillaged, oh! completely pillaged! And in such a filthy condition, too! We at once recognised the mark of the beast, and thought of Bergaz's young friends.'

Already on the previous day Guillaume had read in the newspapers that a band of young Anarchists had entered the Princess's little house by breaking a basement window. She had left it quite deserted, unprotected, even by a caretaker; and the robbers had not merely removed everything from the premises—including even the larger articles of furniture, but had lived there for a couple of days, bringing provisions in from outside, drinking all the wine they found in the cellars, and leaving every room in a most filthy and disgusting condition. On discovering all this, Rosemonde had immediately remembered the evening she had spent at the Chamber of Horrors in the company of Bergaz and his acolytes, Rossi and Sanfaute, who had heard her speak of her intended trip to Norway. The two young men had therefore been arrested, but Bergaz had so far escaped. The Princess was not greatly astonished by it all, for she had already been warned of the presence of dangerous characters among the mixed cosmopolitan set with which she associated. Janzen had told her in confidence of a number of villainous affairs which were attributed to Bergaz and his band. And now the Anarchist leader openly declared that Bergaz had sold himself to the police like Raphanel; and that the burglary at the Princess's residence had been planned by the police officials, who thereby hoped to cover the Anarchist cause with mire. If proof was wanted of this, added Janzen, it could be found in the fact that the police had allowed Bergaz to escape.

'I fancied that the newspapers might have exaggerated matters,' said Guillaume, when the Princess had finished her story. 'They are inventing such abominable things just now, in order to blacken the case of that poor devil Salvat.'

'Oh! they've exaggerated nothing!' Rosemonde gaily rejoined. 'As a matter of fact they have omitted a number of particulars which were too filthy for publication. . . . For my part, I've merely had to go to an hotel. I'm very comfortable there; I was beginning to feel bored in that house of mine. . . . All the same, however, Anarchism is hardly a clean business, and I no longer like to say that I have any connection with it.'

She again laughed, and then passed to another subject, asking Guillaume to tell her of his most recent researches, in order, no doubt, that she might show she knew enough chemistry to understand him. He had been rendered thoughtful, however, by the story of Bergaz and the burglary, and would only answer her in a general way.

Meantime, Hyacinthe was renewing his acquaintance with his schoolfellows, François and Antoine. He had accompanied the Princess to Montmartre against his own inclinations; but since she had taken to whipping him he had become afraid of her. The chemist's little home filled him with disdain, particularly as the chemist was a man of questionable reputation. Moreover, he thought it a duty to insist on his own superiority in the presence of those old schoolfellows of his, whom he found toiling away in the common rut, like other people.

'Ah! yes,' said he to François, who was taking notes from a book spread open before him, 'you are at the École Normale, I believe, and are preparing for your licentiate. Well, for my part, you know, the idea of being tied to anything horrifies me. I become quite stupid when there's any question of examination or competition. The only possible road for one to follow is that of the Infinite. And between ourselves what dupery there is in science, how it narrows our horizon! It's just as well to remain a child with eyes gazing into the invisible. A child knows more than all your learned men.'

François, who occasionally indulged in irony, pretended to share his opinion. 'No doubt, no doubt,' said he, 'but one must have a natural disposition to remain a child. For my part, unhappily, I'm consumed by a desire to learn and know. It's deplorable, as I'm well aware, but I pass my days racking my brain over books. . . . I shall never know very much, that's certain; and perhaps that's the reason why I'm ever striving to learn a little more. You must at all events grant that work like idleness is a means of passing life, though of course it is a less elegant and æsthetic one.'

'Less æsthetic, precisely,' rejoined Hyacinthe. 'Beauty lies solely in the unexpressed, and life is simply degraded when one introduces anything material into it.'

Simpleton though he was in spite of the enormity of his pretensions, he doubtless detected that François had been speaking ironically. So he turned to Antoine, who had remained seated in front of a block he was engraving. It was the one which represented Lise reading in her garden, for he

was ever taking it in hand again and touching it up, in his
desire to improve his indication of the girl's awakening to intelligence and life.

'So you engrave, I see,' said Hyacinthe. 'Well, since I
renounced versification—a little poem I had begun on the
End of Woman—because words seemed to me so gross and
cumbersome, mere paving-stones as it were, fit for labourers,
I myself have had some idea of trying drawing, and perhaps
engraving too. But what drawing can portray the mystery
which lies beyond life, the only sphere that has any real
existence and importance for us? With what pencil and on
what kind of plate could one depict it? We should need
something impalpable, something unheard of, which would
merely suggest the essence of things and beings.'

'But it's only by material means,' Antoine somewhat
roughly replied, 'that art can render the essence of things and
beings, that is their full significance as we understand it. To
transcribe life is my great passion; and briefly life is the only
mystery that there is in things and beings. When it seems
to me that an engraving of mine lives, I'm well pleased, for I
feel that I have created.'

Hyacinthe pouted by way of expressing his contempt of
all fruitfulness. Any fool might beget offspring. It was the
sexless idea, existing by itself, that was rare and exquisite.
He tried to explain this, but became confused, and fell back
on the conviction which he had brought back from Norway,
that literature and art were done for in France, killed by baseness and excess of production.

'It's evident!' said François gaily by way of conclusion.
To do nothing already shows that one has some talent!'

Meantime, Pierre and Marie listened and gazed around
them, somewhat embarrassed by this strange visit which had
set the usually grave and peaceful workroom topsy-turvy.
The little Princess, however, evinced much amiability, and on
drawing near to Marie admired the wonderful delicacy of some
embroidery she was finishing. Before leaving, moreover,
Rosemonde insisted upon Guillaume inscribing his autograph
in an album which Hyacinthe had to fetch from her carriage.
The young man obeyed her with evident boredom. It could
be seen that they were already weary of one another.
Pending a fresh caprice, however, it amused Rosemonde to
terrorise her sorry victim. When she at length led him
away, after declaring to Guillaume that she should always

regard that visit as a memorable incident in her life, she made the whole household smile by saying : ' Oh ! so your sons knew Hyacinthe at college. He's a good-natured little fellow, isn't he ? and he would really be quite nice if he would only behave like other people.'

That same day Janzen and Bache came to spend the evening with Guillaume. Once a week they now met at Montmartre, as they had formerly done at Neuilly. Pierre, on these occasions, went home very late, for as soon as Mère-Grand, Marie, and Guillaume's sons had retired for the night, there were endless chats in the workroom, whence Paris could be seen spangled with thousands of gas-lights. Another visitor at these times was Théophile Morin, but he did not arrive before ten o'clock, as he was detained by the work of correcting his pupils' exercises or some other wearisome labour pertaining to his profession.

As soon as Guillaume had told the others of the Princess's visit that afternoon Janzen hastily exclaimed : ' But she's mad, you know. When I first met her I thought for a moment that I might perhaps utilise her for the cause. She seemed so thoroughly convinced and bold ! But I soon found that she was the craziest of women, and simply hungered for new emotions ! '

Janzen was at last emerging from his wonted frigidity and mysteriousness. His cheeks were quite flushed. In all probability he had suffered from his rupture with the woman whom he had once called ' The Queen of the Anarchists,' and whose fortune and extensive circle of acquaintance had seemed to him such powerful weapons of propaganda.

' You know,' said he, when he had calmed down, ' it was the police who had her house pillaged and turned into a pigstye. Yes, in view of Salvat's trial, which is now near at hand, the idea was to damn Anarchism beyond possibility of even the faintest sympathy on the part of the *bourgeois.*'

' Yes, she told me so,' replied Guillaume, who had become attentive. ' But I scarcely credit the story. If Bergaz had merely acted under such influence as you suggest, he would have been arrested with the others, just as Raphanel was taken with those whom he betrayed. Besides, I know something of Bergaz, he's a freebooter.' Guillaume made a sorrowful gesture, and then in a saddened voice continued : ' Oh, I can understand all claims and all legitimate reprisals.

But theft, cynical theft for the purpose of profit and enjoyment, is beyond me! It lowers my hope of a better and more equitable form of society. Yes, that burglary at the Princess's house has greatly distressed me.'

An enigmatical smile, sharp like a knife, again played over Janzen's lips. 'Oh! it's a matter of heredity with you!' said he. 'The centuries of education and belief that lie behind you compel you to protest. All the same, however, when people won't make restoration things must be taken from them. What worries me is that Bergaz should have sold himself just now. The public prosecutor will use that farcical burglary as a crushing argument when he asks the jury for Salvat's head.'

Such was Janzen's hatred of the police that he stubbornly clung to his version of the affair. Perhaps, too, he had quarrelled with Bergaz, with whom he had at one time freely associated.

Guillaume, who understood that all discussion would be useless, contented himself with replying: 'Ah! yes, Salvat! Everything is against that unhappy fellow, he is certain to be condemned. But you can't know, my friends, what a passion that affair of his puts me into. All my ideas of truth and justice revolt at the thought of it. He's a madman certainly; but there are so many excuses to be urged for him. At bottom he is simply a martyr who has followed the wrong track. And yet he has become the scapegoat, laden with the crimes of the whole nation, condemned to pay for one and all!'

Bache and Morin nodded without replying. They both professed horror of Anarchism; while Morin, forgetting that the word if not the thing dated from his first master Proudhon, clung to his Comtist doctrines, in the conviction that science alone would ensure the happiness and pacification of the nations. Bache, for his part, old mystical humanitarian that he was, claimed that the only solution would come from Fourier, who by decreeing an alliance of talent, labour, and capital, had mapped out the future in a decisive manner. Nevertheless, both Bache and Morin were so discontented with the slow-paced *bourgeoise* Republic of the present day, and so hurt by the thought that everything was going from bad to worse through the flouting of their own particular ideas, that they were quite willing to wax indignant at the manner in which the conflicting parties of the time were striving to make use of Salvat in order to retain or acquire power.

'When one thinks,' said Bache, 'that this ministerial crisis of theirs has now been lasting for nearly three weeks! Every appetite is openly displayed, it's a most disgusting sight! Did you see in the papers this morning that the President has again been obliged to summon Vignon to the Elysée?'

'Oh! the papers,' muttered Morin, in his weary way, 'I no longer read them! What's the use of doing so? They are so badly written, and they all lie!'

As Bache had said, the ministerial crisis was still dragging on. The President of the Republic, taking as his guide the debate in the Chamber of Deputies, by which the Barroux administration had been overthrown, had very properly sent for Vignon, the victor on that occasion, and entrusted him with the formation of a new ministry. It had seemed that this would be an easy task, susceptible of accomplishment in two or three days at the utmost, for the names of the friends whom the young leader of the Radical party would bring to power with him had been freely mentioned for months past. But all sorts of difficulties had suddenly arisen. For ten days or so Vignon had struggled on amidst inextricable obstacles. Then, disheartened and disgusted, fearing, too, that he might use himself up and shut off the future if he persisted in his endeavours, he had been obliged to tell the President that he renounced the task. Forthwith the President had summoned other deputies, and questioned them until he had found one brave enough to make an attempt on his own account; whereupon incidents similar to those which had marked Vignon's endeavours had once more occurred. At the outset a list was drawn up with every prospect of being ratified within a few hours, but all at once hesitation arose, some pulled one way, some another; every effort was slowly paralysed till absolute failure resulted. It seemed as though the mysterious manœuvres which had hampered Vignon had begun again; it was as if some band of invisible plotters was, for some unknown purpose, doing its utmost to wreck every combination. A thousand hindrances arose with increasing force from every side—jealousy, dislike, and even betrayal were secretly prompted by expert agents, who employed every form of pressure, whether threats or promises, besides fanning and casting rival passions and interests into

collision. Thus the President, greatly embarrassed by this
posture of affairs, had again found it necessary to summon
Vignon, who, after reflection and negotiation, now had an
almost complete list in his pocket, and seemed likely to perfect
a new administration within the next forty-eight hours.

'Still it isn't settled,' resumed Bache. 'Well-informed
people assert that Vignon will fail again as he did the first
time. For my part I can't get rid of the idea that Duvillard's
gang is pulling the strings, though for whose benefit is a
mystery. You may be quite sure, however, that its chief
purpose is to stifle the African Railways affair. If Monferrand
were not so badly compromised I should almost suspect some
trick on his part. Have you noticed that the "Globe," after
throwing Barroux overboard in all haste, now refers to Monferrand every day with the most respectful sympathy?
That's a grave sign; for it isn't Fonsègue's habit to show
any solicitude for the vanquished. But what can one expect
from that wretched Chamber! The only point certain is that
something dirty is being plotted there.'

'And that big dunderhead Mège who works for every
party except his own!' exclaimed Morin; 'what a dupe he is
with that idea that he need merely overthrow first one
cabinet and then another, in order to become the leader of
one himself!'

The mention of Mège brought them all to agreement, for they
unanimously hated him. Bache, although his views coincided
on many points with those of the apostle of State Collectivism,
judged each of his speeches, each of his actions, with pitiless
severity. Janzen, for his part, treated the Collectivist leader
as a mere reactionary *bourgeois*, who ought to be swept away
one of the first. This hatred of Mège was indeed the common passion of Guillaume's friends. They could occasionally
show some justice for men who in nowise shared their
ideas; but in their estimation it was an unpardonable crime
for anybody to hold much the same views as themselves,
without being absolutely in agreement with them on every
possible point.

Their discussion continued, their various theories mingling
or clashing till they passed from politics to the press, and
grew excited over the denunciations which poured each
morning from Sagnier's newspaper, like filth from the mouth
of a sewer. Thereupon Guillaume, who had become absorbed
in reverie while pacing to and fro according to his habit,

suddenly exclaimed : ' Ah ! what dirty work it is that Sagnier does ! Before long there won't be a single person, a single thing left on which he hasn't vomited ! You think he's on your side, and suddenly he splashes you with mire ! . . . By the way, he related yesterday that skeleton keys and stolen purses were found on Salvat when he was arrested in the Bois de Boulogne ! It's always Salvat ! He's the inex-haustible subject for articles. The mere mention of him suffices to send up a paper's sales ! The bribe-takers of the African Railways shout " Salvat ! " to create a diversion. And the battles which wreck ministers are waged round his name. One and all set upon him and make use of him and beat him down ! '

With that cry of revolt and compassion, the friends separated for the night. Pierre, who sat near the open window overlooking the sparkling immensity of Paris, had listened to the others without speaking a word. He had once more been mastered by his doubts, the terrible struggle of his heart and mind ; and no solution, no appease-ment had come to him from all the contradictory views he had heard—the views of men who only united in predicting the disappearance of the old world, and could make no joint brotherly effort to rear the future world of truth and justice. In that vast city of Paris stretching below him, spangled with stars, glittering like the sky of a summer's night, Pierre also found a great enigma. It was like chaos, like a dim expanse of ashes dotted with sparks whence the coming aurora would arise. What future was being forged there, he wondered, what decisive word of salvation and happiness would come with the dawn and wing its flight to every point of the horizon ?

When Pierre, in his turn, was about to retire, Guillaume laid his hands upon his shoulders, and with much emotion gave him a long look. ' Ah ! my poor fellow,' said he, ' you've been suffering too for some days past, I have noticed it. But you are the master of your sufferings, for the struggle you have to overcome is simply in yourself, and you can subdue it ; whereas one cannot subdue the world, when it is the world, its cruelty and injustice, that make one suffer ! Good-night ! be brave, act as your reason tells you, even if it makes you weep, and you will find peace surely enough.'

Later on, when Pierre again found himself alone in his little house at Neuilly, where none now visited him save the

shades of his father and mother, he was long kept awake by
a supreme internal combat. He had never before felt so
disgusted with the falsehood of his life, that cassock which
he had persisted in wearing, though he was a priest in name
only. Perhaps it was all that he had beheld and heard at his
brother's, the want and wretchedness of some, the wild,
futile agitation of others, the need of improvement among
mankind which remained paramount amidst every contradic-
tion and form of weakness, that had made him more deeply
conscious of the necessity of living in loyal and normal
fashion in the broad daylight. He could no longer think of
his former dream of leading the solitary life of a saintly priest
when he was nothing of the kind, without a shiver of shame
at having lied so long. And now it was quite decided, he
would lie no longer, not even from feelings of compassion in
order that others might retain their religious illusions. And
yet how painful it was to have to divest himself of that gown
which seemed to cling to his skin, and how heart-rending the
thought that if he did remove it he would be skinless,
lacerated, infirm, unable, do what he might, to become
like other men !

It was this recurring thought which again tortured him
throughout that terrible night. Would life yet allow him to
enter its fold ? Had he not been branded with a mark which
for ever condemned him to dwell apart ? He thought he could
feel his priestly vows burning his very flesh like red-hot iron.
What use would it be for him to dress as men dress, if in
reality he was never to be a man ? He had hitherto lived
in such a quivering state, in a sphere of renunciation and
dreams ! To know manhood never, to be too late for it,
that thought filled him with terror. And when at last he
made up his mind to fling aside his cassock, he did so from a
simple sense of rectitude, for all his anguish remained.

When he returned to Montmartre on the following day
he wore a jacket and trousers of a dark colour. Neither an
exclamation nor a glance that might have embarrassed him
came from Mère-Grand or the three young men. Was not
the change a natural one ? They greeted him therefore in
the quiet way that was usual with them ; perhaps, however,
with some increase of affection, as if to set him the more at
his ease. Guillaume, however, ventured to smile good-
naturedly. In that change he detected his own work. Cure
was coming, as he had hoped it would come, by him and in

his own home, amid the full sunlight, the life which ever streamed in through yonder window.

Marie, who on her side raised her eyes and looked at Pierre, knew nothing of the sufferings which he had endured through her simple and logical inquiry : ' Why not take your cassock off ? '   She merely felt that by removing it he would be more at ease for his work.

' Oh, Pierre, just come and look ! ' she suddenly exclaimed. ' I have been amusing myself with watching all the smoke which the wind is laying yonder over Paris.   One might take it to be a huge fleet of ships shining in the sunlight. Yes, yes, golden ships, thousands of golden ships, setting forth from the ocean of Paris to enlighten and pacify the world ! '

III

THE DAWN OF LOVE

A COUPLE of days afterwards when Pierre was already growing accustomed to his new attire, and no longer gave it a thought, it so happened that on reaching Montmartre he encountered Abbé Rose outside the basilica of the Sacred Heart.   The old priest, who at first was quite thunderstruck and scarcely able to recognise him, ended by taking hold of his hands and giving him a long look.   Then with his eyes full of tears he exclaimed : ' Oh ! my son, so you have fallen into the awful state I feared !   I never mentioned it, but I felt that God had withdrawn from you.   Ah ! nothing could wound my heart so cruelly as this.'

Then, still trembling, he began to lead Pierre away as if to hide such a scandal from the few people who passed by ; and at last, his strength failing him, he sank upon a heap of bricks lying on the grass of one of the adjoining workyards.

The sincere grief which his old and affectionate friend displayed upset Pierre far more than any angry reproaches or curses would have done.   Tears had come to his own eyes, so acute was the suffering he experienced at this meeting which he ought, however, to have foreseen.   There was yet another wrenching, and one which made the best of their blood flow, in that rupture between Pierre and the saintly man, whose charitable dreams and hopes of salvation he had so long shared. There had been so many divine illusions, so many struggles for the relief of the masses, so much renunciation and forgiveness practised in common between them in their desire to hasten the harvest of the future! And now they were parting; he, Pierre, still young in years, was returning to life, leaving his aged companion to his vain waiting and his dreams.

In his turn, taking hold of Abbé Rose's hands, he gave expression to his sorrow. 'Ah, my friend, my father,' said he, 'it is you alone that I regret losing, now that I am leaving my frightful torments behind. I thought that I was cured of them, but it has been sufficient for me to meet you, and my heart is rent again. . . . Don't weep for me, I pray you, don't reproach me for what I have done. It was necessary that I should do it. If I had consulted you, you would yourself have told me that it was better to renounce the priesthood than to remain a priest without faith or honour.'

'Yes, yes,' Abbé Rose gently responded, 'you no longer had any faith left. I suspected it. And your rigidity and saintliness of life, in which I detected such great despair, made me anxious for you. How many hours did I not spend at times in striving to calm you! And you must listen to me again, you must still let me save you. I am not a sufficiently learned theologian to lead you back by discussing texts and dogmas; but in the name of Charity, my child, yes, in the name of Charity alone, reflect and take up your task of consolation and hope once more.'

Pierre had sat down beside Abbé Rose, in that deserted nook, at the very foot of the basilica. 'Charity! charity!' he replied in passionate accents; 'why it is its nothingness and bankruptcy that have killed the priest there was in me. How can you believe that benevolence is sufficient, when you have spent your whole life in practising it without any other result than that of seeing want perpetuated and even increased, and without any possibility of naming the day when such abomination shall cease? . . . You think of the reward after death, do you not? The justice that is to reign in heaven? But that is not justice, it is dupery—dupery that has brought the world nothing but suffering for centuries past.'

Then he reminded the old priest of their life in the Charonne district, when they had gone about together succouring children in the streets and parents in their hovels; the whole of those admirable efforts which, so far as Abbé Rose was concerned, had simply ended in blame from his superiors, and removal from proximity to his poor, under penalty of more severe punishment should he persist in compromising religion by the practice of blind benevolence without reason or object. And now, was he not, so to say, submerged beneath the ever-rising tide of want, aware that he would never, never be able to give enough even should he dispose of millions, and that he could only prolong the agony of the poor, who, even should they eat to-day, would starve again on the morrow? Thus he was powerless. The wound which he tried to dress and heal, immediately reopened and spread, in such wise that all society would at last be stricken and carried off by it.

Quivering as he listened, and slowly shaking his white head, the old priest ended by replying: 'What does that matter, my child? what does that matter? One must give, always give, give in spite of everything! There is no other joy on earth. . . . If dogmas worry you, content yourself with the Gospel, and even of that retain merely the promise of salvation through charity——'

But at this Pierre's feelings revolted. He forgot that he was speaking to one of simple mind, who was all love and nothing else, and could therefore not follow him. 'The trial has been made,' he answered, 'human salvation cannot be effected by charity, nothing but justice can accomplish it. That is the gathering cry which is going up from every nation. For nearly two thousand years now the Gospel has proved a failure. There has been no redemption; the sufferings of mankind are every whit as great and unjust as they were when Jesus came. And thus the Gospel is now but an abolished code, from which society can only draw things that are troublous and hurtful. Men must free themselves from it.'

This was his final conviction. How strange the idea, thought he, of choosing as the world's social legislator one who lived, as Jesus lived, amidst a social system absolutely different from that of nowadays. The age was different, the very world was different. And if it were merely a question of retaining only such of the moral teaching of Jesus as seemed human and eternal, was there not again a danger in applying immutable principles to the society of every age? No society could live under the strict law of the Gospel. Was not all order, all labour, all life destroyed by the teaching of Jesus? Did He not deny woman, the earth, eternal nature, and the eternal fruitfulness of things and beings? Moreover, Catholicism had reared upon His primitive teaching such a frightful edifice of terror and oppression. The theory of original sin, that terrible heredity reviving with each creature born into the world, made no allowance as Science does for the corrective influences of education, circumstances, and environment. There could be no more pessimist conception of man than this one which devotes him to the Devil from the instant of his birth, and pictures him as struggling against himself until the instant of his death. An impossible and absurd struggle, for it is a question of changing man in his entirety, killing the flesh, killing reason, destroying some guilty energy in each and every passion, and of pursuing the Devil to the very depths of the waters, mountains and forests, there to annihilate him with the very sap of the world. If this theory is accepted the world is but sin, a mere Hell of temptation and suffering, through which one must pass in order to merit Heaven. Ah! what an admirable instrument for absolute despotism is that religion of death, which the principle of charity alone has enabled men to tolerate, but which the need of justice will perforce sweep away. The poor man, who is the wretched dupe of it all, no longer believes in Paradise, but requires that each and all should be rewarded according to their deserts upon this earth; and thus eternal life becomes the good goddess, and desire and labour the very laws of the world, while the fruitfulness of woman is again honoured, and the idiotic nightmare of Hell is replaced by glorious Nature whose travail knows no end. Leaning upon modern Science, clear Latin reason sweeps away the ancient Semitic conception of the Gospel.

'For eighteen hundred years,' concluded Pierre, 'Christianity has been hampering the march of mankind towards truth and justice. And mankind will only resume its evolution on the day when it abolishes Christianity, and places the Gospel among the works of the wise, without taking it any longer as its absolute and final law.'

But Abbé Rose raised his trembling hands: 'Be quiet, be quiet, my child!' he cried; 'you are blaspheming! I knew that doubt distracted you; but I thought you so patient, so able to bear suffering, that I relied on your spirit of renunciation and resignation. What can have happened to make you leave the Church in this abrupt and violent fashion? I no longer recognise you. Sudden passion has sprung up in you, an invincible force seems to carry you away. What is it? Who has changed you, tell me?'

Pierre listened in astonishment. 'No,' said he, 'I assure you, I am such as you have known me, and in all this there is but an inevitable result and finish. Who could have influenced me, since nobody has entered my life? What new feeling could transform me, since I find none in me? I am the same as before, the same assuredly.'

Still there was a touch of hesitation in his voice. Was it really true that there had been no change within him? He again questioned himself, and there came no clear answer; decidedly, he could find nothing. It was all but a delightful awakening, an overpowering desire for life, a longing to open his arms widely enough to embrace everyone and everything. Indeed, a breeze of joy seemed to raise him from the ground and carry him along.

Although Abbé Rose was too innocent of heart to understand things clearly, he again shook his head and thought of the snares which the Devil is ever setting for men. He was quite overwhelmed by Pierre's defection. Continuing his efforts to win him back, he made the mistake of advising him to consult Monseigneur Martha, for he hoped that a prelate of such high authority would find the words necessary to restore him to his faith. Pierre, however, boldly replied that if he was leaving the Church it was partly because it comprised such a man as Martha, such an artisan of deception and despotism, one who turned religion into corrupt diplomacy, and dreamt of winning men back to God by dint of ruses. Thereupon Abbé Rose, rising to his feet, could find no other argument in his despair than that of pointing to the basilica which stood beside them, square, huge, and massive, and still waiting for its dome.

'That is God's abode, my child,' said he, 'the edifice of expiation and triumph, of penitence and forgiveness. You have said mass in it, and now you are leaving it sacrilegiously and forswearing yourself!'

But Pierre also had risen; and buoyed up by a sudden rush of health and strength he answered: 'No, no! I am leaving it willingly, as one leaves a dark vault, to return into the open air and the broad sunlight. God does not dwell

there; the only purpose of that huge edifice is to defy
reason, truth, and justice; it has been erected on the highest
spot that could be found like a citadel of error that dominates,
insults, and threatens Paris!'

Then, seeing that the old priest's eyes were again filling
with tears, and feeling on his own side so pained by their
rupture that he began to sob, Pierre wished to go away.
'Farewell! farewell!' he stammered.

But Abbé Rose caught him in his arms and kissed him,
as if he were a rebellious son who yet had remained the
dearest. 'No, not farewell, not farewell, my child,' he
answered; 'say rather till we meet again. Promise me that
we shall see each other again, at least among those who
starve and weep. It is all very well for you to think that
charity has become bankrupt, but shall we not always love
one another in loving our poor?'

Then they parted.

On becoming the companion of his three big nephews,
Pierre had in a few lessons learnt from them how to ride a
bicycle, in order that he might occasionally accompany them
on their morning excursions. He went twice with them and
Marie along the somewhat roughly paved roads in the
direction of the Lake of Enghien. Then one morning when
the young woman had promised to take him and Antoine as
far as the forest of St. Germain, it was found at the last
moment that Antoine could not come. Marie was already
dressed in a chemisette of fawn-coloured silk, and a little
jacket and 'rationals' of black serge, and it was such a
warm, bright April day that she was not inclined to renounce
her trip.

'Well, so much the worse!' she gaily said to Pierre, 'I
shall take you with me, there will only be the pair of us. I
really want you to see how delightful it is to bowl over a
good road between the beautiful trees.'

However, as Pierre was not yet a very expert rider,
they decided that they would take the train as far as Maisons-
Laffitte, whence they would proceed on their bicycles to the
forest, cross it in the direction of St. Germain, and afterwards return to Paris by train.

'You will be here for _déjeuner_, won't you?' asked Guillaume, whom this freak amused, and who looked with a smile
at his brother. The latter, like Marie, was in black: jacket,
breeches, and stockings all of the same hue.

'Oh, certainly!' replied Marie. 'It's now barely eight o'clock, so we have plenty of time. Still you need not wait for us, you know, we shall always find our way back.'

It was a delightful morning. When they started, Pierre could fancy himself with a friend of his own sex, so that this trip together through the warm sunlight seemed quite natural. Doubtless their costumes, which were so much alike, conduced to the gay brotherly feeling he experienced. But beyond all this there was the healthfulness of the open air, the delight which exercise brings, the pleasure of roaming in all freedom through the midst of nature.

On taking the train they found themselves alone in a compartment, and Marie once more began to talk of her college days. 'Ah! you've no idea,' said she, 'what fine games at baseball we used to have at Fénelon! We used to tie up our skirts with string so as to run the better, for we were not allowed to wear rationals like I'm wearing now. And there were shrieks, and rushes, and pushes, till our hair waved about and we were quite red with exercise and excitement. Still that didn't prevent us from working in the class-rooms. On the contrary! Directly we were at study we fought again, each striving to learn the most and reach the top of the class!'

She laughed gaily as she thus recalled her school life, and Pierre glanced at her with candid admiration, so pink and healthy did she look under her little hat of black felt, which a long silver pin kept in position. Her fine dark hair was caught up behind, showing her neck, which looked as fresh and delicate as a child's. And never before had she seemed to him so supple and so strong.

'Ah,' she continued in a jesting way, 'there is nothing like rationals, you know! To think that some women are foolish and obstinate enough to wear skirts when they go out cycling!'

Then, as he declared—just by way of speaking the truth, and without the faintest idea of gallantry—that she looked very nice indeed in her costume, she responded: 'Oh! I don't count. I'm not a beauty. I simply enjoy good health. . . . But can you understand it? To think that women have an unique opportunity of putting themselves at their ease, and releasing their limbs from prison, and yet they won't do so! If they think that they look the prettier in short skirts like schoolgirls they are vastly mistaken! And as for any question of modesty, well it seems to me that it is infinitely less objectionable for women to wear rationals than to bare their bosoms at balls and theatres and dinners as society ladies do.' Then, with a gesture of girlish impulsiveness, she added: 'Besides, does one think of such things when one's rolling along? . . . Yes, rationals are the only things, skirts are rank heresy!'

In her turn, she was now looking at him, and was struck by the extraordinary change which had come over him since the day when he had first appeared to her, so sombre in his long cassock, with his face emaciated, livid, almost distorted by anguish. It was like a resurrection, for now his countenance was bright, his lofty brow had all the serenity of hope, while his eyes and lips once more showed some of the confident tenderness which sprang from his everlasting thirst for love, self-bestowal, and life. All mark of the priesthood had already left him, save that where he had been tonsured his hair still remained rather short.

'Why are you looking at me?' he asked.

'I was noticing how much good has been done you by work and the open air,' she frankly answered, 'I much prefer you as you are. You used to look so poorly. I thought you really ill.'

'So I was,' said he.

The train, however, was now stopping at Maisons-Laffitte. They alighted from it, and at once took the road to the forest. This road rises gently till it reaches the Maisons-gate, and on market days it is often crowded with carts.

'I shall go first, eh?' said Marie, gaily, 'for vehicles still alarm you.'

Thereupon she started ahead, but every now and again she turned with a smile to see if he were following her. And every time they overtook and passed a cart she spoke to him of the merits of their machines, which both came from the Grandidier works. They were 'Lisettes,' examples of those popular bicycles which Thomas had helped to perfect, and which the Bon Marché now sold in large numbers for 250 francs apiece. Perhaps they were rather heavy in appearance, but on the other hand their strength was beyond question. They were just the machines for a long journey, so Marie declared.

'Ah! here's the forest,' she at last exclaimed. 'We have now reached the end of the rise; and you will see what splendid avenues there are. One can bowl along them as on a velvet carpet.'

Pierre had already joined her, and they rode on side by side along the broad straight avenue fringed with magnificent trees.

'I am all right now,' said Pierre, 'your pupil will end by doing you honour, I hope.'

'Oh! I've no doubt of it. You already have a very good seat, and before long you'll leave me behind, for a woman is never a man's equal in a matter like this. At the same time, however, what a capital education cycling is for women!'

'In what way?'

'Oh! I've certain ideas of my own on the subject; and if ever I have a daughter I shall put her on a bicycle as soon as she's ten years old, just to teach her how to conduct herself in life.'

'Education by experience, eh?'

'Yes, why not? Look at the big girls who are brought up hanging to their mothers' apron-strings. Their parents frighten them with everything, they are allowed no initiative, no exercise of judgment or decision, so that at times they hardly know how to cross a street, to such a degree does the traffic alarm them. Well, I say that a girl ought to be set on a bicycle in her childhood, and allowed to follow the roads. She will then learn to open her eyes, to look out for stones and avoid them, and to turn in the right direction at every bend or crossway. If a vehicle comes up at a gallop or any other danger presents itself, she'll have to make up her mind on the instant, and steer her course firmly and properly if she does not wish to lose a limb. Briefly, doesn't all this supply proper apprenticeship for one's will, and teach one how to conduct and defend oneself?'

Pierre had begun to laugh. 'You will all be too healthy,' he remarked.

'Oh, one must be healthy if one wants to be happy. But what I wish to convey is that those who learn to avoid stones and to turn properly along the highways will know how to overcome difficulties, and take the best decisions in after life. The whole of education lies in knowledge and energy.'

'So women are to be emancipated by cycling?'

'Well, why not? It may seem a droll idea; but see what progress has been made already! By wearing rationals women free their limbs from prison; then the facilities which cycling affords people for going out together tend to greater intercourse and equality between the sexes; the wife and the children can follow the husband everywhere, and friends like ourselves are at liberty to roam hither and thither without astonishing anybody. In this lies the greatest advantage of all, one takes a bath of air and sunshine, one goes back to nature, to the earth, our common mother, from whom one derives fresh strength and gaiety of heart! Just look how delightful this forest is. And how healthy the breeze that inflates our lungs! Yes, it all purifies, calms, and encourages one.'

The forest, which was quite deserted on week days, stretched out in quietude on either hand, with sunlight filtering between its deep bands of trees. At that hour the rays only illumined one side of the avenue, there gilding the lofty drapery of verdure; on the other, the shady side, the greenery seemed almost black. It was truly delightful to skim, swallow-like, over that royal avenue in the fresh atmosphere, amidst the waving of grass and foliage, whose powerful scent swept against one's face. Pierre and Marie scarcely touched the soil; it was as if wings had come to them, and were carrying them on with a regular flight, through alternate patches of shade and sunshine, and all the scattered vitality of the far-reaching, quivering forest with its mosses, its sources, its animal and its insect life.

Marie would not stop when they reached the crossway of the Croix de Noailles, a spot where people congregate on Sundays, for she was acquainted with secluded nooks, which were far more charming resting-places. When they reached the slope going down towards Poissy she roused Pierre, and they let their machines rush on. Then came all the joyous intoxication of speed, the rapturous feeling of darting along breathlessly while the grey road flees beneath one, and the trees on either hand turn like the opening folds of a fan. The breeze blows tempestuously, and one fancies that one is journeying yonder towards the horizon, the infinite, which ever and ever recedes. It is like boundless hope, delivery from every shackle, absolute freedom of motion through space. And nothing can inspirit one more gloriously—one's heart leaps as if one were in the very heavens.

'We are not going to Poissy, you know!' Marie suddenly cried, 'we have to turn to the left.'

They took the road from Achères to the Loges, which ascends and contracts, thus bringing one closer together in the shade. Gradually slowing down, they began to exert themselves in order to make their way up the incline. This road was not so good as the others, it had been gullied by the recent heavy rains, and sand and gravel lay about. But then is there not even a pleasure in effort?

'You will get used to it,' said Marie to Pierre, 'it's amusing to overcome obstacles. For my part I don't like roads which are invariably smooth. A little ascent which does not try one's limbs too much rouses and inspirits one. And it is so agreeable to find oneself strong, and able to go on and on in spite of rain, or wind, or hills.'

Her bright humour and courage quite charmed Pierre. 'And so,' said he, 'we are off for a journey round France?'

'No, no, we've arrived. You won't dislike a little rest, eh? And now, tell me, wasn't it worth our while to come on here and rest in such a nice, fresh, quiet spot?'

She nimbly sprang off her machine and, bidding him follow her, turned into a path, along which she went some fifty paces. They placed their bicycles against some trees, and then found themselves in a little clearing, the most exquisite, leafy nest that one could dream of. The forest here assumed an aspect of secluded sovereign beauty. The spring-tide had endowed it with youth, the foliage was light and virginal, like delicate green lace flecked with gold by the sun-rays. And from the herbage and the surrounding thickets arose a breath of life, laden with all the powerful aroma of the earth.

'It's not too warm as yet, fortunately,' exclaimed Marie, as she seated herself at the foot of a young oak tree against which she leant. 'In July ladies get rather red by the time they reach this spot, and all the powder comes off their faces. However, one can't always be beautiful.'

'Well, I'm not cold by any means,' replied Pierre, as he sat at her feet wiping his forehead.

She laughed, and answered that she had never before seen him with such a colour. Then they began to talk like children, like two young friends, finding a source of gaiety in the most puerile things. She was somewhat anxious about his health, however, and would not allow him to remain in the cool shade, as he felt so very warm. In order to tranquillise her, he had to change his place and seat himself with his back to the sun. Then, a little later, he saved her from a large black spider, which had caught itself in the wavy hair on the nape of her neck. At this all her womanly nature reappeared, and she shrieked with terror. 'How stupid it was to be afraid of a spider!' she exclaimed a moment afterwards; yet, in spite of her efforts to master herself, she remained pale and trembling.

Silence at last fell between them, and they looked at one another with a smile. In the midst of that delicate greenery they felt drawn together by frank affection—the affection of brother and sister, so it seemed to them. It made Marie very happy to think that she had taken an interest in Pierre, and that his return to health was largely her own work. However, their eyes never fell, their hands never met, even as they sat there toying with the grass, for they were as pure, as unconscious of all evil as were the lofty oaks around them.

At last Marie noticed that time was flying. 'You know that they expect us back to lunch,' she exclaimed. 'We ought to be off.'

Thereupon they rose, wheeled their bicycles back to the highway, and starting off again at a good pace passed the Loges and reached St. Germain by the fine avenue which conducts to the château. It charmed them to take their course again side by side like birds of equal flight. Their little bells jingled, their chains rustled lightly, and a fresh breeze swept past them as they resumed their talk, quite at ease, and so linked together by friendship that they seemed far removed from all the rest of the world.

They took the train from St. Germain to Paris, and on the journey Pierre suddenly noticed that Marie's cheeks were purpling. There were two ladies with them in the compartment.

'Ah!' said he, 'so you feel warm in your turn now.'

But she protested the contrary, her face glowing more and more brightly as she spoke, as if some sudden feeling of shame quite upset her. 'No, I'm not warm,' said she, 'just feel my hands. . . . But how ridiculous it is to blush like this without any reason for it!'

He understood her. This was one of those involuntary blushing fits which so distressed her, and which, as Mère-

Grand had remarked, brought her heart to her very cheeks. There was no cause for it, as she herself said. After slumbering in all innocence in the solitude of the forest her heart had begun to beat, despite herself.

Meantime, over yonder at Montmartre, Guillaume had spent his morning in preparing some of that mysterious powder, the cartridges of which he concealed upstairs in Mère-Grand's bedroom. Great danger attended this manufacture. The slightest forgetfulness while he was manipulating the ingredients, any delay too, in turning off a tap, might lead to a terrible explosion, which would annihilate the building and all who might be in it. For this reason he preferred to work when he was alone, so that on the one hand, there might be no danger for others, and on the other, less likelihood of his own attention being diverted from his task. That morning, as it happened, his three sons were working in the room, and Mère-Grand sat sewing near the furnace. Truth to tell, she did not count, for she scarcely ever left her place, feeling quite at ease there, however great might be the peril. Indeed, she had become so well acquainted with the various phases of Guillaume's delicate operations, and their terrible possibilities, that she would occasionally give him a helping hand.

That morning, as she sat there mending some house linen—her eyesight still being so keen that in spite of her seventy years she wore no spectacles—she now and again glanced at Guillaume as if to make sure that he forgot nothing. Then feeling satisfied she would once more bend over her work. She remained very strong and active. Her hair was only just turning white, and she had kept all her teeth ; while her face still looked refined, though it was slowly withering with age and had acquired an expression of some severity. As a rule she was a woman of few words ; her life was one of activity and good management. When she opened her lips it was usually to give advice, to counsel reason, energy, and courage. For some time past she had been growing more taciturn than ever, as if all her attention were claimed by the household matters which were in her sole charge ; still her fine eyes would rest thoughtfully on those about her, on the three young men, and on Guillaume, Marie, and Pierre, who all obeyed her as if she were their acknowledged queen. If she looked at them in that pensive way, was it that she foresaw certain changes, and noticed

certain incidents of which the others remained unconscious?
Perhaps so. At all events she became even graver, and more
attentive than in the past. It was as if she were waiting for
some hour to strike when all her wisdom and authority would
be required.

'Be careful, Guillaume,' she at last remarked, as she once
more looked up from her sewing. 'You seem absent-minded
this morning. Is anything worrying you?'

He glanced at her with a smile. 'No, nothing, I assure
you,' he replied. 'But I was thinking of our dear Marie,
who was so glad to go off to the forest in this bright sunshine.'

Antoine, who heard the remark, raised his head, while his
brothers remained absorbed in their work. 'What a pity it
is that I had this block to finish,' said he, 'I would willingly
have gone with her.'

'Oh, no matter,' his father quietly rejoined. 'Pierre is
with her, and he is very cautious.'

For another moment Mère-Grand continued scrutinising
Guillaume; then she once more reverted to her sewing.

If she exercised such sway over the home and all its inmates, it was by reason of her long devotion, her intelligence,
and the kindliness with which she ruled. Uninfluenced by
any religious faith, and disregarding all social conventionalities, her guiding principle in everything was the theory of
human justice which she had arrived at after suffering so
grievously from the injustice which had killed her husband.
She put her views into practice with wonderful courage,
knowing nothing of any prejudices, but accomplishing her
duty, such as she understood it, to the very end. And in the
same way as she had first devoted herself to her husband, and
next to her daughter Marguerite, so at present she devoted
herself to Guillaume and his sons. Pierre, whom she had
first studied with some anxiety, had now, too, become a member
of her family, a dweller in the little realm of happiness which
she ruled. She had doubtless found him worthy of admission
into it, though she did not reveal the reason why. After
days and days of silence she had simply said, one evening to
Guillaume, that he had done well in bringing his brother to
live among them.

Time flew by as she sat sewing and thinking. Towards
noon Guillaume, who was still at work, suddenly remarked
to her: 'As Marie and Pierre haven't come back, we had

better let the lunch wait a little while. Besides, I should like to finish what I'm about.'

Another quarter of an hour then elapsed. Finally, the three young men rose from their work, and went to wash their hands at a tap in the garden.

'Marie is very late,' now remarked Mère-Grand. 'We must hope that nothing has happened to her.'

'Oh ! she rides so well,' replied Guillaume. 'I'm more anxious on account of Pierre.'

At this the old lady again fixed her eyes on him, and said : 'But Marie will have guided Pierre, they already ride very well together.'

'No doubt, still I should be better pleased if they were back home.'

Then all at once, fancying that he heard the ring of a bicycle bell, he called out : 'There they are ! ' And forgetting everything else in his satisfaction, he quitted his furnace and hastened into the garden in order to meet them.

Mère-Grand, left to herself, quietly continued sewing, without a thought that the manufacture of Guillaume's powder was drawing to an end in an apparatus near her. A couple of minutes later, however, when Guillaume came back, saying that he had made a mistake, his eyes suddenly rested on his furnace, and he turned quite livid. Brief as had been his absence the exact moment when it was necessary to turn off a tap in order that no danger might attend the preparation of his powder, had already gone by; and now, unless someone should dare to approach that terrible tap, and boldly turn it, a fearful explosion might take place. Doubtless it was too late already, and whoever might have the bravery to attempt the feat would be blown to pieces.

Guillaume himself had often run a similar risk of death with perfect composure. But on this occasion he remained as if rooted to the floor, unable to take a step, paralysed by the dread of annihilation. He shuddered and stammered in momentary expectation of a catastrophe which would hurl the workshop to the heavens.

'Mère-Grand, Mère-Grand,' he stammered. 'The apparatus, the tap . . . it is all over, all over ! '

The old woman had raised her head without as yet understanding him. 'Eh, what ? ' said she, 'what is the matter with you ? ' Then, on seeing how distorted were his features, how he recoiled as if mad with terror, she glanced at the furnace and realised the danger. 'Well, but it's simple enough,' said she, 'it's only necessary to turn off the tap, eh?'

Thereupon, without any semblance of haste, in the most easy and natural manner possible, she deposited her needle-work on a little table, rose from her chair, and turned off the tap with a light but firm hand. 'There! it's done,' said she. 'But why didn't you do it yourself, my friend?'

He had watched her in bewilderment, chilled to the bones, as if touched by the hand of death. And when some colour at last returned to his cheeks, and he found himself still alive in front of the apparatus whence no harm could now come, he heaved a deep sigh, and again shuddered. 'Why I did not turn it off?' he repeated. 'It was because I felt afraid.'

At that very moment Marie and Pierre came into the workshop all chatter and laughter, delighted with their excursion, and bringing with them the bright joyousness of the sunlight. The three brothers, Thomas, François, and Antoine, were jesting with them, and trying to make them confess that Pierre had at least fought a battle with a cow on the high road, and ridden into a cornfield. All at once, how-ever, they became quite anxious, for they noticed that their father looked terribly upset.

'My lads,' said he, 'I've just been a coward. Ah! it's a curious feeling, I had never experienced it before.'

Thereupon he recounted his fears of an accident, and how quietly Mère-Grand had saved them all from certain death. She waved her hand, however, as if to say that there was nothing particularly heroic in turning off a tap. The young men's eyes nevertheless filled with tears, and one after the other they went to kiss her with a fervour, instinct with all the gratitude and worship they felt for her. She had been devoting herself to them ever since their infancy, she had now just given them a new lease of life. Marie also threw herself into her arms, kissing her with gratitude and emotion. Mère-Grand herself was the only one who did not shed tears. She strove to calm them, begging them to exaggerate nothing and to remain sensible.

'Well, you must at all events let me kiss you as the others have done,' Guillaume said to her, as he recovered his self-possession. 'I at least owe you that. And Pierre, too, shall kiss you, for you are now as good for him as you have always been for us.'

At table, when it was at last possible for them to lunch, he reverted to that attack of fear which had left him both surprised and ashamed. He, who for years had never once thought of death, had for some time past found ideas of caution in his mind. On two occasions recently he had shuddered at the possibility of a catastrophe. How was it that a longing for life had come to him in his decline? Why was it that he now wished to live? At last with a touch of tender affection in his gaiety, he remarked: 'Do you know, Marie, I think it is my thoughts of you that make me a coward. If I've lost my bravery it's because I risk something precious when any danger arises. Happiness has been entrusted to my charge. Just now when I fancied that we were all going to die, I thought I could see you, and my fear of losing you froze and paralysed me.'

Marie indulged in a pretty laugh. Allusions to her coming marriage were seldom made; however, she invariably greeted them with an air of happy affection. 'Another six weeks!' she simply said.

Thereupon Mère-Grand, who had been looking at them, turned her eyes towards Pierre. He, however, like the others was listening with a smile.

'That's true,' said the old lady, 'you are to be married in six weeks' time. So I did right to prevent the house from being blown up.'

At this the young men made merry; and the repast came to an end in very joyous fashion.

During the afternoon, however, Pierre's heart gradually grew heavy. Marie's words constantly returned to him: 'Another six weeks!' Yes, it was indeed true, she would then be married. But it seemed to him that he had never previously known it, never for a moment thought of it. And later on, in the evening, when he was alone in his room at Neuilly, his heart-pain became intolerable. Those words tortured him. Why was it that they had not caused him any suffering when they were spoken, why had he greeted them with a smile? And why had such cruel anguish slowly followed? All at once an idea sprang up in his mind, and became an overwhelming certainty. He loved Marie, he loved her as a lover, with a love so intense that he might die from it.

With this sudden consciousness of his passion everything became clear and plain. He had been going perforce towards

that love ever since he had first met Marie. The emotion
into which the young woman had originally thrown him had
seemed to him a feeling of repulsion, but afterwards he had
been slowly conquered, all his torments and struggles ending in
this love for her.　It was indeed through her that he had at
last found quietude. And the delightful morning which he had
spent with her that day, appeared to him like a betrothal
morning, in the depths of the happy forest. Nature had
resumed her sway over him, delivered him from his sufferings,
made him strong and healthy once more, and given him to
the woman he adored.　The quiver he had experienced, the
happiness he had felt, his communion with the trees, the
heavens, and every living creature—all those things which
he had been unable to explain, now acquired a clear meaning
which transported him.　In Marie alone lay his cure, his
hope, his conviction that he would be born anew and at last
find happiness.　In her company he had already forgotten
all those distressing problems which had formerly haunted
him and bowed him down.　For a week past he had not once
thought of death, which had so long been the companion of
his every hour. All the conflict of faith and doubt, the
distress roused by the idea of nihility, the anger he had felt
at the unjust sufferings of mankind, had been swept away by
her fresh cool hands.　She was so healthy herself, so glad to
live, that she had imparted a taste for life even to him.　Yes,
it was simply that : she was making him a man, a worker, a
lover once more.

Then he suddenly remembered Abbé Rose and his painful
conversation with that saintly man.　The old priest, whose
heart was so ingenuous, and who knew nothing of love and
passion, was nevertheless the only one who had understood
the truth.　He had told Pierre that he was changed, that
there was another man in him.　And he, Pierre, had
foolishly and stubbornly declared that he was the same as he
had always been ; whereas Marie had already transformed
him, bringing all nature back to his breast—all nature, with
its sunlit countrysides, fructifying breezes, and vast heavens,
whose glow ripens its crops.　That indeed was why he had
felt so exasperated with Catholicism, that religion of death ;
why he had shouted that the Gospel was useless, and that the
world awaited another law—a law of terrestrial happiness,
human justice, and living love and fruitfulness !

Ah, but Guillaume ?　Then a vision of his brother rose

before Pierre, that brother who loved him so fondly, and who had carried him to his home of toil, quietude, and affection, in order to cure him of his sufferings. If he knew Marie it was simply because Guillaume had chosen that he should know her. And again Marie's words recurred to him: 'Another six weeks!' Yes, in six weeks his brother would marry the young woman. This thought was like a stab in Pierre's heart. Still, he did not for one moment hesitate: if he must die of his love, he would die of it, but none should ever know it; he would conquer himself, he would flee to the ends of the earth should he ever feel the faintest cowardice. Rather than bring a moment's pain to that brother who had striven to resuscitate him, who was the artisan of the passion now consuming him, who had given him his whole heart, and all he had—he would condemn himself to perpetual torture. And indeed, torture was coming back; for in losing Marie he could but sink into the distress born of the consciousness of his nothingness. As he lay in bed, unable to sleep, he already experienced a return of his abominable torments—the negation of everything, the feeling that everything was useless, that the world had no significance, and that life was only worthy of being cursed and denied. And then the shudder born of the thought of death returned to him. Ah! to die, to die without even having lived!

The struggle was a frightful one. Until daybreak he sobbed in martyrdom. Why had he taken off his cassock? He had done so at a word from Marie; and now another word from her gave him the despairing idea of donning it once more. One could not escape from so fast a prison. That black gown still clung to his skin. He fancied that he had divested himself of it, and yet it was still weighing on his shoulders, and his wisest course would be to bury himself in it for ever. By donning it again he would at least wear mourning for his manhood.

All at once, however, a fresh thought upset him. Why should he struggle in that fashion? Marie did not love him. There had been nothing between them to indicate that she cared for him otherwise than as a charming, tender-hearted sister. It was Guillaume whom she loved, no doubt. Then he pressed his face to his pillow to stifle his sobs, and once more swore that he would conquer himself and turn a smiling face upon their happiness.

IV

TRIAL AND SENTENCE

HAVING returned to Montmartre on the morrow Pierre
suffered so grievously that he did not show himself there on
the two following days. He preferred to remain at home where
there was nobody to notice his feverishness. On the third
morning, however, whilst he was still in bed, strengthless
and full of despair, he was both surprised and embarrassed by
a visit from Guillaume.

'I must needs come to you,' said the latter, 'since you
forsake us. I've come to fetch you to attend Salvat's trial,
which takes place to-day. I had no end of trouble to secure
two places. Come, get up, we'll have *déjeuner* in town, so
as to reach the court early.'

Then, while Pierre was hastily dressing, Guillaume, who
on his side seemed thoughtful and worried that morning,
began to question him : 'Have you anything to reproach us
with ? ' he asked.

'No, nothing. What an idea ! ' was Pierre's reply.

'Then why have you been staying away ? We had got
into the habit of seeing you every day, but all at once you
disappear.'

Pierre vainly sought a falsehood, and all his composure fled. 'I had some work to do here,' said he, 'and then,
too, my gloomy ideas came back to me, and I didn't want to
go and sadden you all.'

At this Guillaume hastily waved his hand. 'If you fancy
that your absence enlivens us you're mistaken,' he replied.
'Marie, who is usually so well and happy, had such a bad
headache on the day before yesterday that she was obliged to
keep her room. And she was ill at ease and nervous and
silent again yesterday. We spent a very unpleasant day.'

As he spoke Guillaume looked Pierre well in the face, his
frank loyal eyes clearly revealing the suspicions which had
come to him, but which he would not express in words.

Pierre, quite dismayed by the news of Marie's indisposition, and frightened by the idea of betraying his secret,
thereupon managed to tell a lie. 'Yes, she wasn't very well
on the day when we went cycling,' he quietly responded. 'But

I assure you that I have had a lot to do here. When you came in just now I was about to get up and go to your house as usual.'

Guillaume kept his eyes on him for a moment longer. Then either believing him or deciding to postpone his search for the truth to some future time, he began speaking affectionately on other subjects. With his keen brotherly love, however, there was blended such a quiver of impending distress, of unconfessed sorrow, which possibly he did not yet realise, that Pierre in his turn began to question him. 'And you,' said he, 'are you ill? You seem to me to have lost your usual serenity.'

'I? Oh! I'm not ill. Only I can't very well retain my composure; Salvat's affair distresses me exceedingly, as you must know. They will all end by driving me mad with the monstrous injustice they show towards that unhappy fellow.'

Thenceforward Guillaume went on talking of Salvat in a stubborn passionate way, as if he wished to find an explanation of all his pain and unrest in that affair. While he and Pierre were partaking of *déjeuner* at a little restaurant on the Boulevard du Palais, he related how deeply touched he was by the silence which Salvat had preserved with regard both to the nature of the explosive employed in the bomb and the few days' work which he had once done at his house. It was, thanks to this silence, that he, Guillaume, had not been worried or even summoned as a witness. Then, in his emotion, he reverted to his invention, that formidable engine which would ensure omnipotence to France, as the great initiatory and liberative power of the world. The results of the researches which had occupied him for ten years past were now out of danger and in all readiness, so that if occasion required they might at once be delivered to the French government. And, apart from certain scruples which came to him at the thought of the unworthiness of French financial and political society, he was simply delaying any further steps in the matter until his marriage with Marie, in order that he might associate her with the gift of universal peace which he imagined he was about to bestow upon the world.

It was through Bertheroy and with great difficulty that Guillaume had managed to secure two seats in court for Salvat's trial. When he and Pierre presented themselves for admission at eleven o'clock they fancied that they would

never be able to enter. The large gates of the Palace of
Justice were kept closed, several passages were fenced off, and
terror seemed to reign in the deserted building, as if indeed
the judges feared some sudden invasion of bomb-laden Anarchists. Each door and barrier, too, was guarded by soldiers
with whom the brothers had to parley. When they at last
entered the Assize Court they found it already crowded with
people, who were apparently quite willing to suffocate there
for an hour before the arrival of the judges, and to remain
motionless for some seven or eight hours afterwards, since it
was reported that the authorities wished to get the case over
in a single sitting. In the small space allotted to the standing
public there was a serried mass of sightseers who had come
up from the streets ; a few companions and friends of Salvat
having managed to slip in among them. In the other compartment, where witnesses are generally huddled together on
oak benches, were those spectators who had been allowed admittance by favour, and these were so numerous and so
closely packed that here and there they almost sat upon one
another's knees. Then, in the well of the court and behind
the bench were rows of chairs set out as for some theatrical
performance, and occupied by privileged members of society,
politicians, leading journalists, and ladies. And meantime a
number of gowned advocates sought refuge wherever chance
offered, crowding into every vacant spot, every available
corner.

Pierre had never before visited the Assize Court, and its
appearance surprised him. He had expected much pomp and
majesty, whereas this temple of human justice seemed to him
small and dismal and of doubtful cleanliness. The bench
was so low that he could scarcely see the arm-chairs of the
presiding judge and his two assessors. Then he was struck
by the profusion of old oak panels, balustrades, and benches,
which helped to darken the apartment, whose wall hangings
were of olive green, while a further display of oak panelling
appeared on the ceiling above. From the seven narrow and
high-set windows with scanty little white curtains there fell
a pale light which sharply divided the court. On one
hand one saw the dock and the defending counsel's seat
steeped in frigid light, while, on the other, was the little,
isolated jury box in the shade. This contrast seemed symbolical of justice, impersonal and uncertain, face to face with
the accused, whom the light stripped bare, probed as it were

to his very soul. Then, through a kind of grey mist above
the bench, in the depths of the stern and gloomy scene, one
could vaguely distinguish the heavy painting of ' Christ
Crucified.' A large white bust of the Republic alone showed
forth clearly against the dark wall just above the dock
where Salvat would presently appear. The only remaining
seats that Guillaume and Pierre could find were on the last
bench of the witnesses' compartment, against the partition
which separated the latter from the space allotted to the
standing public. Just as Guillaume was seating himself, he
saw among the latter little Victor Mathis, who stood
there with his elbows leaning on the partition, while his chin
rested on his crossed hands. The young man's eyes were
glowing in his pale face with thin, compressed lips. Although
they recognised one another, Victor did not move, and
Guillaume on his side understood that it was not safe to exchange greetings in such a place. From that moment,
however, he remained conscious that Victor was there, just
above him, never stirring, but waiting silently, fiercely, and
with flaming eyes, for what was going to happen.

Pierre, meantime, had recognised that most amiable
deputy Duthil, and little Princess Rosemonde seated just in
front of him. Amidst the hubbub of the throng which chatted
and laughed to while away the time, their voices were the
gayest to be heard, and plainly showed how delighted they
were to find themselves at a spectacle to which so many
desired admittance. Duthil was explaining all the arrangements to Rosemonde, telling her to whom or to what purpose
each bench and wooden box was allotted; there was the jury-
box, the prisoner's dock, the seats assigned to counsel for the
defence, the public prosecutor, and the clerk of the court,
without forgetting the table on which material evidence was
deposited and the bar to which witnesses were summoned.
There was nobody as yet in any of these places; one merely
saw an attendant giving a last look round, and advocates passing rapidly. One might indeed have thought oneself in a
theatre, the stage of which remained deserted, while the spectators crowded the auditorium waiting for the play to begin.
To fill up the interval the little Princess ended by looking
about her for persons of her acquaintance among the close-
pressed crowd of sight-seers whose eager faces were already
reddening.

' Oh ! isn't that Monsieur Fonsègue over there behind the

bench, near that stout lady in yellow?' she exclaimed. 'Our friend General de Bozonnet is on the other side, I see. But isn't Baron Duvillard here?'

'Oh! no,' replied Duthil; 'he could hardly come, it would look as if he were here to ask for vengeance.' Then, in his turn questioning Rosemonde, the deputy went on : 'Do you happen to have quarrelled with your handsome friend Hyacinthe? Is that the reason why you've given me the pleasure of acting as your escort to-day?'

With a slight shrug of her shoulders, the Princess replied that poets were beginning to bore her. A fresh caprice, indeed, was drawing her into politics. For a week past she had found amusement in the surroundings of the ministerial crisis, into which the young deputy for Angoulême had initiated her. 'They are all a little bit crazy at the Duvillards', my dear fellow,' said she. 'It's decided, you know, that Gérard is to marry Camille. The Baroness has resigned herself to it, and I've heard from a most reliable quarter that Madame de Quinsac, the young man's mother, has given her consent.'

At this Duthil became quite merry. He also seemed to be well informed on the subject. 'Yes, yes, I know,' said he. 'The wedding is to take place shortly at the Madeleine. It will be a magnificent affair, no doubt. And after all what would you have? There couldn't be a better finish to the affair. The Baroness is really kindness personified, and I said all along that she would sacrifice herself in order to ensure the happiness of her daughter and Gérard. In point of fact that marriage will settle everything, put everything in proper order again.'

'And what does the Baron say?' asked Rosemonde.

'The Baron? Why, he's delighted,' replied Duthil in a bantering way. 'You read no doubt this morning that Dauvergne is given the department of Public Instruction in the new Ministry. This means that Silviane's engagement at the Comédie is a certainty. Dauvergne was simply chosen on that account.'

At this moment the conversation was interrupted by little Massot who, after a dispute with one of the ushers some distance away, had perceived a vacant place by the side of the Princess. He thereupon made her a questioning sign, and she beckoned to him to approach.

'Ah!' said he, as he installed himself beside her, 'I have

not got here without trouble. One's crushed to death on the press bench, and I've an article to write. You are the kindest of women, Princess, to make a little room for your faithful admirer, myself.' Then, after shaking hands with Duthil, he continued without any transition : ' And so there's a new Ministry at last, Monsieur le député. You have all taken your time about it, but it's really a very fine Ministry, which everybody regards with surprise and admiration.'

The decrees appointing the new Ministers had appeared in the 'Journal Officiel' that very morning. After a long deadlock, after Vignon had for the second time seen his plans fail through ever-recurring obstacles, Monferrand, as a last resource, had suddenly been summoned to the Elysée, and in four-and-twenty hours he had found the colleagues he wanted and secured the acceptance of his list, in such wise that he now triumphantly reascended to power after falling from it with Barroux in such wretched fashion. He had also chosen a new post for himself, relinquishing the department of the Interior for that of Finances, with the Presidency of the Council, which had long been his secret ambition. His stealthy labour, the masterly fashion in which he had saved himself while others sank, now appeared in its full beauty. First had come Salvat's arrest, and the use he had made of it, then the wonderful subterranean campaign which he had carried on against Vignon, the thousand obstacles which he had twice set across his path, and finally the sudden *dénouement* with that list he held in readiness, that formation of a Ministry in a single day as soon as his services were solicited.

' It is fine work; I must compliment you on it,' added little Massot by way of a jest.

' But I've had nothing to do with it,' Duthil modestly replied.

' Nothing to do with it ! oh ! yes you have, my dear sir, everybody says so.'

The deputy felt flattered and smiled, while the other rattled on with his insinuations, which were put in such a humorous way that nothing he said could be resented. He talked of Monferrand's followers who had so powerfully helped him on to victory. How heartily had Fonsègue finished off his old friend Barroux in the ' Globe ! ' Every morning for a month past the paper had published an article belabouring Barroux, annihilating Vignon, and preparing the

public for the return of a saviour of society who was not
named. Then, too, Duvillard's millions had waged a secret
warfare, all the Baron's numerous creatures had fought like
an army for the good cause. Duthil himself had played the
pipe and beat the drum, while Chaigneux resigned himself
to the baser duties which others would not undertake. And
so the triumphant Monferrand would certainly begin by
stifling that scandalous and embarrassing affair of the African
Railways, and appointing a committee of inquiry to bury it.

By this time Duthil had assumed an important air.
'Well, my dear fellow,' said he, 'at serious moments when
society is in peril, certain strong-handed men, real men of
government, become absolutely necessary, Monferrand had
no need of our friendship, his presence in office was imperiously required by the situation. His hand is the only one
that can save us!'

'I know,' replied Massot scoffingly. 'I've even been told
that if everything was settled straight off so that the decrees
might be published this morning, it was in order to instil
confidence into the judges and jurymen here, in such wise
that knowing Monferrand's fist to be behind them they would
have the courage to pronounce sentence of death this
evening.'

'Well, public safety requires a sentence of death, and
those who have to ensure that safety must not be left ignorant
of the fact that the government is with them, and will know
how to protect them, if need be.'

At this moment a merry laugh from the Princess broke
in upon the conversation. 'Oh! just look over there!' said
she, 'isn't that Silviane who has just sat down beside
Monsieur Fonsègue?'

'The Silviane Ministry!' muttered Massot in a jesting
way. 'Well, there will be no boredom at Dauvergne's if he
ingratiates himself with actresses.'

Guillaume and Pierre heard this chatter, however little
they cared to listen to it. Such a deluge of society tittle-tattle
and political indiscretion brought the former a keen heart
pang. So Salvat was sentenced to death even before he had
appeared in court. He was to pay for the transgressions of
one and all, his crime was simply a favourable opportunity
for the triumph of a band of ambitious people bent on power
and enjoyment! Ah! what terrible social rottenness there
was in it all; money corrupting one and another, families

sinking to filth, politics turned into a mere treacherous struggle between individuals, and power becoming the prey of the crafty and the impudent! Must not everything surely crumble? Was not this solemn assize of human justice a derisive parody, since all that one found there was an assembly of happy and privileged people defending the shaky edifice which sheltered them, and making use of all the forces they yet retained, to crush a fly—that unhappy devil of uncertain sanity who had been led to that court by his violent and cloudy dream of another superior and avenging justice?

Such were Guillaume's thoughts, when all at once everybody around him started. Noon was now striking, and the jurymen trooped into court in straggling fashion and took their seats in their box. Among them one saw fat fellows clad in their Sunday best and with the faces of simpletons, and thin fellows who had bright eyes and sly expressions. Some of them were bearded and some were bald. However, they all remained rather indistinct, as their side of the court was steeped in shade. After them came the judges, headed by M. de Larombière, one of the Vice-Presidents of the Appeal Court, who in assuming the perilous honour of conducting the trial, had sought to increase the majesty of his long, slender, white face, which looked the more austere as both his assessors, one dark and the other fair, had highly coloured countenances. The public prosecutor's seat was already occupied by one of the most skilful of the advocates-general, M. Lehmann, a broad-shouldered Alsatian Israelite with cunning eyes, whose presence showed that the case was deemed exceptionally important. At last, amidst the heavy tread of gendarmes, Salvat was brought in, at once rousing such ardent curiosity that all the spectators rose to look at him. He still wore the cap and loose overcoat procured for him by Victor Mathis, and everybody was surprised to see his emaciated, sorrowful, gentle face, crowned by scanty reddish hair, which was turning grey. His soft, glowing, dreamy blue eyes glanced around, and he smiled at some one whom he recognised, probably Victor, but perhaps Guillaume. After that he remained quite motionless.

The presiding judge waited for silence to fall, and then came the formalities which attend the opening of a court of law, followed by the perusal of the lengthy indictment, which a subordinate official read in a shrill voice. The scene had now changed, and the spectators listened wearily and somewhat impatiently as, for weeks past, the newspapers had related all that the indictment set forth. At present not a corner of the court remained unoccupied, there was scarcely space enough for the witnesses to stand in front of the bench. The closely packed throng was one of divers hues, the light gowns of ladies alternating with the black gowns of advocates, while the red robes of the judges disappeared from view, the bench being so low that the presiding judge's long face scarcely rose above the sea of heads. Many of those present became interested in the jurors, and strove to scrutinise their shadowy countenances. Others, who did not take their eyes off the prisoner, marvelled at his apparent weariness and indifference, which were so great that he scarcely answered the whispered questions of his counsel, a young advocate with a wide-awake look, who was nervously awaiting the opportunity to achieve fame. Most curiosity, however, centred in the table set apart for the material evidence. Here were to be seen all sorts of fragments, some of the woodwork torn away from the carriage-door of the Duvillard mansion, some plaster that had fallen from the ceiling, a paving stone which the violence of the explosion had split in halves, and other blackened remnants. The more moving sights, however, were the milliner's bonnet-box, which had remained uninjured, and a glass jar in which something white and vague was preserved in spirits of wine. This was one of the poor errand-girl's little hands, which had been severed at the wrist. The authorities had been unable to place her poor ripped body on the table, and so they had brought that hand!

At last Salvat rose, and the presiding judge began to interrogate him. The contrast in the aspect of the court then acquired tragic force: in the shrouding shade upon one hand were the jurors, their minds already made up beneath the pressure of public terror, while in the full, vivid light on the other side was the prisoner, alone and woeful, charged with all the crimes of his race. Four gendarmes watched over him. He was addressed by M. de Larombière in a tone of contempt and disgust. The judge was not deficient in rectitude; he was indeed one of the last representatives of the old, scrupulous, upright French magistracy; but he understood nothing of the new times, and he treated prisoners with the severity of a Biblical Jehovah. Moreover, the infirmity which was the worry of his life; the childish lisp which, in his opinion, had alone prevented him from shining as a public prosecutor, made him ferociously ill-tempered, incapable of any intelligent indulgence. There were smiles, which he divined, as soon as he raised his sharp, shrill little voice, to ask his first questions. That droll voice of his took away whatever majesty might have remained attached to these proceedings, in which a man's life was being fought for in a hall full of inquisitive, stifling, and perspiring folks, who fanned themselves and jested. Salvat answered the judge's earlier questions with his wonted weariness and politeness. While the judge did everything to vilify him, harshly reproaching him with his wretched childhood and youth, magnifying every stain and every transgression in his career, referring to the promiscuity of his life between Madame Théodore and little Céline as something bestial, he, the prisoner, quietly said yes or no, like a man who has nothing to hide and accepts the full responsibility of his actions. He had already made a complete confession of his crime, and he calmly repeated it without changing a word. He explained that if he had deposited his bomb at the entrance of the Duvillard mansion it was to give his deed its true significance, that of summoning the wealthy, the money-mongers who had so scandalously enriched themselves by dint of theft and falsehood, to restore that part of the common wealth which they had appropriated, to the poor, the working classes, their children and their wives, who perished of starvation. It was only at this moment that he grew excited; all the misery that he had endured or witnessed rose to his clouded, semi-educated brain, in which claims and theories and exasperated ideas of absolute justice and universal happiness had gathered confusedly. And from that moment he appeared such as he really was, a sentimentalist, a dreamer transported by suffering, proud and stubborn, and bent on changing the world in accordance with his sectarian logic.

'But you fled!' cried the judge in a voice such as would have befitted a grasshopper. 'You must not say that you gave your life to your cause and were ready for martyrdom!'

Salvat's most poignant regret was that he had yielded in the Bois de Boulogne to the dismay and rage which come upon a tracked and hunted man, and impel him to do all he can to escape capture. And on being thus taunted by the judge he became quite angry. 'I don't fear death, you'll see that,' he replied. 'If all had the same courage as I have, your rotten society would be swept away to-morrow, and happiness would at last dawn.'

Then the interrogatory dealt at great length with the composition and manufacture of the bomb. The judge, rightly enough, pointed out that this was the only obscure point of the affair. 'And so,' he remarked, 'you persist in saying that dynamite was the explosive you employed? Well, you will presently hear the experts, who, it is true, differ on certain points, but are all of opinion that you employed some other explosive, though they cannot say precisely what it was. Why not speak out on the point, as you glory in saying everything?'

Salvat, however, had suddenly calmed down, giving only cautious monosyllabic replies. 'Well, seek for whatever you like if you don't believe me,' he now answered. 'I made my bomb by myself, and under circumstances which I've already related a score of times. You surely don't expect me to reveal names and compromise comrades?'

From this declaration he would not depart. It was only towards the end of the interrogatory that irresistible emotion overcame him on the judge again referring to the unhappy victim of his crime, the little errand girl, so pretty and fair and gentle, whom ferocious destiny had brought to the spot to meet such an awful death. 'It was one of your own class whom you struck,' said M. de Larombière; 'your victim was a work girl, a poor child who, with the few pence she earned helped to support her aged grandmother.'

Salvat's voice became very husky as he answered: 'That's really the only thing I regret. . . . My bomb certainly wasn't meant for her; and may all the workers, all the starvelings remember that she gave her blood as I'm going to give mine!'

In this wise the interrogatory ended amidst profound agitation. Pierre had felt Guillaume shuddering beside him, whilst the prisoner quietly and obstinately refused to say a word respecting the explosive that had been employed, preferring as he did to assume full responsibility for the deed, which was about to cost him his life. Moreover, Guillaume, on turning round, in compliance with an irresistible impulse, had perceived Victor Mathis still motionless behind him: his elbows ever leaning on the rail of the partition, and his chin still resting on his hands, whilst he listened with silent, concentrated passion. His face had become yet paler than before, and his eyes glowed as with an avenging fire, whose flames would never more be extinguished.

The interrogatory of the prisoner was followed by a brief commotion in court.

'That Salvat looks quite nice, he has such soft eyes,' declared the Princess, whom the proceedings greatly amused. 'Oh! don't speak ill of him, my dear deputy. You know that I have Anarchist ideas myself.'

'I speak no ill of him,' gaily replied Duthil. 'Nor has our friend Amadieu any right to speak ill of him. For you know that this affair has set Amadieu on a pinnacle. He was never before talked about to such an extent as he is now; and he delights in being talked about, you know! He has become quite a social celebrity, the most illustrious of our investigating magistrates, and will soon be able to do or become whatever he pleases.'

Then Massot, with his sarcastic impudence, summed up the situation. 'When Anarchism flourishes, everything flourishes, eh? That bomb has helped on the affairs of a good many fine fellows that I know! Do you think that my governor Fonsègue, who's so attentive to Silviane yonder, complains of it? And doesn't Sagnier, who's spreading himself out behind the presiding judge, and whose proper place would be between the four gendarmes—doesn't he owe a debt to Salvat for all the abominable advertisements he has been able to give his paper by using the wretched fellow's back as a big drum? And I need not mention the politicians or the financiers or all those who fish in troubled waters.'

'But I say,' interrupted Duthil, 'it seems to me that you yourself made good use of the affair. Your interview with the little girl Céline brought you in a pot of money.'

Massot, as it happened, had been struck with the idea of ferreting out Madame Théodore and the child, and of relating his visit to them in the 'Globe,' with an abundance of curious and touching particulars. The article had met with prodigious success; Céline's pretty answers respecting her imprisoned father having such an effect on ladies with sensitive hearts that they had driven to Montmartre in their carriages in order to see the two poor creatures. Thus alms had come to them from all sides; and strangely enough the very people who demanded the father's head were the most eager to sympathise with the child.

'Well, I don't complain of my little profits,' said the

journalist in answer to Duthil. 'We all earn what we can, you know.'

At this moment Rosemonde, while glancing round her, recognised Guillaume and Pierre, but she was so amazed to see the latter in ordinary civilian garb that she did not dare to speak to him. Leaning forward she acquainted Duthil and Massot with her surprise, and they both turned round to look. From motives of discretion, however, they pretended that they did not recognise the Froments.

The heat in court was now becoming quite unbearable, and one lady had already fainted. At last the presiding judge again raised his lisping voice, and managed to restore silence. Salvat, who had remained standing, now held a few sheets of paper, and with some difficulty he made the judge understand that he desired to complete his interrogatory by reading a declaration, which he had drawn up in prison, and in which he explained his reasons for his crime. For a moment M. de Larombière hesitated, all surprise and indignation at such a request, but he was aware that he could not legally impose silence on the prisoner, and so he signified his consent with a gesture of mingled irritation and disdain. Thereupon Salvat began his perusal much after the fashion of a schoolboy, hemming and hawing here and there, occasionally becoming confused, and then bringing out certain words with wonderful emphasis, which evidently pleased him. This declaration of his was the usual cry of suffering and revolt already raised by so many disinherited ones. It referred to all the frightful want of the lower spheres; the toiler unable to find a livelihood in his toil; a whole class, the most numerous and worthy of the classes, dying of starvation; whilst, on the other hand, were the privileged ones, gorged with wealth, and wallowing in satiety, yet refusing to part with even the crumbs from their tables, determined as they were to restore nothing whatever of the wealth which they had stolen. And so it became necessary to take everything away from them, to rouse them from their egotism by terrible warnings, and to proclaim to them even with the crash of bombs that the day of justice had come. The unhappy man spoke that word 'justice' in a ringing voice which seemed to fill the whole court. But the emotion of those who heard him reached its highest pitch when, after declaring that he laid down his life for the cause, and expected nothing but a verdict of death from the jury, he added, as if prophetically, that his blood would assuredly give birth to other martyrs. They might send him to the scaffold, said he, but he knew that his example would bear fruit. After him would come another avenger, and yet another, and others still, until the old and rotten social system should have crumbled away so as to make room for the society of justice and happiness of which he was one of the apostles.

The presiding judge, in his impatience and agitation, twice tried to interrupt Salvat. But the other read on and on with the imperturbable conscientiousness of one who fears that he may not give proper utterance to his most important words. He must have been thinking of that perusal ever since he had been in prison. It was the decisive act of his suicide, the act by which he proclaimed that he gave his life for the glory of dying in the cause of mankind. And when he had finished he sat down between the gendarmes with glowing eyes and flushed cheeks, as if he inwardly experienced some great joy.

To destroy the effect which the declaration had produced —a commingling of fear and compassion—the judge at once wished to proceed with the hearing of the witnesses. Of these there was an interminable procession ; though little interest attached to their evidence, for none of them had any revelations to make. Most attention perhaps was paid to the measured statements of Grandidier, who had been obliged to dismiss Salvat from his employ on account of the Anarchist propaganda he had carried on. Then the prisoner's brother-in-law, Toussaint, the mechanician, also seemed a very worthy fellow if one might judge him by the manner in which he strove to put things favourably for Salvat, without, however, departing from the truth. After Toussaint's evidence considerable time was taken up by the discussions between the experts, who disagreed in public as much as they had disagreed in their reports. Although they were all of opinion that dynamite could not have been the explosive employed in the bomb they indulged in the most extraordinary and contradictory suppositions as to this explosive's real nature. Eventually a written opinion given by the illustrious scientist Bertheroy was read ; and this after clearly setting forth the known facts concluded that one found oneself in presence of a new explosive of prodigious power, the formula of which he himself was unable to specify.

Then detective Mondésir and commissary Dupot came in turn to relate the various phases of the man hunt in the Bois

de Boulogne. In Mondésir centred all the gaiety of the proceedings, thanks to the guard-room sallies with which he enlivened his narrative. And in like way the greatest grief, a
perfect shudder of revolt and compassion, was roused by the
errand girl's grandmother, a poor bent, withered old woman,
whom the prosecution had cruelly constrained to attend the
court, and who wept and looked quite dismayed, unable as she
was to understand what was wanted of her. When she had
withdrawn, the only remaining witnesses were those for the
defence, a procession of foremen and comrades, who all
declared that they had known Salvat as a very worthy fellow,
an intelligent and zealous workman, who did not drink, but
was extremely fond of his daughter, and incapable of an act of
dishonesty or cruelty.

It was already four o'clock when the evidence of the
witnesses came to an end. The atmosphere in court was
now quite stifling, feverish fatigue flushed every face, and a
kind of ruddy dust obscured the waning light which fell from
the windows. Women were fanning themselves and men
were mopping their foreheads. However, the passion roused
by the scene still brought a glow of cruel delight to every eye.
And no one stirred.

'Ah!' sighed Rosemonde all at once, 'to think that I
hoped to drink a cup of tea at a friend's at five o'clock. I shall
die of thirst and starvation here.'

'We shall certainly be kept till seven,' replied Massot. 'I
can't offer to go and fetch you a roll, for I shouldn't be re-
admitted.'

Then Duthil, who had not ceased shrugging his shoulders
while Salvat read his declaration, exclaimed: 'What childish
things he said, didn't he? And to think that the fool is going
to die for all that! Rich and poor, indeed! Why, there will
always be rich and poor. And it's equally certain that when
a man is poor his one great desire is to become rich. If that
fellow is in the dock to-day it's simply because he failed to
make money.'

While the others were thus conversing, Pierre for his part
was feeling extremely anxious about his brother, who sat
beside him in silence, pale and utterly upset. Pierre sought
his hand and covertly pressed it. Then in a low voice he
inquired: 'Do you feel ill? Shall we go away?'

Guillaume answered him by discreetly and affectionately
returning his handshake. He was all right, he would remain

till the end, however much he might be stirred by exasperation.

It was now Monsieur Lehmann, the public prosecutor, who rose to address the court. He had a large stern mouth, and was squarely built, with a stubborn Jewish face. Nevertheless he was known to be a man of dexterous, supple nature, one who had a foot in every political camp, and invariably contrived to be on good terms with the powers that were. This explained his rapid rise in life, and the constant favour he enjoyed. In the very first words he spoke he alluded to the new ministry gazetted that morning, referring pointedly to the strong-handed man who had undertaken the task of reassuring peaceable citizens and making evil-doers tremble. Then he fell upon the wretched Salvat with extraordinary vehemence, recounting the whole of his life, and exhibiting him as a bandit expressly born for the perpetration of crime, a monster who was bound to end by committing some abominable and cowardly outrage. Next he flagellated Anarchism and its partisans. The Anarchists were a mere herd of vagabonds and thieves, said he. That had been shown by the recent robbery at the Princess de Harn's house. The ignoble gang that had been arrested for that affair had given the apostles of the Anarchist doctrine as their references! And that was what the application of Anarchist theories resulted in—burglary and filth, pending a favourable hour for wholesale pillage and murder! For nearly a couple of hours the public prosecutor continued in this fashion, throwing truth and logic to the winds, and exclusively striving to alarm his hearers. He made all possible use of the terror which had reigned in Paris, and figuratively brandished the corpse of the poor little victim, the pretty errand girl, as if it were a blood-red flag, before pointing to the pale hand, preserved in spirits of wine, with a gesture of compassionate horror which sent a shudder through his audience. And he ended, as he had begun, by inspiriting the jurors, and telling them that they might fearlessly do their duty now that those at the head of the State were firmly resolved to give no heed to threats.

Then the young advocate entrusted with the defence in his turn spoke. And he really said what there was to say with great clearness and precision. He was of a different school from that of the public prosecutor, his eloquence was very simple and smooth, his only passion seemed to be zeal for truth. Moreover, it was sufficient for him to show Salvat's

life in its proper light, to depict him pursued by social
fatalities since his childhood, and to explain the final action
of his career by all that he had suffered and all that had
sprung up in his dreamy brain. Was not his crime the crime
of one and all? Who was there that did not feel if only in a
small degree responsible for that bomb which a penniless,
starving workman had deposited on the threshold of a wealthy
man's abode—a wealthy man whose name bespoke the
injustice of the social system: so much enjoyment on the
one hand and so much privation on the other? If one of us
happened to lose his head, and felt impelled to hasten the
advent of happiness by violence in such troublous times, when
so many burning problems claimed solution, ought he to be
deprived of his life in the name of justice, when none could
swear that they had not in some measure contributed to his
madness? Following up this question, Salvat's counsel
dwelt at length on the period that witnessed the crime, a
period of so many scandals and collapses, when the old
world was giving birth to a new one amidst the most terrible
struggles and pangs. And he concluded by begging the jury
to show themselves humane, to resist all passion and terror,
and to pacify the rival classes by a wise verdict, instead of
prolonging social warfare by giving the starvelings yet another
martyr to avenge.

It was past six o'clock when M. de Larombière began to
sum up in a partial and flowery fashion, in which one detected
how grieved and angry he was at having such a shrill little
voice. Then the judges and the jurors withdrew, and the
prisoner was led away, leaving the spectators waiting amidst
an uproar of feverish impatience. Some more ladies had
fainted, and it had even been necessary to carry out a gentleman, who had been overcome by the cruel heat. However,
the others stubbornly remained there, not one of them quitting
his place.

'Ah! it won't take long now,' said Massot. 'The jurors
brought their verdict all ready in their pockets. I was looking at them while that little advocate was telling them such
sensible things. They all seemed to be comfortably asleep
in the gloom.'

Then Duthil turned to the Princess and asked her, 'Are
you still hungry?'

'Oh! I'm starving,' she replied. 'I shall never be able
to wait till I get home. You will have to take me to eat a

biscuit somewhere. . . . All the same, however, it's very exciting to see a man's life staked on a yes or a no.'

Meantime Pierre, finding Guillaume still more feverish and grieved, had once again taken hold of his hand. Neither of them spoke, so great was the distress that they experienced for many reasons which they themselves could not have precisely defined. It seemed to them, however, that all human misery —inclusive of their own, the affections, the hopes, the griefs which brought them suffering—was sobbing and quivering in that buzzing hall. Twilight had gradually fallen there, but as the end was now so near it had doubtless been thought unnecessary to light the chandeliers. And thus large vague shadows, dimming and shrouding the serried throng, now hovered about in the last gleams of the day. The ladies in light gowns yonder, behind the bench, looked like pale phantoms with all-devouring eyes, whilst the numerous groups of black-robed advocates formed large sombre patches which gradually spread everywhere. The greyish painting of the Christ had already vanished, and on the walls one only saw the glaring white bust of the Republic, which resembled some frigid death's head starting forth from the darkness.

'Ah!' Massot once more exclaimed, 'I knew that it wouldn't take long!'

Indeed, the jurors were returning after less than a quarter of an hour's absence. Then the judges likewise came back and took their seats. Increased emotion stirred the throng, a great gust seemed to sweep through the court, a gust of anxiety, which made every head sway. Some people had risen to their feet, and others gave vent to involuntary exclamations. The foreman of the jury, a gentleman with a broad red face, had to wait a moment before speaking. At last in a sharp but somewhat sputtering voice he declared: 'On my honour and my conscience, before God and before man, the verdict of the jury is : on the question of Murder, yes, by a majority of votes.'[1]

The night had almost completely fallen when Salvat was once more brought in. In front of the jurors who faded away in the gloom, he stood forth erect with a last ray from the windows lighting up his face. The judges themselves almost disappeared from view, their red robes seemed to have turned

[1] English readers may be reminded that in France the verdict of a majority of the jury suffices for conviction or acquittal. If the jury is evenly divided the prisoner is acquitted.—*Trans.*

black. And how phantom-like looked the prisoner's emaciated face as he stood there listening, with dreamy eyes, while the clerk of the court read the verdict to him.

When silence fell and no mention was made of extenuating circumstances, he understood everything. His face, which had retained a childish expression, suddenly brightened. 'That means death. Thank you, gentlemen,' he said.

Then he turned towards the public, and amidst the growing darkness searched for the friendly faces which he knew were there; and this time Guillaume became fully conscious that he had recognised him, and was again expressing affectionate and grateful thanks for the crust he had received from him on a day of want. He must, however, have also bidden farewell to Victor Mathis, for as Guillaume glanced at the young man, who had not moved, he saw that his eyes were staring wildly, and that a terrible expression rested on his lips.

As for the rest of the proceedings, the last questions addressed to the jury and the counsel, the deliberations of the judges and the delivery of sentence—these were all lost amidst the buzzing and surging of the crowd. A little compassion was unconsciously manifested; and some stupor was mingled with the satisfaction that greeted the sentence of death.

No sooner had Salvat been condemned, however, than he drew himself up to his full height, and as the guards led him away he shouted in a stentorian voice: 'Long live Anarchy!'

Nobody seemed angered by the cry. The crowd went off somewhat quietly, as if weariness had lulled all its passions. The proceedings had really lasted too long and fatigued one too much. It was quite pleasant to inhale the fresh air on emerging from such a nightmare.

In the large waiting hall, Pierre and Guillaume passed Duthil and the Princess, whom General de Bozonnet had stopped while chatting with Fonsègue. All four of them were talking in very loud voices, complaining of the heat and their hunger, and agreeing that the affair had not been a particularly interesting one. However, all was well that ended well. As Fonsègue remarked, the condemnation of Salvat to death was a political and social necessity.

When Pierre and Guillaume reached the Pont Neuf, the latter for a moment rested his elbows on the parapet of the bridge. His brother, standing beside him, also gazed at the grey waters of the Seine, which here and there were fired by the reflections of the gas lamps. A fresh breeze ascended from the river; it was the delightful hour when night steals gently over resting Paris. However, as the brothers stood there breathing that atmosphere which usually brings relief and comfort, Pierre on his side again became conscious of his heart-wound, and remembered his promise to return to Montmartre, a promise that he must keep in spite of the torture there awaiting him; whilst Guillaume on the other hand experienced a revival of the suspicion and disquietude that had come to him on seeing Marie so feverish, changed as it were by some new feeling, of which she herself was ignorant. Were further sufferings, struggles, and obstacles to happiness yet in store for those brothers who loved one another so dearly? At all events their hearts bled once more with all the sorrow into which they had been cast by the scene they had just witnessed: that assize of justice at which a wretched man had been condemned to pay with his head for the crimes of one and all.

Then, as they turned along the quay, Guillaume recognised young Victor going off alone in the gloom, just in front of them. The chemist stopped him and spoke to him of his mother. But the young man did not hear; his thin lips parted, and in a voice as trenchant as a knife-thrust he exclaimed: 'Ah! so it's blood they want. Well, they may cut off his head, but he will be avenged!'

V

SACRIFICE

THE days which followed Salvat's trial seemed gloomy ones up yonder in Guillaume's workroom, which was usually so bright and gay. Sadness and silence filled the place. The three young men were no longer there. Thomas betook himself to the Grandidier works early every morning in order to perfect his little motor; François was so busy preparing for his examination that he scarcely left the École Normale; while Antoine was doing some work at Jahan's, where he delighted to linger and watch his little friend Lise awakening to life. Thus Guillaume's sole companion was Mère-Grand, who sat near the window busy with her needlework; for Marie was ever going about the house, and only stayed in the

workroom for any length of time when Pierre happened to be
there.

Guillaume's gloom was generally attributed to the feelings
of anger and revolt into which the condemnation of Salvat
had thrown him. He had flown into a passion on his return
from the Palace of Justice, declaring that the execution of
the unhappy man would simply be social murder, deliberate
provocation of class warfare. And the others had bowed on
hearing that pain-fraught, violent cry without attempting to
discuss the point. Guillaume's sons respectfully left him
to the thoughts which kept him silent for hours, with his face
pale and a dreamy expression in his eyes. His chemical
furnace remained unlighted, and his only occupation from
morn till night was to examine the plans and documents
connected with his invention, that new explosive and that
terrible engine of war which he had so long dreamt of pre-
senting to France in order that she might impose the
reign of truth and justice upon all the nations. However,
during the long hours which he spent before the papers
scattered over his table, often without seeing them, for his
eyes wandered far away, a multitude of vague thoughts
came to him—doubts respecting the wisdom of his project,
and fears lest his desire to pacify the nations should simply
throw them into an endless war of extermination. Although
he really believed that great city of Paris to be the world's
brain, entrusted with the task of preparing the future, he
could not disguise from himself that with all its folly and
shame and injustice, it still presented a shocking spectacle.
Was it really ripe enough for the work of human salvation
which he thought of entrusting to it? Then, on trying
to re-peruse his notes and verify his formulas, he only
recovered his former energetic determination on thinking of
his marriage, whereupon the idea came to him that it was
now too late for him to upset his life by changing such long
settled plans.

His marriage! Was it not the thought of this which
haunted Guillaume and disturbed him far more powerfully
than his scientific work or his humanitarian passion?
Beneath all the worries that he acknowledged, there was
another which he did not confess even to himself, and which
filled him with anguish. He repeated day by day that he
would reveal his invention to the Minister of War as soon
as he should be married to Marie, whom he wished to asso-

ciate with his glory. Married to Marie! Each time he thought of it, burning fever and secret disquietude came over him. If he now remained so silent and had lost his quiet cheerfulness it was because he had felt new life, as it were, emanating from her. She was certainly no longer the same woman as formerly; she was becoming more and more changed and distant. He had watched her and Pierre when the latter happened to be there, which was now but seldom. He, too, appeared embarrassed, and different from what he had been. On the days when he came, however, Marie seemed transformed; it was as if new life animated the house. Certainly the intercourse between her and Pierre was quite innocent, sisterly on the one hand, brotherly on the other. They simply seemed to be a pair of good friends. And yet a radiance, a vibration emanated from them, something more subtle even than a sun ray or a perfume. After the lapse of a few days Guillaume found himself unable to doubt the truth any longer. And his heart bled, he was utterly upset by it. He had not found them in fault in any way, but he was convinced that these two children, as he so paternally called them, really adored one another.

One lovely morning when he happened to be alone with Mère-Grand, face to face with sunlit Paris, he fell into a yet more dolorous reverie than usual. He seemed to be gazing fixedly at the old lady, as, seated in her usual place, she continued sewing with an air of queenly serenity. Perhaps, however, he did not see her. For her part she occasionally raised her eyes and glanced at him, as if expecting a confession which did not come. At last, finding such silence unbearable, she made up her mind to address him: 'What has been the matter with you, Guillaume, for some time past? Why don't you tell me what you have to tell me?'

He descended from the clouds, as it were, and answered in astonishment: 'What I have to tell you?'

'Yes, I know it as well as you do, and I thought you would speak to me of it, since it pleases you to do nothing here without consulting me.'

At this he turned very pale and shuddered. So he had not been mistaken in the matter, even Mère-Grand knew all about it. To talk of it, however, was to give shape to his suspicions, to transform what, hitherto, might merely have been a fancy on his part into something real and definite.

'It was inevitable, my dear son,' said Mère-Grand. 'I

foresaw it from the outset. And if I did not warn you of it, it was because I believed in some deep design on your part. Since I have seen you suffering, however, I have realised that I was mistaken.' Then, as he still looked at her quivering and distracted, she continued : ' Yes, I fancied that you might have wished it, that in bringing your brother here, you wished to know if Marie loved you otherwise than as a father. There was good reason for testing her—for instance, the great difference between your ages, for your life is drawing to a close, whilst hers is only beginning. And I need not mention the question of your work, the mission which I have always dreamt of for you.'

Thereupon, with his hands raised in prayerful fashion, Guillaume drew near to the old lady and exclaimed : ' Oh ! speak out clearly, tell me what you think. I don't understand, my poor heart is so lacerated; and yet I should so much like to know everything, so as to be able to act and take a decision. To think that you whom I love, you whom I venerate as much as if you were my real mother, you whose profound good sense I know so well that I have always followed your advice—to think that you should have foreseen this frightful thing and have allowed it to happen at the risk of its killing me ! . . . Why have you done so, tell me, why ? '

Mère-Grand was not fond of talking. Absolute mistress of the house as she was, managing everything, accountable to nobody for her actions, she never gave expression to all that she thought or all that she desired. Indeed, there was no occasion for it, as Guillaume, like the children, relied upon her completely, with full confidence in her wisdom. And her somewhat enigmatical ways even helped to raise her in their estimation.

' What is the use of words, when things themselves speak ? ' she now gently answered, while still plying her needle. ' It is quite true that I approved of the plan of a marriage between you and Marie, for I saw that it was necessary that she should be married if she was to stay here. And then, too, there were many other reasons which I needn't speak of. However, Pierre's arrival here has changed everything, and placed things in their natural order. Is not that preferable ? '

He still lacked the courage to understand her. ' Preferable ! When I'm in agony ! When my life is wrecked ! '

Thereupon she rose and came to him, tall and rigid in her

thin black gown, and with an expression of austerity and energy on her pale face. 'My son,' she said, 'you know that I love you, and that I wish you to be very noble and lofty. Only the other morning, you had an attack of fright, the house narrowly escaped being blown up. Then, for some days now, you have been sitting over those documents and plans in an absent-minded, distracted state, like a man who feels weak, and doubts, and no longer knows his way. Believe me, you are following a dangerous path ; it is better that Pierre should marry Marie, both for their sakes and for your own.'

'For my sake ? no, no ! What will become of me ! '

'You will calm yourself and reflect, my son. You have such serious duties before you. You are on the eve of making your invention known. It seems to me that something has bedimmed your sight, and that you will perhaps act wrongly in this respect, through failing to take due account of the problem before you. Perhaps there is something better to be done. . . . At all events, suffer if it be necessary, but remain faithful to your ideal.'

Then, quitting him with a maternal smile, she sought to soften her somewhat stern words by adding : 'You have compelled me to speak unnecessarily ; for I am quite at ease ; with your superior mind, whatever be in question, you can but do the one right thing that none other would do.'

On finding himself alone Guillaume fell into feverish uncertainty. What was the meaning of Mère-Grand's enigmatical words ? He knew that she was on the side of whatever might be good, natural, and necessary. But she seemed to be urging him to some lofty heroism ; and indeed what she had said threw a ray of light upon the unrest which had come to him in connection with his old plan of going to confide his secret to some Minister of War or other, whatever one might happen to be in office at the time. Growing hesitation and repugnance stirred him as he fancied he could again hear her saying that perhaps there might be some better course, that would require search and reflection. But all at once a vision of Marie rose before him, and his heart was rent by the thought that he was asked to renounce her. To lose her, to give her to another ! No, no, that was beyond his strength. He would never have the frightful courage that was needed to pass by the last promised raptures of love with disdain !

For a couple of days Guillaume struggled on. He seemed

to be again living the six years which the young woman had already spent beside him in that happy little house. She had been at first like an adopted daughter there; and later on, when the idea of their marriage had sprung up, he had viewed it with quiet delight in the hope that it would ensure the happiness of all around him. If he had previously abstained from marrying again it was from the fear of placing a strange mother over his children; and if he yielded to the charm of loving yet once more, and no longer leading a solitary life, it was because he had found at his very hearth one of such sensible views, who, in the flower of youth, was willing to become his wife despite the difference in their ages. Then months had gone by, and serious occurrences had compelled them to postpone the wedding, though without undue suffering on his part. Indeed, the certainty that she was waiting for him had sufficed him, for his life of hard work had rendered him patient. Now, however, all at once, at the threat of losing her, his hitherto tranquil heart ached and bled. He would never have thought the tie so close a one. But he was now almost fifty, and it was as if love and woman were being wrenched away from him, the last woman that he could love and desire, one too who was the more desirable as she was the incarnation of youth, from which he must ever be severed, should he indeed lose her. Passionate desire, mingled with rage, flared up within him at the thought that some one should have come to take her from him.

One night, alone in his room, he suffered perfect martyrdom. In order that he might not rouse the house he buried his face in his pillow so as to stifle his sobs. After all, it was a simple matter; Marie had given him her promise, and he would compel her to keep it. She would be his, and his alone, and none would be able to steal her from him. Then, however, there rose before him a vision of his brother, the long-forgotten one, whom, from feelings of affection, he had compelled to join his family. But his sufferings were now so acute that he would have driven that brother away had he been before him. He was enraged, maddened by the thought of him. His brother—his little brother! So all their love was over; hatred and violence were about to poison their lives. For hours Guillaume continued complaining deliriously, and seeking how he might so rid himself of Pierre that what had happened should be blotted out. Now and again, when he recovered self-control, he marvelled at the tempest within him; for was he not a scientist guided by lofty reason, a toiler to whom long experience had brought serenity? But the truth was that this tempest had not sprung up in his mind, it was raging in the child-like soul that he had retained, the nook of affection and dreaminess which remained within him side by side with his principles of pitiless logic and his belief in proven phenomena only. His very genius came from the duality of his nature : behind the chemist was a social dreamer, hungering for justice and capable of the greatest love. And now passion was transporting him, and he was weeping for the loss of Marie as he would have wept over the downfall of that dream of his : the destruction of war *by* war, that scheme for the salvation of mankind at which he had been working for ten years past.

At last, amidst his weariness, a sudden resolution calmed him. He began to feel ashamed of despairing in this wise when he had no certain grounds to go upon. He must know everything, he would question the young woman; she was loyal enough to answer him frankly. Was not this a solution worthy of them both? An explanation in all sincerity, after which they would be able to take a decision. Then he fell asleep ; and, tired though he felt when he rose in the morning, he was calmer. It was as if some secret work had gone on in his heart during his few hours of repose after that terrible storm.

As it happened, Marie was very gay that morning. On the previous day she had gone with Pierre and Antoine on a cycling excursion over frightful roads in the direction of Montmorency, whence they had returned in a state of mingled anger and delight. When Guillaume stopped her in the little garden, he found her humming a song while returning barearmed from the scullery, where some washing was going on.

'Do you want to speak to me?' she asked.

'Yes, my dear child, it's necessary for us to talk of some serious matters.'

She at once understood that their marriage was in question, and became grave. She had formerly consented to that marriage because she regarded it as the only sensible course she could take, and this with full knowledge of the duties which she would assume. No doubt her husband would be some twenty years older than herself, but this circumstance was one of somewhat frequent occurrence, and as a rule such marriages turned out well, rather than other-

wise. Moreover, she was in love with nobody, and was free
to consent. And she had consented with an impulse of gratitude and affection which seemed so sweet that she thought
it the sweetness of love itself. Everybody around her, too,
appeared so pleased at the prospect of this marriage, which
would draw the family yet more closely together. And, on
her side, she had been as it were intoxicated by the idea of
making others happy.

'What is the matter?' she now asked Guillaume in a
somewhat anxious voice. 'No bad news, I hope?'

'No, no,' he answered. 'I've simply something to say to
you.'

Then he led her under the plum trees to the only green
nook left in the garden. An old worm-eaten bench still
stood there against the lilac bushes. And in front of them
Paris spread out its sea of roofs, looking light and fresh in the
morning sunlight.

They both sat down. But at the moment of speaking
and questioning Marie, Guillaume experienced sudden embarrassment, while his heart beat violently at seeing her
beside him, so young and adorable with her bare arms.

'Our wedding-day is drawing near,' he ended by saying.
And then as she turned somewhat pale, perhaps unconsciously, he himself suddenly felt cold. Had not her lips
twitched as if with pain? Had not a shadow passed over
her fresh, clear eyes?

'Oh! we still have some time before us,' she replied.

Then, slowly and very affectionately, he resumed: 'No
doubt; still it is necessary to attend to the formalities. And
it is as well, perhaps, that I should speak of those worries
to-day, so that I may not have to bother you about them
again.'

Then he gently went on telling her all that would have
to be done, keeping his eyes on her whilst he spoke, watching for such signs of emotion as the thought of her promise's early fulfilment might bring to her face. She sat
there in silence, with her hands on her lap, and her features
quite still, thus giving no certain sign of any regret jor
trouble. Still she seemed rather dejected; compliant, as it
were, but in no wise joyous.

'You say nothing, my dear Marie,' Guillaume at last exclaimed. 'Does anything of all this displease you?'

'Displease me? Oh, no!'

'You must speak out frankly, if it does, you know. We will wait a little longer if you have any personal reasons for wishing to postpone the date again.'

'But I've no reasons, my friend. What reasons could I have? I leave you quite free to settle everything as you yourself may desire.'

Silence fell. While answering, she had looked him frankly in the face; but a little quiver stirred her lips, and gloom, for which she could not account, seemed to rise and darken her face, usually as bright and gay as spring water. In former times would she not have laughed and sung at the mere announcement of that coming wedding?

Then Guillaume, with an effort which made his voice tremble, dared to speak out: 'You must forgive me for asking you a question, my dear Marie. There is still time for you to cancel your promise. Are you quite certain that you love me?' At this she looked at him in genuine stupefaction, utterly failing to understand what he could be aiming at. And as she seemed to be deferring her reply, he added: 'Consult your heart. Is it really your old friend or is it another that you love?'

'I? I, Guillaume? Why do you say that to me? What can I have done to give you occasion to say such a thing?'

All her frank nature revolted as she spoke, and her beautiful eyes, glowing with sincerity, gazed fixedly on his.

'I must nevertheless go on to the end,' he resumed with some difficulty, 'for the happiness of all of us is at stake. Question your heart. You love my brother, you love Pierre.'

I love Pierre! I do, I? Well yes, I love him, as I love you all; I love him because he has become one of us, because he shares our life and our joys! I'm happy when he's here certainly; and I should like him to be always here. I'm always pleased to see him and hear him and go out with him. I was very much grieved recently when he seemed to be relapsing into his gloomy ideas. But all that is natural, is it not? And I think that I have only done what you desired I should do, and I cannot understand how my affection for Pierre can in any way exercise an influence respecting our marriage.'

These words, in her estimation, ought to have convinced Guillaume that she was not in love with his brother; but in lieu thereof they brought him painful enlightenment by the very ardour with which she denied the love imputed to her.

'But you unfortunate girl!' he cried. 'You are betraying

yourself without knowing it. . . . It is quite certain you do
not love me, you love my brother ! '

He had caught hold of her wrists and was pressing them
with despairing affection as if to compel her to read her heart.
And she continued struggling. A most loving and tragic contest went on between them, he seeking to convince her by the
evidence of facts, and she resisting him, stubbornly refusing to
open her eyes. In vain did he recount what had happened
since the first day, explaining the feelings which had followed
one upon another in her heart and mind : first covert hostility,
next curiosity regarding that extraordinary young priest, then
sympathy and affection when she had found him so wretched
and had gradually cured him of his sufferings. They were
both young, and mother Nature had done the rest. However,
at each fresh proof and certainty which he put before her,
Marie only experienced growing emotion, trembling at last
from head to foot, but still unwilling to question herself.

' No, no,' said she, ' I do not love him. If I loved him I
should know it and would acknowledge it to you ; for you are
well aware that I cannot tell an untruth.'

Guillaume, however, had the cruelty to insist on the point,
like some heroic surgeon cutting into his own flesh even more
than into that of others, in order that the truth might appear
and everyone be saved. ' Marie,' said he, ' it is not I whom
you love. All that you feel for me is respect and gratitude
and daughterly affection. Remember what your feelings were
at the time when our marriage was decided upon. You were
then in love with nobody, and you accepted the offer like a
sensible girl, feeling certain that I should render you happy,
and that the union was a right and satisfactory one. . . . But
since then my brother has come here ; love has sprung up in
your heart in quite a natural way ; and it is Pierre, Pierre
alone, whom you love as a lover and a husband should be
loved.'

Exhausted though she was, agitated, too, by the light
which, despite herself, was dawning within her, Marie still
stubbornly and desperately protested.

' But why do you struggle like this against the truth, my
child ? ' said Guillaume, ' I do not reproach you. It was I
who chose that this should happen, like the old madman I
am. What was bound to come has come, and doubtless it is for
the best. I only wanted to learn the truth from you in order
that I might take a decision and act uprightly.'

These words vanquished her, and her tears gushed forth. It seemed as though something had been rent asunder within her; and she felt quite overcome as if by the weight of a new truth of which she had hitherto been ignorant. 'Ah! it was cruel of you,' she said, 'to do me such violence so as to make me read my heart. I swear to you again that I did not know I loved Pierre in the way you say. But you have opened my heart, and roused what was quietly slumbering in it. . . . And it is true, I do love Pierre, I love him now as you have said. And so here we are, all three of us supremely wretched through your doing!'

She sobbed, and with a sudden feeling of modesty freed her wrists from his grasp. He noticed, however, that no blush rose to her face. Truth to tell, her virginal loyalty was not in question; she had no cause to reproach herself with any betrayal; it was he alone, perforce, who had awakened her to love. For a moment they looked at one another through their tears: she so strong and healthy, her bosom heaving at each heart-beat, and her white arms—arms that could both charm and sustain—bare almost to her shoulders; and he still vigorous, with his thick fleece of white hair and his black moustaches, which gave his countenance such an expression of energetic youth. But it was all over, the irreparable had swept by, and utterly changed their lives.

'Marie,' he nobly said, 'you do not love me; I give you back your promise.'

But with equal nobility she refused to take it back. 'Never will I do so,' she replied. 'I gave it to you frankly, freely, and joyfully, and my affection and admiration for you have never changed.'

Nevertheless, with more firmness in his hitherto broken voice, Guillaume retorted: 'You love Pierre, and it is Pierre whom you ought to marry.'

'No,' she again insisted, 'I belong to you. A tie which years have tightened cannot be undone in an hour. Once again, if I love Pierre I swear to you that I was ignorant of it this morning. And let us leave the matter as it is; do not torture me any more, it would be too cruel of you.'

Then, quivering like a woman who suddenly perceives that she is bare, in a stranger's presence, she hastily pulled down her sleeves, and even drew them over her hands as if to leave naught of her person visible. And afterwards she rose and walked away without adding a single word.

Guillaume remained alone on the bench in that leafy corner, in front of Paris, to which the light morning sunshine lent the aspect of some quivering, soaring city of dreamland. A great weight oppressed him, and it seemed to him as if he would never be able to rise from the seat. That which brought him most suffering was Marie's assurance that she had till that morning been ignorant of the fact that she was in love with Pierre. She had been ignorant of it, and it was he, Guillaume, who had brought it to her knowledge, compelled her to confess it! He had now firmly planted it in her heart, and perhaps increased it by revealing it to her. Ah! how cruel the thought—to be the artisan of one's own torment! Of one thing he was now quite certain: there would be no more love in his life. At the idea of this, his poor, loving heart sank and bled. And yet amidst the disaster, amidst his grief at realising that he was an old man, and that renunciation was imperative, he experienced a bitter joy at having brought the truth to light. This was very harsh consolation, fit only for one of heroic soul, yet he found lofty satisfaction in it, and from that moment the thought of sacrifice imposed itself upon him with extraordinary force. He must marry his children; there lay the path of duty, the only wise and just course, the only certain means of ensuring the happiness of the household. And when his revolting heart yet leapt and shrieked with anguish, he carried his vigorous hands to his chest in order to still it.

On the morrow came the supreme explanation between Guillaume and Pierre, not in the little garden, however, but in the spacious workroom. And here again one beheld the vast panorama of Paris, a nation as it were at work, a huge vat in which the wine of the future was fermenting. Guillaume had arranged things so that he might be alone with his brother; and no sooner had the latter entered than he attacked him, going straight to the point without any of the precautions which he had previously taken with Marie.

'Haven't you something to say to me, Pierre?' he inquired. 'Why won't you confide in me?'

The other immediately understood him, and began to tremble, unable to find a word, but confessing everything by the confused, entreating expression of his face.

'You love Marie,' continued Guillaume; 'why did you not loyally come and tell me of your love?'

At this Pierre recovered self-possession and defended himself vehemently: 'I love Marie, it's true, and I felt that I could not conceal it, that you yourself would notice it at last. But there was no occasion for me to tell you of it, for I was sure of myself, and would have fled rather than have allowed a single word to cross my lips. I suffered in silence and alone, and you cannot know how great my torture was! It is even cruel on your part to speak to me of it; for now I am absolutely compelled to leave you. . . . I have already, on several occasions, thought of doing so. If I have come back here, it was doubtless through weakness, but also on account of my affection for you all. And what mattered my presence here? Marie ran no risk. She does not love me.'

'She does love you!' Guillaume answered. 'I questioned her yesterday, and she had to confess that she loved you.'

At this Pierre, utterly distracted, caught Guillaume by the shoulders and gazed into his eyes. 'Oh! brother, brother! what is this you say? Why say a thing which would mean terrible misfortune for us all? Even if it were true my grief would far exceed my joy, for I will not have you suffer. Marie belongs to you. To me she is as sacred as a sister. And if there be only my madness to part you, it will pass by, I shall know how to conquer it.'

'Marie loves you,' repeated Guillaume in his gentle, obstinate way. 'I don't reproach you with anything, I well know that you have struggled, and have never betrayed yourself to her either by word or glance. Yesterday she herself was still ignorant that she loved you, and I had to open her eyes. . . . What would you have? I simply state a fact: she loves you.'

This time Pierre, still quivering, made a gesture of mingled rapture and terror, as if some divine and long-desired blessing were falling upon him from heaven and crushing him beneath its weight.

'Well, then,' he said, after a brief pause, 'it is all over. . . . Let us kiss one another for the last time, and then I'll go.'

'Go! Why? You must stay with us. Nothing could be more simple, you love Marie and she loves you. I give her to you.'

A loud cry came from Pierre, who wildly raised his hands again with a gesture of fright and rapture. 'You give me Marie?' he replied. 'You, who adore her, who have been waiting for her for months? No, no, it would overcome me,

it would terrify me, as if you gave me your very heart after
tearing it from your breast. No, no! I will not accept your
sacrifice!'

'But as it is only gratitude and affection that Marie feels
for me,' said Guillaume, 'as it is you whom she really loves,
am I to take a mean advantage of the engagements which she
entered into unconsciously, and force her to a marriage when
I know that she would never be wholly mine? Besides, I
have made a mistake; it isn't I who give her to you, she has
already given herself, and I do not consider that I have any
right to prevent her from doing so.'

'No, no! I will never accept, I will never bring such
grief upon you. . . . Kiss me, brother, and let me go.'

Thereupon Guillaume caught hold of Pierre and compelled
him to sit down by his side on an old sofa near the window.
And he began to scold him almost angrily while still retaining
a smile, in which suffering and kindliness were blended.
'Come,' said he, 'we are surely not going to fight over it.
You won't force me to tie you up so as to keep you here? I
know what I'm about. I thought it all over before I spoke
to you. No doubt, I can't tell you that it gladdens me. I
thought at first that I was going to die; I should have
liked to hide myself in the very depths of the earth. And
then, well, it was necessary to be reasonable, and I understood
that things had arranged themselves for the best in their
natural order.'

Pierre, unable to resist any further, had begun to weep
with both hands raised to his face.

'Don't grieve, brother, either for yourself or for me,' said
Guillaume. 'Do you remember the happy days we lately
spent together at Neuilly after we had found one another
again? All our old affection revived within us, and we remained for hours, hand in hand, recalling the past and loving
one another. And what a terrible confession you made to me
one night, the confession of your loss of faith, your torture,
the void in which you were rolling! When I heard of it my
one great wish was to cure you. I advised you to work, love,
and believe in life, convinced as I was that life alone could
restore you to peace and health. . . . And for that reason I
afterwards brought you here. You fought against it, and it
was I who forced you to come. I was so happy when I found
that you again took an interest in life, and had once more
become a man and a worker! I would have given some of

my blood if necessary to complete your cure. . . . Well, it's done now; I have given you all I had, since Marie herself has become necessary to you, and she alone can save you.'

Then as Pierre again attempted to protest, he resumed: 'Don't deny it. It is so true, indeed, that if she does not complete the work I have begun, all my efforts will have been vain, you will fall back into your misery and negation, into all the torments of a spoilt life. She is necessary to you, I say. And do you think that I no longer know how to love you? Would you have me refuse you the very breath of life that will truly make you a man, after all my fervent wishes for your return to life? I have enough affection for you both to consent to your loving one another. . . . Besides, I repeat it, nature knows what she does. Instinct is a sure guide, it always tends to what is useful and true. I should have been a sorry husband, and it is best that I should keep to my work as an old scientist; whereas you are young and represent the future, all fruitful and happy life.'

Pierre shuddered as he heard this, for his old fears returned to him. Had not the priesthood for ever cut him off from life, had not his long years of chaste celibacy robbed him of his manhood? 'Fruitful and happy life!' he muttered, 'ah! if you only knew how distressed I feel at the idea that I do not perhaps deserve the gift you so lovingly offer me! You are worth more than I am; you would have given her a larger heart, a firmer brain, and perhaps, too, you are really a younger man than myself. . . . There is still time, brother; keep her if with you she is likely to be happier and more truly and completely loved. For my part I am full of doubts. Her happiness is the only thing of consequence. Let her belong to the one who will love her best!'

Indescribable emotion had now come over both men. As Guillaume heard his brother's broken words, the cry of a love that trembled at the thought of possible weakness, he did for a moment waver. With a dreadful heart-pang he stammered despairingly: 'Ah! Marie, whom I love so much! Marie, whom I would have rendered so happy!'

At this Pierre could not restrain himself; he rose and cried: 'Ah! you see that you love her still and cannot renounce her. . . . So let me go! let me go!'

But Guillaume had already caught him round the body, clasping him with an intensity of brotherly love which was increased by the renunciation he was resolved upon: 'Stay!'

said he. 'It wasn't I that spoke, it was the other man that
was in me, he who is about to die, who is already dead! By
the memory of our mother and our father I swear to you
that the sacrifice is consummated, and that if you two refuse to accept happiness from me you will but make me
suffer.'

For a moment the weeping men remained in one another's
arms. They had often embraced before, but never had their
hearts met and mingled as they did now. It was a delightful
moment, which seemed an eternity. All the grief and misery
of the world had disappeared from before them; there remained naught save their glowing love, whence sprang an
eternity of love even as light comes from the sun. And that
moment was compensation for all their past and future tears,
whilst yonder, on the horizon before them, Paris still spread
and rumbled, ever preparing the unknown future.

Just then Marie herself came in. And the rest proved
very simple. Guillaume freed himself from his brother's
clasp, led him forward and compelled him and Marie to take
each other by the hand. At first she made yet another gesture of refusal in her stubborn resolve that she would not take
her promise back. But what could she say face to face with
those two tearful men, whom she had found in one another's
arms, mingling together in such close brotherliness? Did
not those tears and that embrace sweep away all ordinary
reasons, all such arguments as she held in reserve? Even
the embarrassment of the situation disappeared, it seemed as
if she had already had a long explanation with Pierre, and
that he and she were of one mind to accept that gift of love
which Guillaume offered them with so much heroism. A
gust of the sublime passed through the room, and nothing
could have appeared more natural to them than this extraordinary scene. Nevertheless, Marie remained silent, she
dared not give her answer, but looked at them both with her
big soft eyes which, like their own, were full of tears.

And it was Guillaume who, with sudden inspiration, ran
to the little staircase conducting to the rooms overhead, and
called: 'Mère-Grand! Mère-Grand! Come down at once, you
are wanted.'

Then, as soon as she was there, looking slim and pale in
her black gown, and showing the wise air of a queen-mother
whom all obeyed, he said: 'Tell these two children that
they can do nothing better than marry one another. Tell

them that we have talked it over, you and I, and that it is your desire, your will that they should do so.'

She quietly nodded her assent, and then said : 'That is true, it will be by far the most sensible course.'

Thereupon Marie flung herself into her arms, consenting, yielding to the superior forces, the powers of life, that had thus changed the course of her existence. Guillaume immediately desired that the date of the wedding should be fixed, and accommodation provided for the young couple in the rooms overhead. And as Pierre glanced at him with some remaining anxiety and spoke of travelling, for he feared that his wound was not yet healed, and that their presence might bring him suffering, Guillaume responded : 'No, no, I mean to keep you. If I'm marrying you it is to have you both here. Don't worry about me. I have so much work to do, I shall work.'

In the evening when Thomas and François came home and learnt the news they did not seem particularly surprised by it. They had doubtless felt that things would end like this. And they bowed to the *dénouement*, not venturing to say a word, since it was their father himself who announced the decision which had been taken, with his usual air of composure. Antoine, however, who on his own side quivered with love for Lise, gazed with doubting, anxious eyes at his father, who had thus had the courage to pluck out his heart. Could he really survive such a sacrifice, must it not kill him? Then Antoine kissed his father passionately, and the elder brothers in their turn embraced him with all their hearts. Guillaume smiled and his eyes became moist. After his victory over his horrible torments nothing could have been sweeter to him than the embraces of his three big sons.

There was, however, further emotion in store for him that evening. Just as the daylight was departing, and he was sitting at his large table near the window, again checking and classifying the documents and plans connected with his invention, he was surprised to see his old master and friend Bertheroy enter the workroom. The illustrious chemist called on him in this fashion at long intervals, and Guillaume felt the honour thus conferred on him by this old man to whom eminence and fame had brought so many titles, offices, and decorations. Moreover, Bertheroy, with his position as an official *savant* and member of the Institute, showed some courage in thus venturing to call on one whom so-called respectable folks regarded with contumely. On this occasion, however, Guillaume at once understood that it was some feeling of curiosity that had brought him. And so he was greatly embarrassed, for he hardly dared to remove the papers and plans which were lying on the table.

'Oh, don't be frightened,' gaily exclaimed Bertheroy, who, despite his careless and abrupt ways, was really very shrewd. 'I haven't come to pry into your secrets. . . . Leave your papers there, I promise you that I won't read anything.'

Then, in all frankness, he turned the conversation on the subject of explosives, which he was still studying, he said, with passionate interest. He had made some new discoveries which he did not conceal. Incidentally, too, he spoke of the opinion he had given in Salvat's affair. His dream was to discover some explosive of great power, which one might attempt to domesticate and reduce to complete obedience. And with a smile he pointedly concluded: 'I don't know where that madman found the formula of his powder. But if you should ever discover it, remember that the future perhaps lies in the employment of explosives as motive power.'

Then, all at once, he added: 'By the way, that fellow Salvat will be executed on the day after to-morrow. A friend of mine at the Ministry of Justice has just told me so.'

Guillaume had hitherto listened to him with an air of mingled distrust and amusement. But this announcement of Salvat's execution stirred him to anger and revolt, though for some days past he had known it to be inevitable, in spite of the sympathy which the condemned man was now rousing in many quarters.

'It will be a murder!' he cried vehemently.

Bertheroy waved his hand: 'What would you have?' he answered; 'there's a social system and it defends itself when it is attacked. Besides, those Anarchists are really too foolish in imagining that they will transform the world with their squibs and crackers! In my opinion, you know, Science is the only revolutionist. Science will not only bring us truth but justice also, if indeed justice ever be possible on this earth. And that is why I lead so calm a life and am so tolerant.'

Once again Bertheroy appeared to Guillaume as a revolutionist, one who was convinced that he helped on the ruin of the ancient abominable society of nowadays, with its dogmas and laws, even whilst he was working in the depths of his laboratory. He was, however, too desirous of repose, and had too great a contempt for futilities to mingle with the events of the day, and he preferred to live in quietude, liberally paid and rewarded, and at peace with the government whatever it might be, whilst at the same time foreseeing and preparing the formidable parturition of the future.

He waved his hand towards Paris, over which a sun of victory was setting, and then again spoke: 'Do you hear the rumble? It is we who are the stokers, we who are ever flinging fresh fuel under the boiler. Science does not pause in her work for a single hour, and she is the artisan of Paris which—let us hope it—will be the artisan of the future. All the rest is of no account.'

Guillaume, however, was no longer listening to him. He was thinking of Salvat and the terrible engine of war he had invented, that engine which before long would shatter cities. And a new idea was dawning and growing in his mind. He had just freed himself of his last tie, he had created all the happiness he could create around him. Ah! to recover his courage, to be master of himself once more, and, at any rate, derive from the sacrifice of his heart the lofty delight of being free, of being able to lay down even his life, should he some day deem it necessary!

BOOK V

I

THE GUILLOTINE

FOR some reason of his own Guillaume was bent upon witnessing the execution of Salvat. Pierre tried to dissuade him
from doing so; and finding his efforts vain, became somewhat
anxious. He accordingly resolved to spend the night at
Montmartre, accompany his brother and watch over him. In
former times, when engaged with Abbé Rose in charitable
work in the Charonne district, he had learnt that the guillotine could be seen from the house where Mège, the Socialist
deputy, resided at the corner of the Rue Merlin. He therefore offered himself as a guide. As the execution was to take
place as soon as it should legally be daybreak, that is about
half-past four o'clock, the brothers did not go to bed but sat
up in the workroom, feeling somewhat drowsy, and exchanging
few words. Then as soon as two o'clock struck they started
off.

The night was beautifully serene and clear. The full
moon, shining like a silver lamp in the cloudless, far-stretch-
ing heavens, threw a calm, dreamy light over the vague
immensity of Paris, which was like some spell-bound city of
sleep, so overcome by fatigue that not a murmur arose from it.
It was as if beneath the soft radiance which spread over its
roofs, its panting labour and its cries of suffering were lulled
to repose until the dawn. However, in a far, out of the way
district dark work was even now progressing, a knife was being
raised on high in order that a man might be killed.

Pierre and Guillaume paused in the Rue St. Eleuthère, and
gazed at the vaporous, tremulous city spread out below them.
And as they turned they perceived the basilica of the Sacred

Heart, still domeless but already looking huge indeed in the moonbeams, whose clear white light accentuated its outlines and brought them into sharp relief against a mass of shadows. Under the pale nocturnal sky, the edifice showed like a colossal monster, symbolical of provocation and sovereign dominion. Never before had Guillaume found it so huge, never had it appeared to him to dominate Paris, even in the latter's hours of slumber, with such stubborn and overwhelming might.

This wounded him so keenly in the state of mind in which he found himself, that he could not help exclaiming : ' Ah ! they chose a good site for it, and how stupid it was to let them do so ! I know of nothing more nonsensical : Paris crowned and dominated by that temple of idolatry ! How impudent it is, what a buffet for the cause of reason after so many centuries of science, labour, and battle ! And to think of it being reared over Paris, the one city in the world which ought never to have been soiled in this fashion ! One can understand it at Lourdes and Rome ; but not in Paris, in the very field of intelligence which has been so deeply ploughed, and whence the future is sprouting. It is a declaration of war, an insolent proclamation that they hope to conquer Paris also ! '

Guillaume usually evinced all the tolerance of a scientist, for whom religions are simply social phenomena. He even willingly admitted the grandeur or grace of certain Catholic legends. But Marie Alacoque's famous vision, which has given rise to the cult of the Sacred Heart, filled him with irritation and something like physical disgust. He suffered at the mere idea of Christ's open, bleeding breast, and the gigantic heart which the saint asserted she had seen beating in the depths of the wound—the huge heart in which Jesus placed the woman's little heart to restore it to her inflated and glowing with love. What base and loathsome materialism there was in all this ! What a display of viscera, muscles, and blood suggestive of a butcher's shop ! And Guillaume was particularly disgusted with the engraving which depicted this horror, and which he found everywhere, crudely coloured with red and yellow and blue, like some badly executed anatomical plate.

Pierre on his side was also looking at the basilica as, white with moonlight, it rose out of the darkness like a gigantic fortress raised to crush and conquer the city slumbering beneath it. It had already brought him suffering during the last days when he had said mass in it and was struggling with his torments. 'They call it the national votive offering,' he now exclaimed. 'But the nation's longing is for health and strength and restoration to its old position by work. That is a thing the Church does not understand. It argues that if France was stricken with defeat, it was because she deserved punishment. She was guilty, and so to-day she ought to repent. Repent of what? Of the Revolution, of a century of free examination and science, of the emancipation of her mind, of her initiatory and liberative labour in all parts of the world? That indeed is her real transgression; and it is as a punishment for all our labour, search for truth, increase of knowledge, and march towards justice that they have reared that huge pile which Paris will see from all her streets, and will never be able to see without feeling derided and insulted in her labour and glory.'

With a wave of his hand he pointed to the city slumbering in the moonlight as beneath a sheet of silver, and then set off again with his brother, down the slopes, towards the black and deserted streets.

They did not meet a living soul until they reached the outer boulevard. Here, however, no matter what the hour may be, life continues with scarcely a pause. No sooner are the wine shops, music and dancing halls closed, than vice and want, cast into the street, there resume their nocturnal existence. Thus the brothers came upon all the homeless ones: low prostitutes seeking a pallet, vagabonds stretched on the benches under the trees, rogues who prowled hither and thither on the look-out for a good stroke. Encouraged by their accomplice, night, all the mire and woe of Paris had returned to the surface. The empty roadway now belonged to the breadless, homeless starvelings, those for whom there was no place in the sunlight, the vague, swarming, despairing herd which is only espied at night-time. Ah! what spectres of destitution, what apparitions of grief and fright there were! What a sob of agony passed by in Paris that morning, when as soon as the dawn should rise, a man—a pauper, a sufferer like the others—was to be guillotined!

As Guillaume and Pierre were about to descend the Rue des Martyrs, the former perceived an old man lying on a bench with his bare feet protruding from his gaping, filthy shoes. Guillaume pointed to him in silence. Then, a few steps farther on, Pierre in his turn pointed to a ragged girl, crouching, asleep with open mouth, in the corner of a doorway. There was no need for the brothers to express in words all the compassion and anger which stirred their hearts. At long intervals policemen, walking slowly two by two, shook the poor wretches and compelled them to rise and walk on and on. Occasionally, if they found them suspicious or refractory they marched them off to the police-station. And then rancour and the contagion of imprisonment often transformed a mere vagabond into a thief or a murderer.

In the Rue des Martyrs and the Rue du Faubourg-Montmartre, the brothers found night-birds of another kind, women who slunk past them, close to the house-fronts, and men and hussies who belaboured one another with blows. Then, upon the grand boulevards, on the thresholds of lofty black houses, only one row of whose windows flared in the night, pale-faced individuals, who had just come down from their clubs, stood lighting cigars before going home. A lady with a ball-wrap over her evening gown went by accompanied by a servant. A few cabs, moreover, still jogged up and down the roadway, while others, which had been waiting for hours, stood on their ranks in rows, with drivers and horses alike asleep. And as one boulevard after another was reached, the Boulevard Poissonnière, the Boulevard Bonne Nouvelle, the Boulevard St. Denis, and so forth, as far as the Place de la République, there came fresh want and misery, more forsaken and hungry ones, more and more of the human 'waste' that is cast into the streets and the darkness. And on the other hand, an army of street-sweepers was now appearing to remove all the filth of the past four-and-twenty hours, in order that Paris, spruce already at sunrise, might not blush for having thrown up such a mass of dirt and loathsomeness in the course of a single day.

It was, however, more particularly after following the Boulevard Voltaire, and drawing near to the districts of La Roquette and Charonne, that the brothers felt they were returning to a sphere of labour where there was often lack of food, and where life was but so much pain. Pierre found himself at home here. In former days, accompanied by good Abbé Rose, visiting despairing ones, distributing alms, picking up children who had sunk to the gutter, he had a hundred times perambulated every one of those long, densely populated streets. And thus a frightful vision arose before his mind's eye; he recalled all the tragedies he had witnessed, all the shrieks he had heard, all the tears and bloodshed he had seen, all the fathers, mothers and children huddled together and dying of want, dirt, and abandonment: that social hell in which he had ended by losing his last hopes, fleeing from it with a sob in the conviction that Charity was a mere amusement for the rich, and absolutely futile as a remedy. It was this conviction which now returned to him as he again cast eyes upon that want- and grief-stricken district which seemed fated to everlasting destitution. That poor old man whom Abbé Rose had revived one night in yonder hovel, had he not since died of starvation? That little girl whom he had one morning brought in his arms to the Refuge after her parents' death, was it not she whom he had just met, grown but fallen to the streets, and shrieking beneath the fist of a bully? Ah! how great was the number of the wretched! Their name was legion! There were those whom one could not save, those who were hourly born to a life of woe and want, even as one may be born infirm, and those, too, who from every side sank in the sea of human injustice, that ocean which has ever been the same for centuries past, and which though one may strive to drain it, still and for ever spreads. How heavy was the silence, how dense the darkness in those working-class streets where sleep seems to be the comrade of death! Yet hunger prowls, and misfortune sobs; vague spectral forms slink by, and then are lost to view in the depths of the night.

As Pierre and Guillaume went along they became mixed with dark groups of people, a whole flock of inquisitive folk, a promiscuous, passionate tramp, tramp towards the guillotine. It came from all Paris, urged on by brutish fever, a hankering for death and blood. In spite, however, of the dull noise which came from this dim crowd, the mean streets that were passed remained quite dark, not a light appeared at any of their windows; nor could one hear the breathing of the weary toilers stretched on their wretched pallets from which they would not rise before the morning twilight.

On seeing the jostling crowd which was already assembled on the Place Voltaire, Pierre understood that it would be impossible for him and his brother to ascend the Rue de la Roquette. Barriers, moreover, must certainly have been thrown across that street. In order therefore to reach the corner of the Rue Merlin, it occurred to him to take the Rue de la Folie Regnault, which winds round in the rear of the prison, farther on.

Here, indeed, they found solitude and darkness again. The huge, massive prison with its great bare walls on which a moonray fell, looked like some pile of cold stones, dead for centuries past. At the end of the street, however, they once more fell in with the crowd, a dim restless mass of beings, whose pale faces alone could be distinguished. The brothers had great difficulty in reaching the house in which Mège resided at the corner of the Rue Merlin. All the shutters of the fourth floor flat occupied by the Socialist deputy were closed, though every other window was wide open and crowded with surging sightseers. Moreover, the wine shop down below and the first floor room connected with it flared with gas, and were already crowded with noisy customers, waiting for the performance to begin.

'I hardly like to go and knock at Mège's door,' said Pierre.

'No, no, you must not do so!' replied Guillaume. 'Let us go into the wine shop. We may perhaps be able to see something from the balcony.'

The first floor room was provided with a very large balcony, which women and gentlemen were already filling. The brothers nevertheless managed to reach it, and for a few minutes remained there, peering into the darkness before them. The sloping street grew broader between the two prisons, the 'great' and the 'little' Roquette, in such wise as to form a sort of square, which was shaded by four clumps of plane-trees, rising from the footways. The low buildings and scrubby trees, all poor and ugly of aspect, seemed almost to lie on a level with the ground, under a vast sky in which stars were appearing, as the moon gradually declined. And the square was quite empty save that on one spot yonder there seemed to be some little stir. Two rows of guards prevented the crowd from advancing, and even threw it back into the neighbouring streets. On the one hand, the only lofty houses were far away, at the point where the Rue St. Maur intersects the Rue de la Roquette; while, on the other, they stood at the corners of the Rue Merlin and the Rue de la Folie Regnault, so that it was almost impossible to distinguish anything of the execution even from the best placed windows. As for the inquisitive folk on the pavement they only saw the backs of the guards. Still this did not prevent

a crush. The human tide flowed on from all sides with increasing clamour.

Guided by the remarks of some women who, leaning forward on the balcony, had been watching the square for a
long time already, the brothers were at last able to perceive
something. It was now half-past three, and the guillotine
was nearly ready. The little stir which one vaguely espied
yonder under the trees, was that of the headsman's
assistants fixing the knife in position. A lantern slowly
came and went, and five or six shadows danced over the
ground. But nothing else could be distinguished, the square
was like a large black pit, around which ever broke the waves
of the noisy crowd which one could not see. And beyond the
square one could only identify the flaring wine shops, which
showed forth like lighthouses in the night. All the surrounding district of poverty and toil was still asleep, not a gleam
as yet came from workrooms or yards, not a puff of smoke
from the lofty factory chimneys.

'We shall see nothing,' Guillaume remarked.

But Pierre silenced him, for he had just discovered that
an elegantly attired gentleman leaning over the balcony near
him was none other than the amiable deputy Duthil. He
had at first fancied that a woman muffled in wraps who stood
close beside the deputy was the little Princess de Harn, whom
he had very likely brought to see the execution, since he had
taken her to see the trial. On closer inspection, however, he had
found that this woman was Silviane, the perverse creature
with the virginal face. Truth to tell she made no conceal-
ment of her presence, but talked on in an extremely loud
voice, as if intoxicated; and the brothers soon learnt how it
was that she happened to be there. Duvillard, Duthil, and
other friends had been supping with her at one o'clock in the
morning, when on learning that Salvat was about to be
guillotined, the fancy of seeing the execution had suddenly
come upon her. Duvillard, after vainly entreating her to do
nothing of the kind, had gone off in a fury, for he felt that it
would be most unseemly on his part to attend the execution
of a man who had endeavoured to blow up his house. And
thereupon Silviane had turned to Duthil, whom her caprice
greatly worried, for he held all such loathsome spectacles in
horror, and had already refused to act as escort to the Princess.
However, he was so infatuated with Silviane's beauty, and

she made him so many promises, that he had at last consented to take her.

'He can't understand people caring for amusement,' she said, speaking of the Baron. 'And yet this is really a thing to see. . . . But no matter, you'll find him at my feet again to-morrow.'

Duthil smiled and responded: 'I suppose that peace has been signed and ratified now that you have secured your engagement at the Comédie.'

'Peace? No!' she protested. 'No, no. There will be no peace between us until I have made my *début*. After that, we'll see.'

They both laughed; and then Duthil, by way of paying his court, told her how good-naturedly Dauvergne, the new Minister of Public Instruction and Fine Arts, had adjusted the difficulties which had hitherto kept the doors of the Comédie closed upon her. A really charming man was Dauvergne, the embodiment of graciousness, the very flower of the Monferrand ministry. His was the velvet hand in that administration whose leader had a hand of iron.

'He told me, my beauty,' said Duthil, 'that a pretty girl was in place everywhere.' And then as Silviane, as if flattered, pressed closely beside him, the deputy added: 'So that wonderful revival of "Polyeucte," in which you are going to have such a triumph, is to take place on the day after to-morrow. We shall all go to applaud you, remember.'

'Yes, on the evening of the day after to-morrow,' said Silviane, 'the very same day when the wedding of the Baron's daughter will take place. There'll be plenty of emotion that day!'

'Ah! yes, of course!' retorted Duthil, 'there'll be the wedding of our friend Gérard with Mademoiselle Camille to begin with. We shall have a crush at the Madeleine in the morning and another at the Comédie in the evening. You are quite right, too; there will be several hearts throbbing in the Rue Godot de Mauroy.'

Thereupon they again became merry, and jested about the Duvillard family—father, mother, lover and daughter—with the greatest possible ferocity and crudity of language. Then, all at once, Silviane exclaimed: 'Do you know I'm feeling awfully bored here, my little Duthil. I can't distinguish anything, and I should like to be quite near so as to see it all plainly. You must take me over yonder, close to that machine of theirs.'

This request threw Duthil into consternation, particularly as at that same moment Silviane perceived Massot outside the wine shop, and began calling and beckoning to him imperiously. A brief conversation then ensued between the young woman and the journalist: 'I say, Massot!' she called, 'hasn't a deputy the right to pass the guards and take a lady wherever he likes?'

'Not at all!' exclaimed Duthil. 'Massot knows very well that a deputy ought to be the very first to bow to the laws.'

This exclamation warned Massot that Duthil did not wish to leave the balcony. 'You ought to have secured a card of invitation, madame,' said he, in reply to Silviane. 'They would then have found you room at one of the windows of La Petite Roquette. Women are not allowed elsewhere. . . . But you mustn't complain, you have a very good place up there.'

'But I can see nothing at all, my dear Massot.'

'Well, you will in any case see more than Princess de Harn will. Just now I came upon her carriage in the Rue du Chemin Vert. The police would not allow it to come any nearer.'

This news made Silviane merry again, whilst Duthil shuddered at the idea of the danger he incurred, for Rosemonde would assuredly treat him to a terrible scene should she see him with another woman. Then, an idea occurring to him, he ordered a bottle of champagne and some little cakes for his 'beautiful friend,' as he called Silviane. She had been complaining of thirst, and was delighted with the opportunity of perfecting her intoxication. When a waiter had managed to place a little table near her, on the balcony itself, she found things very pleasant, and indeed considered it quite brave to tipple and sup afresh, while waiting for that man to be guillotined close by.

It was impossible for Pierre and Guillaume to remain up there any longer. All that they heard, all that they beheld filled them with disgust. The boredom of waiting had turned all the inquisitive folks of the balcony and the adjoining room into customers. The waiter could hardly manage to serve the many glasses of beer, bottles of expensive wine, biscuits, and plates of cold meat which were ordered of him. And yet the spectators here were all *bourgeois*, rich gentlemen, people of society! On the other hand, time has to be killed somehow when it hangs heavily on one's hands; and thus there were bursts of laughter and paltry and horrible jests, quite a feverish uproar arising amidst the clouds of smoke from the men's cigars. When Pierre and Guillaume passed through the wine shop on the ground floor they there found a similar crush and similar tumult, aggravated by the disorderly behaviour of the big fellows in blouses who were drinking draught wine at the pewter bar which shone like silver. There were people, too, at all the little tables, besides an incessant coming and going of folks who entered the place for a 'wet,' by way of calming their impatience. And what folks they were! All the scum, all the vagabonds who had been dragging themselves about since daybreak on the look-out for whatever chance might offer them, provided it were not work!

On the pavement outside, Pierre and Guillaume felt yet a greater heart pang. In the throng which the guards kept back, one simply found so much mire stirred up from the very depths of Paris life: prostitutes and criminals, the murderers of to-morrow, who came to see how a man ought to die. Loathsome, bareheaded harlots mingled with bands of prowlers or ran through the crowd, howling obscene refrains. Bandits stood in groups chatting and quarrelling about the more or less glorious manner in which certain famous *guillotinés* had died. Among these was one with respect to whom they all agreed, and of whom they spoke as of a great captain, a hero whose marvellous courage was deserving of immortality. Then, as one passed along, one caught snatches of horrible phrases, particulars about the instrument of death, ignoble boasts, and filthy jests reeking with blood. And over and above all else there was bestial fever, a lust for death which made this multitude delirious, an eagerness to see life flow forth fresh and ruddy beneath the knife, so that as it coursed over the soil they might dip their feet in it. As this execution was not an ordinary one, however, there were yet spectators of another kind: silent men with glowing eyes who came and went all alone, and who were plainly thrilled by their faith, intoxicated with the contagious madness which incites one to vengeance or martyrdom.

Guillaume was just thinking of Victor Mathis, when he fancied that he saw him standing in the front row of sight-seers whom the guards held in check. It was, indeed, he, with his thin, beardless, pale, drawn face. Short as he was, he had to raise himself on tip-toes in order to see anything. Near him was a big, red-haired girl who gesticulated; but for his part he never stirred or spoke. He was waiting motionless, gazing yonder with the round, ardent, fixed eyes of a night-bird, seeking to penetrate the darkness. At last a guard pushed him back in a somewhat brutal way; however, he soon returned to his previous position, ever patient though full of hatred against the executioners, wishing indeed to see all he could in order to increase his hate.

Then Massot approached the brothers. This time, on seeing Pierre without his cassock, he did not even make a sign of astonishment, but gaily remarked: 'So you felt curious to see this affair, Monsieur Froment?'

'Yes, I came with my brother,' Pierre replied. 'But I very much fear that we shan't see much.'

'You certainly won't if you stay here,' rejoined Massot. And thereupon in his usual good-natured way—glad, moreover, to show what power a well-known journalist could wield—he inquired: 'Would you like me to pass you through? The inspector here happens to be a friend of mine.'

Then, without waiting for an answer, he stopped the inspector and hastily whispered to him that he had brought a couple of colleagues, who wanted to report the proceedings. At first the inspector hesitated, and seemed inclined to refuse Massot's request; but after a moment, influenced by the covert fear which the police always have of the press, he made a weary gesture of consent.

'Come, quick, then,' said Massot, turning to the brothers, and taking them along with him.

A moment later, to the intense surprise of Pierre and Guillaume, the guards opened their ranks to let them pass. They then found themselves in the large open space which was kept clear. And on thus emerging from the tumultuous throng they were quite impressed by the death-like silence and solitude which reigned under the little plane trees. The night was now paling. A faint gleam of dawn was already falling from the sky.

After leading his companions slantwise across the square, Massot stopped them near the prison and resumed: 'I'm going inside; I want to see the prisoner roused and got ready. In the meantime, walk about here; nobody will say anything to you. Besides, I'll come back to you in a moment.'

A hundred people or so, journalists and other privileged spectators, were scattered about the dark square. Movable wooden barriers—such as are set up at the doors of theatres when there is a press of people waiting for admission, had been placed on either side of the pavement running from the prison gate to the guillotine; and some sight-seers were already leaning over these barriers, in order to secure a close view of the condemned man as he passed by. Others were walking slowly to and fro, and conversing in undertones. The brothers, for their part, approached the guillotine.

It stood there under the branches of the trees, amidst the delicate greenery of the fresh leaves of spring. A neighbouring gas-lamp, whose light was turning yellow in the rising dawn, cast vague gleams upon it. The work of fixing it in position—work performed as quietly as could be, so that the only sound was the occasional thud of a mallet—had just been finished; and the headsman's 'valets' or assistants, in frock coats and tall silk hats, were waiting and strolling about in a patient way. But the instrument itself how base and shameful it looked, squatting on the ground like some filthy beast, disgusted with the work it had to accomplish! What! those few beams lying on the ground, and those others barely nine feet high which rose from it, keeping the knife in position, constituted the machine which avenged Society, the instrument which gave a warning to evil-doers! Where was the big scaffold painted a bright red and reached by a stairway of ten steps, the scaffold which raised high gory arms over the eager multitude, so that everybody might behold the punishment of the law in all its horror? The beast had now been felled to the ground, where it simply looked ignoble, crafty, and cowardly. If on the one hand there was no majesty in the manner in which human justice condemned a man to death at its assizes; on the other, there was merely horrid butchery with the help of the most barbarous and repulsive of mechanical contrivances, on the terrible day when that man was executed.

As Pierre and Guillaume gazed at the guillotine, a feeling of nausea came over them. Daylight was now slowly breaking, and the surroundings were appearing to view: first the square itself with its two low, grey prisons, facing one another; then the distant houses, the taverns, the marble workers' establishments, and the shops selling flowers and wreaths, which are numerous hereabouts, as the cemetery of Père-Lachaise is so near. Before long one could plainly distinguish the black lines of the spectators standing around in a circle, the heads leaning forward from windows and balconies, and the people who had climbed to the very house roofs. The prison of La Petite Roquette over the way had been turned into a kind of tribune for guests; and mounted Gardes de Paris went slowly to and fro across the intervening expanse. Then, as the sky brightened, labour awoke throughout the district beyond the crowd, a district of broad, endless streets lined with factories, workshops, and workyards. Engines began to snort, machinery and appliances were got ready to start once more on their usual tasks, and smoke already curled away from the forest of lofty brick chimneys which, on all sides, sprang out of the gloom.

It then seemed to Guillaume that the guillotine was really in its right place in that district of want and toil. It stood in its own realm, like a *terminus* and a threat. Did not ignorance, poverty, and woe lead to it? And each time that it was set up amidst those toilsome streets, was it not charged to overawe the disinherited ones, the starvelings, who, exasperated by everlasting injustice, were always ready for revolt? It was not seen in the districts where wealth and enjoyment reigned. It would there have seemed purposeless, degrading, and truly monstrous. And it was a tragical and terrible coincidence that the bomb-thrower, driven mad by want, should be guillotined there, in the very centre of want's dominion.

But daylight had come at last, for it was nearly half-past four. The distant noisy crowd could feel that the expected moment was drawing nigh. A shudder suddenly sped through the atmosphere.

'He's coming,' exclaimed little Massot, as he came back to Pierre and Guillaume. 'Ah! that Salvat is a brave fellow after all.'

Then he related how the prisoner had been awakened; how the governor of the prison, magistrate Amadieu, the chaplain, and a few other persons had entered the cell where Salvat lay fast asleep; and then how the condemned man had understood the truth immediately upon opening his eyes. He had risen, looking pale but quite composed. And he had dressed himself without assistance, and had declined the nip of brandy and the cigarette proffered by the good-hearted chaplain, in the same way as with a gentle but stubborn gesture he had brushed the crucifix aside. Then had come the 'toilette' for death. With all rapidity and without a word being exchanged, Salvat's hands had been tied behind his back, his legs had been loosely secured with a cord, and the neckband of his shirt had been cut away. He had smiled when the others exhorted him to be brave. He only feared some nervous weakness, and had but one desire, to die like a hero, to remain the martyr of the ardent faith in truth and justice for which he was about to perish.

'They are now drawing up the death certificate in the register,' continued Massot in his chattering way. 'Come along, come close to the barriers if you wish a good view. . . . I turned paler, you know, and trembled far more than he did. I don't care a rap for anything as a rule; but, all the same, an execution isn't a pleasant business. . . . You can't imagine how many attempts were made to save Salvat's life. Even some of the papers asked that he might be reprieved. But nothing succeeded, the execution was regarded as inevitable, it seems, even by those who consider it a blunder. Still, they had such a touching opportunity to reprieve him, when his daughter, little Céline, wrote that fine letter to the President of the Republic, which I was the first to publish in the "Globe." Ah! that letter, it cost me a lot of running about!'

Pierre, who was already quite upset by this long wait for the horrible scene, felt moved to tears by Massot's reference to Céline. He could again see the child standing beside Madame Théodore in that bare, cold room whither her father would never more return. It was thence that he had set out on a day of desperation with his stomach empty and his brain on fire, and it was here that he would end, between yonder beams, beneath yonder knife.

Massot, however, was still giving particulars. The doctors, said he, were furious because they feared that the body would not be delivered to them immediately after the execution. To this Guillaume did not listen. He stood there with his elbows resting on the wooden barrier and his eyes fixed on the prison gate which still remained shut. His hands were quivering, and there was an expression of anguish on his face as if it were he himself who was about to be executed. The headsman had again just left the prison. He was a little, insignificant looking man, and seemed annoyed, anxious to have done with it all. Then, among a group of frock-coated gentlemen, some of the spectators pointed out Gascogne, the chief of the detective police, who wore a cold official air, and Amadieu, the investigating magistrate, who smiled and looked very spruce, early though the hour was. He had come partly because it was his duty, and partly because he wished to show himself now that the curtain was about to fall on a wonderful tragedy of which he considered himself the author. Guillaume glanced at him, and then as a growing uproar rose from the distant crowd, he looked up for an instant, and again beheld the two grey prisons, the plane trees with their fresh young leaves, and the houses swarming with people beneath the pale blue sky, in which the triumphant sun was about to appear.

'Look out, here he comes!'

Who had spoken? A slight noise, that of the opening gate, made every heart throb. Necks were outstretched, eyes gazed fixedly, there was laboured breathing on all sides. Salvat stood on the threshold of the prison. The chaplain, stepping backwards, had come out in advance of him, in order to conceal the guillotine from his sight, but he had stopped short, for he wished to see that instrument of death, make acquaintance with it, as it were, before he walked towards it. And as he stood there, his long, aged sunken face, on which life's hardships had left their mark, seemed transformed by the wondrous brilliancy of his flaring, dreamy eyes. Enthusiasm bore him up—he was going to his death in all the splendour of his dream. When the executioner's assistants drew near to support him he once more refused their help, and again set himself in motion, advancing with short steps but as quickly and as straightly as the rope, hampering his legs, permitted.

All at once Guillaume felt that Salvat's eyes were fixed upon him. Drawing nearer and nearer the condemned man had perceived and recognised his friend; and as he passed by, at a distance of no more than six or seven feet, he smiled faintly and darted such a deep penetrating glance at Guillaume, that ever afterwards the latter felt its smart. But what last thought, what supreme legacy had Salvat left him to meditate upon, perhaps to put into execution? It was all so poignant that Pierre feared some involuntary call on his brother's part; and so he laid his hand upon his arm to quiet him.

'Long live Anarchy!'

It was Salvat who had raised this cry. But in the deep silence his husky, altered voice seemed to break. The few

who were near at hand had turned very pale; the distant
crowd seemed bereft of life. The horse of one of the Gardes
de Paris was alone heard snorting in the centre of the space
which had been kept clear.

Then came a loathsome scramble, a scene of nameless
brutality and ignominy. The headsman's helps rushed
upon Salvat as he came up slowly with brow erect. Two of them
seized him by the head, but finding little hair there, could
only lower it by tugging at his neck. Next two others
grasped him by the legs and flung him violently upon a
plank which tilted over and rolled forward. Then, by dint of
pushing and tugging, the head was got into the 'lunette,'
the upper part of which fell in such wise that the neck was
fixed as in a ship's port-hole—and all this was accomplished
amidst such confusion and with such savagery that one
might have thought that head some cumbrous thing which
it was necessary to get rid of with the greatest speed. But
the knife fell with a dull, heavy, forcible thud, and two long
jets of blood spurted from the severed arteries, while the dead
man's feet moved convulsively. Nothing else could be seen.
The executioner rubbed his hands in a mechanical way, and
an assistant took the severed blood-streaming head from the
little basket into which it had fallen and placed it in the large
basket into which the body had already been turned.

Ah! that dull, that heavy thud of the knife! It seemed
to Guillaume that he had heard it echoing far away all over
that district of want and toil, even in the squalid rooms where
thousands of workmen were at that moment rising to perform
their day's hard task! And there the echo of that thud
acquired formidable significance; it spoke of man's exasperation with injustice, of zeal for martyrdom, and of the dolorous
hope that the blood then spilt might hasten the victory of the
disinherited.

Pierre, for his part, at the sight of that loathsome butchery,
the abject cut-throat work of that killing machine, had
suddenly felt his chilling shudder become more violent; for
before him arose a vision of another corpse, that of the fair,
pretty child ripped open by a bomb and stretched yonder,
at the entrance of the Duvillard mansion. Blood streamed
from her delicate flesh, just as it had streamed from that
decapitated neck. It was blood paying for blood; it was like
payment for mankind's debt of wretchedness, for which

payment is everlastingly being made, without man ever being
able to free himself from suffering.

Above the square and the crowd all was still silent in the
clear sky. How long had the abomination lasted? An
eternity, perhaps, compressed into two or three minutes.
And now came an awakening: the spectators emerged from
their nightmare with quivering hands, livid faces, and eyes
expressive of compassion, disgust, and fear.

'That makes another one. I've now seen four executions,'
said Massot, who felt ill at ease. 'After all, I prefer to report
weddings. Let us go off, I have all I want for my article.'

Guillaume and Pierre followed him mechanically across
the square, and again reached the corner of the Rue Merlin.
And here they found little Victor Mathis with flaming eyes
and white face, still standing in silence on the spot where
they had left him. He could have seen nothing distinctly;
but the thud of the knife was still echoing in his brain. A
policeman at last gave him a push, and told him to move on.
At this he looked the policeman in the face, stirred by
sudden rage and ready to strangle him. Then, however, he
quietly walked away, ascending the Rue de la Roquette, atop
of which the lofty foliage of Père-Lachaise could be seen,
beneath the rising sun.

The brothers meantime fell upon a scene of explanations,
which they heard without wishing to do so. Now that the
sight was over the Princess de Harn arrived, and she was the
more furious as at the door of the wine shop she could see
her new friend Duthil accompanying a woman.

'I say!' she exclaimed, 'you are nice, you are, to have
left me in the lurch like this! It was impossible for my
carriage to get near, so I've had to come on foot through
all those horrid people who have been jostling and insulting
me.'

Thereupon Duthil, with all promptitude, introduced
Silviane to her, adding, in an aside, that he had taken a
friend's place as the actress's escort. And then Rosemonde,
who greatly wished to know Silviane, calmed down as if by
enchantment, and put on her most engaging ways. 'It would
have delighted me, madame,' said she, 'to have seen this
sight in the company of an *artiste* of your merit, one whom
I admire so much, though I have never before had an opportunity of telling her so.'

'Well, dear me, madame,' replied Silviane, 'you haven't

lost much by arriving late. We were on that balcony there ; and all that I could see were a few men pushing another one about. . . . It really isn't worth the trouble of coming.'

' Well, now that we have become acquainted, madame,' said the Princess, ' I really hope that you will allow me to be your friend.'

' Certainly, madame, my friend ; and I shall be flattered and delighted to be yours.'

Standing there, hand in hand, they smiled at one another. Silviane was very drunk, but her virginal expression had returned to her face ; whilst Rosemonde seemed feverish with vicious curiosity. Duthil, whom the scene amused, now had but one thought, that of seeing Silviane home ; so, calling to Massot who was approaching, he asked him where he should find a cab-rank. Rosemonde, however, at once offered her carriage, which was waiting in an adjacent street. She would set the actress down at her door, said she, and the deputy at his ; and such was her persistence in the matter that Duthil, greatly vexed, was obliged to accept her offer.

' Well, then, till to-morrow at the Madeleine,' said Massot again quite sprightly, as he shook hands with the Princess.

' Yes, till to-morrow, at the Madeleine and the Comédie.'

' Ah ! yes, of course ! ' he repeated, taking Silviane's hand, which he kissed. ' The Madeleine in the morning and the Comédie in the evening. . . . We shall all be there to applaud you.'

' Yes, I expect you to do so,' said Silviane. ' Till to-morrow then ! '

' Till to-morrow ! '

The crowd was now wearily dispersing, to all appearance disappointed and ill at ease. A few enthusiasts alone lingered in order to witness the departure of the van in which Salvat's corpse would soon be removed ; while bands of prowlers and harlots, looking very wan in the daylight, whistled or called to one another with some last filthy expression before returning to their dens. The headsman's assistants were hastily taking down the guillotine, and the square would soon be quite clear.

Pierre for his part wished to lead his brother away. Since the fall of the knife, Guillaume had remained as if stunned, without once opening his lips. In vain had Pierre tried to rouse him by pointing to the shutters of Mège's flat, which still remained closed, whereas every other window of the lofty house was wide open. Although the Socialist deputy hated the Anarchists, those shutters were doubtless closed as a protest against capital punishment. Whilst the multitude had been rushing to that frightful spectacle, Mège, still in bed, with his face turned to the wall, had probably been dreaming of how he would some day compel mankind to be happy beneath the rigid laws of Collectivism. Affectionate father as he was, the recent death of one of his children had quite upset his private life. His cough, too, had become a very bad one; but he ardently wished to live, for as soon as that new Monferrand ministry should have fallen beneath the interpellation which he already contemplated, his own turn would surely come: he would take the reins of power in hand, abolish the guillotine, and decree justice and perfect felicity.

'Do you see, Guillaume,' Pierre gently repeated. 'Mège hasn't opened his windows. He's a good fellow, after all; although our friends Bache and Morin dislike him.' Then, as his brother still refrained from answering, Pierre added, 'Come, let us go, we must get back home.'

They both turned into the Rue de la Folie Regnault, and reached the outer Boulevards by way of the Rue du Chemin Vert. All the toilers of the district were now at work. In the long streets edged with low buildings, workshops and factories, one heard engines snorting and machinery rumbling, while, up above, the smoke from the lofty chimneys was assuming a rosy hue in the sunrise. Afterwards, when the brothers reached the Boulevard de Menilmontant and the Boulevard de Belleville, which they followed in turn at a leisurely pace, they witnessed the great rush of the working classes into central Paris. The stream poured forth from every side; from all the wretched streets of the faubourgs there was an endless exodus of toilers, who having risen at dawn, were now hurrying, in the sharp morning air, to their daily labour. Some wore short jackets and others blouses; some were in velveteen trousers, others in linen overalls. Their thick shoes made their tramp a heavy one; their hanging hands were often deformed by work. And they seemed half asleep, not a smile was to be seen on any of those wan, weary faces turned yonder towards the everlasting task—the task which was begun afresh each day, and which—'twas their only chance— they hoped to be able to take up for ever and ever. There was no end to that drove of toilers, that army of various callings, that human flesh fated to manual labour, upon which

Paris preys in order that she may live in luxury and enjoyment.

Then the procession continued across the Boulevard de la Villette, the Boulevard de la Chapelle, and the Boulevard de Rochechouart, where one reached the height of Montmartre. More and more workmen were ever coming down from their bare cold rooms and plunging into the huge city whence, tired out, they would that evening merely bring back the bread of rancour. And now, too, came a stream of workgirls, some of them in bright skirts, some glancing at the passers-by; girls whose wages were so paltry, so insufficient, that now and again pretty ones among them never more turned their faces homewards, whilst the ugly ones wasted away, condemned to mere bread and water. A little later, moreover, came the *employés*, the clerks, the counter-jumpers, the whole world of frock-coated penury—'gentlemen' who devoured a roll as they hastened onward, worried the while by the dread of being unable to pay their rent, or by the problem of providing food for wife and children until the end of the month should come.[1] And now the sun was fast ascending on the horizon, the whole army of ants was out and about, and the toilsome day had begun with its ceaseless display of courage, energy, and suffering.

Never before had it been so plainly manifest to Pierre that work was a necessity, that it healed and saved. On the occasion of his visit to the Grandidier works, and later still, when he himself had felt the need of occupation, there had come to him the thought that work was really the world's law. And after that hateful night, after that spilling of blood, after the slaughter of that toiler maddened by his dreams, there was consolation and hope in seeing the sun rise once more, and everlasting labour take up its wonted task. However hard it might prove, however unjustly it might be lotted out, was it not work which would some day bring both justice and happiness to the world?

All at once, as the brothers were climbing the steep hillside towards Guillaume's house, they perceived before and above them the basilica of the Sacred Heart rising majestically and triumphantly to the sky. This was no sublunar apparition, no dreamy vision of Domination standing face to face with nocturnal Paris. The sun now clothed the edifice

---

[1] In Paris nearly all clerks and shop-assistants receive monthly salaries; while most workmen are paid once a fortnight.—*Trans.*

with splendour, it looked golden and proud and victorious,
flaring with immortal glory.

Then Guillaume, still silent, still feeling Salvat's last
glance upon him, seemed to come to some sudden and final
decision. He looked at the basilica with glowing eyes, and
pronounced sentence upon it.

II

IN VANITY FAIR

THE wedding was to take place at noon, and for half an hour
already guests had been pouring into the magnificently
decorated church, which was leafy with evergreens and balmy
with the scent of flowers. The high altar in the rear glowed
with countless candles, and through the great doorway which
was wide open one could see the peristyle decked with shrubs,
the steps covered with a broad carpet, and the inquisitive crowd
assembled on the square and even along the Rue Royale,
under the bright sun.

After finding three more chairs for some ladies who had
arrived rather late, Duthil remarked to Massot, who was
jotting down names in his note-book: 'Well, if any more
come, they will have to remain standing.'

'Who were those three?' the journalist inquired.

'The Duchess de Boisemont and her two daughters.'

'Indeed! All the titled people of France, as well as all the
financiers and politicians, are here! It's something more even
than a swell Parisian wedding.'

As a matter of fact all the spheres of 'society' were
gathered together there, and some at first seemed rather embarrassed at finding themselves beside others. Whilst
Duvillard's name attracted all the princes of finance and
politicians in power, Madame de Quinsac and her son were
supported by the highest of the French aristocracy. The
mere names of the witnesses sufficed to indicate what an
extraordinary medley there was. On Gérard's side these
witnesses were his uncle General de Bozonnet and the Marquis
de Morigny; whilst on Camille's they were the great banker
Louvard, and Monferrand, the President of the Council and
Minister of Finances. The quiet bravado which the latter

displayed in thus supporting the bride after being compromised
in her father's financial intrigues, imparted a piquant touch of
impudence to his triumph. And public curiosity was further
stimulated by the circumstance that the nuptial blessing was
to be given by Monseigneur Martha, Bishop of Persepolis, the
Pope's political agent in France, and the apostle of the
endeavours to win the Republic over to the Church by pretending to 'rally' to it.

'But, I was mistaken,' now resumed Massot with a sneer.
'I said a really Parisian wedding, did I not? But in point of
fact this wedding is a symbol. It's the apotheosis of the
bourgeoisie, my dear fellow—the old nobility sacrificing one
of its sons on the altar of the golden calf in order that the
Divinity and the gendarmes, being the masters of France once
more, may rid us of those scoundrelly Socialists!'

Then, again correcting himself, he added: 'But I was
forgetting. There are no more Socialists. Their head was
cut off the other morning.'

Duthil found this very funny. Then in a confidential way
he remarked: 'You know that the marriage wasn't settled
without a good deal of difficulty. . . . Have you read Sagnier's
ignoble article this morning?'

'Yes, yes; but I knew it all before, everybody knew it.'

Then in an undertone, understanding one another's
slightest allusion, they went on chatting. It was only amidst
a flood of tears and after a despairing struggle that Baroness
Duvillard had consented to let her lover marry her daughter.
And in doing so she had yielded to the sole desire of seeing
Gérard rich and happy. She still regarded Camille with all
the hatred of a defeated rival. Then, an equally painful
contest had taken place at Madame de Quinsac's. The
Countess had only overcome her revolt and consented to the
marriage in order to save her son from the dangers which
had threatened him since childhood; and the Marquis de
Morigny had been so affected by her maternal abnegation,
that in spite of all his anger he had resignedly agreed to be
a witness; thus making a supreme sacrifice, that of his
conscience, to the woman whom he had ever loved. And it
was this frightful story that Sagnier—using transparent nick-
names—had related in the 'Voix du Peuple' that morning.
He had even contrived to make it more horrid than it really
was; for, as usual, he was badly informed, and he was
naturally inclined to falsehood and invention, as by sending an

ever thicker and more poisonous torrent from his sewer, he might, day by day, increase his paper's sales. Since Monferrand's victory had compelled him to leave the African Railways scandal on one side, he had fallen back on scandals in private life, stripping whole families bare and pelting them with mud.

All at once Duthil and Massot were approached by Chaigneux, who, with his shabby frock coat badly buttoned, wore both a melancholy and busy air. 'Well, Monsieur Massot,' said he, 'what about your article on Silviane? Is it settled? Will it go in?'

As Chaigneux was always for sale, always ready to serve as a valet, it had occurred to Duvillard to make use of him to ensure Silviane's success at the Comédie. He had handed this sorry deputy over to the young woman, who entrusted him with all manner of dirty work, and sent him scouring Paris in search of applauders and advertisements. His eldest daughter was not yet married, and never had his four women-folk weighed more heavily on his hands. His life had become a perfect hell; they had ended by beating him if he did not bring a thousand-franc note home on the first day of every month.

'My article!' Massot replied; 'no, it surely won't go in, my dear deputy. Fonsègue says that it's written in too laudatory a style for the "Globe." He asked me if I were having a joke with the paper.'

Chaigneux became livid. The article in question was one written in advance, from the society point of view, on the success which Silviane would achieve in 'Polyeucte,' that evening, at the Comédie. The journalist, in the hope of pleasing her, had even shown her his 'copy'; and she, quite delighted, now relied upon finding the article in print in the most sober and solemn organ of the Parisian press.

'Good heavens! what will become of us?' murmured the wretched Chaigneux. 'It's absolutely necessary that the article should go in.'

'Well, I'm quite agreeable. But speak to the governor yourself. He's standing yonder between Vignon and Dauvergne, the Minister of Public Instruction.'

'Yes, I certainly will speak to him—but not here. Byand-bye in the sacristy, during the procession. And I must also try to speak to Dauvergne, for our Silviane particularly wants him to be in the ministerial box this evening. Monferrand will be there ; he promised Duvillard so.'

Massot began to laugh, repeating the expression which had circulated through Paris directly after the actress's engagement : ' The Silviane ministry. . . . Well, Dauvergne certainly owes that much to his godmother ! ' said he.

Just then the little Princess de Harn, coming up like a gust of wind, broke in upon the three men. ' I've no seat, you know ! ' she cried.

Duthil fancied that it was a question of finding her a well-placed chair in the church. ' You mustn't count on me,' he answered. ' I've just had no end of trouble in stowing the Duchess de Boisemont away with her two daughters.'

' Oh, but I'm talking of this evening's performance. Come, my dear Duthil, you really must find me a little corner in somebody's box. I shall die, I know I shall, if I can't applaud our delicious, our incomparable friend ! '

Ever since setting Silviane down at her door on the previous day Rosemonde had been overflowing with admiration for her.

' Oh ! you won't find a single remaining seat, madame,' declared Chaigneux, putting on an air of importance. ' We have distributed everything. I have just been offered three hundred francs for a stall.'

' That's true, there has been a fight even for the bracket seats, however badly they might be placed,' Duthil resumed. ' I am very sorry, but you must not count on me. . . . Duvillard is the only person who might take you in his box. He told me that he would reserve me a seat there. And so far, I think, there are only three of us, including his son. . . Ask Hyacinthe by-and-bye to procure you an invitation.'

Rosemonde, whom Hyacinthe had so greatly bored that she had given him his dismissal, felt the irony of Duthil's suggestion. Nevertheless, she exclaimed with an air of delight : ' Ah, yes ! Hyacinthe can't refuse me that. Thanks for your information, my dear Duthil. You are very nice, you are ; for you settle things gaily even when they are rather sad. . . . And don't forget, mind, that you have promised to teach me politics. Ah ! politics, my dear fellow, I feel that nothing will ever impassion me as politics do ! '

Then she left them, hustled several people, and in spite of the crush ended by installing herself in the front row.

'Ah! what a crank she is!' muttered Massot with an air of amusement.

Then as Chaigneux darted towards magistrate Amadieu to ask him in the most obsequious way if he had received his ticket, the journalist said to Duthil in a whisper: 'By the way, my dear friend, is it true that Duvillard is going to launch his famous scheme for a Trans-Saharian Railway? It would be a gigantic enterprise, a question of hundreds and hundreds of millions this time. . . . At the " Globe " office yesterday evening, Fonsègue shrugged his shoulders and said it was madness, and would never come off!'

Duthil winked, and in a jesting way replied: 'It's as good as done, my dear boy. Fonsègue will be kissing the governor's feet before another forty-eight hours are over.'

Then he gaily gave the other to understand that golden manna would presently be raining down on the press, and all faithful friends and willing helpers. Birds shake their feathers when the storm is over: and he, Duthil, was as spruce and lively, as joyous at the prospect of the presents he now expected, as if there had never been any African Railways scandal to upset him and make him turn pale with fright.

'The deuce!' muttered Massot, who had become serious. 'So this affair here is more than a triumph; it's the promise of yet another harvest. Well, I'm no longer surprised at the crush of people.'

At this moment the organs suddenly burst into a glorious hymn of greeting. The marriage procession was entering the church. A loud clamour had gone up from the crowd, which spread over the roadway of the Rue Royale and impeded the traffic there, while the *cortège* pompously ascended the steps in the bright sunshine. And it was now entering the edifice and advancing beneath the lofty, re-echoing vaults towards the high altar which flared with candles, whilst on either hand crowded the congregation, the men on the right and the women on the left. They had all risen and stood there smiling, with necks outstretched and eyes glowing with curiosity.

First, in the rear of the magnificent beadle, came Camille, leaning on the arm of her father, Baron Duvillard, who wore a proud expression befitting a day of victory. Veiled with superb *point d'Alençon* falling from her diadem of orange blossom, gowned in pleated silk muslin over an underskirt of white satin, the bride looked so extremely happy, so radiant at having conquered, that she seemed almost pretty. Moreover, she held herself so upright that one could scarcely detect that her left shoulder was higher than her right.

Next came Gérard, giving his arm to his mother, the Countess de Quinsac; he looking very handsome and courtly, as was proper, and she displaying impassive dignity in her gown of peacock-blue silk embroidered with gold and steel beads. But it was particularly Eve whom people wished to see, and every neck was craned forward when she appeared on the arm of General Bozonnet, the bridegroom's first witness and nearest male relative. She was gowned in 'old rose' taffetas trimmed with valenciennes of priceless value, and never had she looked younger, more deliciously fair. Yet her eyes betrayed her emotion, though she strove to smile; and her languid grace bespoke her widowhood, her compassionate surrender of the man she loved. Monferrand, the Marquis de Morigny, and banker Louvard, the three other witnesses, followed the Baroness' and General Bozonnet, each giving his arm to some lady of the family. A considerable sensation was caused by the appearance of Monferrand, who seemed on first-rate terms with himself, and jested familiarly with the lady he accompanied, a little brunette with a giddy air. Another who was noticed in the solemn, interminable procession was the bride's eccentric brother Hyacinthe, whose dress coat was of a cut never previously seen, with its tails broadly and symmetrically pleated.

When the affianced pair had taken their places before the prayer-stools awaiting them, and the members of both families and the witnesses had installed themselves in the rear in large armchairs, all gilding and red velvet, the ceremony was performed with extraordinary pomp. The curé of the Madeleine officiated in person; and vocalists from the Grand Opéra reinforced the choir, which chanted the high mass to the accompaniment of the organs, whence came a continuous hymn of glory. All possible luxury and magnificence were displayed, as if to turn this wedding into some public festivity, a great victory, an event marking the apogee of a class. Even the impudent bravado attaching to the loathsome private drama which lay behind it all, and which was known to everybody, added a touch of abominable grandeur to the ceremony. But

the truculent spirit of superiority and domination which cha-
racterised the proceedings became most manifest when Monseigneur Martha appeared in surplice and stole to pronounce
the blessing. Tall of stature, fresh of face, and faintly smiling,
he had his wonted air of amiable sovereignty, and it was
with august unction that he pronounced the sacramental
words, like some pontiff well pleased at reconciling the two
great empires whose heirs he united. His address to the
newly-married couple was awaited with curiosity. It proved
really marvellous—he himself triumphed in it. Was it not in
that same church that he had baptized the bride's mother,
that blonde Eve, who was still so beautiful, that Jewess whom
he himself had converted to the Catholic faith amidst the
tears of emotion shed by all Paris society? Was it not there
also that he had delivered his three famous addresses on the
New Spirit, whence dated, to his thinking, the rout of science,
the awakening of Christian spirituality, and that policy of
rallying to the Republic which was to lead to its conquest?

So it was assuredly allowable for him to indulge in some
delicate allusions, by way of congratulating himself on his
work, now that he was marrying a poor scion of the old aristocracy to the five millions of that *bourgeoise* heiress, in
whose person triumphed the class which had won the victory
in 1789, and was now master of the land. The fourth estate,
the duped, robbed people alone had no place in those festivities.
But by uniting the affianced pair before him in the bonds of
wedlock, Monseigneur Martha sealed the new alliance, gave
effect to the Pope's own policy, that stealthy effort of Jesuitical
Opportunism which would take democracy, power, and wealth
to wife, in order to subdue and control them. When the prelate reached his peroration he turned towards Monferrand,
who sat there smiling; and it was he, the Minister whom he
seemed to be addressing, while he expressed the hope that the
newly-married pair would ever lead a truly Christian life of
humility and obedience in all fear of God, of whose iron hand
he spoke as if it were that of some gendarme charged with main-
taining the peace of the world. Everybody was aware that
there was some diplomatic understanding between the
Bishop and the Minister, some secret pact or other whereby
both satisfied their passion for authority, their craving to in-
sinuate themselves into everything and reign supreme; and
thus when the spectators saw Monferrand smiling in his
somewhat sly, jovial way, they also exchanged smiles.

'Ah!' muttered Massot, who had remained near Duthil, 'how amused old Justus Steinberger would be, if he were here to see his grand-daughter marrying the last of the Quinsacs!'

'But these marriages are quite the thing, quite the fashion, my dear fellow,' the deputy replied. 'The Jews and the Christians, the *bourgeois* and the nobles, do quite right to come to an understanding, so as to found a new aristocracy. An aristocracy is needed, you know, for otherwise we should be swept away by the masses.'

None the less Massot continued sneering at the idea of what a grimace Justus Steinberger would have made if he had heard Monseigneur Martha. It was rumoured in Paris that although the old Jew banker had ceased all intercourse with his daughter Eve since her conversion, he took a keen interest in everything she was reported to do or say, as if he were more than ever convinced that she would prove an avenging and dissolving agent among those Christians, whose destruction was asserted to be the dream of his race. If he had failed in his hope of overcoming Duvillard by giving her to him as a wife, he doubtless now consoled himself with thinking of the extraordinary fortune to which his blood had attained, by mingling with that of the harsh, old-time masters of his race, to whose corruption it gave a finishing touch. Therein perhaps lay that final Jewish conquest of the world, of which people sometimes talked.

A last triumphal strain from the organs brought the ceremony to an end; whereupon the two families and the witnesses passed into the sacristy, where the acts were signed. And forthwith the great congratulatory procession commenced.

The bride and bridegroom at last stood side by side in the lofty but rather dim room, panelled with oak. How radiant with delight was Camille at the thought that it was all over, that she had triumphed and married that handsome man of high lineage, after wresting him with so much difficulty from one and all, her mother especially! She seemed to have grown taller. Deformed, swarthy, and ugly though she was, she drew herself up exultingly, whilst scores and scores of women, friends or acquaintances, scrambled and rushed upon her, pressing her hands or kissing her, and addressing her in words of ecstasy. Gérard, who rose both head and shoulders above his bride, and looked all the nobler and stronger beside

one of such puny figure, shook hands and smiled like some
Prince Charming, who good-naturedly allowed himself to be
loved.   Meanwhile, the relatives of the newly-wedded pair,
though they were drawn up in one line, formed two distinct
groups past which the crowd pushed and surged with
arms outstretched.   Duvillard received the congratulations
offered him, as if he were some king well pleased with his
people ; whilst Eve, with a supreme effort, put on an enchant-
ing mien, and answered one and all with scarcely a sign of
the sobs which she was forcing back.   Then, on the other
side of the bridal pair, Madame de Quinsac stood between
General de Bozonnet and the Marquis de Morigny.   Very
dignified, in fact almost haughty, she acknowledged most of the
salutations addressed to her with a mere nod, only giving her
little withered hand to those people with whom she was well
acquainted.   A sea of strange countenances encompassed
her, and now and again when some particularly murky wave
rolled by, a wave of men whose faces bespoke all the crimes of
money-mongering, she and the Marquis exchanged glances of
deep sadness.   This tide continued sweeping by for nearly
half an hour ; and such was the number of those who wanted
to shake hands with the bridal pair and their relatives, that
the latter soon felt their arms ache.

Meantime, some folks lingered in the sacristy ; little
groups collected, and gay chatter rang out.   Monferrand was
immediately surrounded.   Massot pointed out to Duthil how
eagerly Public Prosecutor Lehmann rushed upon the
Minister to pay him court.   They were immediately joined by
investigating magistrate Amadieu.   And even M. de Larombière, the judge, approached Monferrand, although he hated
the Republic, and was an intimate friend of the Quinsacs.
But then obedience and obsequiousness were necessary on
the part of the magistracy, for it was dependent on those in
power, who alone could give advancement, and appoint even
as they dismissed.   As for Lehmann, it was alleged that he
had rendered assistance to Monferrand by spiriting away
certain documents connected with the African Railways
affair ; whilst with regard to the smiling and extremely
Parisian Amadieu, was it not to him that the government was
indebted for Salvat's head ?

'You know,' muttered Massot, 'they've all come to be
thanked for guillotining that man yesterday.   Monferrand
owes that wretched fellow a fine taper ; for in the first place

his bomb prolonged the life of the Barroux ministry, and later on it made Monferrand prime minister, as a strong-handed man was particularly needed to strangle Anarchism. What a contest, eh? Monferrand on one side and Salvat on the other. It was all bound to end in a head being cut off; one was wanted. . . . Ah! just listen, they are talking of it.'

This was true. As the three functionaries of the law drew near to pay their respects to the all-powerful Minister, they were questioned by lady friends whose curiosity had been roused by what they had read in the newspapers. Thereupon Amadieu, whom duty had taken to the execution, and who was proud of his own importance, and determined to destroy what he called 'the legend of Salvat's heroic death,' declared that the scoundrel had shown no true courage at all. His pride alone had kept him on his feet. Fright had so shaken and choked him that he had virtually been dead before the fall of the knife.

'Ah! that's true!' cried Duthil. 'I was there myself.'

Massot, however, pulled him by the arm, quite indignant at such an assertion, although as a rule he cared a rap for nothing. 'You couldn't see anything, my dear fellow,' said he, 'Salvat died very bravely. It's really stupid to continue throwing mud at that poor devil even when he's dead.'

However, the idea that Salvat had died like a coward was too pleasing a one to be rejected. It was, so to say, a last sacrifice deposited at Monferrand's feet with the object of propitiating him. He still smiled in his peaceful way, like a good-natured man who is stern only when necessity requires it. And he showed great amiability towards the three judicial functionaries, and thanked them for the bravery with which they had accomplished their painful duty to the very end. On the previous day, after the execution, he had obtained a formidable majority in the Chamber on a somewhat delicate matter of policy. Order reigned, said he, and all was for the very best in France. Then, on seeing Vignon —who like a cool gamester had made a point of attending the wedding in order to show people that he was superior to fortune—the Minister detained him, and made much of him, partly as a matter of tactics, for in spite of everything he could not help fearing that the future might belong to that young fellow, who showed himself so intelligent and cautious. When a mutual friend informed them that Barroux' health was now so bad that the doctors had given him up as lost, they both began to express their compassion. Poor Barroux! he had never recovered from that vote of the Chamber which had overthrown him. He had been sinking from day to day, stricken in the heart by his country's ingratitude, dying of that abominable charge of money-mongering and thieving; he who was so upright and so loyal, who had devoted his whole life to the Republic! But then, as Monferrand repeated, one should never confess. The public can't understand such a thing.

At this moment Duvillard, in some degree relinquishing his paternal duties, came to join the others, and the Minister then had to share the honours of triumph with him. For was not this banker the master? Was he not money per-sonified—money, which is the only stable, everlasting force, far above all ephemeral tenure of power, such as attaches to those ministerial portfolios which pass so rapidly from hand to hand? Monferrand reigned, but he would pass away, and a like fate would some day fall on Vignon, who had already had a warning that one could not govern unless the millions of the financial world were on one's side. So was not the only real triumpher himself, the Baron—he who laid out five millions of francs on buying a scion of the aristocracy for his daughter, he who was the personification of the sovereign *bourgeoisie*, who controlled public fortune, and was determined to part with nothing, even were he attacked with bombs? All these festivities really centred in himself, he alone sat down to the banquet, leaving merely the crumbs from his table to the lowly, those wretched toilers who had been so cleverly duped at the time of the Revolution.

That African Railways affair was already but so much ancient history, buried, spirited away by a parliamentary commission. All who had been compromised in it, the Duthils, the Chaigneux, the Fonsègues and others, could now laugh merrily. They had been delivered from their nightmare by Monferrand's strong fist, and raised by Duvillard's triumph. Even Sagnier's ignoble article and miry revelations in the 'Voix du Peuple' were of no real account, and could be treated with a shrug of the shoulders, for the public had been so saturated with denunciation and slander that it was now utterly weary of all noisy scandal. The only thing which aroused interest was the rumour that Duvillard's big affair of the Trans-Saharian Railway was soon to be launched, that millions of money would be handled, and that some of them would rain down upon faithful friends.

Whilst Duvillard was conversing in a friendly way with Monferrand and Dauvergne, the Minister of Public Instruction, who had joined them, Massot encountered Fonsègue, his editor, and said to him in an undertone: 'Duthil has just assured me that the Trans-Saharian business is ready, and that they mean to chance it with the Chamber. They declare that they are certain of success.'

Fonsègue, however, was sceptical on the point. 'It's impossible,' said he, 'they surely won't dare to begin again so soon.'

Although he spoke in this fashion the news had made him grave. He had lately had such a terrible fright through his imprudence in the African Railways affair, that he had vowed he would take every precaution in future. Still this did not mean that he would refuse to participate in matters of business. The best course was to wait and study them, and then secure a share in all that seemed profitable. In the present instance he felt somewhat worried. However, whilst he stood there watching the group around Duvillard and the two ministers, he suddenly perceived Chaigneux, who, flitting hither and thither, was still beating up applauders for that evening's performance. He sang Silviane's praises in every key, predicted a most tremendous success, and did his very best to stimulate curiosity. At last he approached Dauvergne, and with his long figure bent double, exclaimed: 'My dear Minister, I have a particular request to make to you on the part of a very charming person, whose victory will not be complete this evening if you do not condescend to favour her with your vote.'

Dauvergne, a tall, fair, good-looking man, whose blue eyes smiled behind his glasses, listened to Chaigneux with an affable air. He was proving a great success at the Ministry of Public Instruction, although he knew nothing of University matters. However, like a real Parisian of Dijon, as people called him, he was possessed of some tact and skill, gave entertainments at which his young and charming wife outshone all others, and passed as being quite an enlightened friend of writers and artists. Silviane's engagement at the Comédie, which so far was his most notable achievement, and which would have shaken the position of any other minister, had by a curious chance rendered him popular. It was regarded as something original and amusing.

On understanding that Chaigneux simply wished to make sure of his presence at the Comédie that evening, he became yet more affable. 'Why, certainly, I shall be there, my dear deputy,' he replied. 'When one has such a charming god-daughter one mustn't forsake her in a moment of danger.'

At this Monferrand, who had been lending ear, turned round. 'And tell her,' said he, 'that I shall be there too. She may therefore rely on having two more friends in the house.'

Thereupon Duvillard, quite enraptured, his eyes glistening with emotion and gratitude, bowed to the two ministers as if they had granted him some never-to-be-forgotten favour.

When Chaigneux, on his side also, had returned thanks with a low bow, he happened to perceive Fonsègue, and forthwith he darted towards him and led him aside. 'Ah! my dear colleague,' he declared, 'it is absolutely necessary that this matter should be settled. I regard it as of supreme importance.'

'What are you speaking of?' inquired Fonsègue, much surprised.

'Why, of Massot's article, which you won't insert.'

Thereupon, the director of the 'Globe' plumply declared that he could not insert the article. He talked of his paper's dignity and gravity; and declared that the lavishing of much fulsome praise upon a hussy—yes, a mere hussy—in a journal whose exemplary morality and austerity had cost him so much labour, would seem monstrous and degrading. Personally, he did not care a fig about it; if Silviane chose to make an exhibition of herself, well, he would be there to see; but the 'Globe' was sacred.

Disconcerted and almost tearful, Chaigneux nevertheless renewed his attempt. 'Come, my dear colleague,' said he, 'pray make a little effort for my sake. If the article isn't inserted Duvillard will think that it is my fault. And you know that I really need his help. My eldest daughter's marriage has again been postponed, and I hardly know where to turn.' Then perceiving that his own misfortunes in no wise touched Fonsègue, he added: 'And do it for your own sake, my dear colleague, your own sake. For when all is said Duvillard knows what is in the article, and it is precisely because it is so favourable a one that he wishes to see it in the

" Globe." Think it over ; if the article isn't published he will
certainly turn his back on you.'

For a moment Fonsègue remained silent. Was he thinking of the colossal Trans-Saharian enterprise ? Was he
reflecting that it would be hard to quarrel at such a moment
and miss his own share in the coming distribution of millions
among faithful friends ? Perhaps so ; however, the idea that
it would be more prudent to await developments gained the
day with him. 'No, no,' he said; 'I can't, it's a matter of
conscience.'

In the meantime congratulations were still being tendered
to the newly-wedded couple. It seemed as if all Paris were
passing through the sacristy ; there were ever the same smiles
and the same hand shakes. Gérard, Camille, and their
relatives, however weary they might feel, were forced to retain
an air of delight while they stood there against the wall, pent
up by the crowd. The heat was now really becoming unbearable, and a cloud of dust arose as when some big flock
goes by.

All at once little Princess de Harn, who had hitherto
lingered nobody knew where, sprang out of the throng, flung her
arms round Camille, kissed even Eve, and then kept Gérard's
hand in her own while paying him extraordinary compliments.
Then, on perceiving Hyacinthe, she took possession of him
and carried him off into a corner. ' I say,' she exclaimed, ' I
have a favour to ask you.'

The young man was wonderfully silent that day. His
sister's wedding seemed to him a contemptible ceremony, the
most vulgar that one could imagine. So here, thought he,
was another pair accepting the horrid sexual law by which
the absurdity of the world was perpetuated ! For his part, he
had decided that he would witness the proceedings in rigid
silence with a haughty air of disapproval. When Rosemonde
spoke to him, he looked at her rather nervously, for he was glad
that she had forsaken him for Duthil, and feared some fresh
caprice on her part. At last, opening his mouth for the first
time that day, he replied : ' Oh, as a friend, you know, I will
grant you whatever favour you like.'

Forthwith the Princess explained that she should surely
die if she did not witness the *début* of her dear friend Silviane,
of whom she had become such a passionate admirer. So she
begged the young man to prevail on his father to give her a
seat in his box, as she knew that one was left there.

Hyacinthe smiled. ' Oh willingly, my dear,' said he ; ' I'll warn papa, there will be a seat for you.'

Then, as the procession of guests at last drew to an end and the vestry began to empty, the bridal pair and their relatives were able to go off through the chattering throng, which still lingered about to bow to them and scrutinise them once more.

Gérard and Camille were to leave for an estate which Duvillard possessed in Normandy, directly after lunch. This repast, served at the princely mansion of the Rue Godot-de-Mauroy, provided an opportunity for fresh display. The dining-room on the first floor had been transformed into a buffet, where reigned the greatest abundance and the most wonderful sumptuousness. Quite a reception too was held in the drawing-rooms, the large red *salon*, the little blue and silver *salon* and all the others, whose doors stood wide open. Although it had been arranged that only family friends should be invited there were quite three hundred people present. The ministers had excused themselves, alleging that the weighty cares of public business required their presence elsewhere. But the magistrates, the deputies, and the leading journalists who had attended the wedding were again assembled together. And in that throng of hungry folks, longing for some of the spoils of Duvillard's new venture, the people who felt most out of their element were Madame de Quinsac's few guests, whom General de Bozonnet and the Marquis de Morigny had seated on a sofa in the large red *salon*, which they did not quit.

Eve who, for her part, was quite overcome, both her moral and physical strength being exhausted, had seated herself in the little blue and silver drawing-room, which, with her passion for flowers, she had transformed into an arbour of roses. She would have fallen had she remained standing, the very floor had seemed to sink beneath her feet. Nevertheless, whenever a guest approached her she managed to force a smile, and appear beautiful and charming. Unlooked for help at last came to her in the person of Monseigneur Martha, who had graciously honoured the lunch with his presence. He took an armchair near her, and began to talk to her in his amiable, caressing way. He was doubtless well aware of the frightful anguish which wrung the poor woman's heart, for he showed himself quite fatherly, eager to comfort her. She, however, talked on like some inconsolable widow bent on re-

nouncing the world for God, who alone could bring her peace.
Then as the conversation turned on the Asylum for the
Invalids of Labour, she declared that she was resolved to take
her presidency very seriously, and, in fact, would exclusively
devote herself to it, in the future.

'And as we are speaking of this, Monseigneur,' said she, 'I
would even ask you to give me some advice. . . . I shall
need somebody to help me, and I thought of securing the
services of a priest whom I much admire, Monsieur l'Abbé
Pierre Froment.'

At this the Bishop became grave and embarrassed; but
Princess Rosemonde, who was passing by with Duthil, had
overheard the Baroness, and drawing near with her wonted
impetuosity, she exclaimed : 'Abbé Pierre Froment ! Oh ! I
forgot to tell you, my dear, that I met him going about in
jacket and trousers ! And I've been told too that he cycles
in the Bois with some creature or other. Isn't it true, Duthil,
that we met him ? '

The deputy bowed and smiled, whilst Eve clasped her
hands in amazement. 'Is it possible ! A priest who was
all charitable fervour, who had the faith and passion of an
apostle ! '

Thereupon Monseigneur intervened : 'Yes, yes, great
sorrows occasionally fall on the Church. I heard of the madness of the unhappy man you speak of. I even thought it
my duty to write to him, but he left my letter unanswered.
I should so much have liked to stifle such a scandal ! But
there are abominable forces which we cannot always overcome ; and so a day or two ago the archbishop was obliged
to put him under interdict. . . . You must choose somebody
else, madame.'

It was quite a disaster. Eve gazed at Rosemonde and
Duthil, without daring to ask them for particulars, but
wondering what creature could have been so audacious as to
turn a priest from the path of duty. She must assuredly be
some shameless, demented woman ! And it seemed to Eve
as if this crime gave a finishing touch to her own misfortune.
With a wave of the arm, which took in all the luxury around
her, the roses steeping her in perfume, and the crush of
guests around the buffet, she murmured : 'Ah ! decidedly
there's nothing but corruption left ; one can no longer rely
on anybody ! '

Whilst this was going on, Camille happened to be alone in

her own room getting ready to leave the house with Gérard.
And all at once her brother Hyacinthe joined her there. 'Ah!
it's you, youngster!' she exclaimed. 'Well, make haste if you
want to kiss me, for I'm off now, thank goodness!'

He kissed her as she suggested, and then in a doctoral way
replied: 'I thought you had more self-command. The
delight you have been showing all this morning quite
disgusts me.'

A quiet glance of contempt was her only answer.
However, he continued: 'You know very well that she'll
take your Gérard from you again, directly you come back to
Paris.'

At this Camille's cheeks turned white and her eyes flared.
She stepped towards her brother with clenched fists: 'She!
you say that she will take him from me!'

The 'she' they referred to was their own mother.

'Listen, my boy! I'll kill her first!' continued Camilla
'Ah, no! she needn't hope for that. I shall know how to
keep the man that belongs to me. . . . And as for you, keep
your spite to yourself, for I know you, remember; you are a
mere child and a fool!'

He recoiled as if a viper were rearing its sharp, slender,
black head before him; and having always feared her, he
thought it best to beat a retreat.

While the last guests were rushing upon the buffet and
finishing the pillage there, the bridal pair took their leave,
before driving off to the railway-station. General de
Bozonnet had joined a group in order to vent his usual
complaints about compulsory military service, and the
Marquis de Morigny was obliged to fetch him at the moment
when the Countess de Quinsac was kissing her son and
daughter-in-law. The old lady trembled with so much
emotion that the Marquis respectfully ventured to sustain
her. Meantime, Hyacinthe had started in search of his
father, and at last found him near a window with the
tottering Chaigneux, whom he was violently upbraiding, for
Fonsègue's conscientious scruples had put him in a fury.
Indeed, if Massot's article should not be inserted in the
'Globe,' Silviane might lay all the blame upon him, the
Baron, and punish him yet further. However, on being
summoned by his son, he was obliged to don his triumphal
air once more, kiss his daughter on the forehead, shake hands
with his son-in-law, jest and wish them both a pleasant

journey. Then Eve, near whom Monseigneur Martha had remained smiling, in her turn had to say farewell. In this she evinced touching bravery; her determination to remain beautiful and charming until the very end lent her sufficient strength to show both gaiety and motherliness.

She took hold of the slightly quivering hand which Gérard proffered with some embarrassment, and ventured to retain it for a moment in her own, in a good-hearted, affectionate way, instinct with all the heroism of renunciation. 'Good-bye, Gérard,' she said, 'keep in good health, be happy.' Then turning to Camille she kissed her on both cheeks, while Monseigneur Martha sat looking at them with an air of indulgent sympathy. They wished each other 'Au revoir,' but their voices trembled, and their eyes in meeting gleamed like swords; in the same way as beneath the kisses they had exchanged they had felt each other's teeth. Ah! how it enraged Camille to see her mother still so beautiful and fascinating in spite of age and grief! And for Eve how great the torture of beholding her daughter's youth, that youth which had overcome her, and was for ever wresting love from within her reach! No forgiveness was possible between them; they would still hate one another even in the family tomb, where some day they would sleep side by side.

All the same, that evening Baroness Duvillard excused herself from attending the performance of 'Polyeucte' at the Comédie-Française. She felt very tired and wished to go to bed early, said she. As a matter of fact she wept on her pillow all night long. Thus the Baron's stage-box on the first balcony tier only contained himself, Hyacinthe, Duthil, and little Princess de Harn.

At nine o'clock there was a full house, one of the brilliant chattering houses peculiar to great dramatic solemnities. All the society people who had marched through the sacristy of the Madeleine that morning were now assembled at the theatre, again feverish with curiosity, and on the look-out for the unexpected. One recognised the same faces and the same smiles; the women acknowledged one another's presence with little signs of intelligence, the men understood each other at a word, a gesture. One and all had kept the appointment, the ladies with bared shoulders, the gentlemen with flowers in their button-holes. Fonsègue occupied the 'Globe's' box with two friendly families.

Little Massot had his customary seat in the stalls. Amadieu, who was a faithful patron of the Comédie, was also to be seen there, as well as General de Bozonnet and Public Prosecutor Lehmann. The man who was most looked at, however, on account of his scandalous article that morning, was Sagnier, the terrible Sagnier with a bloated, apoplectical face. Then there was Chaigneux, who had merely kept a modest bracket-seat for himself, and who scoured the passages, and climbed to every tier, for the last time preaching enthusiasm. Finally, the two ministers, Monferrand and Dauvergne, appeared in the box facing Duvillard's; whereupon many knowing smiles were exchanged, for everybody was aware that these personages had come to help on the success of the *débutante*.

On the latter point there had still been unfavourable rumours only the previous day. Sagnier had declared that the *début* of such a notorious harlot as Silviane at the Comédie-Française, in such a part too as that of 'Pauline,' which was one of so much moral loftiness, could only be regarded as an impudent insult to public decency. The whole press, moreover, had long been up in arms against the young woman's extraordinary caprice. But then the affair had been talked of for six months past, so that Paris had grown used to the idea of seeing Silviane at the Comédie. And now it flocked thither with the one idea of being entertained. Before the curtain rose one could tell by the very atmosphere of the house that the audience was a jovial, good-humoured one, bent on enjoying itself and ready to applaud should it find itself at all pleased.

The performance really proved extraordinary. When Silviane, chastely robed, made her appearance in the first act, the house was quite astonished by her virginal face, her innocent-looking mouth, and her eyes beaming with immaculate candour. Then, although the manner in which she had understood her part at first amazed people, it ended by charming them. From the moment of confiding in 'Stratonice,' from the moment of relating her dream, she turned 'Pauline' into a soaring mystical creature, some saint, as it were, such as one sees in stained-glass windows, carried along by a Wagnerian Brunhilda riding the clouds. It was a thoroughly ridiculous conception of the part, contrary to reason and truth alike. Still it only seemed to interest people the more, partly on account of mysticism being the fashion, and partly on account of the contrast between Silviane's assumed

candour and real depravity. Her success increased from act
to act, and some slight hissing which was attributed to
Sagnier only helped to make the victory more complete.
Monferrand and Dauvergne, as the newspapers afterwards
related, gave the signal for applause; and the whole house
joined in it partly from amusement and partly perhaps in a
spirit of irony.

During the interval between the fourth and fifth acts there
was quite a procession of visitors to Duvillard's box, where
the greatest excitement prevailed. Duthil, however, after
absenting himself for a moment, came back to say: 'You
remember our influential critic, the one whom I brought to
dinner at the Café Anglais. Well, he's repeating to everybody
that "Pauline" is merely a little *bourgeoise*, and is not transformed by the heavenly grace until the very finish of the
piece. To turn her into a holy virgin from the outset simply
kills the part, says he.'

'Pooh!' retorted Duvillard, 'let him argue if he likes, it
will be all the more advertisement. . . . The important point
is to get Massot's article inserted in the "Globe" to-morrow
morning.'

On this point unfortunately the news was by no means
good. Chaigneux, who had gone in search of Fonsègue,
declared that the latter still hesitated in the matter in spite
of Silviane's success, which he declared to be ridiculous.
Thereupon the Baron became quite angry. 'Go and tell
Fonsègue,' he exclaimed, 'that I insist on it, and that I shall
remember what he does.'

Meantime Princess Rosemonde was becoming quite
delirious with enthusiasm. 'My dear Hyacinthe,' she pleaded,
'please take me to Silviane's dressing-room; I can't wait, I
really must go and kiss her.'

'But we'll all go!' cried Duvillard, who heard her
entreaty.

The passages were crowded, and there were people even
on the stage. Moreover, when the party reached the door
of Silviane's dressing-room, they found it shut. When the
Baron knocked at it, a dresser replied that Madame begged
the gentlemen to wait a moment.

'Oh! a woman may surely go in,' replied Rosemonde,
hastily slipping through the doorway. 'And you may come,
Hyacinthe,' she added, 'there can be no objection to you.'

Silviane was very hot, and a dresser was wiping her

perspiring shoulders when Rosemonde darted forward and
kissed her. Then they chatted together amidst the heat
and glare from the gas and the intoxicating perfumes of all
the flowers which were heaped up in the little room. Finally,
Hyacinthe heard them promise to see one another after the
performance, Silviane even inviting Rosemonde to drink a
cup of tea with her at her house. At this the young man
smiled complacently, and said to the actress : ' Your carriage
is waiting for you at the corner of the Rue Montpensier, is
it not ? Well, I'll take the Princess to it. That will be the
simpler plan, you can both go off together ! '

' Oh ! how good of you,' cried Rosemonde ; ' it's agreed.'

Just then the door was opened, and the men being admitted, began to pour forth their congratulations. However,
they had to regain their seats in all haste so as to witness
the fifth act. This proved quite a triumph ; the whole house
burst into applause when Silviane spoke the famous line,
' I see, I know, I believe, I am undeceived,' with the rapturous enthusiasm of a holy martyr ascending to heaven.
Nothing could have been more soul-like, it was said. And so
when the performers were called before the curtain, Paris
bestowed an ovation on that virgin of the stage who, as
Sagnier put it, knew so well how to act depravity at home.

Accompanied by Duthil, Duvillard at once went behind
the scenes in order to fetch Silviane, while Hyacinthe
escorted Rosemonde to the brougham waiting at the corner
of the Rue Montpensier. Having helped her into it, the
young man stood by waiting. And he seemed to grow
quite merry when his father came up with Silviane, and was
stopped by her just as, in his turn, he wished to get into the
carriage.

' There's no room for you, my dear fellow,' said she. ' I've
a friend with me.'

Rosemonde's little smiling face then peered forth from
the depths of the brougham. And the Baron remained there
open-mouthed while the vehicle swiftly carried the two women
away !

' Well, what would you have, my dear fellow ? ' said
Hyacinthe, by way of explanation to Duthil, who also seemed
somewhat amazed by what had happened. ' Rosemonde was
worrying my life out, and so I got rid of her by packing her
off with Silviane.'

Duvillard was still standing on the pavement and still

looking dazed when Chaigneux, who was going home quite tired out, recognised him, and came up to say that Fonsègue had thought the matter over, and that Massot's article would be inserted. It seemed that in the passages there had been a deal of talk about the famous Trans-Saharian project.

Then Hyacinthe led his father away, trying to comfort him like a sensible friend, who regarded woman as a base and impure creature. 'Let's go home to bed,' said he. 'As that article is to appear, you can take it to her to-morrow. She will see you, sure enough.'

Thereupon they lighted cigars, and now and again exchanging a few words, took their way up the Avenue de l'Opéra, which at that hour was deserted and dismal. Meantime, above the slumbering houses of Paris the breeze wafted a prolonged sigh, the plaint, as it were, of an expiring world.

III

THE GOAL OF LABOUR

EVER since the execution of Salvat, Guillaume had become extremely taciturn. He seemed worried and absent-minded. He would work for hours at the manufacture of that dangerous powder of which he alone knew the formula, and the preparation of which was such a delicate matter that he would allow none to assist him. Then, at other times he would go off, and return tired out by some long solitary ramble. He remained very gentle at home, and strove to smile there. But whenever anybody spoke to him he started as if suddenly called back from dreamland.

Pierre imagined his brother had relied too much upon his powers of renunciation, and found the loss of Marie unbearable. Was it not some thought of her that haunted him now that the date fixed for the marriage drew nearer and nearer? One evening, therefore, Pierre ventured to speak out, again offering to leave the house and disappear.

But at the first words he uttered Guillaume stopped him, and affectionately replied: 'Marie? Oh! I love her, I love her too well to regret what I have done. No, no! you only bring me happiness, I derive all my strength and courage from you now that I know you are both happy. . . . And I assure you that you are mistaken, there is nothing at all the matter with me; my work absorbs me, perhaps, but that is all.'

That same evening he managed to cast his gloom aside, and displayed delightful gaiety. During dinner he inquired if the upholsterer would soon call to arrange the two little rooms which Marie was to occupy with her husband over the workroom. The young woman, who, since her marriage with Pierre had been decided, had remained waiting with smiling patience, thereupon told Guillaume what it was she desired— first, some hangings of red cotton stuff, then some polished pine furniture which would enable her to imagine she was in the country, and finally a carpet on the floor, because a carpet seemed to her the height of luxury. She laughed as she spoke, and Guillaume laughed with her in a gay and fatherly way. His good spirits brought considerable relief to Pierre, who concluded that he must have been mistaken in his surmises.

On the very morrow, however, Guillaume relapsed into a dreamy state. And so disquietude again came upon Pierre, particularly when he noticed that Mère-Grand also seemed to be unusually grave and silent. Not daring to address her, he tried to extract some information from his nephews, but neither Thomas nor François nor Antoine knew anything. Each of them quietly devoted his time to his work, respecting and worshipping his father, but never questioning him about his plans or enterprises. Whatever he might choose to do could only be right and good; and they, his sons, were ready to do the same and help him at the very first call, without pausing to inquire into his purpose. It was plain, however, that he kept them apart from anything at all perilous, that he retained all responsibility for himself, and that Mère-Grand alone was his *confidante*, the one whom he consulted and to whom he perhaps listened. Pierre therefore renounced his hope of learning anything from the sons, and directed his attention to the old lady, whose rigid gravity worried him the more as she and Guillaume frequently had private chats in the room she occupied upstairs. They shut themselves up there all alone, and remained together for hours without the faintest sound coming from the seemingly lifeless chamber.

One day, however, Pierre caught sight of Guillaume as he came out of it, carrying a little valise which appeared to be very heavy. And Pierre thereupon remembered both his brother's powder, one pound weight of which would have sufficed to destroy a cathedral, and the destructive engine which he had purposed bestowing upon France in order that she might be victorious over all other nations, and become the one great initiatory and liberative power. Pierre remembered too that the only person besides himself who knew his brother's secret was Mère-Grand, who, at the time when Guillaume was fearing some perquisition on the part of the police, had long slept upon the cartridges of the terrible explosive. But now why was Guillaume removing all the powder which he had been preparing for some time past? As this question occurred to Pierre a sudden suspicion, a vague dread came upon him, and gave him strength to ask his brother : 'Have you reason to fear anything, since you won't keep things here? If they embarrass you, they can be deposited at my house, nobody will make a search there.'

Guillaume, whom these words astonished, gazed at Pierre fixedly, and then replied : ' Yes, I have learnt that the arrests and perquisitions have begun afresh since that poor devil was guillotined; for they are in terror at the thought that some despairing fellow may avenge him. Moreover, it is hardly prudent to keep destructive agents of such great power here. I prefer to deposit them in a safe place. But not at Neuilly—oh ! no indeed ! they are not a present for you, brother.' Guillaume spoke with outward calmness ; and if he had started with surprise at the first moment, it had scarcely been perceptible.

' So everything is ready ? ' Pierre resumed. 'You will soon be handing your engine of destruction over to the Minister of War, I presume ? '

A gleam of hesitation appeared in the depths of Guillaume's eyes, and he was for a moment about to tell a falsehood. However, he ended by replying : 'No, I have renounced that intention. I have another idea.'

He spoke these last words with so much energy and decision that Pierre did not dare to question him further, to ask him, for instance, what that other idea might be. From that moment, however, he quivered with anxious expectancy. From hour to hour Mère-Grand's lofty silence, and Guillaume's rapt, energetic face seemed to tell him that some huge and terrifying scheme had come into being, and was growing and threatening the whole of Paris.

One afternoon, just as Thomas was about to repair to the

Grandidier works, someone came to Guillaume's with the
news that old Toussaint, the workman, had been stricken
with a fresh attack of paralysis. Thomas thereupon decided
that he would call upon the poor fellow on his way, for he
held him in esteem and wished to ascertain if he could render
him any help. Pierre expressed a desire to accompany his
nephew, and they started off together about four o'clock.

On entering the one room which the Toussaints occupied, the room where they ate and slept, the visitors found
the mechanician seated on a low chair near the table. He
looked half dead, as if struck by lightning. It was a case of
hemiplegia, which had paralysed the whole of his right side,
his right leg and right arm, and had also spread to his face in
such wise that he could no longer speak. The only sound he
could raise was an incomprehensible guttural grunt. His
mouth was drawn to the right, and his once round good-
natured looking face, with tanned skin and bright eyes, had
been twisted into a frightful mask of anguish. At fifty years of
age, the unhappy man was utterly done for. His unkempt
beard was as white as that of an octogenarian, and his knotty
limbs, preyed upon by toil, were henceforth dead. Only his
eyes remained alive, and they travelled around the room, going
from one to another. By his side, eager to do what she could
for him, was his wife, who remained stout even when she had
little to eat, and still showed herself active and clear-headed,
however great her misfortunes.

' It's a friendly visit, Toussaint,' said she. ' It's Monsieur
Thomas who has come to see you with Monsieur l'Abbé.'
Then, quietly correcting herself, she added : ' With Monsieur
Pierre, his uncle. You see that you are not yet forsaken.'

Toussaint wished to speak, but his fruitless efforts only
brought two big tears to his eyes. Then he gazed at his
visitors with an expression of indescribable woe, his jaws
trembling convulsively.

' Don't put yourself out,' repeated his wife. ' The doctor
told you that it would do you no good.'

At the moment of entering the room Pierre had already
noticed two persons who had risen from their chairs and drawn
somewhat on one side. And now to his great surprise he
recognised that they were Madame Théodore and Céline, who
were both decently clad, and looked as if they led a life of
comfort. On hearing of Toussaint's misfortune they had come
to see him, like good-hearted creatures, who, on their own side,

had experienced the most cruel suffering. Pierre, on noticing that they now seemed to be beyond dire want, remembered what he had heard of the wonderful sympathy lavished on the child after her father's execution, the many presents and donations offered her, and the generous proposals that had been made to adopt her. These last had ended in her being adopted by a former friend of Salvat who had sent her to school again, pending the time when she might be apprenticed to some trade ; while, on the other hand, Madame Théodore had been placed as a nurse in a convalescent home ; in such wise that both had been saved.

When Pierre drew near to little Céline in order to kiss her, Madame Théodore told her to thank Monsieur l'Abbé—for so she still respectfully called him—for all that he had previously done for her. 'It was you who brought us happiness, Monsieur l'Abbé,' said she. 'And that's a thing one can never forget. I'm always telling Céline to remember you in her prayers.'

'And so, my child, you are now going to school again,' said Pierre.

'Oh! yes, Monsieur l'Abbé, and I'm well pleased at it. Besides, we no longer lack anything.' Then, however, sudden emotion came over the girl, and she stammered with a sob : 'Ah! if poor papa could only see us ! '

Madame Théodore, meanwhile, had begun to take leave of Madame Toussaint. 'Well, good-bye, we must go,' said she. 'What has happened to you is very sad, and we wanted to tell you how much it grieved us. The worry is that when misfortune falls on one, courage isn't enough to set things right. . . . Céline, come and kiss your uncle. . . . My poor brother, I hope you'll get back the use of your legs as soon as possible.'

They kissed the paralysed man on the cheeks, and then went off. Toussaint had looked at them with his keen and still intelligent eyes, as if he longed to participate in the life and activity into which they were returning. And a jealous thought came to his wife, who usually was so placid and good-natured. 'Ah! my poor old man ! ' she said, after propping him up with a pillow, 'those two are luckier than we are. Everything succeeds with them since that madman Salvat had his head cut off. They're provided for. They've plenty of bread on the shelf.'

Then, turning towards Pierre and Thomas, she continued :

'We others are done for, you know; we're down in the mud, with no hope of getting out of it. But what would you have? My poor husband hasn't been guillotined, he's done nothing but work his whole life long; and now, you see, that's the end of him, he's like some old animal, no longer good for anything.'

Having made her visitors sit down she next answered their compassionate questions. The doctor had called twice already, and had promised to restore the unhappy man's power of speech, and perhaps enable him to crawl round the room with the help of a stick. But as for ever being able to resume real work that must not be expected. And so what was the use of living on? Toussaint's eyes plainly declared that he would much rather die at once. When a workman can no longer work and no longer provide for his wife he is ripe for the grave.

'Savings indeed!' Madame Toussaint resumed. 'There are folks who ask us if we have any savings. . . . Well, we had nearly a thousand francs in the Savings Bank when Toussaint had his first attack. And some people don't know what a lot of prudence one needs to put by such a sum; for, after all, we're not savages, we have to allow ourselves a little enjoyment now and then, a good dish and a good bottle of wine. . . . Well, what with five months of enforced idleness, and the medicines, and the underdone meat that was ordered, we got to the end of our thousand francs; and now that it's all begun again we're not likely to taste any more bottled wine or roast mutton.'

Fond of good cheer as she had always been, this cry, far more than the tears she was forcing back, revealed how much the future terrified her. She was there erect and brave in spite of everything; but what a downfall if she were no longer able to keep her room tidy, stew a piece of veal on Sundays, and gossip with the neighbours while awaiting her husband's return from work! Why, they might just as well be thrown into the gutter and carried off in the scavenger's cart.

However, Thomas intervened: 'Isn't there an Asylum for the Invalids of Labour, and couldn't your husband get admitted to it?' he asked. 'It seems to me that is just the place for him.'

'Oh! dear no,' the woman answered. 'People spoke to me of that place before, and I got particulars of it. They don't take sick people there. When you call they tell you that there are hospitals for those who are ill.'

With a wave of his hand Pierre confirmed her statement: it was useless to apply in that direction. He could again see himself scouring Paris, hurrying from the Lady President, Baroness Duvillard, to Fonsègue, the General Manager, and only securing a bed for Laveuve when the unhappy man was dead!

However, at that moment an infant was heard wailing, and to the amazement of both visitors Madame Toussaint entered the little closet where her son Charles had so long slept, and came out of it carrying a child, who looked scarcely twenty months old. 'Well, yes,' she explained, 'this is Charles's boy. He was sleeping there in his father's old bed, and now you hear him, he's woke up. . . . You see, only last Wednesday, the day before Toussaint had his stroke, I went to fetch the little one at the nurse's at St. Denis, because she had threatened to cast him adrift since Charles had got into bad habits, and no longer paid her. I said to myself at the time that work was looking up, and that my husband and I would always be able to provide for a little mouth like that. . . . But just afterwards everything collapsed! At the same time, as the child's here now, I can't go and leave him in the street.'

While speaking in this fashion she walked to and fro, rocking the baby in her arms. And naturally enough she reverted to Charles's folly with the girl, who had run away, leaving that infant behind her. Things might not have been so very bad if Charles had still worked as steadily as he had done before he went soldiering. In those days he had never lost an hour, and had always brought all his pay home! But he had come back from the army with much less taste for work. He argued, and had ideas of his own. He certainly hadn't yet come to bomb-throwing like that madman Salvat, but he spent half his time with Socialists and Anarchists, who put his brain in a muddle. It was a real pity to see such a strong, good-hearted young fellow turning out badly like that. But it was said in the neighbourhood that many another was inclined the same way; that the best and most intelligent of the younger men felt tired of want and unremunerative labour, and would end by knocking everything to pieces rather than go on toiling with no certainty of food in their old age.

'Ah! yes,' continued Madame Toussaint, 'the sons are

not like the fathers were. These fine fellows won't be as
patient as my poor husband has been, letting hard work wear
him away till he's become the sorry thing you see there. . . .
Do you know what Charles said the other evening when he
found his father on that chair, crippled like that, and unable
to speak ? Why he shouted to him that he'd been a stupid
jackass all his life, working himself to death for those
bourgeois, who now wouldn't bring him so much as a glass of
water. Then, as he none the less has a good heart, he began
to cry his eyes out.'

The baby was no longer wailing, still the good woman
continued walking to and fro, rocking it in her arms and
pressing it to her affectionate heart. Her son Charles could
do no more for them, she said ; perhaps he might be able to
give them a five-franc piece now and again, but even that
wasn't certain. It was of no use for her to go back to her
old calling as a seamstress, she had lost all practice of it.
And it would even be difficult for her to earn anything as
charwoman, for she had that infant on her hands as well
as her infirm husband—a big child, whom she would have to
wash and feed. And so what would become of the three of
them ? She couldn't tell ; but it made her shudder, however
brave and motherly she tried to be.

For their part, Pierre and Thomas quivered with compassion, particularly when they saw big tears coursing down
the cheeks of the wretched, stricken Toussaint, as he sat quite
motionless in that little and still cleanly home of toil and
want. The poor man had listened to his wife, and he looked
at her and at the infant now sleeping in her arms. Voiceless,
unable to cry his woe aloud, he experienced the most awful
anguish. What dupery his long life of labour had been !
how frightfully unjust it was that all his efforts should end
in such sufferings ! how exasperating it was to feel himself
powerless, and to see those whom he loved and who were as
innocent as himself suffer and die by reason of his own
suffering and death ! Ah ! poor old man, cripple that he was,
ending like some beast of burden that has foundered by the
roadside—that goal of labour ! And it was all so revolting
and so monstrous that he tried to put it into words, and his
desperate grief ended in a frightful, raucous grunt.

'Be quiet, don't do yourself harm ! ' concluded Madame
Toussaint. 'Things are like that, and there's no mending
them.

Then she went to put the child to bed again, and on her return, just as Thomas and Pierre were about to speak to her of Toussaint's employer, M. Grandidier, a fresh visitor arrived. Thereupon the others decided to wait.

The new-comer was Madame Chrétiennot, Toussaint's other sister, eighteen years younger than himself. Her husband, the little clerk, had compelled her to break off almost all intercourse with her relatives, as he felt ashamed of them; nevertheless, having heard of her brother's misfortune, she had very properly come to condole with him. She wore a gown of cheap flimsy silk, and a hat trimmed with red poppies, which she had freshened up three times already; but in spite of this display her appearance bespoke penury, and she did her best to hide her feet on account of the shabbiness of her boots. Moreover, she was no longer the beautiful Hortense. Since a recent miscarriage, all trace of her good looks had disappeared.

The lamentable appearance of her brother and the bareness of that home of suffering chilled her directly she crossed the threshold. And as soon as she had kissed Toussaint, and said how sorry she was to find him in such a condition, she began to lament her own fate, and recount her troubles, for fear lest she should be asked for any help.

'Ah! my dear,' she said to her sister-in-law, 'you are certainly much to be pitied! But if you only knew! We all have our worries. Thus in my case, obliged as I am to dress fairly well on account of my husband's position, I have more trouble than you can imagine in making both ends meet. One can't go far on a salary of three thousand francs a year, when one has to pay seven hundred francs rent out of it. You will perhaps say that we might lodge ourselves in a more modest way; but we can't, my dear, I must have a *salon* on account of the visits I receive. So just count! . . . Then there are my two girls. I've had to send them to school; Lucienne has begun to learn the piano and Marcelle has some taste for drawing. . . . By the way, I would have brought them with me, but I feared it would upset them too much. You will excuse me, won't you?'

Then she spoke of all the worries which she had had with her husband on account of Salvat's ignominious death. Chrétiennot, vain, quarrelsome little fellow that he was, felt exasperated at now having a *guillotiné* in his wife's family. And he had lately begun to treat the unfortunate woman

most harshly, charging her with having brought about all
their troubles, and even rendering her responsible for his own
mediocrity, embittered as he was more and more each day by
a confined life of office work. On some evenings they had
serious quarrels; she stood up for herself, and related that
when she was at the confectionery shop in the Rue des
Martyrs she could have married a doctor had she only chosen,
for the doctor found her quite pretty enough. Now, however,
she was becoming plainer and plainer, and her husband felt
that he was condemned to everlasting penury; so that their
life was becoming more and more dismal and quarrelsome,
and as unbearable—despite the pride of being 'gentleman'
and 'lady'—as was the destitution of the working classes.

'All the same, my dear,' at last said Madame Toussaint,
weary of her sister-in-law's endless narrative of worries, 'you
have had one piece of luck. You won't have the trouble of
bringing up a third child, now.'

'That's true,' replied Hortense, with a sigh of relief.
'How we should have managed, I don't know. . . . Still, I was
very ill, and I'm far from being in good health now. The
doctor says that I don't eat enough, and that I ought to have
good food.'

Then she rose for the purpose of giving her brother another
kiss and taking her departure; for she feared a scene on her
husband's part should he happen to come home and find her
absent. Once on her feet, however, she lingered there a
moment longer, saying that she also had just seen her sister
Madame Théodore and little Céline, both of them comfortably
clad and looking happy. And with a touch of jealousy she
added: 'Well, my husband contents himself with slaving
away at his office every day. He'll never do anything to get
his head cut off; and it's quite certain that nobody will think
of leaving an income to Marcelle and Lucienne. . . . Well,
good-bye, my dear, you must be brave, one must always hope
that things will turn out for the best.'

When she had gone off, Pierre and Thomas inquired if M.
Grandidier had heard of Toussaint's misfortune and agreed to
do anything for him. Madame Toussaint answered that he
had so far made only a vague promise; and on learning this
they resolved to speak to him as warmly as they could on
behalf of the old mechanician, who had spent as many as
five-and-twenty years at the works. The misfortune was that
a scheme for establishing a friendly society, and even a

pension fund, which had been launched before the crisis from which the works were now recovering, had collapsed through a number of obstacles and complications. Had things turned out otherwise, Thomas might have had a pittance assured him, even though he was unable to work. But under the circumstances the only hope for the poor stricken fellow lay in his employer's compassion, if not his sense of justice.

As the baby again began to cry, Madame Toussaint went to fetch it, and she was once more carrying it to and fro, when Thomas pressed her husband's sound hand between both his own. 'We will come back,' said the young man, 'we won't forsake you, Toussaint. You know very well that people like you, for you've always been a good and steady workman. So rely on us, we will do all we can.'

Then they left him tearful and overpowered, in that dismal room, while, up and down beside him, his wife rocked the squealing infant—that other luckless creature, who was now so heavy on the old folks' hands, and like them, no doubt, would some day die of want and unjust toil.

Toil, manual toil, panting at every effort, this was what Pierre and Thomas once more found at the works. From the slender pipes above the roofs spurted rhythmical puffs of steam, which seemed like the very breath of all that labour. And in the workshops one found a continuous rumbling, a whole army of men in motion, forging, filing, and piercing, amidst the spinning of leather gearing and the trepidation of machinery. The day was ending, with a final feverish effort to complete some task or other before the bell should ring for departure.

On inquiring for the master, Thomas learnt that he had not been seen since *déjeuner*, which was such an unusual occurrence that the young man at once feared some terrible scene in the silent pavilion, whose shutters were ever closed upon Grandidier's unhappy wife—that mad, but beautiful creature, whom he loved so passionately that he had never been willing to part from her. The pavilion could be seen from the little glazed workshop which Thomas usually occupied, and as he and Pierre stood waiting there, it looked very peaceful and pleasant amidst the big lilac bushes planted round about it. Surely, they thought, it ought to have been brightened by the gay gown of a young woman and the laughter of playful children. But all at once a loud, piercing shriek reached their ears, followed by howls and moans, like

those of an animal that is being beaten or possibly slaughtered.
Ah! those howls ringing out amidst all the stir of the toiling
works, punctuated, it seemed, by the rhythmical puffing of
the steam, accompanied too by the dull rumbling of the
machinery! The receipts of the business had been doubling
and doubling since the last stock-taking; there was increase
of prosperity every month, the bad times were over, far
behind. Grandidier was realising a large fortune with his
famous bicycle for the million, the ' Lisette; ' and the approaching vogue of motor-cars also promised huge gains, should he
again start making little motor-engines, as he meant to do, as
soon as Thomas's long projected motor should be perfected.
But what was wealth when in that dismal pavilion, whose
shutters were ever closed, those frightful shrieks continued,
proclaiming some terrible drama, which all the stir and bustle
of the prosperous works were unable to stifle?

Pierre and Thomas looked at one another, pale and
quivering. And all at once as the cries ceased and the
pavilion sank into death-like silence once more, the latter said
in an undertone:

'The poor young woman is usually very gentle; she will
sometimes spend whole days sitting on a carpet like a little
child. He is fond of her when she is like that; he lays her
down and picks her up, caresses her and makes her laugh as if
she were a baby. Ah! how dreadfully sad it is! When an
attack comes upon her she gets frantic, tries to bite herself, and
kill herself by throwing herself against the walls. And then
he has to struggle with her, for no one else is allowed to touch
her. He tries to restrain her, and holds her in his arms to
calm her. . . . But how terrible it was just now! Did you
hear? I do not think she has ever had such a frightful
attack before.'

For a quarter of an hour longer profound silence prevailed.
Then Grandidier came out of the pavilion, bareheaded and
still ghastly pale. Passing the little glazed workshop on his
way, he perceived Thomas and Pierre there, and at once
came in. But he was obliged to lean against a bench like a
man who is dazed, haunted by a nightmare. His good-
natured, energetic face retained an expression of acute
anguish; and his left ear was scratched and bleeding. However, he at once wished to talk, overcome his feelings, and
return to his life of activity. 'I am very pleased to see you,
my dear Thomas,' said he, 'I have been thinking over what

you told me about our little motor. We must go into the matter again.'

Seeing how distracted he was, it occurred to the young man that some sudden diversion, such as the story of another's misfortunes, might perhaps draw him from his haunting thoughts. 'Of course I am at your disposal,' he replied ; ' but before talking of that matter I should like to tell you that we have just seen Toussaint, that poor old fellow who has been stricken with paralysis. His awful fate has quite distressed us. He is in the greatest destitution, forsaken as it were by the roadside, after all his years of labour.'

Thomas dwelt upon the quarter of a century which the old workman had spent at the factory, and suggested that it would only be just to take some account of his long efforts, the years of his life which he had devoted to the establishment. And he asked that he might be assisted in the name both of equity and compassion.

'Ah ! monsieur,' Pierre in his turn ventured to say, ' I should like to take you for an instant into that bare room, and show you that poor, aged, worn out, stricken man, who no longer has even the power of speech left him to tell people his sufferings. There can be no greater wretchedness than to die in that fashion, despairing of all kindliness and justice.'

Grandidier had listened to them in silence. But big tears had irresistibly filled his eyes, and when he spoke it was in a very low and tremulous voice : 'The greatest wretchedness, who can tell what it is ? Who can speak of it if he has not known the wretchedness of others ? Yes, yes, it's sad undoubtedly that poor Toussaint should be reduced to that state at his age, not knowing even if he will have food to eat on the morrow. But I know sorrows that are just as crushing, abominations which poison one's life in a still greater degree. . . . Ah ! yes, food indeed ! To think that happiness will reign in the world when everybody has food to eat ! What an idiotic hope ! '

The whole grievous tragedy of his life was in the shudder which had come over him. To be the employer, the master, the man who is making money, who disposes of capital and is envied by his workmen, to own an establishment to which prosperity has returned, whose machinery coins gold, apparently leaving one no other trouble than that of pocketing one's profits ; and yet at the same time to be the most wretched of men to know no day exempt from anguish, to find each evening at one's hearth no other reward or prop than the most atrocious torture of the heart! Everything, even success, has to be paid for. And thus that triumpher, that money-maker, whose pile was growing larger at each successive inventory, was sobbing with bitter grief.

However, he showed himself kindly disposed towards Toussaint, and promised to assist him. As for a pension, that was an idea which he could not entertain, as it was the negation of the wage-system such as it existed. He energetically defended his rights as an employer, repeating that the strain of competition would compel him to avail himself of them so long as the present system should endure. His part in it was to do good business in an honest way. However, he regretted that his men had never carried out the scheme of establishing a relief fund, and he said that he would do his best to induce them to take it in hand again.

Some colour had now come back to his cheeks; for on returning to the interests of his life of battle he felt his energy restored. He again reverted to the question of the little motor, and spoke of it for some time with Thomas, while Pierre waited, feeling quite upset. Ah! he thought, how universal was the thirst for happiness! Then, in spite of the many technical terms that were used he caught a little of what the others were saying. Small steam motors had been made at the works in former times; but they had not proved successes. In point of fact a new propelling force was needed. Electricity, though everyone foresaw its future triumph, was at present out of the question on account of the weight of the apparatus which its employment necessitated. So only petroleum remained, and the inconvenience attaching to its use was so great, that victory and fortune would certainly rest with the manufacturer who should be able to replace it by some other hitherto unknown agent. In the discovery and adaptation of the latter lay the whole problem.

'Yes, I am eager about it now,' at last exclaimed Grandidier in an animated way. 'I allowed you to prosecute your experiments without troubling you with any inquisitive questions. But a solution is becoming imperative.'

Thomas smiled: 'Well, you must remain patient just a little longer,' said he, 'I believe that I am on the right road.'

Then Grandidier shook hands with him and Pierre, and

went off to make his usual round through his busy, bustling works, whilst near at hand, awaiting his return, stood the closed pavilion, where every evening he was fated to relapse into endless, uncurable anguish.

The daylight was already waning when Pierre and Thomas, after reascending the height of Montmartre, walked towards the large workshop which Jahan, the sculptor, had set up among the many sheds whose erection had been necessitated by the building of the Sacred Heart. There was here a stretch of ground littered with materials, an extra-ordinary chaos of building stone, beams and machinery; and pending the time when an army of navvies would come to set the whole place in order, one could see gaping trenches, rough flights of descending steps and fences, imperfectly closing doorways which conducted to the substructures of the basilica.

Halting in front of Jahan's workshop, Thomas pointed to one of these doorways by which one could reach the foundation works. 'Have you never had an idea of visiting the foundations?' he inquired of Pierre. 'There's quite a city down there on which millions of money have been spent. They could only find firm soil at the very base of the height, and they had to excavate more than eighty shafts, fill them with concrete, and then rear their church on all those subterranean columns. . . . Yes, that is so. Of course the columns cannot be seen, but it is they who hold that insulting edifice aloft, right over Paris!'

Having drawn near to the fence, Pierre was looking at an open doorway beyond it, a sort of dark landing whence steps descended as if into the bowels of the earth. And he thought of those invisible columns of concrete, and of all the stubborn energy and desire for domination which had set the edifice erect and kept it there.

Thomas was at last obliged to call him. 'Let us make haste,' said he, 'the twilight will soon be here. We shan't be able to see much.'

They had arranged to meet Antoine at Jahan's, as the sculptor wished to show them a new model he had prepared. When they entered the workshop they found the two assistants still working at the colossal angel which had been ordered for the basilica. Standing on a scaffolding they were rough-hewing its symmetrical wings, whilst Jahan, seated on a low chair, with his sleeves rolled up to his elbows, and his hands soiled with clay, was contemplating a figure some three feet high on which he had just been working.

'Ah! it's you,' he exclaimed. 'Antoine has been waiting more than half an hour for you. He's gone outside with Lise to see the sun set over Paris, I think. But they will soon be back.'

Then he relapsed into silence, with his eyes fixed on his work.

This was a bare, erect, lofty female figure of such august majesty, so simple were its lines, that it suggested something gigantic. The figure's abundant, outspread hair suggested rays around its face, which beamed with sovereign beauty like the sun. And its only gesture was one of offer and of greeting; its arms were thrown slightly forward, and its hands were open, for the grasp of all mankind.

Still lingering in his dream Jahan began to speak slowly: 'You remember that I wanted a pendant for my figure of Fecundity. I had modelled a Charity, but it pleased me so little and seemed so commonplace that I let the clay dry and spoil. . . . And then the idea of a figure of Justice came to me. But not a gowned figure with the sword and the scales! That wasn't the Justice that inspired me. What haunted my mind was the other Justice, the one that the lowly and the sufferers await, the one who alone can some day set a little order and happiness among us. And I pictured her like that, quite bare, quite simple, and very lofty. She is the sun as it were, a sun all beauty, harmony and strength; for justice is only to be found in the sun which shines in the heavens for one and all, and bestows on poor and rich alike its magnificence and light and warmth, which are the source of all life. And so my figure, you see, has her hands outstretched as if she were offering herself to all mankind, greeting it and granting it the gift of eternal life in eternal beauty. Ah! to be beautiful and strong and just, one's whole dream lies in that.'

Jahan relighted his pipe and burst into a merry laugh. 'Well, I think the good woman carries herself upright. . . . What do you fellows say?'

His visitors highly praised his work. Pierre for his part was much affected at finding in this artistic conception the very idea that he had so long been revolving in his mind—the idea of an era of Justice rising from the ruins of the world, which Charity after centuries of trial had failed to save.

Then the sculptor gaily explained that he had **prepared**

his model there instead of at home, in order to console himself
a little for his big dummy of an angel, the prescribed triteness of which disgusted him. Some fresh objections had been
raised with respect to the folds of the robe, which gave some
prominence to the thighs, and in the end he had been compelled to modify all the drapery.

'Oh! it's just as they like!' he cried; 'it's no work of
mine, you know; it's simply an order which I'm executing
just as a mason builds a wall. There's no religious art left,
it has been killed by stupidity and disbelief. Ah! if social or
human art could only revive, how glorious to be one of the first
to bear the tidings!'

Then he paused. Where could the youngsters, Antoine
and Lise, have got to? he wondered. He threw the door wide
open, and, a little distance away, among the materials litter-
ing the waste ground, one could see Antoine's tall figure and
Lise's short slender form standing out against the immensity
of Paris, which was all golden amidst the sun's farewell. The
young man's strong arm supported Lise, who with this help
walked beside him without feeling any fatigue. Slender and
graceful, like a girl blossoming into womanhood, she raised
her eyes to his with a smile of infinite gratitude, which proclaimed that she belonged to him for evermore.

'Ah! they are coming back,' said Jahan. 'The miracle is
now complete, you know. I'm delighted at it. I did not
know what to do with her; I had even renounced all attempts
to teach her to read; I left her for days together in a corner,
infirm and tongue-tied like a lack-wit. . . . But your brother
came and took her in hand somehow or other. She listened to
him and understood him, and began to read and write with him,
and grow intelligent and gay. Then, as her limbs still
gained no suppleness, and she remained infirm, ailing, and
puny, he began by carrying her here, and then helped her to
walk in such wise that she can now do so by herself. In a
few weeks' time she has positively grown and become quite
charming. Yes, I assure you, it is second birth, real creation.
Just look at them!'

Antoine and Lise were still slowly approaching. The
evening breeze which rose from the great city, where all was
yet heat and sunshine, brought them a bath of life. If the
young man had chosen that spot with its splendid horizon,
open to the full air which wafted all the germs of life, it was
doubtless because he felt that nowhere else could he instil

more vitality, more soul, more strength into her. And love
had been created by love. He had found her asleep, benumbed,
without power of motion or intellect, and he had awakened
her, kindled life in her, loved her, that he might be loved
by her in return. She was his work, she was part of himself.

'So you no longer feel tired, little one?' said Jahan.

She smiled divinely. 'Oh! no, it's so pleasant, so beautiful to walk straight on like this. . . . All I desire is to go on
for ever and ever with Antoine.'

The others laughed, and Jahan exclaimed in his good-
natured way, 'Let us hope that he won't take you so far.
You've reached your destination now, and I shan't be the
one to prevent you from being happy.'

Antoine was already standing before the figure of Justice,
to which the falling twilight seemed to impart a quiver of
life. 'Oh! how divinely simple, how divinely beautiful!'
said he.

For his own part he had lately finished a new wood-
engraving, which depicted Lise holding a book in her hand, an
engraving instinct with truth and emotion, showing her
awakened to intelligence and love. And this time he had
achieved his desire, making no preliminary drawing, but
tackling the block with his graver, straight away, in presence
of his model. And infinite hopefulness had come upon
him, he was dreaming of great original works in which the
whole period that he belonged to would live anew and for
ever.

Thomas now wished to return home. So they shook
hands with Jahan, who, as his day's work was over, put on
his coat to take his sister back to the Rue du Calvaire.

'Till to-morrow, Lise,' said Antoine, inclining his head
to kiss her.

She raised herself on tip-toes, and offered him her eyes,
which he had opened to life. 'Till to-morrow, Antoine,'
said she.

Outside, the twilight was falling. Pierre was the first
to cross the threshold, and as he did so, he saw so extraordinary a sight that for an instant he felt stupified. But it
was certain enough; he could plainly distinguish his brother
Guillaume emerging from the gaping doorway which conducted to the foundations of the basilica. And he saw him
hastily climb over the palings, and then pretend to be there

by pure chance, as though he had come up from the Rue Lamarck. When he accosted his two sons, as if he were delighted to meet them, and began to say that he had just come from Paris, Pierre asked himself if he had been dreaming. However, an anxious glance which his brother cast at him, convinced him that he had been right. And then he not only felt ill at ease in presence of that man whom he had never previously known to lie; but it seemed to him that he was at last on the track of all he had feared, the formidable mystery that he had for some time past felt brewing around him in the little peaceful house.

When Guillaume, his sons, and his brother reached home and entered the large workroom overlooking Paris, it was so dark that they fancied nobody was there.

'What! nobody in?' said Guillaume.

But in a somewhat low, quiet voice François answered out of the gloom: 'Why, yes, I'm here.'

He had remained at his table, where he had worked the whole afternoon; and as he could no longer read, he now sat in a dreamy mood with his head resting on his hands, his eyes wandering over Paris, where night was gradually falling. As his examination was now near at hand, he was living in a state of severe mental strain.

'What! you are still working there,' said his father. 'Why didn't you ask for a lamp?'

'No, I wasn't working, I was looking at Paris,' François slowly answered. 'It's singular how the night falls over it by degrees. The last district that remained visible was the Montagne Ste Geneviève, the plateau of the Panthéon, where all our knowledge and science have grown up. A sunray still gilds the schools and libraries and laboratories, when the low-lying districts of trade are already steeped in darkness. I won't say that the planet has a particular partiality for us at the École Normale, but it's certain that its beams still linger on our roofs when they are to be seen nowhere else.'

He began to laugh at his jest. Still one could see how ardent was his faith in mental effort, how entirely he gave himself to mental labour, which, in his opinion, could alone bring truth, establish justice, and create happiness.

Then came a short spell of silence. Paris sank more and more deeply into the night, growing black and mysterious, till all at once sparks of light began to appear.

' The lamps are being lighted,' resumed François; ' work
is being resumed on all sides.'

Then Guillaume, who likewise had been dreaming,
immersed in his fixed idea, exclaimed: ' Work, yes, no doubt !
But for work to give a full harvest it must be fertilised by
will. There is something which is superior to work.'

Thomas and Antoine had drawn near. And François,
as much for them as for himself, inquired: ' What is that,
father ? '

' Action.'

For a moment the three young men remained silent,
impressed by the solemnness of the hour, quivering too
beneath the great waves of darkness which rose from the
vague ocean of the city. Then a young voice remarked,
though whose it was one could not tell: ' Action is but
work.'

And Pierre, who lacked the respectful quietude, the silent
faith of his nephews, now felt his nervousness increasing.
That huge and terrifying mystery of which he was dimly
conscious rose before him ; while a great quiver sped by in
the darkness, over that black city where the lamps were now
being lighted for a whole passionate night of work.

IV

THE CRISIS

A GREAT ceremony was to take place that day at the basilica
of the Sacred Heart. Ten thousand pilgrims were to be
present there, at a solemn consecration of the Holy Sacra-
ment ; and pending the arrival of four o'clock, the hour fixed
for the service, Montmartre would be invaded by people. Its
slopes would be black with swarming devotees, the shops
where religious emblems and pictures were sold would be
besieged, the cafés and taverns would be crowded to overflowing. It would all be like some huge fair, and meantime
the big bell of the basilica, ' La Savoyarde,' would be ringing
peal on peal over the holiday-making multitude.

When Pierre entered the workroom in the morning he
perceived Guillaume and Mère-Grand alone there ; and a
remark which he heard the former make caused him to stop

short and listen from behind a tall revolving book-stand. Mère-Grand sat sewing in her usual place near the big window, while Guillaume stood before her, speaking in a low voice.

'Mother,' said he, 'everything is ready, it is for to-day.'

She let her work fall, and raised her eyes, looking very pale. 'Ah!' she said, 'so you have made up your mind.'

'Yes, irrevocably. At four o'clock I shall be yonder, and it will all be over.'

''Tis well—you are the master.'

Silence fell, terrible silence. Guillaume's voice seemed to come from far away, from somewhere beyond the world. It was evident that his resolution was unshakeable, that his tragic dream, his fixed idea of martyrdom wholly absorbed him. Mère-Grand looked at him with her pale eyes, like an heroic woman who had grown old in relieving the sufferings of others, and had ever shown all the abnegation and devotion of an intrepid heart, which nothing but the idea of duty could influence. She knew Guillaume's terrible scheme, and had helped him to regulate the pettiest details of it; but if on the one hand, after all the iniquity she had seen and endured, she admitted that fierce and exemplary punishment might seem necessary, and that even the idea of purifying the world by the fire of a volcano might be entertained; on the other hand, she believed too strongly in the necessity of living one's life bravely to the very end, to be able, under any circumstances, to regard death as either good or profitable.

'My son,' she gently resumed, 'I witnessed the growth of your scheme, and it neither surprised nor angered me. I accepted it as one accepts lightning, the very fire of the skies, something of sovereign purity and power. And I have helped you through it all, and have taken upon myself to act as the mouthpiece of your conscience. . . . But let me tell you once more, one ought never to desert the cause of life.'

'It is useless to speak, mother,' Guillaume replied; 'I have resolved to give my life and cannot take it back. . . . Are you now unwilling to carry out my desires, remain here, and act as we have decided, when all is over?'

She did not answer this inquiry, but in her turn, speaking slowly and gravely, put a question to him: 'So it is useless for me to speak to you of the children, myself, and the house?' said she. 'You have thought it all over, you are quite determined?' And as he simply answered 'Yes,' she added: ''Tis well, you are the master. . . . I will be the one who is to remain behind and act. And you may be without fear, your bequest is in good hands. All that we have decided together shall be done.'

Once more they became silent. Then she again inquired: 'At four o'clock, you say, at the moment of that consecration?'

'Yes, at four o'clock.'

She was still looking at him with her pale eyes, and there seemed to be something superhuman in her simplicity and grandeur as she sat there in her thin black gown. Her glance, in which the greatest bravery and the deepest sadness mingled, filled Guillaume with acute emotion. His hands began to tremble, and he asked: 'Will you let me kiss you, mother?'

'Oh! right willingly, my son,' she responded. 'Your path of duty may not be mine, but you see I respect your views and love you.'

They kissed one another, and when Pierre, whom the scene had chilled to his heart, presented himself as if he were just arriving, Mère-Grand had quietly taken up her needlework once more, while Guillaume was going to and fro, setting one of his laboratory shelves in order with all his wonted activity.

At noon when lunch was ready, they found it necessary to wait for Thomas, who had not yet come home. His brothers François and Antoine complained in a jesting way, saying that they were dying of hunger, while for her part Marie, who had made a *crême*, and was very proud of it, declared that they would eat it all, and that those who came late would have to go without tasting it. When Thomas eventually put in an appearance he was greeted with jeers.

'But it wasn't my fault,' said he; 'I stupidly came up the hill by way of the Rue de la Barre, and you can have no notion what a crowd I fell upon. Quite ten thousand pilgrims must have camped there last night. I am told that as many as possible were huddled together in the St. Joseph Refuge. The others no doubt had to sleep in the open air. And now they are busy eating, here, there, and everywhere, all over the patches of waste ground and even on the pavements. One can scarcely set one foot before the other without risk of treading on somebody.'

The meal proved a very gay one, though Pierre found the gaiety forced and excessive. Yet the young people could surely know nothing of the frightful, invisible thing which to Pierre ever seemed to be hovering around in the bright sunlight of that splendid June day. Was it that the dim presentiment which comes to loving hearts when mourning threatens them, swept by during the short intervals of silence that followed the joyous outbursts? Although Guillaume looked somewhat pale, and spoke with unusual caressing softness, he retained his customary bright smile. But on the other hand, never had Mère-Grand been more silent or more grave.

Marie's *crême* proved a great success, and the others congratulated her on it so fulsomely that they made her blush. Then, all at once, heavy silence fell once more, a deathly chill seemed to sweep by making every face turn pale —even while they were still cleaning their plates with their little spoons.

'Ah! that bell,' exclaimed François; 'it is really intolerable. I can feel my head splitting.'

He referred to 'La Savoyarde,' the big bell of the basilica, which had now begun to toll, sending forth deep sonorous volumes of sound, which ever and ever winged their flight over the immensity of Paris. In the workroom they were all listening to the clang.

'Will it keep on like that till four o'clock?' asked Marie.

'Oh! at four o'clock,' replied Thomas, 'at the moment of the consecration you will hear something much louder than that. The great peals of joy, the song of triumph will then ring out.'

Guillaume was still smiling. 'Yes, yes,' said he, 'those who don't want to be deafened for life had better keep their windows closed. The worst is, that Paris has to hear it whether it will or no, and even as far away as the Panthéon, so I'm told.'

Meantime Mère-Grand remained silent and impassive. Antoine for his part expressed his disgust with the horrible religious pictures for which the pilgrims fought—pictures which in some respects suggested those on the lids of sweetmeat boxes, although they depicted the Christ with His breast ripped open and displaying His bleeding heart. There could be no more repulsive materialism, no grosser or baser art, said Antoine. Then they rose from table, talking at the top of their voices so as to make themselves heard above the incessant din which came from the big bell.

Immediately afterwards they all set to work again. Mère-Grand took her everlasting needlework in hand once more, while Marie, sitting near her, continued some embroidery. The young men also attended to their respective tasks, and now and again raised their heads and exchanged a few words. Guillaume, for his part, likewise seemed very busy; Pierre alone coming and going in a state of anguish, beholding them all as in a nightmare, and attributing some terrible meaning to the most innocent remarks. During *déjeuner*, in order to explain the frightful discomfort into which he was thrown by the gaiety of the meal, he had been obliged to say that he felt poorly. And now he was looking and listening and waiting with ever-growing anxiety.

Shortly before three o'clock, Guillaume glanced at his watch and then quietly took up his hat. 'Well,' said he, 'I'm going out.'

His sons, Mère-Grand and Marie raised their heads.

'I'm going out,' he repeated, '*au revoir*!'

Still he did not go off. Pierre could divine that he was struggling, stiffening himself against the frightful tempest which was raging within him, striving to prevent either shudder or pallor from betraying his awful secret. Ah! he must have suffered keenly; he dared not give his sons a last kiss, for fear lest he might rouse some suspicion in their minds, which would impel them to oppose him and prevent his death! At last with supreme heroism he managed to calm himself.

'*Au revoir*! boys.'

'*Au revoir*! father. Will you be home early?'

'Yes, yes. . . Don't worry about me, do plenty of work.'

Mère-Grand, still majestically silent, kept her eyes fixed upon him. Her he had ventured to kiss, and their glances met and mingled, instinct with all that he had decided and that she had promised: their common dream of truth and justice.

'I say, Guillaume,' exclaimed Marie gaily, 'will you undertake a commission for me if you are going down by way of the Rue des Martyrs?'

'Why, certainly,' he replied.

'Well, then, please look in at my dressmaker's, and tell her that I shan't go to try my gown on till to-morrow morning.'

It was a question of her wedding dress, a gown of light grey silk, the extreme stylishness of which she considered very amusing. Whenever she spoke of it, both she and the others began to laugh.

'It's understood, my dear,' said Guillaume, likewise making merry over it. 'We know it's Cinderella's court robe, eh? The fairy brocade and lace that are to make you very beautiful and for ever happy.'

However, the laughter ceased, and, in the sudden silence which fell, it again seemed as if death were passing by with a great flapping of wings and an icy gust which chilled the hearts of everyone remaining there.

'It's understood; so now I'm really off,' resumed Guillaume. '*Au revoir!* children.'

Then he sallied forth, without even turning round, and for a moment they could hear the firm tread of his feet over the garden gravel.

Pierre having invented a pretext was able to follow him a couple of minutes afterwards. As a matter of fact there was no need for him to dog Guillaume's heels, for he knew where his brother was going. He was thoroughly convinced that he would find him at that doorway, conducting to the foundations of the basilica, whence he had seen him emerge two days before. And so he wasted no time in looking for him among the crowd of pilgrims going to the church. His only thought was to hurry on and reach Jahan's workshop. And in accordance with his expectation, just as he arrived there, he perceived Guillaume slipping between the broken palings. The crush and the confusion prevailing among the concourse of believers favoured Pierre as it had his brother, in such wise that he was able to follow the latter and enter the doorway without being noticed. Once there he had to pause and draw breath for a moment, so greatly did the beating of his heart oppress him.

A precipitous flight of steps, where all was steeped in darkness, descended from the narrow entry. It was with infinite precaution that Pierre ventured into the gloom, which ever grew denser and denser. He lowered his feet gently so as to make no noise, and, feeling the walls with his hands, turned round and round as he went lower and lower into a kind of well. However, the descent was not a very long one. As soon as he found beaten ground beneath his feet he paused, no longer daring to stir for fear of betraying his presence. The darkness was like ink, and there was not a sound, a breath; the silence was complete.

How should he find his way? he wondered. Which direction ought he to take? He was still hesitating when some twenty paces away he suddenly saw a bright spark, the gleam of a lucifer. Guillaume was lighting a candle. Pierre recognised his broad shoulders, and from that moment he simply had to follow the flickering light along a walled and vaulted subterranean gallery. It seemed to be interminable and to run in a northerly direction, towards the nave of the basilica.

All at once, however, the little light stopped, while Pierre, anxious to see what would happen, continued to advance, treading as softly as he could and remaining in the gloom. He found that Guillaume had stood his candle upon the ground in the middle of a kind of low rotunda under the crypt, and that he had knelt down and moved aside a long flagstone which seemed to cover a cavity. They were here among the foundations of the basilica; and one of the columns or piles of concrete poured into shafts in order to support the building could be seen. The gap, which the stone slab removed by Guillaume had covered, was by the very side of the pillar; it was either some natural surface flaw, or a deep fissure caused by some subsidence or settling of the soil. The heads of other pillars could be descried around, and these the cleft seemed to be reaching, for little slits branched out in all directions. Then, on seeing his brother leaning forward, like one who is for the last time examining a mine he has laid before applying a match to the fuse, Pierre suddenly understood the whole terrifying business. Considerable quantities of the new explosive had been brought to that spot. Guillaume had made the journey a score of times at carefully selected hours, and all his powder had been poured into the gap beside the pillar, spreading to the slightest rifts below, saturating the soil at a great depth, and in this wise forming a natural mine of incalculable force. And now the powder was flush with the flagstone which Guillaume had just moved aside. It was only necessary to throw a match there, and everything would be blown into space!

For a moment an acute chill of horror rooted Pierre to the spot. He could neither have taken a step nor raised a cry. He pictured the swarming throng above him, the ten thousand pilgrims crowding the lofty naves of the basilica to witness the solemn consecration of the Host. Peal upon peal flew from 'La Savoyarde,' incense smoked, and ten thousand voices raised a hymn of magnificence and praise. And all at once came thunder and earthquake, and a volcano opening and belching forth fire and smoke, and swallowing up the whole church and its multitude of worshippers. Breaking the concrete piles and rending the unsound soil, the explosion, which was certain to be one of extraordinary violence, would doubtless split the edifice atwain, and hurl one half down the slopes descending towards Paris, whilst the other on the side of the apse would crumble and collapse upon the spot where it stood. And how fearful would be the avalanche: a broken forest of scaffoldings, a hail of stonework, rushing and bounding through the dust and smoke on to the roofs below; whilst the violence of the shock would threaten the whole of Montmartre, which, it seemed likely, must stagger and sink in one huge mass of ruins!

However, Guillaume had again risen. The candle standing on the ground, its flame shooting up, erect and slender, threw his huge shadow all over the subterranean vault. Amidst the dense blackness the light looked like some dismal stationary star. Guillaume drew near to it in order to see what time it was by his watch. It proved to be five minutes past three. So he had nearly another hour to wait. He was in no hurry, he wished to carry out his design punctually, at the precise moment he had selected; and he therefore sat down on a block of stone, and remained there without moving, quiet and patient. The candle now cast its light upon his pale face, upon his towering brow crowned with white hair, upon the whole of his energetic countenance, which still looked handsome and young, thanks to his bright eyes and dark moustaches. And not a muscle of his face stirred; he simply gazed into the void. What thoughts could be passing through his mind at that supreme moment? Who could tell? There was not a quiver; heavy night, the deep eternal silence of the earth reigned all around.

Then Pierre, having quieted his palpitating heart, drew near At the sound of his footsteps Guillaume rose menacingly, but he immediately recognised his brother, and did not seem astonished to see him.

'Ah! it's you,' he said, 'you followed me. . . . I felt that you possessed my secret. And it grieves me that you should have abused your knowledge to join me here. You might have spared me this last sorrow.'

Pierre clasped his trembling hands, and at once tried to entreat him. 'Brother, brother,' he began.

'No, don't speak yet,' said Guillaume, 'if you absolutely wish it I will listen to you by-and-bye. We have nearly an hour before us, so we can chat. But I want you to understand the futility of all you may think needful to tell me. My resolution is unshakeable; I was a long time coming to it, and in carrying it out I shall simply be acting in accordance with my reason and my conscience.'

Then he quietly related that having decided upon a great deed he had long hesitated as to which edifice he should destroy. The opera-house had momentarily tempted him, but he had reflected that there would be no great significance in the whirlwind of anger and justice destroying a little set of enjoyers. In fact, such a deed might savour of jealousy and covetousness. Next he had thought of the Bourse, where he might strike a blow at money, the great agent of corruption, and the capitalist society in whose clutches the wage-earners groaned. Only, here again the blow would fall upon a restricted circle. Then an idea of destroying the Palace of Justice, particularly the assize court, had occurred to him. It was a very tempting thought—to wreak justice upon human justice, to sweep away the witnesses, the culprit, the public prosecutor who charges the latter, the counsel who defends him, the judges who sentence him, and the lounging public which comes to the spot as to the unfolding of some sensational serial. And then too what fierce irony there would be in the summary superior justice of the volcano swallowing up everything indiscriminately, without pausing to enter into details. However, the plan over which he had most lingered was that of blowing up the Arc de Triomphe. This he regarded as an odious monument which perpetuated warfare, hatred among nations, and the false, dearly-purchased, sanguineous glory of conquerors. That colossus raised to the memory of so much frightful slaughter, which had uselessly put an end to so many human lives, ought, he considered, to be slaughtered in its turn. Could he so have arranged things that the earth should swallow it up, he might have achieved the glory of causing no other death than his own, of dying alone, struck down, crushed to pieces beneath that giant of stone. What a tomb, and what a memory might he thus have left to the world!

'But there was no means of approaching it,' he continued, 'no basement, no cellar, so I had to give up the idea. . . . And then, although I'm perfectly willing to die alone, I thought what a loftier and more terrible lesson there would be in the unjust death of an innocent multitude, of thousands of unknown people, of all those that might happen to be passing. In the same way as human society by dint of injustice, want, and harsh regulations causes so many innocent victims, so must punishment fall as the lightning falls, indiscriminately killing and destroying whatever it may encounter in its course. When a man sets his foot on an ant-hill he gives no heed to all the lives which he stamps out.'

Pierre, whom this theory rendered quite indignant, raised a cry of protest: 'Oh! brother, brother, is it you who are saying such things?'

However, Guillaume did not pause: 'If I have ended by choosing this basilica of the Sacred Heart,' he continued, 'it is because I found it near at hand and easy to destroy. But it is also because it haunts and exasperates me, because I have long since condemned it. . . . As I have often said to you, one cannot imagine anything more preposterous than Paris, our great Paris, crowned and dominated by this temple raised to the glorification of the absurd. Is it not outrageous that common sense should receive such a smack after so many centuries of science, that Rome should claim the right of triumphing in this insolent fashion, on our loftiest height in the full sunlight? The priests want Paris to repent and do penitence for its liberative work of truth and justice. But its only right course is to sweep away all that hampers and insults it in its march towards deliverance. And so may the temple fall with its deity of falsehood and servitude! And may its ruins crush its worshippers, so that like one of the old geological revolutions of the world, the catastrophe may resound through the very entrails of mankind, and renew and change it!'

'Brother, brother!' again cried Pierre quite beside himself; 'is it you who are talking? What! you, a great scientist,

a man of great heart, you have come to this! What madness
is stirring you that you should think and say such abominable
things? On the evening when we confessed our secrets one
to the other, you told me of your proud and lofty dream of
ideal anarchy. There would be free harmony in life, which
left to its natural forces would of itself create happiness. But
you still rebelled against the idea of theft and murder. You
would not accept them as right or necessary; you merely
explained and excused them. What has happened then that
you, all brain and thought, should now have become the
hateful hand that acts?'

'Salvat has been guillotined,' said Guillaume simply,
'and I read his will and testament in his last glance. I am
merely an executor. . . . And what has happened, you ask?
Why all that has made me suffer for four months past, the
whole social evil which surrounds us, and which must be
brought to an end'

Silence fell. The brothers looked at one another in the
darkness. And Pierre now understood things; he saw that
Guillaume was changed, that the terrible gust of revolutionary contagion sweeping over Paris had transformed him. It
had all come from the duality of his nature, the presence of
contradictory elements within him. On one side one found a
scientist whose whole creed lay in observation and experiment,
who, in dealing with nature, evinced the most cautious logic;
while on the other side was a social dreamer, haunted by ideas
of fraternity, equality and justice, and eager for universal
happiness. Thence had first come the theoretical anarchist
that he had been, one in whom science and chimeras were
mingled, who dreamt of human society returning to the har-
monious law of the spheres, each man free, in a free association, regulated by love alone. Neither Théophile Morin with
the doctrines of Proudhon and Comte, nor Bache with those
of St. Simon and Fourier, had been able to satisfy his desire
for the absolute. All those systems had seemed to him
imperfect and chaotic, destructive of one another, and tending
to the same wretchedness of life. Janzen alone had occasionally satisfied him with some of his curt phrases which
shot over the horizon, like arrows conquering the whole earth
for the human family. And then in Guillaume's big heart,
which the idea of want, the unjust sufferings of the lowly
and the poor exasperated, Salvat's tragic adventure had suddenly found place, fomenting supreme rebellion. For long

weeks he had lived on with trembling hands, with growing anguish clutching at his throat. First had come that bomb and the explosion which still made him quiver, then the vile cupidity of the newspapers howling for the poor wretch's head, then the search for him and the hunt through the Bois de Boulogne, till he fell into the hands of the police, covered with mud and dying of starvation. And afterwards there had been the Assize Court, the judges, the gendarmes, the witnesses, the whole of France arrayed against one man, and bent on making him pay for the universal crime. And finally, there had come the guillotine, the monstrous, the filthy beast consummating irreparable injustice in human justice's name. One sole idea now remained to Guillaume, that idea of justice which maddened him, leaving naught in his mind save the thought of the just, avenging flare by which he would repair the evil and ensure what was right for all time forward. Salvat had looked at him, and contagion had done its work; he glowed with a desire for death, a desire to give his own blood and set the blood of others flowing, in order that mankind, amidst its fright and horror, should decree the return of the golden age.

Pierre understood the stubborn blindness of such insanity; and he felt utterly upset by the fear that he should be unable to overcome it. 'You are mad, brother!' he exclaimed, 'they have driven you mad! It is a gust of violence passing; they were treated in a wrong way and too relentlessly at the outset, and now that they are avenging one another, it may be that blood will never cease to flow. . . . But, listen, brother, throw off that night-mare. You can't be a Salvat who murders or a Bergaz who steals! Remember the pillage of the Princess's house and remember the fair-haired, pretty child whom we saw lying yonder, ripped open. . . . You do not, you cannot belong to that set, brother——'

With a wave of his hand, Guillaume brushed these vain reasons aside. Of what consequence were a few lives, his own included? No change had ever taken place in the world without millions and millions of existences being stamped out.

'But you had a great scheme in hand,' cried Pierre, hoping to save him by reviving his sense of duty. 'It isn't allowable for you to go off like this!'

Then he fervently strove to awaken his brother's scientific pride. He spoke to him of his secret, of that great engine of warfare which could destroy armies and reduce cities to dust, and which he had intended to offer to France, so that on emerging victorious from the approaching war, she might afterwards become the deliverer of the world. And it was this grand scheme that he had abandoned, preferring to employ his explosive in killing innocent people and over-throwing a church, which would be built afresh, whatever the cost, and become a sanctuary of martyrs!

Guillaume smiled. 'I have not relinquished my scheme,' said he, 'I have simply modified it. Did I not tell you of my doubts, my anxious perplexity? Ah! to believe that one holds the destiny of the world in one's grasp, and to tremble and hesitate and wonder if the intelligence and wisdom that are needful for things to take the one wise course will be forthcoming! At sight of all the stains upon our great Paris, all the errors and transgressions which we lately witnessed, I shuddered. I asked myself if Paris were sufficiently calm and pure for one to entrust her with omni-potence. How terrible would be the disaster if such an in-vention as mine should fall into the hands of a demented nation, possibly a dictator, some man of conquest, who would simply employ it to terrorise other nations and reduce them to slavery. . . . Ah! no, I do not wish to perpetuate warfare, I wish to kill it.'

Then in a clear firm voice he explained his new plan, in which Pierre was surprised to find some of the ideas which General de Bozonnet had one day laid before him in a very different spirit. Warfare was on the road to extinction, threatened by its very excesses. In the old days of mercenaries, and afterwards with conscripts, the percentage of soldiers designated by chance, war had been a profession and a passion. But nowadays, when everybody is called upon to fight, none care to do so. By the logical force of things, the system of the whole nation in arms means the coming end of armies. How much longer will the nations remain on a footing of deadly peace, bowed down by ever increasing 'estimates,' spending millions and millions on holding one another in respect? Ah! how great the deliverance, what a cry of relief would go up on the day when some formidable engine, capable of destroying armies and sweeping cities away, should render war an impossibility and constrain every people to disarm! Warfare would be dead, killed in her own turn, she who has killed so many. This was Guillaume's dream, and he grew quite enthusiastic, so strong was his conviction that he would presently bring it to pass.

'Everything is settled,' said he; 'if I am about to die and disappear it is in order that my idea may triumph. . . . You have lately seen me spend whole afternoons alone with Mère-Grand. Well, we were completing the classification of the documents and making our final arrangements. She has my orders, and will execute them even at the risk of her life, for none has a braver, loftier soul. . . . As soon as I am dead, buried beneath these stones, as soon as she has heard the explosion shake Paris and proclaim the advent of the new era, she will forward a set of all the documents I have confided to her—the formula of my explosive, the drawings of the bomb and gun—to each of the great powers of the world. In this wise I shall bestow on all the nations the terrible gift of destruction and omnipotence which, at first, I wished to bestow on France alone; and I shall do this in order that the nations, being one and all armed with the thunderbolt, may at once disarm, for fear of being annihilated, when seeking to annihilate others.'

Pierre listened to him, gaping, amazed at this extraordinary idea, in which childishness was blended with genius. 'Well,' said he, 'if you give your secret to all the nations, why should you blow up this church, and die yourself?'

'Why! In order that I may be believed!' cried Guillaume with extraordinary force of utterance. Then he added, 'The edifice must lie on the ground, and I must be under it. If the experiment is not made, if universal horror does not attest and proclaim the amazing destructive power of my explosive, people will consider me a mere schemer, a visionary! . . . A lot of dead, a lot of blood, that is what is needed in order that blood may for ever cease to flow!' Then, with a broad sweep of his arm, he again declared that his action was necessary. 'Besides,' he said, 'Salvat left me the legacy of carrying out this deed of justice. If I have given it greater scope and significance, utilising it as a means of hastening the end of war, this is because I happen to be a man of intellect. It would have been better possibly if my mind had been a simple one, and if I had merely acted like some volcano which changes the soil, leaving life the task of renewing humanity.'

Much of the candle had now burnt away, and Guillaume at last rose from the block of stone. He had again consulted his watch, and found that he had ten minutes left him. The little current of air created by his gestures made the light flicker, while all around him the darkness seemed to grow denser. And near at hand ever lay the threatening, open mine, which a spark might at any moment fire.

'It is nearly time,' said Guillaume. 'Come, brother, kiss me and go away. You know how much I love you, what ardent affection for you has been awakened in my old heart. So love me in like fashion, and find love enough to let me die as I want to die, in carrying out my duty. Kiss me, kiss me, and go away without turning your head.'

His deep affection for Pierre made his voice tremble, but he struggled on, forced back his tears, and ended by conquering himself. It was as if he were no longer of the world, no longer one of mankind.

'No, brother, you have not convinced me,' said Pierre, who on his side did not seek to hide his tears, 'and it is precisely because I love you as you love me, with my whole being, my whole soul, that I cannot go away. It is impossible! You cannot be the madman, the murderer you would try to be.'

'Why not? Am I not free? I have rid my life of all responsibilities, all ties. . . . I have brought up my sons, they have no further need of me. But one heart-link remained—Marie, and I have given her to you.'

At this a disturbing argument occurred to Pierre, and he passionately availed himself of it. 'So you want to die because you have given me Marie,' said he. 'You still love her, confess it!'

'No!' cried Guillaume, 'I no longer love her, I swear it. I gave her to you, I love her no more.'

'So you fancied; but you can see now that you still love her, for here you are, quite upset; whereas none of the terrifying things of which we spoke just now could even move you. . . . Yes, if you wish to die it is because you have lost Marie!'

Guillaume quivered, shaken by what his brother said, and in low broken words he tried to question himself. 'No, no, that any love pain should have urged me to this terrible deed would be unworthy—unworthy of my great design. No, no, I decided on it in the free exercise of my reason, and I am accomplishing it from no personal motive, but in the name of justice and for the benefit of humanity, in order that war and want may cease.'

Then, in sudden anguish, he went on: 'Ah! it is cruel of you, brother, cruel of you to poison my delight at dying. I have created all the happiness I could, I was going off well pleased at leaving you all happy, and now you poison my death. No, no! question it how I may, my heart does not ache; if I love Marie it is simply in the same way as I love you.'

Nevertheless, he remained perturbed, as if fearing lest he might be lying to himself; and by degrees gloomy anger came over him: 'Listen, that is enough, Pierre,' he exclaimed, 'time is flying. . . . For the last time, go away! I order you to do so; I will have it!'

'I will not obey you, Guillaume. . . . I will stay, and as all my reasoning cannot save you from your insanity, fire your mine, and I will die with you.'

'You? Die? But you have no right to do so, you are not free!'

'Free, or not, I swear that I will die with you. And if it merely be a question of flinging this candle into that hole, tell me so, and I will take it and fling it there myself.'

He made a gesture at which his brother thought that he was about to carry out his threat. So he caught him by the arm, crying: 'Why should you die? It would be absurd. That others should die may be necessary, but you, no! Of what use could be this additional monstrosity? You are endeavouring to soften me, you are torturing my heart!' Then all at once, imagining that Pierre's offer had concealed another design, Guillaume thundered in a fury: 'You don't want to take the candle in order to throw it there. What you want to do is to blow it out! And you think I shan't be able then—ah! you bad brother!'

In his turn Pierre exclaimed: 'Oh! certainly, I'll use every means to prevent you from accomplishing such a frightful and foolish deed!'

'You'll prevent me!'

'Yes, I'll cling to you, I'll fasten my arms to your shoulders, I'll hold your hands if necessary.'

'Ah! you'll prevent me, you bad brother! You think you'll prevent me!'

Choking and trembling with rage, Guillaume had already caught hold of Pierre, whose ribs he pressed with his powerful, muscular arms. They were closely linked together, their eyes fixed upon one another, and their breath mingling in that kind of subterranean dungeon, where their big dancing shadows looked like ghosts. They seemed to be vanishing into the night; the candle now showed merely like a little yellow tear in the midst of the darkness; and at that moment, in those far depths, a quiver sped through the silence of the earth which weighed so heavily upon them. Distant but sonorous peals rang out, as if death itself were somewhere ringing its invisible bell.

'You hear,' stammered Guillaume, 'it's their bell up there. The time has come, I have vowed to act, and you want to prevent me!'

'Yes, I'll prevent you as long as I'm here alive.'

'As long as you are alive, you'll prevent me!'

Guillaume could hear 'La Savoyarde' pealing joyfully up yonder; he could see the triumphant basilica, overflowing with its ten thousand pilgrims, and blazing with the splendour of the Host amidst the smoke of incense; and blind frenzy came over him at finding himself unable to act, at finding an obstacle suddenly barring the road to his fixed idea.

'As long as you are alive, as long as you are alive!' he repeated, beside himself. 'Well, then, die, you wretched brother!'

A fratricidal gleam had darted from his blurred eyes. He hastily stooped, picked up a large brick forgotten there, and raised it with both hands as if it were a club.

'Ah! I'm willing,' cried Pierre. 'Kill me, then; kill your own brother before you kill the others!'

The brick was already descending, but Guillaume's arms must have deviated, for the weapon only grazed one of Pierre's shoulders. Nevertheless, he sank upon his knees in the gloom. When Guillaume saw him there he fancied he had dealt him a mortal blow. What was it that had happened between them, what had he done? For a moment he remained standing, haggard, his mouth open, his eyes dilating with terror. He looked at his hands, fancying that blood was streaming from them. Then he pressed them to his brow, which seemed to be bursting with pain, as if his fixed idea had been torn from him, leaving his skull open. And he himself suddenly sank upon the ground with a great sob.

'Oh! brother, little brother, what have I done?' he called. 'I am a monster!'

But Pierre had passionately caught him in his arms again. 'It is nothing, nothing, brother, I assure you,' he replied.

'Ah! you are weeping now. How pleased I am! You are saved, I can feel it, since you are weeping. And what a good thing it is that you flew into such a passion, for your anger with me has dispelled your evil dream of violence.'

'I am horrified with myself,' gasped Guillaume, 'to think that I wanted to kill you! Yes, I'm a brute beast that would kill his brother! And the others, too, all the others up yonder. . . . Oh! I'm cold, I feel so cold.'

His teeth were chattering, and he shivered. It was as if he had awakened, half stupified, from some evil dream. And in the new light which his fratricidal deed cast upon things, the scheme which had haunted him and goaded him to madness, appeared like some act of criminal folly, projected by another.

'To kill you!' he repeated almost in a whisper. 'I shall never forgive myself. My life is ended, I shall never find courage enough to live.'

But Pierre clasped him yet more tightly. 'What do you say?' he answered. 'Will there not rather be a fresh and stronger tie of affection between us? Ah! yes, brother, let me save you as you saved me, and we shall be yet more closely united! Don't you remember that evening at Neuilly, when you consoled me and held me to your heart as I am holding you to mine? I had confessed my torments to you, and you told me that I must live and love! . . . And you did far more afterwards, you plucked your own love from your breast and gave it to me. You wished to ensure my happiness at the price of your own! And how delightful it is that, in my turn, I now have an opportunity to console you, save you, and bring you back to life!'

'No, no, the bloodstain is there and it is ineffaceable. I can hope no more!'

'Yes, yes, you can. Hope in life as you bade me do! Hope in love and hope in labour!'

Still weeping and clasping one another, the brothers continued speaking in low voices. The expiring candle suddenly went out unknown to them, and in the inky night and deep silence their tears of redeeming affection flowed freely. On the one hand, there was joy at being able to repay a debt of brotherliness, and on the other, acute emotion at having been led by a fanatical love of justice and mankind to the very verge of crime. And there were yet other things in the depths of those tears which cleansed and purified them; there were protests against suffering in every form, and ardent wishes that the world might some day be relieved of all its dreadful woe.

At last, after pushing the flagstone over the cavity near the pillar, Pierre groped his way out of the vault, leading Guillaume like a child.

Meantime Mère-Grand, still seated near the window of the workroom, had impassively continued sewing. Now and again, pending the arrival of four o'clock, she had looked up at the timepiece hanging on the wall on her left hand, or else had glanced out of the window towards the unfinished pile of the basilica, which a gigantic framework of scaffoldings encompassed. Slowly and steadily plying her needle, the old lady remained very pale and silent, but full of heroic serenity. On the other hand, Marie, who sat near her, embroidering, shifted her position a score of times, broke her thread, and grew impatient, feeling strangely nervous, a prey to unaccountable anxiety, which oppressed her heart. For their part, the three young men could not keep in place at all; it was as if some contagious fever disturbed them. Each had gone to his work; Thomas was filing something at his bench; François and Antoine were on either side of their table, the first trying to solve a mathematical problem, and the other copying a bunch of poppies in a vase before him. It was in vain, however, that they strove to be attentive. They quivered at the slightest sound, raised their heads, and darted questioning glances at one another. What could be the matter? What could possess them? What did they fear? Now and again one or the other would rise, stretch himself, and then resume his place. However, they did not speak; it was as if they dared not say anything, and thus the heavy silence grew more and more terrible.

When it was a few minutes to four o'clock Mère-Grand felt weary, or else desired to collect her thoughts. After another glance at the timepiece, she let her needlework fall on her lap and turned towards the basilica. It seemed to her that she only had enough strength left her to wait; and she remained with her eyes fixed on the huge walls and the forest of scaffolding which rose over yonder with such triumphant pride under the blue sky. Then all at once, however brave and firm she might be, she could not restrain a start, for 'La Savoyarde' had raised a joyful clang. The consecration of the Host was now at hand, the ten thousand pilgrims filled the church, four o'clock was about to strike. And thereupon an irresistible impulse forced the old lady to her feet; she drew herself up quivering, her hands clasped, her eyes ever turned yonder, waiting in mute dread.

'What is the matter?' cried Thomas, who noticed her. 'Why are you trembling, Mère-Grand?'

François and Antoine raised their heads, and in turn sprang forward. 'Are you ill? Why are you turning so pale, you who are so courageous?'

But she did not answer. Ah! might the force of the explosion rend the earth asunder, reach the house and sweep it into the flaming crater of the volcano! Might she and the three young men, might they all die with the father, this was her one ardent wish in order that grief might be spared them. And she remained waiting and waiting, quivering despite herself, but with her brave, clear eyes ever gazing yonder.

'Mère-Grand, Mère-Grand!' cried Marie in dismay; 'you frighten us by refusing to answer us, by looking over there as if some misfortune were coming up at a gallop!'

Then, prompted by the same anguish, the same cry suddenly came from Thomas, François, and Antoine: 'Father is in peril—father is going to die!'

What did they know? Nothing precise certainly. Thomas no doubt had been astonished to see what a large quantity of the explosive his father had recently prepared, and both François and Antoine were aware of the ideas of revolt which he harboured in his mind. But, full of filial deference, they never sought to know anything beyond what he might choose to confide to them. They never questioned him; they bowed to whatever he might do. And yet now a foreboding came to them, a conviction that their father was going to die, that some most frightful catastrophe was impending. It must have been that which had already sent such a quiver through the atmosphere ever since the morning, making them shiver with fever, feel ill at ease, and unable to work.

'Father is going to die, father is going to die!'

The three big fellows had drawn close together, distracted by one and the same anguish, and furiously longing to know what the danger was, in order that they might rush upon it and die with their father if they could not save him. And amidst Mère-Grand's stubborn silence death once more flitted through the room: there came a cold gust such as they had already felt brushing past them during *déjeuner*.

At last four o'clock began to strike, and Mère-Grand raised her white hands with a gesture of supreme entreaty. It was then that she at last spoke : ' Father is going to die. Nothing but the duty of living can save him.'

At this the three young men again wished to rush yonder, whither they knew not; but they felt that they must throw down all obstacles and conquer. Their powerlessness rent their hearts, they were both so frantic and so woeful that their grandmother strove to calm them. ' Father's own wish was to die,' said she, ' and he is resolved to die alone.'

They shuddered as they heard her, and then, on their side, strove to be heroic. But the minutes crept by, and it seemed as if the cold gust had slowly passed away. Sometimes, at the twilight hour, a night-bird will come in by the window like some messenger of misfortune, flit round the darkened room, and then fly off again, carrying its sadness with it. And it was much like that ; the gust passed, the basilica remained standing, the earth did not open to swallow it. Little by little the atrocious anguish which wrung their hearts gave place to hope. And when at last Guillaume appeared, followed by Pierre, a great cry of resurrection came from one and all : ' Father ! '

Their kisses, their tears deprived him of his little remaining strength. He was obliged to sit down. He had glanced round him as if he were returning to life perforce. Mère-Grand, who understood what bitter feelings must have followed the subjugation of his will, approached him smiling, and took hold of both his hands as if to tell him that she was well pleased at seeing him again, and at finding that he accepted his task and was unwilling to desert the cause of life. For his part he suffered dreadfully ; the shock had been so great. The others spared him any narrative of their feelings ; and he, himself, related nothing. With a gesture, a loving word, he simply indicated that it was Pierre who had saved him.

Thereupon, in a corner of the room, Marie flung her arms round the young man's neck. ' Ah ! my good Pierre, I have never yet kissed you,' said she, ' I want it to be for something serious the first time. . . . I love you, my good Pierre, I love you with all my heart.'

Later that same evening, after night had fallen, Guillaume and Pierre remained for a moment alone in the big workroom. The young men had gone out, and Mère-Grand and

Marie were upstairs sorting some house linen, while Madame Mathis, who had brought some work back, sat patiently in a dim corner waiting for another bundle of things which might require mending. The brothers, steeped in the soft melancholy of the twilight hour, and chatting in low tones, had quite forgotten her.

But all at once the arrival of a visitor upset them. It was Janzen with the fair Christ-like face. He called very seldom nowadays; and one never knew from what gloomy spot he had come or into what darkness he would return when he took his departure. He disappeared, indeed, for months together, and was then suddenly to be seen like some momentary passer-by whose past and present life were alike unknown.

'I am leaving to-night,' he said, in a voice sharp like a knife.

'Are you going back to your home in Russia?' asked Guillaume.

A faint, disdainful smile appeared on the Anarchist's lips. 'Home!' said he, 'I am at home everywhere. To begin, I am not a Russian, and then I recognise no other country than the world.'

With a sweeping gesture he gave them to understand what manner of man he was, one who had no fatherland of his own, but carried his gory dream of fraternity hither and thither regardless of frontiers. From some words he spoke the brothers fancied he was returning to Spain, where some fellow-Anarchists awaited him. There was a deal of work to be done there, it appeared. He had quietly seated himself, chatting on in his cold way, when all at once he serenely added: 'By-the-bye, a bomb has just been thrown into the Café de l'Univers on the Boulevard. Three *bourgeois* were killed.'

Pierre and Guillaume shuddered, and asked for particulars. Thereupon Janzen related that he had happened to be there, had heard the explosion, and seen the windows of the café shivered to atoms. Three customers were lying on the floor blown to pieces. Two of them were gentlemen, who had entered the place by chance and whose names were not known, while the third was a regular customer, a petty cit of the neighbourhood, who came every day to play a game at dominoes. And the whole place was wrecked; the marble tables were broken, the chandeliers twisted out of shape, the mirrors studded with projectiles. And how great the terror and the indignation, and how frantic the rush of the crowd! The perpetrator of the deed had been arrested immediately —in fact, just as he was turning the corner of the Rue Caumartin.

'I thought I would come and tell you of it,' concluded Janzen, 'it is well you should know it.'

Then as Pierre, shuddering and already suspecting the truth, asked him if he knew who the man was that had been arrested, he slowly replied : 'The worry is that you happen to know him—it was little Victor Mathis.'

Pierre tried to silence Janzen too late. He had suddenly remembered that Victor's mother had been sitting in a dark corner behind them a short time previously. Was she still there ? Then he again pictured Victor, slight and almost beardless, with a straight, stubborn brow, grey eyes glittering with intelligence, a pointed nose and thin lips expressive of stern will and unforgiving hatred. He was no simple and lowly one from the ranks of the disinherited. He was an educated scion of the *bourgeoisie*, and but for circumstances would have entered the Ecole Normale. There was no excuse for his abominable deed, there was no political passion, no humanitarian insanity in it. He was the destroyer pure and simple, the theorician of destruction, the cold energetic man of intellect who gave his cultivated mind to arguing the cause of murder, in his desire to make murder an instrument of the social evolution. True, he was also a poet, a visionary, but the most frightful of all visionaries : a monster whose nature could only be explained by mad pride, and who craved for the most awful immortality, dreaming that the coming dawn would rise from the arms of the guillotine. Only one thing could surpass him : the scythe of death which blindly mows the world.

For a few seconds, amidst the growing darkness, cold horror reigned in the workroom. 'Ah!' muttered Guillaume, 'he had the daring to do it, he had.'

Pierre, however, lovingly pressed his arm. And he felt that he was as distracted, as upset as himself. Perhaps this last abomination had been needed to ravage and cure him.

Janzen no doubt had been an accomplice in the deed. He was relating that Victor's purpose had been to avenge Salvat, when all at once a great sigh of pain was heard in the darkness, followed by a heavy thud upon the floor. It was Madame Mathis falling like a bundle, overwhelmed by the news which chance had brought her. At that moment it so happened that Mère-Grand came down with a lamp, which lighted up the room, and thereupon they hurried to the help of the wretched woman, who lay there as pale as a corpse in her flimsy black gown.

And this again brought Pierre an indescribable heart-pang. Ah! the poor sad, suffering creature! He remembered her at Abbé Rose's, so discreet, so shamefaced in her poverty, scarce able to live upon the slender resources which persistent misfortunes had left her. Hers had indeed been a cruel lot; first a home with wealthy parents in the provinces, a love story and elopement with the man of her choice; next, illluck steadily pursuing her, all sorts of home troubles, and at last her husband's death. Then, in the retirement of her widowhood, after losing the best part of the little income which had enabled her to bring up her son, naught but this son had been left to her. He had been her Victor, her sole affection, the only one in whom she had faith. She had ever striven to believe that he was very busy, absorbed in work, and on the eve of attaining to some superb position worthy of his merits. And now, all at once, she had learnt that this fondly-loved son was simply the most odious of assassins, that he had flung a bomb into a café, and had there killed three men.

When Madame Mathis had recovered her senses, thanks to the careful tending of Mère-Grand, she sobbed on without cessation, raising such a continuous doleful wail, that Pierre's hand again sought Guillaume's, and grasped it, whilst their hearts, distracted but healed, mingled lovingly one with the other.

V

LIFE'S WORK AND PROMISE

FIFTEEN months later, one fine golden day in September, Bache and Théophile Morin were taking *déjeuner* at Guillaume's, in the big workroom overlooking the immensity of Paris.

Near the table was a cradle with its little curtains drawn.

Behind them slept Jean, a fine boy four months old, the son of Pierre and Marie. The latter, simply in order to protect the child's social rights, had been married civilly at the town-hall of Montmartre. Then, by way of pleasing Guillaume, who wished to keep them with him, and thus enlarge the family circle, they had continued living in the little lodging over the workshop, leaving the sleepy house at Neuilly in the charge of Sophie, Pierre's old servant. And life had been flowing on happily for the fourteen months or so that they had now belonged to one another.

There was simply peace, affection, and work around the young couple. François, who had left the École Normale provided with every degree, every diploma, was now about to start for a college in the west of France, so as to serve his term of probation as a professor, quit to resign his post after-wards and devote himself, if he pleased to science pure and simple. Then Antoine had lately achieved great success with a series of engravings he had executed—some views and scenes of Paris life; and it was settled that he was to marry Lise Jahan in the ensuing spring, when she would have com-pleted her seventeenth year. Of the three sons, however, Thomas was the most triumphant, for he had at last devised and constructed his little motor, thanks to a happy idea of his father's. One morning after the downfall of all his huge chimerical schemes Guillaume, remembering the terrible explosive which he had discovered and hitherto failed to utilise, had suddenly thought of employing it as a motive force in the place of petroleum, in the motor which his eldest son had so long been trying to construct for the Grandidier works. So he had set to work with Thomas, devising a new mechanism, encountering endless difficulties, and labouring for a whole year before reaching success. But now the father and son had accomplished their task; the marvel was created, and stood there riveted to an oak stand, and ready to work as soon as its final toilet should have been per-formed.

Amidst all the changes which had occurred, Mère-Grand, in spite of her great age, continued exercising her active, silent sway over the household, which was now again so gay and peaceful. Though she seldom seemed to leave her chair in front of her work-table, she was really here, there, and everywhere. Since the birth of Jean she had talked of rearing the child in the same way as she had formerly reared Thomas, François, and Antoine. She was indeed full of the bravery of devotion, and seemed to think that she was not at all likely to die so long as she might have others to guide, love, and save. Marie marvelled at it all. She herself, though she was always gay and in good health, felt tired at times now that she was suckling her infant. Little Jean indeed had two vigilant mothers near his cradle; whilst his father Pierre, who had become Thomas's assistant, pulled the bellows, roughened out pieces of metal, and generally completed his apprenticeship as a working mechanician.

On the particular day when Bache and Théophile Morin came to Montmartre, the *déjeuner* proved even gayer than usual, thanks perhaps to their presence. The meal was over, the table had been cleared, and the coffee was being served, when a little boy, the son of a doorkeeper in the Rue Cortot, came to ask for Monsieur Pierre Froment. When they inquired his business, he answered in a hesitating way that Monsieur l'Abbé Rose was very ill, indeed dying, and that he had sent him to fetch Monsieur Pierre Froment at once.

Pierre followed the lad, feeling much affected; and on reaching the Rue Cortot he there found Abbé Rose in a little damp ground-floor room overlooking a strip of garden. The old priest was in bed, dying as the boy had said, but he still retained the use of his faculties, and could speak in his wonted slow and gentle voice. A Sister of Charity was watching beside him, and she seemed so surprised and anxious at the arrival of a visitor whom she did not know, that Pierre understood she was there to guard the dying man and prevent him from having intercourse with others. The old priest must have employed some stratagem in order to send the doorkeeper's boy to fetch him. However, when Abbé Rose in his grave and kindly way begged the Sister to leave them alone for a moment, she dared not refuse this supreme request, but immediately left the room.

'Ah! my dear child,' said the old man, 'how much I wanted to speak to you! Sit down there, close to the bed, so that you may be able to hear me, for this is the end; I shall no longer be here to-night. And I have such a great service to ask of you.'

Quite upset at finding his friend so wasted, with his face white like a sheet, and scarce a sign of life save the sparkle of his innocent, loving eyes, Pierre responded: 'But I would have come sooner if I had known you were in need of me! Why did you not send for me before? Are people being kept away from you?'

A faint smile of shame and confession appeared on the old priest's embarrassed face. 'Well, my dear child,' said he, 'you must know that I have again done some foolish things. Yes, I gave money to some people who, it seems, were not deserving of it. In fact, there was quite a scandal; they scolded me at the Archbishop's palace, and accused me of compromising the interests of religion. And when they heard that I was ill they put that good Sister beside me, because they said that I should die on the floor, and give the very sheets off my bed if I were not prevented.'

He paused to draw breath, and then continued: 'So you understand, that good Sister—oh! she is a very saintly woman—is here to nurse me and prevent me from still doing foolish things. To overcome her vigilance I had to use a little deceit, for which God, I trust, will forgive me. As it happens, it's precisely my poor who are in question; it was to speak to you about them that I so particularly wished to see you.'

Tears had come to Pierre's eyes. 'Tell me what you want me to do,' he answered; 'I am yours, both heart and soul.'

'Yes, yes, I know it, my dear child. It was for that reason that I thought of you—you alone. In spite of all that has happened, you are the only one in whom I have any confidence, who can understand me, and give me a promise which will enable me to die in peace.'

This was the only allusion he would venture to make to the cruel rupture which had occurred after the young man had thrown off his cassock and rebelled against the Church. He had since heard of Pierre's marriage, and was aware that he had for ever severed all religious ties. But at that supreme moment nothing of this seemed of any account to the old priest. His knowledge of Pierre's loving heart sufficed him, for all that he now desired was simply the help of that heart which he had seen glowing with such passionate charity.

'Well,' he resumed, again finding sufficient strength to smile, 'it is a very simple matter. I want to make you my heir. Oh! it isn't a fine legacy I am leaving you; it is the legacy of my poor, for I have nothing else to bestow on you; I shall leave nothing behind me but my poor.'

Of these unhappy creatures, three in particular quite upset his heart. He recoiled from the prospect of leaving them without chance of succour, without even the crumbs which he had hitherto distributed among them, and which had enabled them to live. One was the big Old'un, the aged carpenter whom he and Pierre had vainly sought one night with the object of sending him to the Asylum for the Invalids of Labour. He had been sent there a little later, but he had fled three days afterwards, unwilling as he was to submit to the regulations. Wild and violent, he had the most detestable disposition. Nevertheless, he could not be left to starve. He came to Abbé Rose's every Saturday, it seemed, and received a franc, which sufficed him for the whole week. Then, too, there was a bedridden old woman in a hovel in the Rue du Mont-Cenis. The baker, who every morning took her the bread she needed, must be paid. And in particular there was a poor young woman residing on the Place du Tertre, one who was unmarried but a mother. She was dying of consumption, unable to work, and tortured by the idea that, when she should have gone, her daughter must sink to the pavement like herself. And in this instance the legacy was twofold: there was the mother to relieve until her death, which was near at hand, and then the daughter to provide for until she could be placed in some good household.

'You must forgive me, my dear child, for leaving you all these worries,' added Abbé Rose. 'I tried to get the good Sister, who is nursing me, to take an interest in these poor people, but when I spoke to her of the big Old'un she was so alarmed that she made the sign of the Cross. And it's the same with my worthy friend Abbé Tavernier. I know nobody of more upright mind. Still, I shouldn't be at ease with him, he has ideas of his own. . . . And so, my dear child, there is only you whom I can rely upon, and you must accept my legacy if you wish me to depart in peace.'

Pierre was weeping. 'Ah! certainly, with my whole soul,' he answered. 'I shall regard your desires as sacred.'

'Good! I knew you would accept. . . . So it is agreed: a franc for the big Old'un every Saturday, the bread for the bedridden woman, some help for the poor young mother, and then a home for her little girl. Ah! if you only knew what a weight it is off my heart! The end may come now, it will be welcome to me.'

His kind white face had brightened as if with supreme joy. Holding Pierre's hand within his own, he detained him beside the bed, exchanging a farewell full of serene affection. And his voice weakening, he expressed his whole mind in faint, impressive accents : ' Yes, I shall be pleased to go off. I could do no more, I could do no more ! Though I gave and gave, I felt that it was ever necessary to give more and more. And how sad to find charity powerless, to give without hope of ever being able to stamp out want and suffering ! I rebelled against that idea of yours, as you will remember. I told you that we should always love one another in our poor, and that was true, since you are here, so good and affectionate to me and those whom I am leaving behind. But, all the same, I can do no more, I can do no more ; and I would rather go off, since the woes of others rise higher and higher around me, and I have ended by doing such foolish things, scandalising the faithful and making my superiors indignant with me, without even saving one single poor person from the ever-growing torrent of want. Farewell, my dear child. My poor old heart goes off aching, my old hands are weary and conquered.'

Pierre embraced him with his whole soul, and then departed. His eyes were full of tears and indescribable emotion wrung his heart. Never had he heard a more woeful cry than that confession of the impotence of charity, on the part of that old candid child, whose heart was all simplicity and sublime benevolence. Ah ! what a disaster, that human kindness should be futile, that the world should always display so much distress and suffering in spite of all the compassionate tears that had been shed, in spite of all the alms that had fallen from millions and millions of hands for centuries and centuries ! No wonder that it should bring desire for death, no wonder that a Christian should feel pleased at escaping from the abominations of this earth !

When Pierre again reached the workroom he found that the table had long since been cleared, and that Bache and Morin were chatting with Guillaume, whilst the latter's sons had returned to their customary occupations. Marie, also, had resumed her usual place at the work-table in front of Mère-Grand; but from time to time she rose and went to look at Jean, so as to make sure that he was sleeping peacefully, with his little clenched fists pressed to his heart. And when Pierre, who kept his emotion to himself, had likewise leant over the cradle beside the young woman, whose hair he discreetly kissed, he went to put on an apron in order that he might assist Thomas, who was now, for the last time, regulating his motor.

Then, as Pierre stood there awaiting an opportunity to help, the room vanished from before his eyes; he ceased to see or hear the persons who were there. The scent of Marie's hair alone lingered on his lips amidst the acute emotion into which he had been thrown by his visit to Abbé Rose. A recollection had come to him, that of the bitterly cold morning when the old priest had stopped him outside the basilica of the Sacred Heart, and had timidly asked him to take some alms to that old man Laveuve, who soon afterwards had died of want, like a dog by the wayside. How sad a morning it had been; what battle and torture had Pierre not felt within him, and what a resurrection had come afterwards! He had that day said one of his last masses, and he recalled with a shudder his abominable anguish, his despairing doubts at the thought of nothingness. Two experiments which he had previously made had failed most miserably. First had come one at Lourdes, where the glorification of the absurd had simply filled him with pity for any such attempt to revert to the primitive faith of young nations, who bend beneath the terror born of ignorance; and, secondly, there had been an experiment at Rome, which he had found incapable of any renewal, and which he had seen staggering to its death amidst its ruins, a mere great shadow, which would soon be of no account, fast sinking, as it was, to the dust of dead religions. And, in his own mind, Charity itself had become bankrupt; he no longer believed that alms could cure the sufferings of mankind, he awaited nought but a frightful catastrophe, fire and massacre, which would sweep away the guilty, condemned world. His cassock, too, stifled him; a lie alone kept it on his shoulders—the idea, unbelieving priest though he was, that he could honestly and chastely watch over the belief of others. The problem of a new religion, a new hope, such as was needful to ensure the peace of the coming democracies tortured him, but between the certainties of Science and the need of the Divine, which seemed to consume humanity, he could find no solution. If Christianity crumbled with the principle of Charity there could remain nothing else but Justice, that cry which came from every breast, that battle of Justice against Charity in which his heart must contend in that great city of Paris. It was there that began his third and decisive experiment, the experiment which was to make

truth as plain to him as the sun itself, and give him back
health and strength and delight in life.

At this point of his reverie Pierre was roused by Thomas,
who asked him to fetch a tool. As he did so he heard Bache
remarking: 'The Ministry resigned this morning. Vignon
has had enough of it, he wants to reserve his remaining
strength.'

'Well, he has lasted more than a twelvemonth,' replied
Morin. 'That's already an achievement.'

After the crime of Victor Mathis, who had been tried and
executed within three weeks, Monferrand had suddenly fallen
from power. What was the use of having a strong-handed
man at the head of the Government if bombs still continued
to terrify the country? Moreover, he had displeased the
Chamber by his voracious appetite, which had prevented him
from allowing others more than an infinitesimal share of all
the good things. And this time he had been succeeded by
Vignon, although the latter's programme of reforms had long
made people tremble. He, Vignon, was honest certainly, but
of all these reforms he had only been able to carry out a few
insignificant ones, for he had found himself hampered by a
thousand obstacles. And thus he had resigned himself to
ruling the country as others had done; and people had discovered that after all there were but faint shades of difference
between him and Monferrand.

'You know that Monferrand is being spoken of again?'
said Guillaume.

'Yes, and he has some chance of success. His creatures
are bestirring themselves tremendously,' replied Bache, adding,
in a bitter, jesting way, that Mège, the Collectivist leader,
played the part of a dupe in overthrowing ministry after
ministry. He simply gratified the ambition of each coterie
in turn, without any possible chance of attaining to power
himself.

Thereupon Guillaume pronounced judgment. 'Oh! well,
let them devour one another,' said he. 'Eager as they all are
to reign and dispose of power and wealth, they only fight
over questions of persons. And nothing they do can prevent
the evolution from continuing. Ideas expand, and events
occur, and, over and above everything else, mankind is
marching on.'

Pierre was greatly struck by these words, and he again
recalled the past. His dolorous Parisian experiment had

begun, and he was once more roaming through the city. Paris seemed to him to be a huge vat, in which a world fermented, something of the best and something of the worst, a frightful mixture such as sorceresses might have used; precious powders mingled with filth, from all of which was to come the philter of love and eternal youth. And in that vat Pierre first remarked the scum of the political world: Monferrand who strangled Barroux, who purchased the support of hungry ones such as Fonsègue, Duthil and Chaigneux; who made use of those who only attained to mediocrity, such as Taboureau and Dauvergne; and who employed even the sectarian passions of Mège and the intelligent ambition of Vignon as his weapons. Next came money the poisoner, with that affair of the African Railways, which had rotted the Parliament and turned Duvillard, the triumphant *bourgeois*, into a public perverter, the very cancer as it were of the financial world. Then, as a just consequence of all this there was Duvillard's own home infected by himself, that frightful drama of Eve contending with her daughter Camille for the possession of Gérard, then Camille stealing him from her mother, and Hyacinthe, the son, passing his crazy mistress Rosemonde on to that notorious harlot Silviane, with whom his father publicly exhibited himself. Then there was the old expiring aristocracy, with the pale sad faces of Madame de Quinsac and the Marquis de Morigny; the old military spirit whose funeral was conducted by General de Bozonnet; the magistracy which slavishly served the powers of the day, Amadieu thrusting himself into notoriety by means of sensational cases, Lehmann, the public prosecutor, preparing his speeches in the private room of the Minister whose policy he defended; and finally, the mendacious and cupid press which lived upon scandal, the everlasting flood of denunciation and filth which poured from Sagnier, and the gay impudence shown by the unscrupulous and conscienceless Massot, who attacked all and defended all, by profession and to order! And in the same way as insects, on discovering one of their own kind dying, will often finish it off and fatten upon it, so the whole swarm of appetites, interests, and passions had fallen upon a wretched madman, that unhappy Salvat, whose idiotic crime had brought them all scrambling together, gluttonously eager to derive some benefit from that starveling's emaciated carcass. And all boiled in the huge vat of Paris: the desires, the deeds of violence, the strivings of one and another man's will, the whole nameless medley of the bitterest ferments, whence, in all purity, the wine of the future would at last flow.

Then Pierre became conscious of the prodigious work which went on in the depths of the vat, beneath all the impurity and waste. As his brother had just said, what mattered the stains, the egotism, and greed of politicians if humanity were still on the march, ever slowly and stubbornly stepping forward? What mattered, too, that corrupt and emasculate *bourgeoisie*, nowadays as moribund as the aristocracy, whose place it took, if behind it there ever came the inexhaustible reserve of men who surged up from the masses of the country-sides and the towns? What mattered the debauchery, the perversion arising from excess of wealth and power, the luxuriousness and dissoluteness of life, since it seemed a proven fact that the capitals that had been queens of the world had never reigned without extreme civilisation, a cult of beauty and of pleasure? And what mattered even the venality, the transgressions and the folly of the press, if at the same time it remained an admirable instrument for the diffusion of knowledge, the open conscience, so to say, of the nation, a river which, though there might be horrors on its surface, none the less flowed on, carrying all nations to the brotherly ocean of the future centuries? The human lees ended by sinking to the bottom of the vat, and it was not possible to expect that what was right would triumph visibly every day; for it was often necessary that years should elapse before the realisation of some hope could emerge from the fermentation. Eternal matter is ever being cast afresh into the crucible and ever coming from it improved. And if in the depths of pestilential workshops and factories the slavery of ancient times subsists in the wage-earning system, if such men as Toussaint still die of want on their pallets like broken-down beasts of burden, it is nevertheless a fact that once already, on a memorable day of tempest, Liberty sprang forth from the vat to wing her flight throughout the world. And why in her turn should not Justice spring from it, proceeding from those troubled elements, freeing herself from all dross, flowing forth with dazzling limpidity and regenerating the nations?

However, the voices of Bache and Morin, rising in the course of their chat with Guillaume, once more drew Pierre from his reverie. They were now speaking of Janzen, who after being compromised in a fresh outrage at Barcelona had fled from Spain. Bache fancied that he had recognised him in the street only the previous day. To think that a man with so clear a mind and such keen energy should waste his natural gifts in such a hateful cause!

'When I remember,' said Morin slowly, 'that Barthès lives in exile in a shabby little room at Brussels, ever quivering with the hope that the reign of liberty is at hand—he who has never had a drop of blood on his hands and who has spent two-thirds of his life in prison in order that the nations may be freed!'

Bache gently shrugged his shoulders: 'Liberty, liberty of course,' said he; 'only it is worth nothing if it is not organised.'

Thereupon their everlasting discussion began afresh, with Saint-Simon and Fourier on one side and Proudhon and Auguste Comte on the other. Bache gave a long account of the last commemoration which had taken place in honour of Fourier's memory, how faithful disciples had brought wreaths and made speeches, forming quite a meeting of apostles, who all stubbornly clung to their faith, as confident in the future as if they were the messengers of some new gospel. Afterwards Morin emptied his pockets, which were always full of Positivist tracts and pamphlets, manifestos, answers, and so forth, in which Comte's doctrines were extolled as furnishing the only possible basis for the new, awaited religion. Pierre, who listened, thereupon remembered the disputes in his little house at Neuilly when he himself, searching for certainty, had endeavoured to draw up the century's balance-sheet. He had lost his depth, however, amidst the contradictions and incoherency of the various precursors. Although Fourier had sprung from Saint-Simon he denied him in part, and if Saint-Simon's doctrine ended in a kind of mystical sensuality, the other's conducted to an inacceptable regimenting of society. Proudhon, for his part, demolished without rebuilding anything. Comte, who created method and declared science to be the one and only sovereign, had not even suspected the advent of the social crisis which now threatened to sweep all away, and had finished personally as a mere worshipper of love, overpowered by woman. Nevertheless, these two, Comte and Proudhon, entered the lists and fought against the others, Fourier and Saint-Simon; the combat between them or their disciples becoming so bitter and so blind that the truths common to them all at first seemed obscured and disfigured beyond recognition. Now, however, that evolution had slowly transformed Pierre, those common truths seemed to him as irrefutable, as clear as the sunlight itself. Amidst the chaos of conflicting assertions which was to be found in the gospels of those social messiahs there were certain similar phrases and principles which recurred again and again, the defence of the poor, the idea of a new and just division of the riches of the world in accordance with individual labour and merit, and particularly the search for a new law of labour which would enable this fresh distribution to be made equitably. Since all the precursory men of genius agreed so closely upon those points must they not be the very foundations of to-morrow's new religion, the necessary faith which this century must bequeath to the coming century, in order that the latter may make of it a human religion of peace, solidarity, and love?

Then, all at once, there came a leap in Pierre's thoughts. He fancied himself at the Madeleine once more, listening to the address on the New Spirit delivered by Monseigneur Martha, who had predicted that Paris, now reconverted to Christianity, would, thanks to the Sacred Heart, become the ruler of the world. But no, but no! If Paris reigned it was because it was able to exercise its intelligence freely. To set the cross and the mystic and repulsive symbolism of a bleeding heart above it was simply so much falsehood. Although they might rear edifices of pride and domination as if to crush Paris with their very weight, although they might try to stop Science in the name of a dead ideal and in the hope of setting their clutches upon the coming century, these attempts would be of no avail. Science will end by sweeping away all remnants of their ancient sovereignty, their basilica will crumble beneath the breeze of Truth without any necessity of raising a finger against it. The trial has been made, the Gospel as a social code has fallen to pieces, and human wisdom can only retain account of its moral maxims. Ancient Catholicism is on all sides crumbling into dust, Catholic Rome is a mere field of ruins from which the nations turn aside, anxious as they are for a religion that shall not be a religion of death. In olden times the over-burdened slave, glowing with a new hope and seeking to escape from his gaol, dreamt of a heaven where in return for his earthly misery he would be rewarded with eternal enjoyment. But now that Science has destroyed that false idea of a heaven, and shown what dupery lies in reliance on the morrow of death, the slave, the workman, weary of dying for happiness' sake, demand that justice and happiness shall find place upon this earth. Therein lies the new hope—Justice, after eighteen hundred years of impotent Charity. Ah! in a thousand years from now, when Catholicism will be nought but a very ancient superstition of the past, how amazed men will be to think that their ancestors were able to endure that religion of torture and nihility! How astonished they will feel on finding that God was regarded as an executioner, that manhood was threatened, maimed, and chastised, that nature was accounted an enemy, that life was looked upon as something accursed, and that death alone was pronounced sweet and liberating! For well-nigh two thousand years the onward march of mankind has been hampered by the odious idea of tearing all that is human away from man: his desires, his passions, his free intelligence, his will and right of action, his whole strength. And how glorious will be the awakening when such virginity as is now honoured by the Church is held in derision, when fruitfulness is again recognised as a virtue, amidst the hosannah of all the freed forces of nature—man's desires which will be honoured, his passions which will be utilised, his labour which will be exalted, whilst life is loved and ever and ever creates love afresh!

A new religion! a new religion! Pierre remembered the cry which had escaped him at Lourdes, and which he had repeated at Rome in presence of the collapse of old Catholicism. But he no longer displayed the same feverish eagerness as then—a puerile, sickly desire that a new Divinity should at once reveal himself, an ideal come into being, complete in all respects, with dogmas and form of worship. The Divine certainly seemed to be as necessary to man as were bread and water; he had ever fallen back upon it, hungering for the mysterious, seemingly having no other means of consolation than that of annihilating himself in the unknown. But who can say that Science will not some day quench the thirst for what lies beyond us? If the domain of Science embraces the acquired truths, it also embraces, and will ever do so, the truths that remain to be acquired. And in front of it will there not ever remain a margin for the thirst of knowledge, for the hypotheses which are but so much ideality? Besides, is not the

yearning for the divine simply a desire to behold the Divinity?
And if Science should more and more content the yearning to
know all and be able to do all, will not that yearning be
quieted and end by mingling with the love of acquired truth?
A religion grafted on Science is the indicated, certain, inevitable finish of man's long march towards knowledge. He
will come to it at last as to a natural haven, as to peace in
the midst of certainty, after passing every form of ignorance
and terror on his road. And is there not already some indication of such a religion? Has not the idea of the duality of
God and the Universe been brushed aside, and is not the
principle of unity, *monisme*, becoming more and more evident
—unity leading to solidarity, and the sole law of life proceeding by evolution from the first point of the ether that con-
densed to create the world? But if precursors, scientists, and
philosophers—Darwin, Fourier, and all the others—have sown
the seed of to-morrow's religion by casting the good word to
the passing breeze, how many centuries will doubtless be
required to raise the crop! People always forget that before
Catholicism grew up and reigned in the sunlight, it spent
four centuries in germinating and sprouting from the soil.
Well, then, grant some centuries to this religion of Science of
whose sprouting there are signs upon all sides, and by-and-
bye the admirable ideas of some Fourier will be seen expanding
and forming a new Gospel, with desire serving as the lever to
raise the world, work accepted by one and all, honoured and
regulated as the very mechanism of natural and social life,
and the passions of man excited, contented, and utilised for
human happiness! The universal cry of Justice, which rises
louder and louder, in a growing clamour from the once silent
multitude, the people that have so long been duped and preyed
upon, is but a cry for this happiness towards which human
beings are tending, the happiness that embodies the complete
satisfaction of man's needs, and the principle of life loved for
its own sake, in the midst of peace and the expansion of every
force and every joy. The time will come when this Kingdom
of God will be set up on the earth; so why not close that other
deceptive paradise even if the weak-minded must momentarily
suffer from the destruction of their illusions; for it is necessary to operate even with cruelty on the blind if they are to
be extricated from their misery, from their long and frightful
night of ignorance!

All at once a feeling of deep joy came over Pierre. A

child's faint cry, the wakening cry of his son Jean had drawn him from his reverie. And he had suddenly remembered that he himself was now saved, freed from falsehood and fright, restored to good and healthy nature. How he quivered as he recalled that he had once fancied himself lost, blotted out of life, and that a prodigy of love had extricated him from his nothingness, still strong and sound, since that dear child of his was there, sturdy and smiling. Life had brought forth life; and truth had burst forth, as dazzling as the sun. He had made his third experiment with Paris, and this had been conclusive; it had been no wretched miscarriage with increase of darkness and grief, like his other experiments at Lourdes and Rome. In the first place the law of labour had been revealed to him, and he had imposed upon himself a task, as humble a one as was, that manual calling which he was learning so late in life, but which was, nevertheless, a form of labour, and one in which he would never fail, one too that would lend him the serenity which comes from the accomplishment of duty, for life itself was but labour: it was only by effort that the world existed. And then, moreover, he had loved; and salvation had come to him from woman, and from his child. Ah! what a long and circuitous journey he had made to reach this finish at once so natural and so simple! How he had suffered, how much error and anger he had known before doing what all men ought to do! That eager, glowing love which had contended against his reason, which had bled at sight of the arrant absurdities of the miraculous grotto of Lourdes, which had bled again too in presence of the haughty decline of the Vatican, had at last found contentment now that he was husband and father, now that he had confidence in work and believed in the just laws of life. And thence had come the indisputable truth, the one solution—happiness in certainty.

Whilst Pierre was thus plunged in thought, Bache and Morin had already gone off with their customary handshakes and promises to come and chat again some evening. And as Jean was now crying more loudly, Marie took him in her arms and unhooked her dress-body to give him her breast.

'Oh! the darling, it's his time, you know, and he doesn't forget it!' she said. 'Just look, Pierre, I believe he has got bigger since yesterday.'

She laughed; and Pierre, likewise laughing, drew near to kiss the child. And afterwards he kissed his wife, mastered as he was by emotion at the sight of that pink, gluttonous little creature imbibing life from that lovely breast so full of milk.

'Why! he'll eat you,' he gaily said to Marie. 'How he's pulling!'

'Oh! he does bite me a little,' she replied; 'but I like that the better, it shows that he profits by it.'

Then Mère-Grand, she who as a rule was so serious and silent, began to talk with a smile lighting up her face: 'I weighed him this morning,' said she; 'he weighs nearly a quarter of a pound more than he did the last time. And if you had only seen how good he was, the darling! He will be a very intelligent and well-behaved little gentleman, such as I like. When he's five years old I shall teach him his alphabet, and when he's fifteen, if he likes, I'll tell him how to be a man. . . . Don't you agree with me, Thomas? And you Antoine, and you, too, François?'

Raising their heads the three sons gaily nodded their approval, grateful as they felt for the lessons in heroism which she had given them, and apparently finding no reason why she might not live another twenty years in order to give similar lessons to Jean.

Pierre still remained in front of Marie, basking in all the rapture of love, when he felt Guillaume lay his hands upon his shoulders from behind. And on turning round he saw that his brother was also radiant, like one who felt well pleased at seeing them so happy. 'Ah! brother,' said Guillaume softly, 'do you remember my telling you that you suffered solely from the battle between your mind and your heart, and that you would find quietude again when you loved what you could understand? It was necessary that our father and mother, whose painful quarrel had continued beyond the grave, should be reconciled in you. And now it's done, they sleep in peace within you, since you yourself are pacified.'

These words filled Pierre with emotion. Joy beamed upon his face, which was now so open and energetic. He still had the towering brow, that impregnable fortress of reason, which he had derived from his father, and he still had the gentle chin and affectionate eyes and mouth which his mother had given him, but all was now blended together, instinct with happy harmony and serene strength. Those two experiments of his which had miscarried, were like crises of his maternal heredity, the tearful tenderness which had come to him from his mother, and which for lack of satisfaction had made him desperate; and his third experiment had only ended in happiness because he had contented his ardent thirst for love in accordance with sovereign reason, that paternal heredity which pleaded so loudly within him. Reason remained the queen. And if his sufferings had thus always come from the warfare which his reason had waged against his heart, it was because he was man personified, ever struggling between his intelligence and his passions. And how peaceful all seemed now that he had reconciled and satisfied them both, now that he felt healthy, perfect, and strong, like some lofty oak, which grows in all freedom, and whose branches spread far away over the forest!

'You have done good work in that respect,' Guillaume affectionately continued, 'for yourself and for all of us, and even for our dear parents whose shades, pacified and reconciled, now abide so peacefully in the little home of our childhood. I often think of our dear house at Neuilly, which old Sophie is taking care of for us, and although out of egotism, a desire to set happiness around me, I wished to keep you here, your Jean must some day go and live there, so as to bring it fresh youth.'

Pierre had taken hold of his brother's hands, and looking into his eyes he asked: 'And you—are you happy?'

'Yes, very happy, happier than I have ever been; happy at loving you as I do, and happy at being loved by you as no one else will ever love me.'

Their hearts mingled in ardent brotherly affection, the most perfect and heroic affection that can blend men together. And they embraced one another whilst, with her babe on her breast, Marie, so gay, healthful and loyal, looked at them and smiled, with big tears gathering in her eyes.

Thomas, however, having finished his motor's last toilet, had just set it in motion. It was a prodigy of lightness and strength, of no weight whatever in comparison with the power it displayed. And it worked with perfect smoothness without noise or smell. The whole family was gathered round it in delight when there came a timely visit, one from the learned and friendly Bertheroy, whom indeed Guillaume had asked to call, in order that he might see the motor working.

The great chemist at once expressed his admiration; and when he had examined the mechanism and understood how the explosive was employed as motive power—an idea which he had long recommended—he tendered enthusiastic congratulations to Guillaume and Thomas. 'You have created a little marvel,' said he, 'one which may have far-reaching effects both socially and humanly. Yes, yes, pending the invention of the electrical motor which we have not yet arrived at, here is an ideal one, a system of mechanical traction for all sorts of vehicles. Even aërial navigation may now become a possibility, and the problem of force at home is finally solved. And what a grand step! What sudden progress! Distance again diminished, all roads thrown open, and men able to fraternise! This is a great boon, a splendid gift, my good friends, that you are bestowing on the world.'

Then he began to jest about the new explosive, whose prodigious power he had divined, and which he now found put to such a beneficent purpose. 'And to think, Guillaume,' he said, 'that I fancied you acted with so much mysteriousness, and hid the formula of your powder from me, because you had an idea of blowing up Paris!'

At this Guillaume became grave and somewhat pale. And he confessed the truth. 'Well, I did for a moment think of it.'

However, Bertheroy went on laughing as if he regarded this answer as mere repartee, though, truth to tell, he had felt a slight chill sweep through his hair. 'Well, my friend,' he said, 'you have done far better in offering the world this marvel, which by the way must have been both a difficult and dangerous matter. So here is a powder which was intended to exterminate people, and which in lieu thereof will now increase their comfort and welfare. In the long run things always end well, as I'm quite tired of saying.'

On beholding such lofty and tolerant good-nature, Guillaume felt moved. Bertheroy's words were true. What had been intended for purposes of destruction served the cause of progress, the subjugated, domesticated volcano became labour, peace, and civilisation. Guillaume had even relinquished all idea of his engine of battle and victory, he had found sufficient satisfaction in this last invention of his, which would relieve men of some measure of weariness, and help to reduce their labour to just so much effort as there must always be. In this he detected some little advance towards Justice; at all events it was all that he himself could contribute to the cause. And when on turning towards the window he caught sight of the basilica of the Sacred Heart, he could not explain what insanity had at one moment come over him, and set him dreaming of idiotic and useless destruction. Some miasmal gust must have swept by, something born of want that scattered germs of anger and vengeance. But how blind it was to think that destruction and murder could ever bear good fruit, ever sow the soil with plenty and happiness! Violence cannot last, and all it does is to rouse man's feeling of solidarity even among those on whose behalf one kills. The people, the great multitude, rebel against the isolated individual who seeks to wreak justice. No one man can take upon himself the part of the volcano; this is the whole terrestrial crust, the whole multitude which internal fire compels to rise and throw up either an Alpine chain or a better and freer society. And whatever heroism there may be in their madness, however great and contagious may be their thirst for martyrdom, murderers are never anything but murderers, whose deeds simply sow the seeds of horror. And if on the one hand Victor Mathis had avenged Salvat, he had also slain him, so universal had been the cry of reprobation roused by the second crime, which was yet more monstrous and more useless than the first.

Guillaume, laughing in his turn, replied to Bertheroy in words which showed how completely he was cured: 'You are right,' he said, 'all ends well since all contributes to truth and justice. Unfortunately, thousands of years are sometimes needed for any progress to be accomplished. . . . However, for my part I am simply going to put my new explosive on the market, so that those who secure the necessary authorisation may manufacture it and grow rich. Henceforth it belongs to one and all. . . And I've renounced all idea of revolutionising the world.'

But Bertheroy protested. This great official scientist, this member of the Institute laden with offices and honours, pointed to the little motor, and replied with all the vigour of his seventy years: 'But that is revolution, the true, the only revolution. It is with things like that and not with stupid bombs that one revolutionises the world! It is not by destroying but by creating that you have just done the work of a revolutionist. And how many times already have I not told you that science alone is the world's revolutionary force, the only force which far above all paltry political incidents, the vain agitation of despots, priests, sectarians, and ambitious people of all kinds, works for the benefit of those who will come after us, and prepares the triumph of truth, justice, and peace. . . . Ah, my dear child, if you wish to overturn the world by striving to set a little more happiness in it, you have only to remain in your laboratory here, for human happiness can only spring from the furnace of the scientist.'

He spoke perhaps in a somewhat jesting way, but one could feel that he was convinced of it all, that he held everything excepting science in utter contempt. He had not even shown any surprise when Pierre had cast his cassock aside; and on finding him there with his wife and child he had not scrupled to show him as much affection as in the past.

Meantime, however, the motor was travelling hither and thither, making no more noise than a bluebottle buzzing in the sunshine. The whole happy family was gathered about it, still laughing with delight at such a victorious achievement. And all at once little Jean, Monsieur Jean, having finished sucking, turned round, displaying his milk-smeared lips, and perceived the machine, the pretty plaything which walked about by itself. At sight of it, his eyes sparkled, dimples appeared on his plump cheeks, and stretching out his quivering chubby hands he raised a crow of delight.

Marie, who was quietly fastening her dress, smiled at his glee and brought him nearer, in order that he might have a better view of the toy. 'Ah! my darling, it's pretty, isn't it? It moves and it turns, and it's strong; it's quite alive, you see.'

The others standing around were much amused by the amazed, enraptured expression of the child, who would have liked to touch the machine, perhaps in the hope of understanding it.

'Yes,' resumed Bertheroy, 'it's alive and it's powerful like the sun, like that great sun shining yonder over Paris, and ripening men and things. And Paris too is a motor, a boiler in which the future is boiling, while we scientists keep the eternal flame burning underneath. Guillaume, my good fellow, you are one of the stokers, one of the artisans of the future with that little marvel of yours, which will still further extend the influence of our great Paris over the whole world.'

These words impressed Pierre, and he again thought of a gigantic vat stretching yonder from one horizon to the other, a vat in which the coming century would emerge from an extraordinary mixture of the excellent and the vile. But now, over and above all passions, ambitions, stains and waste, he was conscious of the colossal expenditure of labour which marked the life of Paris, of the heroic manual efforts in work-shops and factories, and the splendid striving of the young men of intellect whom he knew to be hard at work, studying in silence, relinquishing none of the conquests of their elders, but glowing with desire to enlarge their domain. And in all this Paris was exalted, together with the future that was being prepared within it, and which would wing its flight over the world bright like the dawn of day. If Rome, now so near its death, had ruled the ancient world, it was Paris that reigned with sovereign sway over the modern era; and had for the time become the great centre of the nations as they were carried on from civilisation to civilisation, in a sunward course from east to west. Paris was the world's brain. Its past so full of grandeur had prepared it for the part of initiator, civiliser, and liberator. Only yesterday it had cast the cry of Liberty among the nations, and to-morrow it would bring them the religion of Science, the new faith awaited by the democracies. And Paris was also gaiety, kindness, and gentleness, passion for knowledge and generosity without limit. Among the workmen of its faubourgs and the peasants of its country-sides there were endless reserves of men on whom the future might freely draw. And the century ended with Paris, and the new century would begin and spread with it. All the clamour of its prodigious labour, all the light that came from it as from a beacon overlooking the earth, all the thunder and tempest and triumphant brightness that sprang from its entrails, were pregnant with that final splendour, of which human happiness would be compounded.

Marie raised a light cry of admiration as she pointed towards the city. 'Look! just look!' she exclaimed; 'Paris is all golden, covered with a harvest of gold!'

They all re-echoed her admiration, for the effect was really one of extraordinary magnificence. The declining sun was once more veiling the immensity of Paris with golden dust. But this was no longer the city of the sower, a chaos of roofs and edifices suggesting brown land turned up by some huge plough, whilst the sun-rays streamed over it like golden seed, falling upon every side. Nor was it the city whose divisions had one day seemed so plain to Pierre: eastward, the districts of toil, misty with the grey smoke of factories; southward, the districts of study, serene and quiet; westward, the districts of wealth, bright and open; and in the centre the districts of trade with dark and busy streets. It now seemed as if one and the same crop had sprung up on every side, imparting harmony to everything, and making the entire expanse one sole, boundless field, rich with the same fruitfulness. There was corn, corn everywhere, an infinity of corn, whose golden wave rolled from one end of the horizon to the other. Yes, the declining sun steeped all Paris in equal splendour, and it was truly the crop, the harvest, after the sowing.

'Look! just look,' repeated Marie, 'there is not a nook without its sheaf; the humblest roofs are fruitful, and every blade is full-eared wherever one may turn. It is as if there were now but one and the same soil, reconciled and fraternal. Ah! Jean, my little Jean, look! see how beautiful it is!'

Pierre, who was quivering, had drawn close beside her. And Mère-Grand and Bertheroy smiled upon that promise of a future which they would not see, whilst behind Guillaume, whom the sight filled with emotion, were his three big sons, the three young giants, looking quite grave, they who ever laboured and were ever hopeful. Then Marie, with a fine gesture of enthusiasm, stretched out her arms and raised her child aloft, as if offering it in gift to the huge city.

'See, Jean! see, little one,' she cried, 'it's you who'll reap it all, who'll store the whole crop in the barn!'

And Paris flared—Paris which the divine sun had sown with light, and where in glory waved the great future harvest of Truth and of Justice.

THE END

LOURDES

ÉMILE ZOLA

In *The Three Cities*, Zola moves from a study of France's Second Empire past to the Republican present, and directly addresses the religious and social issues of his age. Set at the turn of the century, the three-part itinerary of Lourdes, Rome and Paris can be regarded as an updated pilgrim's progress.

A pilgrim indeed is Pierre Froment, a young Catholic priest in a state of spiritual crisis, when he travels to Lourdes in a train of sufferers and helpers. Here he witnesses the disturbing venality of the spa tourist industry that has developed in the thirty-five years since the vision of Bernadette, and senses the underlying ecclesiastical interests. He is sad but unsurprised that the fond hopes of many, be they devout or superstitious, are sorely deceived, but the pious young woman whom in other circumstances he might well have loved appears to make a miraculous recovery from paralysis.

Will this be the sign that will quell his nagging scepticism and restore his wavering faith in God?

ROME

ÉMILE ZOLA

In *The Three Cities*, Zola moves from a study of France's Second Empire past to the Republican present, and directly addresses the religious and social issues of his age. Set at the turn of the century, the three-part itinerary of Lourdes, Rome and Paris can be regarded as an updated pilgrim's progress.

Three years after his visit to Lourdes, Abbé Pierre Froment has written an ecumenical work, *New Rome*, that has been placed on the Index. In an attempt to have this veto lifted he travels to Rome, where he is subjected to a variety of subtle delaying tactics designed to bring him to contrition and resignation. His enforced wait, which stretches into months, is a pretext for the novelist to develop a finely documented travelogue, as we accompany the priest to every corner of the Eternal City.

Pierre Froment at length obtains an audience with Pope Leo XIII. Will the Holy Father recognize the worth of this book, and the relevance of progressive thought to the priestly vocation?

THE FORTUNE OF THE ROUGONS

ÉMILE ZOLA

This volume is the first of the monumental series of novels with the collective title *Les Rougon-Macquart* which occupied Zola for over twenty years and was to take his chosen family through all the ups and downs of the Second Empire. The rich gallery of characters he created has its origins defined in the self-contained *Fortune of the Rougons*. Set in Plassans (Aix-en-Provence) it evokes the colourful life of this cloistered town, revealed during a period of insurrections, revolutionary movement and violent clashes between peasantry and cavalry.

Aunt Dide, Pierre Rougon, Macquart and all the other members of this ravenous, neurotic and yet humorous family are brought to life in a book which should be read for its own sake. As a bonus it is also the perfect introduction to the whole series of novels which includes *Nana*, *Earth* and *Doctor Pascal*.

THE FAT AND THE THIN

ÉMILE ZOLA

The Fat and the Thin, the third novel in Zola's *Les Rougon-Macquart*, is an epic poem to the physical environment of the Halles, the newly built and technologically advanced central market of Paris, and to the wide range of products that are sold there, enumerated in descriptive passages that have often been likened to symphonies.

It is this setting of coarse, throbbing vitality that greets one of Zola's wide-eyed newcomers. Florent, a political deportee after Louis Bonaparte's *coup d'etat*, returns to the pork butcher's shop presided over by his smug Macquart sister-in-law, and to gainful employment as a market inspector. But the joy of the long-lost brother's homecoming is short-lived on both sides; as one of the eponymous 'thin', he soon feels submerged and asphyxiated beneath the bourgeois complacency of the 'fat', and begins to plot against the regime that has legitimized their plunder.

But is this republican agitator the true villain of the piece?